W9-DCD-437

The Collected Writings of St. Louis Marie de Montfort

God alone

The Collected Writings of St. Louis Marie de Montfort

Montfort Publications Bay Shore, NY 11706

Imprimi Potest
William J. Considine, S.M.M.
Provincial Superior

Censor Librorum
Rev. Msgr. John A. Alesandro, S.T.L., J.C.D.

Imprimatur
Most Reverend John R. McGann, D.D.
Bishop of Rockville Centre, N.Y.

eighth Printing, 2010

Printed in Canada
ISBN 10: 0-910984-55-7
ISBN 13: 978-0-910984-55-3

Library of Congress Cartalog Card Number 87-083345

Design: J. Harding

Frontispiece Detail of small statue, one of many hand carved by de Montfort and used by him in his ministry.

The collected writings for the first time in English.

We present this translation of the collected works of St. Louis Marie de Montfort to the English-speaking public for the first time. Although many of his writings have already been translated and published separately, this volume contains all his works with a few exceptions.

The purpose of the volume is to present a reliable translation of what the saint actually wrote. The translators set out to convey his thought and his message as he conveyed and proclaimed it in the early eighteenth century. Naturally writing at that time would possess a literary form much different from that of our day. Louis Marie used words and expressions which would sound strange in the France of today. His interpretations of many passages of scripture are those current at the time in which he lived and many of them are distinctly personal. But we have endeavored to be faithful to the thought of this saintly missionary whose one aim was to proclaim the Gospel message in its purity to the people of his day. In proclaiming this message he made clear his belief that Mary, the Mother of Jesus, cannot be considered apart from the person and mission of her Son.

We did not deem it expedient to translate all his hymns. (There are 164 of them: many comprising over 30 stanzas.) We have, however, translated a token number of them. We have also confined ourselves to a representative selection of his sermon notes.

When reading reflectively through these writings of St. Louis Marie one feels in contact with a soul which is filled with the Spirit and which lives a life of complete dedication to the person of the Redeemer and to the mission of bringing redemption to his "poor neighbor." One feels the impact of his faith on every page and his burning desire to make Jesus and Mary better known and loved. His doctrine is so spiritually enlightening and stamped with such a personal charism that the reader cannot fail to find inspiration and spiritual enrichment in the writings of this saint.

The Translator Team

What ill or evil, Lord, can harm
This joyous heart that You alone can charm?
I love You more with every breath,
So how can I fear life or death?
To love You, Father, is to live and sing
The songs the angels sing their King.
God alone in every cell of me!
God alone! For all eternity!

St. Louis Marie de Montfort

Introduction

J. Patrick Gaffney, S.M.M.

Since his beatification in 1888 and especially since his canonization in 1947, Saint Louis Mary Grignion de Montfort (1673-1716) has had a remarkable influence upon the Church. Although his writings are truly a catechism of the faith, his popularity, however, seems to be intrinsically linked with that of devotion to Mary. When she is misunderstood and devotion to the Mother of God wanes, the person and teachings of this Breton saint fade into the background of Catholic thought. Now that Christians are showing a renewed and more solidly evangelical respect for Our Lady, so too her troubadour, Father de Montfort, is beginning to experience a resurgence in popularity.

The magisterium of the Church has, however, constantly and repeatedly extolled the preaching of this vagabond missionary. Pius XII designated his writings *flagrans, solida ac recta*—ardent, solid and correct. Pope John, Pope Paul VI continued this praise of Saint Louis' works. However, it is Pope John Paul II who has on several occasions mentioned his high esteem for this preacher, taking as his episcopal motto, retained as Supreme Pontiff, Montfort's short formula of consecration: *Tuus Totus*. His Holiness does not hesitate to declare – with so many others – that "reading this book (the Pope is referring to Montfort's True Devotion) was to be a turning point in my life."

It was Father Faber who in 1862 wrote that Montfort's prestige "bids fair to have a much wider influence in years to come. His preaching, his writing and his conversation were all impregnated with prophecy and with anticipations of the later ages of the Church." The Marian Year with its sequel of the Jubilee Year of Redemption has already stirred new interest in this itinerant French missionary who flourished around the time of the Roi Soleil, Louis XIV. Although Montfort's literary style is not ours, his truly charismatic writings appear to capture the spirit and yearning of our times. Small wonder that many bishops, priests, religious and lay people are continuing to request that this simple priest be named a Doctor of the Church.

So that the teachings of this missionary may be more clearly understood and, as the Church wishes, have a wider influence among the People of God, the Collected Works of Saint Louis de Montfort are now published for the English speaking world. Although primarily because of difficulties in translation, the English Collected Works lacks most of the extremely important "Cantiques" of the saint; nonetheless, what is found in this volume will give the reader a solid understanding of the Sapiential, Christocentric, Marian preachings of Saint Louis Mary.

It is hoped that this short prefatory essay on the life and spirituality of Saint Louis de Montfort may be of some help in understanding the context and basic content of the saint's writings. In no way does this brief introduction intend to probe the varied theological and pastoral implications of the profoundly evangelical charism of Montfort; that is a task which we hope will be spurred on by this English translation of the Collected Works and also by the renewed widespread fascination and respect for this vagabond saint.

An Overview of the Life of Saint Louis de Montfort

The hamlet of Montfort, a Breton village about thirteen miles east of Rennes, is important in any biographical sketch of Louis Mary Grignion. Yet its significance does not lie in the fact that it was there that he was born on January 31, 1673. He linked himself by name to this town because it was there that he was baptized into Christ Jesus. It is for this same reason that as an itinerant preacher he preferred to drop his surname, Grignion, and be called simply, Louis Mary of Montfort, or merely, the Father from Montfort, *le Père de Montfort.* His stress on baptism with its practical consequences of total consecration to the Eternal and Incarnate Wisdom is the root characteristic of his vision of reality.

His stay at the village of Montfort was extremely brief: no more than the first two years of his short life-span of just over forty-three years. His youth was spent at the family's farmhouse, Bois-Marquer, in the town of Iffendic, a few miles from his birthplace. The second of eighteen children, Louis was one of the few who survived to adulthood.

His father, a notary, was known for his fiery temper; his mother, for her deep piety. The Grignion family owned some property but was not considered well-off nor part of the upper class. Louis was born into a family of deep Catholic faith, in an area of France renowned for its dynamic Christian life.

College Days

At the age of eleven, Louis Mary set out for Rennes, the capital of Brittany, to enroll in the Jesuit College of Thomas a Becket. The institution enjoyed an excellent reputation and had, therefore, approximately two thousand young men attending its classes. It was here that Montfort formed lasting friendships, particularly with two fellow students: Claude Poullart des Places, the first founder of the Holy Ghost Fathers, and especially with John Baptist Blain who also became the intimate friend of Saint John Baptist de la Salle, the founder of the Christian Brothers.

Louis Mary's uncle, a priest of the Church of the Holy Savior in Rennes, became the youth's close confidant. His family moved to the city after Louis' first two years at the College, returning to the countryside home at Iffendic during the summers. The young student from the insignificant town of Montfort was considered by his teachers to be intelligent, studious, deeply religious, artistic in nature and somewhat shy. His Jesuit professors and spiritual directors became his life-long friends. Their residences throughout western France would always be his refuge in difficult times, a place where he could find support, rest and spiritual renewal.

It was under the guidance of the Jesuits that Louis' priestly vocation matured. The decision to enter the priesthood was made, so he tells us, at the shrine of Our Lady in the Carmelite Church in Rennes. Thanks especially to his Jesuit directors and those in charge of the Sodality of Our Lady at the College, Montfort's solid devotion to the Mother of the Lord was already an integral part of his spiritual life.

Paris

After eight years at the Jesuit College in Rennes, Louis Mary decided to pursue his theological studies at Saint Sulpice in Paris, thanks to unexpected financial assistance. At the age of nineteen, a new chapter opens in his life. The young man bade goodbye to family and friends at the bridge of Cesson on the outskirts of Rennes. The event takes on deep symbolism. Having left all, he crossed the Cesson bridge to a new life of total dependence upon Divine Providence. So convinced was he that God is truly his loving Father, that he gave to the first beggars he met, his money, baggage and even exchanged clothes with one of them. With total abandon, he gave joyful, free expression to his deep desire to experience the radical demands of the Gospel. Begging for food and shelter along the way, he walked to Paris, arriving in the rags of a mendicant. One of his numerous hymns expresses his deep happiness—in spite of the pain of separation from family and home—in trusting so completely in Providence:

The Lord is my Good Father,
Jesus, my Dear Savior,
Mary, my Good Mother,
Could I have greater joy!

He was beginning to find his freedom in an active and responsible total surrender to God's Love, the Incarnate and Eternal Wisdom, Jesus the Lord.

At Paris, he lodged with communities of poor seminarians who, in one way or another, were connected to the seminary directed by the priests of the parish of Saint Sulpice. For the first two years, Montfort attended classes at the Sorbonne; however, the following six years of theological study were spent under the tutelage of the Sulpicians themselves. Like the Jesuits, they found the student from Montfort talented, a man of deep faith, intensely studious, strongly devoted to Our Lady. His weakness was evident: a practical love for the poor, a desire to serve the outcasts of Paris society, a determination to live the Gospel by identifying with the most neglected.

All his life but especially as a seminarian, Montfort was an avid reader and thoroughly enjoyed his work as librarian at Saint Sulpice. As a young priest he would make this bold statement: "Having read nearly all the books which profess to treat of devotion to Our Lady and having conversed familiarly with the best and wisest men of these latter times . . ." He not only studied the traditional seminarian texts of the time, especially Commentaries on the works of Saint Thomas Aquinas but also knew well the spiritual works of Bernard of Clairvaux, Olier (the founder of the Sulpicians), Vincent de Paul, Boudon, Poiré, Condren, de Bérulle, Francis de Sales, John Eudes, d'Argentan, Vincent Ferrer, Alan de la Roche and many others. It is primarily through these authors that he came into contact with the writings of the Fathers of the Church. However, above all else, he was a man of the Bible. The Sacred Scriptures were his constant companion and his sermons and writings abound with biblical texts, usually interpreted according to the spiritual exegesis of the times.

His goal was also becoming more precise: to be a missionary to the poor, either in France or abroad. He yearned to proclaim the Good News of God's Love to the outcasts, to tell them of the love of Jesus and of the maternal care of Mary. A few years after ordination, he will write to his spiritual director: "I had wished . . . to form myself for the missions and in particular for teaching catechism to the poor . . . I feel a great desire to make Our Lord and His Holy Mother loved, and to go about in a poor and simple way, catechizing poor country people."

First Mass

At the Lady Chapel in the parish church of Saint Sulpice, Father Louis Mary Grignion celebrated his first Mass, June 5, 1700. From the age of eleven, he had completed sixteen years of formal study to reach this goal.

Montfort's priestly ministry itself lasted only sixteen years. After a few years with various mission bands preaching parish renewals, and ministering to the destitute at the poor-house at Poitiers (where with Marie Louise Trichet he began the foundation of a congregation of women, the Daughters of Wisdom) and also serving the sick poor at the immense General Hospital in Paris, Father Louis Mary was far from settled. He found it extremely difficult to discover how to implement his belief that God was calling him to serve the poor and to identify with them.

His solution was simple. This unknown young priest from western

France would seek the advice of the Pope. And so he set out on foot from Poitiers, begging for food and shelter along the arduous and dangerous routes to the Holy City. At the sight of Saint Peter's Basilica, he took off his sandals and continued barefoot to the tomb of Peter. In June, 1706, Montfort met with Clement XI, pouring out his heart to the Vicar of Christ. Strangely, the Holy Father clearly saw in this young priest extraordinary gifts of God. He turned down Louis Mary's offer to proclaim the Gospel in the wilds of Canada or in the Far East. Rather, the Pope named him Apostolic Missionary, telling him to return to his native land and renew the Church there by the proclamation of the baptismal consecration to the Eternal and Incarnate Wisdom, Jesus, the Son of Mary. For this priest from Montfort, it was the seal of approval on his vocation and also of the content and method of his proclamation of the Word of God.

Returning on foot to Poitiers, he spent the rest of his life conducting approximately two hundred missions and retreats throughout the villages and towns of Western France, proclaiming the Gospel of God's Love with Spirit-filled power.

Today, almost three hundred years later, many of the parishes where Father de Montfort preached still hold his visit to their town as a turning point in the faith of the area. His bold, innovative, charismatic proclamation of God's Love was heard in churches, monasteries, barracks, poorhouses, town squares and even in houses of prostitution. His preaching was a source of admiration for many, of resentment and anger for others.

The Vagabond Preacher

Montfort's life-style—a poor, vagabond preacher, his few possessions (Bible, breviary, notebooks) in a knapsack strung across his shoulder—was not considered dignified for a cleric. Several times the episcopal authorities forbade him to preach in one diocese or another. Always obedient, Montfort would move on.

With utter disdain for human respect, Saint Louis Mary identified with the poor and found his greatest joy in serving them with the Word of God and also with any material help he could locate. Typical of his actions was the recorded event—probably one of many similar acts on his part—when the missionary tenderly embraced a dying leprous beggar lying in the streets of Dinan, carried him to a nearby religious house, crying out to the doorkeeper: "Open up to Jesus Christ!" The poor even took up a collection to purchase some warm clothing for this priest whom they proudly called "one of our own."

To the majority of the people, Father Louis Mary was simply the Good Father from Montfort. At times he was named the Father with the big rosary, for he ordinarily had a large rosary attached to the cord-like belt of his cassock. But to some, he was clearly the enemy. His preaching, flowing from his own experience of God's love and Mary's maternal care, attracted thousands back to the faith. In a jansenistic age which harshly stressed the distance between God and people, he recommended even daily communion, a tender devotion to the Mother of God, a lived-out baptismal total surrender to Jesus in Mary.

Because of the style and contents of his preaching, this Elijah-like prophet was regarded by quite a few as at least a strange misfit. He was poisoned and although it did not prove fatal, it caused his health to deteriorate even more rapidly. Other attempts were made on his life, yet Montfort was not deterred. The Jesuits, the Sulpicians, the Dominicans (whose Third Order he joined in 1710) would always be his support. He deeply experienced that his entire life was in the loving hands of Jesus, or as he would put it, he was the "loving slave of Jesus in Mary," always understanding slave in its New Testament sense of total, loving dependence, as Mary calls herself the slave girl of the Lord (Lk 1:38) and as Paul identifies himself as the slave of Jesus Christ (Rom 1:1).

He had so deepened his life in Christ that he had no desire to be a "success," no yearning for any mystical experience, no drive for renown. His only desire was to be the lute the Eternal and Incarnate Wisdom would play, producing whatever melody the Spirit wished. In this active, responsible, lived-out consecration to the Incarnate Wisdom through Mary, he found peace and the power to share the Gospel with all whom he encountered.

Frustration Accepted

This spirit of Montfort is evident especially in what has become known as the Pontchateau Affair. Having preached a mission in the village of Pontchateau, the missionary fulfilled a dream: with the help of thousands, he literally built a hill on which he erected a life-size Calvary to be a permanent site of pilgrimage. The task took well over a year. Only a few days before the scheduled blessing, the Bishop ordered that the Calvary be not blessed but totally demolished. Montfort rushed—on foot—to the Bishop's residence to seek an explanation. Nothing could be done. Again, his detractors had won over the Bishop. The order, so it has been said, had come from the highest officials of the court at Paris who had been informed that the missionary was to use the Calvary at Pontchateau to signal the enemy, the British! The Father from Montfort gave a simple response to the thousands awaiting the blessing: "We had hoped to build a Calvary here; let us build it in our hearts." Father de Montfort could accept this decision with an amazing inner peace, knowing that it was part of the mysterious ways of Divine Providence.

The simple missionary had become a true mystic. He was supple clay in the Potter's hands. An active and responsible living Yes—like Mary—to the Holy Spirit, he was being transformed by the Spirit into the image of the Son. Worn out by his apostolate, weakened by his life of poverty and the attempts on his life, the Father from Montfort collapsed while preaching a mission at the village of Saint Laurent-sur-Sèvre. The theme of his final sermon exemplifies his life: the tenderness of Jesus, the Incarnate Wisdom of the Father.

He died on April 28, 1716, a few months after his forty-third birthday. Some years before, he had written to the first Daughter of Wisdom: "If we do not risk anything for God we will never do anything great for Him." Montfort so joyfully risked everything to live and to proclaim the Gospel. His boldness, his creativity, his lively faith, his utter simplicity of life, his identification with the poor and the oppressed, truly make him a model for Christians of all times.

It is important to note that Saint Louis Mary's sixteen years of priesthood comprise many months of solitude, perhaps as many as a total of four years. At the cave of Mervent, amidst the beauty of the forest, at the hermitage of Saint Lazarus near the village of Montfort, at the hermitage of Saint Eloi in La Rochelle, at Mont Saint-Michel, at various houses of the Jesuits, the missionary found the prayerful solitude needed to become more and more the Spirit filled instrument of the Gospel.

We must also take into account the months Father de Montfort spent walking – at least several thousand miles – when his mind was turned toward his loving Father. As he traveled from one town to the next, whittling little statues and crucifixes (many can be seen in the churches and religious houses of Brittany today) he joyfully sang some of his own hymns of praise to God.

The Founder

Three congregations trace their foundation to Saint Louis de Montfort. The first, the Daughters of Wisdom, live out the loving search of Wisdom for wounded humanity through a variety of ministries, especially among those whom the world rejects and those alienated from the Church.

The missionary also yearned intensely for a company of vagabond preachers, enflamed by the Holy Spirit, totally trusting in Divine Providence, one with Mary in her loving surrender to God. Through this Company, Montfort firmly believed, the renewal of the Church would be brought about. This congregation of priests and brothers was given the name of the Company of the Holy Spirit and also the Company of Mary (which became its official name) for like Mary, the members of this Company are to be filled with the transforming power of the Holy Spirit. Today, this congregation is popularly known as the Montfort Missionaries. In one of his most powerful writings, *Prayer for Missionaries,* Louis Mary begs God to send missionaries to this community, missionaries who would be "as free as the clouds that sail high above the earth . . . but in bondage to your love and your will; men who will range far and wide with the Gospel pouring from their lips like a bright and burning flame, with the Rosary in their hands, baying like watchdogs, burning like fire, dispelling the darkness of this world, lighting it up like the sun . . ."

At times the missionary would place some of the brothers of his small community in charge of teaching catechism to the poor; the group developed into the third community which recognizes Montfort as its founder, the teaching order of the Brothers of Saint Gabriel.

Saint Louis de Montfort typifies the strength of total surrender to the power of the Spirit. Empty of self, he became a dynamo of the Power and Wisdom of the Father. In everything, he breathed deeply of the atmosphere of Mary so that he could be, through the power of the Spirit, more intimately one with Jesus who is forever the fruit of her faith.

An Overview of the Spirituality of Saint Louis de Montfort

Many sources contributed to Saint Louis de Montfort's experience of the Incarnate Wisdom of the Father. His family background, his education, his daily prayerful study of the Bible, the diversity of his readings, his missionary travels, all play a major role in his understanding and expression of the faith. Moreover, he absorbed freely the spirit of the writings and teachings of the Jesuits, Dominicans, Sulpicians, Oratorians, the Hermits of Mont Valerien in Paris and other communities of men. He also had close ties with the Visitation Order, the Benedictine Nuns. From the viewpoint of the variety and diversity of his sources, Montfort's spirituality can be called eclectic. Nonetheless, basing himself primarily upon the French School of spirituality so strongly influenced by Cardinal de Berulle, this itinerant herald of the Good News wove these various strands into a new synthesis which can be rightfully called the Montfort School of spirituality.

The core of this spirituality is the reality of our baptismal insertion into Christ Jesus. So fundamental is this principal thrust of Montfort's thought that he can firmly declare that his preaching "cannot be condemned without overturning the foundations of Christianity" (The True Devotion, 163). His Holiness, Pope John Paul II repeats this thought when he says: "Grignion de Montfort introduces us into the very heart of the mysteries on which our faith lives, grows and bears fruit."

Yet our Baptism into Christ, the Eternal and Incarnate Wisdom of the Father, is not understood in an abstract fashion by this popular and practical preacher. Since we are one in Christ Jesus, we are to trust totally in Divine Providence, we are to imitate the Lord who "emptied himself, taking the form of a slave" (Phil. 2:7). Montfort's teachings abound with the insistence on poverty of spirit, the living to the hilt of the first beatitude, "Blest are the poor in spirit, the Kingdom of heaven is theirs" (Mt 5:3). His writings call, therefore, for a loving, formal acceptance of who we truly are: the slaves of Jesus Christ. The term slave always has, for Montfort, the evangelical connotation that we are the Lord's, that we are loved, that we are redeemed by the Incarnation and total offering of the

Incarnate Wisdom for us. The characteristic then of Montfort's stress on baptismal renewal is "absolute," total. Following the counsel of Pope Clement XI, the vagabond missionary proclaimed the renewal of the vows of our baptism, invigorating the Church wherever he preached.

There is, however, an intrinsic dimension of this baptismal renewal proclaimed by Saint Louis de Montfort. Through baptism we share in the life of the Incarnate Wisdom; but Wisdom seeks a home among us through the consent of a woman of our race, the Immaculate Mary. According to Wisdom's mysterious plan—folly in the eyes of the world—the faith-consent of Mary opens the gates of this sinful universe to the King of Glory. Her representative Yes to the redemptive Incarnation is for Montfort an intrinsic element of salvation history as it is actually planned by God. It is not only part of the "beginning"—the Incarnation—but the never-to-be-repealed plan of the Triune God in *all* His works. Karl Rahner appears to echo this thought of Saint Louis de Montfort when he writes: "The absolutely unique Yes of consent of the Blessed Virgin, which cooperated in determining the whole history of the world, is not a mere happening that has disappeared into the void of the past . . . She still utters her eternal Amen, her eternal Fiat . . ." Devotion to Mary, says Pope Paul VI in *Marialis Cultus* must be based on firm doctrinal foundations. Montfort calls for solid devotion to Mary because of the evangelical doctrine of her divinely-willed role of representative faith in the redemptive Incarnation and all that flows from it. To be inserted by Baptism into the Eternal and Incarnate Wisdom, has a necessary Marian dimension. Jesus is everywhere and forever the Son of Mary, the spokesperson for this universe in actively and responsibly accepting Wisdom's desire to enter into our folly so that we may share in Wisdom.

Montfort's intense devotion to Mary is clearly Christocentric. So strongly does the saint insist upon this point that he forcefully teaches that if devotion to Mary alienated us from Jesus it would have to be rejected as a diabolical temptation (cf. The True Devotion, 62). With Mary we enter into a more intense and more immediate union with Incarnate Wisdom. To wrench Mary from salvation history and therefore from Christian life is, for Montfort, to reject the plan of salvation as decreed by the Father.

The total, lived-out acceptance of the reality of our faith is what Montfort calls "Consecration to the Eternal and Incarnate Wisdom." This loving, free surrender to God's plan renews us in the Spirit so that we may "carry out great things for God and for the salvation of souls" (cf. The True Devotion, 214). His spirituality, founded upon the reality of the redemptive Incarnation and of our insertion into it by Baptism, is eminently apostolic, is essentially missionary. As Wisdom enters into our poverty through Mary's faith, so we must live poverty of spirit as we serve the outcasts of society. And all must be done in the "milieu" of Mary's maternal influence so that we may, like her, be temples of the Holy Spirit and thereby renew the face of the earth.

Living our baptism in the fullest sense of its evangelical meaning,

Montfort concludes that all must be done for God Alone. Everything which opposes God, all the idols of this world are for this vagabond missionary to be destroyed by the omnipotence of our faith in Christ Jesus. "To know Jesus Christ the Eternal and Incarnate Wisdom is to know enough; to know everything and not to know Him, is to know nothing." The missionary's Spirit-filled preaching emphasized the basic opposition between God's Wisdom and the distorted value systems of this world, no matter where they may be found, even if it be within the Christian community itself. He rivets our attention on the precise enemy: making ourselves the center, proudly believing that without God Alone this world can be transformed. No wonder that this vagabond of the Lord begged God for a community of missionaries who would be a "body-guard of hand picked men to protect his House . . ." No wonder that his battle-cry and the one he gave to his religious communities was the simple yet powerful: GOD ALONE!

It is to the glory of this missionary that he is a man of his time, a preacher for the people of his age. It is, of course, in the language and thought patterns of his age, through baroque expressions of the preacher-mystic, of the active-contemplative, that Montfort surfaces what for so many is at best implicit: we are all the evangelical slaves of Jesus in Mary. There are, therefore, expressions and thought-patterns of this saint which must be updated in accord with the on-going experience of the christian community. Verbal fidelity to the teachings of Montfort could lead to a distortion of their true meaning.

The term slave, for example, though definitely scriptural, can in many cultures be so misunderstood that its use would distort Montfort's message. Although it is truly surprising how the saint's Christocentric and ecclesial Mariology dovetails with the thought of the Second Vatican Council and with *Marialis Cultus,* nonetheless, fidelity to the Montfortian charism itself demands that his writings always be read in the light of the present insights and expressions of the Church.

Yet, in conclusion, it must be said that the spirituality of Saint Louis de Montfort – the reform of the Church through a new, lived-out affirmation of our baptism into Christ whereby we willingly and fully accept who we are, the loving slaves of Jesus in Mary – is the Good News itself. Moreover, other aspects of Montfort spirituality which spring from this "baptismal core," especially his charismatic, bold proclamation of the Gospel, his effective love for the poor and oppressed, his joyful trust in Divine Providence, his stress on the Holy Spirit, his practical recognition of Mary's spiritual maternity, a deeply contemplative-active life, all these surely touch a sensitive nerve in today's christians. His life and spirituality appear to be even more relevant today than they have been in the past.

What Father Faber said about Montfort's "True Devotion" can be applied to the entire corpus of his writings: "If I may dare say so, there is a growing feeling of something inspired and supernatural about it as we go on studying it; and with that we cannot help experiencing after repeated readings of it, that its novelty never seems to wear off, nor its fullness to be diminished nor the fresh fragrance and sensible fire of its unction to abate." May this English edition of the Collected Works of Saint Louis de Montfort strengthen us all in the perennial task of the renewal of the Church for which the Father from Montfort so zealously dedicated his life.

J. Patrick Gaffney, s.m.m.
Professor, Theological Studies
Saint Louis University
Saint Louis, Missouri

Foreword

Fr. Gérard Lemire, S.M.M.

For a few hundred years now, the name of Louis Marie de Montfort has been associated in the Church with an important current of spirituality. His doctrine, at once both simple and profound, solidly based on Holy Scripture and sound tradition, has exercised an irresistible attraction on thousands of men and women who have adopted him as their spiritual mentor.

He who was commonly known during his lifetime as "le bon Père de Montfort" (the good Father from Montfort) was an indefatigable preacher of the reign of Jesus through Mary. He put at the service of the mission all the richness of his prolific talent as poet, writer, hymn writer, sculptor and artist. Closely identified with the lot of the poor and outcast, he became one of them. The mystery of suffering, in all its forms, viewed in the light of the Cross, compelled him to discover a treasure of unimaginable value, making him a fervid lover of the Cross. Montfort appears to us as the troubadour of the Blessed Virgin, as one who reveals Mary's primeval role in the plan of salvation. The reading of his works moves us to discover the "secret" which he himself discovered in his research and contemplation of the Eternal Wisdom of God.

In this context, John Paul II acknowledged that: "the reading of the treatise of the True Devotion to the Blessed Virgin was a turning point in my life (at a time when he was secretly studying for the priesthood). Whereas I had initially been afraid lest devotion to Mary might detract from that due to Jesus instead of giving Him his rightful place, I realized, when reading the treatise of Grignion de Montfort, that such was not the case. Our interior relationship with the Mother of God is a result of our association with the mystery of Christ." (André Frossard, "Dialogue avec Jean-Paul II," p. 184-185)

I thank and congratulate those who have translated and edited de Montfort's Collected Works in English. I pray the Lord that this book will encourage many readers to be inspired by the zeal which consumed the soul of St. Louis Marie. The Church and the world have great need of ardent apostles, genuine Marian souls who will spread the love of Jesus Christ, the Eternal and Incarnate Wisdom.

Fr. Gérard Lemire, S.M.M.,

Superior General of the
Company of Mary

Rome, October 7, 1986

Acknowledgments

The publication of this first English edition of the Collected Writings of St. Louis Marie de Montfort, on the 40th anniversary of his canonization, and during the Marian Year, has been truly a work of love and devotion of the Saint's spiritual sons and daughters, both lay and Religious. The title, GOD ALONE, was enthusiastically endorsed by our Religious Superiors not only because they are two words forever recurring in De Montfort's writings, but also because they epitomize the dynamic thrust of his life and writings, of his Trinitarian as well as Christocentric theology and Marian spirituality.

The project of translating all of De Montfort's writings into English originated in the early '70's, when Father Christopher Bennett, S.M.M., of our English Province, came over to America to solicit the help of Father Eugene Moynihan, S.M.M., himself author of an illustrated life of St. Louis de Montfort, here at Montfort Publications. To the original team of translators and collaborators were soon added, Montfort Fathers Joseph Ryan, John Molloy and Joseph Kelly; Brother Julien Rabiller of the Brothers of St. Gabriel; and Sisters Ignatius and Francis of Jesus, both of the Daughters of Wisdom – all from the Montfort Provinces of Great Britain and Ireland.

The enviable task of publishing these collected writings was assigned to us here, at Montfort Publications, in Bay Shore, N.Y. As editor-publisher, my sincere gratitude goes out to those who have worked with me in this sometimes tedious yet always most gratifying undertaking. First of all, to our art director, John Harding, who literally spec'd the book from cover to cover for visual impact and readability; to Father Frank Setzer, S.M.M., for giving up a good portion of his vacation period from the Nicaragua missions to do some of the proof-reading; to Sisters Gertrude Marie O'Brien and Anne Werner of the Daughters of Wisdom of the American Province for the generous gift of their time and literary talent. And last but not least, to our loyal secretary, Miss Therese Thompson, who spent countless hours pouring over the original manuscripts and galley-proofs. To all these must be added the name of the late beloved Clifford J. Laube, Sr., whose poetic rendition of Montfort's poem, THE TRIUMPH OF THE CROSS, appears among the hymns in these pages.

May the dedication and generosity of all these wonderful people (and undoubtedly others not mentioned above) contribute to making St. Louis de Montfort's writings better known and thus broaden his spiritual influence upon the English-speaking world for years to come. May it hasten what he called, the Reign of Jesus through Mary.

Roger Mary Charest, S.M.M.

Illustrations

Chronological Outline of the

Life of Saint Louis Marie

1673	His birth at Montfort-la-Cane
	Baptism in church of Saint-Jean
1675-1685	At Bois-Marquer in Iffendic
1685-1693	Studies at College of St. Thomas à Becket, in Rennes
1693	Trip from Rennes to Paris
1693-1694	Resident at M. de la Barmondière
1694	Resident at M. Boucher
1695-1700	Resident at the "Petit Seminaire" of St. Sulpice
1697	Becomes acquainted with Madam de Montespan
1699	Pilgrimage to Our Lady of Chartres
1700	Ordained to the Priesthood
	Arrives at Nantes
1700-1701	Remains inactive at M. Lévêque's
1701	Trip from Nantes to Fontevrault
	Trip from Fontevrault to Poitiers
	Missions at Grandchamps and surrounding areas
	Trip from Nantes to Poitiers
	Becomes chaplain at General Hospital, there meets Marie-Louise Trichet
1702	Trip to Paris
1703	Ministry at Hospital, Poitiers
	Marie-Louise Trichet receives Religious Habit
	Trip to Paris. Ministry at la Salpêtrière
	Visits with Poullart-des-Places
	At Rue du Pot-de-Fer
	Among the hermits of Mount-Valérien
1704	Returns to Hospital at Poitiers
1705	Final break with Hospital. Missions at Montbernage, Saint-Savin and Calvaire
	Meets Mathurin Rangeard (Brother Mathurin)
1706	Mission at Saint Saturnin
	Pilgrimage to Rome, via Loreto
	Audience with Pope Clement XI
	Returns to Poitiers
	Visits Mount St. Michel
	Stay at Rennes and visit to his home territory
	Missions at Dinan, St. Suliac and Bécherel
1707	Member of M. Leuduger's Mission Band
	Missions in the dioceses of St. Malo and St. Brieuc
	Mission at Montfort-La-Cane

	Mission at Moncontour
	Parts company with M. Leuduger
	Stay at the hermitage of St. Lazare
1708	Missions and Retreats in the area
	Returns to the area of Nantes. Mission at St. Similien
	Mission at Valet
	Missions at: la Renaudière, Landemont, La Chevrolière, Vertou
	Mission at St. Fiacre
1709	Retreat to Penitents (women)
	Mission at Campbon
	Mission at Pontchâteau
	Missions in Grande-Brière region
	Begins construction on Calvary
	Mission at Missillac
1710	Missions at Herbignac, Camoël
	Mission at St. Donatien of Nantes
	Mission at Bouguenais
	Interdict on blessing of Calvary
	Mission at St. Molf. Forbidden to exercise his ministry
	Joins 3rd Order of St. Dominic
1711	Leaves Nantes
	Mission at La Garnache
	Missions at Lhoumeau and La Rochelle
1711-12	Missions in the country places of the diocese of La Rochelle
1712	Mission at the Island of Yeu
	Mission at Sallertaine
	Mission at St. Christophe-du-Ligneron
	Second Mission at La Garnache
	Mission at Thairé-d'Aunis
1712-13	Missions at St. Vivien, Esnandes, Courçon
1713	Missions at Beugnon, Bressuire, Argenton-Chateau
	Mission at La Séguinière
	Trip from La Rochelle to Paris
	Visits Holy Ghost Seminary in Paris
	Mission at Mauzé
	Second Mission at Courçon
1714	Missions in the diocese of Saintes
	Mission at Roussay
	Trip to Nantes
	At Villedieu-les-Poêles, diocese of Avranches
	Mission at St. Lô
	Meeting with Canon Blain at Rouen
	Retreat to Sisters at Ernemont
	Return to Nantes—Trip to Rennes
	Return to La Rochelle
	Missions at Loiré, Le Breuil-Magné, the Island of Aix, St. Laurent-de-la-Prée, Fouras

1715 Meeting with M. Vatel
Mission at Taugon-la-Ronde
Arrival of Marie-Louise Trichet and Catherine Brunet at La Rochelle
Mission at St. Amand-sur-Sèvre
Mission at Mervent and his stay in the grotto
Mission at Fontenay-le-Comte
At the grotto of Mervent
Vocation of M. Mulot
Mission at Vouvant
Mission at St. Pompain

1716 Mission at Villiers-en-Plaine
Pilgrimage to Our Lady of Ardilliers of Saumur by the 33 "Penitents" of St. Pompain
Arrives at St. Laurent-sur-Sevre
Opening of Mission at St. Laurent
Death of Father de Montfort

1838 Declared "Venerable" by Pope Gregory XVI

1869 Pius IX proclaimed his virtues heroic

1888 Beatified by Pope Leo XIII

1947 Canonized by Pope Pius XII

Contents

1 Letters

2 The Love of Eternal Wisdom

3 Letter to the Friends of the Cross

4 The Secret of the Rosary

5 Methods for Saying the Rosary

6 The Secret of Mary

7 True Devotion to the Blessed Virgin

8 Prayer for Missionaries

9 Rule of the Missionary Priests of the Company of Mary

10 Letter to the Members of the Company

11 The Wisdom Cross of Poitiers

12 Original Rule of the Daughters of Wisdom

1 Numbering systems

De Montfort often organized his material by numbering major parts, as well as subdivisions. These divisions he carefully labeled, and the labels plus his numbering system gives an overview of the approach he was taking. At a later date others have added to this, and these additional labels or numbering systems are placed in brackets to show their later origin.
The numbering system of many of De Montfort's books is the work of later scholars and is identified by being set in italics.

2 Abbreviations

used in referring to the works of St. Louis Marie de Montfort

L	Letters
LEW	The Love of Eternal Wisdom
FC	Letter to the Friends of the Cross
SR	The Secret of the Holy Rosary
MR	Methods for Saying the Rosary
SM	The Secret of Mary
TD	True Devotion to the Blessed Virgin
PM	Prayer for Missionaries
RM	Rule of the Missionary Priests of the Company of Mary
LCM	Letter to the Members of the Company of Mary
WC	The Wisdom Cross of Poitiers
RW	Original Rule of the Daughters of Wisdom
MLW	Maxims and Lessons of Divine Wisdom
LPM	Letter to the People of Montbernage
RV	Rule of the Forty-four Virgins
RP	Rule of the White Penitents
PS	Pilgrimage of the Penitents to Our Lady of Saumur
CG	Covenant with God
W	The Last Will of Saint Louis Marie
MP	Morning Prayer
NP	Night Prayer
H	Hymns
RVP	Rules of Voluntary Poverty in the Early Church
MRL	Four Short Meditations on the Religious Life
S	The Book of Sermons
HD	Dispositions for a Happy Death

1 Letters

Introduction

Nothing helps us better to understand an author and his works than his correspondence. It is for this reason that we begin this collection of Montfort's works with his letters.

We do not undertake to make any commentary upon them but confine ourselves simply to prefacing each letter with its historical background and adding, where necessary, a few notes to clarify the text.

Montfort also wrote two lengthy circular letters, one to the people of Montbernage, near Poitiers, and the other to the 'Friends of the Cross'. We do not include them here but place them later on in the volume among his 'missionary' writings.

This collection of letters and fragments of letters is the sum total of all we now possess of his personal correspondence. We can only hazard a guess as to how many letters have been lost. We do not, for example, possess any of the letters he wrote to his personal friend, Fr. Blain, and we know that Mother Marie Louise, the first Daughter of Wisdom, was ordered by her confessor to burn several letters she received from him. Other losses have been pointed out by his biographers. However by all accounts, even if we possessed all his correspondence, we do not think they would fill a book of any appreciable size. Evidently Saint Louis Marie was not a great letter-writer.

The letters and fragments are taken from several sources. There exist only three original manuscripts, which are possessed respectively by the Montfort Fathers, the Daughters of Wisdom, and the Dominican Fathers in Rome. The others are quoted in different biographies of the saint.

God alone

Recipients

Recipients	Letters
Fr. Alain Robert (Louis Marie's uncle)	1 2 3 4
Fr. Leschassier (his confessor)	5 6 8 9 10 11
Guyonne Jeanne (Louise) (his sister)	7 12 17 18 19 24 26
A religious Sister of the Blessed Sacrament	13
A religious Sister	14
Mother Marie Louise of Jesus	15 16 25 27 28 29 34
His mother	20
The parish priest of Bréal	21
Fr. de la Carrière	22
The Master-General of the Dominicans	23
Sister de la Conception	27 29 31
Marie Régnier and Madame Régnier	30
The Community of La Sagesse	32
Mademoiselle Dauvaise	33

Letter 1 [Fragment]

Source Grandet.[1]
To Either the parents of St. Louis Marie or his uncle, Father Alain Robert.[2]
From Paris.
Date Uncertain.

In the autumn of 1693, Louis Marie, at the age of twenty, left Rennes, where his family lived, and took the road to Paris. He was accepted for a year in a seminary for indigent students and directed by Fr. de la Barmondière. It is from there that he wrote the letter of which the following is an extract:[3]

Tell my brother Joseph that I beg him to work hard at his studies and he will be one of the best in his class. Tell him that to achieve this he must seek the help of the Blessed Virgin, who is his good mother. If he continues to show devotion to her she will not fail to supply all his needs. I recommend my sisters to do the same.

Letter 2

Source Besnard.[4]
To Fr. Alain Robert, Louis Marie's uncle.
From Paris.
Date 20th of September, 1694.

Louis Marie was staying at the seminary for students of poor means. Founded in 1686 by Fr. de la Barmondière, a Sulpician, it was closely associated with the seminary of St. Sulpice in spirit, rule and curriculum.

May the perfect love of God reign in our hearts!

It was with great pleasure that I received your letter, coming as it did from one who has great affection for me.

Your letter brought me news of a death and in return I too have to tell you of a death. It is that of Fr. de la Barmondière, my superior and director, who has done so much for me here. He was buried last Sunday, mourned by the whole parish and by everyone who knew him. He lived a saintly life and died a holy death. It was he who founded the seminary here and had the kindness to receive me for nothing. I do not know yet how things will go, whether I shall stay or leave, as his will has not yet been made known. Whatever happens I shall not be worried. I have a Father in heaven who will never fail me. He brought me here, he has kept me here until now and he will continue to treat me with his usual kindness. Although I deserve only punishment for my sins, I never stop praying to him and rely completely on his providence.

I was not able to reply to your letter as soon as I wished because I was making a retreat at St. Sulpice in preparation for the reception of minor orders which, thanks be to God, I have now received.

Letter 3

Source Besnard.
To Fr. Alain Robert.
From Paris.
Date 11th of July, 1695

When Fr. de la Barmondière died, the seminary died with him. The students divided into two groups. Some joined the 'Little' Seminary of St. Sulpice[5] and the others, i.e. the poorest, among whom was Louis Marie, joined a community similar but even poorer than the one he had left. This community was founded by Fr. François Boucher on the grounds of Montaigu college not far from the Sorbonne.

Here the young man began his second year of theology. During his stay he became ill and was taken to the Hôtel-Dieu. After a series of terrible blood-lettings from which no one thought he would recover, he regained his health and then entered the Little Seminary of St. Sulpice. This letter tells of the circumstances surrounding this change.

God alone

11th of July, 1695

My dear uncle,

May the perfect love of God reign in our hearts!

This letter brings you my very best wishes and is to let you know that Providence has placed me in the Little Seminary of St. Sulpice through the kindness of Madame d'Alègre. She is the lady Mademoiselle de Montigny[6] told you about, and Mademoiselle Le Breton lives with her.

This lady has given 160 livres a year for the maintenance of a student for the priesthood. After the death of Fr. de la Barmondière the sum was passed on to the Little Seminary of St. Sulpice where, however, the fee is 260 livres. Madame d'Alègre told Mademoiselle Le Breton and the superior of the Little Seminary that she wanted me to have the place she was helping to provide. Madame d'Alègre heard Mademoiselle Le Breton talking about you and asks you to offer Mass for her at our Lady's altar. I would heartily beg you to do so.

As this money is not enough to cover the fees at the Little Seminary, God in his loving Providence, without my ever having thought of it, has provided me with a benefice of about 100 livres, a few miles from Nantes,[7] from which I will also be provided with a title.

Please in my name thank almighty God for the graces he has given me, not just for the temporal blessings, which are not important, but for the eternal ones. May he not enter into judgement with me, for I do not do justice to his graces; I do nothing but offend him day after day.

Letter 4

Source Grandet.[8]
To Fr. Alain Robert.
From Paris.
Date 6th of March, 1699

Louis Marie was still at the Little Seminary when he wrote this letter. It may have been written as the result of advice given him by his superior, Fr. Brenier, or his director, Fr. Leschassier. It could also have been motivated by his own hostile attitude towards the world and his desire to purify himself of his own selfishness.

Please be kind enough to tell Madame B. that I have received her packet of letters for the Bishop of St. Malo.[9]

I must admit, my dear uncle, that these various errands distress me and make me feel that I am still living in the world. Would to

God that I could be left in peace as the dead are left in their tombs, or the snail in its shell, which, when it is hidden, seems to be something of value, but when it comes out is wretched and disgusting,— which is what I am. Indeed I am worse, for I only spoil things whenever I get involved in them.

So, please, uncle, I beg you to remember me only in your prayers to God. 'Let man not prevail against me; from the unjust and deceitful man deliver me.'[10]

Ever yours in our Lord and in our holy Mother, in time and in eternity.

Letter 5

Source Process of Canonization.[11]
To Fr. Leschassier.
From Nantes.
Date 6th of December, 1700.

Louis Marie was ordained on the 5th of June, 1700. St. Sulpice would have liked him to have stayed on and even expected him to do so, but he had no inclination to stay. He was advised to go to Nantes to a Fr. Lévêque who directed a community of priests destined for parish missions. Louis Marie left for Nantes around September 1700 in the company of Fr. Lévêque who happened to be passing through Paris at that time. This letter was written after he had lived with the community of St. Clément long enough to assess the situation in the house.

To Reverend Fr. Leschassier,
Superior of the Seminary of St. Sulpice,
Paris.

6th of December, 1700

Dear Reverend Father,

May the perfect love of God reign in our hearts!

I cannot tell you how much pleasure your short letter gave me.[12] It shows the bond of charity which unites you and my unworthy self, a bond God has established and wishes to maintain. It is with this in mind that I am writing to tell you briefly about my state of mind at the moment. I have not found here what I had hoped for and what led me to leave such a holy place as St. Sulpice, almost against my better judgement.

My intention was, as yours was too, to prepare for mission-work and especially for teaching catechism to the poor, since this is what attracts me most. But I am not doing that at all and I do not think that I shall ever do it here, for there are very few people in the house and no one has any experience except Fr. Lévêque. He is unable to undertake missions now because of his age and even if his great zeal impelled him to undertake them, Fr. Desjonchères[13] would not allow it as he told me himself. There is not even half the organization and observance here as there was at St. Sulpice and it seems that as things are, there could never be any improvement. It seems to me that there are four types of people here, whose aims and intentions are quite different:—

1. There are five people in the community proper of whom two are incapable of any active work.
2. There are the parish priests, curates, ordinary priests and laymen who come occasionally for retreats.
3. There are a few priests and canons who reside here just for a quiet life.
4. There are some priests and a greater number of young students who go out for theology and philosophy courses—most of them are dressed in lay clothes or without full clerical dress.

All these different people have their own rule which they have made up by taking what suits them from the common rule. I must admit that it is not Fr. Lévêque's fault that the rule is not kept. He does what he can and not what he would like to do, especially with regard to certain members of the community who dislike his simple, saintly ways.

With conditions as they are, I find myself, as time goes on, torn by two apparently contradictory feelings. On one hand, I feel a secret attraction for a hidden life in which I can efface myself and combat my natural tendency to show off. On the other hand, I feel a tremendous urge to make our Lord and his holy Mother loved, to go in a humble and simple way to teach catechism to the poor in country places and to arouse in sinners a devotion to our Blessed Lady. This was the work done by a good priest who died a holy death here recently. He used to go about from parish to parish teaching the people catechism and relying only on what Providence provided for him. I know very well, my dear Father, that I am not worthy to do such honorable work, but when I see the needs of the Church I cannot help pleading continually for a small and poor band of good priests to do this work under the banner and protection of the Blessed Virgin. Though I find it difficult, I try to suppress these desires, good and persistent though they may be. I strive to forget them and self-effacingly place myself in the hands of divine Providence and submit entirely to your advice which will always have the force of law for me.

I still harbor the desire I had in Paris to join Fr. Leuduger, a student of Fr. de St. Brieuc.[14] He is a great missionary and a man of wide experience. Another of my wishes would be to go to Rennes and, with a good priest I know there,[15] work in seclusion at the general hospital, performing charitable services for the poor. But I put aside all these ideas, and always in submission to God's good pleasure I await your advice on whether I should stay here, in spite of having no inclination to do so, or go elsewhere. In the peace of Christ and his holy Mother I am completely at your command.

I take the liberty of asking you to greet Fr. Brenier for me. If you think it useful, I will tell him what I have told you.

Grignion, priest and unworthy slave of Jesus in Mary.

Letter 6

Source Canonization process.
To Fr. Leschassier.
From Poitiers.
Date 4th of May, 1701.

Louis Marie did not find at Nantes the missionary life he was seeking. This letter reveals how providential circumstances led him to the diocese of Poitiers where his missionary vocation was to blossom.

To Reverend Fr. Leschassier,
Superior of the Seminary of St. Sulpice,
Paris.

Poitiers, 4th of May, 1701.

May the perfect love of God reign in our hearts!

His Lordship the Bishop of Poitiers has ordered me to write to you as follows.

On the fourth Sunday in April, I received a letter written at the request of Madame de Montespan,[16] from my sister at Fontevrault, inviting me to be present when she received the Religious habit which was to take place the following Tuesday. I left the same day on foot and arrived at Fontevrault on Wednesday morning, the day after the ceremony.

During the two days I spent at Fontevrault I was privileged to have several private conversations with Madame de Montespan. She asked me about many things, especially about myself. She asked me what I wanted to do. I answered very simply telling her about the attraction you know I feel to work for my brothers, the poor. She told me that she very much approved of my plans, the more so that she knew from her own experience that instruction of the poor on the personal level was much neglected. She was prepared to give me, if I would accept it, a canonry which was under her authority. I thanked her humbly but promptly assured her that I would never exchange divine Providence for a canonry or a benefice. On my refusal, she told me to go and see the Bishop of Poitiers and tell him my plans. Although I had no inclination whatever to satisfy Madame de Montespan's wishes, as much because of the twenty-eight leagues that I should have to travel as for many other reasons, I obeyed her blindly believing this was God's holy will, which was all I wanted.

I arrived at Poitiers the day before the feast of SS. Philip and James and I had to wait four days to see the bishop who was due to return from Niort.

During this time I made a short retreat in a little room where I enclosed myself, in the middle of a large town where I knew nobody. I took it into my head however to go to the poorhouse[17] where I could serve the poor physically even if I could not serve them spiritually. I went into their little church to pray and the four hours I spent there waiting for the evening mealtime seemed all too short. However it seemed so long to some of the poor, who saw me kneeling there dressed in clothes very much like their own, that they went off to tell the others and they all agreed to take up a collection for me. Some gave more, some gave less; the poorer ones a denier, the richer ones a sou. All this went on without my knowing anything about it. Eventually I left the church to ask the time of supper and at the same time to ask permission to serve the poor at table. But I misconceived the situation for I discovered they did not eat together and I was surprised to find out that they wanted to make me an offering and had told the doorkeeper not to let me go away. I blessed God that I had been taken for a poor man wearing the glorious livery of the poor and I thanked my brothers and sisters for their kindness.

Since then, they have become so attached to me that they are going about saying openly that I am to be their priest, that is, their director, for there has not been a regular director in the poorhouse for a considerable time, so abandoned has it become.

Moreover, the poorhouse authorities, in the name of all the inmates, presented a petition to Reverend Father de la Bournat, the Bishop's brother, which impressed both him and the Bishop. So when the Bishop spoke to me again, more cordially this time, he ordered me to write telling you this before I returned to Nantes, so that you can judge what I ought to do. I must tell you, Father, that I do wish most sincerely to work for the spiritual welfare of the poor in general but I am not particularly anxious to settle down and be attached to a poorhouse. However I will remain quite open-minded as I only want to do God's holy will. I am ready to sacrifice my time, my health and my life for the souls of the poor in this neglected house, if you think it the right thing for me to do.

I leave tomorrow, the feast of the Ascension, for Nantes, and trust that I shall never act without your guidance nor ever be without your friendship in Jesus and his holy Mother. In their name I am completely at your disposition.

Grignion, priest and unworthy slave of Jesus in Mary.

P.S. Please allow me to greet Fr. Brenier, Fr. Lefèvre, Fr. Repars[18] and the whole seminary. I have several times been urged to ask your leave to apply for approval for confessions, but I have been most unwilling to do so, because this difficult and dangerous work requires a special calling.

Letter 7

Source Grandet.
To Louis Marie's sister, Guyonne Jeanne (Louise).
From ?
Date 1701.

Guyonne Jeanne was Louis Marie's favorite sister and he always called her 'Louise'. Madame de Montigny had taken eight-year-old Guyonne Jeanne into her care and had arranged for her to be taught to read, write and embroider at a boarding school in Paris. When Madame de Montigny died, Madame de Montespan arranged for her to enter the community of St. Joseph in the Faubourg Saint-Germain. This letter gives the impression that she is a novice and the date indicates that she was twenty or twenty-one years old. It would seem that there was a likelihood of her having to leave the convent and, according to Grandet, one reason among others was that she was not a native of Paris and the convent accepted only Parisians.

My dear sister in Jesus Christ,

May the perfect love of God reign in our hearts!

Even though we are far from each other, we are together in spirit because you are so close to Jesus Christ and his holy Mother, and both you and I are children of divine Providence though I am unworthy to be so called. It would be better to call you a novice of divine Providence because you are just beginning to practise the trust and perfect abandonment which God asks of you. You will be a professed Daughter of Providence only when your abandonment is perfect and your sacrifice complete. God wants you, my dear sister, he wants you to be separated from everything that is not himself, even if it means being deserted by everyone. But be glad and rejoice, you who are the servant and the spouse of Jesus, when you resemble your master and spouse. Jesus is poor; Jesus is abandoned; Jesus is despised and rejected as the refuse of the world. You are indeed happy, Louise Grignion, if you are poor in spirit, abandoned, despised and like refuse cast out from the house of St. Joseph. It is then that you will be truly the servant and spouse of Christ and a truly professed daughter of divine Providence, even if not professed as a religious. What God wants of you, my dear sister, is that you should live each day as it comes, like a bird in the trees, without worrying about tomorrow. Be at peace and trust in divine Providence and the Blessed Virgin, and do not seek anything else but to please God and love him. There is an unshakeable truth, a divine and eternal axiom, as true as the existence of one God (would to God I could engrave it on your mind and heart!): 'Seek first the kingdom of God and his justice and all the rest will be added unto you.' If you fulfil the first part of this declaration, God, who is infinitely faithful, will carry out the second; i.e. if you serve God and his holy Mother faithfully you will want for nothing in this world or the next. You will not even lack a brother-priest for I will always be with you in my sacrifices so that you may more fully belong to Christ in your sacrifice.

I greet your Guardian Angel. 1701

Letter 8

Source Process of canonization.
To Fr. Leschassier.
From Nantes.
Date 5th of July, 1701.

Fr. Leschassier had not yet arrived at a decision concerning Louis Marie's future ministry. Endeavoring to help him Fr. de Montfort wrote informing him of the results of his work in the diocese of Nantes and pointing out the interest Fr. Lévêque and Fr. de Jonchères had shown in his apostolate. But during the interval between this letter and the one he had written on the 4th of May (Letter 6) there was some correspondence between Fr. Leschassier, Msgr. Girard (Bishop of Poitiers) and Fr. de Montfort himself concerning the type of ministry suitable for the young priest.

1 There was the letter of the 6th of May in which the Bishop of Poitiers inquired of Fr. Leschassier if Montfort was suitable for directing a general hospital.

2 There was the reply of the 13th of May from Fr. Leschassier, "I can only tell you what I know of his disposition, leaving to your judgement the decision on the matter."

3 There was a short note from Fr. Leschassier in reply to Montfort's letter of the 4th of May (Letter 6) in which Fr. Leschassier declares that "I am not sufficiently enlightened concerning people whose conduct is out of the ordinary. I am telling you only what I think."

4 There was the (lost) letter of Montfort to Fr. Leschassier of the 11th of June.

5 Finally there was the answer to this letter which Fr. Leschassier begins by saying, "I do not know, Father, how to reply to your letter of the 11th of this month. Like yourself, I await the voice of the divine Pastor to let me know what he is asking of you."

Fr. Leschassier delays his decision. The following letter, written at the request of the Superiors of Nantes brings a few facts to the notice of the director enabling him to come to a definite decision.

5th July 1701

To Reverend Father Leschassier,
Superior of the Seminary of St. Sulpice,
Paris.

Dear Reverend Father,

May the perfect love of God reign in our hearts!

As I must be faithful in telling you everything if you are to arrive at a definite decision, you must know that Fr. (René) Lévêque and Fr. des Jonchères sent me to a very neglected parish in the country. I stayed there for ten days taking the children for catechism twice a day and giving three sermons. God in his goodness and his holy Mother blessed my work.

Because of this work, Fr. des Jonchères and Fr. Lévêque who know of the Poitiers affair[19] told me to write to you and they have offered to give me material help and use their influence[20] to have me sent to the most neglected parishes of the diocese to carry on the work I began so well at Grandchamps (that is the name of the parish) or rather, to carry on the work that divine Providence and the Blessed Virgin began despite my weakness. Dear Father, I find so much wealth in Providence and so much strength in the Blessed Virgin that my poverty is amply enriched and my weakness strengthened. Without these two supports I could do nothing.

Obediently yours in Jesus and Mary,
Grignion, priest and unworthy slave of Jesus in Mary.

Letter 9

Source Canonization process.
To Fr. Leschassier.
From Le Pellerin.
Date 16th of September, 1701.

Louis Marie is confronted with choice of work either in Poitiers or Nantes. He makes known to his director his uncertainty as to which to choose.

God alone

16th of September, 1701

To Reverend Father Leschassier,
Superior of the Seminary of St. Sulpice,
Paris.

Reverend and dear Father in Jesus Christ,

May the perfect love of God reign in our hearts!

The pressing and the repeated requests of the inmates of the poorhouse in Poitiers and the wishes of the Bishop of Poitiers and of Madame de Montespan,[21] upon whom my sisters depend so much, oblige me to trouble you again and express my feelings to you in all simplicity and without any prejudice, as I wish to remain completely impartial to everything except what obedience requires of me.

I have been working without a break for the last three months in the parishes to which Fr. Lévêque and Fr. des Jonchères sent me. At the moment I am writing to you from the parish of Le Pellerin. God and his holy Mother have condescended to use my ministry to do some good. There is a lot to be done here, as indeed there is everywhere, but there are also plenty of workers, besides two retreat houses, one for men and one for women, and three, if not four, missionary societies.

As you know, I have not the slightest inclination to stay in the Saint Clément community. Only obedience keeps me here. Fr. (René) Lévêque, who knows this very well for after you I follow his guidance in all I do, has pointed out to me that since God in his goodness has not called me to be a permanent member of a community which works for priests,[22] I should look for a little place to which I can retire from time to time after the short missions which are assigned to me by obedience. He said at the time that he would willingly give me a small room, but I doubt whether this comes from the heart.

Meanwhile the Bishop, like the poor of Poitiers, has written to ask me to work in his poorhouse. But I have no inclination at all to lead an enclosed life.

The diocese of Poitiers needs workers much more than this one does. I have seen this for myself and it has surprised me. But I am not being asked to help in general ministry but only to do a specific work. The only thing that would make me want to go to the poorhouse at all would be the hope of being able to extend my work later into the town and the countryside and so be able to help more people. When I am teaching catechism to the poor in town and country, I am in my element.

Since I have been here, divine Providence has used me to find a place for another of my poor sisters[23] and has established spiritual ties between me and several other persons who are sinners like myself,[24] as well as with a number of devout souls.[25] This then is the state of my affairs but I consider blind obedience to your wishes as my greatest duty and my greatest desire.

May I assure you, dear Father in Jesus Christ, that I am completely at your command, and entirely yours.

Grignion, priest and unworthy slave of Jesus in Mary.

Letter 10

Source Canonization process.
To Fr. Leschassier.
From Poitiers.
Date 3rd of November, 1701.

Fr. Leschassier answered the preceding letter (Letter 9). He told Fr. de Montfort that since Fr. Lévêque was willing to release him, and the Bishop of Poitiers had petitioned for him, and Madame de Montespan was in favor of his going to work for the poor in Poitiers, that he, Fr. Leschassier, could see no objection to Louis Marie's going to the Poitiers poorhouse. This was the decision Louis Marie was waiting for. The news was a shock to Fr. Lévêque who complained to Fr. Leschassier but to no avail.

Montfort continued reporting to Fr. Leschassier, seeking counsel from him.

Poitiers, 3rd of November, 1701.

To Reverend Father Leschassier,
Superior of the Seminary of St. Sulpice,
Paris.

Reverend and dear Father in Jesus Christ,

May the perfect love of God reign in our hearts!

I am in the junior seminary at Poitiers where the Bishop has found me a place while waiting for the poorhouse authorities to receive me. For almost a fortnight I have been teaching catechism to the beggars of the town with the approval and help of the Bishop. I visit the inmates of the prisons and the sick in the hospitals preaching to them as well as sharing with them the alms I receive.

The poorhouse for which I am destined is a house of discord where there is no peace whatever. It is also a house of privations, lacking temporal and spiritual goods. But I trust that our Lord, through the intercession of my good Mother Mary, will turn it into a holy place, one that will become rich and peaceful. So you see I am in great need of your help.

The matrons of the poorhouse want me to have my meals with them as some of my predecessors did. But I won't hear of it. Am I doing the right thing?

I explained to the Bishop that even in the poorhouse I do not wish to be separated from my mother, divine Providence, and with this in mind I am happy to share the meals of the poor and to have no fixed salary. The Bishop agreed heartily to this and offered to act as a father to me. Have I done the right thing?

I am continuing here several things I did at Nantes. I am sleeping on straw;[26] I do not have any lunch and I do not eat much in the evening. I am keeping very well. Am I doing the right thing? May I take an extra discipline once a week besides the usual three times, or alternatively, may I wear a horsehair belt once or twice?

I take the liberty of greeting Fr. Brenier and humbly thank him. Only God knows all the good he has done for me,[27] and all you have done for me too. I am always your obedient servant in Jesus and Mary.

Grignion, priest and unworthy servant of Jesus in Mary.
I greet your Guardian Angel.

Letter 11

Source Archives of the Dutch Province of the Montfort Fathers.
To Fr. Leschassier.
From Poitiers.
Date 4th of July, 1702.

Fr. de Montfort had written to Fr. Leschassier from Poitiers in November 1701 (Letter 10) asking for guidance in his work at the poorhouse. Fr. Leschassier had replied that he found it difficult to give adequate advice partly because Louis Marie was not like others, which made it difficult to vouch for all he was doing, and partly because, being so far away, it was impossible for him to assess the situations in which Fr. de Montfort found himself. He suggested that Louis Marie should find a good director in the area where he lived, which should not be a problem in a large town. For several months afterwards Louis Marie did not correspond with this priest who had been his director since seminary days. He now takes up his pen to write not so much to an advisor but to one whom he esteems and loves and refers to as a 'father.'

General Hospital, Poitiers, 4th of July, 1702

To Fr. Leschassier,
Superior of the Seminary of St. Sulpice,
Paris.

Letters

Dear Reverend Father in Jesus Christ,

May the pure love of God reign in our hearts!

If I have not written to you for such a long time,[28] it is not because I have forgotten how good you have always been to me nor is it through lack of obedience to the advice I am given here by the priest who takes your place as my spiritual director.[29] The reason is that I was afraid of troubling you, dear Father. I now want to let you know about some of the difficulties and disagreements which are a daily occurrence since I arrived here. Here is a short but truthful account of my conduct and actions. Fr. Lévêque, who is a spiritual father to me, second only to yourself, had given me some extra money to cover the expenses of my journey to Poitiers. This I gave away to the poor before I left Saumur where I stayed to make a novena, and consequently I arrived at Poitiers without a penny. The late bishop[30] gave me a hearty welcome and arranged board and lodging for me in the seminary until he could get me admitted into the poorhouse. In the meantime, for about two months, I gave instructions to the beggars that I encountered in the town and lived entirely at his Lordship's expense. First, I taught them in the church of St. Nicholas and then, as their numbers increased, I gathered them every day in the market hall and heard the confessions of many of them in the church of Saint Porchaire.

The bishop, unable to resist the insistent appeals of the poor any longer, allowed me to go to them shortly after All Saints Day. I entered this poorhouse, or rather this poor Babylon, quite determined to bear in union with Jesus Christ my Savior the cross that would not fail to fall to me if this work was really God's work. All that I had been told by a number of experienced priests of the town to dissuade me from going to this ill-regulated house only increased my determination to undertake this work despite my own inclinations which have always been and still are for mission work.

When I got there, all those connected with the house from the director down to the most humble worker and the entire town rejoiced and looked upon me as a man sent by God to put an end to the prevailing abuses. The directors with whom I was working, not indeed as an equal but as an inferior, gave me full liberty in the drawing up and the observance of the rules[31] I wanted to introduce. Even the Bishop and the committee allowed me to serve the poor in the refectory and to go round the town begging for something extra for them[32] to eat with the dry bread they were usually given. I did this for three months, enduring opposition and snubs, which went on increasing day after day to such an extent that ultimately through the disapproval of a certain gentleman and the matron of the workhouse I was obliged to give up providing food for the dining-room of the poor. In giving this up, I acted in obedience to my director (the one replacing you) although the re-organization of the dining-room had been a great help to the administrators of the establishment. This particular gentleman, embittered against me without any legitimate reason as far as I know, used to snub me and insult me in the house and discredit my behavior in the eyes of the administration and even of the townsfolk. His actions drew upon him the resentment of the poor, who all loved me with the exception of a few perverted ones who backed him against me. During this painful period, I kept silent and lived in retirement putting my cause into the hands of God and relying on his help, in spite of opposite advice given to me. To this end I went for a week's retreat to the Jesuits, confident that our Lord and his holy Mother would take my cause in hand. I was not wrong in my expectation: when I came back I found this gentleman ill and he died a few days later.[33] The matron, a young and sturdy person, also died a short time afterwards. More than eighty of the poor inmates fell ill and some of them died, and the whole town began to say that there was a plague in the poorhouse and that the place was cursed. Through all this period of sickness, and in spite of my involvement with the dying, I was the only one not to be affected with the disease.

Since the death of these two people I have still been subjected to cruel persecution. One of the poor inmates, haughty and full of arrogance, placed himself at the head of a few perverted characters and set himself up in opposition to me, pleading his case with the administrators against me, condemning my behavior because I spoke my mind openly but always kindly to them, concerning their drunkenness and quarrelling and the scandal they were giving.

Though I do not receive anything for my sustenance, not even a piece of bread, being fed by the charity of strangers, scarcely any one among the administrators takes the trouble to correct the vices and disorders in the place. Most of the administrators think of nothing except providing for the temporal state of the house and are quite unconcerned about the spiritual welfare of the inmates.

Yet, to tell the truth, in spite of all these difficulties that I am briefly outlining to you, God has deigned to work wonderful conversions through me both inside and outside the house. Times set for rising and retiring, for prayer together, for Rosary in common, for eating together, for singing hymns, even for mental prayer for those wanting it: all these still subsist in spite of opposition. Since I arrived here it has been like preaching a mission every day. From morning till night I am hearing confessions and giving advice to a constant stream of people. Almighty God, my Father, whom I am serving in spite of my great unworthiness, has enlightened me to a degree I have never experienced before. He has given me the gift of making myself clear, a facility for speaking without preparation, a good health and a great capacity for sympathizing with everyone. This is why I am so highly praised by nearly everyone in the town, which, incidentally, can be a very great danger for my own salvation. I do not allow any woman to enter my room, not even the lady administrators of the poorhouse.

I nearly forgot to tell you that I give a talk to 13 or 14 schoolboys every week for an hour. These boys are the élite of their college.[34] The late bishop approved of this.

In the poorhouse there is a quick-witted girl who is the craftiest and proudest girl I have ever met. She it is who has caused all the trouble. I am afraid that Msgr. de la Poype,[35] like his predecessor, has been greatly deceived by her, because he was too credulous. If you judged it proper you could warn him about this.

Dear Father, I beg you to honor me with a letter. I remain always submissive to you. If I am deprived of your advice, it is only by force of circumstances.

I remain,

Yours very obediently,
L. Grignion, priest and
unworthy slave of Jesus in Mary.

P.S. I greet Fr. Brenier and thank him. I greet Frs. Repars, Lefèvre and everyone in the seminary, especially Fr. Lévêque for whom I have the same sentiments as I have for you.[36]

Letter 12

Source Grandet.
To Guyonne Jeanne (Montfort's sister 'Louise').
From Poitiers.
Date Autumn 1702.

The precarious situation of Guyonne Jeanne (cf. Letter 7) had worsened and was ultimately settled by her departure from the community of St. Joseph during the summer of 1702. She then found herself left entirely to her own devices. Her brother, moved by her plight, left for Paris where his attempts to find her a place were frustrated. In a farewell visit to the Benedictines of the Blessed Sacrament he found unexpectedly a solution to his sister's difficulties. A person of high rank provided a dowry and Louise was accepted as a choir nun into the congregation of the Benedictines of the Blessed Sacrament. She left at once for the novitiate in Lorraine and from there she wrote to her brother thanking him and telling him how happy she was. The following letter is Louis Marie's reply.

My dear sister in Jesus Christ,

God alone

May the perfect love of God reign in our hearts!

Permit my heart to join yours in a flood of joy and my eyes to shed tears of gratitude and my hands to describe on paper the happiness which transports me.

My last visit to Paris was not fruitless and the crosses and rejection you suffered in the past were not in vain for the Lord has been merciful to you. You prayed to him and he has heard you. You are now immolated, truly, deeply and for ever. Let no day pass without offering yourself in sacrifice as a victim.[37] Spend more time before the altar praying than in resting and eating, and be brave, my dear.[38]

Continue asking pardon of God and of Jesus, the eternal High Priest, for the offences I have committed against his divine majesty in the Blessed Sacrament.

I greet your Guardian Angel who is the only one who has stood by you all the way. I am as entirely yours as there are letters in the words I write provided you are just as often sacrificed and crucified with Jesus Christ, your only love, and with Mary, our good Mother.

De Montfort,[39] priest and slave of Jesus in Mary.

Letter 13

Source Grandet.
To A religious of the Blessed Sacrament.
From Poitiers.
Date Autumn 1702?[40]

After Louis Marie's visit to the monastery of the Benedictines of the Blessed Sacrament, the community were favorably impressed by him and several sisters are believed to have written to him.

The following is the only letter of Louis Marie that we possess in answer to these letters. We place it here as a sequel to that of Guyonne Jeanne who henceforth belonged to this Congregation.

A fragment of another letter was placed by Grandet after the one we reproduce. It treats of the same subject and is addressed also to one of the sisters without naming her.

What an inspiring letter! It speaks only of happenings marked with the cross. Whatever human nature and reason may say, without the cross there will never be any real happiness nor any lasting good here below until judgement day.

You are having to bear a large, weighty cross. But what a great happiness for you! Have confidence. For if God, who is all goodness, continues to make you suffer he will not test you more than you can bear. The cross is a sure sign that he loves you. I can assure you of this, that the greatest proof that we are loved by God is when we are despised by the world and burdened with crosses, i.e., when we are made to endure the privation of things we could rightly claim; when our holiest wishes meet with opposition; when we are afflicted with distressing and hurtful insults; when we are subjected to persecution, to having our actions misinterpreted by good people and by those who are our best friends; and when we suffer illnesses which are particularly repugnant, etc.

But why should I tell you things which you know better than I, for you understand and experience all of them.

If Christians only knew the value of the cross, they would walk a hundred miles to obtain it, because enclosed in the beloved cross is true wisdom and that is what I am looking for night and day more eagerly than ever.

O good Cross, come to us for God's greater glory! This is my frequent prayer dictated by my heart in spite of my weakness and my many infidelities. After Jesus, our only love, I place my whole trust in the cross.

Please tell N.[41] that I adore Christ crucified in her, and I pray God that she will think of herself only to offer herself for more painful sacrifices.

Letter 14

Source Grandet.
To A religious.
From Uncertain.
Date Unknown. Cf. Previous letter.

What can I say to you, my dear mother, in reply to your letter except to repeat what the Holy Spirit tells you every day. Love to be humbled and being given scant respect, love the hidden life, love silence, be the silent one who offers Jesus in the Blessed Sacrament, love divine Wisdom, love the Cross. I am opposed and restricted in everything I do. Thank God in my name for the crosses he has given me and which he keeps within limits to suit my weakness, etc.

Letter 15

Source Pauvert.[42]
To Mademoiselle Louise Trichet.[43]
From Paris.
Date End of April—beginning of May 1703?

Around Easter 1703, Fr. de Montfort, encountering so much opposition to his work in the poorhouse, suddenly left Poitiers for Paris. There he hoped to find some support and also the means to further his desire to found a missionary congregation. We possess two letters sent by him while on this Paris visit. They are in response to two letters sent to him by Mademoiselle Trichet.

My dear daughter in our Lord Jesus Christ,

May the perfect love of God reign in our hearts with divine Wisdom.

I know from what I am experiencing more than from your letter that you are continuing to pray to Jesus, your spouse, for this wretched sinner. I can only show my thanks by praying for you in return, especially when I hold the Holy of holies in my unworthy hands each day at the altar. Keep on praying, even increase your prayers for me; ask for extreme poverty, the weightiest cross, abjection and humiliations. I accept them all if only you will beg God to remain with me and not leave me for a moment because I am so weak. What wealth, what glory, what happiness would be mine if from all this I obtained divine Wisdom, which I long for day and night!

I will never cease asking for this boundless treasure and I firmly believe that I shall obtain it even were angels, men and demons to deny it to me. I believe strongly in the efficacy of your prayers, in the loving kindness of our God, in the protection of the Blessed Virgin, our good Mother; I believe too that the needs of the poor are too urgent and the promises of God too explicit for me to be making a mistake in seeking Wisdom. For even if the possession of divine Wisdom were impossible, according to the ordinary workings of divine grace, which is not the case, it would become possible because of the insistence with which we ask for it. Is it not an unchangeable truth that everything is possible to him who believes?

Another thing that makes me say that I shall possess Wisdom is the fact that I have encountered and still encounter so much persecution night and day.

So, my dear daughter, I ask you to enlist some good souls among your friends into a campaign of prayer especially from now until Pentecost, and to pray together for an hour on Mondays from one to two o'clock. I will be praying at the same time. Write and send me their names.

I am at the General Hospital[44] where there are five thousand poor people. I have to make them live for God and I have to die to myself. Do not think that I have become indifferent or grown cold towards the poor of Poitiers, for my Master led me there in spite of myself. He has his plan in all this and I adore his plan, though I do not understand it. Do not think either that material plans or any particular person keep me here; no, my only friend here is God. Those friends I once had in Paris have deserted me.[45]

I have not counted on the goods that were to come to me from Madame de Saint André, nor shall I count on them. I do not even know whether she is in Paris, nor where she lives. I am as happy to die to myself here as I am happy to die in the minds of some people in Poitiers, as long as I find God alone there. I repeat, God alone.

I firmly believe that you will be a religious. Trust and pray.

Letter 16

Source Pauvert.
To Mademoiselle Louise Trichet.
From Paris.
Date 24th of October, 1703?

After four or five months of devoted work at La Salpêtrière, Louis Marie found a note at his place at table asking him to leave. He went to live in a hovel under a staircase in the rue du Pot-de-fer. It would appear that it was from here that he wrote the following letter to Marie Louise.

My dear daughter,

May the perfect love of God reign in our hearts!

Please do not think that the distance between us and my apparent silence mean that I have forgotten your charity towards me and the charity I owe you. Your letter tells me that your wishes[46] are just as strong and eager and as persistent as ever. This is a sure sign that they are from God. So you must put your trust in God. Be sure of this, that you will obtain from him even more than you think.[47] Heaven and earth would pass away before God would break his promises and allow anyone who hoped in him to be frustrated in their hopes.

I feel that you are still asking God that by crosses, humiliations and poverty I may acquire divine Wisdom. Be brave, my dear daughter, be brave. I am grateful to you; I feel the effects of your prayers for I am infinitely more impoverished, crucified and humiliated than ever. Both men and demons in this great city of Paris are waging against me a war that I find sweet and welcome. Let them slander me, scoff at me, destroy my good name, put me into prison;[48] these are precious gifts, tasty morsels, great and wonderful things. They form the accoutrements and retinue of divine Wisdom which he brings into the lives of those in whom he dwells. When shall I possess this lovable and mysterious Wisdom? When will Wisdom come to live in me? When shall I be sufficiently equipped to serve as a place of rest for Wisdom in a world where he is rejected and without a home.

Who will give me this bread of understanding with which Wisdom nourishes great souls? Who will give to drink of the chalice from which Wisdom quenches the thirst of those who serve him? When shall I be crucified and lost to the world?

My dear child in Jesus Christ, do not fail to reply to my requests and fulfil my wishes. You can do it, yes, you can do it, along with some of your chosen friends. Nothing can resist your prayers. Even God himself, great though he be, cannot resist. Fortunately for us, he has shown that he can be moved by a lively faith and a firm hope. So pray, entreat God, plead for me to obtain divine Wisdom. You will obtain it completely for me; of this I am quite convinced.

Letter 17

Source Grandet.
To Sister Catherine of St. Bernard (Guyonne Jeanne).[49]
From Paris.
Date 1703.[50]

Guyonne Jeanne, Montfort's sister, after entering the novitiate of the Benedictines of the Blessed Sacrament at Rambervilliers, fell ill and her brother, hearing about it, wrote the following letter to her.

My dear sister,

May the perfect love of God reign in our hearts!

I am delighted to hear about the illness which God has sent you to purify you like gold in a furnace. You are to become a victim, offered on the altar of the King of kings for his eternal glory.

What a sublime destiny! What a noble calling! I almost envy you your good fortune.

Now how can this victim be entirely acceptable if it is not completely free from every stain, even the smallest? The most Holy One sees stains where creatures only see beauty. His mercy forestalls his justice for he purifies us by sickness which acts as a furnace in which he purifies his chosen ones. You are indeed blessed if God decides to purify you himself, preparing his victim as he himself wishes. Think of the many he leaves to themselves or to others to be cleansed. Think of the many who are accepted as victims without passing through God's trials and his purifying siftings. Be brave then and take courage. Don't be afraid of the devil who will often tell you while you are ill that you will never be professed because of your indisposition, that you will have to leave the monastery and go back to your parents, that you will be left without a home and you will be a burden to everyone. Let your body suffer but let your heart be firm, for nothing is better for you at the moment than sickness. Pray that I may receive divine Wisdom and get others to pray.

I am all yours in Jesus and Mary. Your brother etc.

Letter 18

Source Grandet.
To Sister Catherine of St. Bernard (Guyonne Jeanne).
From Paris.[51]
Date Mid-March 1704.

Guyonne Jeanne is approaching the end of her novitiate and seems to have expressed some apprehension about the outcome. This is her brother's reply.

My very dear sister in Jesus Christ,

May the pure love of God reign in our hearts!

I thank God every day for the mercy he shows you. Try to respond to him by accepting faithfully what he asks of you. If God does not open the door of the convent for you, then you must not go in, for even if you were given a golden key made especially to open the door, it would become for you the door of hell.

To be a Daughter of the Blessed Sacrament is a special vocation for her ideals are very high. The true Sister of the Blessed Sacrament is a real victim, body and soul. Continual and total self-sacrifice is her food; her body is sacrificed by fasting and watching before the Blessed Sacrament and her soul by obedience and self-abandonment. In a word, she dies daily as she lives this life, but by dying she acquires true life. Do all you are asked to do in this house.

All yours. De Montfort.[52]

Letter 19

Source Grandet.[53]
To Catherine of St. Bernard (Guyonne Jeanne).
From Paris.
Date Around mid-March 1704.[54]

Grandet gives us the circumstances of this letter. Sister Catherine of St. Bernard, having recovered from her illness, made profession with two other sisters on the 2nd of February, 1704 in the convent of Rambervilliers. St. Louis Marie wrote this letter to her after the profession.

God alone

Dear Victim in Jesus Christ,

May the pure love of God reign in our hearts!

I cannot thank God enough for the grace he has given you in making you a perfect victim of Jesus Christ, an adorer of the Blessed Sacrament and one who is called to atone for so many bad Christians and unfaithful priests.

What an honor it is for your body to be spiritually sacrificed in the hour of your adoration before the Blessed Sacrament! What a privilege for your soul to do here below what the angels and saints are doing in heaven so sweetly and gloriously although you have not their understanding nor their light of glory but only the feeble light of faith. Faithful adorers give so much glory to God here on earth but they are so few, for even the very spiritual want to taste and see, otherwise they lose interest and slacken off. But 'faith alone suffices'.

But you, faithful child of the Blessed Sacrament, what profit, what wealth, what pleasure is yours kneeling at the feet of this generous and inestimable Lord of lords! Be brave, take courage, enrich yourself and rejoice as you burn yourself out each day like a lamp. The more you give yourself, the more God will give of himself to you. Now that I have congratulated you, don't you think I ought to congratulate myself too—if not because I am your brother, then at least because I am your priest? It is a source of happiness and a great honor for me to have someone so near to me offering loving sacrifices to make up for the faults I have, alas, so often committed against Jesus in the Blessed Sacrament, by half-hearted communions and the times I have forgotten him or neglected him. You and all the good mothers are a source of great rejoicing for me because you have obtained graces for me and for so many other unworthy priests who through their lack of faith have become unworthy to approach the altar.

I am leaving at once for the poorhouse at Poitiers. I beg you, my dear sister, love Jesus in Mary and love God in Jesus through Mary.

Always yours.

Letter 20

Source Grandet.[55]
To Louis Marie's mother.
From Poitiers.
Date 28th of August, 1704.

In August, 1704, St. Louis Marie de Montfort was at Poitiers most probably as chaplain and director of the poorhouse. This letter has to be read in the light of the gospel of St. Matthew (12:46-50) and other gospel texts. Montfort always applied the gospel literally to himself.

You must prepare for death which is closing in upon you through all your trials. Continue to accept them in a Christian spirit, as you are doing. You must suffer and bear your cross every day —this is essential. If it is God's will for you to become so poor that you have to enter the poorhouse, it will be for your greater good to be so despised and to be cast aside by everyone and so to die while still living in the body.

Although I do not write to you, I never forget you in my prayers and sacrifices. I love you and I honor you all the more as flesh and blood have no part in it.

Please do not burden me with my brothers' and sisters' affairs.[56] I have done all God asked me to do for them in a spirit of love. For the moment, I have no worldly goods to give them for I am poorer than all of them. I place them and all the family into the hands of him who created them. Let them think of me as dead. Again I say it, so that they will remember, —let them think of me as dead. I want to receive nothing at all from the family into which God caused me to be born. I give up my right to everything except my patrimony which the Church does not allow me to renounce. My property, home, father and mother are up above. I no longer regard anyone on earth as my kinsfolk.

I know that I owe you and my father a great debt of gratitude for bringing me into the world, for looking after me, bringing me up in the fear of God, and for all the other good things you have done for me. For these I thank you over and over again and pray every day for your salvation and I will go on doing so all during your life and after your death.[57] But I will do nothing else for you and that applies to the rest of the family.

In my new family—the one I belong to now—I have chosen to be wedded to Wisdom and the Cross for in these I find every good, both earthly and heavenly. So precious are these possessions that, if they were but known, Montfort would be the envy of the richest and most powerful kings on earth.

No one knows the secrets I am talking about, or at least very few people do. You will understand them in eternity if you have the happiness to be saved. It could happen that you will not, so fear and love God all the more.

Please tell my father, on behalf of my heavenly Father, not to touch pitch or else he will be defiled; tell him not to indulge in earthly pleasures, for they will suffocate him; and not to be engrossed in worldly affairs, for he will be choked by them. Flee the world and hold it in contempt; love the Blessed Virgin with whom I am all in all to you and my father.

I greet your Guardian Angel and I am all yours in Jesus and Mary.

Montfort, priest and unworthy slave of Jesus living in Mary.

Letter 21

Source Besnard.[58]
To The parish priest of Bréal.[59]
From Saint-Lazare.[60]
Date 17th of February, 1708.

Fr. de Montfort had preached a mission at Bréal in the diocese of Saint Malo around the feast of All Saints, 1707. The parish priest, who was a friend of Louis Marie, was very pleased with the mission and wrote to ask him to return at Shrovetide, 1708. Fr. de Montfort was unable to comply and this was his reply.

My dear Father and friend,

I am very sorry that I cannot do what both you and I would desire. I am already booked for three different places on each of these three days and I must keep to my commitments. However, I will send Mathurin[61] to you on Tuesday to say the Rosary in public and sing hymns and he will bring sixty little crosses of St. Michael for our soldiers.[62] I trust you will have the kindness to distribute them after you have told them on Sunday to meet on Tuesday. This may help a great deal to restrain them from the excesses so frequent during these days. Please remember me to them on Sunday[63] and tell them that I earnestly beg them to be faithful to their rule of life, especially next Monday. Tell them I shall come and see them on one of the Sundays of Lent.

Yours devotedly in Jesus and Mary,

L. Marie de Montfort, priest.

Letter 22

Source Archives of the Daughters of Wisdom, Saint-Laurent-sur-Sèvre.
To Father de la Carrière.[64]
From Nantes.
Date 29th of January, 1711.

In September, 1710, Montfort received an order from Paris requiring him to demolish the monumental calvary he had erected on a wasteland near Pontchâteau, in the diocese of Nantes. He had erected several statues at the foot of an immense crucifix. When they were taken away they were placed in a house confided to the care of Father de la Carrière. These are the statues referred to in this letter.

Dear Reverend Father,

May the perfect love of God reign in our hearts!

Please be kind enough to deliver my statues to the bearer of this letter and to Brother Nicholas.[65] It is necessary to move them, both to relieve me of anxiety[66] and to show obedience[67] because it is God's will. If God did not want them to be moved, he would work a miracle to prevent it. Even when they are brought here, it will only be to await the time when they can be returned to the Calvary with even greater solemnity when the chapel is built.[68] Letters have been sent to Paris about their return and I am more hopeful than ever. But ahead of us there lies still a great deal of work and patient waiting,[69] and much prayer and crosses, for this is destined to be a great work.

With heartfelt regards to you and our good friend,
I remain yours in Jesus and Mary,

L. M. de Montfort, priest.

Letter 23

Source General archives of the Dominican Fathers in Rome.
To The Master-General of the Dominicans.
From Sallertaine?
Date May ? 1712.

The original manuscript of this letter is preserved in the archives of the Dominican Fathers in Rome. It was addressed to the Master-General of the Dominican Order and was probably sent from Sallertaine where Montfort began a mission on the 5th of May, 1712. A letter of recommendation from the French provincial of the Dominicans accompanied Montfort's letter. Montfort had been received as a member of the Third Order of St. Dominic on the 10th of November, 1710 in the monastery of the Dominican Fathers at Nantes.

To the Very Reverend Father General of the Dominican Order,
Minerva,
Rome.

Very Reverend Father,

May the perfect love of God reign in our hearts!

God alone

May I, as the least of your children, ask you for a written permission to preach the Holy Rosary wherever the Lord calls me and to enrol into the Rosary confraternity, with the usual indulgences, as many people as I can. I have already been doing this with the permission of the local Priors and Provincials, inscribing the names of brothers and sisters in the confraternity registers of the places where I have preached missions.

With deepest respect, this is my request.

Your most humble and obedient servant,

Louis Marie de Montfort Grignion,
priest and Apostolic Missionary.[70]

Letter 24

Source Grandet.
To Sister Catherine of St. Bernard (Guyonne Jeanne).
From The Hermitage of Saint Eloi at La Rochelle.
Date 1st of January, 1713.

This letter was sent from the Hermitage of Saint Eloi, near La Rochelle where Montfort retired for a while after the mission of Esnande. He sent it to Guyonne Jeanne, his sister, who had entered the Benedictines at Rambervilliers, in October, 1702. Very little of his correspondence with her has been preserved, just four letters written between 1702 and 1704 and two during 1713.

God takes pleasure in seeing us both struggle and in making us both victorious, you in secret and I in public. Your struggles take place within you and are not seen outside your community, whereas mine ring out through the whole of France, as I fight against the demons of hell or make war on the world and the worldly, the enemies of truth. You would be surprised if you knew all the details of the precious cross which has been sent to me from heaven at the intercession of our good Mother. Please thank my good Lord Jesus and ask your dear community, to whom I send my greetings, to obtain from Jesus the grace for me to carry the roughest and heaviest crosses as I would the light-as-straw ones and to resist with unyielding courage the powers of hell.

Letter 25

Source Besnard.
To Marie Louise of Jesus.
From Paris.
Date July-August, 1713.

After receiving the habit Louise Trichet bore the name of Ma-

rie Louise of Jesus, although she was not yet a religious. Several times she tried to enter religious congregations. One of them was the Sisters of Charity of St. Vincent de Paul, but the Bishop of Poitiers restrained her. Her confessor, Father Carcault, offered to help her enter the Daughters of Calvary but only on condition she wrote to Fr. de Montfort first. In his response, Montfort shows a coolness to Louise's fervent desires.

My daughter,

Providence has recently found a place for a poor girl by providing a dowry for her. His time has not yet come for you. Wait patiently for his time and stay at the hospital.

Letter 26

Source Grandet.
To Sister Catherine of St. Bernard (Guyonne Jeanne).
From Paris.
Date 15th of August, 1713.

In 1703 Montfort had invited Fr. Claude Poullart des Places, who shortly afterwards founded the Congregation of the Missionaries of the Holy Ghost, to join him and work together for the salvation of souls through missionary apostolate. Their dialogue resulted in a promise given by Fr. des Places that if he succeeded in founding a seminary for poor students, Montfort could count on his preparing missionaries for both of them. Fr. des Places died in 1709 and Montfort interrupted his work in the diocese of La Rochelle to go to Paris and seek a continuation of the agreement with the successor of Fr. des Places. It was during this Paris visit that Montfort wrote the following letter to his sister.

May Jesus and his Cross reign for ever!

If only you knew the half of the crosses and humiliations[71] I have to bear, I don't think you would be so eager to see me; for I never seem to go anywhere without bringing something of the Cross to my dearest friends without any fault of mine or theirs. Those who befriend me or support me suffer for doing so, and sometimes draw down upon themselves the wrath of the devil I am fighting against, as well as the world I am protesting against and the flesh I am chastising. This veritable ants' nest of sinners against whom my preaching is directed cannot leave me or my friends in peace. I have forever to be on the alert, treading warily as though on thorns or sharp stones. I am like a ball in a game of tennis; no sooner am I hurled to one side than I am sent back to the other, and the players strike me hard. This is the fate of the poor sinner that I am and I have been like this without rest or respite all the thirteen years since leaving St. Sulpice.

However, my dear sister, thank God for me for I am content and happy in all my troubles. I think there is nothing in the whole world so welcome as the most bitter cross, when it is steeped in the blood of Christ crucified and in the milk of his holy Mother. Besides this inward happiness, there is the great merit of carrying the crosses. I wish you could see mine. I have never had more conversions than after the most painful and unjust prohibitions.[72] Be brave, my dear sister, all three of us must carry our cross to the extreme limits of the kingdom. Carry yours well and I will carry mine well too, with the help of God. Let us not complain or put the burden aside or make excuses or cry like a child who weeps because he is given a load of gold to carry, or a farmer who loses heart when his fields are strewn with pieces of gold by people wanting to make him rich.

Letter 27

Source Besnard.
To Mother Marie Louise of Jesus (Louise Trichet) and Sister Conception (Catherine Brunet).[73]
From La Rochelle.
Date Beginning of 1715.[74]

In agreement with Msgr. de Champflour, Bishop of La Rochelle, Montfort had undertaken to open in the episcopal city a free school for girls and the first Sisters of his Congregation were to take charge of it. There were at that time only two Sisters and these were working in Poitiers serving the poor in the workhouse.

My dear daughters in Jesus Christ, Marie Trichet and Catherine Brunet,[75]

May Jesus and his Cross reign forever!

You have not answered my last letter[76] and I wonder why. I have spoken several times to his Lordship, the Bishop of La Rochelle, about you and about our plans and he thinks you ought to come here and begin the work we want so much. He has rented a house for the purpose until another house can be bought and suitably furnished.

I know you are doing a great deal of good where you are, but you will do infinitely more away from home and we know that since the time of Abraham right up to the time of our Lord and even to our own day, God sends his greatest servants out of their own country because, as our Lord himself says, no prophet is accepted among his own people.

I know you will have many difficulties to overcome[77] but an enterprise which is going to do so much for the glory of God and the salvation of men will have its way strewn with thorns and crosses. If you don't take risks for God, you won't give anything worthwhile. I am writing to you on behalf of the Bishop, so keep this confidential.

I will send you Brother John[78] with some money and a horse to accompany you. Travel as best you can; take a coach or hire a horse. If you have no money, we will try to cover the cost for you.

Please reply as soon as you can as I am leaving here to preach a mission at La Rochelle.

Totally yours in God alone,
God alone.

Letter 28

Source Besnard.
To Marie Louise of Jesus (Louise Trichet).
From La Rochelle.
Date March, 1715.[79]

This fragment of a letter is quoted by Besnard in both the 'Life of Louis Marie Grignion de Montfort' and the 'Life of Sister Marie Louise of Jesus'.

On the 16th of March, 1715 Msgr. de Champflour, Bishop of La Rochelle, wrote to Mother Marie Louise and Sister of the Conception, assuring them (and especially the parents of Marie Louise) that he will provide for their temporal needs, see they lack nothing and that even if the present undertaking fails, he will place them with other Sisters where they could continue to work for the glory of God and in the service of the poor.

Leave as soon as possible, my daughter. The day for the establishment of the Daughters of Wisdom has at last arrived.[80] I only wish you were already at La Rochelle, where I am at the moment; but if you delay you will not find me here as I am in a hurry to leave for a mission.

Letter 29

Source Besnard.

God alone

To Mother Marie Louise of Jesus and Sister of the Conception.
From Taugon-la-Ronde.
Date 4th of April, 1715.

After six days of travel the sisters arrived at La Rochelle on the evening of March 28th. As their journey had been delayed, Montfort had already left to give a mission at Taugon-la-Ronde. Soon after their arrival they wrote to him for advice on certain points. They had only been at La Rochelle eight days when they received the following precisely-numbered instructions from him.

May Jesus and his Cross reign forever!

My dear Daughters,

1 I think that instead of having a poor sinner like myself as your confessor you should choose the senior Canon, provided you keep your rules[81] and the others I will give you[82] and that he does not ask you to do anything contrary to them.

2 From now on, follow all the little rules[83] I have given you and, provided you do not fall into deliberate venial sin, receive holy Communion every day for you both need holy Communion very much.

3 I have been told that you have been going around the town.[84] I find it hard to believe that Daughters of Wisdom should be guilty of such vain curiosity. You ought to be an example of modesty, recollection and humble charity to everyone.

4 Call yourselves the 'Community of the Daughters of Wisdom for the education of children and the care of the poor'.

5 I would very much like to go and see you but I do not think I shall manage to do so after this mission as the Bishop is anxious for me to go on to give another.

6 You may allow the little Geoffroy girl,[85] if she wishes, to follow your rule in what concerns getting up, going to bed, meditation, and the recitation of the Rosary.

7 Learn good handwriting and anything else that is needful for you. Buy some handwriting copy-books to help you.

8 Send me news by Brother John if you cannot manage to come here[86] yourselves.

9 The good God wishes Marie Trichet to be the Mother Superior for three years at least. She is to be both firm and kind.

10 Marie Reine[87] is not to come into the house right away with her apprentices, for they are not at all accustomed to the silence that must be observed.

11 From the beginning you can't be too firm about keeping the

silence and seeing that it is kept in the community and in the school, because if you allow talking to go on uncorrected, all will be lost.

God Alone. This 4th of April, 1715.

Letter 30

Source Besnard.
To Marie Anne Régnier.
From La Rochelle.
Date 12th of August, 1715.

Montfort had told Marie Louise to make the acquaintance of Marie Régnier "because she is a saint." Forty-four years later an incredible number of people, both clergy and lay people, took part in the funeral procession of Marie Régnier. All attested that they had not come to pray for her but in the hope of obtaining her protection in heaven. In 1715 she lived at Saint-Sauveur-de-Nuaillé, in the La Rochelle area, where Montfort had met her, it seems, in 1712. For all of three years then, her religious vocation had been under consideration, which explains the urgent tone of this letter.

La Rochelle, 12th of August, 1715

My dear Daughter,

May Jesus and his Cross reign forever!

The grace of the Holy Spirit does not permit of delay. When God is asking his creatures for anything, he asks gently leaving them entirely free. But the longer we delay in responding to his gentle request the less we hear his voice, and the longer his voice goes unheeded the more his justice is asserted. You must be careful! I spoke to the Bishop a few days ago and he wants you to come here and join the Daughters of Wisdom. I also want you here and I entreat you to come. I am sending this letter by a special messenger[88] who has a means of conveyance for you so that nothing can prevent you following the call of the most high God. Bring only what you need and enough material to supply yourself with a habit as poor as St. Clare's, or rather as poor as that of Christ. The Daughters of Wisdom love you and they are asking for you. A thousand and one reasons, both of grace and nature, which I will not go into now, make it necessary for you to be here tomorrow. I am obliged to leave for a long mission before the feast of the Assumption,[89] and I would like to see you here before I leave.[90] The bishop would like to see you and he too is going away, so come quickly. The more you delay, the less pleasing your sacrifice and your victory are to God. I assure you that if you do not take advantage of this mark of esteem and affection which I have shown you and no other, I never want to see you again. Your troubles will increase every day and this may well lead to the loss of your soul. Don't say: "I will obey the Lord after the grape-gathering," because you will offend this great Lord very much. You will be like the young man in the gospel who lost his vocation because he wanted to go and bury his father before coming to follow Christ.

I am all yours.

The following note is for your father:

Dear Mr. Régnier,[91]

I greet you in the name of the Lord. Please do not oppose God's will concerning the daughter he has confided to you. She was only given to you for you to keep her in baptismal innocence for him and you have done that well. But you cannot hold on to her. She belongs to God and you cannot deprive him of her without suffering for it. If you are ready to offer her to God like those parents we read of in history who sacrificed their only child to God as Abraham did,[92] many blessings will be showered upon you and yours and I forecast that you will receive a glorious crown of honor in eternity. But[93] . . .

Letter 31

Source Besnard.
To Sister of the Conception.
From Fontenay-le-Comte or Vouvant.[94]
Date 24th of October, 1715.

Several days before leaving La Rochelle to preach a mission at Fontenay-le-Comte Montfort decided to send Sister of the Conception to be assistant to the Matron of the general hospital of La Rochelle. The authorities counted upon the zeal of the sister to 'promote the observance of the new rules which had been introduced into the hospital.' Two months later Montfort received a letter from her, telling of all her troubles and asking to leave the hospital. Indeed her troubles were very real for she was considered a reformer who had come to the hospital to change the customs which, they said, were as old as the hospital itself. This letter is Montfort's answer.

May Jesus and his Cross reign forever!

Take heed, my dear daughter, that you do not lose your vocation and allow yourself to be tempted into leaving the hospital. If you do, I never want to see you again.

If you do not wish to go to confession to Fr. Le Tellier,[95] I give you permission to go to the hospital chaplain for three months.

Be faithful to the general and particular rules which your dear spouse Jesus has given you through me. I ask you again to be careful and not to let yourself be led by your own feelings. On my knees I ask Jesus to strengthen you against all evil, for the devil is afraid of any reform in the hospital.

I am all yours, my dear daughter, as long as you remain obedient.[96]

This 24th of October, 1715.

Letter 32

Source Besnard.
To The community of Wisdom at La Rochelle.
From Saint-Pompain.[97]
Date 31st of December, 1715.[98]

After the mission at Vouvant which finished in December, 1715, Montfort journeyed to La Rochelle.

After he had left the Sisters, Marie Louise, always anxious and solicitous, must have written to him asking once more for counsel. Montfort answers by writing to the whole community.

This last day of the year.

My dear daughters in Jesus Christ,

I am sending you a book[99] written especially for you. Read it both in public and in private. What it says is what I have to say to you.

Do not lose your patience in my absence. My wicked self-will, though it may appear good, and my own person spoil everything. I am quite sure that the less I have to do with your foundation, the better it will succeed.

However, I would like each of you to write to me every month and tell me: 1. the main temptations you have had during the month; 2. the main crosses you have been able to accept well; 3. your main victories over yourselves. I would also like to be informed of the principal changes which take place.

You are always in my thoughts. Open your hearts to the Mother Superior, my dear daughters, and to your confessor, if God inspires you to do so.

All yours in God alone.

I wish you a year full of struggles, victories, crosses, poverty and contempt.

Letter 33

Source Grandet.

God alone

To Mademoiselle Dauvaise, matron of a home for incurables at Nantes.
From Saint-Laurent-sur-Sèvre.
Date 4th of April, 1716.

After demolition of the Calvary of Pontchâteau in the autumn of 1710, Montfort remained for a few days at Nantes. A lady, wanting to keep him in the area, offered him quarters in the rue des Hauts-Pavés. He saw the need in the town of Nantes for a home for the incurably sick. He rented a small house quite near to where he was staying and admitted all the incurables it would hold. He placed two good ladies in charge and gave them a rule of life and a grey habit similar to the Daughters of Wisdom.[100] *The matron seemed to want to extend the work and asked Montfort's advice.*

From the mission at Saint-Laurent-sur-Sèvre
4th of April, 1716

May Jesus and his Cross reign forever!

I count on the inexhaustible wealth of the motherly divine Providence which has never failed us in all we have undertaken for the glory of God and I reply quite frankly that I think you ought to obtain the lease for the house in question provided that the persons who are going to care for the poor incurables have the following qualities:

1 They must rely entirely on the unknown and invisible help of divine Providence whether they are rich or poor or whether they have any learning or not. They must not rely on any human help or their own natural talents.

2 They must all follow the same rule in its totality and punctually and have the same spiritual director. If any of the ladies has money and special qualifications she must not expect any privileges, say, exemption from community life or the rule, or the right to choose another director.

3 Finally, if this is God's work, they must be ready to suffer all kinds of crosses cheerfully. For this is the house of the Cross and it must not be given any other name. The first thing you must do is to erect a cross, with the Bishop's permission, so that the name, the grace and the glory of the Cross will always be associated with this house. Erect a very simple cross in the middle of the garden or the courtyard until funds can be found to provide a better one. This cross is the first item to be taken into the new house. Ask our good priest friend[101] to bless it or to send someone to bless it.

When I heard about this new foundation at Nantes, I considered sending you two Daughters of Wisdom[102] who are working among the poor in this diocese. One is about forty years of age, I believe, and both are suitable for this work. Let us pray that God may make his holy will clear to us.

Dear Lord, how very few really obedient, prudent and self-sacrificing young ladies are to be found today! They are all so self-sufficient, or rather each one feels that she is, even if she does not say so openly.

I think young women who present themselves to join the two already mentioned and have the above-mentioned qualities, should be accepted even if they come from other parts of the country. They would be more suitable for the beginning of this new foundation, if it is to be founded on 'living stones'.

I greet with great respect Monsieur Du Portail[103] and those good people who have joined us in this charitable work so dear to the Heart of Jesus who suffered more than any of us.

If the Bishop of Nantes agrees (and I would not arrive without his permission) I will be in Nantes on the evening of the 5th of May.[104] I am enclosing a short letter to his Lordship. I send respectful greetings to Father Barrin and ask him to take my letter to Fr. de Vertamont[105] to present it to the Bishop. If the latter refuses to allow me to stay in Nantes for two weeks resting from my missionary work—and I will go there only if I receive permission to say Mass[106]—then I will know for certain that it is not God's holy will that I go. In submitting to a prohibition, I truly and firmly believe, as if it were an article of faith, that everything will go even better with you than if I were present.

I beg the prayers of all the 'Friends of the Cross'[107] so that God will not punish my sins and refuse true conversion of heart to all the poor who listen to my preaching.

Sincerely yours in Jesus and his holy Mother. I greet all the Guardian Angels of the city of Nantes and yours in particular.

Humility! Humiliations! Humiliations! Thanks be to God for them.[108]

L.M. Grignion

Letter 34

Source Besnard.
To Mother Marie Louise of Jesus.
From Saint-Laurent-sur-Sèvre.
Date Around Easter, 1716.[109]

The sisters were constantly faced with opposition in La Rochelle. They were not wanted in the house where they lived in the rue des Jésuites. They were seeking another house, but it was hard to find a place suitable to their condition and their work, which was the education of children. It would seem that the foundation was on the verge of collapse, so Marie Louise seeks Montfort's advice. At the time he was preaching a mission at Saint-Laurent-sur-Sèvre and he had very little time to answer because he was to die ten or twelve days later. Marie Louise fortunately preserved this letter which contains the last expression of his love for sufferings and the Cross.

My dear Daughter in Jesus Christ,

May Jesus and his Cross reign forever!

I worship the justice and love with which divine Wisdom is treating his little flock, allowing you to live in cramped quarters here on earth so that later you may find spacious dwellings in his divine heart which was pierced for you to enter. How pleasant and safe is this sacred refuge for a soul truly possessing Wisdom! Such a soul came forth with the blood and water which flowed when the lance pierced the divine heart, and it is here that it finds a refuge when persecuted by its enemies. Here it can remain hidden with Jesus Christ in God, more victorious than any hero, crowned with more laurels than any king, shining with greater splendor than the sun and raised higher than the very heavens.

If you truly seek to be a disciple of divine Wisdom and one chosen among so many, then this unkind treatment you are suffering, the contempt, the poverty, the restrictions, all these should be pleasing to you since they are the price you have to pay to obtain Wisdom and true freedom and become partakers of the divinity of the heart of Jesus crucified.

If I were to look at these setbacks from a human standpoint, I would be tempted, like the foolish people of this corrupt world, to complain and be anxious and worried, but that is not how I look at things. Let me tell you that I expect more serious setbacks, more painful ones to test your faith and confidence. We will then found our community of the Daughters of Wisdom, not on quicksands of gold and silver which the devil is always using to adorn his house, nor indeed on the strength and influence of any human being, for no matter how holy and powerful man may be he will always be no more than a wisp of straw. We want to found our Congregation on the Wisdom of the Cross of Calvary. This adorable Cross has been stained with the blood of a God and chosen by Jesus to be the spouse of his heart, his heart's only desire and inspiration, the only object worth his toil, his only arm in combat, his only crown of glory, his only guide in his judgements. It is hard to understand that this great Cross was lost, scorned and hidden in the earth for more than four hundred years.

My dear daughters,[110] apply this to the state in which you find yourselves. I think of you always, especially during holy Mass. I will never forget you, provided you love the precious Cross. I am united with you in bearing the cross as long as you follow the holy will of God and not your own. In this holy will I am all yours . . .

Footnotes to Letters

1 Grandet was the first to publish a life of Louis Marie in 1724.

2 L'Abbé Alain Robert was Louis Marie's uncle on his mother's side.

3 Ten days after his arrival in Paris, Montfort wrote to his parents asking them to thank God for his safe journey. The present text may be part of another written during his first year at the seminary. His brother, Joseph, joined the Dominicans soon after Louis Marie's departure.

4 Besnard was Superior General of the Montfort Fathers (d. 1788). He wrote a life of the saint.

5 The Little Seminary was for poor students. It was called 'Little' to distinguish it from the 'Grand' Seminary of St. Sulpice. Both were theological colleges.

6 Mlle de Montigny was a relative of the Grignion family and it was through her influence that Louis Marie had been received two years earlier into the community of Fr. de la Barmondière. Nothing is known of Mme d'Alègre or Mlle Le Breton.

7 This was the benefice of the chapel of St. Julien in the diocese of Nantes. Louis Marie would renounce this benefice in 1700 after his family had endowed him with the family property of la Bachelleraie which brought him a revenue of 80 livres a year.

8 This letter comes to us through Grandet and Besnard. The latter probably borrowed the text from the former.

9 Montfort-sur-Meu, Louis Marie's home town, belonged in those days to the diocese of St. Malo.

10 Ps. 42:1.

11 This letter is taken from the documents sent to Rome for Montfort's canonization process.

12 The letter referred to was a note of seven lines in which Fr. Leschassier acknowledges a letter from St. Louis Marie which is now lost.

13 M. Desjonchères was vicar-general of the diocese of Nantes.

14 Canon de St. Brieuc was successor to Fr. Maunoir in leading teams of diocesan missionaries. For a short time in 1707, Louis Marie worked under him.

15 This is Fr. Bellier from whom Louis Marie as a student learned to serve the sick so devotedly during his college years.

16 Louis Marie first met Madame de Montespan some time between 1695 and 1697, while he was still a seminarian. She had offered to care for his two sisters, Sylvie and Françoise Marguerite. She sent them to her sister, the abbess of Fontevrault, who received them warmly. Françoise Marguerite was to leave because of an eye affliction but Sylvie went on to be professed and persevered until her death in 1743, 27 years after the death of Louis Marie.

17 This was a hospital founded in 1657 for the invalid poor but which at the same time took in the beggars of the town. The administration was presided over by the bishop.

18 Fr. Brenier and Fr. Repars were in the same community as Fr. Leschassier.

19 The poor of the workhouse at Poitiers had made approaches to Louis Marie asking him to return.

20 His two superiors, Frs. des Jonchères and Lévêque had left Louis Marie inactive for months and Fr. Leschassier had insisted that he be given active apostolic work. But the Poitiers affair worried the two superiors. They did not want him to leave the diocese of Nantes and they offered to send him to the most neglected parishes in order to keep him in the diocese. Louis Marie spent some time at Grandchamps where he worked so well that the two priests wrote to Fr. Leschassier telling him of this successful work in the hope that Fr. Leschassier would counsel Louis to stay in Nantes.

21 The Bishop of Poitiers wrote to Fr. de Montfort on the 25th of August 1701: "Our poor people, dear Father, want you among them and it would seem that Madame de Montespan and Fr. Leschassier are in favor of your moving to Poitiers. It appears to be God's will that you come, if your bishop gives you permission. I pray you to ask him, and if permission is given, come as soon as possible."

22 These words reveal the intentions of Fr. Lévêque concerning Louis Marie. It would seem he had thought of initiating him in the spiritual direction of priests who passed through the house. One wonders if he had the intention of one day putting the whole work of Saint Clement under his direction. Seeing that this first project would not be possible, he accepted as an alternative that Louis Marie undertake full-time work conducting parish missions. Fr. Lévêque was to die at Paris in 1703.

23 This sister has not been identified.

24 Montfort worked in Nantes among a group of students which included a certain M. Arot, a student in law, who after 1716 was invited to write a life of Louis Marie.

25 Among these were two saintly souls, both Sisters of the Visitation of Nantes, Sister Marguerite Thérèse and Sister Marie Madeleine.

26 This was probably a straw mattress as he was a guest at the seminary.

27 Fr. Brenier was a former superior of Louis Marie at the 'Little' seminary of St. Sulpice and for six months his spiritual director. Louis Marie was no doubt thanking him especially for those six months during which Fr. Brenier was particularly hard on Louis Marie. Fr. Blain writes: "No other person would have endured for a moment, let alone six months, the severity of this man who was determined to kill all self-love in him. Louis Marie accepted everything with patience and humility from this priest who sought new ways of mortifying him."

28 Exactly eight months.

29 Fr. Latour, S.J., was his director in Poitiers.

30 Msgr. Girard had died on the 8th of March, 1702.

31 The rules envisaged here are those he speaks of lower down: 'Times for rising, retiring, etc.'

32 He re-established the ancient custom of reminding the rich of the existence of the very poor who were no longer seen in the streets. The chaplain generally accompanied the collectors.

33 The dots seem to indicate that the writer himself was shocked by a death which was considered a 'punishment' by those about him.

34 The Jesuit college. Students of the university joined the college students and Montfort formed them into a 'congregation' with special rules and daily spiritual exercises. A certain number of girls also were grouped into a 'congregation.'

35 He was at that time Vicar-Capitular but afterwards became bishop. He was a former student of the Sulpicians and a great friend of theirs.

36 Fr. Lévêque was doubtless also a confrere of Fr. Leschassier.

37 This letter is full of allusions to the spirituality of the 'Adorers' especially in the terms used: 'Victim,' 'sacrificed,' 'crucified.'

38 The Benedictines of the Blessed Sacrament were engaged in daily adoration of the Blessed Sacrament during which they wore a cord about the neck, held a candle in the hand and made atonement to Jesus Christ for all the sacrileges and profanations he endured in this Mystery.

39 If Grandet, Montfort's biographer, has exactly transmitted the signature, this is the first time this form has been used.

40 Certain biographers identify the recipient of this letter with Mother Saint Joseph. If this is true, Fr. de Montfort must have written from Poitiers around the autumn of 1702, because Mother Saint Joseph died two months after the saint had visited her community. While he was there, God let him see the 'exalted state of perfection and grace attained by one of the religious (Mother Saint Joseph) who received Communion from his hand' (Grandet). This religious in her turn, by a special enlightenment, 'perceived the state of Louis Marie's soul which appeared similar to her own' (Grandet).

41 This is probably another sister of the same community.

42 Although we can accept the general contents of this letter, it would seem that the two Letters 15 and 16 have been touched up. There is a clear difference in the style and phraseology compared with the other letters.

43 Louise Trichet was born in Poitiers of a family of professional magistrates. Montfort became her director from the first day he met her, declaring that the Blessed Virgin had sent her to his confessional. He arranged for her to take up residence in the poorhouse and work among the inmates. Was Montfort aware at this stage of the plans divine Providence had for her? In actual fact she became the first member of his congregation of Sisters.

44 The General Hospital was La Salpêtrière where many priests assisted the chaplains in ministering to the multitude of destitute inmates who had taken refuge there. Louis Marie had joined this band of priests.

45 Among these we must count in the first place Fr. Leschassier, who

had been Montfort's 'oracle' but who was now muted and had ceased to answer his letters. Louis Marie was strongly rebuffed when he went to see him (cf. Blain).

46 I.e. to embrace the religious life.

47 An allusion perhaps to the future congregation of the Daughters of Wisdom which began with Louise Trichet.

48 This alludes to an event not recorded by historians.

49 Guyonne Jeanne had taken the name Catherine of St. Bernard at her clothing.

50 She made profession on the 2nd of February, 1704. She therefore began her novitiate on the 2nd of February, 1703. Around Easter, 1703 Montfort left Poitiers for Paris. Did he write this letter before or after this date? His biographers believe he wrote this letter from Paris.

51 On the date this letter was written, Montfort was resident in Paris. He remained there until mid-March 1704.

52 Grandet is our only source for this letter. He quotes in his biography of the saint seven letters or fragments of letters written to Guyonne Jeanne. There are no signatures given to five of them. Of the other two, one is signed: 'De Montfort, priest and slave of Jesus in Mary' and this present one is simply signed: 'De Montfort.' Grandet seems to attach little importance to signatures!

53 Grandet is the only one among Montfort's first biographers who quotes this letter.

54 On the 9th of March, 1704, the poor of the workhouse at Poitiers wrote to Fr. Leschassier: "We, 400 poor men and women, plead with you to send back to us our much loved and respected pastor." This letter was doubtlessly sent on to Fr. Leschassier by Fr. Blain. It was instrumental in bringing about Montfort's return to Poitiers.

55 Grandet is the source of this letter. Besnard also gives it but leaves out the first paragraph and makes a few corrections.

56 If the list of 18 children in the Grignion family, as given by the biographers, is complete then, in 1704, four daughters and one son still lived at home with their parents. Possibly they were: Renée (aged 29), Françoise Marguerite (aged 25), Françoise Thérèse (aged 23), Jean Baptiste (aged 15), who inherited Bois Marquer, and the youngest, Jeanne Marguerite (aged 13).

57 Louis Marie died in 1716, two years before his mother.

58 Besnard is the only biographer to give this letter.

59 This priest, whose name was Fr. Hindré, was once parish priest of St. John's parish in Montfort and had baptized Louis Marie. He left Montfort in 1698 and became parish priest of Bréal.

60 A place very near Montfort-sur-Meu. Montfort often repaired to the hermitage there during intervals between missions.

61 Mathurin Rangeard (1687-1760) was born at Bouillé-Saint-Paul in the Poitou. At the age of eighteen he joined Montfort and accompanied him in his missions. During the mission at Jaulnay in 1722, Msgr. de Faudras, coadjutor-bishop of Poitiers, conferred the tonsure upon him. Mathurin refrained from taking vows as he was inclined to be scrupulous. He worked for 55 years in the mission min-

istry with Louis Marie and his successors.

62 Bréal was a garrison town. The soldiers had assiduously followed the mission exercises the previous year and a certain number of them were inscribed in the confraternity of St. Michael.

63 In 1708, the 17th of February was a Friday. On the following Sunday, Quinquagesima, the Shrovetide, began.

64 Father de la Carrière was chaplain of Codrosy (Coet-Rosic) near Pontchâteau.

65 Brother Nicholas was a lay-collaborator and worked with Montfort up to the latter's death and became one of the first lay-brothers of the Company of Mary.

66 Montfort was uneasy about the statues and wanted them moved to a safer place.

67 Montfort had to obey an order probably from the bishop, or perhaps from his own spiritual director.

68 Montfort's attempt to have the statues transferred from Pontchâteau to Nantes by Brother Nicholas was doomed to fail. Eventually, three years afterwards, in 1714, Montfort himself made the transfer to Nantes, where they remained until 1748 when they were taken back to the calvary of Pontchâteau. In that year, Fr. Audubon, a missionary of the Company of Mary, restored the calvary chapel.

69 Montfort, in spite of being hopeful, had no illusions about the time which would elapse before the statues could be returned.

70 Montfort was received in audience by Clement XI on the 6th of June 1706, when the pope conferred upon him the title of 'Apostolic Missionary.'

71 Crosses and humiliations had dogged him all his missionary life. His desire for them was fully satisfied at Paris. He was reported to have been preaching in public squares and incurred a prohibition from the Archbishop. He was supposed to have attacked singers and other revellers on the Pont-Neuf and caused a breach of public order and as a result was taken to prison. These reports turned many against him although he was innocent of all the accusations (cf. Fr. Blain).

72 Louis Marie does not accuse anyone but simply states that the cross is the source of blessings.

73 'Montfort sent it to a person of trust with the request to convey it to Sister Marie Louise. This was a necessary measure because her correspondence was often intercepted by the personnel of the poorhouse who did not want her to have any communication with her director' (Besnard).

74 Marie Louise's mother, Madame Trichet, opposed and delayed the departure of her daughter from her home town but resigned herself to it when her husband insisted that his daughter through Louis Marie be given an assurance that the bishop would take her under his protection and approve of the establishment of the Congregation of the Daughters of Wisdom. Msgr. de Champflour gave this assurance by letter of the 6th of March, 1715.

75 One is surprised that Montfort called his daughters by their family names. One questions if they were really given in the original.

76 It would seem that the sisters never received this letter.

77 The founder knew of Madame Trichet's attachment to her daughter. He also foresaw the objections which would be raised by the directors of the workhouse. Indeed Sister Marie Louise had great difficulty in prevailing upon them to let her depart and even the bishop of Poitiers himself did all he could to dissuade her from leaving, and only gave his consent on condition that it should not be publicly known that he had consented to her departure.

78 Brother John was one of Montfort's helpers.

79 Marie Louise left the poorhouse on the 22nd of March, so this letter was written before that date.

80 In Besnard's life of Marie Louise, the expression used is 'taken shape' which would seem to indicate Montfort's desire to give an independent existence to the two sisters once they took up residence in La Rochelle. The events accompanying this new foundation would seem to indicate this. A draft rule was given as early as 1702, and there had been two ceremonies of the Receiving of the Religious habit of two sisters. In the summer that followed this foundation, Montfort wrote a definitive Rule for them. They were guided by him until his death, and then Marie Louise took over the direction of the community.

81 Montfort speaks here of the provisional set of rules that he had drawn up in 1702.

82 The Rules he promises are the definitive set of rules which he gave the Sisters in August, 1715.

83 The 'little rules' probably constitute a daily rule of life which he adapted to their new conditions and work.

84 Sister Marie Louise assured Besnard that this did not happen and that a false report had been spread either through ignorance or through malice.

85 The house that had been rented by the Sisters was not expected to be ready for a month after their arrival and a certain Madame Geoffroy had offered them accommodation. 'Little Geoffroy girl' was the daughter of this lady.

86 Brother John had become a kind of go-between, between Montfort and the Sisters.

87 Marie Reine (whose real name was Marie Roy) was a penitent of Louis Marie. She ran a workshop with a number of apprentices who naturally would not be accustomed to the observance of silence. Montfort had introduced the Sisters to her.

88 Probably again Brother John and a horse for riding.

89 Some authors have changed this to 'after the Assumption' because we know that Montfort was still at La Rochelle after the Assumption, since he presided on the 22nd of August at the ceremony of the Receiving of the Religious habit of Marie Valleau and Marie Régnier in the church of St. Joseph of Providence. But Montfort clearly wanted her at La Rochelle for 'tomorrow' the 13th, i.e. 'before I leave.' Some unforeseen circumstances must have delayed Montfort's departure.

90 This was the mission at Fontenay-le-Comte which began on the

25th of August.

91 Mr. Noêl Régnier was a merchant well known in the parish of St. Sauveur and was godfather at baptism to many children. When he died in 1719, it was said that three neighboring parish priests and practically all the parish assisted at his funeral.

92 Marie Régnier was not an only child. In 1715, M. Régnier had his son, and his son's family, and Marie's elder sister, Marie Anne, living with him.

93 We do not possess the remainder of this letter, but what it tells us is enough to convince us of the holiness of Sister of the Cross.

94 Immediately after the mission of Fontenay-le-Comte, Montfort went to rest for a few days at Mervent. He then went to give a retreat to the Sisters of Notre Dame at Fontenay. The mission at Vouvant began shortly after this retreat and ended in December. On the 24th of October he could have still been with the sisters at Fontenay or perhaps had already arrived at Vouvant.

95 Fr. Le Tellier was a Jesuit and at that time the confessor to the little community. Montfort had suggested earlier (cf. Letter 29) that the Sisters choose the dean of the canons as their confessor. Fr. Le Tellier, a former confessor to Louis XIV, 'took a particular interest in the Daughters of Wisdom. He gave them two ten-day retreats every year in their little chapel. He was a very holy and mortified man and even after three years as their confessor did not know where they lived. The spiritual direction he gave them was simple and consistent, and the five sisters under his direction led a holy and secluded life' (Besnard).

96 Sister of the Conception remained courageously at her post. She was relieved of it on the 1st of May, 1717.

97 The mission of Villiers-en-Plaine opened at the beginning of February 1716. It followed immediately upon that of Saint-Pompain. We can conclude from this that Montfort must have been at Saint-Pompain at the end of December.

98 This can only be the 'last day of the year' 1715. Besnard writes: 'This letter was in a way the last goodbye and the last intimation of Montfort to the Sisters of the crosses that would come their way during the course of the following year—the last of his life.'

99 We have no means of identifying this book.

100 Two ladies, Elizabeth and Marie Dauvaise, took charge of the home in 1710. One of them, it would seem, was still there in 1716.

101 This was Father Barrin, one of the six or seven vicars-general of the diocese of Nantes, who was always a good friend and supporter of Louis Marie. It was he who composed the epitaph engraved on Montfort's tomb.

102 I.e. Sister of the Conception and Sister Michelle who were working in the general hospital of La Rochelle (cf. Letter 31). Saint-Laurent-sur-Sèvre belonged at that time to the diocese of La Rochelle.

103 This gentleman is unknown and was probably involved in work for incurables.

104 In 1749, Madame d'Orion, who attended Montfort's mission at Villiers in February-March 1716, quotes him as telling her that he

would die before the end of the year. He evidently did not expect death to overtake him as early as the 28th of April.

105 M. de Vertamont was one of the vicars-general of Nantes.

106 Msgr. de Beauvau, Bishop of Nantes, had forbidden Louis Marie to preach or hear confessions in his diocese as a consequence of the Pontchâteau affair in 1710. But he did not forbid him to live in the diocese or to celebrate Mass. Montfort wanted to be safe and not risk being forbidden to say Mass during his fortnight's stay there.

107 An association founded by Montfort at Nantes in the parish of Saint Similien in 1708.

108 A certain Brother Alexis who was present at the death of Louis Marie wrote that, as he died, he kissed his cross and murmured Deo Gratias (Crosnier).

109 From certain remarks of Besnard, this letter was written about two weeks before Montfort's death on the 28th of April. Easter that year was on the 12th of April.

110 The last paragraph is addressed to the whole community.

2 The Love of Eternal Wisdom

Introduction

It has rightly been said that this is Montfort's principal book for it alone presents a conspectus of his spirituality and in it we see the true setting of his devotion to Mary and his devotion to the Cross. It is the fruit of study, prayer and experience. He had obviously studied and meditated upon such works as The Holy Way of the Cross *and* The Woes of the World *by* BOUDON *and the* Letters *of* SURIN.

In Montfort's mind, possessing and preserving wisdom was equivalent to seeking union with Jesus Christ and carrying one's cross after him.

1703-1704 has been given as the probable date for the composition of this book and it has been suggested that it represents a series of conferences given by the saint at the seminary of the Holy Ghost Fathers in Paris. As he hoped that several of the seminarians would join him in his missionary work, we can understand his desire to make a contribution towards their spiritual formation.

There is a logical order in the subject-matter of this work as in all Montfort's other works (e.g. the True Devotion, *the* Secret of Mary, *etc.). Its general plan is as follows:*

Introduction: Nos. 1-7 and Chapter 1.

1st Part Necessity of loving Eternal Wisdom.

- *A Eternal Wisdom before the Incarnation: ch. 2-8.*
  - *1 Eternal Wisdom in the Creation and Fall: ch. 2-4.*
  - *2 Eternal Wisdom between the Fall and the Incarnation: ch. 5-6.*
  - *3 Consequences: ch. 7-8.*

B Eternal Wisdom after the Incarnation: ch. 9-14.
1 Incarnation and Life of Wisdom: ch. 9.
2 Motives for loving Wisdom: ch. 10-13.
3 Triumph of Wisdom through the Cross: ch. 14.

2nd Part Means of acquiring Eternal Wisdom.
1 Ardent desire and fervent prayer: ch. 15.
2 Universal mortification: ch. 15.
3 True devotion to Mary: ch. 17.

We possess the entire manuscript of the Love of Eternal Wisdom. *The handwriting is without doubt that of Saint Louis-Marie.*

The Love of Eternal Wisdom

1 Prayer to Eternal Wisdom[1]

1 O divine Wisdom. Lord of heaven and earth, I humbly beg pardon for my audacity in attempting to speak of your perfections, ignorant and sinful as I am. I beg you not to consider the darkness of my mind or the uncleanness of my lips unless it be to take them away with a glance of your eyes and a breath of your mouth.

There is in you so much beauty and delight; you have shielded me from so many evils and showered on me so many favors, and you are moreover so little known and so much slighted. How can I remain silent? Not only justice and gratitude but my own interests urge me to speak about you, even though it be so imperfectly. It is true, I can only lisp like a child, but then I am only a child, anxious to learn how to talk properly through my lisping, once I have attained the fullness of your age.[2]

2 I know there seems to be neither order[3] nor sense in what I write, but because I long so dearly to possess you, I am looking for you everywhere, like Solomon, wandering in all directions.[4] If I am striving to make you known in this world, it is because you yourself have promised that all who explain you and make you known will have eternal life.[5]

Accept, then, my loving Lord, these humble words of mine as though they were a masterly discourse. Look upon the strokes of my pen as so many steps to find you; and from your throne above bestow your blessings and your enlightenment on what I mean to say about you, so that those who read it may be filled with a fresh desire to love you and possess you, on earth as well as in heaven.[6]

2 Admonitions of divine Wisdom to the rulers of this world given in the sixth chapter of the "Book of Wisdom"

3 1 Wisdom is better than strength and prudence is better than courage.

2 Listen, therefore, kings, and understand.
Learn, you judges of the nations.

3 Hear this, you who rule the people and boast of the large number of nations subject to you.

4 Remember you have received your power from the Lord and your authority from the Most High, who will examine your works and scrutinize your thoughts.

5 For, though ministers of his kingdom, you have not judged fairly, nor observed the law of justice, nor walked according to his will.

6 He will appear to you terribly and swiftly, because those who rule others will be judged severely.

7 For God has more compassion for the lowly and they are forgiven more easily, but the mighty will be punished mightily.

8 God shows no partiality; he does not stand in awe of anyone's greatness, because he himself made both the lowly and the great and he is concerned for all alike.[6a]

9 But the great are threatened with greater punishment.

10 To you then, rulers, my words are directed, so that you may learn wisdom and may not go astray.

11 For they who perform just deeds will be considered just and those who have understood what I teach will have a valid defense.

12 Therefore, desire ardently to know my words, love them and you will find instruction in them.

4 13 Wisdom is resplendent and her beauty never fades. Those who love her will have no trouble in recognizing her; and those who seek her will find her.

14 She anticipates those who desire her and makes herself known first to them.

15 He who rises early to look for her will not be disappointed, for she will be found sitting at his gate.

16 To reflect on Wisdom is the highest prudence and he who foregoes sleep to possess her will soon by given repose.

17 For she goes around seeking those worthy of her, graciously

shows her ways to them, guides them and provides for them with loving care.

18 The first step, then, towards acquiring Wisdom is a sincere desire for instruction; the desire for instruction is love; and love is the keeping of her laws.

19 Assiduous obedience to her laws assures a perfect purity of soul.

20 And perfect purity brings one close to God.

21 Thus the desire for Wisdom leads to the everlasting kingdom.

22 If then, rulers of nations, you delight in thrones and scepters, love Wisdom and you will reign eternally.

23 All you who rule over the peoples of the world, love the insight given by Wisdom.

24 I will tell you now what Wisdom is and how she came to be. I will not hide the secrets of God from you but I will trace her right from the beginning. I will throw light upon her and make her known and not hide the truth.

25 I will not imitate the man consumed with envy, for the envious have nothing in common with Wisdom.

26 Multitudes of wise men will bring salvation to the world, and a prudent king is a strong support for his people.

27 Accept, then, instruction from my words and you will draw profit from them.

[3 Preliminary observations]

5 I did not want, my dear reader, to mingle my poor words with the inspired words of the Holy Spirit in this chapter. Yet I make bold to offer a few comments:

1 How gentle, attractive and approachable is Eternal Wisdom who possesses such splendor, excellence and grandeur. He invites men to come to him because he wants to teach them with a smile. He bestows blessings on them many times over and forestalls their needs in a thousand different ways, and even goes as far as to wait at their very doorstep to give them proofs of his friendship.

Who could be so heartless as to refuse to love this gentle conqueror?

6 2 How unfortunate are the rich and powerful if they do not love Eternal Wisdom! How terrifying are the warnings he gives them, so terrifying that they cannot be expressed in human terms: "He will appear to you terribly and swiftly . . . those who rule will be judged severely . . . the mighty will be punished mightily . . . the great are threatened with greater punishment."[7]

To these words can be added those he uttered after he became man: "Woe to you who are rich[8] . . . it is easier for a camel to pass through the eye of a needle than for a rich man to enter the kingdom of heaven" (Mat. 19; Mk. 10, Lk. 18).[9]

So often were these last words repeated by divine Wisdom while on earth that the three evangelists handed them down without the least variation. They ought to make the rich weep and lament: "And now, you rich people, weep and wail over the miseries that are coming upon you" (Jas. 5).[10]

But alas! They find their consolation[11] here on earth; they are as though captivated by the riches and pleasures they enjoy and are blind to the evils that hang over their heads.

7 3 Solomon promises that he will give a faithful and exact description of divine Wisdom and that neither envy nor pride—both contrary to love—can prevent him from making known this heaven-sent knowledge, and he has not the least fear that anyone will surpass him or equal him in knowledge.[12]

Following the example of this great man, I am going, in my simple way, to portray Eternal Wisdom before, during and after his Incarnation and show by what means we can possess and keep him.

But as I do not have Solomon's profound learning nor his insights, I have less to fear from pride and envy than from my own incompetence and ignorance, which I trust, in your kindness, you will overlook.

Chapter One[13]

To love and seek divine Wisdom we need to know him

[1 Our need to acquire knowledge of divine Wisdom]

8 Can we love someone we do not even know? Can we love deeply someone we only know vaguely? Why is Jesus, the adorable, eternal and incarnate Wisdom loved so little if not because he is either too little known or not known at all?

Hardly anyone studies the supreme science of Jesus, as did St. Paul.[14] And yet this is the most noble, the most consoling, the most useful and the most vital of all sciences and subjects in heaven and on earth.

9 1 First, it is the most noble of all sciences because its subject is the most noble and the most sublime: Wisdom uncreated and incarnate. He possesses in himself the fulness of divinity and humanity

alike and all that is great in heaven and on earth, namely, all creatures visible and invisible, spiritual and corporal.

St. John Chrysostom says that our Lord is the summary of all God's works, the epitome of all the perfections to be found in God and in his creatures.[15]

"Jesus Christ is everything that you can and should wish for. Long for him, seek for him, because he is that unique and precious pearl for which you should be ready to sell everything you possess."[16]

"Let the wise man boast no more of his wisdom, nor the strong man of his strength, nor the rich man of his wealth. But if anyone wants to boast, let him boast only of understanding and knowing me and nothing else."[17]

10 2 Nothing is more consoling than to know divine Wisdom. Happy are those who listen to him; happier still are those who desire him and seek him; but happiest of all are those who keep his laws. Their hearts will be filled with that infinite consolation which is the joy and happiness of the eternal Father and the glory of the angels.[18]

If only we knew the joy of a soul that perceives the beauty of divine Wisdom and is nourished with the milk of divine kindness, we would cry out with the bride in the Song of Songs: "Your love is better than wine,"[19] better by far than all created delights. This is especially true when divine Wisdom says to those who contemplate him, "Taste and see,[20] eat and drink, be filled with my eternal sweetness,[21] for you will discover that conversing with me is in no way distasteful, that my companionship is never tedious and in me only will you find joy and contentment."[22]

11 3 This knowledge of eternal Wisdom is not only the most noble and the most consoling of all, it is also the most useful and the most necessary since eternal life consists in knowing God and Jesus Christ, his Son.[23]

Speaking to Eternal Wisdom, the wise man exclaims, "To know you is perfect righteousness and to know your justice and your power is the root of immortality."[24] If we really want to have eternal life let us learn all there is to know about Eternal Wisdom.

If we wish to have roots of immortality deeply embedded in our heart, we must have in our mind knowledge of Eternal Wisdom. To know Jesus Christ incarnate Wisdom, is to know all we need. To presume to know everything and not know him is to know nothing at all.[25]

12 Of what use is it for an archer to hit the outer part of a target if he cannot hit the center? What good will it do us to know all the other branches of knowledge necessary for salvation if we do not learn the only essential one, the knowledge of our Lord Jesus Christ, the center towards which all the other branches of knowledge must tend? Although the great apostle St. Paul was a man of such extensive knowledge and so well versed in human learning, still he said that he did not know anything except Jesus Christ and him nailed to a cross.[26]

Let us then say with him, "I count as loss all the knowledge I have prized so highly until now when I compare it to the knowledge of Jesus Christ, my Savior."[27] Now I see and understand that this knowledge is so excellent, so captivating, so profitable, so admirable that I no longer take any interest in other branches of knowledge that I used to like so much. Everything else is so meaningless, so absurd and a foolish waste of time. "I say this to make sure that no one deceives you with beguiling words. Make sure that no one ensnares you with empty, rational philosophy."[28] I state that Jesus is the abyss of all knowledge so that you do not let yourself be deceived by the fine, glowing words of orators, or by the specious subtleties of philosophers. "Grow in grace and the knowledge of our Lord and Savior Jesus Christ."[29]

That we may all grow in the knowledge and grace of our Lord and Savior, Jesus Christ, incarnate Wisdom, we are going on to speak of him in the following chapters. But first, let us consider the different kinds of wisdom.

[2 Definition and division of the subject]

13 In the general sense of the term wisdom means a delectable knowledge, a taste for God and his truth.[30]

There are several kinds of wisdom.

First: true and false wisdom. True wisdom is a taste for truth without falsehood or deception. False wisdom is a taste for falsehood disguised as truth.[31]

This false wisdom is the wisdom or the prudence of the world, which the Holy Spirit divides into three classes: earthly, sensual, and diabolical.[32]

True wisdom may be divided into natural and supernatural wisdom.

Natural wisdom is the knowledge, in an outstanding degree, of natural things in their principles. Supernatural wisdom is knowledge of supernatural and divine things in their origin.

This supernatural wisdom is divided into substantial or uncreated Wisdom and accidental or created wisdom. Accidental or created wisdom is the communication that uncreated Wisdom makes of himself to mankind. In other words, it is the gift of wisdom. Substantial or uncreated Wisdom is the Son of God, the second person of the most Blessed Trinity. In other words, it is Eternal Wisdom in eternity or Jesus Christ in time.

It is precisely about this Eternal Wisdom that we are going to speak.

14 Starting with his very origin, we shall consider Wisdom in eternity, dwelling in his Father's bosom and object of his Father's love.

Next we shall see him in time, shining forth in the creation of the universe.

Then we shall consider him in the deep abasement of his Incarnation and his mortal life; and then we shall see him glorious and triumphant in heaven.

Finally we shall propose the means to acquire and keep him.

I leave to philosophers their useless philosophical arguments and to scientists the secrets of their worldly wisdom.

Let us now speak to chosen souls seeking perfection[33] of true wisdom, Eternal Wisdom, Wisdom uncreated and incarnate.

Chapter Two

Origin and excellence of Eternal Wisdom

15 Here, with St. Paul, we must declare, "O the depth, the immensity and the incomprehensibility of the Wisdom of God":[35] *Generationem ejus quis enarrabit?*[36] Who is the angel so enlightened, who is the man rash enough as to attempt to give us an adequate explanation of the origin of eternal Wisdom?[37] For here all human beings must close their eyes so as not to be blinded by the vivid brightness of his light.

All should be silent for fear of tarnishing his perfect beauty by attempting to portray him.

Every mind should realize its inadequacy and adore, lest in striving to fathom him, it be crushed by the tremendous weight of his glory.

[1 Wisdom in reference to the Father]

16 Adapting himself to our weakness, the Holy Spirit offers this description of eternal Wisdom in the Book of Wisdom which he composed just for us.[38]

"Eternal Wisdom is a breath of the power of God, a pure emanation of the glory of the Almighty. Hence nothing defiled gains entrance into him. He is the reflection of eternal light, the spotless mirror of God's majesty, the image of his goodness."[39]

17 He is the substantial and eternal idea of divine beauty which was shown to St. John the Evangelist in his ecstatic vision on the island of Patmos, when he exclaimed, "In the beginning was the Word—the Son of God, or Eternal Wisdom—and the Word was in God and the Word was God."[40]

18 This is the Eternal Wisdom of which Solomon often speaks in his books[41] when he says that Wisdom was created—that is, produced—from the very beginning before anything was made or even before the beginning of time.

Speaking of himself, Wisdom says, "I was begotten from eternity, before the creation of the world. The depths did not exist as yet and I was already conceived."[42]

19 God the Father was well pleased with the sovereign beauty of Eternal Wisdom, his Son, throughout time and eternity, as he himself explicitly testified on the day of his Son's baptism and his transfiguration, "This is my beloved Son with whom I am well pleased."[43]

This splendor of dazzling and incomprehensible light of which the apostles caught a glimpse in the Transfiguration, filled them with delight and lifted them to the heights of ecstasy:

Illustre quiddam (cernimus)
Sublime, celsum, interminum,
Antiquius caelo et chao:

This Eternal Wisdom is—

Something resplendent,
Sublime, immense, and infinite,
More ancient than the universe.[44]

My words fail to give even the faintest idea of his beauty and supreme gentleness, and fall infinitely short of his excellence: for who can ever form an adequate idea of him? Who could ever portray him faithfully? You alone, great God, know who he is and can reveal him to all you wish.[45]

[2 The activity of Eternal Wisdom in souls]

20 This is how divine Wisdom himself describes in the 24th chapter of Ecclesiasticus, the effects of his activity in souls. I shall not mingle my poor words with his for fear of diminishing their clarity and sublime meaning.

1 "Wisdom will sing her own praises.
She will be honored in the Lord and will proclaim his glory before his own people.

God alone

2 In the assembly of the Most High she will open her mouth;
she will glorify herself in the armies of the Lord.
3 She will be raised up in the midst of her own people
and will be admired in the assembly of all the saints.
4 In the multitude of the elect she will be praised
and will be blessed by those who are blessed by God.
She will say:
21 5 I came forth from the mouth of the Most High;
I was born before all creatures.
6 I made an unquenchable light to appear in the sky
and I covered the whole earth like a cloud.
7 I had my dwelling in the heights
and my throne was in a pillar of cloud
8 Alone I compassed the vault of heaven; I penetrated into
the deep abyss; I walked on the waves of the sea,
9 And travelled all over the earth.
22 10 I held sway over every people and every nation.
11 By my power I have trodden under foot the hearts of all
men, great and small;
and among all these things I searched for a resting-place and
a dwelling in the heritage of the Lord.
23 12 Then the Creator of the universe commanded me and spoke
to me. He who created me rested in my tent.
13 And he said to me: 'Dwell in Jacob, let Israel be your heritage and take root in my elect.'
24 14 Before all ages, in the beginning, he created me and through
the ages I shall never cease to be,
and in the holy tabernacle I ministered before him.
15 I fixed my abode in Sion;
I found rest in the holy City, and Jerusalem became my domain.
25 16 I took root in the people whom the Lord had honored,
whose heritage is the portion of the Lord;
I fixed my abode in the full assembly of the saints.
17 Like a cedar on Lebanon and like a cypress on Mount Sion
I have grown tall.
18 I raised my branches high like a palm-tree in Engedi
and like the rosebushes of Jericho.
19 I grew tall like a beautiful olive-tree in the field,
like a plane-tree planted along the road near the water.
20 I gave forth fragrance like cinnamon or the most precious
balm;
I gave forth perfume like the most exquisite myrrh.
21 I have filled my house with the sweet fragrance of
galbanum, onycha, myrrh and with the sweet smell of incense;

I exude the scent of the purest balm.
22 I spread out my branches like a terebinth
and my branches are glorious and graceful.
23 I have grown sweet-smelling flowers like the vine;
my blossoms are the fruits of glory and wealth.
26 24 I am the mother of pure love,
of fear, of knowledge and of holy hope.
25 In me is all grace of the way and of the truth;
in me is all hope of life and strength.
27 26 Come to me, all you who yearn for me,
and be filled with my fruits.
27 For my spirit is sweeter than honey
and my inheritance is sweeter than the sweetest honeycomb.
28 My renown will endure down through the ages.
28 29 Those who eat of me will hunger for more; those who drink
of me will thirst for more.
30 Those who listen to me will not be put to shame;
those who work with me will not sin.
31 Those who make me known will possess eternal life.
32 All this is the book of life, the covenant of the Most High
and the knowledge of the truth."

29 Eternal Wisdom compares himself[46] to all these trees and plants, characterized by their varied fruits and qualities which illustrate the great variety of states, functions and virtues of privileged souls. These resemble *cedars* by the loftiness of their hearts raised up towards heaven, or *cypress trees* by their constant meditation on death. They resemble *palm trees* by their humble endurance of labor, or *rosebushes* by martyrdom and the shedding of their blood. They resemble *plane trees* planted along river banks, or *terebinths* with their branches spread out wide, signifying their great love for their fellow-men. They resemble all the other less noticeable but fragrant plants like balm, myrrh and others which symbolize all those retiring souls who prefer to be known by God more than by man.

30 Divine Wisdom shows himself to be the mother and source of all good and he exhorts all men to give up everything and desire him alone. Because, as St. Augustine says,[47] "He gives himself only to those who desire him and seek him with all the zeal such a lofty aim deserves."

In verses 30 and 31, divine Wisdom lists three degrees in holy living, the last of which constitutes perfection:

1 Listen to God with humble submission;
2 Act in him and through him with persevering fidelity;
3 Finally, seek to acquire the light and unction you need to inspire others with that love for Wisdom which will lead them to eternal life.

Chapter Three

The marvelous power of divine Wisdom shown in the creation of the world and man

[1 In the creation of the world]

31 Eternal Wisdom began to manifest himself outside the bosom of God the Father when, after a whole eternity, he made light, heaven and earth. St. John tells us that everything was made through the Word, that is, Eternal Wisdom: "All things were made by him."[48]

Solomon says that Eternal Wisdom is the mother and maker of all things. Notice that Solomon does not call him simply the maker of the universe but also its mother because the maker does not love and care for the work of his hands like a mother does for her child.[49]

32 After creating all things, Eternal Wisdom abides in them to contain, maintain and renew them.[50] It was this supremely perfect beauty who, after creating the universe, established the magnificent order we find there. He it was who separated, arranged, evaluated, augmented and calculated everything.

He spread out the skies; he set the sun, the moon, the stars and the planets in perfect order. He laid the foundations of the earth and assigned limits and laws to the sea and depths to the ocean. He raised mountains and gave moderation to all things even to the springs of water. Finally, he says, "I was with God and I disposed everything with such perfect precision and such pleasing variety that it was like playing a game to entertain my Father and myself."[51]

33 This mysterious game of divine Wisdom is clearly seen in the great variety of all he created. Apart from considering the different species of angels whose number is well-nigh infinite, and the varied brightness of the stars and the different temperaments of men, we are filled with wonderment at the changes we see in the seasons and the weather, at the variety of instincts in animals, at the different species of plants, at the diversified beauty of the flowers and the different tastes of the fruits. "Let him who is wise understand these things."[52] Who is the one to whom Eternal Wisdom has communicated his wisdom? That person alone will understand these mysteries of nature.

34 Eternal Wisdom has revealed these things to the saints, as we learn from their biographies. At times they were so astonished at

the beauty, the harmony and the order that God has put into the smallest things, such as a bee, an ant, an ear of corn, a flower, a worm, that they were carried away in rapture and ecstasy.

[2 In the creation of man]

35 If the power and gentleness of Eternal Wisdom were so luminously evident in the creation, the beauty and order of the universe, they shone forth far more brilliantly in the creation of man. For man is his supreme masterpiece, the living image of his beauty and his perfection, the great vessel of his graces, the wonderful treasury of his wealth and in a unique way his representative on earth. "By your wisdom you appointed man to have dominion over every creature you made" (Wis. 9:2).

36 For the glory of this magnificent and powerful Worker I must describe the original beauty and excellence of man as created by divine Wisdom. But the state of man's grievous sin has fallen upon me, poor miserable child of Eve, dulling my understanding to the point that I can describe only very imperfectly the work of man's creation.

37 We might say that Eternal Wisdom made copies, that is, shining likenesses of his own intelligence, memory, and will, and infused them into the soul of man so that he might become the living image of the Godhead.[53] In man's heart he enkindled the fire of the pure love of God. He gave him a radiant body and virtually enshrined within him a compendium of all the various perfections of angels, animals, and other created things.

38 Man's entire being was bright without shadow, beautiful without blemish, pure without stain, perfectly proportioned without deformity, flaw, or imperfection. His mind, gifted with the light of wisdom, understood perfectly both Creator and creature. The grace of God was in his soul making him innocent and pleasing to the most high God. His body was endowed with immortality. He had the pure love of God in his heart without any fear of death, for he loved God ceaselessly, without wavering and purely for God himself. In short, man was so godlike, so absorbed and rapt in God that he had no unruly passions to subdue and no enemies to overcome.

Such was the generosity shown to man by Eternal Wisdom and such was the happiness that man enjoyed in his state of innocence.

39 But, alas, this vessel of the Godhead was shattered into a thousand pieces. This beautiful star fell from the skies. This brilliant sun lost its light. Man sinned and by his sin lost his wisdom, his innocence, his beauty, his immortality. In a word, he lost all the good things he was given and found himself burdened with a host of evils. His mind was darkened and impaired. His heart turned cold towards the God he no longer loved. His sin-stained soul resembled Satan himself. The passions were in disorder; he is no longer master of himself. His only companions are the devils who have made him their slave and their abode. Even creatures have risen up in warfare against him.

In a single instant, man became the slave of demons, the object of God's anger,[54] the prey of the powers of hell.

He became so hideous in his own sight that he hid himself for shame. He was cursed and condemned to death. He was driven from the earthly paradise and excluded from heaven. With no hope of future happiness, he was doomed to eke out a pitiable life upon an earth under curse.[55] He would eventually die like a criminal and after death, together with all his posterity, share the devil's damnation in body and soul.[56]

Such was the frightful calamity which befell man when he sinned. Such was the well-deserved sentence God in his justice pronounced against him.

40 Seeing himself in such a plight, Adam came close to despair. He could not hope for help from angels or any of God's creatures. Nothing could restore his privileges because he had been so eminently fair, so very magnificently fashioned when he was created, and now by his sin he had become so hideous, so repulsive. He saw himself banished from Paradise and from the presence of God. He could see God's justice pursuing him and all his descendants. He saw heaven closed and no one to open it; he saw hell open and no one to close it.

Chapter Four

Marvels of Wisdom's goodness and mercy before his Incarnation

41 Eternal Wisdom was deeply moved by the plight of Adam and all his descendants. He was profoundly distressed at seeing his vessel of honor shattered, his image torn to pieces, his masterpiece destroyed, his representative in this world overthrown.

He listened tenderly to man's sighs and entreaties and he was moved with compassion when he saw the sweat of his brow, the tears in his eyes, the fatigue of his arms, his sadness of heart, his affliction of soul.

[1 The Incarnation is decreed]

42 I seem to see this lovable Sovereign convoking and assembling the most holy Trinity, a second time, so to speak, for the purpose of rehabilitating man in the state he formerly created him.[57] We can picture a kind of contest going on in this grand council between Eternal Wisdom and God's justice.

43 I seem to hear Eternal Wisdom, in his plea on behalf of man, admit that because of his sin man and all his descendants deserve to be condemned and to spend all eternity with the rebel angels. Still, man should be pitied because he sinned more through ignorance and weakness than through malice. He points out that it would be a pity if such an exquisite masterpiece were to become the slave of the devil forever and millions upon millions of men were to be lost eternally through the sin of only one man. Besides, Eternal Wisdom draws attention to the places left vacant by the fall of the apostate angels. Would it not be fitting to fill these places?[58] And would not God receive great glory in time and in eternity if man were saved?

44 It seems to me that I hear the God of justice replying that the sentence of death and eternal damnation has been pronounced against man and his descendants, and it must be carried out without pardon or mercy, just as happened in the case of Lucifer and his followers. Man has shown himself ungrateful for the gifts he received, has followed the devil in pride and disobedience and should therefore follow him in his punishment, for sin must necessarily be punished.

45 Eternal Wisdom seeing that nothing on earth can expiate man's sin, that nothing can satisfy divine justice and appease God's anger and still, wishing to save unfortunate man whom he cannot help loving, finds a wonderful way of accomplishing this.

Wonder of wonders! With boundless and incomprehensible love, this tender-hearted Lord offers himself in sacrifice to his Father to comply with his justice, to calm the divine anger, to rescue us from the slavery of the devil and from the flames of hell, and to merit for us eternal happiness.

46 His offer is accepted; a decision is reached and made. Eternal Wisdom, the Son of God, will become man at a suitable time and in determined circumstances. For about four thousand years—from the creation of the world and Adam's sin until the Incarnation of divine Wisdom—Adam and his descendants were subject to death, just as God had decreed. But in view of the Incarnation of the Son of God, they received the graces they needed to obey his commandments and do salutary penance for any they might have transgressed. If they died in the state of grace and in God's friendship, their souls went to Limbo, there to await their Savior and Deliverer who would open the gates of heaven for them.

God alone

[2 The time before the Incarnation]

47 During the whole time preceding his Incarnation, Eternal Wisdom proved in a thousand ways his friendship for men and his great desire to bestow his favors on them and to converse with them. "My delight is to be with the children of men."[59] "He went about seeking those worthy of him,"[60] that is those worthy of his friendship, his precious gifts, his very person. He passed through different nations, entering into holy people, making them prophets and friends of God.[61] He it was who instructed all the holy patriarchs, all the friends of God, all the saints and prophets of the old and new testaments (Wis. 7).

This same Wisdom inspired men of God and spoke by the mouths of the prophets. He directed their ways and enlightened them in their doubts. He upheld them in their weakness and freed them from all harm.

48 This is how the Holy Spirit tells it in the 10th chapter of the Book of Wisdom.[62]

1 It was Wisdom who safeguarded Adam, the first man, created alone to be the father of all men.

2 He rescued him from his sin and gave him power to control and rule over all things.

3 When the sinful Cain in anger withdrew from Wisdom, he perished because through his fury he became the murderer of his brother.

4 When the Deluge flooded the earth, because of him, it was Wisdom again who saved it, piloting the just man Noah in a frail wooden ark.

5 When the nations conspired together to do evil, Wisdom discerned the just man, Abraham, preserved him in innocence before God and kept him resolute in overcoming the pity he felt for his son, Isaac.

6 Wisdom rescued the righteous man, Lot, when he fled from the company of wicked men who perished as fire descended upon the Five Cities.

7 Evidence of their wickedness still remains—a smoking wasteland, plants bearing fruit that never ripen, and a pillar of salt standing as a monument to an unbelieving soul.

8 For those who neglected to seek Wisdom were not only kept from the knowledge of good, but they also left to mankind a memorial of their folly, and so their crime could never remain hidden.

49 9 But Wisdom delivered those who served him from all evils.

10 When the just man Jacob fled from the wrath of his brother Esau, Wisdom guided him along straight paths and showed him the kingdom of God. God gave him knowledge of holy things, pros-

pered him in his labors and increased the fruits of his work.

11 He stood by him against the greed of defrauders and made him rich.

12 He protected him from his enemies and saved him from seducers. He gave him victory in his arduous struggle so that he might know that Wisdom is mightier than anything.

13 He did not abandon Joseph, the just man, when he was old, but delivered him from the hands of sinners and went down with him into the well.

14 He did not desert him in his chains until he brought him the scepter of royalty and authority over his oppressors. He showed those who had defamed him to be liars and gave him an eternal renown.

15 He liberated a holy people and a blameless race, the Hebrews, from a nation of oppressors.

16 He entered the soul of God's servant, Moses, and withstood fearsome kings with signs and wonders.

17 He gave the holy ones the reward of their labors, led them along a perfect way, and became a shelter for them by day and shed a starry light upon them by night.

18 He brought them across the Red Sea and led them through the deep waters.

19 He submerged their enemies in the sea and gathered his own people up from the depths of the sea. Thus he carried off the spoils of the wicked.

20 They extolled you in their songs, O Lord, and together praised your conquering hand.

21 For Wisdom opened the mouths of the dumb and made the tongues of the babes speak with fluency.

50 In the next chapter of the Book of Wisdom[63] the Holy Spirit describes the various evils from which eternal Wisdom delivered Moses and the Israelites during the time they lived in the desert. To this we may add those who were delivered from great dangers by eternal Wisdom in the Old and New Testaments. Among them were Daniel who was freed from the lions' den, Susanna from the false crime she was accused of, the three young men from the furnace in Babylon, St. Peter from prison, St. John from the cauldron of boiling oil and numberless martyrs and confessors from the physical torments they were made to suffer and the calumnies which blackened their good name. All these were delivered and healed by Eternal Wisdom. "O Lord, those who have pleased you from the beginning were healed by Wisdom."[64]

[Conclusion]

51 And now let us proclaim: "A thousand times happy is the man into whose soul Wisdom has entered to have his abode! No matter what battles he has to wage, he will emerge victorious. No matter what dangers threaten him, he will escape unharmed. No matter what sorrows afflict him, he will find joy and consolation. No matter what humiliations are heaped upon him, he will be exalted and glorified in time and throughout eternity."

Chapter Five

Marvelous excellence of Eternal Wisdom[65]

52 In the 8th chapter of the Book of Wisdom, the Holy Spirit shows the excellence of Eternal Wisdom in terms so sublime and yet so clear that we need only quote them here, adding a few reflections.

53 1 *"Wisdom reaches mightily from one end of the earth to the other and orders all things graciously."*

Nothing is so gracious as Eternal Wisdom. Of his very nature he is gracious without bitterness; gracious to those who love him, never showing displeasure; gracious in his conduct, never showing severity. He is so gentle and unobtrusive that you might often think he is not present when you meet with accidents and contradictions. But, possessed of invincible power, he quietly but effectively brings all things to a happy issue in ways unknown to men. After his example, the wise man should be graciously firm and firmly gracious—*suaviter fortis et fortiter suavis.*[66]

54 2 *"From my youth I have loved and sought him and desired to take him for my inseparable companion."*

Whoever wishes to find this precious treasure of Wisdom should, like Solomon, search for him, a) early and, if possible, while still young; b) purely and spiritually as a chaste young man seeks a bride; c) unceasingly, to the very end, until he has found him. It is certain that Eternal Wisdom loves souls so much that he even espouses them, contracting with them a true, spiritual marriage which the world cannot understand. History furnishes us with examples of this.[67]

55 3 *"Wisdom shows his glorious origin by being so intimately in union with God and by being loved by him who is Lord of all."*

Wisdom is God himself—such is his glorious origin. God the Father has testified that he is pleased with him, proving how much Wisdom is loved.[68]

56 4 *"Wisdom is the teacher of the knowledge of God and director of all his works."*

Love of Eternal Wisdom

Eternal Wisdom alone enlightens every man that comes into this world.[69] He alone came from heaven to teach the secrets of God.[70] We have no real teacher[71] except the incarnate Wisdom, whose name is Jesus Christ. He alone brings all the works of God to perfection, especially the saints, for he shows them what they must do and teaches them to appreciate and put into practice all he has taught them.

57 5 *"If it is riches we seek in this life, who is richer than divine Wisdom who created all things?"*

6 *"If the mind of man can produce things, who is more able than the fashioner of everything that exists?"*

7 *"If someone loves holiness, again the great virtues are the handiwork of Wisdom, for he teaches temperance and prudence, justice and fortitude, and nothing in this life is more useful than these."*

Solomon clearly shows that since we should love Wisdom alone, then from Wisdom alone we should expect all things—material goods, knowledge of nature's secrets, all spiritual good, the theological and cardinal virtues.[72]

58 8 *"If anyone desires deep knowledge, Eternal Wisdom knows the past and can forecast the future. He understands the subtleties of speech and the lessons of parables. He recognizes signs and wonders and knows all that is going to happen as seasons and ages pass by."*

If anyone desires to possess a deep, holy and special knowledge of the treasures of grace and nature, and not merely dry, common and superficial knowledge, he must make every effort to acquire Wisdom. Without him, man is nothing in the sight of God, no matter how learned he may appear in the eyes of men. "He will count for nothing."[73]

59 9 *"I therefore resolved to take him as my companion in life, knowing that he would share his goods with me and be my consolation in my cares and sorrows."*

Eternal Wisdom is so rich and generous; how can anyone who possesses him be poor? He is so gentle, attractive and tender; how then can anyone who possesses him be unhappy? But among all those who seek Eternal Wisdom, how many can honestly say with Solomon, "I have resolved to possess him?" The majority of men do not make such a resolution with real sincerity. Their decisions are mere wishful thinking or at best weak and wavering resolves. That is why they never find Eternal Wisdom.

60 10 *"Through him, I shall be acclaimed among the people and, although still a youth, honored by the elders."*

11 "I shall be considered shrewd when I sit in judgment. The most powerful will be surprised when they see me and princes will show their admiration for me."

12 *"When I am silent, they will wait for me to speak; when I speak, they will pay attention to what I say. If I speak at some length, they will place their hands on their lips."*

13 *"He it is who will give me immortality, and through him I shall leave an everlasting remembrance to those who come after me."*

14 *"I shall govern people through him, and nations shall be my subjects."*

St. Gregory has this comment to make on Solomon's self-praise, "Those whom God has chosen to write his sacred words are filled with the Holy Spirit. In a way, they seem to rise above themselves and enter into the very one who possesses them. Thus they become mouthpieces of God himself, for they are concerned with God alone in everything they say, and they speak of themselves as though speaking of someone else."

61 15 *"The most formidable kings shall be afraid when they hear of me. I shall show myself kind to my people and valiant in war."*

16 *"When I go home, I shall be at my ease with Wisdom, for his conversation is never disagreeable nor his company unpleasant. With him there is only contentment and joy."*

17 *"I thought about these things and I reflected in my heart that immortality is found in union with Wisdom."*

18 *"I found pure contentment in his friendship, inexhaustible wealth in his accomplishments, understanding in his teaching and conversation, and great joy listening to his counsels; and so I went about seeking him everywhere to make him my companion."*

After summing up his previous commentary, Solomon draws this conclusion: *"I went about seeking for Eternal Wisdom in all directions."* To possess him we must seek ardently; in other words, we must be ready to give up everything, to suffer everything, in order to obtain possession of him. Only a few find him because only a few look for him in a manner worthy of him.

62 In the 7th chapter of the Book of Wisdom, the Holy Spirit speaks of the excellence of Eternal Wisdom in these terms: *"In Wisdom there is a spirit that is intelligent, holy, unique, fruitful, subtle, eloquent, active, unsullied, lucid, gentle, benevolent, keen, irresistible, beneficent, kindly, firm, unfailing, unperturbed, all-powerful, all-seeing, possessing every spirit, understandable, pure and subtle. For Wisdom is more active than any active thing. He is so pure he penetrates all things."*[74]

"Wisdom is an infinite treasure for men. Those who have utilized this treasure have become God's friends, and praiseworthy for their gifts of knowledge."[75]

63 After reading such powerful but tender words which the Holy Spirit uses to show the beauty, the excellence and the treasures of Eternal Wisdom, we cannot but love him and search for him with all our strength. All the more so since he is an inexhaustible source of riches for man who was made for him[76] and infinitely eager to give himself to man.

Chapter Six

Earnest desire of divine Wisdom to give himself to men

64 The bond of friendship between Eternal Wisdom and man is so close as to be beyond our understanding. Wisdom is for man and man is for Wisdom. "He is an infinite treasure for man,"[77] and not for angels or any other creatures.

Wisdom's friendship for man arises from man's place in creation,[78] from his being an abridgement of Eternal Wisdom's marvels, his small yet ever so great world, his living image and representative on earth.[79] Since Wisdom, out of an excess of love, gave himself the same nature by becoming man and delivered himself up to death to save man, he loves man as a brother, a friend, a disciple, a pupil, the price of his own blood and co-heir of his kingdom. For man to withhold his heart from Wisdom or to wrench it away from him would constitute an outrage.

[1 Eternal Wisdom's letter of love]

65 This eternal beauty, ever supremely loving, is so intent on winning man's friendship that for this very purpose he has written a book[80] in which he describes his own excellence and his desire for man's friendship. This book reads like a letter written by a lover to win the affections of his loved one, for in it he expresses such ardent desires for the heart of man, such tender longings for man's friendship, such loving invitations and promises, that you would say he could not possibly be the sovereign Lord of heaven and earth and at the same time need the friendship of man to be happy.

66[81] In his pursuit of man, he hastens along the highways, or scales the loftiest mountain peaks, or waits at the city gates, or goes into the public squares and among the gatherings of people, proclaiming at the top of his voice, "You children of men, it is you I have been calling so persistently; it is you I am addressing; it is you I desire and seek; it is you I am claiming. Listen, draw close to me, for I want to make you happy."[82]

And the better to attract men, Wisdom says to them, "It is through me and through my grace that kings reign, princes rule, monarchs and sovereigns bear the scepter and crown. I inspire legislators with the ability to enact just laws for the good of their people. I give magistrates the courage to administer justice fairly and fearlessly."

67 "I love those who love me and those who seek me diligently find me," and in finding me they will find good things in abundance. "For riches, glory, honors, dignities, real pleasure and true virtue are found in me; and it is far better for a man to possess me than to possess all the gold and silver, all the precious stones, and all the wealth of the whole universe. Those who come to me, I will lead along the paths of justice and prudence. I will enrich them with the inheritance due to rightful children and fulfill their greatest desires.[83] Rest assured, it is my greatest pleasure and purest delight to converse and to abide with the children of men."[84]

68 "And now, my children, listen to me. Happy are those who keep my ways. Hear my instructions, be wise and do not ignore them. Happy is the man who listens to me, watching at my gates every day, waiting beside my door. He who finds me finds life and obtains salvation from the Lord; but he who sins against me, wounds his own soul. All who hate me love death."[85]

69 Even though Eternal Wisdom has spoken so kindly and so reassuringly to win the friendship of men, he still fears that they, filled with awe at his glorious state and sovereign majesty, will not dare approach him. That is why he tells them that "he is easily accessible, is quickly recognized by those who love him and is found by those who seek him; that he hastens to meet those who desire him and that anyone who rises early to look for him will have no trouble, for he will find him sitting at his door, waiting for him."[86]

[2 Incarnation, Death and the Eucharist]

70 Finally, in order to draw closer to men and give them a more convincing proof of his love, Eternal Wisdom went so far as to become man, even to become a little child, to embrace poverty and to die upon a cross for them.

How many times while here on earth could he be heard pleading,[87] "Come to me, come to me, all of you. Do not be afraid, it is I. Why are you afraid? I am just like you; I love you. Are you afraid because you are sinners? But they are the very ones I am looking for; I am the friend of sinners. If it is because you have strayed from the fold through your own fault, then I am the good shepherd. If it is because you are weighed down with sin, covered with grime and utterly dejected, then that is just why you should come to me for I will unburden you, purify you and console you."

71 Eternal Wisdom, on the one hand, wished to prove his love for man by dying in his place in order to save him, but on the other hand, he could not bear the thought of leaving him. So he devised a marvelous way of dying and living at the same time, and of abiding with man until the end of time. So, in order fully to satisfy his love, he instituted the sacrament of Holy Eucharist and went to the extent of changing and overturning nature itself.

He does not conceal himself under a sparkling diamond or some other precious stone, because he does not want to abide with man in an ostentatious manner. But he hides himself under the appearance of a small piece of bread—man's ordinary nourishment—so that when received he might enter the heart of man and there take his delight. *Ardenter amantium hoc est*—Those who love ardently act in this way.[88] "O Eternal Wisdom," says a saint,[89] "O God who is truly lavish with himself in his desire to be with man!"

[3 The ingratitude of those who refuse]

72 How ungrateful and insensitive we would be if we were not moved by the earnest desires of Eternal Wisdom, his eagerness to seek out and the proofs he gives us of his friendship!

How cruel we would be, what punishment would we not deserve even in this world, if, instead of listening to him, we turn a deaf ear; if, instead of seeking him, we flee from him; if, instead of loving him, we spurn and offend him! The Holy Spirit tells us, "Those who neglected to acquire Wisdom not only inherited ignorance of what is good, but they actually left in the world a memorial of their folly in that their sins could not go unnoticed" (Wis. 10:8).

Those who during their lifetime do not strive to acquire Wisdom suffer a triple misfortune. They fall a) into ignorance and blindness, b) into folly, c) into sin and scandal.

But how unhappy they will be at the hour of death when, despite themselves, they hear Wisdom reproach them, "I called you and you did not answer.[90] All the day long I held out my hands to you and you spurned me. Sitting at your door, I waited for you but you did not come to me. Now it is my turn to deride you.[91] No longer do I have ears to hear you weeping, eyes to see your tears, a heart to be moved by your sobs, or hands to help you."

How great will be their misery in hell! Read what the Holy Spirit himself has to say about the miseries, the wailings, the regrets and the despair of the fools in hell who, all too late, realize their folly and misfortune in rejecting the Eternal Wisdom of God. "They are now beginning to speak sensibly—but they are in hell!" (Wis. 5:14).

[4 Conclusion]

73 Above all else let us seek and long for divine Wisdom. "All other things that are desired are not to be compared with Wisdom."[92] And again, "Nothing that you desire can be compared with him."[93] You may desire the gifts of God and even heavenly treasures, but if you do not desire Wisdom, you desire always something of far less worth.

If only we could realize what Wisdom actually is, i.e. an infinite treasure made for man—and I must confess that what I have said about him really amounts to nothing at all—we would be longing for him night and day. We would fly as fast as we could to the ends of the earth, we would cheerfully endure fire and sword, if need be, to merit this infinite treasure.

But we must beware of choosing a wrong wisdom, because there is more than one kind.

Chapter Seven[94]

Choice of true Wisdom

74 God himself has his Wisdom, the one and only true Wisdom which we should love and seek as a great treasure. The corrupt world also has its wisdom which must be condemned and detested, for it is evil and destructive.[95] Philosophers also have their wisdom which must be spurned as useless for it can often endanger our salvation.

So far we have been speaking of God's Wisdom to those who are spiritually mature, as the Apostle calls them,[96] but lest they be deceived by the false glitter of worldly wisdom, let us unmask its hypocrisy and malice.

[1 Wisdom of the world]

75 The wisdom of the world is that of which it is said, "I will destroy the wisdom of the wise,[97] i.e. those whom the world calls wise." "The wisdom of the flesh is an enemy of God,"[98] and does not come from above. It is earthly, devilish and carnal.[99]

This worldly wisdom consists in an exact conformity to the maxims and fashions of the world; a continual inclination towards greatness and esteem; and a subtle and endless pursuit of pleasure and self-interest, not in an uncouth and blatant way by scandalous sin, but in an astute, discreet, and deceitful way. Otherwise the world would no longer label it wisdom but pure licentiousness.

76 In the opinion of the world, a wise man is one with a keen eye to business; who knows how to turn everything to his personal profit without appearing to do so. He excels in the art of duplicity and well-concealed fraud without arousing suspicion. He thinks one thing and says or does another. Nothing concerning the graces and manners of the world is unknown to him. He accommodates himself to everyone to suit his own end, completely ignoring the honor and interests of God. He manages to make a secret but fatal reconciliation of truth and falsehood, of the gospel and the world, of virtue and sin, of Christ and Belial. He wishes to be considered an honest man but not a devout man, and most readily scorns, distorts and condemns devotions he does not personally approve of. In short, a man is worldly-wise who, following solely the lead of his senses and human reasoning, poses as a good Christian and a man of integrity, but makes little effort to please God or atone by penance for the sins he has committed against him.

77 The worldly man bases his conduct on personal honor, on "What will people say?", on convention, on high living, on self-interest, on ceremonious manners, and on witty conversation. These seven principles are irreproachable supports on which, he believes, he can safely depend to enjoy a peaceful life.

The world will canonize him for such virtues as courage, finesse, tactfulness, shrewdness, gallantry, politeness and good humor. It stigmatizes as serious offenses, insensitiveness, stupidity, poverty, boorishness and bigotry.

78 He obeys as faithfully as he can the commandments which the world gives him:

You shall be well acquainted with the world.
You shall be respectable.
You shall be successful in business.
You shall hold on to whatever is yours.
You shall rise above your background.
You shall make friends for yourself.
You shall frequent fashionable society.
You shall seek the good life.
You shall not be a kill-joy.
You shall not be singular, uncouth or over-pious.

79 Never has the world been so corrupt as it is now, for never has it been so cunning, so wise in its own way, and so crafty. It cleverly makes use of the truth to foster untruth, virtue to justify vice, and the very maxims of Jesus Christ to endorse its own, so that even those who are wisest in the sight of God are often deceived.

"Infinite is the number of these men, wise in the sight of the world but foolish in the eyes of God."[100]

80 Earthly wisdom of which St. James speaks, is love for the things of this world. Worldly men secretly subscribe to this wisdom when they set their hearts on worldly possessions and strive to become rich. They institute court proceedings and engage in needless disputes to acquire wealth or hold on to it. Most of the time they are thinking, speaking, acting with the sole aim of acquiring or keeping some temporal possession. They pay little or no attention to their eternal salvation or to the means of saving their souls, such as

Confession, Holy Communion, prayer, etc., except in an offhand way out of routine, once in a while, and for the sake of appearances.

81 The *wisdom of the flesh* is the love of pleasure. This is the wisdom shown by the worldly-wise who seek only the satisfaction of the senses. They want to have a good time. They shun anything that might prove unpleasant or mortifying for the body, such as fasting, and other austerities. Usually they think only of eating, drinking, playing, laughing, enjoying life and having a good time. They must always be comfortable and insist on having entertaining pastimes, the best of food and good company.

They regale themselves with all these pleasures without the least scruple, with no disapproval from the world and no inconvenience to their health. Then they go looking for some broad-minded confessor (that is how they describe lax confessors who shirk their duty) to obtain from him on easy terms the peaceful sanction for their soft and effeminate way of living and a generous pardon for their sins. I say "on easy terms" because these worldly people usually want as a penance only a few prayers or a small offering to the poor. They detest anything that could possibly cause them any bodily discomfort.

82 *Diabolical wisdom* is the love and esteem of honors. This is the wisdom of the worldly-wise who, secretly, of course, long for distinctions, honors, dignities and high offices. They strive to be seen, esteemed, praised and applauded by men. In their studies, their work, their undertakings, their words and actions, all they want is the esteem and praise of men, to be reputed as devout or learned people, as great leaders, eminent lawyers, men of great and distinguished merit or deserving of high consideration. They cannot bear insult or blame and so they hide their shortcomings and parade their better qualities.

83 We must, like our Lord Jesus Christ, incarnate Wisdom, detest and condemn these three kinds of false wisdom if we are to possess the true one, which is not self-seeking, not found in the world nor in the heart of those who lead a comfortable life, and which loathes everything that men consider great and noble.

[2 Natural wisdom]

84 Besides worldly wisdom, which is pernicious and must be condemned, there is the natural wisdom of philosophers.

It was this natural wisdom that the Egyptians and Greeks eagerly sought for: "The Greeks look for wisdom:"[101] Those who had acquired this wisdom were called magi or wise men. This wisdom consists in an eminent knowledge of nature in its primary elements. It was given in full to Adam before the Fall. It was conferred on Solomon, and down through the ages many great men have received it, as history testifies.

85 Philosophers boast that this wisdom is acquired through philosophical argumentation. Alchemists boast of cabalistic secrets for finding the philosopher's stone in which, they imagine, this wisdom is to be found.

It is true that scholastic philosophy, when studied in a truly Christian way, develops the mind and enables it to understand the higher sciences, but it will never confer that so-called natural wisdom which the ancients prided themselves on possessing.

86 The science of alchemists, which purports to teach that natural bodies can be reduced to their basic principles, is still more worthless and dangerous. This science, although valid in itself, has duped and deceived multitudes of people regarding the end it proposes to attain. Judging by my own experience, I am sure that the devil is using this false science to cause a loss of money and time, as well as grace, and even the soul itself, under the pretext of finding the philosopher's stone. No other science claims to accomplish such great effects by such obvious means.

This science claims to produce the philosopher's stone or a powder (which they call "projection") which, when thrown upon any metal in a liquid state, will change it into silver or gold, which will restore health, cure illnesses, even prolong life, and effect countless marvels which ignorant people believe are divine and miraculous.

There is a group of people who consider themselves experts in this science and who are called "Cabalists" and these keep such a close guard on the hidden mysteries of this science that they would rather lose their life than reveal its so-called secrets.

87 They justify what they teach by:

1 The history of Solomon, whom they firmly believe had been given the secret of the philosopher's stone, and as proof they produce a secret book which is false and insidious, entitled "The Clavicle of Solomon."

2 The history of Esdras,[103] to whom God gave a heavenly liquid to drink and which gave him "wisdom," as is related in the seventh book of Esdras.

3 The history of Raymond Lully[104] and of several great philosophers who say they have found this philosopher's stone.

4 Finally, the better to cover their imposture with a cloak of piety, they call it a gift of God, which is given only to those who have persevered in asking for it and who have merited it by their works and prayers.

88 I have given an account of the fantasies or illusions of this futile science so that like many others you may not be deceived. I know that some who, after having spent so much money and wasted so much time, under the most laudable and pious pretexts in the

world and in a most devoted manner, have finally regretted everything and confessed their pretense and their delusions.

I do not admit that the philosopher's stone is a possibility. A learned man named Delrio[105] is certain it is and has given proofs; others deny it. Be that as it may, it is not befitting, it is even dangerous, for a Christian to occupy himself in seeking it. It would be an insult to Jesus Christ, Wisdom incarnate, in whom are found all the treasures of wisdom and knowledge of God[106] as well as every gift of nature, grace and glory. It implies disobedience to the Holy Spirit who tells us in Ecclesiasticus[107] 3: "Do not seek what is beyond your capabilities."[108]

[3 Conclusion]

89 So let us remain with Jesus, the eternal and incarnate Wisdom. Apart from him, there is nothing but aimless wandering, untruth and death. "I am the way, I am the truth, I am the life."[109] Now let us see the effects of Wisdom in souls.

Chapter Eight

Marvelous effects of Wisdom in the souls of those who possess him[110]

90 Eternal Wisdom, ever transcendent in beauty, by nature loves everything that is good, especially the good that is man,[111] and consequently nothing gives him more pleasure than to communicate himself. That is why the Holy Spirit tells us that Wisdom is forever seeking throughout the world for souls worthy of him,[112] and he fills these holy souls with his presence making them "friends of God and prophets."[113]

In former times he entered into the soul of God's servant Moses and filled him with abundant light to see great things, and endowed him with prodigious power to work miracles and gain victories. "He entered the soul of the servant of God and withstood fearsome kings with signs and wonders" (Wisdom 10:16).[114]

When divine Wisdom enters a soul, he brings all kinds of good things with him and bestows vast riches upon that soul. "All good things came to me along with him and untold riches from his hand" (Wisdom 7:11). This is Solomon's own testimony to the truth after he had received Wisdom.

91 Among the countless effects Eternal Wisdom produces in souls, often in such a secret way that the soul is not aware of them,[115] the most usual are the following:

92 1 Eternal Wisdom communicates his Spirit of enlightenment to the soul that possesses him, "I prayed, and understanding was given to me. I pleaded and the spirit of wisdom came upon me."[116] This subtle and penetrating spirit[117] enables a man, as it enabled Solomon, to judge all things with keen discernment and deep penetration. "Because of Wisdom, who communicated his spirit to me, I shall be found keen in judgment and even the great shall be surprised in my presence" (Wisdom 8:11).

93 Eternal Wisdom communicates to man the great science of holiness[118] as well as the natural sciences, and even the most secret ones when they are needed. "If anyone desires deep knowledge, Eternal Wisdom knows the past and can forecast the future. He understands the subtleties of speech and the lessons of parables" (Wisdom 8:8). To Jacob he gave the science of the saints (Wisdom 10:10). To Solomon he gave a true knowledge of the whole of nature (Wisdom 7:17). He revealed to him countless secrets that no one before him had ever known (Wisdom 7:21).

94 From this infinite source of light the great Doctors of the Church, like St. Thomas (as he himself testifies) drew that eminent knowledge for which they are renowned. Note that this enlightened understanding given by Eternal Wisdom is not dry, barren and unspiritual, but radiating splendor, unction, vigor and devotion. It moves and satisfies the heart at the same time as it enlightens the mind.

95 2 Wisdom gives man not only light to know the truth but also a remarkable power to impart it to others. "Wisdom has the voice to convey knowledge.[119] Wisdom knows what we want to say and communicates to us the art of saying it well, for "he opened the mouths of those who were dumb and made the tongues of babies eloquent" (Wisdom 10:21).

He cured Moses of his impediment of speech.[120] He imparted his words to the prophets, enabling them "to root up and to pull down, to destroy and to demolish, to build and to plant" (Jer. 1:10), although they acknowledged that left to themselves they could speak no better than children.[121]

It was Eternal Wisdom who gave the apostles the facility they had to preach the gospel everywhere and to proclaim the wonderful works of God.[122] "He made their mouths a real treasury of words."[123]

Since divine Wisdom is the Word of God throughout time and eternity, he has never ceased speaking and by his word everything was made and everything was restored.[124] He spoke through the mouths of the prophets and apostles[125] and he will go on speaking through the mouths of those to whom he gives himself until the end of time.[126]

96 But the words that divine Wisdom communicates are not just ordinary, natural, human words; they are divine, "truly the words of God."[127] They are powerful, touching, piercing words, "sharper than a two-edged sword,"[128] words that go from the heart of the one through whom he speaks straight to the heart of the listener. Solomon is referring to this gift of Wisdom he himself had received when he said that God gave him the grace to speak according to the feelings of his heart.[129]

97 These are the words which our Lord promised to his apostles, "I will give you an eloquence and a wisdom that none of your adversaries will be able to resist."[130]

How few preachers there are today who possess this most wonderful gift of eloquence and who can say with St. Paul, "We preach the wisdom of God."[131] Most of them speak according to the natural light of their minds, or from what they have taken from books. They do not speak under the impulse[132] of divine Wisdom or from a heart filled to overflowing with wisdom.[133] That is why in these times we see so few conversions made through preaching. If a preacher had truly received from Eternal Wisdom this gift of eloquence, his listeners would hardly be able to resist his words, as happened in the early days of the Church: "They could not resist the wisdom and the Spirit speaking in him."[134] Such a preacher would speak with so much unction and such authority[135] that his words could never be ineffectual and void.[136]

98 3 Eternal Wisdom, besides being the object of the eternal Father's delight, and the joy of the angels,[137] is also the source of purest joy and consolation[138] for man who possesses him. He gives to man a relish for everything that comes from God and makes him lose his taste for things created. He enlightens his mind with the brightness of his own light and pours into his heart an indescribable joy, sweetness and peace even when he is in the midst of the most harrowing grief and suffering, as St. Paul bears witness when he exclaims, "I exceedingly abound with joy in all our tribulations" (2 Cor. 7:4).

Whenever I go into my house, says Solomon, even though I am alone, I will take my rest with Wisdom because Wisdom's company is always pleasing, his companionship is never tedious but always satisfying and joyful.[139] And not only at home did I find joy conversing with him, but everywhere and in everything, because Wisdom went before me.[140] There is a true and holy joy in Wisdom's friendship,[141] while the joys and pleasures we find in created things are illusory, leading only to affliction of spirit.

99 4 When Eternal Wisdom communicates himself to a soul, he gives that soul all the gifts of the Holy Spirit and all the great virtues to an eminent degree. They are: the theological virtues—lively faith, firm hope, ardent charity; the cardinal virtues—well-ordered temperance, complete prudence, perfect justice, invincible fortitude; the moral virtues—perfect religion, profound humility, pleasing gentleness, blind obedience, complete detachment, continuous mortification, sublime prayer, etc. These are the wonderful virtues and heavenly gifts described briefly by the Holy Spirit when he says: "If anyone loves justice, great virtues are again Wisdom's handiwork, for he teaches temperance and prudence, justice and fortitude. Nothing in the world is more useful to man in this life than these" (Wisdom 8:7).

100 5 Finally, as "nothing is more active than Wisdom,"[142] he does not leave those who enjoy his friendship to languish in mediocrity and negligence. He sets them on fire, inspiring them to undertake great things for the glory of God and the salvation of souls. In order to discipline them and make them more worthy of himself, he permits them to engage in strenuous conflicts and in almost everything they undertake they encounter contradictions and disappointments.

At times, he allows the devil to tempt them, the world to calumniate and scorn them, their enemies to defeat and crush them, their friends and relatives to forsake and betray them. Sometimes they may have to suffer illness or loss of possessions, and at other times endure insults, sadness and heartbreak. In short, Wisdom tests them thoroughly in the crucible of tribulation like gold is tested in a furnace.[143]

"But their affliction," says the Holy Spirit, "was light and their reward will be great, for God has put them to the test and found them worthy of himself. He has tried them like gold in a furnace and accepted them as sacrificial victims. When the time comes, he will look upon them with favor" (Wisdom 3:4, 6).

It is Wisdom who enriched the virtuous man in his labors and enabled him to reap the fruit of his toil. He came to his aid against those who were trying to deceive him and made him prosperous. He protected him against his enemies, shielded him against seducers and engaged him in combat so that he might come through victorious and so convince him that Wisdom is more powerful than anything in the world" (Wisdom 10:10).

101 We read in the life of Blessed Henry Suso, a Dominican friar, that in his eagerness to possess Wisdom, he often offered himself to undergo any torment in return for his friendship. One day he said to himself, "Do you not know that lovers endure suffering upon suffering for the sake of the one they love? For them wakeful nights are pleasant, fatigue is delightful, labor is restful, once they are assured that the one they love is pleased and grateful. If men go to such lengths to please a mere mortal, are you not ashamed to show weakness in your resolve to obtain Wisdom? No, Eternal Wisdom, I will never falter in my love for you, even though I have to plunge through thicket and bush to reach you, even though I have to undergo a thousand torments in body and soul. I will always prize your friendship more than anything else on earth and you will always have the first place in my affections."

102 While travelling a few days later, he fell into the hands of robbers who beat him so unmercifully that they themselves could not help pitying him. Seeing himself in such a state, Henry Suso forgot his resolution to be brave no matter what might happen and gave way to deep depression, weeping and wondering why God had afflicted him in this way. As he pondered over his plight, he fell asleep. Early next morning he heard a voice reproaching him, "Look at this warrior of mine! He can scale mountains, climb over rocks, break into strongholds, cut to pieces his enemies when everything is going right for him. But when he meets with adversity his courage fades and he is helpless and useless. In time of consolation he is a fierce lion, but in time of tribulation he is a timid deer. Wisdom does not share his friendship with such faint-hearted cowards."

At this reprimand, Blessed Henry confessed he was wrong in giving way to excessive discouragement, and went on to ask divine Wisdom to allow him to weep and so unburden his heart weighed down by grief.

"No," replied the voice, "all the saints in heaven would lose their respect for you, were you to cry like a baby or a woman. Wipe away your tears and show the world a cheerful face."

103 The cross, then, is the portion and reward of those who desire or already possess Eternal Wisdom.[144] But our loving Savior numbers, weighs and measures everything and sends crosses to his friends in proportion to their strength, and tempers them with divine unction to such an extent that their hearts are filled with joy.

Chapter Nine

The Incarnation and Life of Eternal Wisdom

[1 The Incarnation]

104 The eternal Word, Eternal Wisdom, having decided in the grand council of the Blessed Trinity[145] to become man in order to restore fallen humanity, it is possible he made it known to Adam, and Scripture tells us he promised the patriarchs of the old Law that he would become man in order to redeem the world.

This explains why, during the 4,000 years since the creation of the world, all the holy people of the old Law pleaded earnestly in their prayers for the coming of the Messiah. They groaned, they wept and cried out, "Clouds, rain forth the just one. Earth, bud forth the Savior!"[146] "O Wisdom, who proceeded from the mouth of the Most High, come bring us deliverance."[147]

But their cries, their prayers, and their sacrifices, had not the power to draw the Son of God, Wisdom Eternal, from the bosom of his Father. They reached out towards heaven but their arms were not long enough to reach the throne of the Most High. They offered the sacrifice of their hearts unceasingly to God but they were not worthy enough to obtain the greatest of all graces.[148]

105 At last, when the time appointed for the redemption of mankind had come, Eternal Wisdom built himself a house worthy to be his dwelling-place.[149] He created the most holy Virgin, forming her in the womb of St. Anne with even greater delight than he had derived from creating the universe. It is impossible on the one hand to put into words the gifts with which the Blessed Trinity endowed this most fair creature, or on the other hand to describe the faithful care with which she corresponded to the graces of her Creator.

106 The torrential outpouring of God's infinite goodness which had been rudely stemmed by the sins of men since the beginning of the world, was now released precipitately and in full flood into the heart of Mary. Eternal Wisdom gave to her all the graces which Adam and all his descendants would have received so liberally from him had they remained in their original state of justice.[150] The fulness of God, says a saint, was poured into Mary, insofar as a mere creature is capable of receiving it.[151] O Mary, masterpiece of the Most High, miracle of Eternal Wisdom, prodigy of the Almighty, abyss of grace! I join all the saints in the belief that only the God who created you knows the height, the breadth and the depth of the grace he has conferred on you.[152]

107 During the first fourteen years of her life the most holy Virgin Mary grew so marvelously in the grace and wisdom of God and responded so faithfully to his love that the angels and even God himself were filled with rapturous admiration for her. Her humility, deep as an abyss, delighted him. Her purity so other-worldly drew him down to her. He found her lively faith and her ceaseless entreaties of love so irresistible that he was lovingly conquered by her appeals of love.[153] "So great was the love of Mary," explains St. Augustine, "that it conquered the omnipotent God"—*O quantus amor illius qui vincit omnipotentem.*[154]

Wondrous to relate, this divine Wisdom chose to leave the bosom of his Father and enter the womb of a virgin and there repose amid the lilies of her purity. Desiring to give himself to her by becoming man in her, he sent the archangel Gabriel to greet her on his behalf and to declare to her that she had won his heart and that he would become man within her if she gave her consent. The archangel fulfilled his mission and assured her that she would still remain a virgin while becoming a mother. Notwithstanding her desire to be lowly, Mary wholeheartedly gave the angel that priceless consent which the Blessed Trinity, all the angels and the whole world awaited for so many centuries. Humbling herself before her Creator she said, "Behold the handmaid of the Lord! Let it be done to me according to your word."[155]

108 Notice that at the very moment Mary consented to become the Mother of God, several miraculous events took place. The Holy Spirit formed from the most pure blood of Mary's heart a little body which he fashioned into a perfect living being: God created the most perfect soul that ever could be created. Eternal Wisdom, the Son of God, drew the body and soul into union with his person. Here we have the great wonder of heaven and earth, the prodigious excess of the love of God. "The Word was made flesh."[156] Eternal Wisdom became incarnate. God became man without ceasing to be God. This God-man is Jesus Christ and his name means Savior.[157]

[2 Life of Wisdom Incarnate]

109 Here is a summary of his divine life on earth:

1 He wished to be born of a married woman, though she was indeed a virgin, lest he should be reproached as one born out of wedlock. Other important reasons are given by Fathers of the Church.[158] His conception, as we have just said, was announced to the Blessed Virgin by the angel Gabriel. He became a child of Adam without inheriting Adam's sin.

110 2 His conception took place on Friday, March 25th, and on December 25th, the Savior of the world was born at Bethlehem and was cradled in a manger in a poor stable. An angel brought the news of the Savior's birth to shepherds who were keeping watch over their flocks in the fields. He invited them to go to Bethlehem to adore their Savior. At the same time they heard celestial music, voices of angels singing, "Glory to God in the heavens and peace on earth to men who are God's friends."[159]

111 3 On the eighth day after his birth, as prescribed by the Law of Moses, he was circumcised, even though he was not subject to the law, and he was called Jesus, the name that came from heaven. Three wise men came from the east to adore him, having learned of his birth through the appearance of an extraordinary star which guided them to Bethlehem. This event is celebrated on January 6th, the feast of the Epiphany, that is, the manifestation of God.

112 4 Forty days after his birth he chose to offer himself in the

Temple, observing all that the Law of Moses prescribed for the redeeming of the first-born. Some time later the angel told St. Joseph, spouse of the Blessed Virgin, to take the infant Jesus and his Mother and flee into Egypt to escape the wrath of Herod. This he did. Some authors hold the opinion that our Lord stayed in Egypt for two years; others say for three, and others such as Baronius, think it was as many as eight years. He sanctified the whole of the country by his presence making it worthy to be dwelt in by the holy hermits, as history has shown. Eusebius tells us that at the approach of Jesus the devils took to flight, and St. Athanasius adds that the idols toppled over.

113 5 At the age of twelve the Son of God, sitting among the doctors, questioned them with such wisdom that all his hearers were filled with admiration. After this incident the gospel makes no mention of him until his baptism when he was thirty years old. He then retired into the desert, abstaining from food and drink for forty days. There he fought the devil and vanquished him.

114 6 After this he began to preach in Judea, choosing his apostles and working all the miracles related in the gospels. I need only mention that Jesus, during the third year of his public preaching and at the age of thirty-three, raised Lazarus from the dead, made his triumphant entry into Jerusalem on the 29th day of March, and on the 2nd day of April which was Thursday, the fourteenth day of the month of Nisan, celebrated the Pasch with his disciples, washed the feet of the apostles and instituted the sacrament of the holy Eucharist under the species of bread and wine.

115 On the evening of this day he was apprehended by his enemies with Judas the traitor at their head. The next day, April 3rd, even though it was a feast-day of the Jews, he was condemned to death after being scourged, crowned with thorns, and treated most shamefully.

That same day he was led to Calvary and nailed to a cross between two criminals. The God of all innocence thus chose to die the most shameful of all deaths and undergo the torments which should have been incurred by a robber named Barabbas whom the Jews had preferred to him. The ancient Fathers believed that Jesus was attached to the cross by four nails and that there was in the middle of the cross a wooden support on which his body rested.

116 After languishing for three hours, the Savior of the world died at the age of thirty-three. Joseph of Arimathea had the courage to ask Pilate for the body and laid it in a new sepulchre which he had built. We must not forget that nature showed its sorrow at the death of its maker by many marvelous happenings which took place at the moment of his death. He rose from the dead on the fifth day of April and appeared several times to his Mother and his disciples during forty days. On Thursday, May 14th, he took his disciples to Mount Olivet and there, in their presence, by his own power he ascended into heaven to take his place at the right hand of his Father, leaving on this earth the imprint of his sacred feet.

Chapter Ten

The captivating beauty and the inexpressible gentleness of incarnate Wisdom[160]

117 As the divine Wisdom became man only to stir the hearts of men to love and imitate him, he took pleasure in gracing his human nature with every kind of quality, especially an endearing gentleness and a kindness without any defect or blemish.

[1 Wisdom is gentle in his origin]

118 If we consider him in his origin he is everything that is good and gentle. He is a gift sent by the love of the eternal Father and a product of the love of the Holy Spirit. He was given out of love and fashioned by love.[161] He is therefore all love, or rather the very love of the Father and the Holy Spirit.

He was born of the sweetest, tenderest and the most beautiful of all mothers, Mary, the divinely favored Virgin. To appreciate the gentleness of Jesus we must first consider the gentleness of Mary, his Mother, whom he resembles by his gentle nature. Jesus is Mary's child; consequently there is no haughtiness, or harshness, or unpleasantness in him, and even less, infinitely less, in him than in his Mother, since he is the eternal Wisdom and therefore pure gentleness and beauty.

[2 He is declared gentle by the Prophets]

119 The prophets, who had in advance been shown the incarnate Wisdom, referred to him as a sheep and a lamb because of his gentleness.[162] They foretold that because of his gentleness "He would not break the bruised reed nor quench the smoking flax"[163] (Is. 42:3). He is so full of kindness that even if a poor sinner be weighed-down, blinded, and depraved by his sins, with already, as it were, one foot in hell, he will not condemn him unless the sinner compels him to do so.

St. John the Baptist[164] for almost thirty years lived in the desert practicing austerities to gain the knowledge and love of incarnate Wisdom. No sooner had he seen Jesus approaching than he pointed him out to his disciples, exclaiming, "Behold the Lamb of God. Behold him who takes away the sins of the world."[165] He did not say, as seemingly he should, "Behold the Most High, behold the King of Glory, behold the Almighty!" But knowing him more thoroughly than any man at any time, he said: Behold the Lamb of God, behold that Eternal Wisdom who, to captivate our hearts and to take away our sins, has gathered into his person all that is meek in God and in men, in heaven and on earth.

[3 He is gentle in his name]

120 But what does the name of Jesus, the proper name of incarnate Wisdom, signify to us if not ardent charity, infinite love and engaging gentleness? The distinctive characteristic of Jesus, the Savior of the world, is to love and save men. "No song is sweeter, no voice is more pleasing, no thought is more appealing, than Jesus Son of God."[166] How sweet the name of Jesus sounds to the ear and to the heart of a chosen soul! Sweet as honey to the lips, a delightful melody to the ears, thrilling joy to the heart.[167]

[4 He is gentle in his looks]

121 "Gentle is Jesus in his looks, and in his words and actions."[168] The face of our loving Savior is so serene and gentle that it charmed the eyes and hearts of those who beheld it. The shepherds who came to the stable to see him were so spellbound by the serenity and beauty of his face that they tarried for many days gazing in rapture upon him. The three Kings, proud though they were, had no sooner seen the tender features of this lovely child, than, forgetting their high dignity, they fell down on their knees beside his crib. Time and again they said to one another, "Friend, how good it is to be here! There are no enjoyments in our palaces comparable to those we are experiencing in this stable looking at this dear Infant-God."

When Jesus was still very young, children and people in trouble came from the country around to see him and find comfort and joy. They would say to each other, "Let us go and see young Jesus, the lovely child of Mary." St. John Chrysostom says, "The beauty and majesty of his face were at once so sweet and so worthy of respect that those who knew him could not prevent themselves from loving him, and distant kings, hearing of his beauty, desired to have a painting of him. It is even said that our Lord by special favor sent his portrait to King Abogare.[169] Some writers tell us that the Roman soldiers and the Jews covered his face in order to strike and buffet him more freely because there was in his eyes and face such a kindly and ravishing radiance as would disarm the most cruel of men.

[5 He is gentle in his words]

122 Jesus is also gentle in his words. When he dwelt on earth he won everyone over by his gentle speech. Never was he heard to raise his voice or argue heatedly. The prophets foretold this of him (Isaiah 42:2).[170] Those who listened to him with good intentions were charmed by the words of life which fell from his lips and they exclaimed, "No man has ever spoken as this man" (John 7:46).[171] Even those who hated him were so surprised at his eloquence and wisdom that they asked one another, "Where did he get such wisdom?"[172] No man has ever spoken with such meekness and unction. "Where did he acquire such wisdom in his speech?" they asked.

Multitudes of poor people left their homes and families and went even as far as the desert to hear him, going several days without food or drink, for his gentle words were food enough for them. The apostles were led to follow him by his kindly manner of speaking. His words healed the incurable and comforted the afflicted. He spoke only one word—"Mary"—to the grief-stricken Mary Magdalen and she was overwhelmed with joy and happiness.

Chapter Eleven

The gentleness of the incarnate Wisdom in his actions

[6 He is gentle in his actions]

123 Finally, Jesus is gentle in his actions and in the whole conduct of his life. "He did everything well,"[173] which means that everything he did was done with such uprightness, wisdom, holiness and gentleness that nothing faulty or distorted could be found in him. Let us consider what gentleness our loving Savior always manifested in his conduct.

124 Poor people and little children followed him everywhere seeing him as one of their own. The simplicity, the kindliness, the humble courtesy and the charity they witnessed in our dear Savior made them press close about him. One day when he was preaching in the streets the children, who were usually about him, pressed upon him from behind. The apostles who were nearest to our Lord pushed them back. On seeing this Jesus rebuked his apostles and said to them, "Do not keep the children away from me."[174] When they gathered about him he embraced and blessed them with gentleness and kindness.

The poor, on seeing him poorly dressed and simple in his ways, without ostentation or haughtiness, felt at ease with him. They defended him against the rich and the proud when these calumniated and persecuted him, and he in his turn praised and blessed them on every occasion.

125 But how describe the gentleness of Jesus in his dealings with poor sinners: his gentleness with Mary Magdalen, his courteous solicitude in turning the Samaritan woman from her evil ways, his compassion in pardoning the adulterous woman taken in adultery, his charity in sitting down to eat with the public sinners in order to win them over? Did not his enemies seize upon his great kindness as a pretext to persecute him, saying that his gentleness only encouraged others to transgress the law of Moses, and tauntingly called him the friend of sinners and publicans? With what kindness and concern did he not try to win over the heart of Judas who had decided to betray him, even when Jesus was washing his feet and calling him his friend! With what charity he asked God his Father to pardon his executioners, pleading their ignorance as an excuse.

126 How beautiful, meek and charitable is Jesus, the incarnate Wisdom! Beautiful from all eternity, he is the splendor of his Father, the unspotted mirror and image of his goodness.[175] He is more beautiful than the sun and brighter than light itself. He is beautiful in time, being formed by the Holy Spirit pure and faultless, fair and immaculate, and during his life he charmed the eyes and hearts of men and is now the glory of the angels. How loving and gentle he is with men, and especially with poor sinners whom he came upon earth to seek out in a visible manner, and whom he still seeks in an invisible manner every day.

[7 He continues to be gentle in heaven]

127 Do you think that Jesus, now that he is triumphant and glorious, is any the less loving and condescending? On the contrary, his glory, as it were, perfects his kindness. He wishes to appear forgiving rather than majestic, to show the riches of his mercy rather than the gold of his glory.

128 Read the accounts of his apparitions and you will see that when Wisdom incarnate and glorified showed himself to his friends, he did not appear accompanied by thunder and lightning but in a kindly and gentle manner. He did not assume the majesty of a King or of the Lord of hosts, but the tenderness of a spouse and the kindliness of a friend. On some occasions he has shown himself in the Blessed Sacrament, but I cannot remember having read that he ever did so otherwise than in the form of a gentle and beautiful child.[176]

129 Not long ago an unhappy man, enraged because he had

lost all his money at gambling, drew his sword against heaven, blaming our Lord for the loss of his money. Then, instead of thunderbolts and fiery darts falling upon this man, there came fluttering down from the sky a little piece of paper. Quite taken aback, he caught the paper, opened it and read "O God, have mercy on me."[177] The sword fell from his hands, and, stirred to the depths of his heart, he fell on his knees and begged for mercy.

130 St. Denis the Areopagite relates[178] that a certain bishop, Carpas by name, had, after a great deal of trouble, converted a pagan. On hearing afterwards that a fellow-pagan had lost no time in making the new convert abjure the faith, Carpas earnestly prayed to God all night to wreak vengeance and punishment upon the guilty one for his attack on the supreme authority of God. Suddenly, when his fervor and his entreaties were reaching their peak, he saw the earth opening and on the brink of hell he saw the apostate and the pagan whom the demons were trying to drag down into the abyss. Then lifting up his eyes, he saw the heavens open and Jesus Christ accompanied by a multitude of angels coming to him and saying, "Carpas, you asked me for vengeance, but you do not know me. You do not realize what you are asking for, nor what sinners have cost me. Why do you want me to condemn them? I love them so much that if it were necessary I would be ready to die again for each one of them." Then our Lord approached Carpas and, uncovering his shoulders, said to him, "Carpas, if you want to take vengeance, strike me rather than these poor sinners."

131 With this knowledge of Eternal Wisdom, shall we not love him who has loved us and still loves us more than his own life; and whose beauty and meekness surpass all that is loveliest and most attractive in heaven and on earth?

132 We read in the life of Blessed Henry Suso[179] that one day the Eternal Wisdom, whom he so ardently desired, appeared to him. It happened in this way. Our Lord appeared in human form surrounded by a bright transparent cloud and seated upon a throne of ivory. A brightness like the rays of the sun at noonday radiated from his eyes and face. The crown he wore signified eternity; his robes blessedness; his word, meekness; his embrace, the fulness of bliss possessed by all the blessed. Henry contemplated this spectacle of the divine Wisdom. What surprised him most was to see Jesus at one moment appearing as a young maiden of incomparable beauty and, at the next moment, appearing as a young man who, judging from his face, would seem to have espoused all that is beautiful in God's creation. Sometimes he saw him raise his head higher than the heavens and at the same time tread the chasms of the heart. Sometimes he looked wholly majestic and at other times condescending, gentle, meek and full of tenderness for those who came to him. Then he turned to Henry and said with a smile, "My son, give me your heart."[180] At once Henry threw himself at his feet and offered him for all time the gift of his heart.

Following the example of this holy man, let us offer Eternal Wisdom for all time the gift of our heart. That is all he asks for.

Chapter Twelve

The principal utterances of Wisdom Incarnate which we must believe and practice if we are to be saved[181]

133 1 If anyone wishes to follow me, let him deny himself, take up his cross and follow me. Lk. 9:23.

2 If anyone loves me, he will keep my commandments, and my Father will love him and we will come to him. Jn. 14:23.

3 If you present your gift at the altar and you remember that your brother has something against you, leave your gift before the altar and go make peace with your brother. Mt. 23:24.

134 4 If someone comes to me and does not hate his father, mother, wife, children, brothers and sisters and even his own life, he cannot be my disciple. Lk. 14:26.

5 Whoever has left his house, or brothers, or sisters, or children, or inheritance, out of love for me, will receive a hundredfold reward and will possess eternal life. Mt. 19:29.

6 If you wish to be perfect, go sell what you possess and give to the poor and you will have treasure in heaven. Mt. 19:21.

135 7 Not everyone who cries out to me, "Lord, Lord" will enter the kingdom of heaven, but only he who obeys the will of my heavenly Father will enter there. Mt. 7:21.

8 Whoever hears my words and obeys them is like a wise man who builds upon solid rock. Mt. 7:24.

9 I tell you solemnly, if you do not change and become as children you will not enter the kingdom of heaven. Mt. 18:3.

10 Learn from me, for I am gentle and humble of heart and you will find rest for your souls. Mt. 11:29.

136 11 When you pray, beware of acting like those hypocrites who love to stand and pray in their synagogue so that men may notice them. Mt. 6:5.

12 Of what use is it when you pray to use many words, since your heavenly Father knows your needs before you place them before him. Mt. 6:7.

God alone

13 As you prepare to pray, forgive your neighbor the wrongs he may have committed against you so that your heavenly Father may show mercy to you. Mk. 11:25.

14 When you ask God in prayer for anything, believe that you will receive it, and you will indeed receive it. Mk. 11:24.

137 15 When you are fasting, do not imitate those gloomy hypocrites who go about looking worn out to show others they are fasting. I tell you solemnly, they have already received their reward. Mt. 6:16.

138 16 There will be greater rejoicing in heaven when one sinner is seen to be penitent than when ninety-nine just people show no repentance. Lk. 15:7.

17 I have not come to call the just, but to call sinners and draw them to repentance. Lk. 5:32.

139 18 Blessed are they who suffer persecution for the sake of justice, for theirs is the kingdom of heaven. Mt. 5:10.

19 Blessed are you when men hate you and reject you from their company because of the Son of Man; rejoice, for your reward will be great in heaven. Lk. 6:22.

20 If the world hates you and persecutes you, recall that it hated me before you. If you belonged to the world, the world would love you for its own; but because I have chosen you, it will hate you. Jn. 15:18.

140 21 Come to me all you who are afflicted and heavily-burdened and I will refresh you. Mt. 11:28.

22 I am the bread of life come down from heaven. If anyone eats of this bread he will live forever, and the bread that I give is my flesh. Jn. 6:51.

23 My flesh is the real food and my blood is the real drink. Whoever eats my flesh and drinks my blood lives in me and I live in him. Jn. 6:55, 56.

141 24 You will be hated by all men because of me, but I promise you, not a single hair of your head will be lost. Lk. 21:17-18.

142 25 No one can serve two masters. Either he will hate one and love the other, or he will uphold one and despise the other. Mt. 6:24.

143 26 Evil thoughts which come from the heart make a person unclean; but eating with unwashed hands does not make a person unclean. Mt. 15:19.

27 A good man draws only what is good from his store of goodness; but the wicked man can only draw what is evil from his store. Mt. 12:35.

144 28 No one is worthy of the kingdom of God, if, after putting his hand to the plough, he looks behind him. Lk. 9:62.

29 Every hair of your head is counted; so never fear, you are worth more than many sparrows. Lk. 12:7.

30 God did not send his son into the world to judge and condemn the world, but that he might save the world. Jn. 3:17.

145 31 Every man who does evil avoids the light; he is afraid his evil deeds will be exposed. Jn. 3:20.

32 God is a spirit and those who adore him must do so in spirit and in truth. Jn. 4:24.

33 It is the spirit that gives life to everything; the flesh has nothing to offer. The words I have spoken to you are words of life. Jn. 6:63.

34 Whoever commits sin becomes the servant and slave of sin, and the servant does not remain in the house forever. Jn. 8:34-35.

35 Whoever is faithful in small things will be faithful in the greater; and whoever is dishonest in small things will be dishonest in greater things. Lk. 16:10.

36 It is more likely that heaven and earth should perish than that one detail of the law should not be accomplished. Lk. 16:17.

37 Your light must shine before men so that they will see your good works and they will glorify your Father who is in heaven. Mt. 5:16.

146 38 If your virtue is no better than that of the scribes and pharisees, you will never enter the kingdom of heaven. Mt. 5:20.

39 If your eye causes you to sin, pluck it out; for it is better for you to lose one part of your body than to have your whole body thrown into hell. Mt. 5:29.

40 The kingdom of heaven suffers violence and only those who are violent can take it by force. Mt. 11:12.

41 Do not store up a treasure on earth to be destroyed by moths and rust or stolen by thieves; rather store up a treasure in heaven which no one can steal from you. Mt. 6:19.

42 Do not judge, and you will not be judged; for God will judge you in the same way as you judge others. Mt. 7:1.

147 43 Beware of false prophets who come to you in sheep's clothing but who in their hearts are ravenous wolves; you will recognize them by their fruits. Mt. 7:15.

44 Beware of showing contempt for any of my little ones; their angels see the face of my Father who is in heaven. Mt. 18:10.

45 Be on the watch, for you do not know the day or the hour when the Lord will come. Mt. 25:13.

148 46 Do not be afraid of those who can kill the body; fear rather the one who can kill the body, and then is able to cast the soul into hell. Lk. 12:4, 5.

47 Do not worry over what you are to eat or how you are to clothe your body; your heavenly Father is well aware of all your needs. Lk. 12:22, 30.

48 All that is hidden will be made known and all that is covered up will be revealed. Lk. 8:17.

God alone

149 49 Anyone who aspires to be the greatest among you must become the servant of all, and anyone who wishes to be the first must serve as if he were the last. Mt. 20:26, 27.

50 How difficult it is for those who have riches to enter the kingdom of heaven. Mk. 10:23.

51 It is easier for a camel to pass through the eye of a needle than for a rich person to enter the kingdom of heaven. Lk. 18:25.

52 And I say to you, love your enemies; do good to those who hate you, and pray for those who persecute and calumniate you. Mt. 5:44.

53 Alas for you who are rich; you have your consolation in this world. Lk. 6:24.

150 54 Enter by the narrow gate, for the road that leads to perdition is broad and spacious and many pass along that way. But the gate and the road that lead to eternal life are narrow and only a few find them. Mt. 7:13, 14.

55 The last will be the first and the first will be last; for many are called but few are chosen. Mt. 20:16. There is more happiness in giving than in receiving. Acts 20:35.

56 If anyone strikes you on the right cheek turn to him the other, and if anyone takes you to court to claim your tunic, let him have your cloak as well. Mt. 5:39, 40.

57 You must always pray and never become discouraged. Lk. 18:1. Keep watch and pray, lest you fall into temptation. Mt. 26:41.

58 Everyone who exalts himself will be humbled, and everyone who humbles himself will be exalted. Lk. 14:11.

59 Give alms and everything will be clean for you. Lk. 11:41.

60 If your hand or your foot become a cause of sin for you, cut it off and cast it from you. If your eye is a cause of sin for you, pluck it out and cast it from you. It is better that you enter heaven with only one hand or foot or one eye than to enter hell with two hands, two feet, and two eyes. Mt. 18:8, 9.

The eight beatitudes

151 1 1 Blessed are the poor in spirit, for the kingdom of heaven is theirs.

2 Blessed are the meek, for they shall inherit the earth.

3 Blessed are those who mourn, for they shall find consolation.

4 Blessed are those who hunger and thirst for righteousness, for they will be fully satisfied.

5 Blessed are the merciful, for mercy shall be shown to them.

6 Blessed are the pure of heart, for they shall see God.

7 Blessed are the peacemakers, for they shall be called children of God.
8 Blessed are those who suffer persecution for the sake of righteousness, for the kingdom of heaven is theirs.
Mt. 5:3-10.

152 62 I thank you, Father, Lord of heaven and earth, for having hidden these things from the wise and prudent of this world and for revealing them to humble and little ones; yes, Father, for that is what it has pleased you to do. Mt. 11:25.

153 Such is the summary of the great and important truths which Eternal Wisdom came on earth to teach us, having first put them into practice himself. His aim was to rid us of the blindness and waywardness caused by our sins.

Blessed are those who understand these eternal truths.

Still more blessed are those who believe them.

Most blessed of all are those who believe them, put them into practice and teach them to others; for they will shine in heaven like stars for all eternity.[182]

Chapter Thirteen

Summary of the unbelievable sorrows the Incarnate Wisdom chose to endure out of love for us[183]

[1 The most convincing reason for loving Wisdom]

154 Among all the motives impelling us to love Jesus Christ, the Wisdom Incarnate, the strongest, in my opinion, is the suffering he chose to endure to prove his love for us.

"There is," says St. Bernard, "one motive which excels all others which I feel most keenly and which urges me to love Jesus. It is, dear Jesus, the bitter chalice which you drank for our sakes, and the great work of our Redemption which makes you so lovable to us. Indeed this supreme blessing and incomparable proof of your love makes us want to return your love. This motive attracts us more agreeably, makes most just demands upon us, moves us more pressingly and influences us more forcibly." And he gives the reason in a few words, "Our dear Savior has labored and suffered much to accomplish our redemption. What pain and anguish he has endured!"[184]

[2 The circumstances of his Passion]

155 But what makes us realize more clearly the infinite love of Eternal Wisdom for us is the circumstances surrounding his sufferings.

a The first of these is the perfection of his person. Being infinite he gave infinite value to all the sufferings of his passion. Had God sent a seraph or an angel of the lowest order to become man and die for us, it would have been a stupendous thing and worthy of our eternal gratitude. But that the Creator of heaven and earth, the only Son of God, Eternal Wisdom himself should come and offer up his life! This is inconceivable charity, for, compared with his life, the lives of all angels and all men and all creatures together are of infinitely less value than, say, the life of a gnat when compared with the lives of the kings of this earth. Such an excess of love is shown to us in this mystery that our admiration and our gratitude should be great indeed.

156 b A second circumstance is the condition of the people for whom he suffered. They were human beings—unworthy creatures and his enemies, from whom he has nothing to fear nor anything to hope for. We sometimes hear of people dying for their friends; but are we ever likely to hear of anyone but the Son of God dying for his enemies?

But Jesus Christ proved how well he loved us because though we were sinners—and consequently his enemies—he died for us.[185]

157 c The third circumstance is the amount, the grievousness and the duration of his sufferings. Their extent was so great that he is called "Man of sorrows."[186] "A man of every sorrow in whom there is no soundness from the sole of the foot to the top of the head."[187]

This dear friend of our souls suffered in every way exteriorly and inwardly, in body and soul.[188]

158 He suffered even in material things, apart from the poverty of his birth, of his flight into Egypt and his stay there, and the poverty of his entire life; during his passion he was stripped of his garments by soldiers who shared them among themselves, and then fastened him naked to a cross without as much as a rag to cover his body.

159 He suffered in honor and reputation, for he was overwhelmed with insults and called a blasphemer, a revolutionary, a drunkard, a glutton and a possessed person.

He suffered in his wisdom when they classed him as an ignorant man and an imposter, and treated him as a fool and a madman. He suffered in his power, for his enemies considered him a sorcerer and a magician who worked false miracles through a compact with the devil.

He suffered in his disciples, one of whom bartered him for money and betrayed him; another, their leader, denied him; and the rest abandoned him.

160 He suffered from all kinds of people; from kings, governors, judges, courtiers, soldiers, pontiffs, priests, officials of the temple and lay members; from Jews and gentiles, from men and women; in fact, from everyone. Even his Blessed Mother's presence added painfully to his sufferings for, as he was dying, he saw her standing at the foot of the cross engulfed in a sea of sorrow.

161 Moreover, our dear Savior suffered in every member of his body. His head was pierced with a crown of thorns. His hair and beard were torn out; his cheeks were buffeted; his face covered with spittle; his neck and arms bound with cords; his shoulders weighed down and bruised by the weight of the cross. His hands and feet were pierced by the nails, his side and heart opened by a lance; his whole body lacerated by more than five thousand strokes of the scourge, so that his almost fleshless bones became visible.

All his senses were almost immersed in a sea of sufferings. He suffered in his sight as he beheld the mocking faces of his enemies and the tears of grief of his friends. He suffered in his hearing as he listened to insulting words, false testimonies, calumnious statements and horrible blasphemies which evil tongues vomited against him. He suffered in his sense of smell by the foulness of the filth they spat into his face. He suffered in his taste by a feverish thirst in which he was only given gall and vinegar to drink. He suffered in his sense of touch by the excruciating pain of the lashes, thorns and nails.

162 His most holy soul was grievously tormented because every sin committed by man was an outrage against his Father whom he loved infinitely; because sin was the cause of the damnation of so many souls who would be lost despite his passion and death; and because he had compassion not only for all men in general but for each one in particular, as he knew them all individually.

All these torments were much increased by the length of time they lasted, that is, from the first instant of his conception to the moment of his death, because all the sufferings he was to endure were, in the timeless view of his wisdom, always distinctly present to his mind.

To all these torments we must add the most cruel and the most fearful one, namely his abandonment upon the cross which caused him to cry out, "My God, my God, why have you forsaken me?"[189]

[3 The great love with which he suffered]

163 From all this we must conclude with St. Thomas and the

Fathers of the Church that our good Jesus suffered more than all the martyrs both those of past ages and those of the future up to the end of the world. Now if the smallest pain of the Son of God is more precious and more likely to stir our hearts than all the sufferings of angels and men together had they died and given up everything for us, how deep then should be our grief, our love and our gratitude for our Lord who endured for our sakes freely and with the utmost love all that a man could possibly suffer. "For the joy set before him, he endured the cross."[190] According to the Fathers of the Church,[191] these words mean that Jesus Christ, Eternal Wisdom, could have remained in his heavenly glory, infinitely distant from our misfortunes. But he chose on our account to come down upon earth, take the nature of man and be crucified. Even when he had become man he could have imparted to his body the same joy, the same immortality, the same blessedness which he now enjoys. But he did not choose this because he wanted to be free to suffer.

164 Rupert adds to this that at the Incarnation, the eternal Father proposed to his Son the saving of the world either by joyful means or by suffering, by acquiring honors or by suffering contempt, by richness or by poverty, by living or by dying. Hence while remaining himself glorious and triumphant, he could have redeemed men and taken them with him along a way paved with joys, delights, honors and riches had he wished to do so. But he chose rather to endure the cross and sufferings in order to give to God his Father greater glory and to men a proof of greater love.

165 Further, he loved us so much that instead of shortening his sufferings he chose to prolong them and to suffer even more. That is why when he was hanging on the cross, covered with opprobrium and plunged deep in sorrow, as if not suffering enough, he cried out, "I thirst."[192] For what was he thirsting? St. Laurence Justinian[193] gives us the answer. "His thirst arose from the ardor of his love, from the depth and abundance of his charity. He was thirsting for us, thirsting to give himself to us and suffer for us."

[4 Conclusion]

166 Knowing all this are we not right in exclaiming with St. Francis of Paula, "O God who is love, what excesses of love you have shown us in suffering and in dying!" Or with St. Mary Magdalen of Pazzi, kissing the crucifix, "O Love, how little are you known!" Or St. Francis of Assisi, trudging along the dusty streets, "Jesus, my crucified Love, is not loved."

Holy Church makes us repeat every day, "The world does not know Jesus Christ,"[194] incarnate Wisdom; and in truth, to know what our Lord has endured for us, and yet like the world, not to love him ardently is morally impossible.

Chapter Fourteen

The triumph of Eternal Wisdom in and by the Cross[195]

167 The Cross is according to my belief the greatest secret of the King[196]—the greatest mystery of Eternal Wisdom.

[1 Wisdom and the Cross]

How remote and how different are the thoughts and the ways of eternal Wisdom from those of even the wisest of men.[197] This great God wished to redeem the world, to cast out and chain up the devils, to seal the gates of hell and open heaven to men, and give infinite glory to his eternal Father. Such was his purpose, his arduous task, his great undertaking. What means will be chosen by divine Wisdom, whose knowledge reaches from one end of the universe to the other and orders all things well?[198] His arm is almighty; at a stroke he can destroy all that is opposed to him and do whatever he wills. By a single word he can annihilate and create. What more can I say? He has but to will and all is done.

168 But his power is regulated by his love. He wishes to become incarnate in order to convince men of his friendship; he wishes to come down upon earth to help men to go up to heaven. So be it! It would be expected then that this Wisdom incarnate would appear glorious and triumphant, accompanied by millions and millions of angels, or at least by millions of chosen men and women. With these armies, majestic in his splendor and untouched by poverty, dishonor, humiliations and weaknesses, he will crush all his enemies and win the hearts of men by his attractiveness, his delights, his magnificence and his riches.

Surely nothing less than that. But O wonder! He perceives something which is a source of scandal and horror to Jews and an object of foolishness to pagans.[199] He sees a piece of vile and contemptible wood which is used to humiliate and torture the most wicked and the most wretched of men, called a gibbet, a gallows, a cross. It is upon this cross that he casts his eyes; he takes his delight in it; he cherishes it more than all that is great and resplendent in heaven and on earth. He decides that that will be the instrument of his conquests, the adornment of his royal state. He will make it the wealth and joy of his empire, the friend and spouse of his heart. O the depths of the wisdom and knowledge of God! How amazing is his choice and how sublime and incomprehensible are his ways! But how inexpressible his love for that cross![200]

169 Incarnate Wisdom loved the cross from his infancy.[201] At his coming into the world, while in his Mother's womb, he received it from his eternal Father. He placed it deep in his heart, there to dominate his life, saying, "My God and my Father, I chose this cross when I was in your bosom.[202] I choose it now in the womb of my Mother. I love it with all my strength and I place it deep in my heart to be my spouse and my mistress."[203]

170 Throughout his life he eagerly sought after the Cross. If, like a thirsting deer,[204] he hastened from village to village, from town to town; if with giant strides[205] he pursued his way towards Calvary; if he spoke so frequently of his sufferings and death to his apostles and disciples,[206] and even to his prophets during his Transfiguration;[207] if he so often exclaimed, "I have longed for it, with an infinite desire"[208] it was because all his journeying, all his eagerness, all his pursuits, all his desires were directed towards the cross and because to die in its embrace was for him the very height of glory and success.

He espoused the cross at his Incarnation with indescribable love. He sought it out and carried it with the utmost joy, throughout his whole life, which became but one continuous cross. After having made several efforts to embrace it in order to die upon it on Calvary, he asked, "How great is my distress until it is completed!" How am I hindered? What is delaying me? Why can I not embrace you yet, dear cross of Calvary?[209]

171 At last his wishes were fully satisfied. Bearing a stigma of shame he was attached to the cross, indissolubly joined to it and died joyfully upon it as if in the arms of a dear friend and upon a couch of honor and triumph.

172 Do not think that, wanting to be more triumphant, he rejected the cross after his death. Far from it; he united himself so closely to it that neither angel nor man, nor any creature in heaven or on earth, could separate him from it. The bond between them is indissoluble, their union is eternal. Never the Cross without Jesus, or Jesus without the Cross.

Through his dying upon it the Cross of ignominy became so glorious, its poverty and starkness so enriching, its sorrows so agreeable, its austerity so attractive, that it became as it were deified and an object to be adored by angels and by men. Jesus now requires that all his subjects adore it as they adore him. It is not his wish that the honor even of a relative adoration be given to any other creature however exalted, such as his most Blessed Mother. This special worship is due and given only to his dear Cross. On the day of the last judgment he will bring to an end all veneration to the relics of the saints, even those most venerable, but not to those of his Cross. He will command the chief Seraphim and Cherubim to collect from every part of the world all the particles of the true Cross. By his loving omnipotence he will re-unite them so well that the whole Cross will be re-formed, the very Cross on which he died. He will have his Cross borne in triumph by angels joyfully singing its praises. It will go before him, borne upon the most brilliant cloud that has ever been seen. And with this Cross and by it,[210] he will judge the world.

Great will be the joy of the friends of the Cross on beholding it. Deep will be the despair of its opponents who, not being able to bear the brilliant and fiery sight of this Cross will plead for the mountains to fall upon them and for hell to swallow them.[211]

[2 The Cross and ourselves]

173 While waiting for that great day of the last judgment, Eternal Wisdom has decreed the Cross to be the sign, the emblem and the weapon of his faithful people.

He welcomes no child that does not bear its sign. He recognizes no disciple who is ashamed to display it, or who has not the courage to accept it, or who either drags it reluctantly or rejects it outright. He proclaims, "If anyone wishes to come after me, let him renounce himself and take up his cross and follow me."[212]

He enlists no soldier who does not take up the cross as the weapon to defend himself against all his enemies, to attack, to overthrow and to crush them. And he exclaims, "In this sign you will conquer. Have confidence, soldiers of mine, I am your leader; I have conquered my enemies by the cross,[213] and by it you also will be victorious."

174 He has enclosed in the cross such an abundance of grace, life and happiness that only those who enjoy his special favor know about them. He often reveals to his friends his other secrets, as he did to his Apostles: "All things I have made known to you"[214] but he reveals the secrets of the Cross only to those who make themselves worthy by their great fidelity and great labors. One must be humble, little, self-disciplined, spiritual and despised by the world to learn the mystery of the Cross. The Cross even today is a source of scandal and an object of folly not only to Jews and pagans, Moslems and heretics, the worldly-wise and bad Catholics, but even to seemingly devout and very devout people. Yes, the Cross remains an object of scandal, folly, contempt, and fear: not in theory, for never has so much been spoken or written about its beauty and its excellence than in these times; but in practice, because people lose courage, complain, excuse themselves, and run away as soon as a possibility of suffering arises.

"Father," said this incarnate Wisdom, when beholding in joyful rapture the beauty of the Cross, "I thank you for having hidden these things—the treasures and graces of my cross—from the wise and prudent of this world and revealed them to little ones."[215]

175 If the knowledge of the mystery of the cross is such a special grace, how great must be the enjoyment when one actually possesses it? This is a favor Eternal Wisdom bestows only on his best friends and only after they have prayed for it, longed for it, pleaded for it. However excellent is the gift of faith by which we please God, draw near to him and overcome our enemies, and without which we would be lost, the Cross is an even greater gift.

"It was a greater happiness for Saint Peter," says St. John Chrysostom,[216] "to be imprisoned for Jesus Christ than to be a witness of his glory on Mount Tabor; he was more glorious bound in chains than holding the keys of paradise in his hand."[217] St. Paul esteemed it a greater glory to wear a prisoner's chains for his Savior than to be raised to the third heaven.[218] God bestowed a greater favor on the Apostles and martyrs in giving them his Cross to carry in their humiliations, privations and cruel tortures than in conferring on them the gift of miracles or the grace to convert the world.

All those to whom Eternal Wisdom gave himself have desired the Cross, sought after it, welcomed it. Whenever sufferings came their way, they exclaimed from the depths of their hearts with Saint Andrew, "O wonderful Cross, so long have I yearned for you!"[219]

176 The Cross is precious for many reasons:

1 Because it makes us resemble Jesus Christ;

2 Because it makes us worthy children of the eternal Father, worthy members of Jesus Christ, worthy temples of the Holy Spirit. "God the Father chastises every son he accepts;"[220] Jesus Christ accepts as his own only those who carry their crosses. The Holy Spirit cuts and polishes all the living stones of the heavenly Jerusalem, that is, the elect.[221] These are revealed truths.

3 The Cross is precious because it enlightens the mind and gives it an understanding which no book in the world can give. "He who has not been tried, what can he know?"[222]

4 Because when it is well carried it is the source, the food and the proof of love. The Cross enkindles the fire of divine love in the heart by detaching it from creatures. It keeps this love alive and intensifies it; as wood is the food of flames, so the Cross is the food of love. And it is the soundest proof that we love God. The Cross was the proof God gave of his love for us; and it is also the proof which God requires to show our love for him.

5 The Cross is precious because it is an abundant source of every delight and consolation; it brings joy, peace and grace to our souls.

6 The Cross is precious because it brings the one who carries it "a weight of everlasting glory."[223]

177 If we knew the value of the Cross we would, like St. Peter of Alcantara, have novenas made in order to acquire such a delightful morsel of paradise. We would say, like St. Theresa, "Either to suffer or to die;" or with St. Mary Magdalen of Pazzi, "Not to die but to suffer." Like blessed John of the Cross we would ask only for the grace to suffer and be despised. Heaven esteems nothing in this world except the Cross, he said after his death to a saintly person. And our Lord said to one of his servants, "I have crosses of such great value that my Mother, most powerful as she is, can procure from me nothing more precious for her faithful servants."[224]

178 Wise and honest people living in this world, you do not understand the mysterious language of the Cross. You are too fond of sensual pleasures and you seek your comforts too much. You have too much regard for the things of this world and you are too afraid to be held up to scorn or looked down upon. In short, you are too opposed to the Cross of Jesus. True, you speak well of the Cross in general, but not of the one that comes your way. You shun this as much as you can or else you drag it along reluctantly, grumbling, impatient and protesting. I seem to see in you the oxen that drew the ark of the covenant against their will, bellowing as they went, unaware that what they were drawing contained the most precious treasure upon earth.[225]

179 The number of fools and unhappy people is infinite, says Wisdom,[226] because infinite is the number of those who do not know the value of the Cross and carry it reluctantly. But you, true disciples of eternal Wisdom, if you have trials and afflictions, if you suffer much persecution for justice's sake, if you are treated as the refuse of the world, be comforted, rejoice, be glad, and dance for joy because the cross you carry is a gift so precious as to arouse the envy of the saints in heaven, were they capable of envy. All that is honorable, glorious, and virtuous in God and in his Holy Spirit is vested in you, for your reward is great in heaven and even on earth, because of the spiritual favors it obtains for you.

[3 Practical conclusion]

180 Friends of Jesus Christ, drink of his bitter cup and your friendship with him will increase. Suffer with him and you will be glorified with him. Suffer patiently and your momentary suffering will be changed into an eternity of happiness.

Make no mistake about it; since incarnate Wisdom had to enter heaven by the Cross, you also must enter by the same way. No matter which way you turn, says the *Imitation of Christ,*[227] you will always find the Cross. Like the elect you may take it up rightly, with patience and cheerfulness out of love for God; or else like the reprobate you may carry it impatiently and unwillingly as those doubly unfortunate ones who are constrained to repeat perpetually in hell,

"We have labored and suffered in the world and after it all, here we are with the damned."[228]

True wisdom is not to be found in the things of this world nor in the souls of those who live in comfort. He has fixed his abode in the Cross so firmly that you will not find him anywhere in this world save in the Cross. He has so truly incorporated and united himself with the Cross that in all truth we can say: Wisdom is the Cross and the Cross is Wisdom.

Chapter Fifteen

Means to acquire divine Wisdom[229]

THE FIRST MEANS: AN ARDENT DESIRE

181 Children of men, how long will your hearts remain heavy and earthbound? How long will you go on loving vain things and seeking what is false?[230] Why do you not turn your eyes and your hearts towards divine Wisdom who is supremely desirable and who, to attract our love, makes known his origin, shows his beauty, displays his riches, and testifies in a thousand ways how eager he is that we should desire him and seek him.[231] "Be desirous, therefore, of hearing my words,"[232] he tells us. "Wisdom anticipates those who want her.[233] The desire of Wisdom leads to the everlasting kingdom."[234]

182 The desire for divine wisdom must indeed be a great grace from God because it is the reward for the faithful observance of his commandments. "Son, if you rightly desire wisdom, observe justice and God will give it to you. Reflect on what God requires of you and meditate continually on his commandments and he himself will give you insight, and your desire for wisdom will be granted."[235] "For Wisdom will not enter into a deceitful soul, nor dwell in a body subject to sin."[236]

This desire for Wisdom must be holy and sincere, and fostered by faithful adherence to the commandments of God. There are indeed an infinite number of fools and sluggards moved to be good by countless desires, or rather would-be desires, which, by not bringing them to renounce sin and do violence to themselves, are but spurious and deceitful desires which are fatal and lead to damnation.[237] The Holy Spirit, who is the teacher of true knowledge, shuns what is deceitful and withdraws himself from thoughts that are without understanding; iniquity banishes him from the soul.[238]

183 Solomon, the model given us by the Holy Spirit in the acquiring of Wisdom, only received this gift after he had desired it, sought after it and prayed for it for a long time. "I desired wisdom and it was given to me. I called upon God and the spirit of wisdom came to me."[239] "I have loved and sought wisdom from my youth, and in order to have her as my companion and spouse I went about seeking her."[240] Like Solomon and Daniel we must be men of desire if we are to acquire this great treasure which is wisdom.[241]

THE SECOND MEANS: CONTINUOUS PRAYER

184 The greater the gift of God, the more effort is required to obtain it. Much prayer and great effort, therefore, will be required to obtain the gift of Wisdom, which is the greatest of all God's gifts.

Let us listen to the voice of Wisdom himself: "Seek and you shall find, knock and it shall be opened to you, ask and it shall be given you."[242] It is as if he said: If you wish to find me, you must seek me; if you wish to enter my palace, you must knock at my door; if you wish to receive me, you must ask for me. Nobody finds me unless he searches for me; nobody enters my house unless he knocks at my door; nobody possesses me unless he asks for me. We can only do this by prayer.

Prayer is the usual channel by which God conveys his gifts, especially his Wisdom. The world was asking for the incarnation of divine Wisdom for four thousand years. For fourteen years Mary prepared herself by prayer to receive him in her womb.[243] Solomon received Wisdom only after praying most fervently for a long time: "I went to the Lord and besought him, and I said with all my heart;" ". . . Give me that Wisdom that sits by your throne."[244] "If any of you lacks wisdom let him ask God, and it shall be given him, for God gives his gifts to all men abundantly and ungrudgingly."[245] Note here that the Holy Spirit does not say, "If anyone lacks charity, humility, patience, etc." although these are most excellent virtues, but he says, "If anyone lacks Wisdom." For by asking for Wisdom we ask for all the virtues possessed by incarnate Wisdom.

185 Therefore to possess Wisdom we must pray. But how should we pray?[246]

First, we should pray for this gift with a strong and lively faith, not wavering, because he who wavers in his faith must not expect to receive any gift from the Lord.[247]

186 Secondly, we must pray for it with a pure faith, not counting on consolations, visions or special revelations. Although such things may be good and true, as they have been in some saints, it is always dangerous to rely on them. For the more our faith is dependent on these extraordinary graces and feelings, the less pure and meritorious it is. The Holy Spirit has revealed to us the grandeur and the beauty of Wisdom, and the desire of God to bestow this gift upon us, and our own need of it. Here we find motives strong enough to make us want it and pray God for it with unbounded faith and eagerness.

187 Simple faith is both the cause and the effect of Wisdom in our soul. The more faith we have, the more we shall possess wisdom. The more we possess it, the stronger our faith[248] without seeing, without feeling, without tasting and without faltering. "God has said it or promised it;" these words form the basis of all the prayers and actions of every wise man, although from a natural point of view it may seem that God is blind to his plight, deaf to his prayers, powerless to crush his enemies, seemingly empty-handed when help is needed, even though he may be troubled by distractions and doubts, by darkness of the mind, by illusions of the imagination, by weariness and boredom of the heart, by sadness and anguish of soul.

The wise man does not ask to see extraordinary things such as saints have seen, nor to experience sensible sweetness in his prayers. He asks with faith for divine Wisdom. And he will feel surer that this Wisdom will be given him than if it were vouched for by an angel come down from heaven, because God has said that all who pray in the right manner will receive what they ask for.[249] "If you then, being evil, know how to give good things to your children how much more will your heavenly Father give the good spirit (of Wisdom) to those who ask him?"[250]

188 Thirdly, we must pray perseveringly to obtain this Wisdom. The acquisition of this precious pearl and infinite treasure requires from us a holy importunity in praying to God, without which we shall not obtain it. We ought not to act, as so many do, when praying to God for some grace. After they have prayed for a long time, perhaps for years, and God has not granted their request, they become discouraged and give up praying, thinking that God does not want to listen to them. Thus they deprive themselves of the benefit of their prayers and offend God, who loves to give and who always answers, in some way or another, prayers that are well said.

Whoever then wishes to obtain wisdom must pray for it day and night without wearying or becoming disheartened. Blessings in abundance will be his if, after ten, twenty, thirty years of prayer, or even an hour before he dies, he comes to possess it. And if he does obtain this treasure after having spent his whole life seeking for it and praying for it and meriting it with much toil and suffering, let him remind himself that it is not a gift due to him in justice, a recompense that has been earned, but rather a charitable alms given him simply out of mercy.

189 No, it is not those who are careless and inconstant in their prayers and searchings who obtain Wisdom, but those rather who are like the man in the gospel who goes during the night to knock at the door of a friend, wanting to borrow three loaves of bread (cf. Lk. 11:5). Note that it is divine Wisdom himself who in this parable or story teaches us how we should pray if we wish to be heard. This man knocked and repeated his knockings and entreaties four or five times with increased force and insistence, in spite of the untimely hour, near midnight, and his friend having already gone to bed; and in spite of having been rebuffed and told repeatedly to be off and not make himself a selfish nuisance. At length the friend became so annoyed by the persistence of the man that he got out of bed, opened the door and gave him all he asked for.[251]

190 That is how we must pray to obtain Wisdom. And assuredly God wants to be importuned, will sooner or later rise up, open the door of his mercy and give us the three loaves of Wisdom, that is, the bread of life, the bread of understanding and the bread of angels.[252]

Here is a prayer composed by the Holy Spirit to ask for divine Wisdom:

Prayer of Solomon

191 God of my Fathers, God of mercy, you created all things by your word, and by your wisdom you formed man that he might have dominion over all the creatures you have made; that he might govern the world in fairness and justice and pronounce judgment with an upright heart; give me this Wisdom that sits with you on your throne.

Do not exclude me from the number of your children for I am your servant and the son of your handmaid, a man who is weak and short-lived, with little understanding of judgment and laws. For even though a person be considered perfect among the children of men, he is nonetheless worthless if your Wisdom does not dwell in him.

192 It is your Wisdom who has knowledge of your works, who was with you when you made the world, and who knows what is pleasing in your sight and shows what is right according to your commandments.

Send him then from your sanctuary in heaven and from the throne of your majesty, for him to be with me and work with me so that I may know what is pleasing to you; for he possesses the knowledge and understanding of all things. He will lead me in all my works with true perception, and by his power will guard me. My actions then, will be pleasing to you and I will lead your people with justice and be worthy of the throne of my Father; for what man can know the designs of God, or can discover what is his will?

The thoughts of men are unsure and their plans uncertain, for a perishable body weighs heavily upon their soul, and the earthly dwelling depresses the spirit disturbed by many cares. We understand only with difficulty what is happening upon earth and we find it hard to discern even what is before our eyes. How can we know what is happening in heaven, and how can we know your thoughts unless you give us your Wisdom and send us your Holy Spirit from heaven so that he may straighten out the paths of those living on earth and teach us what is pleasing to you. Lord, it is through your Wisdom that all those who have been pleasing to you since the beginning of time have been saved.[253]

193 To vocal prayer we must add mental prayer, which enlightens the mind, inflames the heart and disposes the soul to listen to the voice of Wisdom, to savor his delights and possess his treasures.

For myself, I know of no better way of establishing the kingdom of God, Eternal Wisdom, than to unite vocal and mental prayer by saying the holy Rosary and meditating on its fifteen mysteries.

Chapter Sixteen

THE THIRD MEANS: UNIVERSAL MORTIFICATION

[1 Necessity of mortification]

194 The Holy Spirit tells us that wisdom is not found in the hearts of those who live in comfort,[254] gratifying their passions and bodily desires, because "they who are of the flesh cannot please God," and "the Wisdom of the flesh is an enemy to God."[255] "My spirit will not remain in man, because he is flesh."[256]

All those who belong to Christ, incarnate Wisdom, have crucified their flesh with its passions and desires. They always bear about in their bodies the dying of Jesus. They continually do violence to themselves, carry their cross daily. They are dead and indeed buried with Christ.[257]

These words of the Holy Spirit show us more clearly than the light of day that, if we are to possess incarnate Wisdom, Jesus Christ, we must practice self-denial and renounce the world and self.

195 Do not imagine that incarnate Wisdom, who is purer than the rays of the sun, will enter a soul and a body soiled by the pleasures of the senses. Do not believe that he will grant his rest and ineffable peace to those who love worldly company and vanities. "To him that overcomes the world and himself, I will give the hidden manna."[258]

Although this lovable prince knows and perceives all things in an instant by his own infinite light, he still looks for persons worthy of him.[259] He has to search because there are so few and he can scarcely find any sufficiently unworldly or sufficiently interior and mortified to be worthy of him, of his treasures, and of union with him.

[2 Qualities required for mortification]

196 Wisdom is not satisfied with half-hearted mortification or mortification of a few days, but requires one that is total, continuous, courageous and prudent if he is to give himself to us.

If we would possess wisdom:

197 1 We must either give up actually our worldly possessions as did the apostles, the disciples, and the first Christians, and as religious do now. This is the quickest, the best and the surest means to possess Wisdom. Or at least we must detach our heart from material things, and possess them as though not possessing them,[260] not eager to acquire more or being anxious to retain any of them, and not complaining or worrying when they are lost. This is something very difficult to accomplish.

198 2 We must not follow the showy fashions of the world in our dress, our furniture, or our dwellings. Neither must we indulge in sumptuous meals or other worldly habits and ways of living. "Be not conformed to this world."[261] Putting this into practice is more necessary than is generally thought.

199 3 We must not believe or follow the false maxims of the world or think, speak or act like people of the world. Their doctrine is as opposed to that of incarnate Wisdom as darkness is to light, and death to life. Look closely at their opinions and their words: they think and speak disparagingly of all the great truths of our religion. True, they do not tell brazen lies, but they cover their falsehood with an appearance of truth; they do not think they are being untruthful, but they lie nonetheless. In general, they do not teach sin openly, but they speak of it as if it were virtuous, or blameless, or a matter of indifference and of little consequence. This guile which the devil has taught the world in order to conceal the heinousness of sin and falsehood is the wickedness spoken of by St. John when he wrote, "The whole world lies in the power of evil"[262] and now more than ever before.

200 4 We must flee as much as possible from the company of others, not only from that of worldly people, which is harmful and dangerous, but even from that of religious people when our association with them would be useless and a waste of time. Whoever wishes to become wise and perfect must put into practice these three golden counsels which eternal Wisdom gave to Saint Arsenius, "Flee, hide, be silent." Flee as much as possible the company of men, as the greatest saints have done.[263] Let your life be hidden with Christ in God.[264] In short, be silent with others, so as to converse with divine Wisdom. "He who knows how to keep silent is a wise man."[265]

201 5 If we would possess Wisdom we must mortify the body, not only by enduring patiently our bodily ailments, the inconveniences of the weather and the difficulties arising from other people's actions, but also by deliberately undertaking some penances and mortifications, such as fasts, vigils and other austerities practiced by holy penitents.

It requires courage to do that because the body naturally idolizes itself, and the world considers all bodily penances as pointless and rejects them. The world does and says everything possible to deter people from practicing the austerities of the saints. Of every saint it can be said, with due allowances, "the wise or the saintly man has brought his body into subjection by vigils, fasts and disciplines, by enduring the cold and nakedness and every kind of austerity, and he has made a compact not to give it any rest in this world" (cf. Rom. Brev. St. Peter of Alcant). The Holy Spirit says of all the saints, that they were enemies of the stained robe of the flesh (Jude 23).

202 6 For exterior and voluntary mortification to be profitable, it must be accompanied by the mortifying of the judgment and the will through holy obedience, because without this obedience all mortification is spoiled by self-will and often becomes more pleasing to the devil than to God.

That is why no exceptional mortification should be undertaken without seeking counsel. "I, Wisdom, dwell in counsel."[266] "He who trusts in himself, trusts in a fool."[267] "The prudent man does all things with counsel."[268] And the great counsel given by the Holy Spirit is this: Do nothing without counsel and you shall have nothing to regret afterwards.[269] Seek counsel always of a wise man.[270]

By holy obedience we do away with self-love, which spoils everything; by obedience the smallest of our actions become meritorious. It protects us from illusions of the devil, enables us to overcome our enemies, and brings us surely, as though while sleeping, into the harbor of salvation.[271]

All that I have just said is contained in this one great counsel: "Leave all things and you will find all things by finding Jesus Christ, incarnate Wisdom."[272]

Chapter Seventeen

FOURTH MEANS: A LOVING AND GENUINE DEVOTION TO THE BLESSED VIRGIN[273]

203 The greatest means of all, and the most wonderful of all

secrets for obtaining and preserving divine Wisdom is a loving and genuine devotion to the Blessed Virgin.

[1 Necessity of genuine devotion to Mary]

No one but Mary ever found favor with God[274] for herself and for the whole human race. To no other person was given the power to conceive and give birth to Eternal Wisdom.[275] No one else had the power to "incarnate" him, so to speak, in the predestinate by the operation of the Holy Spirit.

The patriarchs, prophets and saints of the Old Testament yearned and prayed for the incarnation of Eternal Wisdom, but none of them was able to merit it.[276] Only Mary, by her exalted holiness, could reach the throne of the Godhead and merit this gift of infinite value.[277]

She became the mother, mistress and throne of divine Wisdom.

204 Mary is his most worthy Mother because she conceived him and brought him forth as the fruit of her womb. "Blessed is the fruit of thy womb, Jesus."[278]

Hence it is true to say that Jesus is the fruit and product of Mary wherever he is present, be it in heaven, on earth, in our tabernacles or in our hearts. She alone is the tree of life and Jesus alone is the fruit of that tree.

Therefore anyone who wishes to possess this wonderful fruit in his heart must first possess the tree that produces it; whoever wishes to possess Jesus must possess Mary.

205 Mary is also mistress of divine Wisdom. Not that she is above him who is truly God, or even equal to him. To think or say such a thing would be blasphemous. But because the Son of God, Eternal Wisdom, by making himself entirely subject to her as his Mother, gave her a maternal and natural authority over himself which surpasses our understanding. He not only gave her this power while he lived on earth but still gives it now in heaven, because glory does not destroy nature but makes it more perfect. And so in heaven Jesus is as much as ever the Son of Mary, and Mary, the Mother of Jesus.

As his Mother, Mary has authority over Jesus, who because he wills it, remains in a sense subject to her. This means that Mary by her powerful prayers and because she is the Mother of God, obtains from Jesus all she wishes. It means that she gives him to whom she decides, and produces him every day in the souls of those she chooses.

206 Happy are those who have won Mary's favors! They can rest assured that they will soon possess divine Wisdom, for as she loves those who love her,[279] she generously shares her blessings with them, including that infinite treasure which contains every good,

Jesus, the fruit of her womb.

207 If it is true to say that Mary is, in a sense, mistress of Wisdom incarnate, what control must she have over all the graces and gifts of God, and what freedom must she enjoy in giving them to whom she chooses.

The Fathers of the Church[280] tell us that Mary is an immense ocean of all the perfections of God, the great storehouse of all his possessions, the inexhaustible treasury of the Lord, as well as the treasurer and dispenser of all his gifts.

Because God gave her his Son, it is his will that we should receive all gifts through her, and that no heavenly gift should come down upon earth without passing through her as through a channel.

Of her fulness we have all received, and any grace or hope of salvation we may possess is a gift which comes to us from God through Mary. So truly is she mistress of God's possessions that she gives to whom she wills, all the graces of God, all the virtues of Jesus Christ, all the gifts of the Holy Spirit, every good thing in the realm of nature, grace and glory. These are the thoughts and expressions of the Fathers of the Church, whose words, for the sake of brevity, I do not quote in the Latin.[281]

But whatever gifts this sovereign and lovable Queen bestows upon us, she is not satisfied until she has given us incarnate Wisdom, Jesus her Son; and she is ever on the look-out for those who are worthy of Wisdom,[282] so that she may give him to them.

208 Moreover, Mary is the royal throne of Eternal Wisdom. It is in her that he shows his perfection, displays his treasures and takes his delight. There is no place in heaven or on earth where Eternal Wisdom shows so much magnificence or finds more delight than in the incomparable Virgin Mary.

That is why the Fathers of the Church[283] call her the tabernacle of the divinity, the place of rest and contentment of the Blessed Trinity, the throne of God, the city of God, the altar of God, the temple of God, the world of God and the paradise of God. All these titles are most correct with regard to the different wonders which the most high God has worked in Mary.

209 Only through Mary, then, can we possess divine Wisdom.

But if we do receive this great gift where are we to lodge him? What dwelling, what seat, what throne are we to offer this Prince who is so dazzling that the very rays of the sun are dust and darkness in his presence? No doubt we will be told that he has asked only for our heart, that it is our heart we must offer him, and it is there we must lodge him.

210 But we know that our heart is tainted, carnal, full of unruly inclinations and consequently unfit to house such a noble and holy guest. If we had a thousand hearts like our own and offered him the choice of one of them as his throne, he would rightly reject our offer, turn a deaf ear to our entreaties, and even accuse us of boldness and impertinence in wanting to house him in a place so unclean and so unworthy of his royal dignity.

211 What then can we do to make our hearts worthy of him? Here is the great way, the wonderful secret. Let us, so to speak, bring Mary into our abode by consecrating ourselves unreservedly to her as servants and slaves. Let us surrender into her hands all we possess, even what we value most highly, keeping nothing for ourselves. This good Mistress who never allows herself to be surpassed in generosity will give herself to us in a real but indefinable manner; and it is in her that eternal Wisdom will come and settle as on a throne of splendor.

212 Mary is like a holy magnet attracting Eternal Wisdom to herself with such power that he cannot resist. This magnet drew him down to earth to save mankind, and continues to draw him every day into every person who possesses it. Once we possess Mary, we shall, through her intercession, easily and in a short time possess divine Wisdom.

Mary is the surest, the easiest, the shortest, and the holiest of all the means of possessing Jesus Christ. Were we to perform the most frightful penances, undertake the most painful journeys, or the most fatiguing labors, were we to shed all our blood in order to acquire divine Wisdom, all our efforts would be useless and inadequate if not supported by the intercession of the Blessed Virgin and a devotion to her. But if Mary speaks a word in our favor, if we love her and prove ourselves her faithful servants and imitators, we shall quickly and at little cost possess divine Wisdom.

213 Note that Mary is not only the Mother of Jesus, Head of all the elect, but is also Mother of all his members. Hence she conceives them, bears them in her womb and brings them forth to the glory of heaven through the graces of God which she imparts to them. This is the teaching of the Fathers of the Church, and among them St. Augustine,[284] who says that the elect are in the womb of Mary until she brings them forth into the glory of heaven. Moreover, God has decreed that Mary should dwell in Jacob, make Israel her inheritance and place her roots in his elect and predestinate.[285]

214 From these truths we must conclude:

1 that it is futile for us to compliment ourselves on being the children of God and disciples of Wisdom, if we are not children of Mary;

2 that to be numbered among the elect we must have a loving and sincere devotion to our Lady, so that she may dwell in us and plant the roots of her virtues in us;

3 that Mary must beget us in Jesus Christ and Jesus Christ in us nurturing us towards the perfection and the fulness of his

age,[286] so that she may say more truthfully than St. Paul, "My dear children, I am in travail over you afresh until Jesus Christ, my Son, is perfectly formed in you" (Gal. 4:19).[287]

[2 What genuine devotion to Mary consists in]

215 If I were asked by someone seeking to honor our Lady, "What does genuine devotion to her involve?" I would answer briefly that it consists in a full appreciation of the privileges and dignity of our Lady; in expressing our gratitude for her goodness to us; in zealously promoting devotion to her; in constantly appealing for her help; in being completely dependent on her; and in placing firm reliance and loving confidence in her motherly goodness.

216 We must beware of those false devotions to our Lady which the devil makes use of to deceive and ruin many souls.

I shall not describe them here. I shall only say that genuine devotion to Mary must be *sincere,* free from hypocrisy and superstition; *loving,* not lukewarm or scrupulous; *constant,* not fickle or unfaithful; *holy,* without being presumptuous or extravagant.

217 We must avoid joining those whose devotion is false and *hypocritical,* being only on their lips and in their outward behavior.

Neither must we be among those who are *critical* and *scrupulous,* who are afraid of going too far in honoring our Lady, as if honor given to our Lady could detract from her Son.

We must not be among those who are *lukewarm* or *self-interested,* who have no genuine love for our Lady or filial confidence in her, and who only pray to her to obtain or keep some temporal benefit.

We must not be like those who are *inconstant* and *casual* in their devotion to the Blessed Virgin, who serve her in fits and starts, honor her for a short time and fall away when temptation comes.

Lastly, we must avoid joining those whose devotion is *presumptuous,* who under the cloak of some exterior practices of devotion to Mary, conceal a heart corrupted by sin, and who imagine that because of such devotion to Mary they will not die without the sacraments but will be saved, no matter what sins they commit.

218 We must not neglect to become members of our Lady's confraternities, especially the Confraternity of the Holy Rosary, fulfilling faithfully the duties prescribed which can only make us holy.

219 But the most perfect and most profitable of all devotions to the Blessed Virgin consists in consecrating ourselves entirely to her and to Jesus through her as their slaves. It involves consecrating to her completely and for all eternity our body and soul, our possessions both spiritual and material, the atoning value and the merits of our good actions and our right to dispose of them. In short, it involves the offering of all we have acquired in the past, all we actually possess at the moment, and all we will acquire in the future.

As there are several books treating of this devotion, I will content myself with saying that I have never found a practice of devotion to our Lady more solid than this one, since it takes its inspiration from the example of Jesus Christ. Neither have I found any devotion which redounds more to God's glory, is more salutary to the soul, and more feared by the enemies of our salvation; nor, finally, have I found a devotion that is more attractive and more satisfying.

220 This devotion, if well practiced, not only draws Jesus Christ, Eternal Wisdom, into our soul, but also makes it agreeable to him and he remains there to the end of our life. For, I ask you, what would be the good of searching for secrets of finding divine Wisdom and of making every effort to possess this treasure, if after acquiring it, we were, like Solomon, to have the misfortune to lose it by our unfaithfulness? Solomon was wiser than we perhaps shall ever be, and consequently stronger and more enlightened. He went astray, was overcome by temptation, and fell into sin and folly. Thus he left to all those who came after him a double source of wonderment, that he should be so enlightened and still not see; so wise and still be so foolish in his sins. We can say that, if his example and writings have moved so many who came after him to desire and seek Wisdom, the example of his fall—a fact, as far as we can judge—has kept multitudes of souls from effectively going after something which, although priceless, could easily be lost.

221 To be then in some way wiser than Solomon, we should place in Mary's care all that we possess and the treasure of all treasures, Jesus Christ, that she may keep him for us. We are vessels too fragile to contain this precious treasure, this heavenly manna. We are surrounded by too many cunning and experienced enemies to trust in our own prudence and strength. And we have had too many sad experiences of our fickleness and natural thoughtlessness. Let us be distrustful of our own wisdom and fervor.

222 Mary is wise: let us place everything in her hands. She knows how to dispose of us and all that we have for the greater glory of God.

Mary is charitable: she loves us as her children and servants. Let us offer everything to her and we will lose nothing by it; she will turn everything to our gain.

Mary is liberal: she returns more than we give her. Let us give her unreservedly all that we own without any reservation; she will give us a hundredfold in return.

Mary is powerful: nothing on earth can take from her what we have placed in her keeping. Let us then commit ourselves to her care; she will defend us against our enemies and help us to triumph over them.

God alone

Mary is faithful: she will not permit anything we give her to be lost or wasted. She stands alone as the Virgin most faithful to God and to men. She faithfully guarded and kept all that God entrusted to her, never allowing the least bit to be lost; and she still keeps watch every day, with a special care, over all those who have placed themselves entirely under her protection and guidance.

Let us, then, confide everything to the faithful Virgin Mary, binding ourselves to her as to a pillar that cannot be moved, as to an anchor that cannot slip, or better still, as to Mount Sion which cannot be shaken.

Thus whatever may be our natural blindness, our weakness, and our inconstancy, however numerous and wicked our enemies may be, we shall never go wrong or go astray or have the misfortune to lose the grace of God and that infinite treasure which is Eternal Wisdom.

Consecration of oneself to Jesus Christ, Wisdom incarnate, through the hands of Mary

223 Eternal and incarnate Wisdom, most lovable and adorable Jesus, true God and true man, only Son of the eternal Father and of Mary always Virgin, I adore you profoundly, dwelling in the splendor of your Father from all eternity and in the virginal womb of Mary, your most worthy Mother, at the time of your Incarnation.

I thank you for having emptied yourself in assuming the condition of a slave[288] to set me free from the cruel slavery of the evil one.

I praise and glorify you for having willingly chosen to obey Mary, your holy Mother, in all things, so that through her I may be your faithful slave of love.

But I must confess that I have not kept the vows and promises which I made to you so solemnly at my baptism. I have not fulfilled my obligations, and I do not deserve to be called your child or even your slave.

Since I cannot lay claim to anything except what merits your rejection and displeasure, I dare no longer approach the holiness of your majesty on my own. That is why I turn to the intercession and the mercy of your holy Mother, whom you yourself have given me to mediate with you. Through her I hope to obtain from you contrition and pardon for my sins, and that Wisdom whom I desire to dwell in me always.

224 I turn to you, then, Mary immaculate, living tabernacle of God, in whom Eternal Wisdom willed to receive the adoration of both men and angels.

I greet you as Queen of heaven and earth, for all that is under God has been made subject to your sovereignty.

I call upon you, the unfailing refuge of sinners, confident in your mercy that has never forsaken anyone.

Grant my desire for divine Wisdom and, in support of my petition, accept the promises and the offering of myself which I now make, conscious of my unworthiness.

225 I, an unfaithful sinner, renew and ratify today through you my baptismal promises. I renounce forever Satan, his empty promises, and his evil designs, and I give myself completely to Jesus Christ, the incarnate Wisdom, to carry my cross after him for the rest of my life, and to be more faithful to him than I have been till now.

This day, with the whole court of heaven as witness, I choose you, Mary, as my Mother and Queen. I surrender and consecrate myself to you, body and soul, as your slave, with all that I possess, both spiritual and material, even including the value of all my good actions, past, present, and to come. I give you the full right to dispose of me and all that belongs to me, without any reservations, in whatever way you please, for the greater glory of God in time and throughout eternity.

226 Accept, gracious Virgin, this little offering of my slavery to honor and imitate the obedience which Eternal Wisdom willingly chose to have towards you, his Mother. I wish to acknowledge the authority which both of you have over this little worm and pitiful sinner. By it I wish also to thank God for the privileges bestowed on you by the Blessed Trinity. I declare that for the future I will try to honor and obey you in all things as your true slave of love.

O admirable Mother, present me to your dear Son as his slave now and for always, so that he who redeemed me through you, will now receive me through you.

227 Mother of mercy, grant me the favor of obtaining the true Wisdom of God, and so make me one of those whom you love, teach and guide, whom you nourish and protect as your children and slaves.

Virgin most faithful, make me in everything so committed a disciple, imitator, and slave of Jesus, your Son, incarnate Wisdom, that I may become, through your intercession and example, fully mature with the fulness which Jesus possessed on earth,[289] and with the fulness of his glory in heaven. Amen.

Let those accept it who can.[290]
Who is wise enough to understand these things?[291]

Footnotes for Love of Eternal Wisdom

1 This prayer composed by Saint Louis Marie serves as dedication for the whole book.
2 Cf. Eph. 4:13.
3 As with all Saint Louis Marie's writings this book possesses order and method. Cf. plan of the book in Nos. 7 and 14.
4 Wis. 8:18.
5 Cf. Sir. 8:18.
6 This is precisely the end Montfort is seeking. Cf. the end of Nos. 12 and 226.
6a The preceding numbers in parentheses were not in the original.
7 Wis. 6:6, 7, 9.
8 Lk. 6:24.
9 Mt. 19:24. Cf. Mk. 10:25; Lk. 18:25.
10 Jas. 5:1.
11 Lk. 6:24.
12 Cf. Wis. 6:24-26.
13 In this chapter Montfort resumes bk. 1, c. 3, Nos. 2, 3 of SAINT-JURE'S *On the knowledge and love of the Son of God.*
14 Cf. Eph. 3:19.
15 Cf. Col. 1:16; 2:9.
16 SAINT BERNARD, *Vitis Mystica seu de Passione Domini,* c. 22, No. 75: *"Quia haec est illa una pretiosa margarita . . ."*
17 Jer. 9:23-24.
18 Cf. Prov. 2:1-9.
19 Song 1:3.
20 Ps. 33:9.
21 Song 5:1.
22 Wis. 8:16.
23 Jn. 17:3.
24 Wis. 15:3.
25 Adaptation of a text of SAINT AUGUSTINE, Confessions, 5, c. 4, No. 7.
26 1 Cor. 2:2.
27 Phil. 3:7-8.
28 Col. 2:4,8.
29 2 Pet. 3:18.
30 The explanation of the origin of the word *sapientia* (wisdom) as deriving from sapor (taste) although currently given (by Saint Isidore, Saint Thomas and Saint Bernard) is very much open to question. However it does indicate the basic meaning given to the term by

Christian authors, even though it could not be justified etymologically.

31 Montfort will explain the nature of true wisdom, especially in Chapter 8 where he discusses the wonders produced by Eternal Wisdom in the souls of those who possess him. On the other hand, false wisdom in its different forms will be treated in Chapter 7 where he speaks of the choice to be made of true wisdom.

32 Jas. 3:15.

33 1 Cor. 2:6.

34 The author sets out in this chapter to give an exposition of Wisdom, beginning with his dwelling in the womb of his Father. It is this personal relationship of Wisdom with the Father that constitutes the excellence of his being. This excellence is presented by Montfort as the first in a series of motives which basically inspire the love, the quest and the possession of Wisdom. Cf. No.181: his origin, beauty, richness, desires; and No. 186: his person, his treasures and his covenant. This manner of considering Wisdom under the three headings of excellence, power and goodness recalls the *Triple Crown of the Blessed Virgin,* a prayer dear to Montfort.

35 Rom. 11:33.

36 Is. 53:8; Acts 8:33.

37 In confessing his lack of competence in treating such a sublime subject (cf. Nos. 1 and 19) the author is re-echoing the sentiments of Blessed HENRY SUSO to whom he refers in Nos. 101-103. Cf. HENRY SUSO, *Horologium Sapientiae.*

38 Cf. No. 65: ". . . he has written a book describing his own excellence and his desire for man's friendship."

39 Wis. 7:25, 26.

40 Jn. 1:1.

41 Cf. Sir. 1:4, 8; 24:14.

42 Prov. 8:23, 24.

43 Mt. 17:5; cf. Mt. 3:17. Cf. Nos. 55, 98.

44 Cf. Office hymn of the Transfiguration.

45 Cf. Mt. 11:27; Lk. 10:22.

46 This spiritual commentary, in Nos. 29, 30, has been taken almost literally from the commentary of Sacy on Verses 17 ff.

47 SAINT AUGUSTINE, *De moribus Ecclesiae catholicae,* I, c. 17, No. 31.

48 Jn. 1:3. Cf. Heb. 1:2; Col. 1:16-17.

49 Wis. 7:12, 21.

50 Wis. 1:7; 7:27.

51 Prov. 8:30-31. All this number is a paraphrase of Prov. 8:27-31.

52 Hos. 14:10. Cf. Jer. 9:12; Ps. 106:43.

53 Cf. Gen. 1:26.

54 Cf. Eph. 2:3.

55 Cf. Gen. 3:10, 17-23; 4:11, 12.

56 Montfort here speaks very pessimistically of man but he is really speaking of unredeemed man. Cf. Nos. 43, 46.

57 Cf. Gen. 1:26: "Let us make man in our own image. . . ."

58 Cf. TD 28.

59 Prov. 8:31.
60 Wis. 6:17.
61 Wis. 7:27; cf. 7:14.
62 Wis. 10:1-21.
63 Wis. 11.
64 Wis. 9:19.
65 In the following two chapters Montfort draws from two literary sources: 1) SAINT-JURE, *On the knowledge and love of the Son of God, our Lord Jesus Christ,* Paris 1634.
2) LE MAISTRE DE SACY, from whom he borrows a short commentary on Prov. 8 and Wis. 6-8.
66 Montfort borrows this quotation from SACY who attributes it to SAINT BERNARD.
67 No doubt Montfort has in mind certain saints who were reputed to have arrived at spiritual marriage, e.g. Blessed Henry Suso, Saint Laurence Justinian and Saint Teresa of Avila.
68 Cf. ch. 1 and No. 98.
69 Cf. Jn. 1:9.
70 Cf. Jn. 1:18; Mt. 11:27; 1 Cor. 2:10.
71 Mt. 23:8, 10.
72 The author will consider at length the effects of Wisdom in the souls of the just in Chapter 8.
73 Wis. 3:17.
74 Wis. 7:22-24.
75 This is the most important text of the whole chapter. Montfort considers it as containing in a nutshell all that he has just been explaining. He will return to it at the beginning of the next chapter (No. 64).
76 Cf. SAINT-JURE, I, c. 13: "Ninth motive for loving our Lord: We are made for him."
77 Wis. 7:14.
78 Cf. SAINT-JURE, I, ch. 8: "Fourth motive for loving our Lord: He became man in order to be loved by men" and I, ch. 12: "Eighth motive based upon the rights that God has by creation and redemption."
79 Cf. Nos. 35-38.
80 Does Montfort have in mind the five Wisdom books as they are called in the liturgy? He seems to quote and comment principally upon the eighth chapter of Proverbs. However, because of what he writes here and in No. 16 he would seem to be thinking only of the Book of Wisdom, called also in the Greek, Wisdom of Solomon.
81 Nos. 66 and 67 are taken almost literally from SAINT-JURE, I, ch. 4, Nos. 2, 3.
82 Prov. 8:4.
83 Cf. Prov. 8:15-21.
84 Cf. Prov. 8:31.
85 Prov. 8:32-36.
86 Wis. 6:13b-15.
87 Most of these texts are implicit quotations from the gospels. Cf. Mt. 11:28; 14:27; Mk. 6:50, Jn. 6:20, Lk. 24:36; Mt. 8:26; Mt.

9:13; Mk. 2:17; Lk. 5:32; Mt. 11:19; Jn. 10:11; Mt. 11:28.

88 SAINT JOHN CHRYSOSTOM, *In Joannem homilia.*

89 Blessed GUERRIC, *Sermon 1 for Pentecost.*

90 Prov. 1:24.

91 Prov. 1:26.

92 Prov. 3:15.

93 Prov. 8:11.

94 This chapter contains one of the principal themes of Montfort's preaching as can be gathered from his Book of Sermons. He seems in this matter to have been inspired by a book of BOUDON, *The Woes of the World,* which Montfort had studied during his stay with the community of M. de la Barmondière at Paris.

95 Cf. SAINT-JURE quoting SAINT AUGUSTINE: "What is true philosophy and who is the true philosopher?" in *De civitate Dei,* VIII, ch. 1.

96 Cf. 1 Cor. 2:6.

97 1 Cor. 1:19; cf. Is. 29:14.

98 Rom. 8:7.

99 Jas. 3:15.

100 Eccles. 1:15.

101 1 Cor. 1:22.

103 This is an apocryphal book.

104 RAYMOND LULLY (1235?-1315) and several Christian thinkers of the fifteenth and sixteenth centuries were influenced by the Cabal.

105 MARTIN DEL RIO, S.J. (1551-1608), friend of Justus Lipsius, published in 1599 a book entitled *Six books containing discussions on magic.* In book 1, ch. 5, he gives his opinion on the effectiveness of alchemy.

106 Col. 2:3; also cf. Nos. 57, 58.

107 Sir. 3:22.

108 Cf. LFC 26.

109 Jn. 14:6.

110 It will be noticed in a special way in this chapter that Montfort speaks through personal experience.

111 Wis. 7:22.

112 Cf. Wis. 6:17.

113 Wis. 7:27.

114 Cf. LEW 49.

115 Cf. No. 53. Montfort frequently stresses the secret manner of God's operations. Cf. SM 55.

116 Wis. 7:7.

117 Cf. Wis. 7:22-24.

118 Montfort had personally experienced these gifts of the Holy Spirit during his theological studies at Paris, as Canon Blain remarks in his *Mémoirs:* "He was endowed with a penetrating mind and would have achieved outstanding success if he had continued his studies at the Sorbonne, but he gave greater preference to the science of the saints than to that of theology."

119 Wis. 1:7. The liturgy of Pentecost applies this text to the gift of tongues. Cf. Acts 2:2-4, 11.

120 Cf. Ex. 4:10-12.
121 Jer. 1:6.
122 Acts 2:11.
123 Hymn of the liturgy: "Come, Holy Ghost, come."
124 Cf. Jn. 1:3-13. This is a theme developed in ch. 2-6.
125 Cf. No. 47.
126 Montfort himself enjoyed this gift and wrote about it to his director, Fr. Leschassier (L 11). He also envisaged it for his future missionaries and for the apostles of the "latter times" (cf. TD 57).
127 1 Thess. 2:13.
128 Heb. 4:12.
129 Wis. 7:15.
130 Lk. 21:15.
131 2 Cor. 2:7.
132 Wis. 7:15; cf. No. 96.
133 Mt. 12:34.
134 Acts 6:10.
135 Mk. 1:22.
136 Cf. Is. 55:10-11.
137 Cf. Nos. 10, 19, 55.
138 Cf. No. 10.
139 Wis. 8:16.
140 Wis. 7:12.
141 Wis. 8:18.
142 Wis. 7:24.
143 Here again the author speaks from experience as shown by his letters written about the same time as the LEW (cf. L 15, 16).
144 This theme will be developed in ch. 14 where Montfort identifies Wisdom with the Cross. Cf. FC 26.
145 Cf. Nos. 41-46.
146 Cf. Is. 45:8.
147 Cf. Antiphon of the Advent season.
148 This idea seems to have been inspired by Poiré and Bérulle. Cf. TD 16.
149 Prov. 9:1.
150 Thoughts borrowed from BÉRULLE, *Vie de Jésus,* ch. 4.
151 For further explanation cf. POIRÉ, 12th star: Mary is a true mirror of the divine perfections.
152 Cf. TD 7.
153 Cf. POIRÉ, *Crown of Power,* 1st star: Only Mary had the power of attracting the divine Word down into our world.
154 This text cannot be verified as being of Saint Augustine.
155 Lk. 1:38. Cf. also similar ideas in POIRÉ, *Crown of Power,* 1st star, and in D'ARGENTAN, Conf. 1.
156 Jn. 1:14.
157 Cf. BÉRULLE, *Vie de Jésus,* I, ch. 24; also SAINT JOHN EUDES, *Le coeur admirable,* t. I, bk. 6, ch. 1.
158 Cf. D'ARGENTAN, t. I, conf. 9.
159 Lk. 2:14.
160 Chapters 10 and 11 together cover one theme. They present one

special motive for loving Eternal Wisdom, namely, the gentleness of Jesus. The last sermon of his life was given on this subject at Saint-Laurent-sur-Sèvre. NOUET and SAINT-JURE are the main sources used in these chapters, although, as usual, he was inspired very much by Holy Scripture.

161 Jn. 3:16.

162 Jer. 11:19. This text refers to Jeremiah himself but is applied to the suffering Messiah in the Holy Week liturgy.

163 Is. 42:3. Cf. Mt. 12:20.

164 For Saint Louis Marie, the example of Saint John the Baptist shows clearly that the third means of obtaining and preserving Wisdom (universal mortification, Nos. 194-202) attains its end.

165 Jn. 1:29.

166 *Nil canitur suavius, Nil auditur jucundius, Nil cogitatur dulcius, Quam Jesus Dei Filius.* Hymn wrongly attributed to ST. BERNARD.

167 ST. BERNARD, *Sermo 15 in Cantica:* Mel in ore *in aure melos, in corde jubilus.*

168 Cf. ST. AUGUSTINE, *Enarratio in Ps. 44, 3.*

169 This legend is borrowed from an ancient Syrian manuscript called *Doctrina Addai.* Cf. G. PHILIPS, *The Doctrine of Addai the Apostle,* London, 1876, sp. 5.

170 Mt. 12:19. Cf. Is. 42:2.

171 Jn. 7:46.

172 Mt. 13:54.

173 Mk. 7:37.

174 Mt. 19:14.

175 Cf. Wis. 7:26. See also No. 16.

176 NOUET relates this as having happened to Hugh of Saint-Victor.

177 Ps. 50:3.

178 DIONYSIUS AREOPAGITA, *Epistola* 8.

179 Cf. HENRY SUSO, *Horologium Sapientiae,* I, c. 1.

180 Prov. 23:26.

181 The first forty-nine "utterances" or "oracles" have almost literally been taken from A. BONNEFONS, S.J. We have given the complete scriptural references where, in most cases, Montfort only indicated the chapters where these texts are found. These utterances provide an incentive for increasing in love of Wisdom and are found in other writings of Montfort, especially in the "Maxims."

182 Dan. 12:3.

183 This chapter was inspired by SAINT-JURE's *On the Knowledge and Love of the Son of God, our Lord Jesus Christ,* 7th motive: his sufferings and his death.

184 Cf. SAINT BERNARD, *Sermon 20 on the Song of Songs.*

185 Rom. 5:8, 9.

186 Is. 53:3.

187 This text in its literal sense refers to the people of Judah but it is applied by the Church of Jesus in his Passion.

188 What follows is taken from the *Summa Theologica* of SAINT THOMAS, III, qu. 46, art. 5-7.

189 Mt. 27:46.
190 Heb. 12:2.
191 Montfort has borrowed these considerations on Tradition from SAINT-JURE, who in turn summarized them from the commentary of CORNELIUS A LAPIDE on Heb. 12:2.
192 Jn. 19:28.
193 SAINT LAURENCE JUSTINIAN, *De triumphali Christi agone,* c. 19.
194 Jn. 1:10.
195 This chapter was inspired by the two works of HENRI BOUDON, *The Holy Pathways of the Cross* and *God Alone, or the Holy Slavery of the Admirable Mother of God.* Cf. also FC.
196 Tob. 12:7.
197 Cf. Is. 55:8.
198 Cf. Wis. 8:1.
199 Cf. Cor. 1:23.
200 Rom. 11:33.
201 Cf. Wis. 8:2.
202 Ps. 39:9.
203 Cf. Wis. 8:2.
204 Cf. Ps. 41:2.
205 Cf. Ps. 18:6.
206 Cf. Mt. 16:21; 17:12, 22, 23; 20:17-19.
207 Cf. Lk. 9:31.
208 Lk. 22:15.
209 Lk. 12:50: *Quomodo coarctor usque dum perficiatur.*
210 This idea is expressed by several Fathers, e.g. SAINT JOHN CHRYSOSTOM, *Homily 2: The Cross and the Thief,* No. 4.
211 Cf. Lk. 23:30.
212 Mt. 16:24; Lk. 9:23.
213 Jn. 16:33.
214 Jn. 15:15.
215 Lk. 10:21.
216 SAINT JOHN CHRYSOSTOM, *Homily 8 on Ephesians* Nos. 1, 2.
217 Acts 12:3-7; Mt. 16:19.
218 Eph. 3:1, 4:1; 2 Cor. 12:2.
219 Cf. SAINT BERNARD, *Sermo in vigilia Sancti Andreae,* No. 3.
220 Heb. 12:6.
221 Cf. 1 Pet. 2:5; Apoc. 21:2, 10.
222 Sir. 34:9.
223 2 Cor. 4:17.
224 The author has possibly found these sentiments in BOUDON's books *The Holy Pathways of the Cross,* I, ch. 5, and *The Holy Slavery,* ch. 12.
225 1 Kgs. 6:12.
226 Ecc. 1:15.
227 *Imitation of Christ,* bk. 2, c. 12, No. 3.
228 Wis. 5:7.
229 The matter of the following two chapters, already touched upon in No. 175, would seem to have been taken from SAINT-JURE,

L'homme spirituel.
230 Ps. 4:3.
231 The author sums up here all the motives for loving Eternal Wisdom that he has already propounded in the preceding chapters; these therefore make up the first part of the work.
232 Wis. 6:12.
233 Wis. 6:14.
234 Wis. 6:21.
235 Sir. 1:26; 6:37.
236 Wis. 1:4.
237 Prov. 21:25.
238 Wis. 1:5.
239 Wis. 7:7.
240 Wis. 8:2, 18.
241 Cf. Dan. 9:23.
242 Mt. 7:7; Lk. 11:9.
243 Cf. Nos. 105-107, 203; TD 16.
244 Wis. 8:21; 9:4.
245 Jas. 1:5.
246 Cf. SR 11th Rose, Nos. 34, 35.
247 Jas. 1:6, 7.
248 Cf. Rom. 1:17.
249 Lk. 11:10.
250 Lk. 11:13.
251 Cf. Lk. 11:5-8.
252 Cf. Sir. 15:3; Jn. 6:35; the hymn *Lauda Sion;* L 16; SM 20.
253 Wis. 9:1-6, 9-19.
254 Job 28:13.
255 Rom. 8:8, 7.
256 Gen. 6:3.
257 Gal. 5:24; 2 Cor. 4:10; Lk. 9:23. Rom. 6:4, 8..
258 Apoc. 2:17.
259 Wis. 6:17.
260 Cf. 1 Cor. 7:30.
261 Rom. 12:2.
262 1 Jn. 5:19.
263 *Imitation of Christ,* I, c. 20, No. 1.
264 Col. 3:3.
265 Sir. 20:5.
266 Prov. 8:12.
267 Prov. 28:26.
268 Prov. 13:16.
269 Sir. 32:24.
270 Tob. 4:19.
271 Cf. SAINT JOHN CLIMACUS, *Scala Paradisi,* gradus 4.
272 *Imitation of Christ,* III, c. 32, No. 1.
273 The teaching of Saint Louis Marie as propounded in this chapter occupies an important place in the spiritual doctrine of the saint. He considers that devotion to Mary is the most efficacious way of arriving at union with Christ-Wisdom.

God alone

274 Cf. Lk. 1:30.
275 Cf. SM 7; TD 16; POIRÉ, *Crown of Power,* 1st star.
276 Cf. No. 104.
277 Cf. SAINT GREGORY THE GREAT, *In librum primum Regum expositio,* I, c. 1, No. 5, and SAINT BERNARD, *Sermo de aquaeductu,* PL 183, 441.
278 Lk. 1:42.
279 Cf. Prov. 8:17.
280 Cf. TD 23-26.
281 Cf. TD 26.
282 Wis. 6:17.
283 Cf. TD 262.
284 Cf. TD 30-33.
285 Cf. Sir. 24:13.
286 Eph. 4:13.
287 GA 4:19. Cf. B. GUERRICUS, *Sermo 1 in Assumptione B. Mariae,* No. 3.
288 Cf. Phil. 2:7.
289 Eph. 4:13.
290 Mt. 19:12.
291 Hos. 14:9. Cf. Jer. 9:12; Ps. 106:43.

3 Letters to the Friends of the Cross

Introduction

The Cross occupied an important place in St. Louis Marie's concept of the Christian life. He presents it as essential in living an evangelical programme. We find him stressing the Cross in several chapters of the "Love of the Eternal Wisdom," in his hymns, and in the manuscripts of his sermons. He writes to a religious Sister, "If Christians only knew the value of the Cross they would walk miles to find it, for in the beloved Cross is the true Wisdom that I am searching for more eagerly than ever" (Letter 13). He founded associations of people who, attracted by love of the Cross, had taken to heart the words of our Lord, "If anyone wants to be a follower of mine let him renounce himself and take up his cross every day and follow me" (Lk. 9:24).

He wrote the "Letter to the Friends of the Cross" during a visit to Rennes at a time when he was not engaged in active work and was making a retreat. He composed it whilst meditating on the sufferings of Jesus, and had it printed and circulated.

The manuscript of the letter has not survived and the earliest existing copy was published in 1839 by Fr. Dalin, Superior General of the Montfort Fathers. The authenticity of the letter is beyond all question but as the manuscript does not exist it is not possible to guarantee the accuracy of the complete text.

To gather material for it Montfort went to Holy Scripture and the Fathers of the Church, and drew from his own spiritual experiences. He certainly consulted a book by Fr. Boudon entitled, "The Holy Ways of the Cross," for passages from this book are easily recognizable. Fr. Blain, Montfort's friend from seminary days, testifies that Louis Marie had read this book and was deeply impressed by it.

God alone

1 Since the divine Cross keeps me in retirement and prevents me from speaking to you personally, I cannot, and I do not even desire to express by word of mouth the feelings of my heart on the excellence and the practices[1] of your Association in the sacred Cross of Christ.

However, on this last day of my retreat, I leave the delights of the interior life to develop on paper a few little points on the Cross with which to pierce your generous hearts. Would to God I could use the blood of my veins rather than the ink of my pen! But, alas, even if blood were required, mine would not be good enough. I pray rather that the Spirit of the living God may be the life, strength, and guiding hand of this letter; that his unction may be my ink, the holy Cross my pen, and your hearts my book.

[I Excellence of the Association]

2 Friends of the Cross, you are like crusaders united to fight against the world; not like Religious who retreat from the world lest they be overcome, but like brave and valiant warriors on the battlefield, who refuse to retreat or even yield an inch. Be brave and fight courageously.

You must be joined together in a close union of mind and heart, which is stronger and far more formidable to the world and to hell than are the armed forces of a great nation to its enemies. Evil spirits are united to destroy you; you must be united to crush them. The avaricious are united to make money and amass gold and silver; you must combine your efforts to acquire the eternal treasures hidden in the Cross. Pleasure-seekers unite to enjoy themselves; you must be united to suffer.[2]

[A Greatness of Your Title]

3 You call yourselves "Friends of the Cross." What a glorious title! I must confess that I am charmed and captivated by it. It is brighter than the sun, higher than the heavens, more magnificent and resplendent than all the titles given to kings and emperors. It is the glorious title of Jesus Christ, true God and true man. It is the genuine title of a Christian.[3]

4 But, if I am captivated by its splendor, I am no less frightened by its responsibility, for it is a title that embraces difficult and

inescapable obligations, summed up in the words of the Holy Spirit, "A chosen race, a royal priesthood, a people set apart."[4]

A Friend of the Cross is one chosen by God, from among thousands who live only according to their reason and senses, to be wholly divine, raised above mere reason and completely opposed to material things, living in the light of pure faith, and inspired by a deep love of the Cross.

A Friend of the Cross is an all-powerful king, a champion who triumphs over the devil, the world, and the flesh in their three-fold concupiscence. He crushes the pride of Satan by his love of humiliations; he overcomes the greed of the world by his love of poverty; he restrains the sensuality of the flesh by his love of suffering.

A Friend of the Cross is one who is holy and set apart from the things that are visible, for his heart is raised above all that is transient and perishable, and his homeland is in heaven;[5] he travels through this world like a visitor and a pilgrim,[6] and, far from setting his heart on it, he looks on it with indifference and tramples it underfoot with contempt.

A Friend of the Cross is a glorious trophy gained by the crucified Christ on Calvary, in union with his holy Mother. He is a Benoni or Benjamin, a child of sorrow and of the right hand,[7] conceived in the suffering heart of Jesus, born from his pierced side, and baptized in his blood.[8] True to his origin, his life embraces the cross, and death to the world, the flesh, and sin,[9] so as to live here below a life hidden with Christ in God.[10]

In short, a perfect Friend of the Cross is a true Christ-bearer, or rather another Christ, so that he can truly say, "I live now not with my own life but with the life of Christ who lives in me."[11]

5 My dear Friends of the Cross, do you live in accordance with the noble title you bear? Or at least, have you a real desire and a sincere determination to do so with the help of God's grace, under the shelter of Christ's Cross and of our Lady of Sorrows? Are you taking the means necessary for this? Are you walking along the true way of life,[12] which is the narrow and stony way of Calvary? Or are you, without perhaps realizing it, on the wide road of the world which leads to perdition? Are you aware that there is a highway which is to all appearances a straight and safe road, but which really leads to eternal death?[13]

6 Do you clearly distinguish the voice of God and his grace from that of the world and of human nature? Do you listen to the voice of God, our heavenly Father, pronouncing his threefold malediction on all who follow the desires of the world: "Woe, woe, woe to all the people on earth;"[14] the Father who stretches out his arms to you in loving appeal, "Come out, my chosen people,"[15] dear friends of my Son's Cross, away from worldlings, who have been cursed by myself, rejected by my Son,[16] and condemned by my Holy Spirit.[17] Beware of following their counsels, of sitting in their company, or even lingering on the road they take.[18] Hasten away from the infamous Babylon.[19] Listen only to the voice of my beloved Son and follow only him, whom I have given you to be your way, your truth, your life,[20] and your model. *(Ipsum audite.)* "Listen to him."[21]

Do you listen to the voice of Jesus who, burdened with his Cross, calls out to you, "Come after me;[22] anyone who follows me will not be walking in the dark;[23] be brave; I have conquered the world."[24]

[B The Two Companies]

7 My dear brothers and sisters, there are two companies[25] that appear before you each day: the followers of Christ and the followers of the world.

Our dear Savior's company is on the right,[26] climbing up a narrow road, made all the narrower by the world's immorality. Our Master leads the way, barefooted, crowned with thorns, covered with blood, and laden with a heavy cross. Those who follow him, though most valiant, are only a handful, either because his quiet voice is not heard amid the tumult of the world, or because people lack the courage to follow him in his poverty, sufferings, humiliations and other crosses which his servants must carry all the days of their life.

8 On the left hand is the company of the world or of the devil. This is far more numerous, more imposing and more illustrious, at least in appearance. Most of the fashionable people run to join it, all crowded together, although the road is wide and is continually being made wider than ever by the crowds that pour along it like a torrent. It is strewn with flowers, bordered with all kinds of amusements and attractions, and paved with gold and silver.[28]

9 On the right, the little groups which follow Jesus[29] speak about sorrow and penance, prayer and indifference to worldly things. They continually encourage one another saying, "Now is the time to suffer and to mourn, to pray and do penance, to live in retirement and poverty, to humble and mortify ourselves;[30] for those who do not possess the spirit of Christ, which is the spirit of the cross, do not belong to Him.[31] Those who belong to Christ have crucified all self-indulgent passions and desires.[32] We must be true images of Christ[33] or be eternally lost."

"Have confidence," they say to each other. If God is on our side, within us and before us, who can be against us?[34] He who is within us is stronger than the one who is in the world. The servant is not greater than his master.[35] This slight and temporary distress we suffer will bring us a tremendous and everlasting glory.[36] The number of those who will be saved is not as great as some people imagine.[37] It is only the brave and the daring who take heaven by storm,[38] where only those are crowned who strive to live according to the law of the Gospel[39] and not according to the maxims of the world. Let us fight with all our strength, let us run with all speed, that we may attain our goal and win the crown.[40]

Such are some of the heavenly counsels with which the Friends of the Cross inspire each other.

10 Those who follow the world, on the contrary, urge each other to continue in their evil ways without scruple, calling to one another day after day, "Let us eat and drink, sing and dance and enjoy ourselves.[42] God is good; He has not made us to damn us. He does not forbid us to amuse ourselves. We shall not be damned for so little. We are not to be scrupulous. No, you will not die."[43]

11 Dear brothers and sisters, remember that our loving Savior has his eyes on you at this moment, and he says to each one of you individually, "See how almost everyone deserts me on the royal road of the Cross. Pagans in their blindness ridicule my Cross as foolishness; obstinate Jews are repelled by it[44] as by an object of horror; heretics pull it down and break it to pieces as something contemptible.

"Even my own people—and I say this with tears in my eyes and grief in my heart—my own children whom I have brought up and instructed in my ways, my members whom I have quickened with my own spirit, have turned their backs on me and forsaken me by becoming enemies of my Cross.[45] 'Will you also go away?'[46] Will you also desert me by running away from my Cross like the worldlings, who thus become so many antichrists?[47] Will you also follow the world;[48] despise the poverty of my Cross, in order to seek after wealth; shun the sufferings of my Cross, to look for enjoyment; avoid the humiliations of my Cross in order to chase after the honors of the world? 'There are many who pretend they are friends of mine and protest that they love me, but in their hearts they hate me. I have many friends of my table, but very few of my Cross'" (Imit. II, 11, 1).

12 At this loving appeal of Jesus, let us rise above our human nature; let us not be seduced by our senses, as Eve was;[49] but keep our eyes fixed on Jesus crucified, who leads us in our faith and brings it to perfection (Heb. 12:2). Let us keep ourselves apart from the evil practices of the world;[50] let us show our love for Jesus in the best way, that is, through all kinds of crosses. Reflect well on these remarkable words of our Savior, "If anyone wants to be a follower of mine, let him renounce himself, and take up his cross and follow me" (Mt. 16:24; Lk. 9:23).

[II The Practices of Christian Perfection]

13 Christian holiness consists in this:

1 Resolving to become a saint: "If anyone wants to be a follower of mine;"
2 Self-denial: "Let him renounce himself;"
3 Suffering: "Let him take up his cross;"
4 Acting: "Let him follow me."[51]

[A If anyone wants to follow me]

14 "If *anyone,*" says our Lord, to point out the small number of chosen ones[52] willing to conform themselves to Christ crucified by carrying their cross. Their number is so small that we would be dumbfounded if we knew it.

It is so small that there is scarcely one in ten thousand, as has been revealed to several saints, including St. Simon Stylites (as is related by Abbot Nilus), St. Basil, St. Ephrem, and others. It is so small that, should it please God to gather them together, He would have to call them one by one as He did of old through his prophet, "You will be gathered one by one;"[53] one from this country, one from that province.

15 "If anyone *wants,*" if anyone has a genuine desire, a determination, not prompted by nature, habit, self-love, self-interest, or human respect, but by the all-conquering grace of the Holy Spirit, which is not given to everyone. "It is not given to all men to know this mystery."[54]

In fact, only a few people have the knowledge of how to live out the mystery of the cross in daily life. For a man to climb Mount Calvary and allow himself to be nailed to the cross with Christ in the midst of his own people, he must be courageous, heroic, resolute; one who is close to God, and treats with indifference the world and the devil, his own body and his own desires; one who is determined to leave all things, to undertake all things, and to suffer all things for Christ.

You must realize, my dear Friends of the Cross, that should there be anyone among you without this determination, he is only walking on one foot, flying with one wing. He is not worthy to be one of your company, since he is not worthy to be called a Friend of the Cross, which we must, like Jesus, love "with a generous mind and a willing heart."[55]

It only needs one half-hearted member to spoil the whole group, like a mangy sheep. If such a one has entered your fold through the evil door of the world, then in the name of Christ crucified drive him out as you would a wolf from the flock.[56]

16 "If anyone wants to be a follower of mine." If anyone wants to follow Me Who so humbled and emptied Myself[57] that I became a worm rather than a man;[58] Who came into the world only to embrace the Cross,[59] to set it in my heart,[60] to love it from my youth,[61] to long for it all the days of my life,[62] to carry it joyfully, preferring it to all the joys and delights that heaven and earth could offer,[63] and not being content till I had died in its divine embrace.

[B Let him Renounce Himself]

17 If anyone, therefore, wants to follow Me thus abased and crucified,[64] he must glory, as I did, only in the poverty, humiliations and sufferings of my Cross. "Let him renounce himself."

Excluded, then, from the company of the Friends of the Cross are those who take pride in their sufferings; the worldly-wise, the intellectuals and the sceptics who are attached to their own ideas and puffed up with their own talents. Away from you those endless talkers who make a great show but produce nothing but vanity. Away from you those so-called devout Catholics who in their pride display the self-sufficiency of proud Lucifer[65] wherever they go, saying, "I am not like the rest of men;" who cannot endure being blamed without making some excuse, being attacked without answering back, being humbled without exalting themselves.

Be careful not to admit into your society those delicate and sensitive people who are afraid of the slightest pin-prick, who cry out and complain at the least pain, who know nothing of the hair-shirt, the discipline or other instruments of penance, and who mingle, with their fashionable devotions, a most refined fastidiousness and a most studied lack of mortification.

[C Let Him Take up His Cross]

18 "Let him take up *his* cross," the one that is his. Let that man (or woman) so rare "far beyond the price of pearls,"[66] take up his cross joyfully, embrace it lovingly, and carry it courageously on his shoulders, his own cross, and not that of another—his own cross which I, in my wisdom, designed for him in every detail of number, measure and weight;[67] his own cross which I have fashioned with my own hands and with great exactness as regards its four dimensions[68] of length, breadth, thickness and depth;[69] his own cross, which out of love for him I have carved from a piece of the one I bore to Calvary; his own cross, which is the greatest gift I can bestow upon my chosen ones on earth; his own cross, whose *thickness* is made up of the loss of one's possessions, humiliations, contempt, sufferings, illnesses and spiritual trials, which come to him daily till his death in accordance with my providence; his own cross, whose *length* consists of a certain period of days or months enduring slander, or lying on a sick-bed, or being forced to beg, or suffering from temptations, dryness, desolation, and other interior trials; his own cross, whose *breadth* is made up of the most harsh and bitter circumstances brought about by relatives, friends, servants; his own cross, whose *depth* is made up of the hidden trials I shall inflict on him without his being able to find any comfort from other people, for they also, under my guidance, will turn away from him and join with me in making him suffer.

19 "Let him *take up,*" that is, let him carry his cross and not drag it, or shake it off, or lighten it, or hide it. Instead, let him lift it on high and carry it without impatience or annoyance, without intentional complaint or grumbling, without hesitation or concealment, without shame or human respect.

"Let him take it up" and set it on his brow, saying with St. Paul, "The only thing I can boast about is the Cross of our Lord Jesus Christ."[70]

Let him carry it on his shoulders like our Lord, that it may become the source of his victories and the scepter of his power: "Dominion is laid upon his shoulders."[71]

Let him set it in his heart, where it may, like the burning bush of Moses, burn day and night with the pure love of God without being consumed![72]

20 *"The cross"*: let him carry it, for nothing is so necessary, so beneficial, so agreeable, or so glorious as to suffer something for Jesus Christ.[73]

[1 Nothing is so necessary]

21 Dear Friends of the Cross, we are all sinners; there is not one of us who has not deserved hell,[74] and I more than anyone. Our offenses have to be punished either in this world or in the next. If we suffer for them now, we shall not suffer for them after death. If we willingly accept punishment for them, this punishment will be an act of God's love; for it is mercy which holds sway and chastises in this world, and not strict justice. This punishment will be light and temporary, accompanied by consolation and merit, and followed by rewards both here and in eternity.

22 But if the punishment due for our sins is put off till the next world, then it will be God's avenging justice, which puts everything to fire and sword, which will inflict the punishment, a dreadful, indescribable punishment:[75] "Who understands the power of your anger?"[76] Judgment without mercy,[77] without relief, without merit, without limit and without end. Yes, without end. That serious sin you committed in a few brief moments, that deliberate evil thought which now escapes your memory,[78] that word carried away by the wind, that brief action against the law of God—they shall all be punished for eternity, in the company of the devils in hell, so long as God is God. And this avenging God will have no pity on your torments, on your cries and tears, violent enough to cleave the rocks. To suffer forever, without merit, without mercy, and without end.

23 Do we think of this, my dear brothers and sisters, when we have to suffer some trial in this world? How fortunate we are to be able to exchange a never-ending and unprofitable punishment for a temporary and rewarding one just by bearing our cross with patience! How many of our debts are still unpaid! How many sins have we committed which, despite a sincere confession and heartfelt contrition, will have to be atoned for in purgatory for many years, simply because in this world we contented ourselves with a few slight penances!

Ah, let us settle our debts with good grace in this life by cheerfully carrying our cross. In the next, a strict account is demanded down to the last penny,[79] to the last idle word.[80] If we were able to snatch from the devil the book of death[81] in which he has entered all our sins and the punishment due to them, what a heavy debit we should find, and how delighted we should be to suffer for long years on earth rather than a single day in the world to come!

24 Friends of the Cross, do you not flatter yourselves that you are, or desire to become, the friends of God? Well then, resolve to drink the cup that you must drink in order to become his friends: "They drank the cup of the Lord and became the friends of God." Benjamin, the beloved son of Jacob, was given the cup, while his other brothers received nothing but wheat.[84] The beloved disciple of Christ, so dear to his Master's heart, went up to Calvary and drank of his cup. "Can you drink the cup that I am going to drink?"[83] To desire God's glory is excellent, but to desire and pray for it without resolving to suffer all things is both foolish and extravagant: "You do not know what you are asking. . . ." We must experience many hardships before we enter the kingdom of heaven.[84] To enter this kingdom, you must suffer many crosses and tribulations.

25 Rightly you glory in being God's children. You should glory, then, in the correction your heavenly Father has given you and will give you in the future, for he chastises all his children.[85] If you are not included among his beloved children, you are, alas, included among those who are lost, as St. Augustine points out.[86] He also tells us, "The one who does not mourn in this world like a stranger and a pilgrim will not rejoice in the world to come as a citizen of heaven."

If your heavenly Father does not send you some worthwhile crosses from time to time, it is because He no longer cares about you and is angry with you; He is treating you as an outsider, no longer belonging to his family and deserving his protection, or as an illegitimate child,[87] who, having no claim to a share of the inheritance, deserves neither care nor correction.[88]

26 Friends of the Cross, disciples of a crucified God, the mystery of the Cross[89] is a mystery unknown to the Gentiles, rejected by the Jews,[90] and despised by heretics and bad Catholics. But it is the great mystery you must learn to practice in the school of Christ, and which can only be learnt from him. You will look in vain in all the schools of ancient times for a philosopher who taught it; in vain will you appeal to the senses or to reason to throw some light on it. It is only Jesus, through his all-powerful grace, who can teach you this mystery and give you the ability to appreciate it.

Strive then to become proficient in this all-important science under your great Master, and you will understand all other sciences, for it contains them all in an eminent degree. It is our natural and supernatural philosophy, our divine and mystic theology, our philosopher's stone, which by patience transforms the basest metals into precious ones, the bitterest pains into delight, poverty into riches, the most profound humiliations into glory. The one among you who knows best how to carry his cross, even though in other things he does not know A from B, is the most learned of all.[91]

The great St. Paul returned from the third heaven, where he learned mysteries hidden even from the angels, and he proclaimed that he did not know, nor did he want to know anything but Christ crucified.[92] Rejoice, then, you ordinary Christian, man or woman, without any schooling or intellectual abilities, for if you know how to suffer cheerfully, you know more than a doctor of Sorbonne University who does not know how to suffer as you do.[93]

27 You are the members of Christ,[94] a wonderful honor indeed, but one which entails suffering. If the Head is crowned with thorns, can the members expect to be crowned with roses? If the Head is jeered[95] at and covered with dust on the road to Calvary, can the members expect to be sprinkled with perfumes on a throne? If the Head has no pillow on which to rest,[96] can the members expect to recline on feathers and down? That would be unthinkable!

No, no, my dear Companions of the Cross, do not deceive yourselves. Those Christians you see everywhere, fashionably dressed, fastidious in manner, full of importance and dignity, are not real disciples, real members of Christ crucified. To think they are would be an insult to our thorn-crowned Head and to the truth of the Gospel. How many so-called Christians imagine they are members of our Savior when in reality they are his treacherous persecutors, for while they make the sign of the cross with their hand, in their hearts they are its enemies!

If you are guided by the same spirit, if you live the same

life as Jesus, your thorn-crowned Head, you must expect only thorns, lashes and nails; that is, nothing but the cross; for the disciple must be treated like the master and the members like the head.[97] And if you were to be offered, as was St. Catherine of Siena, a crown of thorns and one of roses, you should, like her, choose the crown of thorns without hesitation and press it upon your head, so as to be like Christ.[98]

28 You know that you are living temples of the Holy Spirit[99] and that, like living stones,[100] you are to be set by the God of love into the building of the heavenly Jerusalem.[101] And so you must expect to be shaped, cut, and chiseled under the hammer of the cross; otherwise, you would remain rough stones, good for nothing but to be cast aside. Be careful that you do not cause the hammer to recoil when it strikes you; respect the chisel that is carving you and the hand that is shaping you. It may be that this skillful and loving craftsman wants you to have an important place in his eternal edifice, or to be one of the most beautiful works of art in his heavenly kingdom. So let him do what he pleases; he loves you, he knows what he is doing, he has had experience. His strokes are skillful and directed by love; not one will miscarry unless your impatience makes it do so.

29 The Holy Spirit compares the cross sometimes to a winnowing-fan which separates the grain from the chaff and the dust.[102] Like the grain before the fan, let yourselves be shaken up and tossed about without resisting; for the Father of the household is winnowing you and will soon put you in his granary. At other times the Holy Spirit compares the cross to a fire which removes the rust from the iron by the intensity of its heat.[103] Our God is a consuming fire[104] dwelling in our souls through His cross in order to purify them without consuming them, as He did of old in the burning bush.[105]

Again, he likens the cross to the crucible of a forge in which the good metal is refined[106] and the dross vanishes in smoke; the metal is purified by fire, while the impurities disappear in the heat of the flames. And it is in the crucible of tribulation and temptation that the true friends of the cross are purified by their constancy in sufferings, while its enemies are swept away[107] through their impatience and murmurings.

30 My dear Friends of the Cross, see before you a great cloud of witnesses[108] who, without saying a word, prove what I have been saying. Consider, for example, that upright man Abel, who was killed by his brother;[109] and Abraham, an upright man who was a stranger on earth;[110] Lot, an upright man driven from his own country;[111] Jacob, an upright man persecuted by his brother;[112] Tobit, an upright man stricken with blindness;[113] Job, an upright man who was impoverished, humbled, and covered with sores from head to foot.[114]

31 Consider the countless apostles and martyrs who were bathed in their own blood; the virgins and confessors who were reduced to poverty, humbled, persecuted, or exiled. They can all say with St. Paul, "Look upon Jesus, the pioneer and perfecter of our faith,"[115] the faith we have in him and in his Cross; it was necessary that he should suffer and so enter through the Cross into his glory.[116]

At the side of Jesus, see Mary his Mother, who was never stained with any sin, original or actual, yet whose pure and loving heart was pierced through.[117] If I had time to dwell on the sufferings of Jesus and Mary, I could show that what we suffer is nothing compared to theirs.

32 Who, then, would dare claim to be exempt from the cross? Which of us would not hasten to the place where he knows the cross awaits him? Who would refuse to say with St. Ignatius of Antioch, "Come, fire and gibbet, wild beast and all the torments of hell, that I may delight in the possession of Christ."

33 But if you are not willing to suffer patiently and carry your cross with resignation like God's chosen ones, then you will have to carry it, grumbling and complaining like those on the road to damnation. You will be like the two oxen that drew the Ark of the Covenant, lowing as they went;[118] like Simon of Cyrene who unwillingly took up the very cross of Christ[119] and did nothing but complain while he carried it. And in the end, you will be like the impenitent thief,[120] who from the summit of his cross plunged into the abyss.

No, this accursed earth on which we live is not destined to make us happy; in this land of darkness we cannot expect to see clearly; there is no perfect calm on this stormy sea; we can never avoid conflicts on this field of trial and battle; we cannot escape being scratched on this thorn-covered earth.[121] Willingly or unwillingly, all must carry their cross, both those who serve God and those who do not. Keep in mind the words of the hymn:

Three crosses stand on Calvary's height;
One must be chosen, so choose aright;
You must suffer like a saint or repentent thief,
Or like a reprobate, in endless grief.

That is to say, if you are not willing to suffer gladly like Jesus, or patiently like the penitent thief, then you will have to suffer like the unrepentent thief. You will have to drink the cup of bitterness to the dregs[122] without the consoling help of grace, and you will have to bear the whole weight of your cross, deprived of the powerful support of Christ. You will even have to carry the deadly weight which the devil will add to it by means of the impatience it will cause you. And after sharing the unhappiness of the impenitent thief on earth, you will share his misery in eternity.

[2 Nothing is so useful and so agreeable]

34 But if, on the contrary, you suffer in the right way, the cross will become a yoke that is easy and light,[123] since Christ himself will carry it with you. It will give you wings, as it were, to lift you to heaven;[124] it will become your ship's mast, bringing you smoothly and easily to the harbor of salvation.

Carry your cross *patiently* and it will be a light in your spiritual darkness, for the one who has never suffered trials is ignorant.[125]

Carry your cross *cheerfully* and you will be filled with divine love; for only in suffering can we dwell in the pure love of Christ.[126]

Roses are only found among thorns. It is the cross alone which nourishes our love of God, as wood is the fuel which feeds the fire. Remember the beautiful saying in the *Imitation of Christ,* "In proportion as you do violence to yourself, by suffering patiently, so will you make progress"[127] in divine love.

Do not expect anything from those sensitive and slothful people who reject the cross when it approaches them, and who are careful not to seek out crosses. What are they but an untilled soil which will produce nothing but thorns because it has not been dug up, harrowed and turned over by an experienced farmer. They are like stagnant water, which is unfit for either washing or drinking.

Carry your cross cheerfully and you will draw from it an all-powerful strength which none of your enemies will be able to resist,[128] and you will find in it a delight beyond anything you have known. Indeed, brethren, the true earthly paradise is found in suffering for Christ.

Ask any of the saints, and they will tell you they have never tasted a banquet more delicious for the spirit than when undergoing the severest torments. "Let all the torments of the devil come upon me," said St. Ignatius the Martyr.[129] "Let me suffer or die," said St. Teresa of Avila. "Not death but suffering," said St. Mary Magdalen of Pazzi. "May I suffer and be despised for your sake," said Blessed John of the Cross. And many others have spoken in the same terms, as we read in their lives.[130]

My dear brothers and sisters, have faith in the word of God, for the Holy Spirit tells us that when we suffer cheerfully for God, the cross is the source of every kind of joy for all kinds of people. The joy that comes from the cross[131] is greater than that of a poor man who suddenly comes into a fortune, or of a peasant who is raised to the throne; greater than the joy of a trader who becomes a millionaire; than of a military leader over the victories he has won; than of prisoners released from their chains. In short, imagine the greatest joys that can be experienced on earth, and then realize that the happiness of the one who bears his sufferings in the right way contains, and even surpasses, all of them.

[3 Nothing is so glorious]

35 So rejoice and be glad when God favors you with one of his choicest crosses; for without realizing it, you are blessed with the greatest gift of heaven, the greatest gift of God. If you really appreciated that, you would have Masses offered, you would make novenas at the shrines of the saints, you would undertake long pilgrimages, as did the saints, to obtain from heaven this divine gift.[132]

36 The world calls this madness, degradation, stupidity, a lack of judgment and of common sense. They are blind: let them say what they like. This blindness, which makes them view the cross in a human and distorted way, is a source of glory to us. Every time they cause us to suffer by their ridicule and insults, they are presenting us with jewels, setting us on a throne, and crowning us with laurels.[133]

37 More than that . . . as St. John Chrysostom says, "All the wealth and honors and scepters and jeweled crowns of kings and emperors are not to be compared with the splendor of the cross."[134] It is greater even than the glory of an apostle or evangelist. "If I had the choice," continues this holy man, enlightened by the Holy Spirit, "I would willingly leave heaven in order to suffer for the God of heaven.[135] I would prefer dungeons and prisons to the thrones of the highest heaven, and the heaviest of crosses to the glory of the seraphim. I value the honor of suffering more than the gift of miracles, giving me the power to command evil spirits, shake the elements of the world, halt the sun in its course, or raise the dead to life. St. Peter and St. Paul are more glorious in their prison chains[136] than in being caught up into the third heaven[137] or receiving the keys of heaven."[138]

38 Indeed, is it not the Cross which has given to Jesus Christ "the name which is above all other names, so that all beings in the heavens, on earth and in the underworld should bend the knee at the name of Jesus?"[139] The glory of one who knows how to suffer is so great that heaven, angels and men, and even God himself, gaze on him with joy as a most glorious sight. And if the saints in heaven desired anything, it would be to return to earth so as to bear some crosses.

39 But if this glory is so great even on earth, what will it be in heaven? Who could describe it? Who could ever understand fully that eternal weight of glory[140] which a single moment spent in cheerfully carrying a cross obtains for us? Who could understand the glory gained in heaven by a year, and sometimes a whole lifetime, of crosses and suffering?

40 You can be sure, my dear Friends of the Cross, that something wonderful is awaiting you, since the Holy Spirit has united you so intimately to that which everyone so carefully avoids. And you can be sure, too, that God will make of you as many saints as there are Friends of the Cross if you are faithful to your vocation and willingly carry your cross as Christ did.

[D Let Him Follow Me]

41 But to suffer is not enough: the evil one and the world have their martyrs. We must suffer and carry our cross in the footsteps of Christ: "Let him follow me,"[141] that is to say, we must suffer the way Jesus did. To help you to do that, here are the rules to be followed:

42 1 Do not deliberately contrive to bring crosses upon yourself. We must not do what is wrong in order to bring about something good; nor must we, without a special inspiration of God, do things badly so as to draw down ridicule upon ourselves. Rather, we ought to imitate our Lord, of whom it was said, "He did all things well,"[142] not indeed out of self-esteem or vanity, but to please God and win over our fellow-men. And if you fulfill your duties as well as you can, you will find no lack of opposition, criticism and ridicule, which will be sent by divine providence without your choosing or wanting it.

43 2 If you happen to do something which is neither good nor bad in itself, and your neighbor takes scandal at it—although without reason—refrain from doing it, out of charity to him, so as to avoid the scandal of the weak.[143] Such an heroic act of charity will be of greater worth in God's sight than the action you were doing or intending to do. However, if what you are doing is necessary or beneficial to your neighbor, and some hypocritical or evil-minded person takes scandal without reason, refer the matter to some prudent adviser to find out whether it is really necessary or advantageous to others. If he judges it is, then carry on without worrying about what people say, so long as they do not stop you. And you can say to them what our Lord said to some of his disciples when they told him that the scribes and Pharisees were scandalized at what he said and did: "Leave them alone. They are blind men leading the blind."[144]

44 3 Although certain great and holy men have sought and asked for crosses, and even by their peculiar behavior have brought sufferings, scorn and humiliations upon themselves, let us be content with admiring and praising the marvelous work of the Holy Spirit in their souls. Let us humble ourselves at the sight of such sublime virtue without attempting to reach such heights ourselves.

Compared with those swift eagles and strong lions, we are timid and faint-hearted sheep.

45 4 You may, and should, pray for the wisdom of the cross, that knowledge of the truth which we experience within ourselves and which by the light of faith deepens our knowledge of the most hidden mysteries, including that of the cross. But this is obtained only by much labor, great humiliations and fervent prayer. If you stand in need of this strengthening spirit[145] which enables us to carry the heaviest crosses courageously; of this gracious and consoling spirit,[146] which enables us, in the higher part of the soul, to take delight in things that are bitter and repulsive; of this sound and upright spirit[147] which seeks God alone; of this science of the cross which embraces all things; in short, of this inexhaustible treasure by which those who make good use of it win God's friendship[148]—if you stand in need of such, pray for wisdom, ask for it continually and fervently, without wavering[149] or fear of not obtaining it, and it will be yours. Then you will clearly understand from your own experience how it is possible to desire, seek and find joy in the cross.

46 5 If you make a blunder which brings a cross upon you, whether it be inadvertently or even through your own fault, bow down under the mighty hand of God[150] without delay, and as far as possible do not worry over it. You might say within yourself, "Lord, here is a sample of my handiwork." If there is anything wrong in what you have done, accept the humiliation as a punishment for it; if it was not sinful, accept it as a means of humbling your pride. Frequently, even very frequently, God allows his greatest servants, those far advanced in holiness, to fall into the most humiliating faults so as to humble them in their own eyes and in the eyes of others. He thus keeps them from thoughts of pride in which they might indulge because of the graces they have received, or the good they are doing, so that "no one can boast in God's presence."[157]

47 6 You must realize that through the sin of Adam and through the sins we ourselves have committed, everything in us has become debased,[152] not only our bodily senses, but also the powers of our soul. And so the moment our corrupt minds reflect with self-complacency on any of God's gifts within us, that gift, that action, that grace becomes tarnished and spoilt, and God no longer looks on it with favor. If the thoughts and reflections of the mind can so spoil man's best actions and God's greatest gifts, how much worse will be the evil effects of man's self-will, which are even more corrupt than those of the mind?

So we need not be surprised that God is pleased to hide his friends in the shelter of his presence,[153] that they may not be defiled by the scrutiny of men or by their own self-awareness. And to keep them hidden, what does this jealous God not permit and even bring about! How often he humiliates them! How many faults he allows them to fall into! By what temptations he permits them to be attacked, as St. Paul was![154] In what uncertainty, darkness, and perplexity he leaves them! Oh, how wonderful is God in his saints, and in the means he adopts to lead them to humility and holiness!

48 7 Do not be like those proud and self-conceited churchgoers, imagining that your crosses are heavy, that they are proofs of your fidelity and marks of God's exceptional love for you. This temptation, arising from spiritual pride, is most deceptive, subtle and full of poison. You must believe (1) that your pride and sensitiveness make you magnify splinters into planks, scratches into wounds, molehills into mountains, a passing word meaning nothing into an outrageous insult or a cruel slight; (2) that the crosses God sends you are loving punishments for your sins rather than marks of God's special favor; (3) that whatever cross or humiliation he sends you is exceedingly light in comparison with the number and the greatness of your offenses, for you should consider your sins in the light of God's holiness, who can tolerate nothing that is defiled, and against whom you have set yourself; in the light of a God suffering death while overwhelmed with sorrow at the sight of your sins; in the light of an everlasting hell which you have deserved time and again; (4) that the patience with which you bear your sufferings is tinged more than you think with natural and human motives. Witness those little ways of looking after yourself, that unobtrusive seeking for sympathy, those confidences you make in such a natural way to your friends, and perhaps to your spiritual director, those specious excuses you are so ready with, those complaints, or rather criticisms of those who have done you an injury, expressed in such pleasant words and charitable manner, that keen satisfaction you feel on considering your troubles, that self-complacency of Lucifer which makes you imagine you are somebody,[155] and so on. I should never finish if I were to describe here all the twists and turns of human nature, even in suffering.

49 8 Take advantage of little sufferings, even more than of great ones. God considers not so much what we suffer as how we suffer. To suffer a great deal, but badly, is to suffer like the damned; to suffer much even bravely, but for an evil cause, is to suffer as a disciple of the devil; to suffer little or much for God's sake is to suffer like a saint.

If it is true to say that we may have a preference for certain crosses, let it be particularly for small, obscure ones when they come to us at the same time as great and spectacular ones. To seek and ask for great and dazzling crosses, and even to choose and welcome them, may be the result of our natural pride; but to choose small and insignificant ones and bear them cheerfully can only come from a special grace and a great fidelity to God. So do what a shopkeeper does in regard to his business: turn everything to profit. Do not allow the tiniest piece of the true Cross to be lost, even though it be only an insect sting or a pin-prick, a little eccentricity of your neighbor or some unintentional slight, the loss of some money, some little anxiety, a little bodily weariness, or a slight pain in your limbs. Turn everything to profit, as the grocer does in his shop, and you will soon become rich before God, just as the grocer becomes rich in money by adding penny to penny in his till. At the least annoyance say "Thank you, Lord. Your will be done."[156] Then store up in God's memory-bank, so to speak, the profitable cross you have just gained, and think no more about it except to repeat your thanks.

50 9 When we are told to love the cross, that does not refer to emotional love, impossible to our human nature.

There are three kinds of love: emotional love, rational love, and the supernatural love of faith. In other words, the love that resides in the lower part of man, in his body; the love in the higher part, his reason; and the love in the highest part of man, in the summit of the soul, that is, the intelligence enlightened by faith.

51 God does not ask you to love the cross with the will of the flesh. Since the flesh is subject to sin and corruption, all that proceeds from it is perverted[157] and, of itself, cannot be submissive to the will of God and his crucifying law. It was this human will our Lord referred to in the Garden of Olives when He cried out, "Father, let your will be done, not mine."[158] If the lower part of Christ's human nature, although so holy, could not love the cross continuously, then with still greater reason will our tainted nature reject it. It is true that we may sometimes experience even a sensible joy in our sufferings, as many of the Saints have done; but that joy does not come from the body, even though it is experienced in the body. It comes from the soul, which is so overwhelmed with the divine joy of the Holy Spirit that it overflows into the body. In that way, someone who is suffering greatly can say with the psalmist, "My heart and my flesh ring out their joy to God, the living God."[159]

52 There is another love of the cross which I have called rational love and which is in the higher part of man, the mind. This love is entirely spiritual; it springs from the knowledge of how happy we can be in suffering for God, and so it can be experienced by the soul, to which it gives interior joy and strength. But although this rational and perceptible joy is good, in fact, excellent, it is not always necessary in order to suffer joyfully for God's sake.

53 And so there is a third kind of love, which is called by the masters of the spiritual life the love of the summit of the soul, and which is known to philosophers as the love of the intellect. In this, without any feeling of joy in the senses or pleasure in the mind, we love the cross we are carrying, by the light of pure faith, and take delight in it, even though the lower part of our nature may often be in a state of conflict and disturbance, groaning and complaining, weeping and longing for relief. In this case, we can say with our Lord, "Father, let your will be done, not mine;"[160] or with our Lady, "I am the slave of the Lord: let what you have said be done to me."[161]

It is with one of these two higher loves that we should love and accept the cross.

54 10 My dear Friends of the Cross, make the resolution to suffer any kind of cross without excluding or choosing any: any poverty, injustice, loss, illness, humiliation, contradiction, slander, spiritual dryness, desolation, interior and exterior trials, saying always, "My heart is ready, O God, my heart is ready."[162] Be prepared, then, to be forsaken by men and angels, and seemingly by God himself; to be persecuted, envied, betrayed, slandered, discredited and abandoned by everyone; to suffer hunger, thirst, poverty, nakedness, exile, imprisonment, the gallows, and all kinds of torture, even though you have done nothing to deserve it.

Finally, imagine that you have been deprived of your possessions and your good name, and turned out of your home, like Job and St. Elizabeth of Hungary; that you are thrown into the mire, like St. Elizabeth, or dragged on to the dung heap, like Job,[163] all covered with ulcers, without a bandage for your sores or a piece of bread to eat—something people would not refuse to a horse or a dog. Imagine that, in addition to all these dreadful misfortunes, God leaves you a prey to every assault of the devil, without imparting to your soul the least feeling of consolation.

You should firmly believe that this is the highest point of heavenly glory and of genuine happiness for the true and perfect Friend of the Cross.

55 11 To help you to suffer in the right spirit, acquire the good habit of reflecting on these four points:

Firstly, the eye of God, who, like a great king from the height of a tower, observes with satisfaction his soldier in the midst of battle, and praises his courage. What is it that attracts God's attention on earth? Is it kings and emperors on their thrones? He often regards them only with contempt. Is it great victories of armies, precious stones, or whatever is great in the eyes of men? No, "what is thought highly of by men is loathsome in the sight of God."[164] What, then, does He look upon with pleasure and satisfaction, and about which He inquires of the angels and even the devils? It is the one who is struggling with the world, the devil, and himself for the love of God, the one who carries his cross cheerfully. As the Lord said to Satan, "Did you not see on earth a great wonder, at which all heaven is filled with admiration? Have you seen my servant

Job,[165] who is suffering for my sake?"

56 Secondly, consider the hand of God. All natural evils which befall us, from the smallest to the greatest, come from the hand of God. The same hand that killed an army of a hundred thousand men on the spot[166] also causes a leaf to fall from the tree and a hair from your head;[167] the hand which pressed so heavily on Job[168] gently touches you with a light tribulation. It is the same hand which makes both day and night, sunshine and darkness, good and evil. He has permitted the sinful actions which hurt you; he is not the cause of their malice, but he permits the actions.

If anyone, then, treats you as Shimei treated King David, heaping you with insults and throwing stones at you,[169] say to yourself, "We must not take revenge. Let him carry on, for the Lord has commanded him to act in this way. I know I deserve every kind of insult, and that it is only right that God should punish me. My hands, keep yourselves from violence; refrain, my tongue, from speaking; do not strike, do not say a word. It is true this man attacks me, that woman reviles me, but they are God's representatives, who have come on behalf of his mercy to punish me as his love alone knows how. Let us not offend his justice by usurping his rights to vengeance. Let us not slight his mercy by resisting the loving strokes of his lash, lest he should deliver me, instead, to the absolute justice of eternity."

On the one hand, God in his infinite power and wisdom bears you up, while with the other He afflicts you. With one hand He deals out death, while with the other He dispenses life. He humbles you to the dust and raises you up, and with both arms he reaches from one end of your life to the other with kindness and power:[170] with kindness, by not allowing you to be tempted and afflicted beyond your strength; with power, by supporting you with his grace in proportion to the violence and duration of the temptation or affliction; with power again, by coming himself, as he tells us through his holy Church, "to support you on the edge of the precipice, to guide you on the uncertain road, to shade you in the scorching heat, to protect you in the drenching rain and biting cold, to carry you in your weariness, to aid you in your difficulties, to steady you on slippery paths, to be your refuge in the midst of storms" *(Prayer for a Journey)*.

57 Thirdly, reflect on the wounds and sufferings of Christ crucified. He himself has told us, *All you who pass by the way* of thorns and the cross, *look and see.*[171] Look with the eyes of your body, and see through the eyes of your contemplation, whether your poverty, destitution, disgrace, sorrow, desolation are like mine; look upon me who am innocent, and lament, you who are guilty!"

The Holy Spirit also tells us, through the Apostles, to contemplate the crucified Christ.[172] He bids us arm ourselves with this thought,[173] for it is the most powerful and formidable weapon against our enemies. When you are assailed by poverty, disrepute, sorrow, temptation and other crosses, arm yourselves with the shield, breastplate, helmet and two-edged sword,[174] which is the remembrance of Christ crucified. It is there you will find the solution of every problem and the means to conquer all your enemies.

58 Fourthly, look *upwards* and see the beautiful crown that awaits you in heaven if you carry your cross well. It was this reward which sustained the patriarchs and prophets in their faith and persecutions; which inspired the apostles and martyrs in their labors and torments. The patriarchs could say with Moses, *"We would rather by afflicted with the people of God,* and be happy with him forever, *than enjoy for a time the pleasures of sin."*[175] And the prophets could say with David, "We suffer persecution for the reward."[176] The Apostles and Martyrs could say with St. Paul, *"We are as men sentenced to death, put on show in front of the whole universe, angels as well as men* by our suffering, and *as the offal of the world, the scum of the earth,*[177] *for the sake of a weight of eternal glory, which this small and temporary suffering will produce in us."*[178]

Let us look *upward* and see the angels, who exclaim, "Be careful not to forfeit the crown which is marked out for the cross you have received, if you bear it well. If you do not bear it well, another will carry it in the right spirit and will take your crown with it. Fight bravely and suffer patiently, we are told by all the saints, and you will receive an eternal kingdom." Finally, listen to our Lord himself, who says to you, "I will give my reward only to the one who suffers and is victorious through his patience."[179]

Now let us look *downward* to the place we have deserved and which awaits us in hell in the company of the bad thief and all who have not repented, if we suffer as they did, with feelings of resentment, ill-will and revengefulness. Let us say with St. Augustine, "Lord, treat me as you will in this world for my sins, so long as you pardon them in eternity."

59 12 Never willingly complain against any person or thing that God may use to afflict you. There are three kinds of complaints we may make in times of distress. The first is natural and spontaneous, as when the body groans and complains, weeps and laments. There is no fault in this, provided, as I have said, that the heart is resigned to the will of God. The second kind of complaint is that of the mind, as when we make known our ills to someone who can give us some relief, such as a doctor or a superior. There may be some imperfection in this if we are too eager to tell our troubles, but there is no sin in it. The third kind is sinful: that is when we criticize our neighbor either to get rid of an evil which afflicts us or to take revenge on him; or when we willfully complain of what we suffer with impatience and murmurings.

60 13 Whenever you receive any cross, always welcome it with humility and gratitude. And when God favors you with a cross of some importance, show your gratitude in a special way, and get others to thank him for you. Follow the example of the poor woman who lost all that she had in an unjust law-suit and immediately offered her few remaining coins to have a Mass said in thanksgiving for her good fortune.[180]

61 14 If you want to make yourself worthy of the best kind of crosses, that is, those which come to you without your choosing, then under the guidance of a prudent director, take up some of your own accord.

For example, suppose you have a piece of furniture you are fond of, but which is of no use to you. You could give it away to someone who needs it, saying to yourself, "Why should I have things I don't need when Jesus is so poor?"

Or if you have a distaste for a certain kind of food, an aversion for the practice of some particular virtue, or a dislike for some offensive odor, you could take the food, practice the virtue, accept the odor, and thus conquer yourself.

Or again, your fondness for a certain person or thing may be immoderate. Why not see less of that person, or keep away from those things that attract you?

If you have a natural inclination never to miss what is going on, to be always doing things, to be in the limelight, to frequent popular places, then guard your eyes, watch your tongue, and stay where you are.

Have you a natural aversion for certain persons or things? Then overcome it by not avoiding them.

62 If you are truly Friends of the Cross, then without your knowing it, love, which is ever ingenious, will discover thousands of little crosses to enrich you. And you will not need to have any fear of vainglory, which so often spoils the patience which people exhibit under spectacular crosses. And because you have been faithful in little things, the Lord will place you in charge of greater,[181] according to his promise. That is to say, in charge of the greater graces He will bestow on you, of the greater crosses He will send you, of the greater glory He will prepare for you. . . .[182]

Footnotes to Letter to the Friends of the Cross

1 These two words "excellence" and "practices" indicate the two divisions of this letter which Montfort wrote to his dear Friends of the Cross. Not being able to visit them and speak to them on this sub-

ject dear to his heart he conveys his thoughts to them in this letter.
2 Cf. SR 127; PM 27-29.
3 Cf. Gal. 6:14.
4 Cf. 1 Pet. 2:9.
5 Cf. Phil. 3:20.
6 Cf. 1 Pet. 2:11.
7 Cf. Gen. 35:18.
8 Cf. Jn. 19:34.
9 Cf. Rom. 6:2; 8, 11; 1 Pet. 2:24.
10 Cf. Col. 3:3.
11 Gal. 2:20.
12 Cf. Prov. 6:23; 10:17; Jer. 21:8.
13 Cf. Prov. 14:12.
14 Apoc. 88:13.
15 Cf. Numb. 16:21; Is. 52:11; Apoc. 18:4.
16 Cf. Jn. 17:9.
17 Cf. Jn. 16:8-11.
18 Cf. Ps. 1:1.
19 Cf. Is. 48:20; Jer. 50:8; 51:6, 9, 45.
20 Cf. Jn. 14:6.
21 Mt. 17:5; Lk. 9:35; 2 Pet. 1:17; also cf. Mk. 9:6.
22 Mt. 4:19; Mk. 1:17.
23 Jn. 8:12.
24 Jn. 16:33.
25 Cf. Mt. 6:24; Lk. 16:13. Montfort wrote this letter to the Friends of the Cross on the last day of his retreat. He may have been influenced here by his recollection of the Exercises of St. Ignatius.
26 Cf. Mt. 25:33; cf. Nos. 8, 9.
27 Cf. Mt. 25:33.
28 Cf. Mt. 7:13, 14.
29 Cf. Mt. 25:33.
30 Cf. Jn. 16:20.
31 Cf. Rom. 8:9.
32 Gal. 5:24.
33 Cf. Rom. 8:29.
34 Rom. 8:31.
35 Jn. 13:16; 15:20.
36 Cf. 2 Cor. 4:17; cf. Nos. 39, 58.
37 Cf. Mt. 20:16; Lk. 13:23, 24.
38 Cf. Mt. 11:12.
39 Cf. 2 Tim. 2:5.
40 Cf. 1 Cor. 9:24, 25.
41 Same as 42.
42 Cf. Is. 22:13; Mt. 24:37-39; Lk. 17:26-28; 1 Cor. 15:32.
43 Gen. 3:4.
44 Cf. 1 Cor. 1:23.
45 Cf. Is. 1:2; Phil. 3:18.
46 Jn. 6:68.
47 1 Jn. 2:18.
48 Cf. Rom. 12:2.
49 Cf. Gen. 3:6.

50 Cf. 2 Pet. 1:4.
51 The following numbers constitute a commentary upon this text.
52 Cf. Mt. 20:16; Lk. 13:23, 24. Also No. 9.
53 Is. 27:12.
54 Mt. 13:11; Mk. 4:11.
55 2 Mac. 1:3.
56 Cf. Mt. 7:15; Jn. 10:1.
57 Cf. Phil. 2:6-8.
58 Ps. 21:7.
59 Ps. 39:8; Heb. 10:7, 9.
60 Ps. 39:9.
61 Wis. 8:2.
62 Lk. 12:50.
63 Heb. 12:2.
64 Cf. Phil. 2:6-8; also No. 16.
65 Lk. 18:11.
66 Prov. 31:10.
67 Cf. Wis. 11:21.
68 Cf. BOUDON, *"The Holy Pathways of the Cross,"* bk. 4, ch. 7: "One must be ready to carry one's cross, whatever its size."
69 Cf. Eph. 3:18.
70 Gal. 6:14.
71 Cf. Is. 9:6.
72 Cf. Exod. 3:2.
73 Cf. Acts 5:41.
74 Cf. Prov. 24:16; 1 Jn. 1:10.
75 Heb. 10:31.
76 Ps. 89:11.
77 Jas. 2:13.
78 Without the original it is difficult to confirm the authenticity of this passage.
79 Cf. Mt. 5:26.
80 Cf. Mt. 12:36.
81 Montfort is probably alluding here to the canceling of "every record of the debt that we had to pay." Col. 2:14.
82 Cf. Gen. 44:1-12.
83 Mt. 20:22; Mk. 10; 38.
84 Acts 14:21.
85 Cf. Prov. 3:11, 12; Heb. 12:5-8; Apoc. 3:19.
86 Cf. SAINT AUGUSTINE, *Sermone 31, De Verbis Psalmi* 125, 5, 6.
87 Cf. Heb. 12:8.
88 Cf. BOUDON, *op. cit.,* bk. 1, ch. 6: "Crosses are a sign of predestination and even of the highest predestination."
89 Cf. BOUDON, *op. cit.,* bk. 1, ch. 1: "The knowledge of the Cross is a hidden mystery."
90 Cf. 1 Cor. 1:23.
91 Cf. LEW, ch. 7: Choice of true Wisdom, especially Nos. 85-88.
92 1 Cor. 2:2.
93 Cf. Mt. 11:25; Lk. 10:21.
94 Cf. 1 Cor. 6:15; 12:27; Eph. 5:30.

95 Cf. Mt. 14:65; Jn. 18;22; 19:3.
96 Cf. Mt. 8:20; Lk. 9:58.
97 Cf. BOUDON, *op. cit.*, bk. 1, ch. 4: One must necessarily walk the way of the Cross.
98 The story of the two crowns is well known among the biographers of St. Catherine of Siena. (Cf. her life by Joergensen.) Pictures of St. Catherine generally represent her as wearing a crown of thorns.
99 Cf. 1 Cor. 6:19.
100 1 Pet. 2:5.
101 Cf. Apoc. 21; 2, 10; also the office of the Dedication of a church.
102 Is. 41:16; Jer. 15:7; Mt. 3:12; Lk. 3:17.
103 Cf. 1 Pet. 1:7.
104 Heb. 12:29; Cf. Deut. 4:24; 9:3.
105 Cf. Exod. 3:2, 3.
106 Cf. Prov. 17:3; Sir. 2:5.
107 Cf. Ps. 37:20; 67:2.
108 Heb. 12:1.
109 Cf. Gen. 4:4, 8.
110 Cf. Gen. 12:1-9.
111 Cf. Gen. 19:1, 17.
112 Cf. Gen. 25:27; 27:41.
113 Cf. Tob. 2:9-11.
114 Cf. Jb. ch. 1 and 2.
115 Heb. 12:2.
116 Lk. 24:26.
117 Cf. Lk. 2:35.
118 Cf. 1 Kgs. 6:12.
119 Cf. Mt. 27:32; Mk. 15:21.
120 Cf. Mt. 27:38; Mk. 15:27.
121 Cf. Gen. 3:18.
122 Cf. Is. 51:17; Mt. 20, 22, 23.
123 Cf. Mt. 11:30.
124 A comparison borrowed from St. Augustine and St. Bernard.
125 Cf. Sir. 34:9.
126 Imitation of Christ, bk. 3, ch. 5, No. 7.
127 Cf. Imitation of Christ, bk. 1, ch. 25, No. 3.
128 Cf. Lk. 21:15.
129 Cf. No. 32, Note.
130 Cf. SAINT JOHN CHRYSOSTOM, *Monitum in homiliam de gloria in tribulationibus.* Among the saints who have expressed these same sentiments is Montfort himself whose greatest suffering was to be without suffering. His well-known exclamation, "No cross, what a cross," uttered when his mission at Vertou met with success in 1708, accurately describes him and entitles him to be associated with those of the saints mentioned.
131 Cf. Jas. 1:2.
132 Cf. Letters 13.
133 Cf. 1 Cor. ch. 1 and 2. Montfort re-echoes here in his own way the ideas developed by St. Paul in these two chapters.
134 Montfort sums up here the inspired words of St. John Chrysostom

as expressed in his homilies.
135 Montfort quotes Boudon almost literally in all this No. 37.
136 Cf. Acts 12:3-7.
137 Cf. 2 Cor. 12:2.
138 Cf. Mt. 16:19.
139 Phil. 2:9, 10.
140 Cf. 2 Cor. 4:17; cf. Nos. 9, 58.
141 Mt. 16:24; Lk. 9:23.
142 Mk. 7:37.
143 1 Cor. 8:13.
144 Mt. 15:14.
145 Ps. 50:14.
146 Lk. 11:13.
147 Ps. 50:12.
148 Cf. Wis. 7:14.
149 Cf. Jas. 1:5, 6.
150 1 Pet. 5:6.
151 1 Cor. 1:29.
152 Montfort refers often to this idea of "corruption" entering into us through sin. Cf. No. 51; TD 78, 79, 83, 173, etc.
153 Cf. Ps. 30:21.
154 Cf. 2 Cor. 12:7.
155 Cf. Acts 8:9.
156 Montfort wrote a hymn of twenty-two stanzas on the theme of thanking God for the crosses which come our way.
157 Cf. No. 47.
158 Lk. 22:42.
159 Ps. 83:3.
160 Lk. 22:42.
161 Lk. 1:38.
162 Ps. 56:8; 107:2.
163 Cf. Job 2:7, 8.
164 Lk. 16:15.
165 Job 2:3.
166 Cf. Kgs. 19:35. Montfort presumably alludes to the passage where it is stated that the angel of the Lord went forth and slew one hundred and eighty-five thousand men in the Assyrian camp.
167 Cf. Lk. 21:18.
168 Cf. Job 1:13-22.
169 Cf. 2 Kgs. 16:5-14.
170 Cf. Wis. 8:1.
171 Lam. 1:12.
172 Cf. Gal. 3:1.
173 Cf. 1 Pet. 4:1.
174 Cf. Eph. 6:11-18.
175 Cf. Heb. 11:24-26.
176 Cf. Ps. 68:8; 118, 112.
177 Cf. 1 Cor. 4:9, 13.
178 Cf. 2 Cor. 4:17. Also Nos. 9, 39.
179 Cf. Apoc. 2:7.

180 Cf. BOUDON, *op. cit.*, bk. 4, ch. 6: "We must receive crosses with joy and thanksgiving."

181 Mt. 25:21, 23; Mk. 10; 30.

182 Is this really the end of the letter? It could naturally finish at this point. Dalin, whose text we are following, ends with a line of dots which gives the impression that there is more. Quérard in his "Providential Mission of Venerable Montfort" writes on page 357: "It is regrettable that the ending of this excellent instruction on the Cross has been lost." As we do not possess the original or even the first edition we cannot know whether the text is complete or not.

S. LUIS GRIGNION DE MONTFORT
QUE VENHA O TEU REINO
QUE VENHA O REINO DE MARIA

4 The Secret of the Holy Rosary

Introduction

One of the most honorable titles given to St. Louis Marie de Montfort ("the priest with the big rosary") is that of "Apostle of the Cross and the holy Rosary." The Rosary occupied an important place in his own spiritual life and in his apostolate. The "Secret of the Holy Rosary" is not as original in its composition as his other books for here he is demonstrating the value of one particular devotional practice and at the same time borrowing extensively from many authors.

As he was primarily a missionary of the ordinary people, concentrating especially on the poor and abandoned, he set out to renew in them the spirit of Christianity, believing that this could be achieved by devotion to Mary which could only lead men to Jesus and holiness. He believed that the Rosary was a wonderfully secret way of knowing Mary and finding Jesus through her. He saw how much more fervent were those parishes whose people had maintained the practice of saying the Rosary than those whose people had abandoned it (cf. No. 113). He established the devotion of the Rosary wherever he preached and had it recited publicly every day during his missions.

Although this book was not published during his lifetime, he certainly intended it to be made available to the faithful. The "Little Roses" which form an introduction to the book indicate that he destined it for all classes of people, priests, sinners, mystical souls, children. The "mystical" souls may constitute a problem but the saint points out (No. 149) that the Rosary and contemplation are quite compatible, as is proved in the lives of many saints. He is naturally anxious that priests should recite it and then go on to counsel it to the faithful and establish a Confraternity of the Rosary.

One may ask, "How does Montfort propose to convince his readers?" He follows the classical method: The marvelous origin of this form of Marian devotion and the climate of miracles in which it developed over the centuries. He was aware that critics would express doubts about some of his stories but he points out simply that he has quoted them from reputable authors. He has used extensively the "Mystical Rosary" of Antonin Thomas O.P., a book containing 400 pages and divided into fifteen decades, each decade covering ten chapters. Montfort's book is much smaller and is divided into five decades, each containing ten "Roses." The first four decades show generous borrowings from Thomas, but when quoting him Montfort is implicitly returning to the common source of all material for the Rosary: the Dominican, Alan de la Roche.

The Secret of the Rosary for Renewal and Salvation

A White Rose

1 [1]Dear ministers of the most high God, you my fellow priests who preach the truth of God and who teach the gospel to all nations, let me give you this little book as a white rose that I would like you to keep. The truths contained in it are set forth in a very simple and straightforward manner, as you will see.

Please keep them in your heart so that you yourselves may make a practice of the Rosary and taste its fruits.

Please have them always on your lips too, so that you will always preach the Rosary and thus convert others by teaching them the excellence of this holy devotion.

I beg of you to beware of thinking of the Rosary as something of little importance—as do ignorant people, and even several great but proud scholars. Far from being insignificant, the Rosary is a priceless treasure which is inspired by God.

Almighty God has given it to you because he wants you to use it as a means to convert the most hardened sinners and the most obstinate heretics. He has attached to it grace in this life and glory in the next. The saints have said it faithfully and the Popes have endorsed it.

When the Holy Spirit has revealed this secret to a priest and director of souls, how blessed is that priest! For the vast majority of people fail to know this secret or else only know it superficially. If such a priest really understands this secret, he will say the Rosary each day and will encourage others to say it. God and his blessed Mother will pour abundant grace into his soul, so that he may become God's instrument for his glory; and his word, though simple, will do more good in one month than that of other preachers in several years.

2 Therefore, my dear brothers and fellow priests, it will not be enough for us to preach this devotion to others; we must practice it ourselves, for if we firmly believed in the importance of the holy Rosary but never said it ourselves, people could hardly be expected to act upon our advice, since no one can give what he does not have: "Jesus began to do and to teach."[2] We ought to pattern ourselves on our Lord, who began practicing what he preached. We ought to emulate St. Paul, who knew and preached nothing but Jesus crucified.

I could tell you at great length of the grace God has given me to know by experience the effectiveness of the preaching of the holy Rosary, and of how I have seen, with my own eyes, the most wonderful conversions it has brought about. I would gladly tell you all these things if I thought that it would move you to preach this beautiful devotion, in spite of the fact that priests are not in the habit of doing so these days. But instead of all this, I think it will be quite enough for this little summary that I am writing if I tell you a few ancient but authentic stories about the holy Rosary. These excerpts really go to prove what I have outlined for the faithful.

A Red Rose

3 Poor men and women who are sinners, I, a greater sinner than you, wish to give you this rose, a crimson one, because the precious blood of our Lord has fallen upon it. Please God that it may bring true fragrance into your lives—but above all, may it save you from the danger that you are in. Every day unbelievers and unrepentant sinners cry, "Let us crown ourselves with roses."[3] But our cry should be, "Let us crown ourselves with the roses of the holy Rosary."

How different are theirs from ours! Their roses are pleasures of the flesh, worldly honors and passing riches which wilt and decay in no time, but ours, which are the Our Father and Hail Mary which we have said devoutly over and over again, and to which we have added good penitential acts, will never wilt or die, and they will be just as exquisite thousands of years from now as they are today.

On the contrary, sinners' roses only look like roses, while in point of fact they are cruel thorns which prick them during life by giving them pangs of conscience, at their death they pierce them with bitter regret and, still worse, in eternity they turn to burning shafts of anger and despair. But if our roses have thorns, they are the thorns of Jesus Christ, who changes them into roses. If our roses prick us, it is only for a short time, and only in order to cure the illness of sin and to save our souls.

4 So by all means we should eagerly crown ourselves with these roses from heaven, and recite the entire Rosary every day, that is to say, three rosaries each of five decades, which are like three little wreaths or crowns of flowers. There are two reasons for doing this: first of all, to honor the three crowns of Jesus and Mary—Jesus' crown of grace at the time of his Incarnation, his crown of thorns during his passion, and his crown of glory in heaven, and of course the three-fold crown which the Blessed Trinity gave Mary in heaven. Secondly, we should do this so that we ourselves may receive three crowns from Jesus and Mary, the first a crown of merit during our lifetime; the second, a crown of peace at our death; and the third, a crown of glory in heaven.

If you say the Rosary faithfully until death, I do assure you that, in spite of the gravity of your sins "you shall receive a never-fading crown of glory."[4] Even if you are on the brink of damnation, even if you have one foot in hell, even if you have sold your soul to the devil as sorcerers do who practice black magic, and even if you are a heretic as obstinate as a devil, sooner or later you will be converted and will amend your life and save your soul, if—and mark well what I say—if you say the Rosary devoutly every day until death for the purpose of knowing the truth and obtaining contrition and pardon for your sins.

In this book there are several stories of great sinners who were converted through the power of the Rosary. Please read and meditate upon them.

A Mystical Rose Tree

5 Good and devout souls, who walk in the light of the Holy Spirit, I do not think you will mind my giving you this little mystical rose tree which comes straight from heaven and which is to be planted in the garden of your soul. It cannot possibly harm the sweet-smelling flowers of your contemplations; for it is a heavenly tree and its scent is very pleasant. It will not in the least interfere with your carefully planned flower-beds; for, being itself all pure and well-ordered, it inclines all to order and purity. If it is carefully watered and properly attended to every day, it will grow to such a marvelous height, and its branches will have such a wide span that, far from hindering your other devotions, it will maintain and perfect them. Of course, you understand what I mean, since you are spiritually minded; this mystical rose tree is Jesus and Mary in life, death and eternity.

6 Its green leaves are the Joyful Mysteries, the thorns the Sorrowful ones, and the flowers the Glorious Mysteries of Jesus and Mary. The buds are the childhood of Jesus and Mary, and the open blooms show us both of them in their sufferings, and the full-blown roses symbolize Jesus and Mary in their triumph and glory.

A rose delights us because of its beauty: so here we have Jesus and Mary in the Joyful Mysteries. Its thorns are sharp, and they prick, which makes us think of them in the Sorrowful Mysteries, and last of all, its perfume is so sweet that everyone loves it, and this fragrance symbolizes their Glorious Mysteries.

So please do not scorn this beautiful and heavenly tree, but plant it with your own hands in the garden of your soul, by making the resolution to say your Rosary every day. By saying it daily and by doing good works you will be tending your tree, watering it, hoeing the earth around it. Eventually you will see that this little seed which I have given you, and which seems so small now, will grow into a tree so great that the birds of heaven, that is, predestinate and contemplative souls, will dwell in it and make their nests there. Its shade will shelter them from the scorching heat of the sun and its height will keep them safe from the wild beasts on the ground. And best of all, they will feed upon the tree's fruit, which is none other than our adorable Jesus, to whom be honor and glory forever and ever. Amen.

God Alone

A Rosebud

7 Dear little friends, this beautiful rosebud is for you; it is one of the beads of your Rosary, and it may seem to you to be such a tiny thing. But if you only knew how precious this bead is! This wonderful bud will open out into a gorgeous rose if you say your Hail Mary really well.

Of course it would be too much to expect you to say the whole fifteen mysteries every day, but do say at least five mysteries, and say them properly with love and devotion. This Rosary will be your little wreath of roses, your crown for Jesus and Mary. Please pay attention to every word I have said, and listen carefully to a true story that I want to tell you, and that I would like you to remember.

8 Two little girls, who were sisters, were saying the Rosary very devoutly in front of their house. A beautiful lady suddenly appeared, walked towards the younger girl, who was only about six or seven, took her by the hand, and led her away. Her elder sister was very startled and looked for the little girl everywhere. At last, still not having found her, she went home weeping and told her parents that her sister had been kidnapped. For three whole days the poor father and mother sought the child without success.

At the end of the third day they found her at the front door looking extremely happy and pleased. Naturally they asked her where on earth she had been, and she told them that the lady to whom she had been saying the Rosary had taken her to a lovely place where she had given her delicious things to eat. She said that the lady had also given her a baby boy to hold, that he was very beautiful, and that she had kissed him again and again.

The father and mother, who had been converted to the Catholic faith only a short time before, sent at once for the Jesuit Father who had instructed them for their reception into the Church and who had also taught them devotion to the Rosary. They told him everything that had happened, and it was this priest himself who told me this story. It all took place in Paraguay.[5]

So, dear children, imitate these little girls and say your Rosary every day as they always did. If you do this, you will earn the right to go to heaven to see Jesus and Mary. If it is not their wish that you should see them in this life, at any rate after you die you will see them for all eternity. Amen.

Therefore let all men, the learned and the ignorant, the just and the sinners, the great and the small, praise and honor Jesus and Mary night and day, by saying the holy Rosary. "Greet Mary who has labored much among you."[6]

FIRST DECADE

The surpassing merit of the Rosary as seen in its origin and name.

First Rose

9 The Rosary is made up of two things: mental prayer and vocal prayer. In the Rosary mental prayer is none other than meditation of the chief mysteries of the life, death and glory of Jesus Christ and of his blessed Mother. Vocal prayer consists in saying fifteen decades of the Hail Mary, each decade headed by an Our Father, while at the same time meditating on and contemplating the fifteen principal virtues which Jesus and Mary practiced in the fif-

teen mysteries of the Rosary.

In the first five decades we must honor the five Joyful Mysteries and meditate on them; in the second five decades, the Sorrowful Mysteries; and in the third group of five, the Glorious Mysteries. So the Rosary is a blessed blending of mental and vocal prayer by which we honor and learn to imitate the mysteries and the virtues of the life, death, passion and glory of Jesus and Mary.

Second Rose

10 Since the Rosary is composed, principally and in substance, of the prayer of Christ and the Angelic Salutation, that is, the Our Father and the Hail Mary, it was without doubt the first prayer and the principal devotion of the faithful and has been in use all through the centuries, from the time of the apostles and disciples down to the present.

11 It was only in the year 1214, however, that the Church received the Rosary in its present form and according to the method we use today. It was given to the Church by St. Dominic, who had received it from the Blessed Virgin as a means of converting the Albigensians and other sinners.

I will tell you the story of how he received it, which is found in the very well-known book *De Dignitate Psalterii,* by Blessed Alan de la Roche. Saint Dominic, seeing that the gravity of people's sins was hindering the conversion of the Albigensians, withdrew into a forest near Toulouse, where he prayed continuously for three days and three nights. During this time he did nothing but weep and do harsh penances in order to appease the anger of God. He used his discipline so much that his body was lacerated, and finally he fell into a coma.

At this point our Lady appeared to him, accompanied by three angels, and she said, "Dear Dominic, do you know which weapon the Blessed Trinity wants to use to reform the world?"

"Oh, my Lady," answered Saint Dominic, "you know far better than I do, because next to your Son Jesus Christ you have always been the chief instrument of our salvation."

Then our Lady replied, "I want you to know that, in this kind of warfare, the principal weapon has always been the Angelic Psalter, which is the foundation-stone of the New Testament. Therefore, if you want to reach these hardened souls and win them over to God, preach my Psalter."

So he arose, comforted, and burning with zeal for the conversion of the people in that district, he made straight for the cathedral. At once unseen angels rang the bells to gather the people together, and Saint Dominic began to preach.

At the very beginning of his sermon, an appalling storm broke out, the earth shook, the sun was darkened, and there was so much thunder and lightning that all were very much afraid. Even greater was their fear when, looking at a picture of our Lady exposed in a prominent place, they saw her raise her arms to heaven three times to call down God's vengeance upon them if they failed to be converted, to amend their lives, and seek the protection of the holy Mother of God.

God wished, by means of these supernatural phenomena, to spread the new devotion of the holy Rosary and to make it more widely known.

At last, at the prayer of Saint Dominic, the storm came to an end, and he went on preaching. So fervently and compellingly did he explain the importance and value of the Rosary that almost all the people of Toulouse embraced it and renounced their false beliefs. In a very short time a great improvement was seen in the town;[7] people began leading Christian lives and gave up their former bad habits.

Third Rose

12 The miraculous way in which the devotion to the holy Rosary was established is something of a parallel to the way in which God gave his law to the world on Mount Sinai, and it obviously proves its value and importance.

Inspired by the Holy Spirit, instructed by the Blessed Virgin as well as by his own experience, Saint Dominic preached the Rosary for the rest of his life. He preached it by his example as well as by his sermons, in cities and in country places, to people of high station and low, before scholars and the uneducated, to Catholics and to heretics.

The Rosary, which he said every day, was his preparation for every sermon and his little tryst with our Lady immediately after preaching.

13 One day he had to preach at Notre Dame in Paris, and it happened to be the feast of St. John the Evangelist. He was in a little chapel behind the high altar prayerfully preparing his sermon by saying the Rosary, as he always did, when our Lady appeared to him and said: "Dominic, even though what you have planned to say may be very good, I am bringing you a much better sermon."

Saint Dominic took in his hands the book our Lady proffered, read the sermon carefully and, when he had understood it and meditated on it, he gave thanks to her.

When the time came, he went up into the pulpit and, in spite of the feast day, made no mention of Saint John other than to say that he had been found worthy to be the guardian of the Queen of Heaven. The congregation was made up of theologians and other eminent people, who were used to hearing unusual and polished discourses; but Saint Dominic told them that it was not his desire to give them a learned discourse, wise in the eyes of the world, but that he would speak in the simplicity of the Holy Spirit and with his forcefulness.

So he began preaching the Rosary and explained the Hail Mary word by word as he would to a group of children, and used the very simple illustrations which were in the book given him by our Lady.

14 Carthagena, the great scholar, quoting Blessed Alan de la Roche in *De Dignitate Psalterii,* describes how this took place.

"Blessed Alan writes that one day Father Dominic said to him in a vision, 'My son, it is good to preach; but there is always a danger of looking for praise rather than the salvation of souls. Listen carefully to what happened to me in Paris, so that you may be on your guard against this kind of mistake. I was to preach in the great church dedicated to the Blessed Virgin and I was particularly anxious to give a fine sermon, not out of pride, but because of the high intellectual stature of the congregation.

"'An hour before the time I had to preach, I was dutifully saying my Rosary—as I always did before giving a sermon—when I fell into ecstasy. I saw my beloved friend, the Mother of God, coming towards me with a book in her hand. "Dominic," she said, "your sermon for today may be very good indeed, but no matter how good it is, I have brought you one that is very much better."

"'Of course I was overjoyed, and I took the book and read every word of it. Just as our Lady had said, I found exactly the right things to say in my sermon, so I thanked her with all my heart.

"'When it was time to begin, I saw that the University of Paris had turned out in full force, as well as a large number of noblemen. They had all seen and heard of the great things that the good Lord had been doing through me.

"'I went up into the pulpit. It was the feast of Saint John the Evangelist but all I said about him was that he had been found worthy to be the guardian of the Queen of Heaven. Then I addressed the congregation:

"'My Lords and illustrious doctors of the University, you are accustomed to hearing learned sermons suited to your refined tastes. Now I do not want to speak to you in the scholarly language of human wisdom but, on the contrary, to show you the Spirit of God and his greatness.'"

Here ends the quotation from Blessed Alan, after which Carthagena goes on to say in his own words, "Then Saint Dominic explained the Angelic Salutation to them, using simple comparisons and examples from everyday life."[8]

15 Blessed Alan, according to Carthagena, mentioned several other occasions when our Lord and our Lady appeared to Saint Dominic to urge him and inspire him to preach the Rosary more and more in order to wipe out sin and convert sinners and heretics.

In another passage Carthagena says, "Blessed Alan said our Lady revealed to him that, after she had appeared to Saint Dominic, her blessed Son appeared to him and said, 'Dominic, I rejoice to see that you are not relying on your own wisdom and that, rather than seek the empty praise of men, you are working with great humility for the salvation of souls.

"'But many priests want to preach thunderously against the worst kinds of sin at the very outset, failing to realize that before a sick person is given bitter medicine, he needs to be prepared by being put into the right frame of mind to really benefit by it.

"'That is why, before doing anything else, priests should try to kindle a love of prayer in people's hearts and especially a love of my Angelic Psalter. If only they would all start saying it and would really persevere, God in his mercy could hardly refuse to give them his grace. So I want you to preach my Rosary.'"[9]

16 In another place Blessed Alan says, "All priests say a Hail Mary with the faithful before preaching, to ask for God's grace.[10] They do this because of a revelation that Saint Dominic had from our Lady. 'My son,' she said one day, 'do not be surprised that your sermons fail to bear the results you had hoped for. You are trying to cultivate a piece of ground which has not had any rain. Now when God planned to renew the face of the earth, he started by sending down rain from heaven—and this was the Angelic Salutation. In this way God reformed the world.

"'So when you give a sermon, urge people to say my Rosary, and in this way your words will bear much fruit for souls.'

"Saint Dominic lost no time in obeying, and from then on he exerted great influence by his sermons." (This last quotation is from "The Book of Miracles of the Holy Rosary," written in Italian, also found in Justin's works, Sermon 143.)[11]

17 I have been very pleased to quote these well-known authors word for word for the benefit of those who might otherwise have doubts as to the marvelous power of the Rosary.

As long as priests followed Saint Dominic's example and preached devotion to the holy Rosary, piety and fervor thrived throughout the Christian world and in those religious orders which were devoted to the Rosary. But since people have neglected this gift from heaven, all kinds of sin and disorder have spread far and wide.

Fourth Rose

 18 All things, even the holiest, are subject to change, especially when they are dependent on man's free will. It is hardly to be wondered at, then, that the Confraternity of the Holy Rosary only retained its first fervor for a century after it was instituted by Saint Dominic. After this it was like a thing buried and forgotten.

Doubtless, too, the wicked scheming and jealousy of the devil were largely responsible for getting people to neglect the Rosary, and thus block the flow of God's grace which it had drawn upon the world.

Thus, in 1349 God punished the whole of Europe with the most terrible plague that had ever been known. Starting in the east, it spread throughout Italy, Germany, France, Poland and Hungary, bringing desolation wherever it went, for out of a hundred men hardly one lived to tell the tale. Big cities, towns, villages and monasteries were almost completely deserted during the three years that the epidemic lasted.

This scourge of God was quickly followed by two others, the heresy of the Flagellants and a tragic schism in 1376.

19 Later on, when these trials were over, thanks to the mercy of God, our Lady told Blessed Alan to revive the former Confraternity of the Holy Rosary. Blessed Alan was one of the Dominican Fathers at the monastery at Dinan, in Brittany. He was an eminent theologian and a famous preacher. Our Lady chose him because, since the Confraternity had originally been started in that province, it was fitting that a Dominican from the same province should have the honor of re-establishing it.[12]

Blessed Alan began this great work in 1460, after a special warning from our Lord. This is how he received that urgent message, as he himself tells it:

One day when he was offering Mass, our Lord, who wished to spur him on to preach the holy Rosary, spoke to him in the Sacred Host. "How can you crucify me again so soon?" Jesus said. "What did you say, Lord?" asked Blessed Alan, horrified. "You crucified me once before by your sins," answered Jesus, "and I would willingly be crucified again rather than have my Father offended by the sins you used to commit. You are crucifying me again now because you have all the learning and understanding that you need to preach my Mother's Rosary, and you are not doing it. If you only did that, you could teach many souls the right path and lead them away from sin. But you are not doing it, and so you yourself are guilty of the sins that they commit."

This terrible reproach made Blessed Alan solemnly resolve to preach the Rosary unceasingly.[13]

20 Our Lady also said to him one day to inspire him to preach the Rosary more and more, "You were a great sinner in your youth, but I obtained the grace of your conversion from my Son. Had such a thing been possible, I would have liked to have gone through all kinds of suffering to save you, because converted sinners are a glory to me.[14] And I would have done that also to make you worthy of preaching my Rosary far and wide."

Saint Dominic[15] appeared to Blessed Alan as well and told him of the great results of his ministry: he had preached the Rosary unceasingly, his sermons had borne great fruit and many people had been converted during his missions.

He said to Blessed Alan, "See what wonderful results I have had through preaching the Rosary. You and all who love our Lady ought to do the same so that, by means of this holy practice of the Rosary, you may draw all people to the real science of the virtues."[16]

Briefly, then, this is the history of how Saint Dominic established the holy Rosary and of how Blessed Alan de la Roche restored it.

[Fifth Rose]

21 Strictly speaking, there can be only one kind of Confraternity of the Rosary, that is, one whose members agree to say the entire Rosary of 150 Hail Marys every day. However, considering the fervor of those who say it, we may distinguish three kinds: Ordinary Membership, which entails saying the complete Rosary once a week; Perpetual Membership, which requires it to be said only once a year; Daily Membership, which obliges one to say it all every day, that is, the fifteen decades made up of 150 Hail Marys.

None of these oblige under pain of sin. It is not even a venial sin to fail in this duty because such an undertaking is entirely voluntary and supererogatory. Needless to say, people should not join the Confraternity if they do not intend to fulfill their obligation by saying the Rosary as often as is required, without, however, neglecting the duties of their state in life.

So whenever the Rosary clashes with a duty of one's state in life, holy as the Rosary is, one must give preference to the duty to be performed. Similarly, sick people are not obliged to say the whole Rosary or even part of it if this effort might tire them and make them worse.

If you have been unable to say it because of some duty required by obedience or because you genuinely forgot, or because of some urgent necessity, you have not committed even a venial sin. You will then receive the benefits of the Confraternity just the same, sharing in the graces and merits of your brothers and sisters in the Rosary, who are saying it throughout the world.

And, my dear Catholic people, even if you fail to say your Rosary out of sheer carelessness or laziness, as long as you do not have any formal contempt for it, you do not sin, absolutely speaking, but you forfeit your participation in the prayers, good works and merits of the Confraternity. Moreover, because you have not been faithful in things that are little and of supererogation, almost without knowing it you may fall into the habit of neglecting big things, such as those duties which bind under pain of sin; for "He that scorns small things shall fall little by little."[17]

Sixth Rose

22 From the time Saint Dominic established the devotion to the holy Rosary up to the time when Blessed Alan de la Roche re-established it in 1460, it has always been called the Psalter of Jesus and Mary. This is because it has the same number of Hail Marys as there are psalms in the Book of the Psalms of David. Since simple and uneducated people are not able to say the Psalms of David, the Rosary is held to be just as fruitful for them as David's Psalter is for others.

But the Rosary can be considered to be even more valuable than the latter for three reasons:

1 Firstly, because the Angelic Psalter bears a nobler fruit, that of the Word incarnate, whereas David's Psalter only prophesies his coming;

2 Just as the real thing is more important than its prefiguration and the body surpasses the shadow, so the Psalter of our Lady is greater than David's Psalter, which did no more than pre-figure it;

3 Because our Lady's Psalter or the Rosary made up of the Our Father and Hail Mary is the direct work of the Blessed Trinity.

Here is what the learned Carthagena says about it:

The scholarly writer of Aix-la-Chapelle says in his book, The Rose Crown, dedicated to the Emperor Maximilian: "It cannot be maintained that Salutation of Mary is a recent innovation. It spread almost with the Church itself. For at the very beginnings of the Church the more educated members of the faithful celebrated the praises of God in the 150 psalms of David. The ordinary people, who encountered more difficulty in divine service, thus conceived a holy emulation of them. . . . They considered, which is indeed true, that the heavenly praises of the Rosary contained all the divine secrets of the psalms, for, if the psalms sing of the one who is to come, the Rosary proclaims him as having come.

"That is how they began to call their prayer of 150 Salutations 'The Psalter of Mary,' and to precede each decade with an Our Father, as was done by those who recited the psalms."[18]

23 The Psalter or Rosary of our Lady is divided into three chaplets of five decades each, for the following reasons:

1 to honor the three persons of the Blessed Trinity;

2 to honor the life, death and glory of Jesus Christ;
3 to imitate the Church triumphant, to help the members of the Church militant, and to bring relief to the Church suffering;
4 to imitate the three groups into which the psalms are divided, the first being for the purgative life, the second for the illuminative life, and the third for the unitive life;
5 to give us graces in abundance during life, peace at death, and glory in eternity.

Seventh Rose

24 Ever since Blessed Alan de la Roche re-established this devotion, the voice of the people, which is the voice of God, gave it the name of the Rosary, which means "crown of roses." That is to say that every time people say the Rosary devoutly they place on the heads of Jesus and Mary 153 white roses and sixteen red roses. Being heavenly flowers, these roses will never fade or lose their beauty.

Our Lady has approved and confirmed this name of the Rosary; she has revealed to several people that each time they say a Hail Mary they are giving her a beautiful rose, and that each complete Rosary makes her a crown of roses.[19]

25 The Jesuit brother, Alphonsus Rodriguez, used to say his Rosary with such fervor that he often saw a red rose come out of his mouth at each Our Father, and a white rose at each Hail Mary, both equal in beauty and differing only in color.

The chronicles of St. Francis tell of a young friar who had the praiseworthy habit of saying this crown of our Lady every day before dinner. One day, for some reason or other, he did not manage to say it. The refectory bell had already been rung when he asked the Superior to allow him to say it before coming to the table, and, having obtained permission, he withdrew to his cell to pray.

After he had been gone a long time, the Superior sent another friar to fetch him, and he found him in his room bathed in a heavenly light in the presence of our Lady and two angels. Beautiful roses kept issuing from his mouth at each Hail Mary, and the two angels were taking them one by one and placing them on our Lady's head, while she smilingly accepted them. Finally, two other friars who had been sent to find out what had happened to the first two saw the same scene, and our Lady did not leave until the whole Rosary had been said.[20]

So the complete Rosary is a large crown of roses and each chaplet of five decades is a little wreath of flowers or a little crown of heavenly roses which we place on the heads of Jesus and Mary. The rose is the queen of flowers, and so the Rosary is the rose of devotions and the most important one.

Eighth Rose

26 It is scarcely possible for me to put into words how our Lady esteems the Rosary and how she prefers it to all other devotions. Nor can I sufficiently express how wonderfully she rewards those who work to make known the devotion, to establish it and spread it nor, on the other hand, how strictly she punishes those who work against it.

St. Dominic had nothing more at heart during his life than to praise our Lady, to preach her greatness, and to inspire everybody to honor her by saying her Rosary. As a reward he received countless graces from her. This powerful Queen of heaven crowned his labors with many miracles and prodigies. God always granted him what he asked through our Lady. The greatest favor of all was that she helped him to crush the Albigensian heresy and made him the founder and patriarch of a great religious order.[21]

27 As for Blessed Alan de la Roche, who restored the devotion of the Rosary, he received many privileges from our Lady; she graciously appeared to him several times to teach him how to work out his salvation, to become a good priest and perfect religious, and how to pattern himself on our Lord.

He used to be horribly tempted and persecuted by devils, and then a deep sadness would fall upon him and sometimes he would be near to despair. But our Lady always comforted him by her presence, which banished the clouds of darkness from his soul.

She taught him how to say the Rosary, explaining its value and the fruits to be gained by it; and she gave him a great and glorious privilege, which was the honor of being called her new spouse. As a token of her chaste love for him, she placed a ring upon his finger and a necklace made of her own hair about his neck and gave him a Rosary.[22]

Fr. Tritème, the learned Carthagena and Martin of Navarre, as well as others, have spoken of him in terms of highest praise. Blessed Alan died at Zwolle, in Flanders, on September 8th, 1475, after having brought more than a hundred thousand people into the Confraternity.[23]

28 Blessed Thomas of St. John was well known for his sermons on the holy Rosary, and the devil, jealous of his success, tortured him so much that he fell ill and was sick for such a long time that the doctors gave him up. One night, when he really thought he was dying, the devil appeared to him in the most terrible form imaginable. There was a picture of our Lady near his bed; he looked at it and cried with all his heart and soul and strength, "Help me, save me, my dearest Mother." No sooner had he said this than the picture seemed to come alive and our Lady put out her hand, took him by the arm and said, "Do not be afraid, Thomas my son, here

I am and I am going to save you; get up now and go on preaching my Rosary as you used to do. I promise to shield you from your enemies."

When our Lady said this, the devil fled and Blessed Thomas got up, finding himself in perfect health. He then thanked our Lady with tears of joy. He resumed his Rosary apostolate, and his sermons were wonderfully successful.[24]

29 Our Lady not only blesses those who preach her Rosary but she highly rewards all those who, by their example, get others to say it.

Alphonsus, King of Leon and Galicia, very much wanted all his servants to honor the Blessed Virgin by saying the Rosary, so he used to hang a large rosary on his belt, though he never said it himself. Nevertheless, his wearing it encouraged his courtiers to say the Rosary devoutly.

One day the King fell seriously ill and when he was given up for dead he found himself, in spirit, before the judgment-seat of our Lord. Many devils were there accusing him of all the sins he had committed, and our Lord was about to condemn him when our Lady came forward to speak in his favor. She called for a pair of scales and had his sins placed in one of the balances, while she put the large rosary which he had always worn on the other scale, together with all the rosaries that had been said through his example. It was found that the Rosaries weighed more than his sins.

Looking at him with great kindness, our Lady said, "As a reward for the little service you did for me in wearing my rosary, I have obtained a great grace for you from my Son. Your life will be spared for a few more years. See that you spend those years wisely, and do penance."

When the King regained consciousness he cried out, "Blessed be the Rosary of the most holy Virgin Mary, by which I have been delivered from eternal damnation."

After he had recovered his health, he spent the rest of his life in spreading devotion to the Rosary, and said it faithfully every day.

People who love the Blessed Virgin ought to follow the example of King Alphonsus and that of the saints whom I have mentioned, so that they too may win other souls for the Confraternity of the Holy Rosary. They will receive great graces here on earth and finally eternal life.[25] "Those who explain me will have life everlasting."[26]

Ninth Rose

30 It is very wicked indeed and unjust to hinder the progress of the Confraternity of the Holy Rosary. God has severely punished many of those who have been so benighted as to scorn the Confraternity and have sought to destroy it.

Even though God has set his seal of approval on the Rosary by many miracles, and though it has been approved by the Church in many papal bulls, there are only too many people who are against the holy Rosary today. Such are free-thinkers and those who scorn religion, who either condemn the Rosary or try to turn others away from it.

It is easy to see that they have absorbed the poison of hell and that they are inspired by the devil; for no one can condemn devotion to the holy Rosary without condemning all that is most holy in the Catholic faith, such as the Lord's prayer, the Hail Mary and the mysteries of the life, death and glory of Jesus Christ and his holy Mother.

These freethinkers, who cannot bear to have people saying the Rosary, often fall into an heretical state of mind without realizing it and come to hate the Rosary and its mysteries.

To have a loathing for confraternities is to fall away from God and true piety, for our Lord himself has told us that he is always in the midst of those who are gathered together in his name. No good Catholic would neglect the many great indulgences which the Church has granted to confraternities. Finally, to dissuade others from joining the Rosary Confraternity is to be an enemy of souls, because the Rosary is a means of avoiding sin and leading a good life.

St. Bonaventure says in his "Psalter"[27] that whoever neglects our Lady will die in his sins. What, then, must be the punishment in store for those who turn people away from devotion to her?[28]

Tenth Rose

31 While St. Dominic was preaching the Rosary in Carcassone, a heretic made fun of his miracles and the fifteen mysteries of the Rosary, and this prevented other heretics from being converted. As a punishment God allowed fifteen thousand devils to enter the man's body.

His parents took him to Father Dominic to be delivered from the evil spirits. He started to pray and he begged everyone who was there to say the Rosary out loud with him, and at each Hail Mary our Lady drove a hundred devils out of the man, and they came out in the form of red-hot coals.

After he had been delivered, he abjured his former errors, was converted and joined the Rosary Confraternity. Several of his associates did the same, having been greatly moved by his punishment and by the power of the Rosary.[24]

32 The learned Franciscan, Carthagena, as well as several other authors, says that an extraordinary event took place in 1482. The venerable Fr. James Sprenger and the religious of his order were zealously working to re-establish devotion to the Rosary and its

Confraternity in the city of Cologne. Unfortunately, two priests who were famous for their preaching ability were jealous of the great influence they were exerting through preaching the Rosary. These two Fathers spoke against this devotion whenever they had a chance, and as they were very eloquent and had a great reputation, they persuaded many people not to join the Confraternity.

One of them, the better to achieve his wicked end, wrote a special sermon against the Rosary and planned to give it the following Sunday. But when the time came for the sermon he did not appear and, after a certain amount of waiting, someone went to fetch him. He was found to be dead, and he had evidently died without anyone to help him.

After persuading himself that this death was due to natural causes, the other priest decided to carry out his friend's plan and give a similar sermon on another day, hoping to put an end to the Confraternity of the Rosary. However, when the day came for him to preach and it was time to give the sermon, God punished him by striking him down with paralysis which deprived him of the use of his limbs and of his power of speech.

At last he admitted his fault and that of his friend and in his heart he silently besought our Lady to help him. He promised that if only she would cure him, he would preach the Rosary with as much zeal as that with which he had formerly fought against it. For this end he implored her to restore his health and his speech, which she did, and finding himself instantaneously cured he rose up like another Saul, a persecutor turned defender of the holy Rosary. He publicly acknowledged his former error and ever afterwards preached the wonders of the Rosary with great zeal and eloquence.[30]

33 I am quite sure that freethinkers and ultra-critical people of today will question the truth of the stories in this little book, as they question most things, but all I have done has been to copy them from very good contemporary authors and, in part, from a book written a short time ago, *The Mystical Rose-tree,* by Fr. Antonin Thomas, O.P.

Everyone knows that there are three different kinds of faith by which we believe different kinds of stories. To stories from Holy Scripture we owe divine faith; to stories on non-religious subjects which are not against common sense and are written by trustworthy authors, we pay the tribute of human faith; and to stories about holy subjects which are told by good authors and are not in any way contrary to reason, to faith or to morals[31] (even though they may sometimes deal with happenings which are above the ordinary), we pay the tribute of a pious faith.

I agree that we must be neither too credulous nor too critical, and that we should keep a happy medium in all things in order to find just where truth and virtue lie. But on the other hand, I know equally well that charity easily leads us to believe all that is not contrary to faith or morals: "Charity believes all things," in the same way as pride induces us to doubt even well authenticated stories on the plea that they are not to be found in Holy Scripture.

This is one of the devil's traps; heretics of the past who denied tradition have fallen into it, and over-critical people of today are falling into it too, without even realizing it. People of this kind refuse to believe what they do not understand or what is not to their liking, simply because or their own spirit of pride and independence.

SECOND DECADE

The surpassing merit of the Rosary as seen in the prayers which compose it.

Eleventh Rose [The Creed]

34 The Creed or the Symbol of the Apostles, which is said on the crucifix of the rosary, is a holy summary of all the Christian truths. It is a prayer that has great merit, because faith is the root, foundation and beginning of all Christian virtues, of all eternal virtues, and of all prayers that are pleasing to God. "Anyone who comes to God must believe,"[32] and the greater his faith the more merit his prayer will have, the more powerful it will be, and the more it will glorify God.

I shall not take time here to explain the Creed word for word, but I cannot resist saying that the first words, "I believe in God," are wonderfully effective as a means of sanctifying our souls and putting the devils to rout, because these words contain the acts of the three theological virtues of faith, hope and charity.

It was by saying these words that many saints overcame temptations, especially those against faith, hope or charity, either during their lifetime or at the hour of their death. They were also the last words of St. Peter, Martyr. A heretic had cleft his head in two by a blow of his sword, and although St. Peter was at his last gasp, he managed to trace these words in the sand with his finger.

35 The holy Rosary contains many mysteries of Jesus and Mary, and since faith is the only key which opens up these mysteries for us, we must begin the Rosary by saying the Creed very devoutly, and the stronger our faith the more merit our Rosary will have.

This faith must be lively and informed by charity; in other words, to recite the Rosary properly it is necessary to be in God's grace, or at least seeking it. This faith must be strong and constant, that is, one must not be looking for sensible devotion and spiritual consolation in the recitation of the Rosary; nor should one give it up because the mind is flooded with countless involuntary distractions, or because one experiences a strange distaste in the soul or an almost continual and oppressive fatigue of the body. Neither feelings, nor consolation, nor sighs, nor transports, nor the continual attention of the imagination are needed; faith and good intentions are quite enough. *Sola fides sufficit.*[33]

Twelfth Rose [The Our Father]

36 The Our Father or the Lord's Prayer derives its great value above all from its author, who is neither a man nor an angel, but the King of angels and of men, our Lord Jesus Christ. St. Cyprian says[34] it was necessary that he who came to give us the life of grace as our Savior should teach us the way to pray as our heavenly Master.

The beautiful order, the tender forcefulness and the clarity of this divine prayer pay tribute to our divine Master's wisdom. It is a short prayer but can teach us so very much, and it is well within the grasp of uneducated people, while scholars find it a continual source of investigation into the mysteries of God.

The Our Father contains all the duties we owe to God, the acts of all the virtues and the petitions for all our spiritual and corporal needs. Tertullian says[35] that the Our Father is a summary of the New Testament. Thomas a Kempis says that it surpasses all the desires of all the saints; that it is a condensation of all the beautiful sayings of all the psalms and canticles; that in it we ask God for everything that we need; that by it we praise him in the very best way; that by it we lift up our souls from earth to heaven and unite them closely to God.[36]

37 St. John Chrysostom says[37] that we cannot be our Master's disciples unless we pray as he did and in the way that he showed us. Moreover, God the Father listens more willingly to the prayer that we have learned from his Son rather than those of our own making, which have all our human limitations.

We should say the Our Father with the certitude that the eternal Father will hear us because it is the prayer of his Son, whom he always hears, and because we are his members. God will surely grant our petitions made through the Lord's Prayer because it is impossible to imagine that such a good Father could refuse a request couched in the language of so worthy a Son, reinforced by his merits, and made at his behest.

St. Augustine[38] assures us that whenever we say the Our Father devoutly our venial sins are forgiven. The just man falls seven times, and in the Lord's Prayer he will find seven petitions which will both help him to avoid lapses and protect him from his spiritual enemies. Our Lord, knowing how weak and helpless we are, and how many difficulties we endure, made his prayer short and easy to say, so that if we say it devoutly and often, we can be sure that God will quickly come to our aid.

38 I have a word for you, devout souls who pay little attention to the prayer that the Son of God gave us himself and asked us all to say: It is high time for you to change your way of thinking. You only esteem prayers that men have written, as though anybody, even the most inspired man in the whole world, could possibly know more about how we ought to pray than Jesus Christ himself! You look for prayers in books written by other men almost as though you were ashamed of saying the prayer that our Lord told us to say.

You have managed to convince yourself that the prayers in those books are for scholars and for the rich, and that the Rosary is only for women and children and the poor people. As if the prayers and praises you have been reading were more beautiful and more pleasing to God than those which are to be found in the Lord's Prayer! It is a very dangerous temptation to lose interest in the prayer that our Lord gave us and to take up prayers that men have written instead.

Not that I disapprove of prayers that saints have written to encourage the faithful to praise God, but it is not to be endured that they should prefer these to the prayer which was uttered by Wisdom incarnate. If they ignore this prayer, it is as though they passed by the spring to go to the brook, and refusing the clear water, they drink instead that which is dirty. For the Rosary, made up of the Lord's Prayer and the Hail Mary, is this clear and ever-flowing water which comes from the fountain of grace, whereas other prayers which they look for in books are nothing but tiny streams which spring from this fountain.

39 People who say the Lord's Prayer carefully, weighing every word and meditating on them, may indeed call themselves blessed, for they find therein everything that they need or can wish for.

When we say this wonderful prayer, we touch God's heart at the very outset by calling him by that sweet name of Father.

"Our Father," he is the dearest of fathers: all-powerful in his creation, wonderful in the way he maintains the world, completely lovable in his divine Providence, all good and infinitely so in the Redemption. We have God for our Father, so we are all brothers, and heaven is our homeland and our heritage. This should be more than enough to teach us to love God and our neighbor, and to be detached from the things of this world.

So we ought to love our heavenly Father and say to him over

and over again: "Our Father who art in heaven"—

Thou who dost fill heaven and earth
with the immensity of thy being,
Thou who art present everywhere:
Thou who art in the saints by thy glory,
in the damned by thy justice,
in the good by thy grace,
in sinners by the patience
with which thou dost tolerate them,
grant that we may always remember
that we come from thee;
grant that we may live as thy true children;
that we may direct our course towards thee alone
with all the ardor of our soul.

"Hallowed be thy name." The name of the Lord is holy and to be feared, said the prophet-king David, and heaven, according to Isaiah, echoes with the praises of the seraphim who unceasingly praise the holiness of the Lord, God of hosts.

We ask here that all the world may learn to know and adore the attributes of our God, who is so great and so holy. We ask that he may be known, loved and adored by pagans, Turks, Jews, barbarians and all infidels; that all men may serve and glorify him by a living faith, a staunch hope, a burning charity, and by the renouncing of all erroneous beliefs. In short, we pray that all men may be holy because our God himself is holy.

"Thy kingdom come." That is to say: May you reign in our souls by your grace, during life, so that after death we may be found worthy to reign with thee in thy kingdom, in perfect and unending bliss; that we firmly believe in this happiness to come; we hope for it and we expect it, because God the Father has promised it in his great goodness, and because it was purchased for us by the merits of God the Son; and it has been made known to us by the light of the Holy Spirit.

"Thy will be done on earth as it is in heaven." As Tertullian says, this sentence does not mean in the least that we are afraid of people thwarting God's designs, because nothing whatsoever can happen without divine Providence having foreseen it and having made it fit into his plans beforehand. No obstruction in the whole world can possibly prevent the will of God from being carried out.

Rather, when we say these words, we ask God to make us humbly resigned to all that he has seen fit to send us in this life. We also ask him to help us to do, in all things and at all times, his holy will, made known to us by the commandments, promptly, lovingly and faithfully, as the angels and the blessed do in heaven.

40 "Give us this day our daily bread." Our Lord teaches us to ask God for everything that we need, whether in the spiritual or the temporal order. By asking for our *daily bread,* we humbly admit our own poverty and insufficiency, and pay tribute to our God, knowing that all temporal goods come from his Providence. When we say *bread* we ask for that which is necessary to live; and, of course that does not include luxuries.

We ask for this bread *today,* which means that we are concerned only for the present, leaving the morrow in the hands of Providence.

And when we ask for our daily bread, we recognize that we need God's help every day and that we are entirely dependent upon him for his help and protection.

"Forgive us our trespasses as we forgive those who trespass against us." Every sin, says St. Augustine and Tertullian, is a debt which we contract with God, and he in his justice requires payment down to the last farthing. Unfortunately we all have these sad debts.

No matter how many they may be, we should go to God with all confidence and with true sorrow for our sins, saying, "Our Father who art in heaven, forgive us our sins of thought and those of speech, forgive us our sins of commission and of omission which make us infinitely guilty in the eyes of thy justice.

"We dare to ask this because thou art our loving and merciful Father, and because we have forgiven those who have offended us, out of obedience to you and out of charity.

"Do not permit us, in spite of our infidelity to thy graces, to give in to the temptations of the world, the devil, and the flesh.

"But deliver us from evil." The evil of sin, from the evil of temporal punishment and of everlasting punishment, which we have rightly deserved.

"Amen." This word at the end of the Our Father is very consoling, and St. Jerome says that it is a sort of seal of approbation that God puts at the end of our petitions to assure us that he will grant our requests, as though he himself were answering:

"Amen! May it be as you have asked, for truly you have obtained what you asked for." That is what is meant by this word: Amen.

Thirteenth Rose

41 Each word of the Lord's Prayer is a tribute we pay to the perfections of God. We honor his fecundity by the name of Father.

Father,
thou who throughout eternity
dost beget a Son
who is God like thee,
eternal, consubstantial with thee,

who is of the very same essence as thee;
and is of like power
and goodness
and wisdom
as thou art. . . .
Father and Son,
who, from your mutual love,
produce the Holy Spirit,
who is God like unto you;
three persons
but one God.

Our Father. This means that he is the Father of mankind, because he has created us and continues to sustain us, and because he has redeemed us. He is also the merciful Father of sinners, the Father who is the friend of the just, and the glorious Father of the blessed in heaven.

When we say *Who art,* we honor by these words the infinity and immensity and fulness of God's essence. God is rightly called "He who is;[39]" that is to say, he exists of necessity, essentially, and eternally, because he is the Being of beings and the cause of all beings. He possesses within himself, in a supereminent degree, the perfections of all beings, and he is in all of them by his essence, by his presence and by his power, but without being bounded by their limitations. We honor his sublimity and his glory and his majesty by the words *Who art in heaven,* that is to say, seated as on thy throne, holding sway over all men by thy justice.

When we say *Hallowed be thy name,* we worship God's holiness; and we make obeisance to his kingship and bow to the justice of his laws by the words *Thy kingdom come,* praying that men will obey him on earth as the angels do in heaven.

We show our trust in his Providence by asking for our daily bread, and we appeal to his mercy when we ask for the forgiveness of our sins.

We look to his great power when we beg him *not to lead us into temptation,* and we show our faith in his goodness by our hope that he will *deliver us from evil.*

The Son of God has always glorified his Father by his works, and he came into the world to teach men to give glory to him. He showed men how to praise him by this prayer, which he taught us with his own lips. It is our duty, therefore, to say it often, with attention, and in the same spirit as he composed it.

Fourteenth Rose

42 We make as many acts of the noblest Christian virtues as we pronounce words when we recite this divine prayer attentively.

In saying "Our Father, who art in heaven," we make acts of faith, adoration and humility. When we ask that his name be hallowed, we show a burning zeal for his glory. When we ask for the spread of his kingdom, we make an act of hope; by the wish that his will be done on earth as it is in heaven, we show a spirit of perfect obedience. In asking for our daily bread, we practice poverty of spirit and detachment from worldly goods. When we beg him to forgive us our sins, we make an act of sorrow for them. By forgiving those who have trespassed against us, we give proof of the virtue of mercy in its highest degree. Through asking God's help in all our temptations, we make acts of humility, prudence and fortitude. As we wait for him to deliver us from evil, we exercise the virtue of patience.

Finally, while asking for all these things, not only for ourselves but also for our neighbor and for all members of the Church, we are carrying out our duty as true children of God, we are imitating him in his love which embraces all men and we are keeping the commandment of love of our neighbor.

43 If we mean in our hearts what we say with our lips, and if our intentions are not at variance with those expressed in the Lord's Prayer, then, by reciting this prayer, we hate all sin and we observe all of God's laws. For whenever we think that God is in heaven, that is to say, infinitely removed from us by the greatness of his majesty, we place ourselves in his presence filled with overwhelming reverence. Then the fear of the Lord will chase away all pride and we will bow down before God in utter nothingness.

When we pronounce the name "Father" and remember that we owe our existence to God, by means of our parents, and even the instruction we have received by means of our teachers, who take the place of God and are his living images, we cannot help paying them honor and respect, or, to be more exact, to honor God in them. And nothing would be farther from our thoughts than to be disrespectful to them or hurt them.

When we pray that God's holy name be glorified, we cannot be farther from profaning it. If we really look upon the kingdom of God as our heritage, we cannot possibly be attached to the things of this world.

If we sincerely ask God that our neighbor may have the same blessings that we ourselves stand in need of, it goes without saying that we will give up all hatred, quarrelling and jealousy. And if we ask God for our daily bread, we shall learn to hate gluttony and sensual pleasures which thrive in rich surroundings.

While sincerely asking God to forgive us as we forgive those who trespass against us, we no longer give way to anger and revenge, we return good for evil and we love our enemies.

To ask God to save us from falling into sin when we are tempted is to give proof that we are fighting laziness and that we are genuinely seeking means to root out vicious habits and to work out our salvation.

To pray God to deliver us from evil is to fear his justice, and this will give us true happiness, for the fear of God is the beginning of wisdom. It is through the virtue of the fear of God that men avoid sin.

Fifteenth Rose

44 The Angelic Salutation, or Hail Mary, is so heavenly and so beyond us in its depth of meaning, that Blessed Alan de la Roche[40] held that no mere creature could ever understand it, and that only our Lord Jesus Christ, born of the Virgin Mary, can really explain it.

Its enormous value is due, first of all, to our Lady to whom it was addressed, to the purpose of the Incarnation of the Word, for which reason this prayer was brought from heaven, and also to the archangel Gabriel who was the first ever to say it.

The Angelic Salutation is a most concise summary of all that Catholic theology teaches about the Blessed Virgin. It is divided into two parts, that of praise and that of petition. The first shows all that goes to make up Mary's greatness; and the second, all that we need to ask her for, and all that we may expect to receive through her goodness.

The most Blessed Trinity revealed the first part of it to us; St. Elizabeth, inspired by the Holy Spirit, added the second; and the Church gave us the conclusion in the year 430 when she condemned the Nestorian heresy at the Council of Ephesus and defined that the Blessed Virgin is truly the Mother of God. At this time she ordered us to pray to our Lady under this glorious title by saying, "Holy Mary, Mother of God, pray for us sinners, now and at the hour of our death."

45 The greatest event in the whole history of the world was the Incarnation of the eternal Word by whom the world was redeemed and peace was restored between God and men. Our Lady was chosen as his instrument for this tremendous event, and it was put into effect when she was greeted with the Angelic Salutation. The archangel Gabriel, one of the leading princes of the heavenly court, was chosen as ambassador to bear these glad tidings.

In the Angelic Salutation can be seen the faith and hope of the patriarchs, the prophets and the apostles. Furthermore, it gives to martyrs their unswerving constancy and strength, it is the wisdom of the doctors of the Church, the perseverance of the holy confessors and the life of all religious (Blessed Alan).[41] It is the new hymn of the law of grace, the joy of angels and men, and the hymn which terrifies devils and puts them to shame.

By the Angelic Salutation God became man, a virgin became the Mother of God, the souls of the just were delivered from Limbo, the empty thrones in heaven have been filled, sin has been pardoned, grace been given to us, the sick been made well, the dead brought back to life, exiles brought home, the Blessed Trinity has been appeased, and men obtained eternal life.

Finally, the Angelic Salutation is the rainbow in the sky, a sign of the mercy and grace which God has given to the world (Blessed Alan).[42]

Sixteenth Rose

46 Even though there is nothing so great as the majesty of God and nothing so low as man in so far as he is a sinner, Almighty God does not despise our poor prayers. On the contrary, he is pleased when we sing his praises.

And the Angel's greeting to our Lady is one of the most beautiful hymns which we could possibly sing to the glory of the Most High. "To you will I sing a new song.[43] This new hymn, which David foretold would be sung at the coming of the Messiah, is none other than the Angelic Salutation.

There is an old hymn and a new hymn: the first is that which the Jews sang out of gratitude to God for creating them and maintaining them in existence, for delivering them from captivity and leading them safely through the Red Sea, for giving them manna to eat, and for all his other blessings.

The new hymn is that which Christians sing in thanksgiving for the graces of the Incarnation and the Redemption. As these marvels were brought about by the Angelic Salutation, so also do we repeat the same salutation to thank the most Blessed Trinity for the immeasurable goodness shown to us.

We praise God the Father because he so loved the world that he gave us his only Son as our Savior. We bless the Son because he deigned to leave heaven and come down upon earth, because he was made man and redeemed us. We glorify the Holy Spirit because he formed our Lord's pure body in the womb of our Lady, that body which was the victim for our sins. In this spirit of deep thankfulness should we, then, always say the Hail Mary, making acts of faith, hope, love and thanksgiving for the priceless gift of salvation.

47 Although this new hymn is in praise of the Mother of God and is sung directly to her, it is nevertheless most glorious to the Blessed Trinity, for any honor we pay to our Lady returns inevitably to God, the source of all her perfections and virtues. God the Father is glorified when we honor the most perfect of his creatures; God the Son is glorified when we praise his most pure Mother; the Holy Spirit is glorified when we are lost in admiration at the graces with which he has filled his spouse.

When we praise and bless our Lady by saying the Angelic Salutation, she always refers these praises to God in the same way as she did when she was praised by St. Elizabeth. The latter blessed her in her high dignity as Mother of God and our Lady immediately returned these praises to God in her beautiful *Magnificat.*

48 Just as the Angelic Salutation gave glory to the Blessed Trinity, it is also the very highest praise that we can give to Mary.

One day, when St. Mechtilde was praying and was trying to think of some way in which she could express her love of the Blessed Virgin better than before, she fell into ecstasy. Our Lady appeared to her with the Angelic Salutation written in letters of gold upon her breast and said to her, "My daughter, I want you to know that no one can please me more than by saying the greeting which the most adorable Trinity presented to me and by which I was raised to the dignity of the Mother of God.

"By the word *Ave,* which is the name of Eve, *Eva,* I learned that God in his infinite power had preserved me from all sin and its attendant misery which the first woman had been subject to.

"The name *Mary,* which means 'lady of light,' shows that God has filled me with wisdom and light, like a shining star, to light up heaven and earth.

"The words, *full of grace,* remind me that the Holy Spirit has showered so many graces upon me that I am able to give these graces in abundance to those who ask for them through my mediation.

"When people say, *The Lord is with thee,* they renew the indescribable joy that was mine when the eternal Word became incarnate in my womb.

"When you say to me, *Blessed art thou among women,* I praise the mercy of God who has raised me to this exalted degree of happiness.

"And at the words, *Blessed is the fruit of thy womb, Jesus,* the whole of heaven rejoices with me to see my Son Jesus adored and glorified for having saved mankind."[44]

Seventeenth Rose

49 Blessed Alan de la Roche, who was so deeply devoted to the Blessed Virgin, had many revelations from her, and we know that he confirmed the truth of these revelations by a solemn oath. Three of them stand out with special emphasis: the first, that if people fail to say the Hail Mary, which has saved the world, out of carelessness, or because they are lukewarm, or because they hate it, this is an indication that they will probably be condemned to eternal punishment.

The second truth is that those who love this divine salutation bear the very special stamp of predestination.

The third is that those to whom God has given this favor of loving our Lady and of serving her out of love must take very great care to continue to love and serve her until the time when she shall have had them placed in heaven by her Son in the degree of glory which they have earned (Blessed Alan).[45]

50 Heretics, all of whom are children of the devil and who clearly bear the sign of God's reprobation, have a horror of the Hail Mary. They still say the Our Father, but never the Hail Mary; they would rather carry a poisonous snake about them than a rosary.[46]

Among Catholics, those who bear the mark of God's reprobation think but little of the Rosary. They either neglect to say it or only say it quickly and in a lukewarm manner.

Even if I did not believe what was revealed to Blessed Alan de la Roche, even then my own experience would be enough to convince me of this terrible but consoling truth. I do not know, nor do I see clearly, how it can be that a devotion which seems to be so small can be the infallible sign of eternal salvation, and how its absence can be the sign of God's eternal displeasure; nevertheless, nothing could be more true.

In our own day we see that people who hold new doctrines that have been condemned by the Church, with all their would-be piety, ignore the devotion to the Rosary and often dissuade their acquaintances from saying it with all sorts of fine pretexts. They are very careful not to condemn the Rosary and the Scapular, as the Calvinists do, but the way they set about attacking them is all the more deadly because it is the more cunning. I shall refer to it again later on.[47]

51 The Hail Mary, the Rosary, is the prayer and the infallible touchstone by which I can tell those who are led by the Spirit of God from those who are deceived by the devil. I have known souls who seemed to soar like eagles to the heights by their sublime contemplation and yet were pitifully led astray by the devil. I only found out how wrong they were when I learned that they scorned the Hail Mary and the Rosary, which they considered as being far beneath them.

The Hail Mary is a blessed dew that falls from heaven upon the souls of the predestinate. It gives them a marvelous spiritual fertility so that they can grow in all virtues. The more the garden of the soul is watered by this prayer, the more enlightened in mind we become, the more zealous in heart, the stronger against all our enemies.

The Hail Mary is a sharp and flaming shaft which, joined to the Word of God, gives the preacher the strength to pierce, move, and convert the most hardened hearts, even if he has little or no natural gift for preaching.

As I have already said, this was the great secret that our Lady taught St. Dominic and Blessed Alan for the conversion of heretics and sinners. Saint Antoninus tells us that that is why many priests acquired the habit of saying a Hail Mary at the beginning of their sermons.[48]

Eighteenth Rose

52 This heavenly salutation draws down upon us the blessings of Jesus and Mary in abundance, for it is an infallible truth that Jesus and Mary reward in a marvelous way those who glorify them. "I love those who love me. I enrich them and fill their treasures."[49] That is what Jesus and Mary say to us. "Those who sow blessings will also reap blessings."[50]

Now if we say the Hail Mary properly, is not that a way to love, bless and glorify Jesus and Mary? In each Hail Mary we bless both Jesus and Mary: "Blessed art thou among women, and blessed is the fruit of thy womb, Jesus."

By each Hail Mary we give our Lady the same honor that God gave her when he sent the archangel Gabriel to greet her for him. How could anyone possibly think that Jesus and Mary, who often do good to those who curse them, could ever curse those who bless and honor them by the Hail Mary?

Both Saint Bernard and Saint Bonaventure say that the Queen of Heaven is certainly no less grateful and good than gracious and well-mannered people of this world. Just as she excels in all other perfections, she surpasses us all in the virtue of gratitude; so she will never let us honor her with respect without repaying us a hundredfold. Saint Bonaventure says that Mary will greet us with grace if we greet her with the Hail Mary.[51]

Who could possibly understand the graces and blessings which the greeting and tender regard of the Virgin Mary effect in us? From the very first instant that Saint Elizabeth heard the greeting given her by the Mother of God, she was filled with the Holy Spirit and the child in her womb leaped for joy. If we make ourselves worthy of the greeting and blessing of our Lady, we shall certainly be filled with graces and a flood of spiritual consolations will flow into our souls.

Nineteenth Rose

53 It is written, "Give, and it shall be given to you."[52] To take Blessed Alan's illustration of this: "Supposing I were to give you a hundred and fifty diamonds every day, even if you were an enemy of mine, would you not forgive me? Would you not treat me as a friend and give me all the graces that you were able to give? If you

want to gain the riches of grace and of glory, salute the Blessed Virgin, honor your good Mother.[53]

"He who honors his Mother (the Blessed Virgin) is as one who lays up a treasure."[54] Present her every day with at least fifty Hail Marys, for each one is worth fifteen precious stones, which are more pleasing to her than all the riches of this world put together.

And you can then expect great things from her generosity. She is our Mother and our friend. She is the empress of the universe and loves us more than all the mothers and queens of the world have ever loved any one human being, for, as St. Augustine says, the charity of the Blessed Virgin far surpasses the natural love of all mankind and even of all the angels.[55]

54 One day Saint Gertrude had a vision of our Lord counting gold coins. She summoned the courage to ask him what he was doing, and he answered, "I am counting the Hail Marys that you have said; this is the money with which you purchase heaven."[56]

The holy and learned Jesuit, Father Suarez, was so deeply aware of the value of the Angelic Salutation that he said he would gladly give all his learning for the price of one Hail Mary well said.[57]

55 Blessed Alan de la Roche said, "Let everyone who loves you, O most holy Mary, listen to this and drink it in:

"Whenever I say Hail, Mary, the court of heaven rejoices and earth is lost in wonderment; I despise the world and my heart is filled with the love of God, when I say 'Hail, Mary.' All my fears wilt and die and my passions are quelled, if I say 'Hail, Mary'; devotion grows within me and sorrow for sin awakens, when I say 'Hail, Mary.'

"Hope is made strong in my breast and the dew of consolation falls on my soul more and more, because I say, 'Hail, Mary.' And my spirit rejoices and sorrow fades away, when I say 'Hail, Mary.'

"For the sweetness of this blessed salutation is so great that there are no words to explain it adequately, and even when its wonders have been sung, we still find it so full of mystery and so profound that its depths can never be plumbed. It has but few words but is exceeding rich in mystery; it is sweeter than honey and more precious than gold. We should often meditate on it in our hearts, and have it ever on our lips so as to say it devoutly again and again."[58]

Blessed Alan also relates that a nun who had always had a great devotion to the Rosary appeared after her death to one of her sisters in religion and said to her, "If I were able to return in my body to have the chance of saying just a single Hail Mary, even without great fervor, I would gladly go through the sufferings that I had during my last illness all over again, in order to gain the merit of this prayer."[59] It is to be noted that she had been bedridden and suffered agonizing pains for several years before she died.

56 Michel de Lisle, Bishop of Salubre, who was a disciple and co-worker of Blessed Alan de la Roche in the re-establishment of the holy Rosary, said that the Angelic Salutation is the remedy for all ills that we suffer as long as we say it devoutly in honor of our Lady.[60]

Twentieth Rose Brief explanation of the Hail Mary

57 Are you in the miserable state of sin? Then call on Mary and say to her, *"Ave,"* which means "I greet thee with the most profound respect, thou who art without sin," and she will deliver you from the evil of your sins.

Are you groping in the darkness of ignorance and error? Go to Mary and say to her, "Hail Mary," which means "Hail, thou who art bathed in the light of the Sun of Justice," and she will give you a share in her light.

Have you strayed from the path leading to heaven? Then call on Mary, for her name means "Star of the Sea, the Polar Star which guides the ships of our souls during the voyage of this life," and she will guide you to the harbor of eternal salvation.

Are you in sorrow? Turn to Mary, for her name means also "Sea of Bitterness which has been filled with bitterness in this world but which is now turned into a sea of purest joy in heaven," and she will turn your sorrow into joy and your affliction into consolation.

Have you lost the state of grace? Praise and honor the numberless graces with which God has filled the Blessed Virgin and say to her, Thou art full of grace and filled with all the gifts of the Holy Spirit, and she will give you some of these graces.

Are you alone, having lost God's protection? Pray to Mary and say, *The Lord is with thee,* in a nobler and more intimate way than he is with the saints and the just, because thou art one with him. He is thy Son and his flesh is thy flesh; thou art united to the Lord because of thy perfect likeness to him and by your mutual love, for thou art his Mother. And then say to her, "The three persons of the Godhead are with thee because thou art the Temple of the Blessed Trinity," and she will place you once more under the protection and care of God.

Have you become an outcast and been accursed by God? Then say to our Lady, "Blessed art thou above all women and above all nations by thy purity and fertility; thou hast turned God's maledictions into blessings for us." She will bless you.

Do you hunger for the bread of grace and the bread of life? Draw near to her who bore the living Bread which came down from heaven, and say to her, "Blessed be the fruit of thy womb, whom thou hast conceived without the slightest loss to thy virginity, whom thou didst carry without discomfort and brought forth without pain. Blessed be Jesus who redeemed our suffering world when we were in the bondage of sin, who has healed the world of its sickness, who has raised the dead to life, brought home the banished, restored sinners to grace, and saved men from damnation. Without doubt, your soul will be filled with the bread of grace in this life and of eternal glory in the next. Amen."[61]

58 Conclude your prayer with the Church and say, *"Holy Mary,"* holy because of thy incomparable and eternal devotion to the service of God, holy in thy great rank as Mother of God, who has endowed thee with eminent holiness, in keeping with this great dignity.

"*Mother of God,* and our Mother, our Advocate and Mediatrix, Treasurer and dispenser of God's graces, obtain for us the prompt forgiveness of our sins and grant that we may be reconciled with the divine majesty.

"*Pray for us sinners,* thou who art always filled with compassion for those in need, who never despise sinners or turn them away, for without them you would never have been Mother of the Redeemer.

"*Pray for us now,* during this short life, so fraught with sorrow and uncertainty; now, because we can be sure of nothing except the present moment; now that we are surrounded and attacked night and day by powerful and ruthless enemies.

"*And at the hour of our death,* so terrible and full of danger, when our strength is waning and our spirits are sinking, and our souls and bodies are worn out with fear and pain; at the hour of our death when the devil is working with might and main to ensnare us and cast us into perdition; at that hour when our lot will be decided forever and ever, heaven or hell.

"Come to the help of your poor children, gentle Mother of pity, Advocate and Refuge of sinners, at the hour of our death drive far from us our bitter enemies, the devils, our accusers, whose frightful presence fills us with dread. Light our path through the valley of the shadow of death. Lead us to thy Son's judgment-seat and remain at our side. Intercede for us and ask thy Son to pardon us and receive us into the ranks of thy elect in the realms of everlasting glory. Amen."[62]

59 No one could help admiring the excellence of the holy Rosary, made up as it is of these two divine parts: the Lord's Prayer and the Angelic Salutation. How could there be any prayers more pleasing to God and to the Blessed Virgin, or any that are easier, more precious, or more helpful than these two prayers? We should always have them in our hearts and on our lips to honor the most Blessed Trinity, Jesus Christ our Savior and his most holy Mother.

In addition, at the end of each decade it is good to add the *Gloria Patri,* that is: Glory be to the Father, and to the Son, and to the

Holy Spirit. As it was in the beginning, is now, and ever shall be, world without end. Amen.[63]

THIRD DECADE

The surpassing merit of the holy Rosary as a meditation on the life and passion of our Lord Jesus Christ

Twenty-first Rose The Fifteen Mysteries of the Rosary

60 A mystery is a sacred thing which is difficult to understand. The works of our Lord Jesus Christ are all sacred and divine because he is God and man at one and the same time. The works of the Blessed Virgin are very holy because she is the most perfect and the most pure of God's creatures. The works of our Lord and of his blessed Mother can rightly be called mysteries because they are so full of wonders, of all kinds of perfections, and of deep and sublime truths, which the Holy Spirit reveals to the humble and simple souls who honor these mysteries.

The works of Jesus and Mary can also be called wonderful flowers, but their fragrance and beauty can only be appreciated by those who approach them, who breathe in their fragrance, and who discover their beauty by diligent and serious meditation.[64]

61 St. Dominic divided the lives of our Lord and our Lady into fifteen mysteries, which stand for their virtues and their most important actions. These are fifteen pictures whose every detail must rule and inspire our lives. They are fifteen flaming torches to guide our steps throughout this earthly life; fifteen shining mirrors to help us to know Jesus and Mary, to know ourselves and to light the fire of their love in our hearts; fifteen fiery furnaces to consume us completely in their heavenly flames.

Our Lady taught Saint Dominic this excellent method of praying and ordered him to preach it far and wide so as to reawaken the fervor of Christians and to revive in their hearts a love for our Blessed Lord. She also taught it to Blessed Alan de la Roche and said to him in a vision, "When people say 150 Hail Marys, that prayer is very helpful to them and a most pleasing tribute to me. But they will do better still and will please me more if they say these salutations while meditating on the life, death, and passion of Jesus Christ, for this meditation is the soul of this prayer." For the Rosary said without the meditation on the sacred mysteries of our salvation would almost be a body without a soul, excellent matter, but without the form, which is the meditation, and which distinguishes it from other devotions.[65]

62 The first part of the Rosary contains five mysteries: the first, the *Annunciation* of the archangel Gabriel to our Lady; the second, the *Visitation* of our Lady to Saint Elizabeth; the third, the *Nativity* of Jesus Christ; the fourth, the *Presentation* of the Child Jesus in the Temple and the purification of the Blessed Virgin; the fifth, the *Finding* of Jesus in the Temple among the doctors.

These are called the *Joyful Mysteries* because of the joy which they gave to the whole universe. Our Lady and the angels were overwhelmed with joy the moment the Son of God became incarnate. Saint Elizabeth and St. John the Baptist were filled with joy by the visit of Jesus and Mary. Heaven and earth rejoiced at the birth of the Savior. Holy Simeon felt great consolation and was filled with joy when he took the holy child into his arms. The doctors were lost in admiration and wonderment at the replies which Jesus gave; and who could express the joy of Mary and Joseph when they found Jesus after three days' absence?

63 The second part of the Rosary is also composed of five mysteries, which are called the *Sorrowful Mysteries* because they show us our Lord weighed down with sadness, covered with wounds, laden with insults, sufferings and torments.

The first of these mysteries is our Lord's prayer and his *Agony* in the Garden of Olives; the second, his *Scourging*; the third, his being *Crowned* with thorns; the fourth, his *Carrying of the Cross*; the fifth, his *Crucifixion* and death on Calvary.

64 The third part of the Rosary contains five more mysteries, which are called the *Glorious Mysteries,* because when we say them we meditate on Jesus and Mary in their triumph and glory. The first is the *Resurrection* of Jesus; the second, his *Ascension* into heaven; the third, the *Descent of the Holy Spirit* upon the apostles; the fourth, our Lady's *Assumption* in glory; the fifth, her *Coronation.*

Such are the fifteen fragrant flowers of the mystical Rose-tree, on which devout souls linger, like discerning bees, to gather their nectar and make the honey of a solid devotion.

Twenty-second Rose The Meditation of the Mysteries makes us resemble Jesus

65 The chief concern of the Christian should be to tend to perfection. "Be faithful imitators of God, as his well-beloved children," the great Apostle tells us.[66] This obligation is included in the eternal decree of our predestination, as the one and only means prescribed by God to attain everlasting glory.

Saint Gregory of Nyssa makes a delightful comparison when he says that we are all artists and that our souls are blank canvasses which we have to fill in. The colors which we use are the Christian virtues, and the original which we have to copy is Jesus Christ, the perfect living image of God the Father. Just as a painter who wants to do a life-like portrait places the model before his eyes and looks at it before making each stroke, so the Christian must always have before his eyes the life and virtues of Jesus Christ, so as never to say, think or do anything which is not in conformity with his model.[67]

66 It was because our Lady wanted to help us in the great task of working out our salvation that she ordered Saint Dominic to teach the faithful to meditate upon the sacred mysteries of the life of Jesus Christ. She did this, not only that they might adore and glorify him, but chiefly that they might pattern their lives and actions on his virtues.

Children copy their parents through watching them and talking to them, and they learn their own language through hearing them speak. An apprentice learns his trade through watching his master at work; in the same way the faithful members of the Confraternity of the Holy Rosary can become like their divine Master if they reverently study and imitate the virtues of Jesus which are shown in the fifteen mysteries of his life. They can do this with the help of his grace and through the intercession of his blessed Mother.[68]

67 Long ago, Moses was inspired by God to command the Jewish people never to forget the graces which had been showered upon them. The Son of God has all the more reason to command us to engrave the mysteries of his life, passion and glory upon our hearts and to have them always before our eyes, since each mystery reminds us of his goodness to us in some special way and it is by these mysteries that he has shown us his overwhelming love and desire for our salvation. "Oh, all you who pass by, pause a while," he says, "and see if there has ever been any sorrow like to the sorrow I have endured for love of you.[69] Be mindful of my poverty and humiliations; think of the gall and wormwood I took for you in my bitter passion."[70]

These words and many others which could be given here should be more than enough to convince us that we must not only say the Rosary with our lips in honor of Jesus and Mary, but also meditate upon the sacred mysteries while we are saying it.[71]

Twenty-third Rose The Rosary is a Memorial of the Life and Death of Jesus

68 Jesus Christ, the divine spouse of our souls and our very dear friend, wishes us to remember his goodness to us and to prize his gifts above all else. Whenever we meditate devoutly and lovingly upon the sacred mysteries of the Rosary, he receives an added joy, as also do our Lady and all the saints in heaven. His gifts are the most outstanding results of his love for us and the richest presents he could possibly give us, and it is by virtue of such presents that the Blessed Virgin herself and all the saints are glorified in heaven.

One day Blessed Angela of Foligno begged our Lord to let her know by which religious exercise she could honor him best. He appeared to her nailed to his cross and said, "My daughter, look at my wounds." She then realized that nothing pleases our dear Lord more than meditating upon his sufferings. Then he showed her the wounds on his head and revealed still other sufferings and said to her, "I have suffered all this for your salvation. What can you ever do to return my love for you?"[72]

69 The holy sacrifice of the Mass gives infinite honor to the most Blessed Trinity because it represents the passion of Jesus Christ and because through the Mass we offer to God the merits of our Lord's obedience, of his sufferings, and of his precious blood. All the heavenly court also receive an added joy from the Mass. Several doctors of the Church, including St. Thomas, tell us that, for the same reason, all the blessed in heaven rejoice in the communion of the faithful because the Blessed Sacrament is a memorial of the passion and death of Jesus Christ, and that by means of it men share in its fruits and work out their salvation.

Now the holy Rosary, recited with the meditation on the sacred mysteries, is a sacrifice of praise to God for the great gift of our redemption and a holy reminder of the sufferings, death and glory of Jesus Christ. It is therefore true that the Rosary gives glory and added joy to our Lord, our Lady and all the blessed, because they cannot desire anything greater, for the sake of our eternal happiness, than to see us engaged in a practice which is so glorious for our Lord and so salutary for ourselves.[73]

70 The Gospel teaches us that a sinner who is converted and who does penance gives joy to all the angels. If the repentance and conversion of one sinner is enough to make the angels rejoice, how great must be the happiness and jubilation of the whole heavenly court and what glory for our Blessed Lord himself to see us here on earth meditating devoutly and lovingly on his humiliations and torments and on his cruel and shameful death! Is there anything that could touch our hearts more surely and bring us to sincere repentance?[74]

A Christian who does not meditate on the mysteries of the Rosary is very ungrateful to our Lord and shows how little he cares for all that our divine Savior has suffered to save the world. This attitude seems to show that he knows little or nothing of the life of Jesus Christ, and that he has never taken the trouble to find out what he has done and what he went through in order to save us. A Christian of that kind ought to fear that, not having known Jesus Christ or having put him out of his mind, Jesus will reject him on the day of judgment with the reproach, "I tell you solemnly, I do not know you."[75]

Let us meditate, then, on the life and sufferings of our Savior by means of the holy Rosary; let us learn to know him well and to be grateful for all his blessings, so that, on the day of Judgment, he may number us among his children and his friends.[76]

Twenty-fourth Rose Meditation on the Mysteries of the Rosary is a great means of perfection

71 The saints made our Lord's life the principal object of their study; they meditated on his virtues and his sufferings, and in this way arrived at Christian perfection.

Saint Bernard began with this meditation and he always kept it up. "At the very beginning of my conversion," he said, "I made a bouquet of myrrh fashioned from the sorrows of my Savior. I placed this bouquet upon my heart, thinking of the lashes, the thorns and the nails of his passion. I applied my whole mind to the meditation on these mysteries every day."

This was also the practice of the holy martyrs; we admire how they triumphed over the most cruel sufferings. Where could this admirable constancy of the martyrs come from, says Saint Bernard, if not from the wounds of Jesus Christ, on which they meditated so frequently? Where was the soul of these generous athletes when their blood gushed forth and their bodies were wracked with cruel torments? Their soul was in the wounds of Christ and those wounds made them invincible.[77]

72 During her whole life, our Savior's holy Mother was occupied in meditating on the virtues and the sufferings of her Son. When she heard the angels sing their hymn of joy at his birth and saw the shepherds adore him in the stable, her heart was filled with wonder and she meditated on all these marvels. She compared the greatness of the Word incarnate to the way he humbled himself in this lowly fashion; the straw of the crib, to his throne in the heart of his Father; the might of God, to the weakness of a child; his wisdom, to his simplicity.

Our Lady said to Saint Bridget one day, "Whenever I used to contemplate the beauty, modesty, and wisdom of my Son, my heart was filled with joy; and whenever I considered his hands and feet which would be pierced with cruel nails, I wept bitterly and my heart was rent with sorrow and pain."[78]

73 After our Lord's Ascension, our Blessed Lady spent the rest of her life visiting the places that had been hallowed by his presence and by his sufferings. There, she meditated on his boundless love and on his terrible passion.

Saint Mary Magdalen continually performed the same religious exercises during the last thirty years of her life, when she lived at Sainte-Baume.

Saint Jerome tells us that this was the devotion of the faithful in the early centuries of the Church. From all the countries of the world they came to the Holy Land to engrave more deeply on their hearts a great love and remembrance of the Savior of mankind by seeing the places and things he had made holy by his birth, his work, his sufferings, and his death.[79]

74 All Christians have but one faith and adore one and the same God, and hope for the same happiness in heaven; they know only one mediator, who is Jesus Christ; all must imitate their divine model, and in order to do this they must meditate on the mysteries of his life, of his virtues and of his glory.

It is a great mistake to think that only priests and religious and those who have withdrawn from the turmoil of the world are supposed to meditate upon the truths of our faith and the mysteries of the life of Christ. If priests and religious have an obligation to meditate on the great truths of our holy religion in order to live up to their vocation worthily, the same obligation is just as much incumbent on the laity, because of the fact that every day they meet with spiritual dangers which might cause them to lose their souls. Therefore they should arm themselves with the frequent meditation on the life, virtues, and sufferings of our Blessed Lord, which are presented to us in the fifteen mysteries of the holy Rosary.[80]

Twenty-fifth Rose The Riches of Holiness contained in the Prayers and Meditations of the Rosary

75 Never will anyone be able to understand the marvelous riches of sanctification which are contained in the prayers and mysteries of the holy Rosary. This meditation on the mysteries of the life and death of our Lord Jesus Christ is the source of the most wonderful fruits for those who make use of it.

Today people want things that strike and move them, that leave deep impressions on the soul. Now has there ever been anything in the history of the world more moving than the wonderful story of the life, death, and glory of our Savior which is contained in the holy Rosary? In the fifteen tableaux, the principal scenes or mysteries of his life unfold before our eyes. How could there be any prayers more wonderful and sublime than the Lord's Prayer and the *Ave* of the angel? All our desires and all our needs are found expressed in these two prayers.

76 The meditation on the mysteries and prayers of the Rosary is the easiest of all prayers, because the diversity of the virtues of our Lord and the different situations of his life which we study, refresh and fortify our mind in a wonderful way and help us to avoid distractions. For the learned, these mysteries are the source of the most profound doctrine, while simple people find in them a means of instruction well within their reach.

We need to learn this easy form of meditation before progressing to the highest state of contemplation. That is the view of Saint Thomas Aquinas,[81] and the advice that he gives when he says that, first of all, one must practice on a battlefield, as it were, by acquiring all the virtues of which we have the perfect model in the mysteries of the Rosary; for, says the learned Cajetan, that is the way we arrive at a really intimate union with God, since without that union contemplation is nothing but an illusion which can lead souls astray.[82]

77 If only the Illuminists or the Quietists of these days had followed this piece of advice, they would never have fallen so low or caused such scandals among spiritual people. To think that it is possible to say prayers that are finer and more beautiful than the Our Father and the Hail Mary is to fall a prey to a strange illusion of the devil, for these heavenly prayers are the support, the strength and the safeguard of our souls.

I admit it is not always necessary to say them as vocal prayers and that interior prayer is, in a sense, more perfect than vocal. But believe me, it is really dangerous, not to say fatal, to give up saying the Rosary of your own accord under the pretext of seeking a more perfect union with God. Sometimes a soul that is proud in a subtle way and who may have done everything that he can do interiorly to rise to the sublime heights of contemplation that the saints have reached may be deluded by the noonday devil into giving up his former devotions which are good enough for ordinary souls. He turns a deaf ear to the prayers and the greeting of an angel and even to the prayer which God has composed, put into practice, and commanded: Thus shall you pray: Our Father.[83] Having reached this point, such a soul drifts from illusion to illusion, and falls from precipice to precipice.

78 Believe me, dear brother of the Rosary Confraternity, if you genuinely wish to attain a high degree of prayer in all honesty and without falling into the illusions of the devil so common with those who practice mental prayer, say the whole Rosary every day, or at least five decades of it.[84]

If you have already attained, by the grace of God, a high degree of prayer, keep up the practice of saying the holy Rosary if you wish to remain in that state and by it to grow in humility. For never will anyone who says his Rosary every day become a formal heretic or be led astray by the devil. This is a statement which I would sign with my blood.

On the other hand, if God in his infinite mercy draws you to himself as forcibly as he did some of the saints while saying the Rosary, make yourself passive in his hands and let yourself be drawn towards him. Let God work and pray in you and let him say your Rosary in his way, and that will be sufficient for the day.

But if you are still in the state of active contemplation or the ordinary prayer of quietude, of the presence of God, affective prayer, you have even less reason for giving up the Rosary. Far from making you lose ground in mental prayer or stunting your spiritual growth, it will be a wonderful help to you. You will find it a real Jacob's ladder with fifteen rungs by which you will go from virtue to virtue and from light to light. Thus, without danger of being misled, you will easily arrive at the fulness of the age of Jesus Christ.

Twenty-sixth Rose

79 Whatever you do, do not be like a certain pious but self-willed lady in Rome, so often referred to by speakers on the Rosary. She was so devout and fervent that she put to shame by her holy life even the strictest religious in the Church.

Having decided to ask St. Dominic's advice about her spiritual life, she made her confession to him. For penance he gave her one Rosary to say and advised her to say it every day. She excused herself, saying that she had her regular exercises, that she made the Stations of Rome every day, that she wore sack-cloth as well as a hair-shirt, that she gave herself the discipline several times a week, that she often fasted and did other penances. Saint Dominic urged her over and over again to take his advice and say the Rosary, but she would not hear of it. She left the confessional, horrified at the methods of this new spiritual director who had tried so hard to persuade her to take up a devotion for which she had no taste.

Later on, when she was at prayer she fell into ecstasy and had a vision of her soul appearing before the Supreme Judge. Saint Michael put all her penances and other prayers on one side of the scales and all her sins and imperfections on the other. The tray of her good works were greatly outweighed by that of her sins and imperfections.

Filled with alarm, she cried for mercy, imploring the help of the Blessed Virgin, her gracious advocate, who took the one and only Rosary she had said for her penance and dropped it on the tray of her good works. This one Rosary was so heavy that it weighed more than all her sins as well as all her good works. Our Lady then reproved her for having refused to follow the counsel of her servant Dominic and for not saying the Rosary every day.

As soon as she came to herself she rushed and threw herself at the feet of Saint Dominic and told him all that had happened, begged his forgiveness for her unbelief, and promised to say the Rosary faithfully every day. By this means she rose to Christian perfection and finally to the glory of everlasting life.[85]

You who are people of prayer, learn from this the power, the value and the importance of this devotion of the holy Rosary when it is said with meditation on the mysteries.

80 Few saints have reached the same heights of prayer as Saint Mary Magdalen, who was lifted up to heaven by angels each day, and who had the privilege of learning at the feet of Jesus and his holy Mother. Yet one day, when she asked God to show her a sure way of advancing in his love and arriving at the heights of perfection, he sent the archangel St. Michael to tell her, on his behalf, that there was no other way for her to reach perfection than to meditate on our Lord's passion. So he placed a cross in the front of her cave and told her to pray before it, contemplating the sorrowful mysteries which she had seen take place with her own eyes.[86]

The example of Saint Francis de Sales, the great spiritual director of his time, should spur you on to join the holy confraternity of the Rosary, since, great saint though he was, he bound himself by vow to say the whole Rosary every day for as long as he lived.

Saint Charles Borromeo also said it every day and strongly recommended this devotion to his priests and clerics in seminaries and to all his people.

Blessed Pius V, one of the greatest popes who have ever ruled the Church, used to say the Rosary every day. Saint Thomas of Villanova, Archbishop of Valencia, Saint Ignatius, Saint Francis Xavier, Saint Francis Borgia, Saint Teresa and Saint Philip Neri, as well as many other great men whom I do not mention, were greatly devoted to the Rosary.[87]

Follow their example; your spiritual directors will be very pleased, and if they are aware of the benefits which you can derive from this devotion, they will be the first to urge you to adopt it.

Twenty-seventh Rose

81 To encourage you still more in this devotion practiced by so many holy people, I should like to add that the Rosary recited with the meditation of the mysteries brings about the following marvelous results:

1 it gradually brings us a perfect knowledge of Jesus Christ;
2 it purifies our souls from sin;
3 it gives us victory over all our enemies;
4 it makes the practice of virtue easy;
5 it sets us on fire with the love of our Lord;
6 it enriches us with graces and merits;
7 it supplies us with what is needed to pay all our debts to

God and to our fellow-men, and finally, it obtains all kinds of graces from God.

82 The knowledge of Jesus Christ is the science of Christians and the science of salvation; it surpasses, says Saint Paul,[88] all human sciences in value and perfection:

1 because of the dignity of its object, which is a God-man, compared to whom the whole universe is but a drop of dew or a grain of sand;

2 because of its utility to us; human sciences only fill us with the wind and emptiness of pride;

3 because of its necessity; for no one can be saved without the knowledge of Jesus Christ, while a person who knows absolutely nothing of any other science will be saved as long as he is enlightened by the knowledge of Jesus Christ.

Blessed is the Rosary which gives us this science and knowledge of our Blessed Lord through our meditations on his life, death, passion and glory.

The Queen of Sheba, lost in admiration at Solomon's wisdom, cried out, "Blessed are your attendants and your servants who are always in your presence and hear your wisdom." But happier still are the faithful who carefully meditate on the life, virtues, sufferings and glory of our Savior, because by this means they can gain perfect knowledge of him,[89] in which eternal life consists.[90]

83 Our Lady revealed to Blessed Alan that no sooner had Saint Dominic begun preaching the Rosary than hardened sinners were touched and wept bitterly over their grievous sins. Young children performed unbelievable penances, and everywhere he preached the Rosary such fervor was aroused that sinners changed their lives and edified everyone by their penances and the amendment of their lives.

If by chance your conscience is burdened with sin, take your Rosary and say at least a part of it in honor of some of the mysteries of the life, passion, and glory of Jesus Christ, and you can be sure that, while you are meditating on these mysteries and honoring them, he will show his sacred wounds to his Father in heaven. He will plead for you and obtain for you contrition and the forgiveness of your sins. One day our Lord said to Blessed Alan,[91] "If only these poor wretched sinners would say my Rosary often, they would share in the merits of my passion, and I would be their Advocate and would appease the justice of God."[92]

84 This life is a continual war and a series of temptations; we do not have to contend with enemies of flesh and blood, but with the very powers of hell.[93] What better weapon could we possibly use to combat them than the prayer which our great Leader has taught us, than the Angelic Salutation which has put the devils to flight, destroyed sin and renewed the world? What better weapon could we use than meditation on the life and passion of Jesus Christ? For, as Saint Peter tells us, it is with this thought that we must arm ourselves, in order to defend ourselves against the very same enemies whom he has conquered and who molest us every day.

"Ever since the devil was crushed by the humility and the passion of Jesus Christ," says Cardinal Hugues, "he has been practically unable to attack a soul that is armed with meditation on the mysteries of our Lord's life, and, if he does trouble such a soul, he is sure to be shamefully defeated." "Put on the armor of God so as to be able to resist the attacks of the devil."[94]

85 So arm yourself with the arms of God, with the holy Rosary, and you will crush the devil's head and stand firm in the face of all his temptations. That is why even a pair of rosary beads is so terrible to the devil, and why the saints have used them to fetter him and drive him from the bodies of those who were possessed. Such happenings have been recorded more than once.

86 Blessed Alan relates that a man he knew had tried desperately all kinds of devotions to rid himself of the evil spirit which possessed him, but without success. Finally, he thought of wearing his rosary round his neck, which eased him considerably. He discovered that whenever he took it off the devil tormented him cruelly, so he resolved to wear it night and day. This drove the evil spirit away forever because he could not bear such a terrible chain. Blessed Alan also testifies that he delivered a great number of those who were possessed by putting a rosary round their necks.

87 Father Jean Amât, of the Order of St. Dominic, was giving a series of Lenten sermons in the Kingdom of Aragon one year, when a young girl was brought to him who was possessed by the devil. After he had exorcised her several times without success, he put his rosary round her neck. Hardly had he done so when the girl began to scream and cry out in a fearful way, shrieking, "Take it off, take it off; these beads are tormenting me." At last, the priest, filled with pity for the girl, took his rosary off her.

The very next night, when Fr. Amât was in bed, the same devils who had possession of the girl came to him, foaming with rage and tried to seize him. But he had his rosary clasped in his hand and no efforts of theirs could wrench it from him. He beat them with it very well indeed and put them to flight, crying out, "Holy Mary, Our Lady of the Rosary, come to my help."

The next day on his way to the church, he met the poor girl, still possessed; one of the devils within her started to jeer at him, saying, "Well, brother, if you had been without your rosary, we should have made short shrift of you." Then the good Father threw his rosary round the girl's neck without more ado, saying, "By the sacred names of Jesus and Mary his holy Mother, and by the power of the holy Rosary, I command you, evil spirits, to leave the body of this girl at once." They were immediately forced to obey him, and she was delivered from them.

These stories show the power of the holy Rosary in overcoming all sorts of temptations from the evil spirits and all sorts of sins, because these blessed beads of the Rosary put devils to rout.

Twenty-eighth Rose

88 St. Augustine[95] assures us that there is no spiritual exercise more fruitful or more useful than the frequent reflection on the sufferings of our Lord. Blessed Albert the Great, who had St. Thomas Aquinas as his student, learned in a revelation that by simply thinking of or meditating on the passion of Jesus Christ, a Christian gains more merit than if he had fasted on bread and water every Friday for a year, or had beaten himself with the discipline once a week till blood flowed, or had recited the whole Book of Psalms every day. If this is so, then how great must be the merit we can gain from the Rosary, which commemorates the whole life and passion of our Lord?

Our Lady one day revealed to Blessed Alan de la Roche[96] that, after the holy sacrifice of the Mass, which is the first and most living memorial of our Lord's passion, there was indeed no more excellent devotion or one of greater merit than that of the Rosary, which is like a second memorial and representation of the life and passion of Jesus Christ.[97]

89 Fr. Dorland[98] relates that in 1481[99] our Lady appeared to the Venerable Dominic, a Carthusian devoted to the holy Rosary, who lived at Treves, and said to him:

"Whenever one of the faithful, in a state of grace, says the Rosary while meditating on the mysteries of the life and passion of Christ, he obtains full and entire remission of all his sins."

She also said to Blessed Alan, "I want you to know that, although there are numerous indulgences already attached to the recitation of my Rosary, I shall add many more to every five decades for those who, free from serious sin, say them with devotion, on their knees. And whosoever shall persevere in the devotion of the holy Rosary, with its prayers and meditations, shall be rewarded for it; I shall obtain for him full remission of the penalty and the guilt of all his sins at the end of his life.

"And let this not seem incredible to you; it is easy for me because I am the Mother of the King of heaven, and he calls me full of grace. And being filled with grace, I am able to dispense it freely to my dear children."

90 St. Dominic was so convinced of the efficacy of the Rosary and its great value that, when he heard confessions, he hardly ever gave any other penance, as we have seen in the story I told you of the lady in Rome to whom he gave only a single Rosary.

St. Dominic was a great saint and other confessors also ought to walk in his footsteps by asking their penitents to say the Rosary with meditation on the sacred mysteries, rather than giving them other penances which are less meritorious and less pleasing to God, less likely to help them to advance in virtue, and not as efficacious in helping them to avoid sin. Moreover, while saying the Rosary, people gain numerous indulgences which are not attached to many other devotions.[100]

91 As Abbot Blosius says, "The Rosary, with meditation on the life and passion of Christ, is certainly most pleasing to our Lord and his blessed Mother and is a very successful means of obtaining all graces; we can say it for ourselves as well as for those who have been recommended to our prayers and for the whole Church. Let us turn, then, to the holy Rosary in all our needs, and we shall infallibly obtain the graces we ask for from God to attain our salvation.[101]

Twenty-ninth Rose

92 There is nothing more divine, according to the mind of St. Denis, nothing more noble or agreeable to God than to cooperate in the work of saving souls and to frustrate the devil's plans for ruining them. The Son of God came down to earth for no other reason than to save us. He upset Satan's empire by founding the Church, but the devil rallied his strength and wreaked cruel violence on souls by the Albigensian heresy, by the hatred, dissensions and abominable vices which he spread throughout the world in the eleventh century.

Only severe remedies could possibly cure such terrible disorders and repel Satan's forces. The Blessed Virgin, protectress of the Church, has given us a most powerful means for appeasing her Son's anger, uprooting heresy and reforming Christian morals, in the Confraternity of the Holy Rosary, as events have shown. It has brought back charity[102] and the frequent reception of the sacraments as in the first golden centuries of the Church, and it has reformed Christian morals.

93 Pope Leo X said in his bull that this Confraternity had been founded in honor of God and of the Blessed Virgin as a wall to hold back the evils that were going to break upon the Church.

Gregory XIII said that the Rosary was given us from heaven as a means of appeasing God's anger and of imploring the intercession of our Lady.

Julius III said that the Rosary was inspired by God that heaven might be more easily opened to us through the favors of our Lady.

Paul III and Blessed Pius V declared that the Rosary was given to the faithful in order that they might have spiritual peace and consolation more easily. Surely everyone will want to join a confraternity which was founded for such noble purposes.[103]

94 Father Dominic, a Carthusian, who was deeply devoted to the holy Rosary, had a vision in which he saw heaven opened and the whole heavenly court assembled in magnificent array. He heard them sing the Rosary in an enchanting melody, and each decade was in honor of a mystery of the life, passion, or glory of Jesus Christ and his holy Mother. Fr. Dominic noticed that whenever they pronounced the holy name of Mary they bowed their heads, and at the name of Jesus they genuflected and gave thanks to God for the great good he had wrought in heaven and on earth through the holy Rosary. He also saw our Lady and the Saints present to God the Rosaries which the Confraternity members say here on earth. He noticed too that they were praying for those who practice this devotion. He also saw beautiful crowns without number, which were made of sweet-smelling flowers, for those who say the Rosary devoutly. He learned that by every Rosary that they say they make a crown for themselves which they will be able to wear in heaven.

This holy Carthusian's vision is very much like that which the Beloved Disciple had, in which he saw a great multitude of angels and saints, who continually praised and blessed Jesus Christ for all that he had done and suffered on earth for our salvation. And is not this what the devout members of the Rosary Confraternity do?[104]

95 It must not be imagined that the Rosary is only for women, and for simple and unlearned people; it is also for men and for the greatest of men. As soon as St. Dominic acquainted Pope Innocent III with the fact that he had received a command from heaven to establish the Confraternity of the Holy Rosary, the Holy Father gave it his full approval, urged St. Dominic to preach it, and said that he wished to become a member himself.[105] Even Cardinals embraced the devotion with great fervor, which prompted Lopez to say, "Neither sex nor age nor any other condition has kept anyone from devotion to the Rosary."[106]

Members of this Confraternity have come from all walks of life: dukes, princes, kings, as well as prelates, cardinals and Sovereign Pontiffs. It would take too long to list them in this little book. If you join this Confraternity, dear reader, you will share in their devotion and their graces on earth and their glory in heaven. "Since you are united to them in their devotion, you will share in their dignity."

Thirtieth Rose

96 If privileges, graces and indulgences of a confraternity make it valuable to us, then that of the Rosary is the one to be most recommended, since it is the most favored and enriched with indulgences, and ever since its inception there has hardly been a pope who has not opened the treasures of the Church to enrich it with further privileges. And since example is more persuasive than words and favors, the Holy Fathers have found that there was no better way to show their high regard for this holy Confraternity than to join it themselves.[104]

Here is a short summary of the indulgences which they wholeheartedly granted to the Confraternity of the Holy Rosary, and which were confirmed again by our Holy Father Pope Innocent XI on 31st July 1679, and received and made public by the Archbishop of Paris on 25th September of the same year:

1 Members may gain a plenary indulgence on the day of joining the Confraternity;

2 A plenary indulgence at the hour of death;

3 For each rosary of five decades recited: ten years and ten quarantines;

4 Each time that members say the holy names of Jesus and Mary devoutly: seven days' indulgence;

5 For those who assist with devotion at the procession of the holy Rosary: seven years and seven quarantines of indulgence;

6 Members who have made a good confession and are genuinely sorry for their sins may gain a plenary indulgence on certain days by visiting the Rosary Chapel in the church where the Confraternity is established. This may be gained on the first Sunday of every month, and on the feasts of our Lord and our Lady;

7 To those who assist at the *Salve Regina:* a hundred days' indulgence;

8 To those who openly wear the rosary out of devotion and to set a good example: a hundred days' indulgence;

9 Sick members who are unable to go to church may gain a plenary indulgence by going to confession and Communion and by saying that day the whole Rosary, or at least five decades;

10 The Sovereign Pontiffs have shown their generosity towards members of the Rosary Confraternity by allowing them to gain the indulgences attached to the Stations of the Cross by visiting five altars in the church where the Rosary Confraternity is established, and by saying the Our Father and Hail Mary five times before each altar, for the well-being of the Church. If there are only one or two altars in the Confraternity church, they should say the Our Father and Hail Mary twenty-five times before one of them.[108]

97 This is a wonderful favor granted to Confraternity members, for in the Station Churches in Rome plenary indulgences can be obtained, souls can be delivered from purgatory, and many other important remissions can be gained, and these are available to members without trouble, without expense, and without leaving their own country. And even if the Confraternity is not established in the place where the members live, they can gain the very same indulgences by visiting five altars in any church. This concession was granted by Leo X.

The Sacred Congregation of Indulgences drew up a list of certain definite days on which those outside the city of Rome could gain the indulgences of the Stations of Rome. The Holy Father approved this list on March 7th, 1678, and commanded that it be strictly observed. These indulgences can be gained on the following days:

All the Sundays of Advent; each of the three Ember Days; Christmas Eve, and the Masses of midnight, of the Dawn and of the Day; the feasts of St. Stephen, St. John the Evangelist, the Holy Innocents, the Circumcision and the Epiphany; the Sundays of Septuagesima, Sexagesima, Quinquagesima, and every day from Ash Wednesday to Low Sunday inclusively; each of the three Rogation days; Ascension; the vigil of Pentecost, and every day of its octave; and the three days of the September Ember Days.[109]

Dear brothers and sisters of the Confraternity, there are numerous other indulgences which you can gain. If you want to know about them, read the complete list of indulgences which have been granted to the members of the Confraternity. You will see there the names of the popes, the year in which they granted the indulgence, and many other particulars which I have not been able to include in this little summary.

FOURTH DECADE

The surpassing merit of the holy Rosary as seen in the wonders God has worked through it.

Thirty-first Rose

98 The saintly Blanche of Castille, Queen of France, was deeply grieved because twelve years after her marriage she was still childless. When St. Dominic went to see her he advised her to say the Rosary every day to ask God for the grace of motherhood, and she faithfully carried out his advice. In the year 1213 she gave birth to her eldest child, who was called Philip. But when the child died in infancy, the Queen sought our Lady's help more than ever, and had a large number of rosaries given out to all members of the court and to people in several towns in the Kingdom, asking them to pray to God for a blessing which this time would be complete. This was granted to her, for in 1215 St. Louis was born, the prince who was to become the glory of France and the model of Christian kings.[110]

99 Alphonsus VIII, King of Aragon and Castille, had been leading a disorderly life and had been punished by God in several ways, and he was forced to take refuge in a town belonging to one of his allies.

St. Dominic happened to be in this town on Christmas Day and he preached on the Rosary as he usually did, and spoke of the graces that we obtain through this devotion. He mentioned, among other things, that those who said the Rosary devoutly would overcome their enemies and regain all they had lost.

The King listened attentively and sent for St. Dominic to ask whether what he had said about the Rosary was really true. The Saint assured him that nothing was more true, and that if only he would practice this devotion and join the Confraternity, he would see for himself. The King resolved to say the Rosary every day and persevered for a year in doing so. The very next Christmas, our Lady appeared to him at the end of his Rosary and said, "Alphonsus, you have served me for a year by saying my Rosary devoutly every day, so I have come to reward you. I have obtained the forgiveness of your sins from my Son. Here is a rosary, which I present to you; wear it, and I promise you that none of your enemies will be able to harm you."

Our Lady vanished, leaving the King overjoyed and greatly encouraged; he immediately went in search of the Queen and told her all about our Lady's gift and the promise that went with it. He touched her eyes with this rosary, for she had lost her sight, and she was cured.

Shortly afterwards the King rallied some troops and with the help of his allies boldly attacked his enemies. He forced them to give back the territory they had taken from him and make reparation for his losses. They were completely routed, and he became so successful in war that soldiers came from all sides to fight under his standard, because it seemed that, whenever he went into battle, the victory was sure to be his.

This is not surprising because he never went into battle without first saying his Rosary on his knees. He made certain that the whole of his court joined the Confraternity of the Rosary and he saw to it that all his officials and servants were devoted to it.

The Queen also joined the Confraternity, and they both persevered in the service of Blessed Virgin and lived very holy lives.[111]

Thirty-second Rose

100 St. Dominic had a cousin named Don Perez or Pedro,[112] who was leading a highly immoral life. When he heard that his cousin was preaching on the wonders of the Rosary and learned that several people had been converted and had amended their lives by

means of it, he said, "I had given up all hope of being saved but now I am beginning to take heart again. I really must hear this man of God."

So one day he went to hear one of St. Dominic's sermons. When the latter caught sight of him, he struck out against sin more zealously than ever before, and from the depths of his heart he besought God to enlighten his cousin and let him see what a deplorable state his soul was in.

At first, Don Perez was somewhat alarmed, but he still did not resolve to change his ways. He came once more to hear the Saint preach and his cousin, realizing that a heart as hardened as his could only be moved by something extraordinary, cried out with a loud voice, "Lord Jesus, grant that this whole congregation may see the state of the man who has just come into your house."

Then everyone suddenly saw that Don Perez was completely surrounded by a band of devils in the form of hideous beasts, who were holding him in great iron chains. People fled in all directions in abject terror, and Don Perez himself was even more appalled when he saw how everyone shunned him. St. Dominic told them all to stand still and said to his cousin, "Unhappy man that you are, acknowledge the deplorable state you are in and throw yourself at our Lady's feet. Take this rosary, say it with devotion and with true sorrow for all your sins, and make a resolution to amend your life."

Don Perez knelt down and said the Rosary; he then felt the desire to make his confession, which he did with heartfelt contrition. St. Dominic ordered him to say the Rosary every day; he promised to do this and he entered his own name in the register of the Confraternity. When he left the church his face was no longer horrible to behold but shining like that of an angel. Thereafter he persevered in devotion to the Rosary, led a well-ordered life and died a happy death.[113]

Thirty-third Rose

101 When St. Dominic was preaching the Rosary near Carcassone, an Albigensian[114] was brought to him who was possessed by the devil. The Saint exorcised him in the presence of a great crowd of people; it appears that over twelve thousand had come to hear him speak. The devils who were in possession of this wretched man were forced to answer St. Dominic's questions in spite of themselves. They said:

1 that there were fifteen thousand of them in the body of that poor man, because he had attacked the fifteen mysteries of the Rosary;

2 that by the Rosary which he preached, he put fear and

horror into the depths of hell, and that he was the man they hated most throughout the world because of the souls he snatched from them by the devotion of the Rosary.

3 They revealed several other things.

St. Dominic put his rosary round the neck of the possessed man and asked them who, of all the saints in heaven, was the one they feared most, who should therefore be the most loved and revered by men.

At this they let out such unearthly screams that most of the people fell to the ground, seized with fear. Then, using all their cunning so as not to answer, the devils wept and wailed in such a pitiful way that many of the people wept also, out of pure natural pity. The devils, speaking through the mouth of the Albigensian, pleaded in a heart-rending voice, "Dominic, Dominic, have pity on us, we promise you we will never harm you.

"You have always had compassion for sinners and those in distress; have pity on us, for we are in grievous straits. We are suffering so much already, why do you delight in increasing our pains? Can't you be satisfied with the pains we now endure? Have mercy on us, have mercy on us!"

102 St. Dominic was not in the least moved by the pathetic words of those wretched spirits, and told them he would not let them alone until they had answered his question. Then they said they would whisper the answer in such a way that only St. Dominic would be able to hear. The latter firmly insisted upon their answering clearly and audibly. Then the devils kept quiet and would not say another word, completely disregarding St. Dominic's orders.

So he knelt down and said this prayer to our Lady:[115] "Oh, most glorious Virgin Mary, I implore you by the power of the holy Rosary command these enemies of the human race to answer my question."

No sooner had he said this prayer than a glowing flame leaped out of the ears, nostrils and mouth of the possessed man. Everyone shook with fear, but the fire did not hurt anyone. Then the devils cried, "Dominic, we beseech you, by the passion of Jesus Christ and the merits of his holy Mother and of all the saints, let us leave the body of this man without speaking further; for the angels will answer your question whenever you wish. After all, are we not liars—so why should you want to believe us? Do not torment us any more, have pity on us."

"Woe to you, wretched spirits, who do not deserve to be heard," St. Dominic said, and kneeling down he prayed to the Blessed Virgin:[116] "O most worthy Mother of Wisdom, I am praying for the people assembled here, who have already learned how to say the Angelic Salutation properly. I beg you for the salvation of those here present, compel these adversaries of yours to proclaim the whole truth here and now before the people."

St. Dominic had scarcely finished this prayer when he saw the Blessed Virgin near at hand surrounded by a multitude of angels. She struck the possessed man with a golden rod that she held and said, "Answer my servant Dominic at once." (It must be noted that the people neither saw nor heard our Lady, only St. Dominic.)

103 Then the devils started screaming:

104 "Oh, you who are enemy, our downfall and our destruction, why have you come from heaven to torture us so grievously? O advocate of sinners, you who snatch them from the very jaws of hell, you who are a most sure path to heaven, must we, in spite of ourselves, tell the whole truth and confess before everyone who it is who is the cause of our shame and our ruin? Oh, woe to us, princes of darkness.

"Then listen, you Christians. This Mother of Jesus is most powerful in saving her servants from falling into hell. She is like the sun which destroys the darkness of our wiles and subtlety. It is she who uncovers our hidden plots, breaks our snares, and makes our temptations useless and ineffective.

"We have to say, however, reluctantly, that no soul who has really persevered in her service has ever been damned with us; one single sigh that she offers to the Blessed Trinity is worth far more than all the prayers, desires, and aspirations of all the saints. We fear her more than all the other saints in heaven together, and we have no success with her faithful servants.

"Many Christians who call on her at the hour of death and who really ought to be damned according to our ordinary standards are saved by her intercession. And if that Marietta (it is thus in their fury they called her) did not counter our plans and our efforts, we should have overcome the Church and destroyed it long before this, and caused all the Orders in the Church to fall into error and infidelity.

"Now that we are forced to speak, we must also tell you that nobody who perseveres in saying the Rosary will be damned, because she obtains for her servants the grace of true contrition for their sins by which they obtain pardon and mercy."[117]

Then St. Dominic had all the people say the Rosary very slowly and with great devotion, and a wonderful thing happened: at each Hail Mary which he and the people said, a large number of devils issued forth from the wretched man's body under the guise of red-hot coals. When the devils had all been expelled and the heretic completely delivered from them, our Lady, although invisible, gave her blessing to the assembled company, and they were filled with joy.

A large number of heretics were converted because of this miracle and joined the Confraternity of the Holy Rosary.

Thirty-fourth Rose

105 It is almost impossible to do credit sufficiently to the victories that Count Simon de Montfort[118] won against the Albigensians under the patronage of Our Lady of the Rosary. They are so famous that the world has never seen anything to match them. One day he defeated ten thousand heretics with a force of five hundred men; on another occasion he overcame three thousand with only thirty men; finally, with eight hundred horsemen and one thousand infantrymen he completely routed the army of the King of Aragon, which was a hundred thousand strong, and this with the loss on his side of only one horseman and eight soldiers.

106 Our Lady also protected Alan de l'Anvallay, a Breton knight, from great perils. He too was fighting for the faith against the Albigensians. One day, when he found himself surrounded by enemies on all sides, our Lady let fall a hundred and fifty rocks upon his enemies and he was delivered from their hands.

Another day, when his ship had foundered and was about to sink, this good Mother caused a hundred and fifty small hills to appear miraculously above the water and by means of them they reached Brittany in safety. In thanksgiving to our Lady for the miracles she had worked on his behalf in answer to his daily Rosary, he built a monastery at Dinan for the religious of the new Order of St. Dominic and, having become a religious himself, he died a holy death at Orleans.[119]

107 Othère, also a Breton soldier, from Vaucouleurs, often put whole companies of heretics or robbers to flight, wearing his rosary on his arm and on the hilt of his sword. Once when he had beaten his enemies, they admitted that they had seen his sword shining brightly, and another time had noticed a shield on his arm on which our Lord, our Lady and the saints were depicted. This shield made him invisible and gave him the strength to attack well.

Another time he defeated twenty thousand heretics with only ten companies without losing a single man. This so impressed the general of the heretics' army that he sought out Othère, abjured his heresy and declared that he had seen him surrounded by flaming swords during the battle.[120]

Thirty-fifth Rose

108 Blessed Alan[121] relates that a certain Cardinal Pierre, whose titular church was that of St. Mary-beyond-the-Tiber, was a great friend of St. Dominic's and had learned from him to have a great devotion to the holy Rosary. He grew to love it so much that he never ceased singing its praises and encouraging everyone he met to embrace it. Eventually he was sent as legate to the Holy Land to the Christians who were fighting against the Saracens. So successfully did he convince the Christian army of the power of the Rosary that they all started saying it and stormed heaven for help in a battle in which they knew they would be pitifully outnumbered. And in fact, their three thousand triumphed over an enemy of one hundred thousand.[122]

As we have seen, the devils have an overwhelming fear of the Rosary. St. Bernard says that the Angelic Salutation puts them to flight and makes all hell tremble. Blessed Alan assures us that he has seen several people delivered from Satan's bondage after taking up the holy Rosary, even though they had previously sold themselves to him, body and soul, by renouncing their baptismal vows and their allegiance to Jesus Christ.

[Thirty-sixth Rose]

109 In 1578, a woman of Antwerp had given herself to the devil and signed a contract with her own blood. Shortly afterwards she was stricken with remorse and had an intense desire to make amends for this terrible deed. So she sought out a kind and wise confessor to find out how she could be set free from the power of the devil.

She found a wise and holy priest, who advised her to go to Fr. Henry, director of the Confraternity of the Holy Rosary, at the Dominican Friary, to be enrolled there and to make her confession. Accordingly, she asked to see him but met, not Fr. Henry, but the devil disguised as a friar. He reproved her severely and said she could never hope to receive God's grace, and there was no way of revoking what she had signed. This grieved her greatly but she did not lose hope in God's mercy and sought out Fr. Henry once more, only to find the devil a second time, and to meet with a second rebuff. She came back a third time and then at last, by divine providence, she found Fr. Henry in person, the priest whom she had been looking for, and he treated her with great kindness, urging her to throw herself on the mercy of God and to make a good confession. He then received her into the Confraternity and told her to say the Rosary frequently.

One day, while Fr. Henry was celebrating Mass for her, our Lady forced the devil to give her back the contract she had signed. In this way she was delivered from the devil by the authority of Mary and by devotion to the holy Rosary.[123]

[Thirty-seventh Rose]

110 A nobleman[124] who had several daughters placed one of them in a lax monastery where the nuns were concerned only with vanity and pleasures. Their confessor, on the other hand, was a zealous priest with a great devotion to the holy Rosary. Wishing to guide this nun into a better way of life, he ordered her to say the

Rosary every day in honor of the Blessed Virgin, while meditating on the life, passion and glory of Jesus Christ.

She joyously undertook this devotion, and little by little she grew to have a repugnance for the wayward habits of her sisters in religion. She developed a love of silence and prayer, in spite of the fact that the others despised and ridiculed her and called her a fanatic.

It was at this time that a holy priest, who was making the visitation of the convent, had a strange vision during his meditation: he saw a nun in her room, rapt in prayer, kneeling in front of a Lady of great beauty who was surrounded by angels. The latter had flaming spears with which they repelled a crowd of devils who wanted to come in. These evil spirits then fled to the other nuns' rooms under the guise of vile animals.

By this vision the priest became aware of the lamentable state of that monastery and was so upset that he thought he might die of grief. He sent for the young religious and exhorted her to persevere. As he pondered on the value of the Rosary, he decided to try and reform the Sisters by means of it. He bought a supply of beautiful rosaries and gave one to each nun, imploring them to say it every day and promising them that, if they would only say it faithfully, he would not try to force them to alter their lives. Wonderful and strange though it may seem, the nuns willingly accepted the rosaries and promised to say the prayer on that condition. Little by little they began to give up their empty and worldly pursuits, letting silence and recollection come into their lives. In less than a year they all asked that the monastery be reformed.

The Rosary worked more changes in their hearts than the priest could have done by exhorting and commanding them.[125]

Thirty-eighth Rose

111 A Spanish countess[126] who had been taught the holy Rosary by St. Dominic used to say it faithfully every day, with the result that she was making marvelous progress in her spiritual life. Since her only desire was to attain to perfection, she asked a bishop who was a renowned preacher for some practices that would help her to become perfect. The bishop told her that, before he could give her any advice, she would have to let him know the state of her soul and what her religious exercises were. She answered that her most important exercise was the Rosary, which she said every day, meditating on the Joyful, Sorrowful and Glorious Mysteries, and that she had profited greatly by so doing.

The Bishop was overjoyed to hear her explain what priceless lessons the mysteries contain. "I have been a doctor of theology for twenty years," he exclaimed, "and I have read many excellent books on various devotional practices. But never before have I come across one better than this or more conformed to the Christian life. From now on I shall follow your example, and I shall preach the Rosary."

He did so with such success that in a short while he saw his diocese changed for the better. There was a notable decline in immorality and worldliness of all kinds as well as in gambling. There were several instances of people being brought back to the faith, of sinners making restitution for their crimes, and of others sincerely resolving to give up their lives of vice. Religious fervor and Christian charity began to flourish. These changes were all the more remarkable because this bishop had been striving to reform his diocese for some time but with hardly any results.

To inculcate the devotion of the Rosary all the more, the bishop also wore a beautiful rosary at his side and always showed it to his congregation when he preached. He used to say, "My dear brethren, I am a doctor of theology, and of canon and civil law, but I say to you, as your bishop, that I take more pride in wearing the rosary of the Blessed Virgin than in any of my episcopal regalia or academic robes."[127]

Thirty-ninth Rose

112 A Danish priest[128] used to love to tell how the very same improvement that the Spanish bishop noticed in his diocese had occurred in his own parish. He always told his story with great joy of heart because it gave such glory to God.

"I had," he said, "preached as compellingly as I could, touching on many aspects of our holy Faith, and using every argument I could possibly think of to get people to amend their way of life, but in vain. Finally, I decided to preach the holy Rosary. I told my congregations how precious it was and taught them how to say it, and I affirm that having taught them to appreciate this devotion, I saw a manifest change within six months.

"How true it is that this God-given prayer has a divine power to touch our hearts and inspire them with a horror of sin and a love of virtue!"

One day our Lady said to Blessed Alan, "Just as God chose the Angelic Salutation to bring about the incarnation of his Word and the redemption of mankind, so those who want to bring about moral reforms and regenerate them in Jesus Christ must honor me and greet me with the same salutation. I am the channel by which God came to men, and so, next to Jesus Christ, it is through me that men must obtain grace and virtue."[129]

113 I, who write this, have learnt from my own experience that the Rosary has the power to convert even the most hardened hearts.

I have known people who have gone to missions and heard sermons on the most terrifying subjects without being in the least moved; and yet, after they had, on my advice, started to say the Rosary every day, they eventually became converted and gave themselves completely to God.

When I have gone back to parishes where I had given missions, I have seen tremendous differences between them; in those parishes where the people had given up the Rosary, they had generally fallen back into their sinful ways, whereas in places where the Rosary was said faithfully I found the people were persevering in the grace of God and advancing in virtue day by day.

Fortieth Rose

114 Blessed Alan de la Roche, Fr. Jean Dumont, Fr. Thomas, the chronicles of St. Dominic and other writers who have seen these things with their own eyes speak of the marvelous conversions that are brought about by this wonderful devotion. Great sinners, both men and women, have been converted after twenty, thirty or forty years of sin and unspeakable vice. I will not even relate those which I have seen myself because I do not want to make this book too long; there are several reasons why I would rather not talk about them.

Dear reader, if you practice and preach this devotion, you will learn more, by your own experience, than from spiritual books, and you will have the happiness of being rewarded by our Lady in accordance with the promises she made to St. Dominic, to Blessed Alan de la Roche, and to those who encourage this devotion which is so dear to her. For the Rosary teaches people about the virtues of Jesus and Mary, and leads them to mental prayer, to the imitation of Jesus Christ, to the frequentation of the sacraments, the practice of genuine virtue and of all kinds of good works. It also helps us to gain many wonderful indulgences, which people are unaware of because those who preach this devotion hardly ever mention them and content themselves with giving a popular sermon on the Rosary which very often produces admiration but not instruction.

115 Finally, I shall content myself with saying, in company with Blessed Alan de la Roche, that the Rosary is a source and a storehouse of countless blessings.

1 Sinners obtain pardon;
2 Those who thirst are refreshed;
3 Those who are fettered are set free;
4 Those who weep find joy;
5 Those who are tempted find peace;
6 Those in need find help;
7 Religious are reformed;

8 The ignorant are instructed;
9 The living learn to resist spiritual decline;
10 The dead have their pains eased by suffrages.[130]

Our Lady once said to Blessed Alan, "I want those who are devoted to my Rosary to have my Son's grace and blessing during their lifetime, at death and after their death. I want them to be freed from all slavery so that they will be like kings, with crowns on their heads, scepters in their hands and to reign in eternal glory. Amen.

FIFTH DECADE

How to say the Rosary worthily

Forty-first Rose

116 It is not so much the length of a prayer as the fervor with which it is said which pleases God and touches his heart. A single Hail Mary said properly is worth more than a hundred and fifty said badly. Most Catholics say the Rosary, either the whole fifteen mysteries or five of them, or at least a few decades. Why is it then that so few of them give up their sins and make progress in virtue, if not because they are not saying them as they should.

117 It is a good thing to think over how we should pray if we want to please God and become more holy.

1 Firstly, to say the holy Rosary with advantage one must be in a state of grace or at least be fully determined to give up sin, for all our theology teaches us that good works and prayers are dead works if they are done in a state of mortal sin. Therefore, they can neither be pleasing to God nor help us to gain eternal life. As Scripture says, "Praise is not seemly in the mouth of a sinner" (Eccles. 15).[131]

The praise and greeting of the angel and the very prayer of Jesus Christ are not pleasing to God when they are said by unrepentant sinners.

"These people honor me with their lips, but their heart is far from me" (Mark 7:6).

Those who join my confraternities (says Jesus Christ), who say the Rosary every day, without any contrition for their sins, offer me lip service only and their hearts are far from me.

2 I have just said that a person must "at least be fully determined to give up sin," 1) because if it were true that God only heard the prayers of those in a state of grace, it would follow that those who are in a state of serious sin should not pray at all. This is an erroneous teaching which has been condemned by the Church,

because sinners, of course, need to pray far more than good people. Were this horrible doctrine true, it would be useless and futile to tell a sinner to say the Rosary, because it would never help him; 2) because they join one of our Lady's confraternities, or say the Rosary or some other prayer, without having the slightest intention of giving up sin, they join the ranks of her false devotees. These presumptuous and impenitent devotees,[132] hiding under her mantle, with the scapular round their necks and the rosary in their hands, cry out, "Blessed Virgin, good Mother, Hail Mary," and yet at the same time they are crucifying Jesus Christ and tearing his flesh anew by their sins. It is a great tragedy, but from the ranks of our Lady's most holy confraternities souls are falling into the fires of hell.

118 We earnestly advise everyone to say the Rosary: the virtuous, that they may persevere and grow in the grace of God; sinners, that they may rise from their sins. But God forbid we should ever encourage a sinner to think that our Lady will protect him with her mantle if he continues to love sin, for it will turn into a mantle of damnation which will hide his sins from the public eye. The Rosary, which is a remedy for all ills, would then be turned into a deadly poison. *Corruptio optimi pessima.*

The learned Cardinal Hugues tells us that one should be as pure as an angel to approach the Blessed Virgin and say the Angelic Salutation. One day, our Lady showed herself to an immoral man who used to say the Rosary regularly every day. She showed him a bowl of beautiful fruit, but the bowl itself was covered with filth. The man was horrified to see this, and our Lady said to him, "This is the way you are honoring me. You are giving me beautiful roses in a dirty bowl. Do you think I can find them pleasing to me?[133]

Forty-second Rose

119 In order to pray well, it is not enough to give expression to our petitions by means of that most excellent of all prayers, the Rosary, but we must also pray with great attention, for God listens more to the voice of the heart than that of the mouth. To be guilty of willful distractions during prayer would show a great lack of respect and reverence; it would make our Rosaries unfruitful and make us guilty of sin.

How can we expect God to listen to us if we ourselves do not pay attention to what we are saying? How can we expect him to be pleased if, while in the presence of his tremendous majesty, we give in to distractions, like a child running after a butterfly? People who do that forfeit God's blessing, which is changed into a curse for having treated the things of God disrespectfully: "Cursed be the one who does God's work negligently." Jer. 48:10.[134]

120 Of course, you cannot say your Rosary without having a few involuntary distractions; it is even difficult to say a Hail Mary without your imagination troubling you a little, for it is never still; but you can say it without voluntary distractions, and you must take all sorts of precautions to lessen involuntary distractions and to control your imagination.

To do this, put yourself in the presence of God and imagine that God and his Blessed Mother are watching you, and that your guardian angel is at your right hand, taking your Hail Marys, if they are well said, and using them like roses to make crowns for Jesus and Mary. But remember that at your left hand is the devil, ready to pounce on every Hail Mary that comes his way and to write it down in his book of death, if they are not said with attention, devotion, and reverence. Above all, do not fail to offer up each decade in honor of one of the mysteries, and try to form a picture in your mind of Jesus and Mary in connection with that mystery.

121 We read in the life of Blessed Hermann[135] of the Order of the Premonstratensians, that at one time when he used to say the Rosary attentively and devoutly while meditating on the mysteries, our Lady used to appear to him resplendent in breathtaking majesty and beauty. But, as time went on, his fervor cooled and he fell into the way of saying his Rosary hurriedly and without giving it his full attention. Then one day our Lady appeared to him again, but this time she was far from beautiful, and her face was furrowed and drawn with sadness. Blessed Hermann was appalled at the change in her, and our Lady explained, "This is how I look to you, Hermann, because this is how you are treating me; as a woman to be despised and of no importance. Why do you no longer greet me with respect and attention while meditating on my mysteries and praising my privileges?"[136]

Forty-third Rose

122 When the Rosary is well said, it gives Jesus and Mary more glory and is more meritorious for the soul than any other prayer. But it is also the hardest prayer to say well and to persevere in, owing especially to the distractions which almost inevitably attend the constant repetition of the same words.

When we say the Little Office of Our Lady, or the Seven Penitential Psalms, or any prayers other than the Rosary, the variety of words and expressions keeps us alert, prevents our imagination from wandering, and so makes it easier for us to say them well. On the contrary, because of the constant repetition of the Our Father and Hail Mary in the same unvarying form, it is difficult, while saying the Rosary, not to become wearied and inclined to sleep, or to turn to other prayers that are more refreshing and less tedious. This shows that one needs much greater devotion to persevere in saying the Rosary than in saying any other prayer, even the psalter of David.

123 Our imagination, which is hardly still a minute, makes our task harder, and then of course there is the devil who never tires of trying to distract us and keep us from praying. To what ends does not the evil one go against us while we are engaged in saying our Rosary against him.

Being human, we easily become tired and slipshod, but the devil makes these difficulties worse when we are saying the Rosary. Before we even begin, he makes us feel bored, distracted, or exhausted; and when we have started praying, he oppresses us from all sides, and when after much difficulty and many distractions, we have finished, he whispers to us, "What you have just said is worthless. It is useless for you to say the Rosary. You had better get on with other things. It is only a waste of time to pray without paying attention to what you are saying; half-an-hour's meditation or some spiritual reading would be much better. Tomorrow, when you are not feeling so sluggish, you'll pray better; leave the rest of your Rosary till then." By tricks of this kind the devil gets us to give up the Rosary altogether or to say it less often, and we keep putting it off or change to some other devotion.

124 Dear friend of the Rosary Confraternity, do not listen to the devil, but be of good heart, even if your imagination has been bothering you throughout your Rosary, filling your mind with all kinds of distracting thoughts, so long as you tried your best to get rid of them as soon as you noticed them. Always remember that the best Rosary is the one with the most merit, and there is more merit in praying when it is hard than when it is easy. Prayer is all the harder when it is, naturally speaking, distasteful to the soul and is filled with those annoying little ants and flies running about in your imagination, against your will, and scarcely allowing you the time to enjoy a little peace and appreciate the beauty of what you are saying.

125 Even if you have to fight distractions all through your whole Rosary, be sure to fight well, arms in hand: that is to say, do not stop saying your Rosary even if it is difficult to say and you have no sensible devotion. It is a terrible battle, but one that is profitable to the faithful soul. If you put down your arms, that is, if you give up the Rosary, you will be admitting defeat and then the devil, having got what he wanted, will leave you in peace, and on the day of judgment will taunt you because of your faithlessness and lack of courage. "He who is faithful in little things will also be faithful in those that are greater." Luke 16:10.

He who is faithful in rejecting the smallest distractions when he says even the smallest prayer, will also be faithful in great things. Nothing is more certain, since the Holy Spirit has told us so.

So all of you, servants and handmaids of Jesus Christ and the

Blessed Virgin, who have made up your minds to say the Rosary every day, be of good heart. Do not let the multitude of flies (as I call the distractions that make war on you during prayer) make you abandon the company of Jesus and Mary, in whose holy presence you are when saying the Rosary. In what follows I shall give you suggestions for diminishing distractions in prayer.

Forty-fourth Rose

126 After you have invoked the Holy Spirit, in order to say your Rosary well, place yourself for a moment in the presence of God and make the offering of the decades in the way I will show you later.

Before beginning a decade, pause for a moment or two, depending on how much time you have, and contemplate the mystery that you are about to honor in that decade. Always be sure to ask, by this mystery and through the intercession of the Blessed Virgin, for one of the virtues that shines forth most in this mystery or one of which you are in particular need.

Take great care to avoid the two pitfalls that most people fall into during the Rosary. The first is the danger of not asking for any graces at all, so that if some good people were asked their Rosary intention they would not know what to say. So, whenever you say your Rosary, be sure to ask for some special grace or virtue, or strength to overcome some sin.

The second fault commonly committed in saying the Rosary is to have no intention other than that of getting it over with as quickly as possible. This is because so many look upon the Rosary as a burden, which weighs heavily upon them when it has not been said, especially when we have promised to say it regularly or have been told to say it as a penance more or less against our will.

127 It is sad to see how most people say the Rosary. They say it astonishingly fast, slipping over part of the words. We could not possibly expect anyone, even the most important person, to think that a slipshod address of this kind was a compliment, and yet we imagine that Jesus and Mary will be honored by it!

Small wonder, then, that the most sacred prayers of our holy religion seem to bear no fruit, and that, after saying thousands of Rosaries, we are still no better than we were before.

Dear friend of the Confraternity, I beg you to restrain your natural precipitation when saying your Rosary, and make some pauses in the middle of the Our Father and Hail Mary, and a smaller one after the words of the Our Father and Hail Mary which I have marked with a cross, as follows:

Our Father who art in heaven, + hallowed by thy name, + thy kingdom come, + thy will be done + on earth as it is in heaven. +

Give us this day + our daily bread, + and forgive us our trespasses + as we forgive those who trespass against us, + and lead us not into temptation, + but deliver us from evil. Amen. +

Hail, Mary, full of grace, + the Lord is with thee, + blessed art thou among women, + and blessed is the fruit of thy womb, Jesus. +

Holy Mary, Mother of God, + pray for us sinners, now + and at the hour of our death. Amen. +

At first, you may find it difficult to make these pauses because of your bad habit of saying prayers in a hurry; but a decade said recollectedly in this way will be worth more than thousands of Rosaries said in a hurry, without pausing or reflecting.

128 Blessed Alan de la Roche and other writers, including Robert Bellarmine, tell the story of how a good priest advised three of his penitents, who happened to be sisters, to say the Rosary every day without fail for a whole year. This was so that they might make a beautiful robe of glory for the Blessed Virgin out of their Rosaries. This was a secret that the priest had received from heaven.

So the three sisters said the Rosary faithfully for a year, and on the feast of the Purification our Lady appeared to them at night when they had retired. St. Catherine and St. Agnes were with her, and she was wearing a dress brilliant with light, on which was written in letters of gold the words "Hail, Mary, full of grace." Our Lady approached the eldest sister and said, "I greet you, my daughter, who have greeted me so often and so well. I want to thank you for the beautiful robes you have made me." The two virgin saints who accompanied our Lady also thanked her and all three disappeared.

An hour later, our Lady, with the same two companions, entered the room again, but this time she was wearing a green dress which had no gold lettering and did not shine. She went to the second sister and thanked her for the robe she had made by saying her Rosary. But since this sister had seen our Lady appear to the eldest sister much more magnificently dressed, she asked the reason why. Our Lady answered, "Your sister made me more beautiful clothes because she has been saying the Rosary better than you."

About an hour after this, she appeared to the youngest of the sisters wearing tattered and dirty rags. "My daughter," she said, "I want to thank you for these clothes you have made me." The young girl, feeling ashamed, cried out, "O my lady, how could I have dressed you so badly! I beg you to forgive me. Please grant me a little more time to make you a beautiful robe by saying my Rosary better." Our Lady and the two saints vanished, leaving the girl heartbroken. She told her confessor everything that had happened and he urged them to say the Rosary for another year and to say it with more devotion than ever.

At the end of this second year, on the same day of the Purification, our Lady, clothed in a magnificent robe, and again attended by St. Catherine and St. Agnes, wearing crowns, appeared to them in the evening. She said to them, "I have come to tell you that you have earned heaven at last, and you will all have the great joy of going there tomorrow." The three of them cried, "Our hearts are ready, dearest Queen, our hearts are ready." Then the vision faded. That same night they became ill and sent for their confessor, and received the last sacraments, after having thanked him for the holy practice he had taught them. After Compline, our Lady appeared with a large company of virgins and had the three sisters clothed in white robes. While angels were singing, "Come, spouses of Jesus Christ, receive the crowns which have been prepared for you for all eternity,"[137] they departed from this life.

Some important truths can be learned from this story:
1) How important it is to have a good director who will counsel holy practices, especially that of the holy Rosary; 2) How important it is to say the Rosary with attention and devotion; 3) How kind and merciful is the Blessed Virgin to those who are sorry for the past and are firmly resolved to do better; 4) How generous she is in rewarding us in life, at death, and in eternity for the little services that we render her with fidelity.

Forty-fifth Rose

129 I would like to add that the Rosary ought to be said reverently, that is to say, it ought to be said as much as possible, kneeling, with hands joined, clasping the rosary. However, if you are ill, you can, of course, say it in bed; or if one is travelling it can be said while walking; if, on account of some infirmity, you cannot kneel you can say it standing or sitting. You can even say it while working if your duties do not allow you to leave your job, for work with one's hands is not always incompatible with vocal prayer.

I agree that, since the soul has its limitations and can only do so much, when we are concentrating on manual work we are less attentive to the activities of the spirit, such as prayer. But when we cannot do otherwise, this kind of prayer is not without its value in our Lady's eyes, and she rewards our good-will more than our exterior actions.

130 I advise you to divide up your Rosary into three parts and to say each group of five decades at different times of the day. This is much better than saying the whole fifteen decades at once.

If you cannot find the time to say five decades all together, say a decade here and a decade there; you will thus be able, in spite of your work and the calls upon your time, to complete the whole Rosary before going to bed.

St. Francis de Sales set us a very good example of fidelity in this respect: once when he was extremely tired from the visits he had made during the day and remembered, towards midnight, that he had left a few decades of his Rosary unsaid, he knelt down and said them before going to bed, notwithstanding all the efforts of his secretary, who saw he was tired and begged him to leave the rest of his prayers till the next day.

Imitate also the faithfulness, reverence and devotion of the holy friar, mentioned in the chronicles of St. Francis, who always said five decades of the Rosary with great reverence and attention before dinner. I have mentioned this earlier.[138]

Forty-sixth Rose

131 Of all the ways of saying the holy Rosary, the most glorious to God, most salutary to our souls, and the most terrible to the devil is that of saying or chanting the Rosary publicly in two choirs.

God is very pleased to have people gathered together in prayer. All the angels and the blessed unite to praise him unceasingly. The just on earth, gathered together in various communities, pray in common, night and day. Our Lord expressly recommended this practice to his apostles and disciples, and promised that whenever there would be at least two or three gathered in his name he would be there in the midst of them.[139]

What a wonderful thing to have Jesus Christ in our midst! And all we have to do to have him with us is to come together to say the Rosary. That is why the first Christians met so often to pray together, in spite of the persecutions of the Emperors, who had forbidden them to assemble. They preferred to risk death rather than to miss their gatherings where our Lord was present.

132 This way of praying is of the greatest benefit to us:

1 because our minds are usually more alert during public prayer than when we pray alone;

2 when we pray in common, the prayer of each one belongs to the whole group and make all together but one prayer, so that if one person is not praying well, someone else in the same gathering who is praying better makes up for his deficiency. In the same way, those who are strong uphold the weak, those who are fervent inspire the lukewarm, the rich enrich the poor, the bad are merged with the good. How can a measure of cockle be sold? This can be done very easily by mixing it with four or five bushels of good wheat.

3 One who says his Rosary alone only gains the merit of one Rosary; but if he says it with thirty other people he gains the merit of thirty Rosaries. This is the law of public prayer. How profitable, how advantageous this is!

4 Urban VIII, who was very pleased to see how the devotion of the holy Rosary had spread to Rome and how it was being said in two groups or choirs, particularly at the convent of Santa Maria sopra Minerva, attached a hundred days' extra indulgence *toties quoties,* whenever the Rosary was said in two choirs. This is set out in his brief *Ad perpetuam rei memoriam,* of the year 1626. So every time you say the Rosary in common, you gain a hundred days' indulgence.

5 Public prayer is more powerful than private prayer to appease the anger of God and call down his mercy, and the Church, guided by the Holy Spirit, has always advocated it in times of disasters and general distress.

In his Bull on the Rosary, Pope Gregory XIII declares that we must believe, on pious faith, that the public prayers and processions of the members of the Confraternity of the Holy Rosary were largely responsible for the great victory over the Turkish navy at Lepanto,[140] which God granted to the Christians on the first Sunday of October 1571.

133 When King Louis the Just, of blessed memory, was besieging La Rochelle, where the rebellious heretics had their strongholds, he wrote to his mother to beg her to have public prayers offered for a victorious outcome. The Queen-Mother decided to have the Rosary recited publicly in Paris in the Dominican church of Faubourg Saint-Honoré, and this was carried out by the Archbishop of Paris. It was begun on May 20th, 1628.

Both the Queen and the Queen-Mother were present, with the Duke of Orleans, Cardinal de la Rochefoucault, Cardinal de Bérulle, and several prelates. The court turned out in full force as well as a great number of the general populace. The Archbishop read the meditations on the mysteries aloud and then began the Our Father and Hail Mary of each decade, while the congregation of religious and lay-folk answered. At the end of the Rosary a statue of the Blessed Virgin was carried solemnly in procession while the Litany of our Lady was sung.

This devotion was continued every Saturday with admirable fervor and resulted in a manifest blessing from heaven, for the King triumphed over the English at the Island of Ré and made his triumphant entry into La Rochelle on All Saints Day of the same year.[144] This shows us the power of public prayer.

134 Finally, when the Rosary is said in common, it is far more formidable to the devil, because in this public prayer it is an army that is attacking him. He can often overcome the prayer of an individual, but if it is joined to that of others, the devil has much more trouble in getting the best of it. It is easy to break a single stick; but if you join it to others to make a bundle, it cannot be broken. *Vis unita fit fortior.* Soldiers join together in an army to overcome their enemies; immoral people often come together for parties of debauchery and dancing; evil spirits join forces in order to make us lose our souls. Why, then, should not Christians join forces to have Jesus Christ present with them, to appease the anger of God, to draw down his grace and mercy on us, and to frustrate and overcome the devil more forcefully?

Dear friend of the Confraternity, whether you live in the town or the country, near the parish church or a chapel, go there at least every evening, with the approval of the parish priest, together with all those who want to recite the Rosary in two choirs. If a church or chapel is not available, say the Rosary together in your own or a neighbor's house.

135 This is a holy practice, which God, in his mercy, has set up in places where I have preached missions, in order to safeguard and increase the good brought about by the mission and to prevent further sin. Before the Rosary was established in these little towns and villages, dances and parties of debauchery went on; dissoluteness, wantonness, blasphemy, quarrels and feuds flourished; one heard nothing but evil songs and double-meaning talk. But now nothing is heard but hymns and the chant of the Our Father and Hail Mary. The only gatherings to be seen are those of twenty, thirty or a hundred or more people who, at a fixed time, sing the praises of God as religious do.

There are even places where the Rosary is said in common every day, at three different times of the day. What a blessing from heaven that is! As there are wicked people everywhere, do not expect to find that the place you live in is free of them; there will be people who avoid going to church for the Rosary, who may even make fun of it and do all they can, by what they do and say, to stop you from going. But do not give up. As those wretched people will have to be separated from God and heaven forever, already here on earth they have to be separated from the company of Jesus and his servants.

Forty-seventh Rose

136 People of God, cut yourselves adrift from those who are damning themselves by their impious lives, laziness and lack of devotion without delay, and say the Rosary often with faith, humility, confidence and perseverance.

1 Our Lord told us to pray always, after the example he has given us, because of our endless need of prayer, on account of the darkness of our minds, our ignorance, and weakness, and the number of our enemies. Anyone who really gives heed to this commandment of our Master will surely not be satisfied with saying the Rosary once a year, as the Perpetual Members do, or once a week,

like the Ordinary Members, but will say it every day without fail, as a member of the Daily Rosary, even though the only obligation he has is that of his own salvation. "We ought always to pray and not lose heart."[142]

137 These are the eternal words of our Blessed Lord himself. And we must believe his words and abide by them if we do not want to be damned. You can explain them as you wish so long as you do not interpret them as the world does and observe them in a worldly way. Our Lord gave us the true explanation of his words in the examples he left us: "I have given you an example that as I have done to you, so you do also." (Jn. 13:5.) And "he spent the whole night in prayer to God," (Luke 6:12) as if the day was not sufficient for it.

Often he repeated to his Apostles these two words, "Watch and pray."[143] The flesh is weak, temptation is everywhere and always around you. If you do not keep up your prayers, you will fall. And because some of them evidently thought that these words of our Lord constituted only a counsel, they completely missed the point. That is why they fell into temptation and sin, even though they were in the company of Jesus Christ.

138 Dear friend of the Confraternity, if you want to lead a fashionable life and belong to the world—by this I mean if you do not mind falling into mortal sin from time to time and then going to confession, and avoiding conspicuous sins which the world considers vile, while keeping up the "respectable" ones—then, of course, there is no need for you to say so many prayers and Rosaries. To be "respectable" you only need to say a little prayer morning and evening, an occasional Rosary given to you for your penance, a few decades said in a casual way, when the fancy takes you—that is quite enough for any good-living person. If you did less, you might be branded as a freethinker or profligate; if you do more, you are becoming an eccentric or a fanatic.

139 But if you want to lead a true Christian life and genuinely want to save your soul and walk in the footsteps of the saints and not fall into serious sin, if you wish to break all the snares of the devil and extinguish all his flaming darts, you must pray always as our Lord taught and commanded you to do.

If you really have this wish at heart, then you should at least say your Rosary every day, or its equivalent.

I repeat "at least," because probably all that you will accomplish through your Rosary will be to avoid mortal sin and temptation. This is because you are exposed to the strong current of the world's wickedness by which many a strong soul is swept away; you are in the midst of the thick, clinging darkness which often blinds even the most enlightened souls; you are surrounded by evil spirits who, being more experienced than ever and knowing that their time is short, are more subtle and more effective in tempting you.

It will indeed be a marvel of grace wrought by the holy Rosary if you manage to keep out of the clutches of the world, the devil and the flesh and sin, and gain eternal life.

140 If you do not want to believe what I say, at least learn from your own experience. I should like to ask you if, when you were in the habit of saying no more prayers than people usually say in the world, and saying them in the way they usually say them, you were able to avoid serious faults and sins that were grievous but seemed of little account to you in your blindness. Now at last you must wake up, and if you want to live and die without sin, at least serious sin, pray always; say your Rosary every day, as all members used to do in the early days of the Confraternity. (See the end of this book for proof of what I say.)[144]

When our Blessed Lady gave the Rosary to St. Dominic, she ordered him to say it every day and to get others to say it daily. St. Dominic never let anyone join the Confraternity unless he were fully determined to say it every day. If nowadays people are allowed to be Ordinary members through saying the Rosary once a week, it is because fervor has dwindled and charity grown cold. You get what you can from one who is poor in prayer. "It was not so in the beginning."[145]

Three things must be noted here.

141 The first is that if you want to be enrolled in the Confraternity of the Daily Rosary and share in the prayers and merits of its members, it is not enough to be enrolled in the Ordinary Rosary or simply to make a resolution to say it every day. In addition, you must give your name to those who have the power of enrolling. It is also a very good thing to go to confession and communion for this intention. The reason for this is that the Ordinary Rosary membership does not include that of the Daily Rosary, but this latter does include the former.

The second point I want to make is that, absolutely speaking, it is not even a venial sin to fail to say the Rosary every day, or every week, or every year.

The third point is that whenever illness, or obedience to a lawful superior, or necessity, or involuntary forgetfulness has prevented you from saying the Rosary, you do not forfeit your share in the merits and you do not lose your participation in the Rosaries of the other Confraternity members. So it is not absolutely necessary for you to say two Rosaries on the following day to make up for the one you missed, as I suppose, through no fault of your own. If, however, when you are ill, your sickness is such that you are still able to say part of your Rosary, you have to say that part.

"Blessed are those who stand before you always." "Happy those who dwell in your house, O Lord, they praise you continually."[146]

Lord Jesus, blessed are the brothers and sisters of the Daily Rosary Confraternity who, day after day, are present in and around your throne in heaven, so that they may meditate and contemplate your joyful, sorrowful and glorious mysteries. How happy they are on earth because of the wonderful graces you bestow on them, and how blessed shall they be in heaven where they will praise you in a special way forever and ever.

142 2 The Rosary should be said with faith, for our Blessed Lord said, "Believe that you will receive and it will be granted."[147] If you believe that you will receive what you ask from God, he will grant your petitions. He will say to you, "As you have believed, so be it done to you."[148] "If anyone needs wisdom, let him ask God with faith, and without hesitating, and—through his Rosary—it will be given him."

143 3 Thirdly, we must pray with humility, like the publican; he was kneeling on the ground, on two knees, not on one knee as proud and worldly people do, or one knee on the bench. He was at the back of the church and not in the sanctuary as the Pharisee was; his eyes were cast down, for he dared not look up to heaven; he did not hold his head up and look about him like the Pharisee; he beat his breast, confessing himself a sinner and asking for forgiveness: "Be merciful to me, a sinner," and not like the Pharisee who boasted of his good works, who despised others in their prayers. Do not imitate the prayer of the proud Pharisee which only hardened his heart and increased his guilt; imitate rather the humility of the tax-collector, whose prayer obtained him the remission of his sins.

You must be on your guard against giving yourself to what is extraordinary and asking or even desiring knowledge of extraordinary things, visions, revelations, or other miraculous graces which God has occasionally given to some of the saints while they were saying the Rosary. *Sola fides sufficit:* Faith alone suffices now that the Gospel and all the devotions and pious practices are sufficiently established.

Even if you suffer from dryness of soul, distaste for prayer and interior discouragement, never give up the least part of your Rosary; this would be a sign of pride and infidelity; but like a brave champion of Jesus and Mary, say your Our Fathers and Hail Marys in your dryness, without seeing, feeling, or appreciating, and concentrating as best you can on the mysteries.

You ought not to look for sweets or jam to eat with your daily bread, as children do; but to imitate Jesus more perfectly in his agony you could say your Rosary more slowly sometimes when you find it particularly hard to say: "Being in agony, he prayed the longer," so that what was said of our Lord when he was in his agony of prayer may be said of you: he prayed all the longer.

144 4 Pray with great confidence, with confidence based on the goodness and infinite generosity of God and on the promises of Jesus Christ. God is the spring of living water which flows unceasingly into the hearts of those who pray. The eternal Father yearns for nothing so much as to share the life-giving waters of his grace and mercy with us. He entreats us, "All you who thirst, come to the waters,"[149] that is, come and drink of my spring through prayer, and when we do not pray to him he sorrowfully says that we are forsaking him, "They have forsaken me, the fountain of living water."

We please our Lord when we ask him for graces, and if we do not ask he makes a loving complaint, "Until now you have not asked anything. . . . Ask and you will receive, seek and you will find, knock and the door will be opened to you."[150]

Furthermore, to give us more confidence in praying to him, he has bound himself by a promise: that his eternal Father would grant everything we ask in his name.

Forty-eighth Rose

145 As a fifth point, I must add perseverance and prayer. Only he who perseveres in asking, seeking, and knocking, will receive, will find and will enter. It is not enough to ask God for certain graces for a month, a year, ten or twenty years; we must never tire of asking. We must keep on asking until the very moment of death, and even in this prayer, which shows our confidence in God, we must join the thought of death to that of perseverance and say, "Although he should kill me, I will trust in him,"[151] will trust him to give me what I ask.

146 Prominent and rich people of the world show their generosity by foreseeing people's wants and ministering to them, even before they are asked for anything. God's munificence, on the other hand, is shown by his making us seek and ask, over a long period of time, for the graces which he wishes to bestow, and the more precious the grace, the longer he takes to grant it:

1 in order to increase the grace still more;

2 in order that the recipient may more deeply appreciate it;

3 in order that the one who receives it may guard against losing it; for people do not appreciate very much what they obtain quickly and at little cost.

So, dear members of the Confraternity, persevere in asking God for all your needs, both spiritual and material, through the holy Rosary; especially should you pray for divine Wisdom, which is "an infinite treasure,"[152] and there can be no possible doubt that you will receive it sooner or later, provided you do not give up and do not lose courage in the middle of your journey. "You still have a great way to go."[153]

You have a long way to travel, there will be bad times to weather, many difficulties to overcome, and many enemies to defeat before you will have stored up enough treasures for eternity, enough Our Fathers and Hail Marys with which to buy your way to heaven and win the glorious crown which awaits each faithful brother and sister of the Confraternity.

"Let no one take your crown":[154] take care that your crown is not appropriated by another who has been more faithful than you in saying his Rosary every day. "Your crown": it was yours, God had prepared it for you; it was yours, you had already half obtained it by your Rosaries well said. But because you stopped on the way when you were running so well,[155] another has left you behind and got there first; another who is more diligent and more faithful has paid, by his Rosaries and good works, what was required to obtain that crown.

"You began your race well; who has hindered you?"[155] Who has prevented you from having the crown of the holy Rosary? Alas, none other than the enemies of the Rosary, who are so numerous.

147 Believe me, it is only the violent who take it by force.[157] These crowns are not for the timid who are afraid of this world's taunts and threats, neither are they for the lazy and indolent who only say their Rosary carelessly, or hastily, just for the sake of geting it over with. The same applies to people who say it intermittently, as the spirit moves them. These crowns are not for cowards who lose heart and lay down their arms as soon as they see hell is let loose against their Rosary.

Dear fellow-members, if you want to serve Jesus and Mary by saying the Rosary every day, you must be prepared for temptation: "If you aspire to serve the Lord, prepare yourself for temptation."[158] Heretics, licentious people, the so-called respectable people of the world, persons of superficial piety, and false prophets, hand in glove with your fallen nature and all hell itself—all will wage terrible battles against you in an endeavor to make you give up this holy practice.

148 To help you to be better armed against their onslaught—not so much of acknowledged heretics and profligates as those who are considered "respectable" in the eyes of the world, and even those who are devout but have no use for the Rosary—I am going to tell you simply some of the things these people are always saying and thinking.

"What does this babbler want to say?" "Come, let us attack him, for he is against us."[159] What is he doing, saying so many Rosaries? What is it he is always mumbling? Such laziness! He does nothing but keep on sliding those beads along, he would do much better to work without amusing himself with such foolishness. Oh yes, it's quite true, all you have to do is to say the Rosary and a fortune will fall from heaven into your lap. The Rosary brings you all you need without lifting a finger. But hasn't it been said, "God helps those who help themselves"? Why load yourself with so many prayers? *Brevis oratio penetrat coelos;* an Our Father and a Hail Mary well said are quite sufficient. God has never commanded us to say the Rosary; of course it's all right, it's not a bad devotion when you've got the time, but don't think for one minute that people who say the Rosary are any more sure of heaven than we are. Just look at the saints who never said it!

Far too many people want everyone to see through their own eyes, people who lack prudence and carry everything to extremes, scrupulous people who see sin almost everywhere, who say that those who do not say the Rosary will be damned.

Oh yes, the Rosary is all right for old women who can't read. But surely the Little Office of our Lady is much more worthwhile, or the seven penitential psalms? Is there anything more beautiful than those psalms which have been inspired by the Holy Spirit?

You say you have undertaken to say the Rosary every day; that's just a flash in the pan, you know it won't last. Wouldn't it be better to undertake less and be more faithful about it? Come, my friend, take my word for it, say your morning and night prayers, work hard during the day and offer it up. God does not ask any more than that. If you didn't have your living to earn, as you have, you could commit yourself to saying your Rosary. But as it is, say your Rosary on Sundays and Holydays when you have plenty of time, but not on days when you have to work.

But really and truly, what are you doing with that enormous pair of beads? I've seen a rosary of only one decade, it's just as good as one of fifteen decades. Why on earth are you wearing it on your belt, fanatic that you are? Why don't you go the whole way and wear it round your neck like the Spaniards? They are great lovers of rosaries; they carry a big rosary in one hand, while in the other they have a dagger to give a treacherous stab. For goodness' sake drop these exterior devotions; true devotion is in the heart. And so on.

149 Similarly, not a few clever people and learned scholars may occasionally try to dissuade you from saying the Rosary, proud and critical people, I mean. They would rather you said the seven penitential psalms or some other prayers. If a good confessor has given you a Rosary for your penance, to be said for a fortnight or a month, all you have to do to get your penance changed to a few other prayers, fasts, alms or Masses, is to go to confession to one of those gentlemen.

If you consult even some people who live lives of prayer in the world, but who have never tried the Rosary, they will not only not encourage it but will turn people away from it to get them to learn contemplation, as if the Rosary and contemplation were incompatible, as if all the saints who have been devoted to the Rosary had not reached the heights of contemplation.

Your closest enemies will attack you all the more cruelly because they are within you. I mean the powers of your soul and your bodily senses, the distractions of the mind, distress and uncertainty of the will, dryness of the heart, exhaustion and illness of the body—all that will combine with the evil spirits to say to you, "Give up your Rosary, that is what is giving you such a headache; give up your Rosary, there is no obligation under pain of sin; at least say only a part of it; the difficulties you are having are a sign that God does not want you to say it; you can say it tomorrow when you are more in the mood. And so on."

150 Finally, my dear brothers and sisters, the daily Rosary has so many enemies that I look upon the grace of persevering in it until death as one of the greatest favors God can give us.

Persevere in it and your fidelity will be rewarded with the wonderful crown which is prepared for you in heaven: "Be faithful until death and I will give you the crown of life."[160]

Forty-ninth Rose

151 This is the time to say a little about the indulgences which have been granted to Rosary Confraternity members, so that you may gain as many as possible.

An indulgence, in general, is a remission or relaxation of temporal punishment due to actual sins, by the application of the superabundant satisfactions of Jesus Christ, of the Blessed Virgin and all the saints, which are contained in the treasury of the Church.

A plenary indulgence is a remission of the whole punishment due to sin; a partial indulgence of, for instance, a hundred or a thousand years can be explained as the remission of as much punishment as could have been expiated during a hundred or a thousand years, if one had been given a corresponding number of the penances prescribed by the Church's ancient Canons.

Now these Canons exacted seven and sometimes ten or fifteen years' penance for a single mortal sin, so that a person who was guilty of twenty mortal sins would probably have had to perform a seven year penance at least twenty times, and so on.[161]

152 Members of the Rosary Confraternity who want to gain the indulgences must:

1 Be truly repentant and go to confession and communion, as the Papal Bull of indulgences states.

2 Be entirely free from affection for venial sin, because if affection for sin remains, the guilt also remains, and if the guilt re-

mains the punishment cannot be lifted.

3 Say the prayers and perform the good works designated by the Bull. If, in accordance with what the Popes have said, one can gain a partial indulgence (for instance, of a hundred years) without gaining a plenary indulgence, it is not always necessary to go to confession and communion in order to gain it. Many such partial indulgences are attached to the Rosary (either of five or fifteen decades), to processions, blessed rosaries, etc. Do not neglect these indulgences.

153 Flammin and a great number of other writers tell the story of a young girl of noble station named Alexandra, who had been miraculously converted and enrolled by St. Dominic in the Confraternity of the Rosary. After her death, she appeared to him and said she had been condemned to seven hundred years in purgatory because of her own sins and those she had caused others to commit by her worldly ways. So she implored him to ease her pains by his prayers and to ask the Confraternity members to pray for the same end. St. Dominic did as she had asked.

Two weeks later she appeared to him, more radiant than the sun, having been quickly delivered from purgatory by the prayers of the Confraternity members. She also told St. Dominic that she had come on behalf of the souls in purgatory to beg him to go on preaching the Rosary and to ask their relations to offer their Rosaries for them, and that they would reward them abundantly when they entered into glory.[162]

154 To make the recitation of the Rosary easier for you, here are several methods which will help you to say it in a good and holy way, with the meditation on the joyful, sorrowful and glorious mysteries of Jesus and Mary. Choose whichever method pleases you and helps you the most: or you can make up one for yourself, as several holy people have done.[163]

Footnotes to The Secret of the Rosary

1 In the manuscript, Nos. 1-8 come at the end of the volume; Montfort probably wrote his introduction after he had set out the details. It has been thought useful to transfer these numbers to their proper place, at the beginning.

2 Acts 1:1.

3 Wis. 2:8.

4 1 Pet. 5:4.

5 Antoine BOISSIEU, S.J., *Le Chrétien prédestiné par la dévotion à la Sainte Vierge.*

6 Cf. Rom. 16:6.

7 Antonin THOMAS, *Rosier mystique,* 1st decade, ch. 3.

8 ALAN DE LA ROCHE, *De dignit. Psalt.,* ch. 18; quoted by CAR-

THAGENA in *De Sacris Arcanis Deiparae,* bk. 16, hom. 1. Montfort gives this quotation in Latin, as well as those in Nos. 15 and 16.

9 ALAN DE LA ROCHE, *De Dignit. Psalt.,* ch. 17; CARTHAGENA, *De Sacris Arcanis,* bk. 16, hom. 1.

10 ST. ANTONINUS, Part 4, Tit. 15, ch. 14, quoted by P. A. SPINELLI in *Maria Deipara Thronus Dei,* ch. 29, No. 38.

11 P.A. SPINELLI, *ibid.,* who quotes a text borrowed from Alan de la Roche.

12 *Rosier mystique,* 9th decade, ch. 4.

13 *Rosier mystique,* 9th decade, ch. 7. ALAN DE LA ROCHE, *De Dignit. Psalt.* Part 2, ch. 9.

14 *Rosier mystique,* 9th decade, ch. 8.

15 ALAN DE LA ROCHE, *De Dignit. Psalt.,* Part 2, ch. 7.

16 *Ibid.,* ch. 13; quoted by CARTHAGENA in *De Sacris Arcanis Deiparae,* bk. 2, ch. 17.

17 Sir. 19:1.

18 CARTHAGENA, *De Sacris Arcanis,* bk. 16, hom. 1.

19 *Rosier mystique,* 1st decade, ch. 6.

20 ANTOINE BOISSIEU, S.J., *Le Chrétien prédestiné,* p. 752.

21 ALAN DE LA ROCHE, *Apologia,* ch. 22. *Rosier mystique,* 9th decade, ch. 8.

22 ALAN DE LA ROCHE, *Ibid.,* ch. 7.

23 *Rosier mystique,* 9th decade, ch. 8.

24 *Rosier mystique,* 9th decade, ch. 8.

25 *Ibid.*

26 Sir. 24:31.

27 SAINT BONAVENTURE, *Psalterium,* lectio 4.

28 *Rosier mystique,* 9th decade, ch. 9.

29 Cf. Rose 33. *Rosier mystique,* 9th decade, ch. 10.

30 JOANNES LOPEZ, *Liber Miraculorum Sancti Rosarii;* quoted by CARTHAGENA in *De Sacris Arcanis Deiparae,* last book. *Rosier mystique,* 9th decade, ch. 10.

31 1 Cor. 13:7.

32 Heb. 11:6.

33 Hymn "Pange lingua."

34 SAINT CYPRIAN, *De Oratione Dominica,* Nos. 1, 2.

35 TERTULLIAN, *Liber de Oratione "Evangelii Breviarium,"* ch. 1.

36 THOMAS A KEMPIS, *Enchiridium Monachorum,* ch. 3.

37 SAINT JOHN CHRYSOSTOM, *Homilia XIX in Mattheum,* ch. 6.

38 SAINT AUGUSTINE, *Sermo 182 De Tempore.*

39 Exod. 3:14.

40 ALAN DE LA ROCHE, *De Dignit. Psalt.,* Part 2, ch. 10.

41 *Ibid.*

42 *Ibid.,* Part 4, ch. 49.

43 Ps. 143:9.

44 *Rosier mystique,* 2nd decade, ch. 9.

45 ALAN DE LA ROCHE, *De Dignit. Psalt.,* ch. 11.

46 Cf. TD 249-253.

47 Cf. 48th Rose, Nos. 147, 148.

48 Cf. 3rd Rose, No. 16.
49 Prov. 8:17, 21.
50 2 Cor. 9:6.
51 SAINT BONAVENTURE, *Psalterium,* lectio 4.
52 Lk. 6:38.
53 ALAN DE LA ROCHE, *De Dignit. Psalt.,* Part 4, ch. 1.
54 Sir. 3:5.
55 *Rosier mystique, 2nd decade, ch. 10.*
56 *Revelations,* ch. 53.
57 Cf. FRANÇOIS POIRÉ, *The Triple Crown,* treatise 3, ch. 13.
58 ALAN DE LA ROCHE, *De Dignit. Psalt.,* ch. 70.
59 *Ibid.,* ch. 69.
60 *Rosier mystique,* 2nd decade, ch. 10.
61 *Ibid.*
62 *Ibid.*
63 *Ibid.*
64 *Ibid.,* 4th decade, ch. 3.
65 *Ibid.,* ch. 3 and 1.
66 Eph. 5:1.
67 *Rosier mystique,* 4th decade, ch. 5.
68 *Ibid.*
69 Lam. 1:12.
70 Lam. 3:19.
71 *Rosier mystique,* 4th decade, ch. 6.
72 *Ibid.,* 4th decade, ch. 7.
73 *Ibid.*
74 *Ibid.*
75 Mt. 25:12.
76 *Rosier mystique,* 4th decade, ch. 9.
77 *Ibid.,* ch. 10.
78 *Ibid.*
79 *Ibid.*
80 *Ibid.,* 5th decade, ch. 3.
81 SAINT THOMAS, II-II, qu. 182, art. 3.
82 *Rosier mystique,* 5th decade, ch. 9.
83 Mt. 6:9.
84 Montfort adds a footnote quoting the following text taken from SAINT CATHERINE OF SIENA in her *Revelations: Quicumque justus vel peccator recurrit ad Eam cum devota reverentia, nullo modo decipitur vel devorabitur ab infernali daemone.* Anyone, either just or sinner, who turns to her with reverence and devotion will be neither deceived nor devoured by the demon of hell.
85 CAVANAC, O.P., *Les merveilles du Sacré Rosaire,* ch. II, p. 450.
86 The former office of Saint Martha, 2nd nocturn.
87 *Rosier mystique,* 10th decade, ch. 5.
88 Phil. 3:8.
89 1 Kgs. 10:8.
90 *Rosier mystique,* 6th decade, ch. 1.
91 ALAN DE LA ROCHE, *De Dignit. Psalt.,* Part 2, ch. 3.
92 *Rosier mystique,* 6th decade, ch. 2.

93 Eph. 6:12.
94 *Rosier mystique,* 6th decade, ch. 3.
95 SAINT AUGUSTINE, *Sermo 23 ad fratres in eremo.*
96 ALAN DE LA ROCHE, *De Dignit. Psalt.,* Part 2, ch. 17.
97 *Rosier mystique,* 6th decade, ch. 8.
98 DORLAND, *Chronica,* bk. 7, ch. 2.
99 The date given in the manuscript is 1481, but it should be 1431.
100 *Rosier mystique,* 6th decade, ch. 9.
101 *Ibid.,* ch. 10.
102 *Ibid.,* 10th decade, ch. 2.
103 *Ibid.*
104 *Ibid.,* ch. 3.
105 *Ibid.,* ch. 8.
106 JOANNES LOPEZ, *De Beatae Virginis Rosario.*
107 *Rosier mystique,* 10th decade, ch. 8.
108 *Ibid.,* 11th decade, ch. 8.
109 *Ibid.*
110 *Ibid.,* 7th decade, ch. 1.
111 *Ibid.,* ch. 8.
112 ALAN DE LA ROCHE, *De Dignit. Psalt.,* ch. 53.
113 *Rosier mystique,* 7th decade, ch. 1.
114 Cf. TD 42.
115 O excellentissima Virgo Maria, per virtutem psalterii et rosarii tui, compelle hos humani generis hostes questioni meae satisfacere.
116 O Mater sapientiae dignissima et de cujus salutatione quomodo illa fieri debeat jam edoctus est populus; pro salute populi circumstantis rogo. Coge hosce tuos adversarios, ut plenam et sinceram veritatem palam hic profiteantur.
117 Cf. THEODORICUS APOLDIANUS, *Vita S. Dominici.* "O inimica nostra, ô nostra damnatrix, ô nostra inimica, ô nostra damnatrix, ô confusio nostra, quare de caelo descendisti, ut nos hic ita torqueres? Per te quae infernum evacuas et pro peccatoribus tanquam potens advocata exoras; ô Via caeli certissima et securissima, cogimur sine mora et intermissione ulla, nobis quamvis invitis, et contra nitentibus, totam rei proferre veritatem. Nunc declarandum nobis est simulque publicandum ipsum medium et modus quo ipsimet confundamur, unde vae et maledictio in aeternum nostris tenebrarum principibus. Audite igitur vos, christiani. Haec christi Mater potentissima est in preservandis suis servis quominus precipites ruant in baratrum nostrum inferni. Illa est quae dissipat et enervat, ut sol, tenebras omnium machinarum et astutiarum nostrarum, detegit omnes fallacias nostras et ad nihilum redigit omnes nostras tentationes. Coactique fatemur neminem nobiscum damnari qui ejus sancto cultui et pio obsequio devotus perseverat. Unicum ipsius suspirium, superat et excedit omnium sanctorum preces, atque pium et sanctum eorum votum et desiderium, magisque eum formidamus quam omnes paradisi sanctos; nec contra fideles ejus famulos quidquam praevalere possumus.
Notum sit etiam vobis plurimos christianos in hora mortis ipsam invocantes contra nostra jura salvari, et nisi Marietta illa obstitisset

nostrosque conatus repressisset, a longo jam tempore totam Ecclesiam exterminassemus, nam saepissime universos Ecclesiae status et ordines a fide deficere fecissemus. Imo planius et plenius vi et necessitate compulsi, adhuc vobis dicimus, nullum in exercitio Rosarii sive psalterii ejus perseverantem aeternos inferni subire cruciatus. Ipsa enim devotis servis suis veram impetrat contritionem qua fit ut peccata sua confiteantur, et eorum indulgentiam a Deo consequantur."

118 ALAN DE LA ROCHE, *De Dignit. Psalt.*, Part 2, ch. 17.
119 ALAN DE LA ROCHE, *De Dignit. Psalt.*, Part 4, ch. 41.
120 *Rosier mystique,* 7th decade, ch. 8.
121 ALAN DE LA ROCHE, *De Dignit. Psalt.*, Part 4, ch. 40.
122 *Rosier mystique,* 7th decade, ch. 8.
123 *Ibid.*
124 ALAN DE LA ROCHE, *De Dignit. Psalt.*, Part 4, ch. 65.
125 *Rosier mystique,* 7th decade, ch. 5.
126 ALAN DE LA ROCHE, *De Dignit. Psalt.*, Part 4, ch. 64.
127 *Rosier mystique,* 7th decade, ch. 6.
128 ALAN DE LA ROCHE, *Apologia,* ch. 15.
129 *Rosier mystique,* 7th decade, ch. 6.
130 1* P Peccatoribus praestat paenitentiam;
2* S Sitientibus stillat satietatem;
3* A Alligatis adducit absolutionem;
4* L Lugentibus largitur laetitiam;
5* T Tentatis tradit tranquillitatem;
6* E Egenis expellit egestatem;
7* R Religiosis reddit reformationem;
8* I Ignorantibus inducit intelligentiam;
9* V Vivis vincit vastitatem;
10* M Mortuis mittit misericordiam per modum suffragii.
J.A. COPPENSTEIN, *B.F. Alani Redivivi Tractatus Mirabilis,* ch. 1.
131 Sir. 15:9.
132 Cf. TD 97.
133 *Rosier mystique,* 8th decade, ch. 1.
134 *Ibid.,* ch. 2.
135 *Chronica Virginis, anno* 1235.
136 *Rosier mystique,* 8th decade, ch. 2.
137 J.A. COPPENSTEIN, *B.F. Alani Redivivi Tractatus Mirabilis,* ch. 7.
138 Cf. 7th Rose, No. 25.
139 Mt. 18:19.
140 *Rosier mystique,* 7th decade, ch. 8.
141 *Ibid.*
142 Lk. 18:1.
143 Mt. 26:41.
144 Cf. No. 158.
145 Mt. 19:8.
146 1 Kgs. 10:8; Ps. 83:5.
147 Mk. 11:24.
148 Mt. 8:13.
149 Is. 55:1; Jer. 2:13.

150 Mt. 7:7.
151 Job 13:15.
152 Wis. 7:14.
153 1 Kgs. 19:7.
154 Apoc. 3:11.
155 Gal. 5:7.
156 *Ibid.*
157 Mt. 11:12.
158 Sir. 2:1.
159 Acts 17:18; Exod. 1:10; Wis. 2:12.
160 Apoc. 2:10.
161 *Rosier mystique,* 11th decade, ch. 1, 4.
162 CAVANAC, *Merveilles du S. Rosaire, ch. 8.*
163 The 50th Rose is not found in the manuscript. It may be due to a distraction of the author, or possibly he considered the following *Methods* as forming the final Rose.

5 Methods for Saying the Rosary

Introduction

As would be expected from a popular missionary, Montfort's book: "The Secret of the Holy Rosary," was meant to serve a practical apostolate and with this in mind he added to his book two methods for saying the Rosary. We also include a third which he composed for the Daughters of Wisdom.

He gives two further methods in his book of sermons and they too are included here.

It was thought useful to reproduce some passages on the Rosary which Montfort quotes verbatim from other authors and these are placed after the methods. (See Nos. 48-56.)

Methods of saying the Rosary

to draw into our souls the Graces of the Mysteries of the Life, Passion and Glory of Jesus and Mary

God alone

First Method

1 Say the "Come Holy Spirit" and then make this offering of the Rosary: I unite with all the saints in heaven and with all the just on earth; I unite with you, my Jesus, to praise your holy Mother worthily and to praise you in her and by her. I renounce all the distractions that may come to me while I am saying this Rosary. O Blessed Virgin Mary, we offer you this creed to honor the faith you had upon earth and to ask you to permit us to share in that same faith. O Lord, we offer you this Our Father to adore you in your oneness and to acknowledge you as the first cause and the last end of all things. Most Holy Trinity, we offer you these three Hail Marys to thank you for all the graces which you have given to Mary and which you have given to us through her intercession.

Our Father, three Hail Marys, Glory be to the Father. . . .

Offering of the Decades

Joyful Mysteries

2 *First decade* We offer you, Lord Jesus, this first decade in honor of your Incarnation. Through this mystery and the intercession of your holy Mother we ask for humility of heart.

Our Father, ten Hail Marys, Glory be to the Father. May the grace of the mystery of the Incarnation come into me and make me truly humble.

Second decade We offer you, Lord Jesus, this second decade in honor of the Visitation of your holy Mother to her cousin Saint Elizabeth. Through this mystery and the intercession of Mary we ask for a perfect love of our neighbor.

Our Father, ten Hail Marys, Glory be to the Father. May the grace of the mystery of the Visitation come into me and make me truly charitable.

Third decade We offer you, Child Jesus, this third decade in honor of your holy Birth. Through this mystery and the intercession of your blessed Mother we ask for detachment from the things of this world, love of poverty and love of the poor.

Our Father, ten Hail Marys, Glory be to the Father. May the

grace of the Birth of Jesus come into me and make me truly poor in spirit.

Fourth decade We offer you, O Lord Jesus, this fourth decade in honor of your presentation in the temple by the hands of Mary. Through this mystery and the intercession of your blessed Mother we ask for the gift of wisdom and purity of heart and body.

Our Father, ten Hail Marys, Glory be to the Father. May the grace of the mystery of the presentation come into me and make me truly wise and pure.

Fifth decade We offer you, Lord Jesus, this fifth decade to honor Mary's finding you in the temple among the learned men after she had lost you. Through this mystery and the intercession of your blessed Mother we ask you to convert us and all sinners, heretics, schismatics and pagans.

Our Father, ten Hail Marys, Glory be to the Father. May the grace of the mystery of the Finding of Jesus in the temple come into me that I may be truly converted.

Sorrowful Mysteries

3 *Sixth decade* We offer you, Lord Jesus, this sixth decade in honor of your intense agony in the garden of Olives. Through this mystery and the intercession of your holy Mother we ask for perfect sorrow for our sins and perfect conformity to your holy will.

Our Father, ten Hail Marys, Glory be to the Father. May the grace of the Agony of Jesus come into me and make me truly contrite and perfectly obedient to the will of God.

Seventh decade We offer you, Lord Jesus, this seventh decade in honor of your cruel Scourging. Through this mystery and the intercession of your holy Mother we ask for the grace to mortify our senses.

Our Father, ten Hail Marys, Glory be to the Father. May the grace of the Scourging of Jesus come into me and make me truly mortified.

Eighth decade We offer you, Lord Jesus, this eighth decade in honor of being crowned with Thorns. Through this mystery and the intercession of your holy Mother we ask for a deep contempt of the world.

Our Father, ten Hail Marys, Glory be to the Father. May the grace of the mystery of Our Lord's Crowning with Thorns come into me and make me truly opposed to the world.

Ninth decade We offer you, Lord Jesus, this ninth decade in honor of your carrying the Cross. Through this mystery and the intercession of your holy Mother we ask for great patience in carrying our cross after you all the days of our life.

Our Father, ten Hail Marys, Glory be to the Father. May the grace of the mystery of the carrying of the Cross come into me and make me truly patient.

Tenth decade We offer you, Lord Jesus, this tenth decade in honor of your Crucifixion on Mount Calvary. Through this mystery and the intercession of your holy Mother we ask for a great horror of sin, a love for the Cross and the grace of a holy death for us and for those who are now in their last agony.

Our Father, ten Hail Marys, Glory be to the Father. May the grace of the Death and Passion of Our Lord and Savior Jesus Christ come into me and make me truly holy.

Glorious Mysteries

4 *Eleventh decade* We offer you, Lord Jesus, this eleventh decade in honor of your triumphant Resurrection. Through this mystery and through the intercession of your holy Mother we ask for a lively faith.

Our Father, ten Hail Marys, Glory be to the Father. May the grace of the Resurrection come into me and make me truly faithful.

Twelfth decade We offer you, Lord Jesus, this twelfth decade in honor of your glorious Ascension. Through this mystery and the intercession of your holy Mother we ask for a firm hope and a great longing for heaven.

Our Father, ten Hail Marys, Glory be to the Father. May the grace of the mystery of the Ascension of Our Lord come into me and prepare me for heaven.

[*Thirteenth decade*] We offer you, O Holy Spirit, this thirteenth decade in honor of the mystery of Pentecost. Through this mystery and the intercession of Mary, your most holy spouse, we ask for your holy wisdom that we may know, taste and practice your truth and share it with everyone.

Our Father, ten Hail Marys, Glory be to the Father. May the grace of Pentecost come into me and make me truly wise in the eyes of God.

Fourteenth decade We offer you, Lord Jesus, this fourteenth decade in honor of the Immaculate Conception of your holy Mother and her assumption into heaven body and soul. Through these two mysteries and her intercession we ask for the gift of true devotion to her in order to live a good life and have a happy death.

Our Father, ten Hail Marys, Glory be to the Father. May the grace of the Immaculate Conception and the Assumption of Mary come into me and make me truly devoted to her.

[*Fifteenth decade*] We offer you, Lord Jesus, this fifteenth and last decade in honor of the Crowning in glory of your holy Mother in heaven. Through this mystery and her intercession we ask for perseverance and an increase in virtue up to the moment of our death and thereafter the eternal crown that is prepared for us. We ask for the same grace for all the just and all our benefactors.

Our Father, ten Hail Marys, Glory be to the Father.

5 We beseech you, Lord Jesus, by the fifteen mysteries of your life, death, passion and glory, and the merits of your holy Mother, to convert sinners, to help the dying, to free the souls in purgatory, and to give all of us your grace so that we may live well and die well. We pray also for the light of glory to see you face to face and love you during all eternity. Amen.

[Second,] Shorter Method

Of Celebrating the life, death and heavenly glory of Jesus and Mary in the Holy Rosary and a method of restraining our imagination and lessening distractions.

6 To do this a word or two is added to each Hail Mary of the decade reminding us of the mystery we are celebrating. This addition follows the name of Jesus in the middle of the Hail Mary: and blessed is the fruit of thy womb,

Decade	1st	"Jesus becoming man"
	2nd	"Jesus sanctifying"
	3rd	"Jesus born in poverty"
	4th	"Jesus sacrificed"
	5th	"Jesus holy of holies"
	6th	"Jesus in his agony"
	7th	"Jesus scourged"
	8th	"Jesus crowned with thorns"
	9th	"Jesus carrying his Cross"
	10th	"Jesus crucified"
	11th	"Jesus risen from the dead"
	12th	"Jesus ascending to heaven"
	13th	"Jesus filling thee with the Holy Spirit"
	14th	"Jesus raising thee up"
	15th	"Jesus crowning thee"

At the end of the first five mysteries we say:

May the grace of the joyful mysteries come into our souls and make us really holy.

At the end of the second:

May the grace of the sorrowful mysteries come into our souls and make us truly patient.

At the end of the third:

May the grace of the glorious mysteries come into our souls and make us eternally happy. Amen.

[Third Method]

Of Fr. de Montfort for saying fruitfully the holy Rosary, for the use of the Daughters of Wisdom.

7 I unite with all the saints in heaven, with all the just on earth, and with all the faithful here present. I unite with you, my Jesus, in order to praise your holy Mother worthily and to praise you in her and through her. I renounce all distractions which may arise during this Rosary. I desire to say it with attention and devotion as if it were the last of my life. Amen. We offer you, Lord Jesus, this Creed in honor of all the mysteries of our faith, the Our Father and three Hail Marys in honor of the unity of your being and the Trinity of your persons. We ask of you a lively faith, a firm hope and an ardent charity. Amen.

I believe in God; Our Father; three Hail Marys.

In each mystery, after the word Jesus, add a word to recall and honor the particular mystery. For example: Jesus incarnate, Jesus sanctifying, etc. as it is indicated at each decade.

The Joyful Mysteries

The Incarnation

8 We offer you, Lord Jesus, this first decade in honor of your Incarnation in Mary's womb; through this mystery and her intercession we ask for deep humility. Amen.

Our Father. Hail Mary ten times, adding Jesus becoming man. May the grace of the mystery of the Incarnation come into our souls. Amen.

The Visitation

We offer you, Lord Jesus, this second decade in honor of the Visitation of your holy Mother to her cousin Saint Elizabeth and of the sanctification of Saint John the Baptist; through this mystery and the intercession of your holy Mother we ask for charity towards our neighbor. Amen.

Our Father. Hail Mary ten times. Jesus sanctifying. May the grace of the Visitation come into our souls. Amen.

The Birth of Jesus

We offer you, Lord Jesus, this third decade in honor of your Birth in the stable at Bethlehem; through this mystery and the intercession of your holy Mother, we ask for detachment from worldly things, contempt of riches and a love of poverty. Amen.

Our Father. Hail Mary ten times. Jesus being born. May the grace of the mystery of the Birth of Jesus come into our souls. Amen.

The Presentation in the Temple

We offer you, Lord Jesus, this fourth decade in honor of your presentation in the temple and the purification of Mary; through this mystery and her intercession we ask for purity in body and mind. Amen.

Our Father. Hail Mary ten times. Jesus sacrificed. May the grace of the mystery of the Presentation come into our souls. Amen.

The Finding of Jesus

We offer you, Lord Jesus, this fifth decade in honor of your being found in the temple by Mary; through this mystery and her intercession we ask for true wisdom. Amen.

Our Father. Hail Mary ten times. Jesus Holy of holies. May the grace of the mystery of the Finding of Jesus come into our souls. Amen.

At the end of this first Rosary the Magnificat is said.

The Sorrowful Mysteries

The Agony

9 We offer you, Lord Jesus, this sixth decade in honor of your Agony in the Garden of Olives; through this mystery and the intercession of your holy Mother we ask for sorrow for our sins. Amen.

Our Father. Hail Mary ten times. Jesus in Agony. May the grace of the mystery of the Agony of Jesus come into our souls. Amen.

The Scourging

We offer you, Lord Jesus, this seventh decade in honor of your cruel Scourging; through this mystery and the intercession of your holy Mother we ask for the grace to mortify our senses. Amen.

Our Father. Hail Mary ten times. Jesus being scourged. May the grace of the mystery of the Scourging of Jesus come into our souls. Amen.

The Crowning with Thorns

We offer you, Lord Jesus, this eighth decade in honor of your being Crowned with Thorns; through this mystery and the intercession of your holy Mother we ask for contempt of the world. Amen.

Our Father. Hail Mary ten times. Jesus crowned with thorns. May the grace of the mystery of the Crowning with Thorns come into our souls. Amen.

The Carrying of the Cross

We offer you, Lord Jesus, this ninth decade in honor of your carrying the Cross; through this mystery and the intercession of your holy Mother we ask for patience in all our crosses. Amen.

Our Father. Hail Mary ten times. Jesus carrying his Cross. May the grace of the mystery of the Carrying of the Cross come into our souls. Amen.

The Crucifixion

We offer you, Lord Jesus, this tenth decade in honor of your Crucifixion and shameful Death on Calvary; through this mystery and the intercession of your holy Mother we ask for the conversion of sinners, perseverance for the just and relief for the souls in Purgatory. Amen.

Our Father. Hail Mary ten times. Jesus crucified.

10 In this decade before each Hail Mary we ask God through the intercession of the nine choirs of angels for the graces we stand in need of.

Holy Seraphim, ask God etc. Hail Mary etc.
Holy Cherubim, ask etc.
Holy Thrones, ask etc.
Holy Dominations, ask etc.
Holy Virtues, ask etc.
Holy Powers, ask etc.
Holy Principalities, ask etc.
Holy Archangels, ask etc.
Holy Angels, ask etc.
All the Saints of Paradise, ask etc.
Glory be to the Father, etc.

May the grace of the mystery of the Crucifixion of Jesus come down into our souls. Amen.

11 At the end of the second rosary the following prayers are said kneeling:

Prayer composed by Fr. de Montfort asking God for divine Wisdom

O God of our fathers, Lord of mercy, Spirit of truth, I, a mere worm of the earth, prostrate before your divine Majesty, acknowledging the great need I have of your divine wisdom which I have lost through my sins and trusting in the unfailing promise you have made to all those who ask with confidence, I come before you today to beg this grace of you with all possible earnestness and the greatest humility. Send us, O Lord, this wisdom which sits by your throne to strengthen our weakness, to enlighten our minds, to inflame our hearts, to speak and to act, to work and suffer in union with you, to direct our footsteps and to fill our souls with the virtues of Jesus Christ and the gifts of the Holy Spirit, for only Wisdom can bring us these gifts. O Father of mercy, God of all consolation, we ask you for this infinite treasure of your divine wisdom, through the tender heart of Mary, through the Precious Blood of your dear Son and through the intense desire you have to bestow your gifts on your poor creatures. Hear and grant our prayers. Amen.

12 Prayer to Saint Joseph

Hail Joseph the just, Wisdom is with you; blessed are you among all men and blessed is Jesus, the fruit of Mary, your faithful spouse. Holy Joseph, worthy foster-father of Jesus Christ, pray for us sinners and obtain divine Wisdom for us from God, now and at the hour of our death. Amen.

This prayer is said three times.

The Glorious Mysteries

The Resurrection

13 We offer you, Lord Jesus, this eleventh decade in honor of your glorious Resurrection; through this mystery and the intercession of your holy Mother, we ask for love of God and fervor in your service. Amen.

Our Father. Hail Mary ten times. Jesus risen from the dead. May the grace of the mystery of the Resurrection come into our souls. Amen.

The Ascension

We offer you, Lord Jesus, this twelfth decade in honor of your triumphant Ascension; through this mystery and the intercession of your holy Mother we ask for an ardent desire for heaven, our true home. Amen.

Our Father. Hail Mary ten times. Jesus ascending to heaven. May the grace of the mystery of the Ascension come into our souls. Amen.

The Pentecost

We offer you, Lord Jesus, this thirteenth decade in honor of the mystery of Pentecost; through this mystery and the intercession of your holy Mother we ask that the Holy Spirit may come into our souls. Amen.

Our Father. Hail Mary ten times. Jesus filling us with the Holy Spirit. May the grace of the mystery of Pentecost come into our souls. Amen.

The Assumption of the Blessed Virgin

We offer you, Lord Jesus, this fourteenth decade in honor of the Resurrection and triumphant Assumption of your holy Mother into heaven; through this mystery and her intercession we ask for a tender devotion to so good a Mother. Amen.

Our Father. Hail Mary ten times. Jesus raising thee up. May the grace of the mystery of the Assumption come into our souls. Amen.

The Coronation of Mary

We offer you, Lord Jesus, this fifteenth and last decade in honor of the Coronation of your holy Mother; through this mystery and her intercession we ask for perseverance in grace and the crown of glory. Amen.

Our Father. Hail Mary ten times. Jesus crowning thee.

In this decade before each Hail Mary we ask God through the intercession of all the saints for the graces we stand in need of.

St. Michael the Archangel and all the holy angels, ask of God etc.

Hail Mary etc.

St. Abraham and all the holy Patriarchs, ask of God etc.

St. John Baptist and all the holy Prophets, ask of God etc.

St. Peter and St. Paul and all the holy Apostles, ask of God etc.

St. Stephen, St. Lawrence and all the Martyrs, ask of God etc.

St. Hilary and all the holy Pontiffs, ask of God etc.

St. Joseph and all the holy Confessors, ask of God etc.

St. Catherine, St. Therese and all the holy Virgins, ask of God etc.

St. Anne and all holy Women, ask of God etc.

Glory be to the Father etc.

May the grace of the mystery of the Crowning in glory of Mary come into our souls. Amen.

At the end of the third Rosary the following prayer is said:

Prayer to the Blessed Virgin

Hail Mary, well-beloved daughter of the eternal Father, admirable Mother of the Son, most faithful spouse of the Holy Spirit, glorious temple of the Blessed Trinity. Hail, sovereign Queen, to whom everyone is subject in heaven and on earth. Hail sure Refuge of sinners, our Lady of mercy, who has never repelled anyone. Sinner as I am, I cast myself at your feet and beg you to obtain from Jesus, your dear Son, contrition and pardon for all my sins and the gift of divine wisdom. I consecrate myself to you with all that I have. I choose you today as my Mother and Mistress; treat me then as the weakest of your children and the most submissive of your servants. Hear, O my Queen, the prayers of a heart that desires to love and serve you faithfully. Let it not be said that of all who have ever had recourse to you, I was the first to be unheeded. O my hope, my life, my faithful and immaculate Virgin Mary, hear me, protect me, strengthen me, instruct me, save me. Amen.

Praised, adored and loved be Jesus in the most holy sacrament of the altar. Forever and ever.

O Jesus, my dear Jesus, O Mary, Mother of Jesus, my beloved Mother, give us your holy blessing. Amen.

Support us in our troubles, hear us when we pray, preserve us from the world and the devil. Amen.

The superior says, Nos cum prole pia benedicat Virgo Maria. Amen.

[Fourth Method]

Summary of the life, death and passion and heavenly glory of Jesus and Mary in the holy Rosary.

16 Credo: 1) Faith in the presence of God. 2) Faith in the gospel. 3) Faith and obedience to the pope as Vicar of Jesus Christ.

1		Our Father	Unity of one, living and true God.
	1	Hail Mary	To honor the eternal Father who conceives his Son in contemplating himself.
	2	Hail Mary	The eternal Word, equal to his Father and who with him produces the Holy Spirit by their mutual love.
	3	Hail Mary	The Holy Spirit who proceeds from the Father and the Son by the way of love.
2		Our Father	Immense charity of God.

The Incarnation

17	1	Hail Mary	To deplore the unhappy state of disobedient Adam; his just condemnation and that of all his descendants.
	2	Hail Mary	To honor the desires of the patriarchs and

prophets who pleaded for the coming of the Messiah.

3 [Hail Mary] To honor the desires and prayers of the Blessed Virgin Mary to bring forward the coming of the Messiah; and her marriage with Saint Joseph.

4 [Hail Mary] The love of the eternal Father in giving us his Son.

5 Hail Mary The love of the Son who gave himself up for us.

6 Hail Mary The mission and the greeting of the angel Gabriel.

7 Hail Mary The maidenly fear of Mary.

8 Hail Mary The faith and consent of the Virgin Mary.

9 Hail Mary The creation of the soul and the formation of the body of Jesus in the womb of Mary by the Holy Spirit.

10 Hail Mary The angels adoring the Word Incarnate in the womb of Mary.

3 Our Father The most adorable majesty of God.

The Visitation

18 1 Hail Mary To honor the joy in the heart of Mary at the Incarnation and the dwelling for nine months of the eternal Word in her womb.

2 Hail Mary The sacrifice of himself that Jesus Christ offered to his Father on coming into the world.

3 Hail Mary The contentment of Jesus Christ in the humble and Virginal womb of Mary and that of Mary in the enjoyment of her God.

4 Hail Mary The doubts of St. Joseph on discovering that Mary was with child.

5 Hail Mary The agreement between Jesus and Mary in her womb on the choice of the elect.

6 Hail Mary The fervor of Mary when visiting her cousin.

7 Hail Mary The greeting of Mary and the sanctification of St. John Baptist and of his mother St. Elizabeth.

8 [Hail Mary] Mary's thanksgiving to God expressed in her Magnificat.

9 Hail Mary Her charity and humility in the service of her cousin.

10 Hail Mary The mutual dependence of Jesus and Mary

			and the dependence we should have upon them both.
4		Our Father	The infinite richness of God.

The Birth of Jesus

19	1	Hail Mary	To honor the contempt and the rebuffs which Mary and Joseph encountered at Bethlehem.
	2	Hail Mary	The poverty of the Stable where God came into the world.
	3	Hail Mary	The deep recollection of the exceeding love of Mary when she was about to give birth to her child.
	4	Hail Mary	The coming forth of the eternal Word from the womb of Mary without breaking the seal of her Virginity.
	5	Hail Mary	The adoration and the singing of the angels when Jesus was born.
	6	Hail Mary	The ravishing beauty of her divine child.
	7	Hail Mary	The coming of the shepherds into the stable with their humble gifts.
	8	Hail Mary	The circumcision of Jesus and his suffering accepted in love.
	9	Hail Mary	The giving of the name of Jesus and the nobility of this name.
	10	Hail Mary	The adoration of the kings and the gifts they brought.
5		Our Father	The eternal wisdom of God.

The Purification

20	1	Hail Mary	Obedience of Jesus and Mary to the Law.
	2	Hail Mary	The sacrifice that Jesus made of his humanity to the Law.
	3	[Hail Mary]	The sacrifice of her honor the Virgin Mary made to the Law.
	4	Hail Mary	The joy and the songs of Simeon and Anna the prophetess.
	5	Hail Mary	The ransoming of Jesus by the offering of two turtledoves.
	6	Hail Mary	The massacre of the Holy Innocents by Herod the Cruel.
	7	Hail Mary	The flight of Jesus to Egypt through St. Joseph's obedience to the voice of the angel.
	8	Hail Mary	The mystery of his abode in Egypt.
	9	Hail Mary	His return to Nazareth.
	10	Hail Mary	His growth in age and wisdom.

6 Our Father — The incomprehensible holiness of God.

21 The Finding of Jesus in the Temple

1 Hail Mary — To honor his hidden, hardworking and obedient life at Nazareth.
2 Hail Mary — His preaching and his being found in the temple among the doctors.
3 Hail Mary — His fasting and his temptations in the desert.
4 Hail Mary — His baptism by St. John Baptist.
5 Hail Mary — His wonderful preaching.
6 Hail Mary — His astounding miracles.
7 Hail Mary — The choice of the twelve apostles and the powers he gave them.
8 Hail Mary — His marvelous transfiguration.
9 Hail Mary — The washing of the feet of the apostles.
10 Hail Mary — The institution of the Holy Eucharist.
7 Our Father — The essential happiness of God.

The Agony of Jesus

22 1 Hail Mary — To honor the places of retreat that Jesus Christ chose during his life, especially that of the Garden of Olives.
2 Hail Mary — His humble and fervent prayers offered during his life and on the eve of his passion.
3 Hail Mary — His patience and gentleness towards his apostles during his life and especially in the Garden of Olives.
4 Hail Mary — His weariness of soul during all his life and especially in the Garden of Olives.
5 Hail Mary — The outpouring of blood in which his sorrows bathed him.
6 Hail Mary — The comfort he consented to receive from an angel in his agony.
7 Hail Mary — His conformity to the will of his Father in spite of his natural reluctance.
8 Hail Mary — The courage with which he went to meet his executioners and the power of his words with which he crushed them and then uplifted them.
9 Hail Mary — His betrayal by Judas and his arrest by the Jews.
10 Hail Mary — His desertion by his apostles.
8 Our Father — Wonderful patience of God.

The Scourging

23		1	Hail Mary	To honor the chains and ropes with which Jesus was bound.
		2	Hail Mary	The blow that he received in the house of Caiphas.
		3	Hail Mary	The three denials of St. Peter.
		4	Hail Mary	The shameful treatment he received at the house of Herod when he was dressed in a white robe.
		5	Hail Mary	His being stripped of all his clothes.
		6	Hail Mary	The scorn and insults he received from his tormenters because of his nakedness.
		7	Hail Mary	His being beaten and flayed with rods of thorn and cruel whips.
		8	Hail Mary	The pillar to which he was bound.
		9	Hail Mary	The blood he shed and the wounds he received.
		10	Hail Mary	His collapse through weakness into a pool of his own blood.
	9		Our Father	Unspeakable beauty of God.

The Crowning with Thorns of Jesus Christ

24		1	Hail Mary	To honor his being stripped a third time.
		2	Hail Mary	To honor His crown of thorns.
		3	Hail Mary	The veil with which they blindfolded him.
		4	Hail Mary	The blows and the spittle rained upon his face.
		5	Hail Mary	The old robe they put over his shoulders.
		6	Hail Mary	The reed they put into his hand.
		7	Hail Mary	The rough stone upon which he was made to sit.
		8	Hail Mary	The abuse and insults that were hurled at him.
		9	Hail Mary	The blood which poured from his adorable head.
		10	Hail Mary	His hair and beard which they tore at.
	10		Our Father	Limitless omnipotence of God.

25 The Carrying of the Cross

	1	Hail Mary	To honor Our Lord being presented to the people at the "Ecce Homo."
	2	Hail Mary	The preferring of Barabbas to Jesus.
	3	Hail Mary	The false testimonies given against him.
	4	Hail Mary	His being condemned to death.
	5	Hail Mary	The love with which he embraced and kissed the Cross.

6 Hail Mary — The dreadful sufferings he endured in carrying it.
7 Hail Mary — His falling through weakness under its weight.
8 Hail Mary — His sorrow on meeting his Mother.
9 Hail Mary — The veil of Veronica on which his face was imprinted.
10 Hail Mary — His tears and those of his Mother and the pious women who followed him to Calvary.
11 Our Father — Fearful justice of God.

The Crucifixion of Jesus Christ

26 1 Hail Mary — To honor the five wounds of Jesus Christ and the shedding of his blood on the Cross.
2 Hail Mary — His pierced heart and the Cross upon which he was crucified.
3 Hail Mary — The nails and the lance which pierced him, the sponge, the gall and the vinegar which he was given to drink.
4 Hail Mary — The shame and the ignominy he endured in being crucified naked between two thieves.
5 Hail Mary — The compassion of his Blessed Mother.
6 Hail Mary — His seven last words.
7 Hail Mary — His abandonment and his silence.
8 Hail Mary — The distress of the whole universe.
9 Hail Mary — His painful and shameful death.
10 Hail Mary — His being taken down from the Cross and his burial.
12 Our Father — The eternity of God without a beginning.

The Resurrection

27 1 Hail Mary — To honor the descent of the soul of Our Lord into hell.
2 Hail Mary — The joy and the release of the ancient fathers who were in limbo.
3 Hail Mary — The re-uniting of his body and soul in the tomb.
4 Hail Mary — His miraculous emergence from the tomb.
5 Hail Mary — His victories over death and sin, the world and the devil.
6 Hail Mary — The four qualities of his glorious body.
7 [Hail Mary] — The power that he received from his Father in heaven and on earth.
8 Hail Mary — His appearances to his Mother, his apostles and disciples.
9 Hail Mary — His discourses on heaven and the meal that

he had with his disciples.

10 Hail Mary The peace, the authority and the mission he gave them to go out into the whole world.

13 Our Father The unlimited omnipresence of God.

The Ascension of Jesus Christ

28 1 Hail Mary To honor the promise that Jesus Christ made to his apostles to send them the Holy Spirit and the command he gave them to prepare to receive him.

2 Hail Mary The gathering of all his disciples on the Mount of Olives.

3 Hail Mary The blessings he gave them as he rose from the earth towards heaven.

4 Hail Mary His glorious ascension by his own power into heaven.

5 Hail Mary The welcome and triumphant acclaim which he received from God, his Father and from all the heavenly court.

6 Hail Mary The triumphant power with which he opened the gates of heaven through which no mortal had passed.

7 Hail Mary His being seated at the right hand of his Father as his beloved Son equal to his Father.

8 Hail Mary The power he received to judge the living and the dead.

9 Hail Mary His last coming upon earth when his power and majesty will appear in all their magnificence.

10 Hail Mary The justice he will mete out at the last judgment when he rewards the just and punishes the wicked for all eternity.

14 Our Father The all-embracing Providence of God.

Pentecost

29 1 Hail Mary To honor the truth of God the Holy Spirit proceeding from the Father and the Son and who is the love of the Godhead.

2 Hail Mary The sending of the Holy Spirit upon the apostles by the Father and the Son.

3 Hail Mary His descent accompanied by the sound of a great wind which shows his might and power.

4 Hail Mary The tongues of fire he sent to the apostles giving them an understanding of the scrip-

tures and love of God and neighbor.

5 Hail Mary — The fullness of grace which the heart of Mary, his faithful spouse, was privileged to receive.

6 Hail Mary — The marvelous guidance he gave to all the saints and even to the person of Jesus Christ during all his life.

7 Hail Mary — The twelve fruits of the Holy Spirit.

8 Hail Mary — The seven gifts of the Holy Spirit.

9 Hail Mary — To ask especially for the gift of wisdom and the coming of his kingdom into men's hearts.

10 [Hail Mary] — To be victorious over the three evil spirits that are opposed to him, namely the spirit of the flesh, of the world and of the devil.

15 Our Father — The unspeakable generosity of God.

The Assumption of Mary

30 1 Hail Mary — To honor the eternal predestination of Mary to be the masterpiece of God's hands.

2 Hail Mary — Her Immaculate Conception and her fullness of grace and reason in the very womb of St. Anne.

3 Hail Mary — Her birth which gladdened the whole world.

4 Hail Mary — Her presentation and her abode in the temple.

5 Hail Mary — Her wonderful life and her exemption from all sin.

6 Hail Mary — Her fullness of pre-eminent virtue.

7 Hail Mary — Her fruitful virginity and her painless childbearing.

8 [Hail Mary] — Her divine Motherhood and her relationship with the three persons of the most holy Trinity.

9 [Hail Mary] — Her precious and loving death.

10 [Hail Mary] — Her resurrection and triumphant Assumption.

16 Our Father — The unattainable glory of God.

The Crowning of Mary

31 1 Hail Mary — To honor the triple crown which Mary received from the Holy Trinity.

2 Hail Mary — The joy and the added glory that heaven received through her triumphant entry.

3 Hail Mary — To acknowledge her as queen of heaven

and earth, of angels and men.

4 Hail Mary As treasurer and dispenser of the graces of God, the merits of Jesus Christ and the gifts of the Holy Spirit.

5 Hail Mary Mediatrix and advocate of men.

6 Hail Mary Exterminator and destroyer of the devil and of heresies.

7 Hail Mary Safe refuge of sinners.

8 Hail Mary Nurturing Mother of sinners.

9 Hail Mary The joy and delight of the just.

10 Hail Mary Refuge for all the living, all-powerful relief for the afflicted, for the dying and for the souls in purgatory.

God Alone

[Fifth Method]

150 Motives Impelling us to say the Rosary.

32 Creed definition and essence of the Rosary

1 Our Father Eminence of the Rosary

1 Hail Mary the daily Rosary

2 Hail Mary the ordinary Rosary

3 Hail Mary perpetual Rosary

33 2 Our Father excellence of the holy Rosary as prefigured in the Old Testament and the parables of the New.

1 Hail Mary the strength of the holy Rosary against the world, as prefigured by that small stone, which, thrown by no hand of man, fell upon the statue of Nebuchadnezzar and broke it into pieces.

2 Hail Mary its strength against the devil, as prefigured by the sling of David with which he overcame Goliath.

3 Hail Mary its power against all sorts of enemies of salvation, as prefigured by the power of David which contained innumerable kinds of defensive and offensive arms.

4 [Hail Mary] its miracles as prefigured in the rod of Moses which caused water to flow from the rock, calmed the waters, divided the seas and performed miracles.

5 [Hail Mary] its holiness as prefigured by the Ark of the Covenant which contained the law, the manna and the rod and also by the psalter

of David which prefigured the Rosary.

6 [Hail Mary] its light as shown in the columns of fire during the night and the shining cloud during the day which guided the Israelites.

7 [Hail Mary] its sweetness as shown in the honey found in the mouth of the lion.

8 [Hail Mary] its fruitfulness as shown in the net that St. Peter by order of Our Lord threw into the sea and which though filled with 153 fish did not break.

9 [Hail Mary] its marvelous fruitfulness as shown in the parable of the mustard seed which, although so small in appearance, becomes a great tree in which the birds of the air make their nests.

10 [Hail Mary] its richness as shown in the parable of the treasure hidden in a field for which a wise man must give up all he has to possess it.

34 3 Our Father It is a gift come down from heaven; a great present that God gives to his most faithful servants.

1 Hail Mary God is the author of the prayers of which it is composed and of the mysteries which it contains.

2 Hail Mary it is the Blessed Virgin who gave the Rosary its form.

3 [Hail Mary] St. Dominic preached and although he was a saint he converted hardly any sinners.

4 [Hail Mary] he was accompanied in his missions by several holy bishops and still his efforts were without fruit.

5 [Hail Mary] by the power of prayer and mortification, he received the holy Rosary in the forest of Toulouse.

6 [Hail Mary] he entered Toulouse and preached the Rosary and great wonders and great blessings accompanied his preaching.

7 [Hail Mary] he continued all his life preaching the Rosary with results never seen before.

8 [Hail Mary] the marvelous effects the Rosary has had wherever it was preached.

9 [Hail Mary] the decline of the Rosary.

10 [Hail Mary] the restoration of the Rosary by Blessed Alan de la Roche.

35 4 Our Father The Rosary is the triple crown that we

			place on the heads of Jesus and Mary and he who recites it every day will receive the same crown.
	1	Hail Mary	Mary possesses three kinds of crown.
	2	Hail Mary	The daily Rosary is her great crown.
	3	Hail Mary	The reprobate crown themselves with faded roses.
	4	[Hail Mary]	The predestinate crown Jesus and Mary with eternal roses.
	5	[Hail Mary]	The Jews crown Jesus with piercing crowns.
	6	[Hail Mary]	True Christians crown him with fragrant roses.
	7	Hail Mary	The first is the bridal crown or crown of excellence which we place on Mary's head by the joyful mysteries.
	8	[Hail Mary]	The second is the crown of triumph or of power that we give her by the sorrowful mysteries.
	9	[Hail Mary]	The third is the royal crown or crown of goodness that we give her by the glorious mysteries.
	10	[Hail Mary]	There are three crowns for the one who recites the Holy Rosary every day: 1 crown of graces during life 2 crown of peace at death 3 crown of glory in eternity
36	5	Our Father	The Rosary is a mystical summary of all the most beautiful prayers of the Church.
	1	Hail Mary	The Creed is a summary of the gospel.
	2	Hail Mary	It is the prayer of believers.
	3	Hail Mary	The shield of the soldiers of Jesus Christ.
	4	[Hail Mary]	The Our Father—prayer of which Jesus Christ is the sole author.
	5	Hail Mary	Prayer he used when praying to his Father and through which he obtained what he desired.
	6	Hail Mary	Prayer which contains a summary of all we must ask of God.
	7	[Hail Mary]	Prayer in which are found all our duties towards God.
	8	Hail Mary	Prayer which contains a summary of all we must ask of God.
	9	Hail Mary	Prayer whose value is unknown and which is said very badly by the majority of Christians.
	10	Hail Mary	Paraphrase of the Our Father.

God alone

37 6		Our Father	The Rosary contains the angelic greeting which is the most pleasing prayer we can offer our Blessed Lady.
	1	Hail Mary	The Hail Mary is a divine compliment which wins over the heart of the Blessed Virgin.
	2	Hail Mary	It is the new song of the New Testament which the faithful sing as they escape from the captivity of the devil.
	3	[Hail Mary]	It is the hymn of the angels and saints in heaven.
	4	[Hail Mary]	It is the prayer of the predestinate and of Catholics.
	5	[Hail Mary]	It is a mysterious rose which is a source of joy to the Blessed Virgin and to the soul.
	6	[Hail Mary]	It is a precious stone which embellishes and sanctifies the soul.
	7	[Hail Mary]	It is a valuable piece of money with which to purchase heaven.
	8	[Hail Mary]	It is the prayer which distinguishes the predestinate from the reprobate.
	9	[Hail Mary]	It is the terror of the devil, the blow which crushes him, the nail of Sisera which pierces his head.
	10	Hail Mary	Paraphrase of the Hail Mary.
38 7		Our Father	The Rosary is a divine Summary of the mysteries of Jesus and Mary in which we proclaim and commemorate their life, passion and glory.
	1	Hail Mary	Men's misfortune and ruin come from ignorance and neglect of the mysteries of Jesus Christ.
	2	Hail Mary	The Rosary provides the knowledge of the mysteries of Jesus and Mary and recalls them to mind in view of applying them to one's life.
	3	Hail Mary	The greatest desire of Jesus Christ was and still is that we remember him. With this in mind he instituted the sacrifice of the Mass.
	4	[Hail Mary]	After holy Mass the Rosary is the holiest action and prayer that we can offer because it is a remembrance and a celebration of what Jesus Christ has done and suffered for us.
	5	Hail Mary	The Rosary is the prayer of the angels and

			saints in heaven because they are engaged in celebrating the life, death and glory of Jesus Christ.
	6	Hail Mary	When we say the Rosary we celebrate in one day or one week all the mysteries that the Church celebrates in a year for the sanctification of her children.
	7	[Hail Mary]	Those who say the holy Rosary every day have a share in what the saints are doing in heaven which is the same as they were doing upon earth meritoriously, for they who are on earth are doing what the saints are doing in heaven.
	8	Hail Mary	The mysteries of the Holy Rosary are like mirrors for the predestinate in which they see their faults and like torches which guide them in this world of darkness.
	9	Hail Mary	They see springs of living water from the Savior to whom one may go with joy to draw the saving waters of grace.
	10	Hail Mary	They are the 15 steps of the temple of Solomon and the 15 rungs of the ladder of Jacob by which the angels descend to them and return to heaven and by which they ascend to heaven.
39	8	Our Father	The Rosary is the tree of life which bears marvelous fruits all the year round.
	1	Hail Mary	The Rosary enlightens blind and hardened sinners.
	2	Hail Mary	It brings back obstinate heretics.
	3	Hail Mary	It sets prisoners free.
	4	Hail Mary	It heals the incurable.
	5	Hail Mary	It enriches the poor.
	6	Hail Mary	It supports the weak.
	7	[Hail Mary]	It consoles the afflicted and the dying.
	8	Hail Mary	It reforms lax religious orders.
	9	Hail Mary	It checks the effects of God's anger.
	10	Hail Mary	It makes good people better.
40	9	Our Father	The Rosary is a practice that God has sanctioned by many miracles.
	1	Hail Mary	Miracles in the conversion of sinners.
	2	Hail Mary	In the conversion of heretics.
	3	Hail Mary	In the cure of all sorts of diseases.
	4	[Hail Mary]	In favor of the dying brethren.

	5	[Hail Mary]	In the sanctification of devout people.
	6	[Hail Mary]	In the release of souls from purgatory.
	7	[Hail Mary]	In the reception into the Confraternity.
	8	[Hail Mary]	For the procession of the holy Rosary and the oil lamp of the holy Rosary.
	9	Hail Mary	For its devout recitation.
	10	[Hail Mary]	To carry it on one's person with devotion.
41	10	Our Father	The holy Rosary is most excellent because it was established for very noble ends which give great glory to God and are very salutory for the soul.
	1	Hail Mary	By being enrolled in this Confraternity we are strengthened in a wonderful way by joining millions of brothers and sisters.
	2	Hail Mary	We thus preserve a continuous remembrance of the mysteries of Jesus and Mary.
	3	Hail Mary	We are able to praise God at every moment of the day and night and in every place on earth, which one could not do on one's own.
	4	[Hail Mary]	To thank Our Lord for all the graces he is giving us at every moment.
	5	[Hail Mary]	To be ever asking pardon for our daily sins.
	6	Hail Mary	To make our prayers more powerful by being united with others.
	7	Hail Mary	For mutual help at the hour of death which is so difficult and so important.
	8	Hail Mary	To be supported at the hour of judgment by as many intercessors as there are members of the confraternity of the Rosary.
	9	Hail Mary	To be given relief after death and speedily released from the pains of purgatory by the Masses and prayers which are offered up.
	10	Hail Mary	To form an army arrayed as for battle to destroy the empire of the devil and establish that of Jesus Christ.
42	11	Our Father	The Rosary is a great store of indulgence accorded by popes outdoing one another.
	1	Hail Mary	Plenary indulgences of the stations of Rome and Jerusalem by going to Communion on certain days.
	2	Hail Mary	Plenary indulgence on enrollment in the confraternity.
	3	Hail Mary	Plenary indulgence at the hour of death.
	4	Hail Mary	Indulgence for the recitation of the Rosary.

	5	Hail Mary	Indulgence for those who organize the saying of the Rosary.
	6	Hail Mary	Indulgence for those who receive communion in the church of the Rosary on the first Sunday of the month.
	7	Hail Mary	Indulgence on the occasion of the procession.
	8	Hail Mary	Indulgence for those who say the Mass of the Rosary.
	9	Hail Mary	Indulgence for certain good works.
	10	Hail Mary	Indulgence for those who are unable to visit the church of the Rosary, or receive Communion, or take part in a procession.
43	12	Our Father	The Rosary is sanctioned by the example given to us by the saints.
	1	Hail Mary	St. Dominic, its origination.
	2	Hail Mary	Blessed Alan de la Roche who restored it.
	3	Hail Mary	The saintly Dominicans who propagated it.
	4	Hail Mary	Among the popes: Pius V, Innocent III, and Boniface VIII who had it embroidered in satin.
	5	Hail Mary	Among the cardinals: St. Charles Borromeo.
	6	[Hail Mary]	Among the bishops: St. Francis de Sales.
	7	[Hail Mary]	Among religious: St. Ignatius, St. Philip Neri, St. Felix of Cantalice.
	8	[Hail Mary]	Among kings and queens: St. Louis, Philip I, King of Spain, Queen Blanche.
	9	Hail Mary	Among the learned: Albert the Great, Navarre, etc.
	10	Hail Mary	Among saintly people: the famous holy women of Rome, Sister Mary of the Incarnation.
44	13	Our Father	The vanquished enemies of the Rosary prove its fame to us.
	1	Hail Mary	Those who neglect it.
	2	Hail Mary	Those who say it with indifference and without attention.
	3	Hail Mary	Those who say it in haste and to get it over with.
	4	Hail Mary	Those who say it with unrepentant mortal sin.
	5	Hail Mary	Those who say it out of hypocrisy, lacking any devotion.

6 Hail Mary — Critics who strive ingeniously to do away with it.
7 Hail Mary — The impious who speak against it.
8 Hail Mary — The cowardly who accept it and then abandon it.
9 Hail Mary — Heretics who attack it and run it down.
10 Hail Mary — The devils who hate it and strive to destroy it by numerous tricks.

45 14 Our Father — The overcoming of objections that heretics, critics, libertines and those who neglect and ignore the Rosary generally make either to do away with it or to avoid saying it.

1 Hail Mary — It is a new religious practice.
2 Hail Mary — It is an invention of Religious to make money.
3 Hail Mary — It is a devotion of ignorant women who do not know how to read.
4 [Hail Mary] — It is superstitious being based on counting prayers.
5 Hail Mary — It is preferable to say the penitential psalms.
6 Hail Mary — It is preferable to make a meditation.
7 Hail Mary — It is too long and too tiresome a prayer.
8 Hail Mary — One cannot be saved without saying the Rosary.
9 Hail Mary — We sin if we fail to say it.
10 Hail Mary — It is good, but I have not the time to say it.

46 15 Our Father — Manner of saying the Rosary well.
1 Hail Mary — It must be said with a pure heart without attachment to grave sin.
2 Hail Mary — In a worthy manner with good intentions.
3 Hail Mary — With attention avoiding voluntary distractions.
4 Hail Mary — Slowly and calmly with pauses in the prayers.
5 Hail Mary — Devout whilst meditating on the mysteries.
6 Hail Mary — Modestly and in a respectful attitude whether standing or kneeling.
7 Hail Mary — Wholeheartedly and every day.
8 Hail Mary — Inwardly when it is said alone.
9 Hail Mary — Publicly and in two responding groups.
10 Hail Mary — Perseveringly until death.

47 16 Our Father — Different methods of saying the holy Rosary.

1	Hail Mary	The holy Rosary can be said in a straightforward manner, saying only the Our Fathers and Hail Marys with the intentions of the mysteries.
2	Hail Mary	We can add a word to each mystery of the decade.
3	Hail Mary	We can make a little offering at each decade.
4	[Hail Mary]	We can make a more important offering at each decade.
5	[Hail Mary]	We can have a special intention for each Hail Mary.
6	[Hail Mary]	We can recite it inwardly without speaking.
7	Hail Mary	We can genuflect at each Hail Mary.
8	Hail Mary	We can prostrate at each Hail Mary.
9	Hail Mary	We can give ourselves a stroke of the discipline.
10	Hail Mary	We can commemorate the saints at each decade and blend with one of the abovementioned methods as the holy spirit inspires.

[Appendix]

The Principal Rules Of The Confraternity of the Holy Rosary

48 Members should:

1 Have their names written in the register of the confraternity and, if possible, go to Confession and Communion and say the Rosary on the day they are enrolled.
2 Possess a blessed rosary.
3 Say the Rosary every day or at least once a week.
4 Whenever possible, go to Confession and Communion on the first Sunday of every month and take part in the Rosary processions.

Remember that none of these rules binds under pain of sin.

On the Power and Dignity of the Rosary[1]

49 "Through the Rosary, hardened sinners of both sexes became converted and began to lead a holy life, regretting their past sins with genuine tears of sorrow. Even children performed unbelievable penances, and devotion to my Son and to me spread so much that it seemed almost as though angels were living on earth. Faith was increasing and many of the faithful longed to shed their blood for it and fight against heretics. . . .

50 "Thus, through the sermons of my very dear Dominic and through the power of the Rosary the heretical regions became submissive to the Church. Almsgiving became widespread; churches and hospitals were built; people led pure and honorable lives; real wonders were accomplished. Holiness and unworldliness were seen everywhere; the church was seen as honorable; princes were just; people lived at peace with one another and justice and equity reigned in the guilds and in the home. More impressive still, workmen did not take up their tools until after they had greeted me by saying my Rosary and they did not retire at night without again praying to me on their knees. If they remembered in the middle of the night that they had not offered me this tribute, they would immediately rise from their bed and greet me with even greater respect, and with sorrow for their lapse. The Rosary became so well-known that people who were devout were considered by others as being obviously confraternity members. If a man lived openly in sin or blasphemed, it was commonly said: "This man cannot possibly be a brother of St. Dominic." I must not fail to mention the signs and wonders that I have wrought and put in different lands through the holy Rosary.

"I have stopped pestilences and put an end to horrible wars and averted bloodshed, besides strengthening those who said the Rosary in order to avoid sin. When you say the Rosary the angels rejoice in it, the holy Trinity delights in it, my son finds joy in it and I myself am happier than you can possibly imagine. After the holy Sacrifice of the Mass there is nothing that I love so much as the holy Rosary." (Cf. Blessed Alan de la Roche). . . .

51 "Having been strongly urged to do so by St. Dominic, all the brothers and sisters of his Order honored my Son and me unceasingly and in an indescribably beautiful way by saying this psalter of the Holy Trinity. Every day each one of them said at least one complete Rosary. If anybody failed to say it he felt that the whole of his day was spoiled. The brothers of St. Dominic had so great a love for this holy devotion that it made them hurry to church or choir more willingly. If one of them was seen to carry out his duties carelessly the others would say with assurance, "Dear brother, you must not be saying Mary's psalter any more or else you are saying it badly."

52 On the Dignity of the Hail Mary

"The holy angels in heaven salute the most Blessed Virgin with the Hail Mary not audibly but with their angelic mind. For they are fully aware that through it reparation was made for the fallen angels' sin, God became man and the world was renewed"

(Blessed Alan). "I myself, knowing the power of this greeting by the Lord, repeated it with great fervor. Indeed, realizing my own human nature, I begged Mary for a share in her divine life of grace and glory" (Blessed Alan). "One night when a woman member of the Confraternity had retired, Our Lady appeared to her and said, 'My daughter, do not be afraid of me. I am your loving Mother whom you praise so faithfully every day. Be steadfast and persevere. I want you to know that the Hail Mary gives me so much joy that no man could ever really describe it'" (Guillaume Pepin, In Rosario aureo, Sermon 47).

53 "This was corroborated by a vision of St. Gertrude. In her revelations, Book IV, chapter XI, we find this story:

"On the morning of the feast of the Annunciation of the Blessed Virgin Mary while the Ave Maria was being sung in Gertrude's monastery, she had a vision in which three streams gushed forth from the Father, the Son and the Holy Spirit and gently flowed into the heart of the Virgin Mary. From this heart these streams flowed back impetuously to their source. From this, Gertrude learned that the Blessed Trinity has allowed Our Lady to be the most powerful after God the Father, the wisest after God the Son and the most loving after God the Holy Spirit. She also learned that every time the Hail Mary is said by the faithful the three mysterious streams surround Our Lady in a mighty current rush to her heart. After they have completely bathed her in happiness they gush back into the bosom of God. The saints and angels share in this abundance of joy, as do the faithful on earth who say this prayer, for the Hail Mary is the source of all good for God's children.

54 "Listen to what Our Lady herself said to Saint Mechtilde: 'Never has any man composed anything more beautiful than the Hail Mary. No greeting could be dearer to my heart than those beautiful and dignified words that God the Father addressed to me himself.' Our Lady one day said to Saint Mechtilde, 'All the Hail Marys you have given me are blazoned on my cloak. She then held out a portion of her mantle, saying, 'When this part of my cloak is full of Hail Marys I shall gather you up and take you into the Kingdom of my beloved Son.'" Denis the Carthusian, speaking of a vision of Our Lady to one of her clients, said, "We should greet the Blessed Virgin with our hearts, our lips and our deeds, so that she will not be able to say to us, 'These people honor me with their lips but their hearts are far from me.'"

55 Richard of St. Laurence lists the reasons why it is good to say a Hail Mary at the beginning of a sermon:

1 The Church militant should follow the example of Saint Gabriel who saluted Mary with great respect saying "Hail Mary," before he told her the joyous news: "Behold you shall conceive and bear a Son. . . ." Thus the Church greets

the Virgin before announcing the gospel.

2 The congregation will derive more fruit from a sermon that is prefaced by the Hail Mary. The priest who gives the sermon has the angel's role. But in order that the congregation may give birth to Christ in their souls (by faith) they must first obtain this grace from the Blessed Virgin who gave birth to him the first time, and so together with her, they will become mothers of the Son of God. For without Mary they cannot produce Jesus in their souls.

3 The gospel shows us the effectiveness of the Hail Mary and people will receive help from Our Lady through this prayer.

4 Through the Hail Mary, priests avoid pitfalls in their preaching, for Mary gives enlightenment to preachers.

5 The congregation, following Our Lady's example, listens more attentively and is more apt to remember the Word of God.

6 The devil, who is the enemy of the human race and of the preaching of the gospel, is driven off by the Hail Mary. This is most necessary because, to quote Our Lord's words, there is a danger of his coming to take the Word of God out of people's hearts, "lest believing they might be saved."

56 In his first sermon on the holy Rosary Clement Losow says: "After St. Dominic had gone to heaven, devotion to the Rosary waned and it was nearly extinct, when a terrible pestilence broke out in several parts of the country. The afflicted people sought the advice of a saintly hermit who lived a very austere life in the desert. They besought him to pray to God for them. The holy man called upon the Mother of the Savior, imploring her as advocate of sinners to come to the aid of the people. Mary appeared and said, 'These people have stopped singing my praises; that is why these misfortunes have come upon them. Let them return to the devotion of the Rosary and they will again enjoy my protection. I shall obtain the graces of salvation for them if they honor me by saying the Rosary for this psalter is very pleasing to me.' So the people did what Mary asked and made themselves rosaries which they said with all their heart."

1 Paragraphs 49 to 56 is a direct quotation by de Montfort of a book of sermons on the Litany of Loreto, Sermon 313, No. 6, by Justinus Miechovius, O.P.

6

The Secret of Mary

Introduction

The Secret of Mary is a presentation in the form of a spiritual letter of the theme developed in the "True Devotion to the Blessed Virgin." Its authenticity is convincingly established by its long-standing acceptance by the Montfort families, by the style of the composition and by the ideas and even the expressions it contains.

The title itself, "The Secret of Mary," is not St. Louis Marie's but was given by the first publishers who were no doubt inspired by a text of the book: "Happy, indeed sublimely happy, is the person to whom the Holy Spirit reveals the secret of Mary thus imparting to him true knowledge of her" (No. 20).

The original manuscript of this letter has not survived. The present text is that of a copy which dates back to the first half of the eighteenth century. Sister Florence, an early historian of the Daughters of Wisdom, wrote in 1761, "It is through the same channel that we possess this wonderful letter that Father de Montfort wrote to a religious Sister of Nantes on the devotion of the Holy Slavery of Jesus in Mary and to which he added three prayers, one addressed to Jesus, a second for those preaching the Holy Slavery and a third which he entitled, 'the multiplication of the philosopher's stone' or 'the cultivation of the Tree of Life.' "

The "same channel" referred to is believed to be a layman named Joseau and a certain Brother Jacques. The latter, a companion of Montfort, settled at St. Laurent-sur-Sevre in 1716 and became friendly with a young man named Joseau to whom he gave the writings of Fr. de Montfort to be copied. The internal evidence of the document leaves us without any doubt that it was based on the copy made by Joseau and consequently goes back to the first half of the eighteenth century.

A nearly-complete text of the "Secret" was published in 1868. Later in 1898, Fr. Lhoumeau, Superior-General of the Montfort Fathers, published the complete text, leaving out only that part dealing with the "small chains." Further improvements were made in 1926 when Fr. Huré, also a Superior-General, published a standard edition conformed to the original copy and including many footnotes.

The text presented here is based upon the original copy of the manuscript and contains a number of corrections of textual mistakes found in other editions.

The Secret of Mary

concerning the Holy Servitude of the Blessed Virgin

[Introduction]

1 Here is a secret,[1] chosen soul, which the most High God taught me and which I have not found in any book, ancient or modern.[2] Inspired by the Holy Spirit, I am confiding it to you, with these conditions:

1 That you share it only with people who deserve to know it because they are prayerful, give alms to the poor, do penance, suffer persecution, are unworldly, and work seriously for the salvation of souls.

2 That you use this secret to become holy and worthy of heaven, and the more you make use of it the more benefit you will derive from it. Under no circumstances must you let this secret make you idle and inactive. It would then become harmful and lead to your ruin.[3]

3 That you thank God every day of your life for the grace he has given you in letting you into a secret that you do not deserve to know.

As you go on using this secret in the ordinary actions of your life, you will come to understand its value and its excellent quality. At the beginning, however, your understanding of it will be clouded because of the seriousness and number of your sins, and your unconscious love of self.

2 Before you read any further, in an understandable impatience to learn this truth, kneel down and say devoutly the *Ave Maris Stella* ("Hail, thou star of ocean"), and the "Come Holy Spirit," to ask God to help you understand and appreciate this secret given by him. As I have not much time for writing and you have little time for reading, I will be brief in what I have to say.

[1 Necessity of Having a True Devotion to Mary]

[A The Grace of God is absolutely necessary]

3 Chosen soul, living image of God and redeemed by the precious blood of Jesus Christ, God wants you to become holy like him in this life, and glorious like him in the next.[4]

It is certain that growth in the holiness of God is your vocation. All your thoughts, words, actions, everything you suffer or undertake must lead you towards that end. Otherwise you are resisting God in not doing the work for which he created you and for which he is even now keeping you in being. What a marvelous transformation is possible! Dust into light, uncleanness into purity, sinfulness into holiness, creature into Creator, man into God! A marvelous work, I repeat, so difficult in itself, and even impossible for a mere creature to bring about, for only God can accomplish it by giving his grace abundantly and in an extraordinary manner. The very creation of the universe is not as great an achievement as this.

4 Chosen soul, how will you bring this about? What steps will you take to reach the high level to which God is calling you? The means of holiness and salvation are known to everybody, since they are found in the gospel; the masters of the spiritual life have explained them; the saints have practiced them and shown how essential they are for those who wish to be saved and attain perfection. These means are: sincere humility, unceasing prayer, complete self-denial, abandonment to divine Providence, and obedience to the will of God.[5]

5 The grace and help of God are absolutely necessary for us to practice all these, but we are sure that grace will be given to all, though not in the same measure. I say "not in the same measure," because God does not give his graces in equal measure to everyone,[6] although in his infinite goodness he always gives sufficient grace to each. A person who corresponds to great graces performs great works, and one who corresponds to lesser graces performs lesser works. The value and high standard of our actions corresponds to the value and perfection of the grace given by God and responded to by the faithful soul. No one can contest these principles.

God alone

[B To find the grace of God, we must discover Mary]

6 It all comes to this, then. We must discover a simple means to obtain from God the grace needed to become holy. It is precisely this I wish to teach you. My contention is that you must first discover Mary if you would obtain this grace from God.

7 I explain:

1 Mary alone found grace with God for herself and for every individual person.[7] No patriarch nor prophet nor any other holy person of the Old Law could manage to find this grace.

8 2 It was Mary who gave existence and life to the author of all grace, and because of this she is called the "Mother of Grace."[8]

9 3 God the Father, from whom, as from its essential source, every perfect gift and every grace come down to us,[9] gave her every grace when he gave her his Son. Thus, as St. Bernard says, the will of God is manifested to her in Jesus and with Jesus.[10]

10 4 God chose her to be the treasurer, the administrator and the dispenser of all his graces, so that all his graces and gifts pass through her hands. Such is the power that she has received from him that, according to St. Bernardine,[11] she gives the graces of the eternal Father, the virtues of Jesus Christ, and the gifts of the Holy Spirit to whom she wills, as and when she wills, and as much as she wills.[12]

11 5 As in the natural life a child must have a father and a mother, so in the supernatural life of grace a true child of the Church must have God for his Father and Mary for his mother. If he prides himself on having God for his Father but does not give Mary the tender affection of a true child, he is an imposter and his father is the devil.[13]

12 6 Since Mary produced the head of the elect, Jesus Christ, she must also produce the members of that head, that is, all true Christians. A mother does not conceive a head without members, nor members without a head.[14] If anyone, then, wishes to become a member of Jesus Christ, and consequently be filled with grace and truth,[15] he must be formed in Mary through the grace of Jesus Christ, which she possesses with a fullness enabling her to communicate it abundantly to true members of Jesus Christ, her true children.

13 7 The Holy Spirit espoused Mary[16] and produced his greatest work, the incarnate Word, in her, by her and through her. He has never disowned her and so he continues to produce every day, in a mysterious but very real manner, the souls of the elect in her and through her.[17]

14 8 Mary received from God a unique dominion over souls en-

abling her to nourish them and make them more and more godlike.[18] St. Augustine[19] went so far as to say that even in this world all the elect are enclosed in the womb of Mary, and that their real birthday is when this good mother brings them forth to eternal life. Consequently, just as an infant draws all its nourishment from its mother, who gives according to its needs, so the elect draw all their spiritual nourishment and all their strength from Mary.

15 9 It was to Mary that God the Father said, "Dwell in Jacob,"[20] that is, dwell in my elect who are typified by Jacob. It was to Mary that God the Son said, "My dear Mother, your inheritance is in Israel," that is, in the elect. It was to Mary that the Holy Spirit said, "Place your roots in my elect." Whoever, then, is of the chosen and predestinate will have the Blessed Virgin living within him, and he will let her plant in his very soul[21] the roots of every virtue, but especially deep humility and ardent charity.

16 10 Mary is called by St. Augustine, and is indeed, the "living mold of God."[22] In her alone the God-man was formed in his human nature without losing any feature of the Godhead. In her alone, by the grace of Jesus Christ, man is made godlike as far as human nature is capable of it.

A sculptor can make a statue or a life-like model in two ways: 1) By using his skill, strength, experience and good tools to produce a statue out of hard, shapeless matter; 2) By making a cast of it in a mold. The first way is long and involved and open to all sorts of accidents. It only needs a faulty stroke of the chisel or hammer to ruin the whole work. The second is quick, easy, straightforward, almost effortless and inexpensive, but the mold must be perfect and true to life and the material must be easy to handle and offer no resistance.

17 Mary is the great mold of God, fashioned by the Holy Spirit to give human nature to a Man who is God by the hypostatic union, and to fashion through grace men who are like to God. No godly feature is missing from this mold. Everyone who casts himself into it and allows himself to be molded will acquire every feature of Jesus Christ, true God, with little pain or effort, as befits his weak human condition. He will take on a faithful likeness to Jesus with no possibility of distortion, for the devil has never had and never will have any access to Mary, the holy and immaculate Virgin, in whom there is not the least suspicion of a stain of sin.

18 Dear friend, what a difference there is between a soul brought up in the ordinary way to resemble Jesus Christ by people who, like sculptors, rely on their own skill and industry, and a soul thoroughly tractable, entirely detached, most ready to be molded in her by the working of the Holy Spirit. What blemishes and defects, what shadows and distortions, what natural and human imperfections are found in the first soul, and what a faithful and divine likeness to

Jesus is found in the second!

19 There is not and there never will be, either in God's creation or in his mind, a creature in whom he is so honored as in the most Blessed Virgin Mary, not excepting even the saints, the cherubim or the highest seraphim in heaven.

Mary is God's garden of Paradise,[23] his own unspeakable world, into which his Son entered to do wonderful things, to tend it and to take his delight in it. He created a world for the wayfarer, that is, the one we are living in. He created a second world – Paradise – for the Blessed. He created a third for himself, which he named Mary. She is a world unknown to most mortals here on earth. Even the angels and saints in heaven find her incomprehensible, and are lost in admiration of a God who is so exalted and so far above them, so distant from them, and so enclosed in Mary, his chosen world, that they exclaim: "Holy, holy, holy" unceasingly.[24]

20 Happy, indeed sublimely happy, is the person to whom the holy Spirit reveals the secret[25] of Mary, thus imparting to him true knowledge of her. Happy the person to whom the Holy Spirit opens this enclosed garden[26] for him to enter, and to whom the Holy Spirit gives access to this sealed fountain where he can draw water and drink deep draughts of the living waters of grace. That person will find only God and no creature in the most lovable Virgin Mary. But he will find that the infinitely holy and exalted God is at the same time infinitely solicitous for him and understands his weaknesses. Since God is everywhere, he can be found everywhere, even in hell. But there is no place where God can be more present to his creature and more sympathetic to human weakness than in Mary. It was indeed for this very purpose that he came down from heaven. Everywhere else he is the Bread of the strong and the Bread of angels, but living in Mary he is the Bread of children.[27]

21 Let us not imagine, then, as some misguided teachers do, that Mary being simply a creature would be a hindrance to a union with the Creator.[28] Far from it, for it is no longer Mary who lives but Jesus Christ himself, God alone, who lives in her. Her transformation into God far surpasses that experienced by St. Paul[29] and other saints, more than heaven surpasses the earth.

Mary was created only for God, and it is unthinkable that she should reserve even one soul for herself. On the contrary she leads every soul straight to God and to union with him. Mary is the wonderful echo of God.[30] The more a person joins himself to her, the more effectively she unites him to God. When we say "Mary," she re-echoes "God."

When, like St. Elizabeth, we call her blessed,[31] she gives the honor to God. If those misguided ones who were so sadly led astray by the devil, even in their prayer-life, had known how to discover Mary, and Jesus through her, and God through Jesus,[32] they would not have had such terrible falls. The Saints tell us that when we have once found Mary, and through Mary, Jesus, and through Jesus, God the father, then we have discovered every good. When we say "every good," we except nothing. "Every good" includes every grace, continuous friendship with God, every guarantee against the enemies of God, possession of truth to counter every falsehood, endless benefits and unfailing headway against the hazards we meet on the way to salvation, and finally every consolation and joy amid the bitter afflictions of life.

22 This does not mean that one who has discovered Mary through a genuine devotion is exempt from crosses and sufferings.[33] Far from it! One is tried even more than others, because Mary, as Mother of the living, gives to all her children splinters of the tree of life, which is the Cross of Jesus.[34] But while meting out crosses to them she gives the grace to bear them with patience, and even with joy. In this way, the crosses she sends to those who trust themselves to her are rather like sweetmeats, i.e., "sweetened" crosses rather than "bitter" ones. If from time to time they do taste the bitterness of the chalice from which we must drink to become proven friends of God, the consolation and joy which their Mother sends in the wake of their sorrows creates in them a strong desire to carry even heavier and still more bitter crosses.

[C A True Devotion to the Blessed Virgin is indispensable]

23 The difficulty, then, is how to arrive at the true knowledge of the most holy Virgin and so find grace in abundance through her. God, as the absolute Master, can give directly what he ordinarily dispenses only through Mary, and it would be rash to deny that he sometimes does so. However, St. Thomas[35] assures us that, following the order established by his divine Wisdom, God ordinarily imparts his graces to men through Mary. Therefore, if we wish to go to him, seeking union with him, we must use the same means which he used in coming down from heaven to assume our human nature and to impart his graces to us. That means was a complete dependence on Mary his Mother, which is true devotion to her.

[2 What Perfect Devotion to Mary Consists In]

[A Some true devotions to the Blessed Virgin Mary]

24 There are indeed several true devotions to our Lady. I do not intend treating of those which are false.[36]

25 The first[37] consists in fulfilling the duties of our Christian state, avoiding all mortal sin, performing our actions for God more through love than through fear, praying to our Lady occasionally, and honoring her as the Mother of God, but without our devotion to her being exceptional.

26 The second consists in entertaining for our Lady deeper feelings of esteem and love, of confidence and veneration. This devotion inspires us to join the Confraternities of the Holy Rosary and the Scapular, to say the five or fifteen decades of the Rosary, to venerate our Lady's pictures and shrines, to make her known to others, and to enroll in her sodalities. This devotion, in keeping us from sin, is good, holy and praiseworthy, but it is not as perfect as the third, nor as effective in detaching us from creatures, or in practicing that self-denial necessary for union with Jesus Christ.

27 The third devotion to our Lady is one which is unknown to many and practiced by very few. This is the one I am about to present to you.

[B The Perfect Practice of Devotion to Mary]

[1 What it consists in]

28 Chosen soul, this devotion consists in surrendering oneself in the manner of a slave to Mary, and to Jesus through her, and then performing all our actions with Mary, in Mary, through Mary, and for Mary.[38]

Let me explain this statement further.

29 We should choose a special feastday on which to give ourselves. Then, willingly and lovingly and under no constraint, we consecrate and sacrifice to her unreservedly our body and soul. We give to her our material possessions, such as house, family, income, and even the inner possessions of our soul, namely, our merits, graces, virtues and atonements.[39]

Notice that in this devotion we sacrifice to Jesus through Mary all that is most dear to us, that is, the right to dispose of ourselves, of the value of our prayers and alms, of our acts of self-denial and atonements. This is a sacrifice which no religious order[40] would require of its members. We leave everything to the free disposal of our Lady, for her to use as she wills for the greater glory of God, of which she alone is perfectly aware.[41]

30 We leave to her the right to dispose of all the satisfactory and prayer value of our good deeds, so that, after having done so and without going so far as making a vow, we cease to be master over

any good we do. Our Lady may use our good deeds either to bring relief or deliverance to a soul in purgatory, or perhaps to bring a change of heart to a poor sinner.

31 By this devotion we place our merits in the hands of our Lady, but only that she may preserve, increase and embellish them, since merit for increase of grace and glory cannot be handed over to any other person. But we give to her all our prayers and good works, inasmuch as they have intercessory and atonement value, for her to distribute and apply to whom she pleases. If, after having thus consecrated ourselves to our Lady, we wish to help a soul in purgatory, rescue a sinner, or assist a friend by a prayer, an alms, an act of self-denial or an act of self-sacrifice, we must humbly request it of our Lady, abiding always by her decision, which of course remains unknown to us. We can be fully convinced that the value of our actions, being dispensed by that same hand which God himself uses to distribute his gifts and graces to us, cannot fail to be applied for his greatest glory.[42]

32 I have said that this devotion consists in adopting the status of a slave with regard to Mary. We must remember that there are three kinds of slavery.[43]

There is, first, a slavery based on nature. All men, good and bad alike, are slaves of God in this sense.

The second is a slavery of compulsion. The devils and the damned are slaves of God in this second sense.

The third is a slavery of love and free choice. This is the kind chosen by one who consecrates himself to God through Mary, and this is the most perfect way for us human beings to give ourselves to God, our Creator.

33 Note that there is a vast difference between a servant and a slave. A servant claims wages for his services, but a slave can claim no reward. A servant is free to leave his employer when he likes and serves him only for a time, but a slave belongs to his master for life and has no right to leave him. A servant does not give his employer a right of life and death over him, but a slave is so totally committed that his master can put him to death without fearing any action by the law.

It is easy to see, then, that no dependence is so absolute as that of a person who is a slave by compulsion. Strictly speaking, no man should be dependent to this extent on anyone except his Creator. We therefore do not find this kind of slavery among Christians, but only among Muslims and pagans.

34 But happy, very happy indeed, will the generous person be who, prompted by love, consecrates himself entirely to Jesus through Mary as their slave, after having shaken off by baptism the tyrannical slavery of the devil.[44]

[2 The Excellence of this practice of devotion]

35 I would need much more enlightenment from heaven to describe adequately the surpassing merit of this devotional practice.[45] I shall limit myself to these few remarks:

1 In giving ourselves to Jesus through Mary's hands, we imitate God the Father, who gave us his Son only through Mary, and who imparts his graces to us only through Mary.[46] Likewise we imitate God the Son, who by giving us his example for us to follow, inspires us to go to him using the same means he used in coming to us, that is, through Mary. Again, we imitate the Holy Spirit, who bestows his graces and gifts upon us only through Mary. "Is it not fitting," remarks St. Bernard, "that grace should return to its author by the same channel that conveyed it to us?"[47]

36 2 In going to Jesus through Mary, we are really paying honor to our Lord, for we are showing that, because of our sins, we are unworthy to approach his infinite holiness directly on our own. We are showing that we need Mary, his holy Mother, to be our advocate and mediatrix with him who is our Mediator. We are going to Jesus as Mediator and Brother, and at the same time humbling ourselves before him who is our God and our Judge. In short, we are practicing humility, something which always gladdens the heart of God.[48]

37 3 Consecrating ourselves in this way to Jesus through Mary implies placing our good deeds in Mary's hands. Now, although these deeds may appear good to us, they are often defective, and not worthy to be considered and accepted by God, before whom even the stars lack brightness.

Let us pray, then, to our dear Mother and Queen that having accepted our poor present, she may purify it, sanctify it, beautify it, and so make it worthy of God.[49] Any good our soul could produce is of less value to God our Father, in winning his friendship and favor, than a worm-eaten apple would be in the sight of a king, when presented by a poor peasant to his royal master as payment for the rent of his farm. But what would the peasant do if he were wise and if he enjoyed the esteem of the queen? Would he not present his apple first to her, and would she not, out of kindness to the poor man and out of respect for the king, remove from the apple all that was maggoty and spoilt, place it on a golden dish, and surround it with flowers? Could the king then refuse the apple? Would he not accept it most willingly from the hands of his queen who showed such loving concern for that poor man?[50] "If you wish to present something to God, no matter how small it may be," says St. Bernard,[51] "place it in the hands of Mary to ensure its certain acceptance."

38 Dear God, how everything we do comes to so very little! But let us adopt this devotion and place everything in Mary's hands. When we have given her all we possibly can, emptying ourselves completely to do her honor, she far surpasses our generosity and gives us very much for very little. She enriches us with her own merits and virtues. She places our gift on the golden dish of her charity[52] and clothes us, as Rebecca clothed Jacob,[53] in the beautiful garments of her first-born and only son, Jesus Christ, which are his merits, and which are at her disposal. Thus, as her servants and slaves, stripping ourselves of everything to do her honor, we are clad by her in double garments[54]—namely, the garments, adornments, perfumes, merits and virtues of Jesus and Mary. These are imparted to the soul of the slave who has emptied himself and is resolved to remain in that state.

39 4 Giving ourselves in this way to our Lady is a practice of charity towards our neighbor[55] of the highest possible degree, because in making ourselves over to Mary, we give her all that we hold most dear and we let her dispose of it as she wishes in favor of the living and the dead.[56]

40 5 In adopting this devotion, we put our graces, merits and virtues into safe keeping by making Mary the depositary of them.[57] It is as if we said to her, "See, my dear Mother, here is the good that I have done through the grace of your dear Son. I am not capable of keeping it, because of my weakness and inconstancy, and also because so many wicked enemies are assailing me day and night. Alas, every day we see cedars of Lebanon fall into the mire, and eagles which had soared towards the sun become birds of darkness, a thousand of the just falling to the left and ten thousand to the right.[58] But, most powerful Queen, hold me fast lest I fall. Keep a guard on all my possessions lest I be robbed of them. I entrust all I have to you,[59] for I know well who you are, and that is why I confide myself entirely to you. You are faithful to God and man, and you will not suffer anything I entrust to you to perish. You are powerful, and nothing can harm you or rob you of anything you hold.

"When you follow Mary you will not go astray; when you pray to her, you will not despair; when your mind is on her, you will not wander; when she holds you up, you will not fall; when she protects you, you will have no fear; when she guides you, you will feel no fatigue; when she is on your side, you will arrive safely home" (St. Bernard). And again, "She keeps her Son from striking us; she prevents the devil from harming us; she preserves virtue in us; she prevents our merits from being lost and our graces from receding." These words of St. Bernard[60] explain in substance all that I have said. Had I but this one motive to impel me to choose this devotion, namely, that of keeping me in the grace of God and increasing that grace in me, my heart would burn with longing for it.

41 This devotion makes the soul truly free by imbuing it with the liberty of the children of God.[61] Since we lower ourselves willingly to a state of slavery out of love for Mary, our dear Mother, she out of gratitude opens wide our hearts enabling us to walk with giant strides in the way of God's commandments.[62] She delivers our soul from weariness, sadness and scruples. It was this devotion that our Lord taught to Mother Agnes of Langeac,[63] a religious who died in the odor of sanctity, as a sure way of being freed from the severe suffering and confusion of mind which afflicted her. "Make yourself," he said, "my Mother's slave and wear her little chain." She did so, and from that time onwards her troubles ceased.

42 To prove that this devotion is authoritatively sanctioned, we need only recall the bulls of the popes and the pastoral letters of bishops recommending it, as well as the indulgences accorded to it, the confraternities founded to promote it, and the examples of many saints and illustrious people who have practiced it. But I do not see any necessity to record them here.[64]

[3 The Interior Constituents of This Consecration and Its Spirit]

43 I have already said that this devotion consists in performing all our actions with Mary, in Mary, through Mary, and for Mary.[65]

44 It is not enough to give ourselves just once as a slave to Jesus through Mary; nor is it enough to renew that consecration once a month or once a week. That alone would make it just a passing devotion and would not raise the soul to the level of holiness which it is capable of reaching. It is easy to enroll in a confraternity; easy to undertake the devotion; easy to say every day the few vocal prayers prescribed. The chief difficulty is to enter into its spirit, which requires an interior dependence on Mary, and effectively becoming her slave and the slave of Jesus through her. I have met many people who with admirable zeal have set about practicing exteriorly this holy slavery of Jesus and Mary, but I have met only a few who have caught its interior spirit, and fewer still who have persevered in it.

[Act with Mary]

45 1 The essential practice of this devotion is to perform all our actions with Mary. This means that we must take her as the accomplished model for all we have to do.[66]

46 Before undertaking anything, we must forget self and abandon our own views.[67] We must consider ourselves as a mere nothing before God, as being personally incapable of doing anything supernaturally worthwhile or anything conducive to our salvation. We must have habitual recourse to our Lady, becoming one with her and adopting her intentions, even though they are unknown to us. Through Mary we must adopt the intentions of Jesus. In other words, we must become an instrument in Mary's hands for her to act in us and do with us what she pleases, for the greater glory of her Son; and through Jesus for the greater glory of the Father. In this way, we pursue our interior life and make spiritual progress only in dependence on Mary.

[Act in Mary]

47 2 We must always act in Mary,[68] that is to say, we must gradually acquire the habit of recollecting ourselves interiorly and so form within us an idea or a spiritual image of Mary. She must become, as it were, an Oratory for the soul where we offer up our prayers to God without fear of being ignored. She will be as a Tower of David[69] for us where we can seek safety from all our enemies. She will be a burning lamp[70] lighting up our inmost soul and inflaming us with love for God. She will be a sacred place of repose where we can contemplate God in her company. Finally, Mary will be the only means we will use in going to God, and she will become our intercessor for everything we need. When we pray we will pray in Mary. When we receive Jesus in Holy Communion we will place him in Mary for him to take his delight in her. If we do anything at all, it will be in Mary, and in this way Mary will help us to forget self everywhere and in all things.

[Act through Mary]

48 3 We must never go to our Lord except through Mary, using her intercession and good standing with him.[71] We must never be without her when praying to Jesus.

[Act for Mary]

49 4 We must perform all our actions for Mary,[72] which means that as slaves of this noble Queen we will work only for her, promoting her interests and her high renown, and making this the first aim in all our acts, while the glory of God will always be our final end. In everything we must renounce self-love because more often than not, without our being aware of it, selfishness sets itself up as the end of all we work for. We should often repeat from the depths of our heart: "Dear Mother, it is to please you that I go here or there, that I do this or that, that I suffer this pain or that injury."

50 Beware, chosen soul, of thinking that it is more perfect to direct your work and intention straight to Jesus or straight to God.

Without Mary, your work and your intention will be of little value. But if you go to God through Mary, your work will become Mary's work, and consequently will be most noble and most worthy of God.

51 Again, beware of doing violence to yourself, endeavoring to experience pleasure in your prayers and good deeds. Pray and act always with something of that pure faith which Mary showed when on earth, and which she will share with you as time goes on. Poor little slave, let your sovereign Queen enjoy the clear sight of God, the raptures, delights, satisfactions and riches of heaven. Content yourself with a pure faith, which is accompanied by aversions, distractions, weariness and dryness. Let your prayer be: "To whatever Mary my Queen does in heaven, I say Amen, so be it." We cannot do better than this for the time being.

52 Should you not savor immediately the sweet presence of the Blessed Virgin within you, take great care not to torment yourself. For this is a grace not given to everyone, and even when God in his great mercy favors a soul with this grace, it remains none the less very easy to lose it, except when the soul has become permanently aware of it through the habit of recollection. But should this misfortune happen to you, go back calmly to your sovereign Queen[73] and make amends to her.

[4 The effects that this devotion produces in a faithful soul]

53 Experience will teach you much more about this devotion than I can tell you, but, if you remain faithful to the little I have taught you, you will acquire a great richness of grace that will surprise you and fill you with delight.

54 Let us set to work, then, dear soul, through perseverance in the living of this devotion, in order that Mary's soul may glorify the Lord in us and her spirit be within us to rejoice in God her Savior.[74] Let us not think that there was more glory and happiness in dwelling in Abraham's bosom—which is another name for Paradise[75]—than in dwelling in the bosom of Mary where God has set up his throne. (Abbot Guerric).

55 This devotion faithfully practiced produces countless happy effects in the soul.[76] The most important of them is that it establishes, even here on earth, Mary's life in the soul, so that it is no longer the soul that lives, but Mary who lives in it. In a manner of speaking, Mary's soul becomes identified with the soul of her servant. Indeed when by an unspeakable but real grace Mary most holy becomes Queen of a soul, she works untold wonders in it. She is a great wonder-worker especially in the interior of souls. She works there in secret, unsuspected by the soul,[77] as knowledge of it might destroy the beauty of her work.

56 As Mary is everywhere the fruitful Virgin, she produces in the depths of the soul where she dwells a purity of heart and body, a singleness of intention and purpose, and a fruitfulness in good works. Do not think, dear soul, that Mary, the most fruitful of all God's creatures, who went as far as to give birth to a God-man, remains idle in a docile soul. She causes Jesus to live continuously in that soul and that soul to live in continuous union with Jesus. If Jesus is equally the fruit of Mary for each individual soul as for all souls in general, he is even more especially her fruit and her masterpiece in the soul where she is present.

57 To sum up, Mary becomes all things for the soul that wishes to serve Jesus Christ. She enlightens his mind with her pure faith. She deepens his heart with her humility. She enlarges and inflames his heart with her charity, makes it pure with her purity, makes it noble and great through her motherly care. But why dwell any longer on this? Experience alone will teach us the wonders wrought by Mary in the soul, wonders so great that the wise and the proud, and even a great number of devout people find it hard to credit them.

58 As it was through Mary that God came into the world the first time in a state of self-abasement and privation, may we not say that it will be again through Mary that he will come the second time? For does not the whole Church expect him to come and reign over all the earth and to judge the living and the dead? No one knows how and when this will come to pass, but we do know that God, whose thoughts are further from ours than heaven is from earth,[78] will come at a time and in a manner least expected, even by the most scholarly of men and those most versed in Holy Scripture, which gives no clear guidance on this subject.

59 We are given reason to believe that, towards the end of time and perhaps sooner than we expect, God will raise up great men filled with the Holy Spirit and imbued with the spirit of Mary. Through them Mary, Queen most powerful, will work great wonders in the world, destroying sin and setting up the kingdom of Jesus her Son upon the ruins of the corrupt kingdom of the world. These holy men will accomplish this by means of the devotion of which I only trace the main outlines and which suffers from my incompetence.

[5 Exterior Practices]

60 Besides interior practices, which we have just mentioned, this devotion has certain exterior practices which must not be omitted or neglected.[79]

God alone

[Consecration and its renewal]

61 The first is to choose a special feastday to consecrate ourselves through Mary to Jesus, whose slaves we are making ourselves. This is an occasion for receiving Holy Communion and spending the day in prayer. At least once a year on the same day, we should renew the act of consecration.[80]

[Offering of a tribute in submission to the Blessed Virgin]

62 The second is to give our Lady every year on that same day some little tribute[81] as a token of our servitude and dependence. This has always been the customary homage paid by slaves to their master. This tribute could consist of an act of self-denial or an alms, or a pilgrimage, or a few prayers. St. Peter Damian tells us that his brother, Blessed Marino,[82] used to give himself the discipline in public on the same day every year before the altar of our Lady. This kind of zeal is not required, nor would we counsel it. But what little we give to our Lady we should at least offer with a heart that is humble and grateful.

[A Special Celebration of the Feast of the Annunciation]

63 The third practice is to celebrate every year with special fervor the feast of the Annunciation of our Lord.[93] This is the distinctive feast of this devotion and was chosen so that we might honor and imitate that dependence which the eternal Word accepted on this day out of love for us.

[The Saying of the Little Crown and the Magnificat]

64 The fourth practice is to say every day, without the obligation of sin, the prayer entitled "The Little Crown of the Blessed Virgin," which comprises three Our Fathers and twelve Hail Marys,[84] and to say frequently the Magnificat, which is the only hymn composed by our Lady. In the Magnificat we thank God for favoring us in the past, and we beg further blessings from him in the future. One special time when we should not fail to say it is during thanksgiving after Holy Communion. A person so scholarly as Gerson informs us that our Lady herself used to recite it in thanksgiving after Holy Communion.

[The Wearing of a little chain]

65 The fifth is the wearing of a small blessed chain either around the neck, on the arm, on the foot, or about the body.[85] Strictly speaking, this practice can be omitted without affecting the essential nature of the devotion, but just the same it would be wrong to despise or condemn it, and foolhardy to neglect it.

Here are the reasons for wearing this external sign:

1 It signifies that we are free from the baneful chains of original and actual sin which held us in bondage.

2 By it we show our esteem for the cords and bonds of love with which our Lord let himself be bound that we may be truly free.

3 As these bonds are bonds of love,[86] they remind us that we should do nothing except under the influence of love.

4 Finally, wearing this chain recalls to us once more that we are dependent on Jesus and Mary as their slaves. Eminent people[87] who had become slaves of Jesus and Mary valued these little chains so much that they were unhappy at not being allowed to trail them publicly like the slaves of the Muslims.

These chains of love are more valuable and more glorious than the necklaces of gold and precious stones worn by emperors, because they are the illustrious insignia of Jesus and Mary, and signify the bonds uniting us to them.

It should be noted that if the chains are not of silver, they should for convenience sake at least be made of iron.

They should never be laid aside at any time, so that they may be with us even to the day of judgment. Great will be the joy, glory and triumph of the faithful slave on that day when, at the sound of the trumpet, his bones rise from the earth still bound by the chain of holy bondage, which to all appearance has not decayed. This thought alone should convince a devout slave never to take off his chain, however inconvenient it may be.

[Supplement]

Prayer to Jesus

66 Most loving Jesus, permit me to express my heartfelt gratitude to you for your kindness in giving me to your holy Mother through the devotion of holy bondage, and so making her my advocate to plead with your Majesty on my behalf, and make up for all that I lack through my inadequacy.

Alas, O Lord, I am so wretched that without my dear Mother I would certainly be lost. Yes, I always need Mary when I am approaching you. I need her to calm your just indignation at the many offenses I have committed every day. I need her to save me from the just sentence of eternal punishment I have deservedly incurred. I need her to turn to you, speak to you, pray to you, approach you and please you. I need her to help me save my soul and the souls of others. In a word, I need her so that I may always do your holy will and seek your greater glory in everything I do.

Would that I could publish throughout the whole world the mercy which you have shown me! Would that the whole world could know that without Mary I would now be doomed! If only I could offer adequate thanks for such a great benefit as Mary! She is within me.[88] What a precious possession and what a consolation for me. Should I not in return be all hers? If I were not, how ungrateful would I be. My dear Savior, send me death rather than I should be guilty of such a lapse, for I would rather die than not belong to Mary.

Like St. John the Evangelist at the foot of the Cross,[89] I have taken her times without number as my total good and as often have I given myself to her. But if I have not done so as perfectly as you, dear Jesus, would wish, I now do so according to your desire. If you still see in my soul or body anything that does not belong to this noble Queen, please pluck it out and cast it far from me, because anything of mine which does not belong to Mary is unworthy of you.

67 Holy Spirit, grant me all these graces. Implant in my soul the tree of true life,[90] which is Mary. Foster it and cultivate it so that it grows and blossoms and brings forth the fruit of life in abundance. Holy Spirit, give me a great love and a longing for Mary, your exalted spouse. Give me a great trust in her maternal heart and a continuous access to her compassion, so that with her you may truly form Jesus, great and powerful, in me until I attain the fullness of his perfect age.[91] Amen.

Prayer to Mary
for her faithful slaves

68 Hail, Mary, most beloved daughter of the eternal Father; hail, Mary, most admirable mother of the Son; hail, Mary, most faithful spouse of the Holy Spirit; hail, Mary, Mother most dear, Lady most lovable. Queen most powerful! Hail, Mary, my joy, my glory, my heart and soul.[92] You are all mine through God's mercy, but I am all yours in justice. Yet I do not belong sufficiently to you, and so once again, as a slave who always belongs to his master, I give myself wholly to you, reserving nothing for myself or for others.

If you still see anything in me which is not given to you, please take it now. Make yourself completely owner of all my capabilities. Destroy in me everything that is displeasing to God. Uproot it and bring it to nothing. Implant in me all that you deem to be good; improve it and make it increase in me.

May the light of your faith dispel the darkness of my mind. May your deep humility take the place of my pride. May your heavenly contemplation put an end to the distractions of my wandering imagination. May your continuous vision of God fill my memory with his presence. May the burning love of your heart inflame the coldness of mine. May your virtues take the place of my sins. May your merits be my adornment and make up for my unworthiness before God.[93] Finally, most dearly beloved Mother, grant, if it be possible, that I may have no other spirit but yours to know Jesus and his divine will. May I have no soul but yours to praise and glorify the Lord. May I have no heart but yours to love God purely and ardently as you love him.

69 I do not ask for visions or revelations, for sensible devotion or even spiritual pleasures.[94] It is your privilege to see God clearly in perpetual light. It is your privilege to savor the delights of heaven where nothing is without sweetness. It is your privilege to triumph gloriously in heaven at the right hand of your Son without further humiliation, and to command angels, men, and demons, with readiness on their part. It is your privilege to dispose at your own choice of all the good gifts of God with no exception.

Such, most holy Mary, is the excellent portion which the Lord has given you, and which will never be taken from you,[95] and which gives me great joy. As for my portion here on earth, I wish only to have a share in yours, that is, to have simple faith without seeing or tasting, to suffer joyfully without the consolations of men, to die daily to myself without flinching, to work gallantly for you even until death without any self-interest, as the most worthless of your slaves. The only grace I beg you in your kindness to obtain for me is that every day and moment of my life I may say this threefold Amen: Amen, so be it, to all you did upon earth; Amen, so be it, to all you are doing now in heaven; Amen, so be it, to all you are doing in my soul. In that way, you and you alone will fully glorify Jesus in me during all my life and my eternity. Amen.

The Care and Growth of the
Tree of Life,
or, in other words, how best to cause
Mary to Live and Reign
in our souls

[1 The Holy Slavery of Love. The Tree of Life]

70 Have you understood with the help of the Holy Spirit what I have tried to explain in the preceding pages? If so, be thankful to God. It is a secret of which very few people are aware. If you have discovered this treasure in the field of Mary, this pearl of great price,[96] you should sell all you have to purchase it. You must offer yourself to Mary, happily lose yourself in her, only to find God in her.

If the Holy Spirit has planted in your soul the true Tree of Life,[97] which is the devotion that I have just explained, you should see carefully to its cultivation, so that it will yield its fruit in due season. This devotion is like the mustard seed of the Gospel,[98] which is indeed the smallest of all seeds, but nevertheless it grows into a big plant, shooting up so high that the birds of the air, that is, the elect, come and make their nest in its branches. They repose there, shaded from the heat of the sun, and safely hidden from beasts of prey.

[2 How to cultivate it]

Here is the best way, chosen soul, to cultivate it:

71 1 This tree, once planted in a docile heart, requires fresh air and no human support. Being of heavenly origin, it must be uninfluenced by any creature, since a creature might hinder it from rising up towards God who created it. Hence you must not rely on your own endeavors or your natural talents or your personal standing or the guidance of men. You must resort to Mary, relying solely on her help.

72 2 The person in whose soul this tree has taken root must, like a good gardener, watch over it and protect it. For this tree, having life and capable of producing the fruit of life, should be raised and tended with enduring care and attention of soul. A soul that desires to be holy will make this its chief aim and occupation.

73 Whatever is likely to choke the tree or in the course of time prevent its yielding fruit, such as thorns and thistles, must be cut away and rooted out. This means that by self-denial and self-discipline you must sedulously cut short and even give up all empty pleasures and useless dealings with other creatures. In other words, you must crucify the flesh, keep a guard over the tongue, and mortify the bodily senses.

74 3 You must guard against grubs doing harm to the tree. These parasites are love of self and love of comfort, and they eat away the green foliage of the Tree and frustrate the fair hope it offered of yielding good fruit; for love of self is incompatible with love of Mary.

75 4 You must not allow this Tree to be damaged by destructive animals, that is, by sins, for they may cause its death simply by their contact. They must not be allowed even to breathe upon the Tree, because their mere breath, that is, venial sins, which are most dangerous when we do not trouble ourselves about them.

76 5 It is also necessary to water this Tree regularly with your Communions, Masses and other public and private prayers. Otherwise it will not continue bearing fruit.

77 6 Yet you need not be alarmed when the winds blow and shake this tree, for it must happen that the storm-winds of temptation will threaten to bring it down, and snow and frost tend to smother it. By this we mean that this devotion to our Blessed Lady will surely be called into question and attacked. But as long as we continue steadfastly in tending it, we have nothing to fear.

[3 Its lasting fruit: Jesus Christ]

78 Chosen soul, provided you thus carefully cultivate the Tree of Life, which has been freshly planted in your soul by the Holy Spirit, I can assure you that in a short time it will grow so tall that the birds of the air will make their home in it. It will become such a good tree that it will yield in due season the sweet and adorable Fruit of honor and grace, which is Jesus, who has always been and will always be the only fruit of Mary.

Happy is that soul in which Mary, the tree of life,[99] is planted. Happier still is the soul in which she has been able to grow and blossom. Happier again is the soul in which she brings forth her fruit. But happiest of all is the soul which savors the sweetness of Mary's fruit and preserves it up till death and then beyond to all eternity. Amen.

"Let him who possesses this, hold fast to it."[100]

Footnotes to The Secret of Mary

1 Frequently in his writings Montfort speaks of a "secret." In SM 20 and TD 11, 248, 264, he uses the term in referring to the knowledge of Mary and the marvels of grace operated in her by God. Elsewhere "secret" is applied by him to the knowledge and practice of a marvelous means of acquiring holiness.

We may say that in Montfort's mind the term "secret" should be understood as meaning:

1) that the place and function of Mary in the saving work of God have not been sufficiently understood or inserted into the reality of the Christian life;

2) that we need a special grace from God to "understand and relish" (No. 2) the nature of this Marian devotion which enables us in our spiritual life to respond as perfectly as possible to the divine plan of salvation;

3) that this special Marian way of life does not just consist in a number of practices but in a disposition of the soul producing interior acts which constitute its essential element and are a rich source of grace.

2 Montfort writes in LEW 219, TD 118, 159, and SM 42 that he had read almost all the books on the subject of devotion to Mary and

had never found a form of devotion to her like the one he is proposing. This devotion, he states, goes so far back into the history of the Church that it is impossible to see where it began (cf. TD 159, SM 42).

Cf. PIUS XII: *Discourse of the pilgrims gathered for the Canonization of St. Louis Marie de Montfort,* 21 July 1947: "He attracted the enlightenment of God more by his life of prayer than by his active work. It was by this interior guidance that he understood and explained in his unique way what he found in the deposit of Revelation and in the Church's traditional devotion."

3 This "caution" recalls the parable of the talents.

4 Cf. Mt. 5:48.

5 Montfort enlarges upon these means in other places, for example, Humility of heart: TD 143, 144; Continual prayer: LEW 184-193; Universal mortification: LEW 194-202; Abandonment to Providence: ACM 3-4; Conformity to the will of God: FC 51-53.

6 Cf. Rom. 12:6.

7 Cf. Lk. 1:30; SAINT BERNARD, *On the Annunciation, sermon 3.*

8 This is a Marian title found frequently in spiritual authors. Montfort's text evokes the ideas expressed in *Lumen Gentium* No. 61: Mary's unique cooperation in the Savior's work for the restoration of supernatural life to souls. . . . This is the reason why she has been our Mother in the order of grace.

9 Cf. Jas. 1:17.

10 Cf. TD 25, 141.

11 Cf. TD 25.

12 This whole number is a résumé of TD 23-25.

13 Cf. TD 30.

14 Cf. TD 32.

15 Cf. Jn. 1:14.

16 Cf. TD 4.

17 This whole number is a résumé of TD 34-36.

18 Cf. TD 37.

19 Cf. TD 33.

20 These three quotations are taken from Sir. 24:8, 12, and a fuller commentary is given in TD 29, 31, 34.

21 Mary can be said to be present in us 1) by seeing and knowing us in the beatific vision; 2) by her influence as our spiritual Mother; 3) by our mystical union with her by love.

22 Attributed to St. Augustine but the true author of the sermon where it appears is Ambroise Autpert.

23 This expression is unique in the works of Montfort. Generally he uses the phrase "Paradise of the new Adam" (cf. TD 6, Note).

24 Is. 6:3.

25 SM 1, Note 1.

26 Song 4:12; TD 263, Note

27 Cf. LEW 190; TD 208.

28 Cf. TD 164-165.

29 Cf. Gal. 2:20.

30 Cf. TD 225.

31 Cf. Lk. 1:45.
32 Cf. TD 86.
33 Cf. TD 153-154.
34 Cf. SM 70. Note
35 This is a difficult text. Montfort is certainly teaching the universality of the mediation of Mary in the distribution of graces *according to God's plan.* This teaching must be placed alongside the teaching of Vatican II, No. 60: In the words of the Apostle our Mediator is unique. There is only one God and only one mediator between God and man, Christ Jesus . . . (1 Tim. 2:5). Mary's function as Mother of men makes for no dimming or diminution of this unique mediation of Christ but rather demonstrates his power. All the Blessed Virgin's salutary influence on men has its origin not in real necessity but in the divine decision; his mediation is its support, it is wholly dependent on that mediation, draws all its strength from it. Later in No. 62 the document makes a more general statement: "The unique mediation of the Redeemer does not exclude but rather stimulates among creatures a participation and cooperation which is varied but which originates from a single source."

The interpretation of this text can be reduced to three simple questions:

1) What is the order established by God in communicating himself to men? Montfort answers by saying that in the order of grace divine Wisdom does this ordinarily through Mary.

2) Absolutely speaking, can God communicate himself directly to men? Montfort answers, Yes, since God as the absolute Master can give to men directly what he ordinarily gives through Mary.'

3) Does it actually happen that God gives graces directly to men independently of Mary? Montfort says it would be rash to say No.

36 Cf. TD 92, Note
37 Compare these three numbers 25-27 with TD 99, 115-117.
38 Cf. TD 257 where this order is given differently.
39 Cf. TD 121.
40 That is, Order or religious Congregation.
41 Cf. TD 123-124, 136.
42 Cf. TD 122, 132.
43 Cf. TD 69, 71.
44 Cf. TD 126. Montfort presents his consecration as a perfect renewal of baptismal vows.
45 Cf. TD 135, ff., where Montfort treats at length of the motives which recommend this devotion.
46 Cf. TD 139-140.
47 Cf. TD 142, Note
48 Cf. TD 83-86, 143.
49 This whole passage is developed in TD 146-150.
50 The same example is given in TD 147.
51 Cf. TD 149, Note
52 TD 144, 216.
53 In TD 183-212 Montfort gives a long commentary on the biblical figure of Rebecca and Jacob.

54 Prov. 31:21; cf. TD 206.
55 Cf. TD 171-172.
56 In TD 132, Montfort answers objections on this point.
57 This number is a résumé of the 8th motive of TD 173-178.
58 Cf. Ps. 19:7.
59 1 Tim. 6:20; 2 Tim. 1:12.
60 SAINT BERNARD, *Hom. 2 super Missus est.* Cf. TD 174.
61 Cf. Rom. 8:21. This motive is developed in TD 169-170, 215.
62 Cf. Ps. 18:6.
63 AGNES DE LANGEAC (1602-1634), Prioress of the Dominican Sisters of the community of St. Catherine of Langeac. Cf. TD 170.
64 Cf. TD 159-163 where Montfort gives a quick historical survey of eminent people who have practiced this devotion over the centuries.
65 The order of these acts is given differently in TD 257.
66 Cf. TD 260.
67 Montfort gives here two very important preconditions: to renounce oneself and to give oneself to Mary. In SM we find them here in the formula "With." In the TD it is placed in the formula "Through," No. 259.
68 In explaining this formula Montfort uses here, as in TD 261-264, a series of symbols signifying the activity of our Lady and the cooperation of the soul in a life of intimate union which goes as far as identification.
69 Cf. Song 4:4.
70 Cf. Mt. 5:15; Lk. 8:16; 11:33.
71 Cf. TD 258.
72 Cf. TD 265.
73 Montfort speaks here of a very high degree of grace, not given to everybody.
74 Cf. SAINT AMBROSE, *Exposit. in Luc II,* No. 26.
75 Cf. Lk. 16:22-23.
76 Montfort explains these effects in TD 213-225.
77 Accommodation to Mary of Gal. 2:20.
78 Reference to Is. 55:8, 9.
79 Cf. TD 226-256.
80 Cf. TD 227-231.
81 Cf. TD 232.
82 Cf. TD 159. Note
83 Cf. TD 243-248.
84 Cf. TD 234, 235. The Montfortian version of the "Little Crown" is given among the Morning and Night Prayers.
85 Concerning the little chains cf. TD 236-242.
86 Hos. 11:4; cf. also TD 237, 241.
87 In TD 242 Montfort quotes the examples of Fr. Vincent Caraffa and Mother Agnes of Jesus.
88 Ps. 118:56, quoted also in TD 179.
89 Cf. Jn. 19:27; TD 179. Note 295.
90 Cf. SM 70. Note 97 below.
91 Cf. TD 33. Note 59. This text (Eph. 4:13) is very dear to Montfort and is met frequently in his writings. Cf. Act of Consecration in

LEW 223.

92 This greeting to Mary recalls that of the final prayer of the "Little Crown" (Morning Prayer) and can be considered as a renewal of the act of Consecration.

93 These two phrases should be understood in the sense given in SM 37.

94 Cf. SM 51.

95 Allusion made to Lk. 10:42.

96 Allusion to Mt. 13:44-46.

97 The expression "Tree of Life" was first spoken of in Genesis 2:9. Montfort used the term in SM 22 in reference to the Cross of Jesus. Here, however, and in LEW and TD he identifies it with perfect devotion to Mary and describes the way to cultivate it.

98 Marian accommodation of Mk. 4:31.

99 Cf. SM 70. Note 97 above.

100 These words seem to be inspired by 2 Thess. 2:7. The text of Montfort signifies: Let him who possesses this precious doctrine preserve it with care and faithfulness.

C'est par la tres sainte vierge Marie que Jesus-Christ est venu au monde, et c'est aussi par elle qu'il doit regner dans le monde.

Marie a été tres cachée dans sa vie c'est pourquoi elle est appellée par le St esprit et l'église, alma mater, mere cachée, et secrette. Son humilité a été si profonde qu'elle n'a point eu sur la terre d'attrait plus puissant et plus continuel que de se cacher a elle même et a toute creature pour n'être connue que de Dieu seul. Dieu pour l'exaucer dans les demandes qu'elle lui fit de la cacher, appauvrir et humilier, a pris plaisir a la cacher dans sa conception dans sa naissance, dans sa vie, dans ses mysteres, dans sa resurrection et assomption a l'égard de presque toute creature humaine. Ses parents même ne la connoissoint pas et les anges se demandoint souvent les uns aux autres, quae est ista qui est celle la, parce que le tres haut la leur cachoit ou s'il leur en decouvroit quelque chose, il leur en cachoit infiniment

7 True Devotion to the Blessed Virgin

Introduction

This is the best known although not the most important work of Saint Louis-Marie de Montfort. In No. 110, we are given the nature of the work, the people it was written for and some idea of the date of the manuscript: "I have taken up my pen to write down what for many years I have been teaching with success both publicly and in private in my missions."

Montfort's aim was to show the role of Mary in the plan of God, in one's life as a baptized person and in one's apostolic life. He addressed himself therefore to all baptized Catholics and especially to the "poor and simple" among them (No. 26).

Nothing in the text would indicate the exact date of the work. All we know is that he had preached its message for "many years" and therefore must have written the book towards the end of his missionary career. He mentions, in No. 159, that Fr. Boudon had died "a short time ago" and it is known that this good priest died in 1702.

Three dates have been suggested for its composition:

1 The winter of 1710-1711 when Montfort was obliged to rest for a few months at Nantes.

2 The autumn of 1712 when he stayed at the hermitage of Saint Eloi, near La Rochelle.

3 During the second half of 1715 when he spent several months in the forest of Mervent.

Tradition has favored the year 1712.

No one has ever questioned the authenticity of the manuscript. During the French Revolution it was buried for safety with other books and documents, "in the darkness and silence of a chest" (No. 114) and hidden in a field at Saint-Laurent-sur-Sèvre. After the rev-

olution it remained forgotten until it was found on April 29th, 1842. The handwriting was immediately recognized as that of Saint Louis-Marie, but there are some misgivings about a number of corrections made to the text although some of them have evidently been made by the saint himself.

The manuscript, as found, comprised a number of detached leaves with evidently many missing at the beginning and at the end. The author speaks in Nos. 227, 228 and 256, of a first part which contains a method of spending at least 12 days in emptying oneself of the spirit of the world which is opposed to that of Jesus Christ, the Litany of the Holy Spirit with an accompanying prayer and practices implying rejection of the world. These are missing. Then, in No. 230, he speaks of a second part containing the prayer of Saint Augustine (which in fact he gives in No. 67). Again, he mentions in Nos. 231 and 236 the formula of Consecration and blessing of little chains which we will find "further on." These also are missing. We cannot know for sure what else is contained in the missing pages but we know that what we actually possess is an adequate presentation of the Marian theme.

Almost immediately after the finding, i.e., 127 years after the death of its author, the manuscript was printed and published. Since then the "True Devotion" has run into hundreds of editions in over 20 languages.

As the first pages of the manuscript were missing, the first publishers had to choose a title for the work. They decided upon "True Devotion to the Blessed Virgin," and this title has been maintained in all subsequent editions. In recent times, however, it has been thought fitting to add as sub-title the definition Montfort gives of his work in No. 227: "Preparation for the Reign of Jesus Christ."

Where did Montfort find the inspiration for this work? He himself gives us some indications. In No. 118 he writes: "Having read nearly every book on devotion to the Blessed Virgin and talked to the most saintly and learned people of the day, I can now state with conviction that I have never known or heard of any devotion to our Lady which is comparable to the one I am about to speak of." It is certain that one of the persons he consulted was Fr. Tronson, the superior of the seminary of Saint Sulpice in Paris, a priest renowned for exceptional prudence and holiness.

Reading the "True Devotion," we cannot help being impressed by the author's familiarity with the Bible and the Fathers of the Church. The work is a tissue of scriptural texts and allusions. He had a remarkable knowledge of spiritual authors, due no doubt to his work in the library of the seminary of Saint Sulpice when he was a student there. Although he owes many of his ideas to the Jesuits, Poiré and Crasset, he was really a spiritual son of the French School of spirituality of the seventeenth century. Authors such as

Bérulle, Olier, John Eudes, Boudon and de Renty, who belonged to that school, certainly influenced him, as did the classical Marian writers. He intended his doctrine to be rooted in the tradition of Church teaching and he goes as far as to state in No. 163, that this devotion "could not be condemned without overthrowing the foundations of Christianity." He had found no devotion like the one he is teaching and stresses that it makes for a deep interior life. "No other devotion," he declares, "keeps us more firmly in the grace of God in us" (No. 118). It was a devotion that already existed but he gave it a new shape and clothed it with helpful practices, both interior and exterior, and, strengthened by his own experience in living it, he declares it to be a "secret that the Spirit of Jesus Christ will reveal" (No. 119).

Today this shape may appear outmoded. The "True Devotion" is a work that was conceived and written in an age and milieu far different from those of the twentieth century. Many of its expressions, illustrations and biblical interpretations may not be acceptable to the modern mentality and erudition. But the earnest reader, understanding the main thrust and substance of the work, will have the joy of encountering a solid doctrine which continues to engage the attention of theologians and the interest of truly spiritual people.

[Introduction of St. Louis Marie de Montfort]

1 It is through the blessed Virgin Mary that Jesus Christ came into the world, and it is also through her that he must reign in the world.

2 Because Mary remained hidden during her life, she is called by the Holy Spirit and the Church, *Alma Mater,* Mother hidden and unknown.[1] So great was her humility that she desired nothing more upon earth than to remain unknown to herself and to others, and to be known only to God.

3 In answer to her prayers to remain hidden, poor and lowly, God was pleased to conceal her from nearly every other human creature in her conception, her birth, her life, her mysteries, her resurrection and assumption. Her own parents did not really know her; and the angels would often ask one another, "Who can she possibly be?"[2] for God had hidden her from them, or if he did reveal anything to them, it was nothing compared with what he withheld.

4 God the Father willed that she should perform no miracle during her life, at least no public one, although he had given her the power to do so.[3] God the Son willed that she should speak very little although he had imparted his wisdom to her.

Even though Mary was his faithful spouse,[4] God the Holy Spirit willed that his apostles and evangelists should say very little about her and then only as much as was necessary to make Jesus known.

5 Mary is the supreme masterpiece of Almighty God and he has reserved the knowledge and possession of her for himself.[5] She is the glorious Mother of God the Son, who chose to humble and conceal her during her lifetime in order to foster her humility. He called her, "Woman,"[6] as if she were a stranger, although in his heart he esteemed and loved her above all men and angels. Mary is the sealed fountain[7] and the faithful spouse of the Holy Spirit where only he may enter. She is the sanctuary and resting-place of the Blessed Trinity where God dwells in greater and more divine splendor than anywhere else in the universe, not excluding his dwelling above the cherubim and seraphim. No creature, however pure, may enter there without being specially privileged.[8]

6 I declare with the saints: Mary is the earthly paradise of Jesus Christ the new Adam,[9] where he became man by the power of the Holy Spirit, in order to accomplish in her wonders beyond our understanding. She is the vast and divine world of God where unutterable marvels and beauties are to be found. She is the magnificence of the Almighty[10] where he hid his only Son, as in his own bosom, and with him everything that is most excellent and precious. What great and hidden things the all-powerful God has done for this wonderful creature, as she herself had to confess in spite of her great humility, "The Almighty has done great things for me."[11] The world does not know these things because it is incapable and unworthy of knowing them.

7 The saints have said wonderful things of Mary, the holy City of God, and, as they themselves admit, they were never more eloquent and more pleased than when they spoke of her. And yet they maintain that the height of her merits rising up to the throne of the Godhead cannot be perceived;[12] the breadth of her love which is wider than the earth cannot be measured; the greatness of the power which she wields over one who is God[13] cannot be conceived; and the depths of her profound humility and all her virtues and graces cannot be sounded. What incomprehensible height! What indescribable breadth! What immeasurable greatness! What an impenetrable abyss![14]

8 Every day, from one end of the earth to the other, in the highest heaven and in the lowest abyss, all things preach, all things proclaim the wondrous Virgin Mary. The nine choirs of angels, men and women of every age, rank and religion, both good and evil, even the very devils themselves are compelled by the force of truth, willingly or unwillingly, to call her blessed.

According to St. Bonaventure, all the angels in heaven unceasingly call out to her: "Holy, holy, holy Mary, Virgin Mother of God."[15] They greet her countless times each day with the angelic greeting, "Hail, Mary," while prostrating themselves before her, begging her as a favor to honor them with one of her requests. According to St. Augustine, even St. Michael, though prince of all the heavenly court, is the most eager of all the angels to honor her and lead others to honor her. At all times he awaits the privilege of going at her word to the aid of one of her servants.[16]

9 The whole world is filled with her glory,[17] and this is especially true of Christian peoples, who have chosen her as guardian and protectress of kingdoms, provinces, dioceses, and towns. Many cathedrals are consecrated to God in her name. There is no church without an altar dedicated to her, no country or region without at least one of her miraculous images where all kinds of afflictions are cured and all sorts of benefits received. Many are the confraternities and associations honoring her as patron; many are the orders under her name and protection; many are the members of sodalities and religious of all congregations who voice her praises and make known her compassion. There is not a child who does not praise her by lisping a Hail, Mary. There is scarcely a sinner, however hardened, who does not possess some spark of confidence in her. The very devils in hell, while fearing her, show her respect.

10 And yet in truth we must still say with the saints: *De Maria numquam satis:* We have still not praised, exalted, honored, loved and served Mary adequately. She is worthy of even more praise, respect, love and service.[18]

11 Moreover, we should repeat after the Holy Spirit, "All the glory of the king's daughter is within,"[19] meaning that all the external glory which heaven and earth vie with each other to give her is nothing compared to what she has received interiorly from her Creator, namely, a glory unknown to insignificant creatures like us, who cannot penetrate into the secrets of the king.[20]

12 Finally, we must say in the words of the apostle Paul, "Eye has not seen, nor has ear heard, nor has the heart of man understood"[21] the beauty, the grandeur, the excellence of Mary, who is indeed a miracle of miracles[22] of grace, nature and glory. "If you wish to understand the mother," says a saint, "then understand the Son. She is a worthy Mother of God." *Hic taceat omnis lingua:* Here let every tongue be silent.

13 My heart has dictated with special joy all that I have written to show that Mary has been unknown up till now, and that that is one of the reasons why Jesus Christ is not known as he should be.[23] If then, as is certain, the knowledge and the kingdom of Jesus Christ must come into the world, it can only be as a necessary consequence of the knowledge and reign of Mary. She who first gave him to the world will establish his kingdom in the world.

[I True Devotion to our Lady in General]

[Chapter 1 Necessity of Devotion to Our Lady]

[1 *Mary's part in the Incarnation*]

14 With the whole Church I acknowledge that Mary, being a mere creature fashioned by the hands of God is, compared to his infinite majesty, less than an atom, or rather is simply nothing, since he alone can say, "I am he who is."[24] Consequently, this great Lord, who is ever independent and self-sufficient, never had and does not now have any absolute need of the Blessed Virgin for the accomplishment of his will and the manifestation of his glory. To do all things he has only to will them.[25]

15 However, I declare that, considering things as they are, because God has decided to begin and accomplish his greatest works through the Blessed Virgin ever since he created her, we can safely believe that he will not change his plan in the time to come, for he is God and therefore does not change in his thoughts or his way of acting.[26]

16 God the Father gave his only Son to the world only through Mary. Whatever desires the patriarchs may have cherished, whatever entreaties the prophets and saints of the Old Law may have made for 4,000 years to obtain that treasure, it was Mary alone who merited it and found grace before God[27] by the power of her prayers and the perfection of her virtues. "The world being unworthy," said St. Augustine, "to receive the Son of God directly from the hands of the Father, he gave his son to Mary for the world to receive him from her."

The Son of God became man for our salvation but only in Mary and through Mary.

God the Holy Spirit formed Jesus Christ in Mary but only after having asked her consent[28] through one of the chief ministers of his court.

17 God the Father imparted to Mary his fruitfulness[29] as far as a mere creature was capable of receiving it, to enable her to bring forth his Son and all the members of his mystical body.

18 God the Son came down into her virginal womb as a new Adam into his earthly paradise,[30] to take his delight there and produce hidden wonders of grace.

God-made-man found freedom in imprisoning himself in her womb. He displayed power in allowing himself to be borne by this young maiden. He found his glory and that of his Father in hiding his splendors from all creatures here below and revealing them only to Mary. He glorified his independence and his majesty in depending upon this lovable virgin in his conception, his birth, his presentation in the temple, and in the thirty years of his hidden life. Even at his death she had to be present so that he might be united with her in one sacrifice and be immolated with her consent to the eternal Father,[31] just as formerly Isaac was offered in sacrifice by Abraham when he accepted the will of God.[32] It was Mary who nursed him, fed him, cared for him, reared him, and sacrificed him for us.

The Holy Spirit could not leave such wonderful and inconceivable dependence of God unmentioned in the Gospel,[33] though he concealed almost all the wonderful things that Wisdom Incarnate did during his hidden life in order to bring home to us its infinite value and glory. Jesus gave more glory to God his Father by submitting to his Mother for thirty years than he would have given him had he converted the whole world by working the greatest miracles.[34] How highly then do we glorify God when to please him we submit ourselves to Mary, taking Jesus as our sole model!

19 If we examine closely the remainder of the life of Jesus Christ, we see that he chose to begin his miracles through Mary. It was by her word that he sanctified St. John the Baptist in the womb of his mother, St. Elizabeth; no sooner had Mary spoken than John was sanctified. This was his first and greatest miracle of grace.[35] At the wedding in Cana he changed water into wine at her humble prayer,[36] and this was his first miracle in the order of nature. He began and continued his miracles through Mary and he will continue them through her until the end of time.

20 God the Holy Spirit, who does not produce any divine person, became fruitful through Mary whom he espoused.[37] It was with her, in her and of her that he produced his masterpiece, God-made-man, and that he produces every day until the end of the world the members of the body of this adorable Head. For this reason the more he finds Mary his dear and inseparable spouse in a soul the more powerful and effective he becomes in producing Jesus Christ in that soul and that soul in Jesus Christ.

21 This does not mean that the Blessed Virgin confers on the Holy Spirit a fruitfulness which he does not already possess. Being God, he has the ability to produce just like the Father and the Son, although he does not use this power and so does not produce another divine person. But it does mean that the Holy Spirit chose to make use of our Blessed Lady, although he had no absolute need of her, in order to become actively fruitful in producing Jesus Christ and his members in her and by her. This is a mystery of grace unknown even to many of the most learned and spiritual of Christians.

[2 *Mary's part in the sanctification of souls*]

22 The plan adopted by the three persons of the Blessed Trinity in the Incarnation, the first coming of Jesus Christ, is adhered to each day in an invisible manner throughout the Church and they will pursue it to the end of time until the last coming of Jesus Christ.

23 God the Father gathered all the waters together and called them the seas. He gathered all his graces together and called them Mary.[38] The great God has a treasury or storehouse full of riches in which he has enclosed all that is beautiful, resplendent, rare, and precious, even his own Son. This immense treasury is none other than Mary whom the saints call the "treasury of the Lord."[39] From her fullness all men are made rich.

24 God the Son imparted to his mother all that he gained by his life and death, namely, his infinite merits and his eminent virtues. He made her the treasurer of all his Father had given him as heritage. Through her he applies his merits to his members and through her he transmits his virtues and distributes his graces.[40] She is his mystic channel, his aqueduct,[41] through which he causes his mercies to flow gently and abundantly.

25 God the Holy Spirit entrusted his wondrous gifts to Mary, his faithful spouse, and chose her as the dispenser of all he possesses, so that she distributes all his gifts and graces[42] to whom she wills, as much as she wills, how she wills and when she wills. No heavenly gift is given to men which does not pass through her virginal hands. Such indeed is the will of God, who has decreed that we should have all things through Mary, so that, making herself poor and lowly, and hiding herself in the depths of nothingness during her whole life, she might be enriched, exalted and honored by almighty God. Such are the views of the Church and the early Fathers.[43]

26 Were I speaking to the so-called intellectuals of today, I would prove at great length by quoting Latin texts taken from Scripture and the Fathers of the Church all that I am now stating so simply. I could also instance solid proofs which can be read in full in Fr. Poiré's book *The Triple Crown of the Blessed Virgin.*[44] But I am speaking mainly for the poor and simple who have more good will and faith than the common run of scholars. As they believe more simply and more meritoriously, let me merely state the truth to them quite plainly without bothering to quote Latin passages

which they would not understand. Nevertheless, I shall quote some texts as they occur to my mind as I go along.

27 Since grace enhances our human nature and glory adds a still greater perfection to grace, it is certain that our Lord remains in heaven just as much the Son of Mary as he was on earth. Consequently, he has retained the submissiveness and obedience of the most perfect of all children towards the best of all mothers.

We must take care, however, not to consider this dependence as an abasement or imperfection in Jesus Christ. For Mary, infinitely inferior to her Son, who is God, does not command him in the same way as an earthly mother would command her child who is beneath her. Since she is completely transformed in God by that grace and glory which transforms all the saints in him, she does not ask or wish to do anything which is contrary to the eternal and unchangeable will of God. When therefore we read in the writings of St. Bernard, St. Bernardine, St. Bonaventure, and others that all in heaven and on earth, even God himself, is subject to the Blessed Virgin,[45] they mean that the authority which God was pleased to give her is so great that she seems to have the same power as God. Her prayers and requests are so powerful with him that he accepts them as commands in the sense that he never resists his dear mother's prayer because it is always humble and conformed to his will.

Moses by the power of his prayer curbed God's anger against the Israelites so effectively that the infinitely great and merciful Lord was unable to withstand him and asked Moses to let him be angry and punish that rebellious people.[46] How much greater, then, will be the prayer of the humble Virgin Mary, worthy Mother of God, which is more powerful with the King of heaven than the prayers and intercession of all the angels and saints in heaven and on earth.[47]

28 Mary has authority over the angels and the blessed in heaven. As a reward for her great humility, God gave her the power and the mission of assigning to saints the thrones made vacant by the apostate angels who fell away through pride.[48]

Such is the will of almighty God who exalts the humble,[49] that the powers of heaven, earth and hell, willingly or unwillingly, must obey the commands of the humble Virgin Mary.[50] For God has made her queen of heaven and earth, leader of his armies, keeper of his treasures, dispenser of his graces, worker of his wonders, restorer of the human race, mediatrix on behalf of men, destroyer of his enemies, and faithful associate in his great works and triumphs.[51]

29 God the Father wishes Mary to be the mother of his children until the end of time and so he says to her, "Dwell in Jacob,"[51] that is to say, take up your abode permanently in my children, in my holy ones represented by Jacob, and not in the children of the devil and sinners represented by Esau.

30 Just as in natural and bodily generation there is a father and a mother, so in the supernatural and spiritual generation there is a father who is God and a mother who is Mary. All true children of God have God for their father and Mary for their mother; anyone who does not have Mary for his mother does not have God for his father.[53] This is why the reprobate, such as heretics and schismatics, who hate, despise or ignore the Blessed Virgin, do not have God for their father though they arrogantly claim they have, because they do not have Mary for their mother. Indeed if they had her for their mother they would love and honor her as good and true children naturally love and honor the mother who gave them life.

An infallible and unmistakable sign by which we can distinguish a heretic, a man of false doctrine, an enemy of God, from one of God's true friends is that the heretic and the hardened sinner show nothing but contempt and indifference for our Lady. He endeavors by word and example, openly or insidiously—sometimes under specious pretexts[54]—to belittle the love and veneration shown to her. God the Father has not told Mary to dwell in them because they are, alas, other Esaus.

31 God the Son wishes to form himself, and, in a manner of speaking, become incarnate every day in his members through his dear Mother. To her he said, "Take Israel for your inheritance."[55] It is as if he said, God the Father has given me as heritage all the nations of the earth, all men good and evil, predestinate and reprobate. To the good I shall be father and advocate, to the bad a just avenger, but to all I shall be a judge. But you, my dear Mother, will have for your heritage and possession only the predestinate represented by Israel. As their loving mother, you will give them birth, feed them and rear them. As their queen, you will lead, govern and defend them.

32 "This one and that one were born in her."[56] According to the explanation of some of the Fathers, the first man born of Mary is the God-man, Jesus Christ. The second is simply man, child of God and Mary by adoption. If Jesus Christ, the head of mankind, is born of her, the predestinate, who are members of this head, must also as a necessary consequence be born of her.[57]

One and the same mother does not give birth to the head without the members nor to the members without the head, for these would be monsters in the order of nature. In the order of grace likewise the head and the members are born of the same mother. If a member of the mystical body of Christ, that is, one of the predestinate, were born of a mother other than Mary who gave birth to the head, he would not be one of the predestinate, nor a member of Jesus Christ, but a monster in the order of grace.

33 Moreover, Jesus is still as much as ever the fruit of Mary, as heaven and earth repeat thousands of times a day, "Blessed is the fruit of thy womb, Jesus." It is therefore certain that Jesus is the fruit and gift of Mary for every single man who possesses him, just as truly as he is for all mankind. Consequently, if any of the faithful have Jesus formed in their heart they can boldly say, "It is thanks to Mary that what I possess is Jesus, her fruit, and without her I would not have him." We can attribute more truly to her what St. Paul said of himself,[58] "I am in labor again with all the children of God until Jesus Christ, my Son, is formed in them to the fullness of his age."[59] St. Augustine,[60] surpassing himself as well as all that I have said so far, affirms that in order to be conformed to the image of the Son of God all the predestinate, while in the world, are hidden in the womb of the Blessed Virgin where they are protected, nourished, cared for and developed by this good Mother, until the day she brings them forth to a life of glory after death, which the Church calls the birthday of the just. This is indeed a mystery of grace unknown to the reprobate and little known even to the predestinate!

34 God the Holy Spirit wishes to fashion his chosen ones in and through Mary. He tells her, "My well-beloved, my spouse, let all your virtues take root in my chosen ones[61] that they may grow from strength to strength and from grace to grace. When you were living on earth, practicing the most sublime virtues, I was so pleased with you that I still desire to find you on earth without your ceasing to be in heaven. Reproduce yourself then in my chosen ones, so that I may have the joy of seeing in them the roots of your invincible faith,[62] profound humility, total mortification, sublime prayer, ardent charity, your firm hope and all your virtues.[63] You are always my spouse, as faithful, pure, and fruitful as ever. May your faith give me believers; your purity, virgins; your fruitfulness, elect and living temples."

35 When Mary has taken root in a soul she produces in it wonders of grace which only she can produce; for she alone is the fruitful virgin who never had and never will have her equal in purity and fruitfulness. Together with the Holy Spirit Mary produced the greatest thing that ever was or ever will be: a God-man. She will consequently produce the marvels which will be seen in the latter times. The formation and the education of the great saints who will come at the end of the world are reserved to her,[64] for only this singular and wondrous virgin can produce in union with the Holy Spirit singular and wondrous things.

36 When the Holy Spirit, her spouse, finds Mary in a soul, he hastens there and enters fully into it. He gives himself generously to that soul according to the place it has given to his spouse. One of the main reasons why the Holy Spirit does not now work striking wonders in souls is that he fails to find in them a sufficiently close union with his faithful and inseparable spouse. I say "inseparable spouse," for from the moment the substantial love of the Father and the Son espoused Mary to form Jesus, the head of the elect, and Jesus in the elect, he has never disowned her, for she has always been faithful and fruitful.

[3 *Consequences*]

37 We must obviously conclude from what I have just said: First, that Mary has received from God a far-reaching dominion over the souls of the elect. Otherwise she could not make her dwelling-place in them as God the Father has ordered her to do, and she could not conceive them, nourish them, and bring them forth to eternal life as their mother. She could not have them for her inheritance and her possession and form them in Jesus and Jesus in them. She could not implant in their heart the roots of her virtues, nor be the inseparable associate of the Holy Spirit in all these works of grace. None of these things, I repeat, could she do unless she had received from the Almighty rights and authority over their souls.[65]

For God, having given her power over his only-begotten and natural Son, also gave her power over his adopted children, not only in what concerns their body—which would be of little account—but also in what concerns their soul.

38 Mary is the Queen of heaven and earth by grace as Jesus is king by nature and by conquest.[66] But as the kingdom of Jesus Christ exists primarily in the heart or interior of man, according to the words of the Gospel, "The kingdom of God is within you,"[67] so the kingdom of the Blessed Virgin is principally in the interior of man, that is, in his soul. It is principally in souls that she is glorified with her Son more than in any visible creatures. So we may call her, as the saints do, Queen of all hearts.[68]

39 Secondly, we must conclude that, being necessary to God by a necessity which is called "hypothetical," (that is, because God so willed it),[69] the Blessed Virgin is all the more necessary for men to attain their final end. Consequently, we must not place devotion to her on the same level as devotion to the other saints as if it were merely something optional.

40 The pious and learned Jesuit, Suarez, Justus Lipsius, a devout and erudite theologian of Louvain, and many others have proved incontestably that devotion to Our Blessed Lady is necessary to attain salvation.[70] This they show from the teaching of the Fathers, notably St. Augustine, St. Ephrem, deacon of Edessa, St. Cyril of Jerusalem, St. Germanus of Constantinople, St. John Damascene, St. Anselm, St. Bernard, St. Bernardine, St. Thomas and St. Bonaventure. Even according to Oecolampadius and other heretics, lack of esteem and love for the Virgin Mary is an infallible sign of God's disapproval. On the other hand, to be entirely and genuinely devoted to her is a sure sign of God's approval.

41 The types and texts of the Old and New Testaments prove the truth of this, the opinions and examples of the saints confirm it, and reason and experience teach and demonstrate it. Even the devil and his followers, forced by the evidence of the truth, were frequently obliged against their will to admit it. For brevity's sake, I shall quote one only of the many passages which I have collected[71] from the Fathers and Doctors of the Church to support this truth. "Devotion to you, O Blessed Virgin, is a means of salvation which God gives to those whom he wishes to save" (St. John Damascene).

42 I could tell many stories in evidence of what I have just said.

1 One is recorded in the chronicles of St. Francis.[72] The saint saw in ecstasy an immense ladder reaching to heaven, at the top of which stood the Blessed Virgin. This is the ladder, he was told, by which we must all go to heaven.

2 There is another related in the Chronicles of St. Dominic.[73] Near Carcassonne, where St. Dominic was preaching the Rosary, there was an unfortunate heretic who was possessed by a multitude of devils. These evil spirits to their confusion were compelled at the command of Our Lady to confess many great and consoling truths concerning devotion to her. They did this so clearly and forcibly that, however weak our devotion to Our Lady may be, we cannot read this authentic story containing such an unwilling tribute paid by the devils to devotion to Our Lady without shedding tears of joy.

43 If devotion to the Blessed Virgin is necessary for all men simply to work out their salvation, it is even more necessary for those who are called to a special perfection. I do not believe that anyone can acquire intimate union with Our Lord and perfect fidelity to the Holy Spirit without a very close union with the most Blessed Virgin and an absolute dependence on her support.

44 Mary alone found grace before God without the help of any other creature.[74] All those who have since found grace before God have found it only through her. She was full of grace when she was greeted by the Archangel Gabriel[75] and was filled with grace to overflowing by the Holy Spirit when he so mysteriously overshadowed her.[76] From day to day, from moment to moment, she increased so much this two-fold plenitude that she attained an immense and inconceivable degree of grace. So much so, that the Almighty made her the sole custodian of his treasures and the sole dispenser of his graces. [77] She can now ennoble, exalt and enrich all she chooses. She can lead them along the narrow path to heaven and guide them through the narrow gate to life. She can give a royal throne, scepter and crown to whom she wishes. Jesus is always and everywhere the fruit and Son of Mary and Mary is everywhere the genuine tree that bears that Fruit of life, the true Mother who bears that Son.[78]

God alone

45 To Mary alone God gave the keys of the cellars[79] of divine love and the ability to enter the most sublime and secret ways of perfection, and lead others along them. Mary alone gives to the unfortunate children of unfaithful Eve entry into that earthly paradise where they may walk pleasantly with God and be safely hidden from their enemies. There they can feed without fear of death on the delicious fruit of the tree of life and the tree of the knowledge of good and evil. They can drink copiously the heavenly waters of that beauteous fountain which gushes forth in such abundance. As she is herself the earthly paradise, the virgin and blessed land from which sinful Adam and Eve were expelled, she lets only those whom she chooses enter her domain in order to make them saints.[80]

46 All the rich among the people, to use an expression of the Holy Spirit as explained by St. Bernard,[81] all the rich among the people will look pleadingly upon your countenance throughout all ages and particularly as the world draws to its end. This means that the greatest saints, those richest in grace and virtue, will be the most assiduous in praying to the most Blessed Virgin, looking up to her as the perfect model to imitate and as a powerful helper to assist them.

47 I said that this will happen especially towards the end of the world, and indeed soon, because Almighty God and his holy Mother are to raise up great saints who will surpass in holiness most other saints as much as the cedars of Lebanon tower above little shrubs. This has been revealed to a holy soul whose life has been written by M. de Renty.[82]

48 These great souls filled with grace and zeal will be chosen to oppose the enemies of God who are raging on all sides. They will be exceptionally devoted to the Blessed Virgin. Illumined by her light, strengthened by her food, guided by her spirit, supported by her arm, sheltered under her protection, they will fight with one hand and build with the other.[83] With one hand they will give battle, overthrowing and crushing heretics and their heresies, schismatics and their schisms, idolaters and their idolatries, sinners and their wickedness. With the other hand they will build the temple of the true Solomon and the mystical city of God, namely, the Blessed Virgin, who is called by the Fathers of the Church the *Temple of Solomon* and the *City of God.* By word and example they will draw all men to a true devotion to her and though this will make many enemies, it will also bring about many victories and much glory to God alone. This is what God revealed to St. Vincent Ferrer,[84] that outstanding apostle of his day, as he has amply shown in one of his works.

This seems to have been foretold by the Holy Spirit in Psalm 58: "The Lord will reign in Jacob and all the ends of the earth. They will be converted towards evening and they will be as hungry as dogs and they will go around the city to find something to eat."[85] This city around which men will roam at the end of the world seeking conversion and the appeasement of the hunger they have for justice is the most Blessed Virgin, who is called by the Holy Spirit the *City of God.*[86]

[4 *Mary's part in the latter times*]

49 The salvation of the world began through Mary and through her it must be accomplished. Mary scarcely appeared in the first coming of Jesus Christ[87] so that men, as yet insufficiently instructed and enlightened concerning the person of her Son, might not wander from the truth by becoming too strongly attached to her. This would apparently have happened if she had been known, on account of the wondrous charms with which the Almighty had endowed even her outward appearance. So true is this that St. Denis the Areopagite tells us in his writings[88] that when he saw her he would have taken her for a goddess, because of her incomparable beauty, had not his well-grounded faith taught him otherwise. But in the second coming of Jesus Christ, Mary must be known and openly revealed by the Holy Spirit so that Jesus may be known, loved and served through her. The reasons which moved the Holy Spirit to hide his spouse during her life and to reveal but very little of her since the first preaching of the gospel exist no longer.

[1 *God wishes to make Mary better known in the latter times.*]

50 God wishes therefore to reveal Mary, his masterpiece, and make her more known in these latter times:

1 Because she kept herself hidden in this world and in her great humility considered herself lower than dust, having obtained from God, his apostles and evangelists the favor of not being made known.

2 Because, as Mary is not only God's masterpiece of glory in heaven, but also his masterpiece of grace on earth, he wishes to be glorified and praised because of her by those living upon earth.

3 Since she is the dawn which precedes and discloses the Sun of Justice, Jesus Christ, she must be known and acknowledged so that Jesus may be known and acknowledged.

4 As she was the way by which Jesus first came to us, she will again be the way by which he will come to us the second time though not in the same manner.

5 Since she is the sure means, the direct and immaculate way to Jesus and the perfect guide to him, it is through her that souls who are to shine forth in sanctity, must find him. He who finds Mary finds life,[89] that is, Jesus Christ who is the way, the truth and

the life.[90] But no one can find Mary who does not look for her. No one can look for her who does not know her, for no one seeks or desires something unknown. Mary then must be better known than ever for the deeper understanding and the greater glory of the Blessed Trinity.

6 In these latter times Mary must shine forth more than ever in mercy, power and grace: *in mercy,* to bring back and welcome lovingly the poor sinners and wanderers who are to be converted and return to the Catholic Church; *in power,* to combat the enemies of God who will rise up menacingly to seduce and crush by promises and threats all those who oppose them; finally, she must shine forth *in grace* to inspire and support the valiant soldiers and loyal servants of Jesus Christ who are fighting for his cause.

7 Lastly, Mary must become as terrible as an army in battle array[91] to the devil and his followers, especially in these latter times. For Satan, knowing that he has little time[92]—even less now than ever—to destroy souls, intensifies his efforts and his onslaughts every day. He will not hesitate to stir up savage persecutions and set treacherous snares for Mary's faithful servants and children whom he finds more difficult to overcome than others.

51 It is chiefly in reference to these last wicked persecutions of the devil, daily increasing until the advent of the reign of anti-Christ, that we should understand that first and well-known prophesy and curse of God uttered against the serpent in the garden of paradise. It is opportune to explain it here for the glory of the Blessed Virgin, the salvation of her children and the confusion of the devil. "I will place enmities between you and the woman, between your race and her race; she will crush your head and you will lie in wait for her heel" (Gen. 3:15).

52 God has established only one enmity—but it is an irreconcilable one[93] which will last and even go on increasing to the end of time. That enmity is between Mary, his worthy Mother, and the devil, between the children and the servants of the Blessed Virgin and the children and followers of Lucifer.

Thus the most fearful enemy that God has set up against the devil is Mary, his holy Mother. From the time of the earthly paradise, although she existed then only in his mind, he gave her such a hatred for his accursed enemy, such ingenuity in exposing the wickedness of the ancient serpent and such power to defeat, overthrow and crush this proud rebel, that Satan fears her not only more than angels and men but in a certain sense more than God himself. This does not mean that the anger, hatred and power of God are not infinitely greater than the Blessed Virgin's, since her attributes are limited. It simply means that Satan, being so proud, suffers infinitely more in being vanquished and punished by a lowly and humble servant of God, for her humility humiliates him more than the power of God. Moreover, God has given Mary such great power over the evil spirits that, as they have often been forced unwillingly to admit through the lips of possessed persons,[94] they fear one of her pleadings for a soul more than the prayers of all the saints, and one of her threats more than all their other torments.

53 What Lucifer lost by pride Mary won by humility. What Eve ruined and lost by disobedience Mary saved by obedience.[45] By obeying the serpent, Eve ruined her children as well as herself and delivered them up to him. Mary by her perfect fidelity to God saved her children with herself and consecrated them to his divine majesty.

54 God has established not just one enmity but "enmities," and not only between Mary and Satan but between her race and his race. That is, God has put enmities, antipathies and hatreds between the true children and servants of the Blessed Virgin and the children and slaves of the devil. They have no love and no sympathy for each other. The children of Belial, the slaves of Satan, the friends of the world—for they are all one and the same—have always persecuted and will persecute more than ever in the future those who belong to the Blessed Virgin, just as Cain of old persecuted his brother Abel,[96] and Esau his brother Jacob.[97] These are the types of the wicked and of the just. But the humble Mary will always triumph over Satan, the proud one, and so great will be her victory that she will crush his head, the very seat of his pride. She will always unmask his serpent's cunning and expose his wicked plots. She will scatter to the winds his devilish plans and to the end of time will keep her faithful servants safe from his cruel claws.

But Mary's power over the evil spirits will especially shine forth in the latter times, when Satan will lie in wait for her heel, that is, for her humble servants and her poor children whom she will rouse to fight against him. In the eyes of the world they will be little and poor and, like the heel, lowly in the eyes of all, down-trodden and crushed as is the heel by the other parts of the body. But in compensation for this they will be rich in God's graces, which will be abundantly bestowed on them by Mary. They will be great and exalted before God in holiness. They will be superior to all creatures by their great zeal and so strongly will they be supported by divine assistance that, in union with Mary, they will crush the head of Satan with their heel, that is, their humility, and bring victory to Jesus Christ.

[2 *We must conclude that devotion to Mary is especially necessary in the latter times.*]

55 Finally, God in these times wishes his Blessed Mother to be more known, loved and honored than she has ever been. This will certainly come about if the elect, by the grace and light of the Holy Spirit, adopt the interior and perfect practice of the devotion which I shall later unfold. Then they will clearly see that beautiful Star of the Sea, as much as faith allows. Under her guidance they will come safely to port in spite of storms and pirates. They will perceive the splendors of this Queen and will consecrate themselves entirely to her service as subjects and slaves of love. They will experience her motherly kindness and affection for her children. They will love her tenderly and will appreciate how full of compassion she is and how much they stand in need of her help. In all circumstances they will have recourse to her as their advocate and mediatrix with Jesus Christ. They will see clearly that she is the safest, easiest, shortest and most perfect way of approaching Jesus[98] and will surrender themselves to her, body and soul, without reserve in order to belong entirely to Jesus.

56 But what will they be like, these servants, these slaves, these children of Mary?

They will be ministers of the Lord[99] who, like a flaming fire, will enkindle everywhere the fires of divine love. They will become, in Mary's powerful hands, like sharp arrows,[100] with which she will transfix her enemies.

They will be as the children of Levi, thoroughly purified by the fire of great tribulations and closely joined to God.[101] They will carry the gold of love in their heart, the frankincense of prayer in their mind and the myrrh of mortification in their body. They will bring to the poor and lowly everywhere the sweet fragrance of Jesus,[102] but they will bring the odor of death to the great, the rich and the proud of this world.

57 They will be like thunder-clouds[103] flying through the air at the slightest breath of the Holy Spirit. Attached to nothing, surprised at nothing, troubled at nothing, they will shower down the rain of God's word and of eternal life. They will thunder against sin, they will storm against the world, they will strike down the devil and his followers and for life and for death, they will pierce through and through with the two-edged sword of God's word[104] all those against whom they are sent by almighty God.

58 They will be true apostles of the latter times to whom the Lord of Hosts will give eloquence and strength to work wonders and carry off glorious spoils from his enemies. They will sleep without gold or silver and, more important still, without concern in the midst of other priests,[105] ecclesiastics and clerics. Yet they will have the silver wings of the dove enabling them to go wherever the Holy Spirit calls them, filled as they are, with the resolve to seek the glory of God and the salvation of souls. Wherever they preach, they will leave behind them nothing but the gold of love, which is the fulfillment of the whole law.[106]

59 Lastly, we know they will be true disciples of Jesus Christ, imitating his poverty, his humility, his contempt of the world and his love. They will point out the narrow way to God in pure truth according to the holy Gospel, and not according to the maxims of the world. Their hearts will not be troubled, nor will they show favor to anyone;[107] they will not spare or heed or fear any man, however powerful he may be. They will have the two-edged sword of the Word of God[108] in their mouths and the blood-stained standard of the Cross on their shoulders. They will carry the crucifix in their right hand and the rosary in their left,[109] and the holy names of Jesus and Mary on their heart. The simplicity and self-sacrifice of Jesus will be reflected in their whole behavior.

Such are the great men who are to come. By the will of God Mary is to prepare them to extend his rule over the impious and unbelievers. But when and how will this come about? Only God knows. For our part we must yearn and wait for it in silence and in prayer: "I have waited and waited."[110]

[Chapter 2 In what Devotion to Mary consists]

[A *Basic principles of devotion to Mary*]

60 Having spoken briefly of the necessity of devotion to the Blessed Virgin, I must now explain what this devotion consists in. This I will do with God's help after I have laid down certain basic truths which throw light[111] on the remarkable and sound devotion which I propose to unfold.

First truth: [Christ must be the ultimate end of all devotions.]

61 Jesus, our Savior, true God and true man must be the ultimate end of all our other devotions; otherwise they would be false and misleading. He is the Alpha and the Omega,[112] the beginning and end of everything. "We labor," says St. Paul, "only to make all men perfect in Jesus Christ."

For in him alone dwells the entire fullness of the divinity and the complete fullness of grace, virtue and perfection. In him alone we have been blessed with every spiritual blessing; he is the only teacher from whom we must learn; the only Lord on whom we should depend; the only Head to whom we should be united and the only model that we should imitate. He is the only Physician that can heal us; the only Shepherd that can feed us; the only Way that can lead us; the only Truth that we can believe; the only Life that can animate us. He alone is everything to us and he alone can satisfy all our desires.

We are given no other name under heaven by which we can be saved. God has laid no other foundation for our salvation, perfection and glory than Jesus. Every edifice which is not built on that firm rock, is founded upon shifting sands and will certainly fall sooner or later. Every one of the faithful who is not united to him is like a branch broken from the stem of the vine. It falls and withers and is fit only to be burnt. If we live in Jesus and Jesus lives in us, we need not fear damnation. Neither angels in heaven nor men on earth, nor devils in hell, no creature whatever can harm us, for no creature can separate us from the love of God which is in Christ Jesus. Through him, with him and in him, we can do all things and render all honor and glory to the Father in the unity of the Holy Spirit;[113] we can make ourselves perfect and be for our neighbor a fragrance of eternal life.

62 If then we are establishing sound devotion to Our Blessed Lady, it is only in order to establish devotion to Our Lord more perfectly, by providing a smooth but certain way of reaching Jesus Christ. If devotion to Our Lady distracted us from Our Lord, we would have to reject it as an illusion of the devil. But this is far from being the case. As I have already shown and will show again later on,[114] this devotion is necessary, simply and solely because it is a way of reaching Jesus perfectly, loving him tenderly, and serving him faithfully.

63 Here I turn to you for a moment, dear Jesus, to complain lovingly to your divine Majesty that the majority of Christians, and even some of the most learned among them, do not recognize the necessary bond that unites you and your Blessed Mother. Lord, you are always with Mary and Mary is always with you. She can never be without you because then she would cease to be what she is. She is so completely transformed into you by grace that she no longer lives, she no longer exists, because you alone, dear Jesus, live and reign in her more perfectly than in all the angels and saints. If we only knew the glory and the love given to you by this wonderful creature, our feelings for you and for her would be far different from those we have now. So intimately is she united to you that it would be easier to separate light from the sun, and heat from the fire. I go further, it would even be easier to separate all the angels and saints from you than Mary; for she loves you more ardently, and glorifies you more perfectly than all your other creatures put together.

64 In view of this, my dear Master, is it not astonishing and pitiful to see the ignorance and shortsightedness of men with regard to your holy Mother? I am not speaking so much of idolators and pagans who do not know you and consequently have no knowledge of her. I am not even speaking of heretics and schismatics who have left you and your holy Church and therefore are not interested in your holy Mother. I am speaking of Catholics, and even of educated Catholics, who profess to teach the faith to others but do not know you or your Mother except speculatively, in a dry, cold and sterile way.[115]

These people[116] seldom speak of your Mother or devotion to her. They say they are afraid that devotion to her will be abused and that you will be offended by excessive honor paid to her. They protest loudly when they see or hear a devout servant of Mary speak frequently with feeling, conviction and vigor of devotion to her. When he speaks of devotion to her as a sure means of finding and loving you without fear of illusion, or when he says this devotion is a short road free from danger, or an immaculate way free from imperfection, or a wondrous secret[117] of finding you, they put before him a thousand specious reasons to show him how wrong he is to speak so much of Mary. There are, they say, great abuses in this devotion which we should try to stamp out and we should refer people to you rather than exhort them to have devotion to your Mother, whom they already love adequately.

If they are sometimes heard speaking of devotion to your Mother, it is not for the purpose of promoting it or convincing people of it but only to destroy the abuses made of it. Yet all the while these persons are devoid of piety or genuine devotion to you, for they have no devotion to Mary. They consider the Rosary and the Scapular as devotions suitable only for simple women or ignorant people. After all, they say, we do not need them to be saved. If they come across one who loves our Lady, who says the Rosary or shows any devotion towards her, they soon move him to a change of mind and heart. They advise him to say the seven penitential psalms instead of the Rosary, and to show devotion to Jesus instead of to Mary.

Dear Jesus, do these people possess your spirit? Do they please you by acting in this way? Would it please you if we were to make no effort to give pleasure to your Mother because we are afraid of offending you? Does devotion to your holy Mother hinder devotion to you? Does Mary keep for herself any honor we pay her? Is she a rival of yours? Is she a stranger having no kinship with you? Does pleasing her imply displeasing you? Does the gift of oneself to her constitute a deprivation for you? Is love for her a lessening of our love for you?

65 Nevertheless, my dear Master, the majority of learned scholars could not be further from devotion to your Mother, or show more indifference to it even if all I have just said were true. Keep me from their way of thinking and acting and let me share your feelings of gratitude, esteem, respect and love for your holy Mother. I can then love and glorify you all the more, because I will be imitating and following you more closely.

66 As though I had said nothing so far to further her honor, grant me now the grace to praise her more worthily,[118] in spite of all her enemies who are also yours. I can then say to them boldly with the saints, "Let no one presume to expect mercy from God, who offends his holy Mother."[119]

67 So that I may obtain from your mercy a genuine devotion to your blessed Mother and spread it throughout the whole world, help me to love you wholeheartedly, and for this intention accept the earnest prayer I offer with St. Augustine and all who truly love you.[120]

[Prayer of St. Augustine]

O Jesus Christ, you are my Father, my merciful God, my great King, my good Shepherd, my only Master, my best helper, my beloved friend of overwhelming beauty, my living Bread, my eternal priest. You are my guide to my heavenly home, my one true light, my holy joy, my true way, my shining wisdom, my unfeigned simplicity, the peace and harmony of my soul, my perfect safeguard, my bounteous inheritance, my everlasting salvation.

My loving Lord, Jesus Christ, why have I ever loved or desired anything else in my life but you, my God? Where was I when I was not in communion with you? From now on, I direct all my desires to be inspired by you and centered on you. I direct them to press forward for they have tarried long enough, to hasten towards their goal, to seek the one they yearn for.

O Jesus, let him who does not love you be accursed, and filled with bitterness. O gentle Jesus, let every worthy feeling of mine show you love, take delight in you and admire you. O God of my heart and my inheritance, Christ Jesus, may my heart mellow before the influence of your spirit and may you live in me. May the flame of your love burn in my soul. May it burn incessantly on the altar of my heart. May it glow in my innermost being. May it spread its heat into the hidden recesses of my soul and on the day of my consummation may I appear before you consumed in your love. Amen.

Second truth: [We belong to Jesus and Mary as their slaves.]

68 From what Jesus Christ is in regard to us we must conclude, as St. Paul says,[121] that we belong not to ourselves but entirely to him as his members and his slaves, for he bought us at an infinite price—the shedding of his Precious Blood. Before baptism, we belonged to the devil as slaves,[122] but baptism made us in very truth slaves of Jesus. We must therefore live, work and die for the sole purpose of bringing forth fruit for him, glorifying him in our body and letting him reign in our soul. We are his conquest, the people he has won, his heritage.[123]

It is for this reason that the Holy Spirit[124] compares us: 1) to trees which are planted along the waters of grace in the field of the Church and which must bear their fruit when the time comes; 2) to branches of the vine of which Jesus is the stem, which must yield good grapes; 3) to a flock of sheep of which Jesus is the Shepherd, which must increase and give milk; 4) to good soil cultivated by God, where the seed will spread and produce crops up to thirty-fold, sixty-fold, or a hundred-fold. Our Lord cursed the barren fig-tree and condemned the slothful servant who wasted his talent.[125]

All this proves that he wishes to receive some fruit from our wretched selves, namely, our good works, which by right belong to him alone, "created in Christ Jesus for good works."[126] These words of the Holy Spirit show that Jesus is the sole source and must be the sole end of all our good works, and that we must serve him not just as paid servants but as slaves of love. Let me explain what I mean.

69 There are two ways of belonging to another person and being subject to his authority. One is by ordinary service and the other is by slavery. And so we must use the terms "servant" and "slave." Ordinary service in Christian countries is when a man is employed to serve another for a certain length of time at a wage which is fixed or agreed upon. When a man is totally dependent on another for life, and must serve his master without expecting any wages or recompense, when he is treated just like a beast of the field over which the owner has the right of life and death, then it is slavery.

70 Now there are three kinds of slavery:[127] natural slavery, enforced slavery, and voluntary slavery. All creatures are slaves of God in the first sense, for "the earth and its fullness belong to the Lord."[128] The devils and the damned are slaves in the second sense. The saints in heaven and the just on earth are slaves in the third sense. Voluntary slavery is the most perfect of all three states, for by it we give the greatest glory to God, who looks into the heart and wants it to be given to him. Is he not indeed called the God of the heart[129] or of the loving will? For by this slavery we freely choose God and his service before all things, even if we were not by our very nature obliged to do so.

71 There is a world of difference between a servant and a slave.[130] 1) A servant does not give his employer all he is, all he has, and all he can acquire by himself or through others. A slave, however, gives himself to his master completely and exclusively with all he has and all he can acquire. 2) A servant demands wages for the services rendered to his employer. A slave, on the other hand, can expect nothing, no matter what skill, attention or energy he may have put into his work. 3) A servant can leave his employer whenever he pleases, or at least when the term of his service expires, whereas the slave has no such right. 4) An employer has no right of life and death over a servant. Were he to kill him as he would a beast of burden, he would commit murder. But the master of a slave has by law the right of life and death over him, so that he can sell him to anyone he chooses or—if you will pardon the comparison—kill him as he would kill his horse. 5) Finally, a servant is in his employer's service only for a time: a slave for always.

72 No other human state involves belonging more completely to another than slavery.[131] Among Christian peoples, nothing makes a person belong more completely to Jesus and his holy Mother than voluntary slavery. Our Lord himself gave us the example of this when out of love for us he "took the form of a slave."[132] Our Lady gave us the same example when she called herself the handmaid or slave of the Lord.[133] The Apostle considered it an honor to be called "slave of Christ."[134] Several times in Holy Scripture, Christians are referred to as "slaves of Christ."[135]

The Latin word *servus* at one time[136] signified only a slave because servants as we know them did not exist. Masters were served either by slaves or by freedmen. The Catechism of the Council of Trent leaves no doubt about our being slaves of Jesus Christ, using the unequivocal term *Mancipia Christi,* which plainly means: slaves of Christ.[137]

73 Granting this, I say that we must belong to Jesus and serve him not just as hired servants but as willing slaves who, moved by generous love, commit themselves to his service after the manner of slaves for the honor of belonging to him. Before we were baptized we were the slaves of the devil, but baptism made us the slaves of Jesus. Christians can only be slaves of the devil or slaves of Christ.[138]

74 What I say in an absolute sense of our Lord, I say in a relative sense of our Blessed Lady. Jesus, in choosing her as his inseparable associate in his life, death, glory and power in heaven and on earth, has given her by grace in his kingdom all the same rights and privileges that he possesses by nature.[139] "All that belongs to God by nature belongs to Mary by grace," say the saints,[140] and, according to them, just as Jesus and Mary have the same will and the same power, they have also the same subjects, servants and slaves.[141]

75 Following therefore the teaching of the saints and of many great men we can call ourselves, and become, the loving slaves of our Blessed Lady in order to become more perfect slaves of

Jesus.[142] Mary is the means Our Lord chose to come to us and she is also the means we should choose to go to him, for she is not like other creatures who tend rather to lead us away from God than towards him, if we are over-attached to them. Mary's strongest inclination is to unite us to Jesus,[143] her Son, and her Son's strongest wish is that we come to him through his Blessed Mother. He is pleased and honored just as a king would be pleased and honored if a citizen, wanting to become a better subject and slave of the king, made himself the slave of the queen. That is why the Fathers of the Church, and St. Bonaventure after them,[144] assert that the Blessed Virgin is the way which leads to Our Lord.

76 Moreover, if, as I have said,[145] the Blessed Virgin is the Queen and Sovereign of heaven and earth, does she not then have as many subjects and slaves as there are creatures? "All things, including Mary herself, are subject to the power of God. All things, God included, are subject to the Virgin's power," so we are told by St. Anselm, St. Bernard, St. Bernardine and St. Bonaventure. Is it not reasonable to find that among so many slaves there should be some slaves of love, who freely choose Mary as their Queen? Should men and demons have willing slaves, and Mary have none? A king makes it a point of honor that the queen, his consort, should have her own slaves, over whom she has right of life and death,[146] for honor and power given to the queen is honor and power given to the king. Could we possibly believe that Jesus, the best of all sons, who shared his power with his blessed Mother, would resent her having her own slaves? Has he less esteem and love for his Mother than Ahasuerus had for Esther, or Solomon for Bathsheba?[147] Who could say or even think such a thing?

77 But where is my pen leading me? Why am I wasting my time proving something so obvious? If people are unwilling to call themselves slaves of Mary, what does it matter? Let them become and call themselves slaves of Jesus Christ, for this is the same as being slaves of Mary, since Jesus is the fruit and glory of Mary.[148] This is what we do perfectly in the devotion we shall discuss later.[149]

Third truth: [We must rid ourselves of what is evil in us.]

78 Our best actions are usually tainted and spoiled by the evil that is rooted in us. When pure, clear water is poured into a foul-smelling jug, or wine into an unwashed cask that previously contained another wine, the clear water and the good wine are tainted and readily acquire an unpleasant odor. In the same way when God pours into our soul, infected by original and actual sin, the heavenly waters of his grace or the delicious wines of his love, his gifts are usually spoiled and tainted by the evil sediment left in us by sin.

God alone

Our actions, even those of the highest virtue, show the effects of it.[150] It is therefore of the utmost importance that, in seeking the perfection that can be attained only by union with Jesus, we rid ourselves of all that is evil in us. Otherwise our infinitely pure Lord, who has an infinite hatred for the slightest stain in our soul, will refuse to unite us to himself and will drive us from his presence.

79 To rid ourselves of selfishness, we must first become thoroughly aware, by the light of the Holy Spirit, of our tainted nature. Of ourselves we are unable to do anything conducive to our salvation. Our human weakness is evident in everything we do and we are habitually unreliable. We do not deserve any grace from God. Our tendency to sin is always present. The sin of Adam has almost entirely spoiled and soured us, filling us with pride and corrupting every one of us, just as leaven sours, swells and corrupts the dough in which it is placed. The actual sins we have committed, whether mortal or venial, even though forgiven, have intensified our base desires, our weakness, our inconsistency and our evil tendencies, and have left a sediment of evil in our soul.

Our bodies are so corrupt that they are referred to by the Holy Spirit[151] as bodies of sin, as conceived and nourished in sin, and capable of any kind of sin. They are subject to a thousand ills, deteriorating from day to day and harboring only disease, vermin and corruption.

Our soul, being united to our body, has become so carnal that it has been called flesh. "All flesh had corrupted its way."[152] Pride and blindness of spirit, hardness of heart, weakness and inconstancy of soul, evil inclinations, rebellious passions, ailments of the body—these are all we can call our own. By nature we are prouder than peacocks, we cling to the earth more than toads, we are baser than goats, more envious than serpents, greedier than pigs, fiercer than tigers, lazier than tortoises, weaker than reeds, and more changeable than weather-cocks. We have in us nothing but sin,[153] and deserve only the wrath of God and the eternity of hell.[154]

80 Is it any wonder then that Our Lord laid down that anyone who aspires to be his follower must deny himself and hate his very life? He makes it clear that anyone who loves his life shall lose it and anyone who hates his life shall save it.[155] Now, Our Lord, who is infinite Wisdom, and does not give commandments without a reason, bids us hate ourselves only because we richly deserve to be hated. Nothing is more worthy of love than God and nothing is more deserving of hatred than self.

81 Secondly, in order to empty ourselves of self, we must die daily to ourselves. This involves our renouncing what the powers of the soul and the senses of the body incline us to do. We must see as if we did not see, hear as if we did not hear and use the things of this world as if we did not use them.[156] This is what St. Paul calls "dying daily."[157] Unless the grain of wheat falls to the ground and dies, it remains only a single grain and does not bear any good fruit.[158] If we do not die to self and if our holiest devotions do not lead us to this necessary and fruitful death, we shall not bear fruit of any worth and our devotions will cease to be profitable. All our good works will be tainted by self-love and self-will so that our greatest sacrifices and our best actions will be unacceptable to God. Consequently when we come to die we shall find ourselves devoid of virtue and merit and discover that we do not possess even one spark of that pure love which God shares only with those who have died to themselves and whose life is hidden with Jesus Christ in him.[159]

82 Thirdly, we must choose among all the devotions to the Blessed Virgin the one which will lead us most surely to this dying to self. This devotion will be the best and the most sanctifying for us. For we must not believe that all that glitters is gold, all that is sweet is honey, or all that is easy to do and is done by the majority of people is the most sanctifying. Just as in nature there are secrets enabling us to do certain natural things quickly, easily and at little cost, so in the spiritual life there are secrets which enable us to perform supernatural works rapidly, smoothly and with facility. Such works are, for example, emptying ourselves of self-love, filling ourselves with God, and attaining perfection.[160]

The devotion that I propose to explain is one of these secrets of grace,[161] for it is unknown to most Christians. Only a few devout people know of it and it is practiced and appreciated by fewer still. To begin the explanation of this devotion here is a fourth truth which is a consequence of the third.

Fourth truth: [It is more humble to have an intermediary with Christ.]

83 It is more perfect because it supposes greater humility to approach God through a mediator rather than directly by ourselves. Our human nature, as I have just shown,[162] is so spoilt that if we rely on our own work, effort and preparedness to reach God and please him, it is certain that our good works will be tainted and carry little weight with him. They will not induce him to unite himself to us or answer our prayers. God had his reasons for giving us mediators with him. He saw our unworthiness and helplessness and had pity on us. To give us access to his mercies he provided us with powerful advocates, so that to neglect these mediators and to approach his infinite holiness directly and without help from any one of them, is to be lacking in humility and respect towards God who is so great and so holy. It would mean that we have less esteem for the King of kings than for an earthly king or ruler, for we would not dare approach an earthly king without a friend to speak for us.[163]

84 Our Lord is our Advocate and our Mediator of redemption with God the Father. It is through him that we must pray with the whole Church, triumphant and militant. It is through him that we have access to God the Father. We should never appear before God, our Father, unless we are supported by the merits of his Son, and, so to speak, clothed in them, as young Jacob was clothed in the skin of the young goats when he appeared before his father Isaac to receive his blessing.[164]

85 But have we no need at all of a mediator with the Mediator himself? Are we pure enough to be united directly to Christ without any help? Is Jesus not God, equal in every way to the Father? Therefore is he not the Holy of Holies, having a right to the same respect as his Father? If in his infinite love he became our security and our Mediator with his Father, whom he wished to appease in order to redeem us from our debts, should we on that account show him less respect and have less regard for the majesty and holiness of his person?

Let us not be afraid to say with St. Bernard[165] that we need a mediator with the Mediator himself and the divinely-honored Mary is the one most able to fulfill this office of love. Through her, Jesus came to us; through her, we should go to him. If we are afraid of going directly to Jesus, who is God, because of his infinite greatness, or our lowliness, or our sins, let us implore without fear the help and intercession of Mary, our Mother. She is kind, she is tender, and there is nothing harsh or forbidding about her, nothing too sublime or too brilliant. When we see her, we see our own human nature at its purest. She is not the sun, dazzling our weak sight by the brightness of its rays. Rather, she is fair and gentle as the moon, which receives its light from the sun and softens it and adapts it to our limited perception.

She is so full of love that no one who asks for her intercession is rejected, no matter how sinful he may be. The saints[166] say that it never has been known since the world began that anyone had recourse to our Blessed Lady, with trust and perseverance, and was rejected. Her power is so great that her prayers are never refused. She has but to appear in prayer before her Son and he at once welcomes her and grants her requests. He is always lovingly conquered by the prayers of the dear Mother who bore him and nourished him.

86 All this is taken from St. Bernard and St. Bonaventure. According to them, we have three steps to take in order to reach God. The first, nearest to us and most suited to our capacity, is Mary; the second is Jesus Christ; the third is God the Father. To go to Jesus, we should go to Mary, our mediatrix of intercession. To go to God the Father, we must go to Jesus, our Mediator of redemption.[167] This order is perfectly observed in the devotion I shall speak about further on.[168]

Fifth truth: [It is difficult to keep the graces received from God.]

87 It is very difficult, considering our weakness and frailty, to keep the graces and treasures we have received from God.

1 We carry this treasure, which is worth more than heaven and earth, in fragile vessels,[169] that is, in a corruptible body and in a weak and wavering soul which requires very little to depress and disturb it.

88 2 The evil spirits, cunning thieves that they are, can take us by surprise and rob us of all we possess. They are watching day and night for the right moment. They roam incessantly seeking to devour us[170] and to snatch from us in one brief moment of sin all the grace and merit we have taken years to acquire. Their malice and their experience, their cunning and their numbers ought to make us ever fearful of such a misfortune happening to us. People, richer in grace and virtue, more experienced and advanced in holiness than we are, have been caught off their guard and robbed and stripped of everything. How many cedars of Lebanon, how many stars of the firmament have we sadly watched fall and lose in a short time their loftiness and their brightness!

What has brought about this unexpected reverse? Not the lack of grace, for this is denied no one. It was a lack of humility; they considered themselves stronger and more self-sufficient than they really were. They thought themselves well able to hold on to their treasures. They believed their house secure enough and their coffers strong enough to safeguard their precious treasure of grace. It was because of their unconscious reliance on self—although it seemed to them that they were relying solely on the grace of God—that the most just Lord left them to themselves and allowed them to be despoiled. If they had only known of the wonderful devotion that I shall later explain,[171] they would have entrusted their treasure to Mary, the powerful and faithful Virgin. She would have kept it for them as if it were her own possession and even have considered that trust an obligation of justice.

89 3 It is difficult to persevere in holiness because of the excessive corrupting influence of the world. The world is so corrupt that it seems almost inevitable that religious hearts be soiled, if not by its mud, at least by its dust.[172] It is something of a miracle for anyone to stand firm in the midst of this raging torrent and not be swept away; to weather this stormy sea and not be drowned, or robbed by pirates; to breathe this pestilential air and not be contaminated by

it. It is Mary, the singularly faithful Virgin over whom Satan had never any power, who works this miracle for those who truly love her.

[B *Marks of false and authentic devotion to Mary.*]

90 Now that we have established these five basic truths, it is all the more necessary to make the right choice of the true devotion to our Blessed Lady,[173] for now more than ever there are false devotions to her which can easily be mistaken for true ones. The devil, like a counterfeiter and crafty, experienced deceiver, has already misled and ruined many Christians by means of fraudulent devotions to our Lady. Day by day he uses his diabolical experience to lead many more to their doom, fooling them, lulling them to sleep in sin and assuring them that a few prayers, even badly said, and a few exterior practices inspired by himself, are authentic devotions. A counterfeiter usually makes coins only of gold and silver, rarely of other metals, because these latter would not be worth the trouble. Similarly, the devil leaves other devotions alone and counterfeits mostly those directed to Jesus and Mary, as for example, devotion to the Holy Eucharist and to the Blessed Virgin, because these are to other devotions what gold and silver are to other metals.

91 It is therefore very important, first, to recognize false devotions to our Blessed Lady so as to avoid them, and to recognize true devotion in order to practice it. Second, among so many different forms of true devotion to our Blessed Lady we should choose the one most perfect and the most pleasing to her, the one that gives greater glory to God and is most sanctifying for us.[174]

[1 *False devotion to our Lady.*]

92 There are, I find, seven kinds of false devotion[175] to Mary, namely, the devotion of (1) the critical, (2) the scrupulous, (3) the superficial, (4) the presumptuous, (5) the inconstant, (6) the hypocritical, (7) the self-interested.

93 *Critical* devotees are for the most part proud scholars, people of independent and self-satisfied minds, who deep down in their hearts have a vague sort of devotion to Mary. However, they criticize nearly all those forms of devotion to her which simple and pious people use to honor their good Mother just because such practices do not appeal to them. They question all miracles and stories which testify to the mercy and power of the Blessed Virgin, even those recorded by trustworthy authors or taken from the chronicles of religious orders. They cannot bear to see simple and humble people on their knees before an altar or statue of Our Lady, or at prayer before some outdoor shrine. They even accuse them of idolatry as if they were adoring the wood or the stone. They say that as far as they are concerned they do not care for such outward display of devotion and that they are not so gullible as to believe all the fairy tales and stories told of our Blessed Lady. When you tell them how admirably the Fathers of the Church praised Our Lady, they reply that the Fathers were exaggerating as orators do, or that their words are misrepresented.[176] These false devotees, these proud worldly people are greatly to be feared. They do untold harm to devotion to Our Lady. While pretending to correct abuses, they succeed only too well in turning people away from this devotion.

94 *Scrupulous* devotees are those who imagine they are slighting the Son by honoring the Mother. They fear that by exalting Mary they are belittling Jesus. They cannot bear to see people giving to Our Lady the praises due to her and which the Fathers of the Church have lavished upon her. It annoys them to see more people kneeling before Mary's altar than before the Blessed Sacrament, as if these acts were at variance with each other, or as if those who were praying to Our Lady were not praying through her to Jesus. They do not want us to speak too often of her or to pray so often to her.

Here are some of the things they say: "What is the good of all these rosaries, confraternities and exterior devotions to our Lady? There is a great deal of ignorance in all this. It is making a mockery of religion. Tell us about those who are devoted to Jesus (and they often pronounce his name without uncovering their heads). We should go directly to Jesus, since he is our sole Mediator. We must preach Jesus; that is sound devotion." There is some truth in what they say, but the inference they draw to prevent devotion to Our Lady is very insidious. It is a subtle snare of the evil one under the pretext of promoting a greater good. For we never give more honor to Jesus than when we honor his Mother, and we honor her simply and solely to honor him all the more perfectly. We go to her only as a way leading to the goal we seek—Jesus, her Son.

95 The Church, with the Holy Spirit,[177] blesses our Lady first, then Jesus, "Blessed art thou among women and blessed is the fruit of thy womb, Jesus." Not that Mary is greater than Jesus, or even equal to him—that would be an intolerable heresy. But in order to bless Jesus more perfectly we should first bless Mary.[178] Let us say with all those truly devoted to her, despite these false and scrupulous devotees: "O Mary, blessed art thou among women and blessed is the fruit of thy womb, Jesus."

96 *Superficial* devotees are people whose entire devotion to our Lady consists in exterior practices. Only the externals of devotion appeal to them because they have no interior spirit. They say many rosaries with great haste and assist at many Masses distractedly. They take part in processions of our Lady without inner fervor. They join her confraternities without reforming their lives or restraining their passions or imitating Mary's virtues. All that appeals to them is the emotional aspect of this devotion, but the substance of it has no appeal at all. If they do not *feel* a warmth in their devotions, they think they are doing nothing; they become upset, and give up everything, or else do things only when they feel like it. The world is full of these shallow devotees, and there are none more critical of men of prayer who regard the interior devotion as the essential aspect and strive to acquire it without, however, neglecting a reasonable external expression which always accompanies true devotion.

97 *Presumptuous* devotees are sinners who give full reign to their passions or their love of the world, and who, under the fair name of Christian and servant of our Lady, conceal pride, avarice, lust, drunkenness, anger, swearing, slandering, injustice and other vices. They sleep peacefully in their wicked habits, without making any great effort to correct them, believing that their devotion to our Lady gives them this sort of liberty. They convince themselves that God will forgive them, that they will not die without confession, that they will not be lost for all eternity. They take all this for granted because they say the Rosary, fast on Saturdays, are enrolled in the Confraternity of the Holy Rosary or the Scapular, or a sodality of our Lady, wear the medal or the little chain of Our Lady.

When you tell them that such a devotion is only an illusion of the devil and a dangerous presumption which may well ruin them, they refuse to believe you. God is good and merciful, they reply, and he has not made us to damn us. No man is without sin. We will not die without confession, and a good act of contrition at death is all that is needed. Moreover, they say they have devotion to our Lady; that they wear the scapular; that they recite faithfully and humbly every day the seven Our Fathers and seven Hail Marys in her honor; that sometimes they even say the Rosary and the Office of our Lady, as well as fasting and performing other good works.

Blinding themselves still more, they quote stories they have heard or read—whether true or false does not bother them—which relate how people who had died in mortal sin were brought back to life again to go to confession, or how their soul was miraculously retained in their bodies until confession, because in their lifetime they said a few prayers or performed a few pious acts, in honor of our Lady. Others are supposed to have obtained from God at the moment of death, through the merciful intercession of the Blessed Virgin, sorrow and pardon for their sins, and so were saved. Accordingly, these people expect the same thing to happen to them.

98 Nothing in our Christian religion is so deserving of condemnation as this diabolical presumption. How can we truthfully claim to love and honor the Blessed Virgin when by our sins we pitilessly wound, pierce, crucify and outrage her Son? If Mary made it a rule to save by her mercy this sort of person, she would be condoning wickedness and helping to outrage and crucify her Son. Who would even dare to think of such a thing?

99 I declare that such an abuse of devotion to her is a horrible sacrilege and, next to an unworthy Communion, is the greatest and the least pardonable sin, because devotion to our Lady is the holiest and best after devotion to the Blessed Sacrament.

I admit that to be truly devoted to Our Lady, it is not absolutely necessary to be so holy as to avoid all sin, although this is desirable. But at least it is necessary (note what I am going to say), (i) to be genuinely determined to avoid at least all mortal sin, which outrages the Mother as well as the Son; (ii) to practice great self-restraint in order to avoid sin; (iii) to join her confraternities, say the Rosary or other prayers, fast on Saturdays, and so on.[179]

100 Such means are surprisingly effective in converting even the hardened sinner. Should you be such a sinner, with one foot in the abyss, I advise you to do as I have said. But there is an essential condition. You must perform these good works solely to obtain from God, through the intercession of Our Lady, the grace to regret your sins, obtain pardon for them and overcome your evil habits, and not to live complacently in the state of sin, disregarding the warning voice of conscience, the example of our Lord and the saints, and the teaching of the holy gospel.

101 *Inconstant* devotees are those whose devotion to Our Lady is practiced in fits and starts. Sometimes they are fervent and sometimes they are lukewarm. Sometimes they appear ready to do anything to please Our Lady, and then shortly afterwards they have completely changed. They start by embracing every devotion to Our Lady. They join her confraternities, but they do not faithfully observe the rules. They are as changeable as the moon,[180] and like the moon Mary puts them under her feet. Because of their fickleness they are unworthy to be included among the servants of the Virgin most faithful, because faithfulness and constancy are the hallmarks of Mary's servants. It is better not to burden ourselves with a multitude of prayers and pious practices but rather adopt only a few and perform them with love and perseverance in spite of opposition from the devil and the world and the flesh.

102 There is another category of false devotees of Our Lady—*hypocritical* ones. These hide their sins and evil habits under the mantle of the Blessed Virgin so as to appear to their fellow-men different from what they are.

103 Then there are the *self-interested* devotees who turn to her only to win a court-case, to escape some danger, to be cured of some ailment, or have some similar need satisfied. Except when in need they never think of her. Such people are acceptable neither to God nor to his Mother.

104 We must, then, carefully avoid joining the *critical* devotees, who believe nothing and find fault with everything; the *scrupulous* ones who, out of respect for our Lord, are afraid of having too much devotion to his Mother; the *exterior* devotees whose devotion consists entirely in outward practices; the *presumptuous* devotees who under cover of a fictitious devotion to our Lady wallow in their sins; the *inconstant* devotees who, being unstable, change their devotional practices or abandon them altogether at the slightest temptation; the *hypocritical* ones who join confraternities and wear emblems of our Lady only to be thought of as good people; finally, the *self-interested* devotees who pray to our Lady only to be rid of bodily ills or to obtain material benefits.

[2 Marks of authentic devotion to our Lady.]

105 After having explained and condemned false devotions to the Blessed Virgin we shall now briefly describe what true devotion is. It is *interior, trustful, holy, constant* and *disinterested.*[181]

106 **First, true devotion to our Lady is interior,** that is, it comes from within the mind and the heart and follows from the esteem in which we hold her, the high regard we have for her greatness, and the love we bear her.

107 **Second, it is trustful,** that is to say, it fills us with confidence in the Blessed Virgin, the confidence that a child has for its loving Mother. It prompts us to go to her in every need of body and soul with great simplicity, trust and affection. We implore our Mother's help always, everywhere, and for everything. We pray to her to be enlightened in our doubts, to be put back on the right path when we go astray, to be protected when we are tempted, to be strengthened when we are weakening, to be lifted up when we fall into sin, to be encouraged when we are losing heart, to be rid of our scruples, to be consoled in the trials, crosses and disappointments of life. Finally, in all our afflictions of body and soul, we naturally turn to Mary for help, with never a fear of importuning her or displeasing our Lord.

108 **Third, true devotion to our Lady is holy,** that is, it leads us to avoid sin and to imitate the virtues of Mary. Her ten principal virtues are:[182] deep humility, lively faith, blind obedience, unceasing prayer, constant self-denial, surpassing purity, ardent love, heroic patience, angelic kindness, and heavenly wisdom.

109 **Fourth, true devotion to our Lady is constant.** It strengthens us in our desire to do good and prevents us from giving up our devotional practices too easily. It gives us the courage to oppose the fashions and maxims of the world, the vexations and unruly inclinations of the flesh and the temptations of the devil. Thus a person truly devoted to our Blessed Lady is not changeable, fretful, scrupulous or timid. We do not say however that such a person never sins or that his sensible feelings of devotion never change. When he has fallen, he stretches out his hand to his Blessed Mother and rises again. If he loses all taste and feeling for devotion, he is not at all upset because a good and faithful servant of Mary is guided in his life by faith[183] in Jesus and Mary, and not by feelings.

110 **Fifth, true devotion to Mary is disinterested.** It inspires us to seek God alone in his Blessed Mother and not ourselves. The true subject of Mary does not serve his illustrious Queen for selfish gain. He does not serve her for temporal or eternal well-being but simply and solely because she has the right to be served and God alone in her. He loves her not so much because she is good to him or because he expects something from her, but simply because she is lovable. That is why he loves and serves her just as faithfully in weariness and dryness of soul as in sweet and sensible fervor. He loves her as much on Calvary as at Cana. How pleasing and precious in the sight of God and his holy Mother must these servants of Mary be, who serve her without any self-seeking. How rare they are nowadays! It is to increase their number that I have taken up my pen to write down what I have been teaching with success both publicly and in private in my missions for many years.

111 I have already said many things about the Blessed Virgin and, as I am trying to fashion a true servant of Mary and a true disciple of Jesus, I have still a great deal to say, although through ignorance, inability, and lack of time, I shall leave infinitely more unsaid.

112 But my labor will be well rewarded if this little book falls into the hands of a noble soul, a child of God and of Mary, born not of blood nor the will of the flesh nor of the will of man.[184] My time will be well spent if, by the grace of the Holy Spirit, after having read this book he is convinced of the supreme value of the solid devotion to Mary I am about to describe. If I thought that my guilty blood could help the reader to accept in his heart the truths that I set down in honor of my dear Mother and Queen, I, her most unworthy child and slave, would use it instead of ink to write these words. I would hope to find faithful souls who, by their perseverance in the devotion I teach, will repay her for the loss she has suffered through my ingratitude and infidelity.

113 I feel more than ever inspired to believe and expect the complete fulfillment of the desire that is deeply engraved on my heart and what I have prayed to God for over many years, namely, that in the near or distant future the Blessed Virgin will have more children, servants and slaves of love than ever before,[185] and that through them Jesus, my dear Lord, will reign more than ever in the hearts of men.

114 I clearly foresee that raging beasts will come in fury to tear to pieces with their diabolical teeth this little book and the one the Holy Spirit made use of to write it, or they will cause it at least to lie hidden[186] in the darkness and silence of a chest and so prevent it from seeing the light of day.

They will even attack and persecute those who read it and put into practice what it contains. But no matter! So much the better! It even gives me encouragement to hope for great success at the prospect of a mighty legion of brave and valiant soldiers of Jesus and Mary, both men and women, who will fight the devil, the world, and corrupt nature in the perilous times that are sure to come.

"Let the reader understand. Let him accept this teaching who can."[187]

[3 *Principal practices of devotion to Mary.]*

115 There are several *interior* practices of true devotion to the Blessed Virgin. Here briefly are the main ones:[188]

1 Honoring her, as the worthy Mother of God, by the cult of hyperdulia, that is, esteeming and honoring her more than all the other saints as the masterpiece of grace and the foremost in holiness after Jesus Christ, true God and true man.

2 Meditating on her virtues, her privileges and her actions.

3 Contemplating her sublime dignity.

4 Offering to her acts of love, praise and gratitude.

5 Invoking her with a joyful heart.

6 Offering ourselves to her and uniting ourselves to her.

7 Doing everything to please her.

8 Beginning, carrying out and completing our actions through her, in her, with her and for her in order to do them through Jesus, in Jesus, with Jesus, and for Jesus, our last end. We shall explain this last practice later.

116 True devotion to Our Lady has also several *exterior* practices. Here are the principal ones:

1 Enrolling in her confraternities and joining her sodalities.

2 Joining religious orders dedicated to her.

3 Making her privileges known and appreciated.

4 Giving alms, fasting, performing interior and exterior acts of self-denial in her honor.

5 Carrying such signs of devotion to her as the rosary, the scapular, or a little chain.

6 Reciting with attention, devotion and reverence the fifteen decades of the Rosary in honor of the fifteen principal mysteries of our Lord, or at least five decades in honor of the Joyful mysteries—the Annunciation, the Visitation, the Birth of our Lord, the Purification, the Finding of the Child Jesus in the temple; or the Sorrowful mysteries: the Agony in the Garden, the Scourging, the Crowning with thorns, the Carrying of the Cross, and the Crucifixion; or the Glorious mysteries: the Resurrection of our Lord, the Ascension, the Descent of the Holy Spirit, the Assumption of our Lady, body and soul, into heaven, the Crowning of Mary by the Blessed Trinity.

One may also choose any of the following prayers: the Rosary of six or seven decades in honor of the years our Lady is believed to have spent on earth; the Little Crown of the Blessed Virgin, composed of three Our Fathers and twelve Hail Marys in honor of her crown of twelve stars or privileges; the Little Office of Our Lady so widely accepted and recited in the Church; the Little Psalter of the Blessed Virgin, composed in her honor by St. Bonaventure, which is so heartwarming, and so devotional that you cannot recite it without being moved by it; the fourteen Our Fathers and Hail Marys in honor of her fourteen joys. There are various other prayers and hymns of the Church, such as, the hymns of the liturgical seasons, the *Ave Maris Stella,* the *O Gloriosa Domina;* the *Magnificat* and other prayers which are found in all prayer-books.

7 Singing hymns to her or teaching others to sing them.

8 Genuflecting or bowing to her each morning while saying for example sixty or a hundred times, "Hail Mary, Virgin most faithful," so that through her intercession with God we may faithfully correspond with his graces throughout the day; and in the evening saying "Hail Mary, Mother of Mercy," asking her to obtain God's pardon for the sins we have committed during the day.

9 Taking charge of her confraternities, decorating her altars, crowning and adorning her statues.

10 Carrying her statues or having others carry them in procession, or keeping a small one on one's person as an effective protection against the evil one.

11 Having statues made of her, or her name engraved and placed on the walls of churches or houses and on the gates and entrances of towns, churches and houses.

12 Solemnly giving oneself to her by a special consecration.

117 The Holy Spirit has inspired saintly souls with other practices of true devotion to the Blessed Virgin, all of which are conducive to holiness. You can read of them in detail in *Paradise opened to Philagia,* a collection of many devotions practiced by holy people to honor the Blessed Virgin, compiled by Fr. Paul Barry of the Society of Jesus. These devotions are a wonderful help for souls seeking holiness provided they are performed in a worthy manner, that is:

1 With the right intention of pleasing God alone, seeking union with Jesus, our last end, and giving edification to our neighbor.

2 With attention, avoiding willful distractions.

3 With devotion, avoiding haste and negligence.

4 With decorum and respectful bodily posture.

[4 *The Perfect Practice*]

118 Having read nearly every book on devotion to the Blessed Virgin[189] and talked to the most saintly and learned people of the day, I can now state with conviction that I have never known or heard of any devotion to our Lady which is comparable to the one I am going to speak of. No other devotion calls for more sacrifices for God, none empties us more completely of self and self-love, none keeps us more firmly in the grace of God and the grace of God in us. No other devotion unites us more perfectly and more easily to Jesus. Finally no devotion gives more glory to God, is more sanctifying for ourselves or more helpful to our neighbor.

119 As this devotion essentially consists in a state of soul, it will not be understood in the same way by everyone. Some—the great majority—will stop short at the threshold and go no further. Others—not many—will take but one step into its interior. Who will take a second step? Who will take a third? Finally who will remain in it permanently? Only the one to whom the Spirit of Jesus reveals the secret.[190] The Holy Spirit himself will lead this faithful soul from strength to strength, from grace to grace, from light to light, until at length he attains transformation into Jesus in the fullness of his age on earth and of his glory in heaven.[191]

[II The Perfect Devotion to Our Lady]

[Chapter 3: The Perfect Consecration to Jesus Christ]

 [1 A complete consecration to Mary]

120 As all perfection consists in our being conformed, united and consecrated to Jesus it naturally follows that the most perfect of all devotions is that which conforms, unites, and consecrates us most completely to Jesus. Now of all God's creatures Mary is the most conformed to Jesus. It therefore follows that, of all devotions, devotion to her makes for the most effective consecration and conformity to him.[193] The more one is consecrated to Mary, the more one is consecrated to Jesus.

That is why perfect consecration to Jesus is but a perfect and complete consecration of oneself to the Blessed Virgin, which is the devotion I teach; or in other words, it is the perfect renewal of the vows and promises of holy baptism.[194]

121 This devotion consists in giving oneself entirely to Mary in order to belong entirely to Jesus through her. It requires us to give:

1 Our body with its senses and members;

2 Our soul with its faculties;

3 Our present material possessions and all we shall acquire in the future.

4 Our interior and spiritual possessions, that is, our merits, virtues and good actions of the past, the present and the future.

In other words, we give her all that we possess both in our natural life and in our spiritual life as well as everything we shall acquire in the future in the order of nature, of grace, and of glory in heaven. This we do without any reservation, not even of a penny, a hair, or the smallest good deed. And we give for all eternity without claiming or expecting, in return for our offering and our service, any other reward than the honor of belonging to Our Lord through Mary and in Mary, even though our Mother were not—as in fact she always is—the most generous and appreciative of all God's creatures.

122 Note here that two things must be considered regarding our good works, namely, satisfaction and merit or, in other words, their satisfactory or prayer value and their meritorious value. The satisfactory or prayer value of a good work is the good action in so far as it makes condign atonement for the punishment due to sin or obtain some new grace. The meritorious value or merit is the good action in so far as it merits grace and eternal glory. Now by this consecration of ourselves to the Blessed Virgin we give her all satisfactory and prayer value as well as the meritorious value of our good works, in other words, all the satisfactions and the merits. We give her our merits, graces and virtues, not that she might give them to others, for they are, strictly speaking, not transferable, because Jesus alone, in making himself our surety with his Father, had the power to impart his merits to us. But we give them to her that she

may keep, increase and embellish them for us, as we shall explain later,[195] and we give her our acts of atonement that she may apply them where she pleases for God's greater glory.

123 1 It follows then that by this devotion we give to Jesus all we can possibly give him, and in the most perfect manner, that is, through Mary's hands. Indeed we give him far more than we do by other devotions which require us to give only part of our time, some of our good works or acts of atonement and penances. In this devotion everything is given and consecrated, even the right to dispose freely of one's spiritual goods and the satisfactions earned by daily good works. This is not done even in religious orders. Members of religious orders give God their earthly goods by the vow of poverty, the goods of the body by the vow of chastity, their free will by the vow of obedience, and sometimes their freedom of movement by the vow of enclosure. But they do not give him by these vows the liberty and right to dispose of the value of their good works. They do not despoil themselves of what a Christian considers most precious and most dear—his merits and satisfactions.

124 2 It follows then that anyone who in this way consecrates and sacrifices himself voluntarily to Jesus through Mary may no longer dispose of the value of any of his good actions. All his sufferings, all his thoughts, words, and deeds belong to Mary. She can then dispose of them in accordance with the will of her Son and for his greater glory. This dependence, however, is without detriment to the duties of a person's present and future state of life. One such duty, for example, would be that of a priest who, by virtue of his office or otherwise, must apply the satisfactory or prayer value of the Holy Mass to a particular person. For this consecration can only be made in accordance with the order established by God and in keeping with the duties of one's state of life.

125 3 It follows that we consecrate ourselves at one and the same time to Mary and to Jesus. We give ourselves to Mary because Jesus chose her as the perfect means to unite himself to us and unite us to him. We give ourselves to Jesus because he is our last end. Since he is our Redeemer and our God we are indebted to him for all that we are.

[2 *A Perfect Renewal of Baptismal Promises*]

126 I have said[196] that this devotion could rightly be called a perfect renewal of the vows and promises of holy baptism. Before baptism every Christian was a slave of the devil because he belonged to him. At baptism he has either personally or through his sponsors solemnly renounced Satan, his seductions and his works.[197] He has chosen Jesus as his Master and sovereign Lord and undertaken to depend upon him as a slave of love. This is what is done in the devotion I am presenting to you. We renounce the devil, the world, sin and self, as expressed in the act of consecration,[198] and we give ourselves entirely to Jesus through Mary.[199] We even do something more than at baptism, when ordinarily our godparents speak for us and we are given to Jesus only by proxy. In this devotion we give ourselves personally and freely and we are fully aware of what we are doing.

In holy baptism we do not give ourselves to Jesus explicitly through Mary, nor do we give him the value of our good actions. After baptism we remain entirely free either to apply that value to anyone we wish or keep it for ourselves. But by this consecration we give ourselves explicitly to Jesus through Mary's hands and we include in our consecration the value of all our actions.

127 "Men," says St. Thomas, "vow in baptism to renounce the devil and all his seductions."[200] "This vow," says St. Augustine,[201] "is the greatest and the most indispensable of all vows." Canon Law experts say the same thing: "The vow we make at baptism is the most important of all vows."[202]But does anyone keep this great vow? Does anyone fulfill the promises of baptism faithfully? Is it not true that nearly all Christians prove unfaithful to the promises made to Jesus in baptism? Where does this universal failure come from, if not from man's habitual forgetfulness of the promises and responsibilities of baptism and from the fact that scarcely anyone makes a personal ratification of the contract made with God through his sponsors?

128 This is so true that the Council of Sens,[203] convened by order of the Emperor Louis the Debonair to remedy the grave disorders of Christendom, came to the conclusion that the main cause of this moral breakdown was man's forgetfulness of his baptismal obligations and his disregard for them. It could suggest no better way of remedying this great evil than to encourage all Christians to renew the promises and vows of baptism.

129 The Catechism of the Council of Trent, faithful interpreter of that holy Council, exhorts priests to do the same and to encourage the faithful to remember and to hold fast to the belief that they are bound and consecrated as slaves to Jesus, their Redeemer and Lord. "The parish priest shall exhort the faithful never to lose sight of the fact that they are bound in conscience to dedicate and consecrate themselves forever to their Lord and Redeemer as his slaves."[204]

130 Now the Councils, the Fathers of the Church and experience itself, all indicate that the best remedy for the frequent lapses of Christians is to remind them of the responsibilities of their baptism and have them renew the vows they made at that time. Is it not reasonable therefore to do this in our day and in a perfect manner by adopting this devotion with its consecration to Our Lord through his Blessed Mother? I say, "in a perfect manner," for in making this consecration to Jesus they are adopting the perfect means of giving themselves to him, which is the most Blessed Virgin Mary.

131 No one can object that this devotion is novel or of no value. It is not new, since the Councils, the Fathers of the Church, and many authors both past and present, speak of consecration to Our Lord or renewal of baptismal vows as something going back to ancient times and recommended to all the faithful. Nor is it valueless, since the chief source of moral disorders and the consequent eternal loss of Christians spring from forgetfulness of this practice and indifference to it.

132 Some may object that this devotion makes us powerless to help the souls of our relatives, friends and benefactors, since it requires us to give our Lord, through Mary, the value of our good works, prayers, penances, and almsgiving.

To them I reply:[205]

1 It is inconceivable that our friends, relatives and benefactors should suffer any loss because we have dedicated and consecrated ourselves unconditionally to the service of Jesus and Mary; it would be an affront to the power and goodness of Jesus and Mary who will surely come to the aid of our relatives, friends and benefactors whether from our meager spiritual assets or from other sources.

2 This devotion does not prevent us from praying for others, both the living and the dead, even though the application of our good works depends on the will of our Blessed Lady. On the contrary, it will make us pray with even greater confidence. Imagine a rich man, who, wanting to show his esteem for a great prince, gives his entire fortune to him. Would not that man have greater confidence in asking the prince to help one of his friends who needed assistance? Indeed the prince would only be too happy to have such an opportunity of proving his gratitude to one who had sacrificed all that he possessed to enrich him, thereby impoverishing himself to do him honor. The same must be said of our Lord and our Lady. They will never allow themselves to be outdone in gratitude.

133 Some may say, perhaps, if I give our Lady the full value of my actions to apply it to whom she wills, I may have to suffer a long time in purgatory. This objection, which arises from self-love and from an unawareness of the generosity of God and his holy Mother, refutes itself.

Take a fervent and generous soul who values God's interests more than his own. He gives God all he has without reserve till he can give no more. He desires only that the glory and the kingdom of Jesus may come through his Mother, and he does all he can to bring this about. Will this generous and unselfish soul, I ask, be punished more in the next world for having been more generous and unselfish than other people? Far from it! For we shall see later[206] that our Lord and his Mother will prove most generous to such a soul with gifts of nature, grace and glory in this life and in the next.

134 We must now consider[207] as briefly as possible:
1) The *motives* which commend this devotion to us, 2) the wonderful *effects* it produces in faithful souls, and 3) the *practices* of this devotion.

[Chapter 4: Motives Which Recommend This Devotion]

[First Motive. By it we give ourselves completely to God]

135 This first motive shows us the excellence of the consecration of ourselves to Jesus through Mary.

We can conceive of no higher calling than that of being in the service of God and we believe that the least of God's servants is richer, stronger and nobler than any earthly monarch who does not serve God. How rich and strong and noble then must be the good and faithful servant, who serves God as unreservedly and as completely as he possibly can! Just such a person is the faithful and loving slave of Jesus in Mary. He has indeed surrendered himself entirely to the service of the King of kings through Mary, his Mother, keeping nothing for himself. All the gold of the world and the beauties of the heavens could not recompense him for what he has done.

136 Other congregations, associations, and confraternities set up in honor of our Lord and our Blessed Lady, which do so much good in the Church, do not require their members to give up absolutely everything. They simply prescribe for them the performance of certain acts and practices in fulfillment of their obligations. They leave them free to dispose of the rest of their actions as well as their time. But this devotion makes us give Jesus and Mary all our thoughts, words, actions, and sufferings and every moment of our lives without exception. Thus, whatever we do, whether we are awake or asleep, whether we eat or drink, whether we do important or unimportant work, it will always be true to say that everything is done for Jesus and Mary. Our offering always holds good, whether we think of it or not, unless we explicitly retract it.[208] How consoling this is!

137 Moreover, as I have said before,[209] no other act of devotion enables us to rid ourselves so easily of the possessiveness which slips unnoticed even into our best actions. This is a remarkable grace which our dear Lord grants us in return for the heroic and selfless surrender to him through Mary of the entire value of our good works. If even in this life he gives a hundredfold reward to those who renounce all material, temporal and perishable things[210] out of love for him, how generously will he reward those who give up even interior and spiritual goods for his sake!

138 Jesus, our dearest friend, gave himself to us without reserve, body and soul, graces and merits. As St. Bernard says,[211] "He won me over entirely by giving himself entirely to me." Does not simple justice as well as gratitude require that we give all we possibly can? He was generous with us first, so let us be generous to him in return and he will prove still more generous to us during life, at the hour of death, and throughout eternity. "He will be generous towards the generous."

[Second Motive. It helps us to imitate Christ]

139 Our good Master stooped to enclose himself in the womb of the Blessed Virgin, a captive but loving slave, and to make himself subject to her for thirty years. As I said earlier,[212] the human mind is bewildered when it reflects seriously upon this conduct of Incarnate Wisdom. He did not choose to give himself in a direct manner to the human race though he could easily have done so. He chose to come through the Virgin Mary. Thus he did not come into the world independently of others in the flower of his manhood, but he came as a frail little child dependent on the care and attention of his Mother. Consumed with the desire to give glory to God, his Father, and save the human race, he saw no better or shorter way to do so than by submitting completely to Mary.

He did this not just for the first eight, ten or fifteen years of his life like other children, but for thirty years. He gave more glory to God, his Father, during all those years of submission and dependence than he would have given by spending them working miracles, preaching far and wide, and converting all mankind. Otherwise he would have done all these things.

What immeasurable glory then do we give to God when, following the example of Jesus, we submit to Mary! With such a convincing and well-known example before us, can we be so foolish as to believe that there is a better and shorter way of giving God glory than by submitting ourselves to Mary, as Jesus did?

140 Let me remind you again[213] of the dependence shown by the three divine Persons on our Blessed Lady. Theirs is the example which fully justifies our dependence on her. The Father gave and still gives his Son only through her. He raises children for himself only through her. He dispenses his graces to us only through her. God the Son was prepared for mankind in general by her alone.

Mary, in union with the Holy Spirit, still conceives him and brings him forth daily. It is through her alone that the Son distributes his merits and virtues. The Holy Spirit formed Jesus only through her, and he forms the members of the Mystical Body and dispenses his gifts and his favors only through her.

With such a compelling example of the three divine Persons before us, we would be extremely perverse to ignore her and not consecrate ourselves to her. Indeed we would be blind if we did not see the need for Mary in approaching God and making our total offering to him.

141 Here are a few passages from the Fathers of the Church which I have chosen to prove what I have just said: "Mary has two sons, the one a God-man, the other, mere man. She is Mother of the first corporally and of the second spiritually" (St. Bonaventure and Origen).[214]

"This is the will of God who willed that we should have all things through Mary. If then, we possess any hope or grace or gift of salvation, let us acknowledge that it comes to us through her" (St. Bernard).[215]

"All the gifts, graces, virtues of the Holy Spirit are distributed by the hands of Mary, to whom she wills, when she wills, as she wills, and in the measure she wills" (St. Bernardine).[216]

"As you were not worthy that anything divine should be given to you, all graces were given to Mary so that you might receive through her all graces you would not otherwise receive" (St. Bernard).[217]

142 St. Bernard tells us that God, seeing that we are unworthy to receive his graces directly from him, gives them to Mary so that we might receive from her all that he decides to give us. His glory is achieved when he receives through Mary the gratitude, respect and love we owe him in return for his gifts to us. It is only right then that we should imitate his conduct, "in order," as St. Bernard again says, "that grace might return to its author by the same channel through which it came to us."[218]

This is what we do by this devotion. We offer and consecrate all we are and all we possess to the Blessed Virgin in order that Our Lord may receive through her as intermediary the glory and gratitude that we owe to him. We deem ourselves unworthy and unfit to approach his infinite majesty on our own, and so we avail ourselves of Mary's intercession.

143 Moreover, this devotion is an expression of great humility, a virtue which God loves above all others. A person who exalts himself debases God, and a person who humbles himself exalts God. "God opposes the proud, but gives his graces to the humble."[219] If you humble yourself, convinced that you are unworthy to appear before him, or even to approach him, he condescends to come down to you. He is pleased to be with you and exalts you in spite of yourself. But, on the other hand, if you venture to go towards God boldly without a mediator, he vanishes and is nowhere to be found. How dearly he loves the humble of heart! It is to such humility that this devotion leads us, for it teaches us never to go alone directly to Our Lord, however gentle and merciful though he may be, but always to use Mary's power of intercession, whether we want to enter his presence, speak to him, be near him, offer him something, seek union with him or consecrate ourselves to him.

[Third Motive. It obtains many blessings from our Lady]

144 The Blessed Virgin, mother of gentleness and mercy, never allows herself to be surpassed in love and generosity. When she sees someone giving himself entirely to her in order to honor and serve her, and depriving himself of what he prizes most in order to adorn her, she gives herself completely in a wondrous manner to him. She engulfs him in the ocean of her graces, adorns him with her merits, supports him with her power, enlightens him with her light, and fills him with her love. She shares her virtues with him—her humility, faith, purity, etc.[220] She makes up for his failings and becomes his representative with Jesus. Just as one who is consecrated belongs entirely to Mary, so Mary belongs entirely to him. We can truthfully say of this perfect servant and child of Mary what St. John in his gospel says of himself, "He took her for his own."[221]

145 This produces in his soul, if he is persevering, a great distrust, contempt, and hatred of self, and a great confidence in Mary with complete self-abandonment to her.[222] He no longer relies on his own dispositions, intentions, merits, virtues and good works, since he has sacrificed them completely to Jesus through his loving Mother. He has now only one treasury, where all his wealth is stored. That treasury is not within himself: it is Mary. That is why he can now go to Our Lord without any servile or scrupulous fear and pray to him with great confidence. He can also share the sentiments of the devout and learned Abbot Rupert, who, referring to the victory which Jacob won over an angel,[223] addressed Our Lady in these words, "O Mary, my Queen, Immaculate Mother of the God-man, Jesus Christ, I desire to wrestle with this man, the Divine Word, armed with your merits and not my own."[224]

How much stronger and more powerful are we in approaching Our Lord when we are armed with the merits and prayers of the worthy Mother of God, who, as St. Augustine says, has conquered the Almighty by her love![225]

146 Since by this devotion we give to Our Lord, through the hands of his holy Mother, all our good works, she purifies them, making them beautiful and acceptable to her Son.

1 She purifies them of every taint of self-love and of that unconscious attachment to creatures which slips unnoticed into our best actions. Her hands have never been known to be idle or uncreative. They purify everything they touch. As soon as the Blessed Virgin receives our good works, she removes any blemish or imperfection she may find in them.

147 2 She enriches our good works by adorning them with her own merits and virtues. It is as if a poor peasant, wishing to win the friendship and favor of the king, were to go to the queen and give her an apple—his only possession—for her to offer it to the king. The queen, accepting the peasant's humble gift, puts it on a beautiful golden dish and presents it to the king on behalf of the peasant. The apple in itself would not be a gift worthy of a king, but presented by the queen in person[226] on a dish of gold, it becomes fit for any king.

148 3 Mary presents our good works to Jesus. She does not keep anything we offer for herself, as if she were our last end, but unfailingly gives everything to Jesus. So by the very fact we give anything to her, we are giving it to Jesus. Whenever we praise and glorify her, she immediately praises and glorifies Jesus. When anyone praises and blesses her, she sings today as she did on the day Elizabeth praised her, "My soul glorifies the Lord."[227]

149 At Mary's request, Jesus accepts the gift of our good works, no matter how poor and insignificant they may be for one who is the King of kings, the Holiest of the holy. When we present anything to Jesus by ourselves, relying on our own dispositions and efforts, he examines our gift and often rejects it because it is stained with self-love, just as he once rejected the sacrifices of the Jews because they were imbued with selfish motives.

But when we present something to him by the pure, virginal hands of his beloved Mother, we take him by his weak side, in a manner of speaking. He does not consider so much the present itself as the person who offers it. Thus Mary, who is never slighted by her Son but is always well received, prevails upon him to accept with pleasure everything she offers him, regardless of its value. Mary has only to present the gift for Jesus graciously to accept it. This is what St. Bernard strongly recommended to all those he was guiding along the pathway to perfection. "When you want to offer something to God, to be welcomed by him, be sure to offer it through the worthy Mother of God, if you do not wish to see it rejected."[228]

150 Does not human nature itself, as we have seen,[229] suggest this mode of procedure to the less important people of this world with regard to the great? Why should grace not inspire us to do likewise with regard to God? He is infinitely exalted above us. We are less than atoms in his sight. But we have an advocate so powerful that she is never refused anything. She is so resourceful that she knows every secret way to win the heart of God. She is so good and kind that she never passes over anyone no matter how lowly and sinful.

Further on, I shall relate the story of Jacob and Rebecca[230] which exemplifies the truths I have been setting before you.

[Fourth Motive. It is an excellent means of giving glory to God]

151 This devotion, when faithfully undertaken, is a perfect means of ensuring that the value of all our good works is being used for the greater glory of God.[231] Scarcely anyone works for that noble end, in spite of the obligation to do so, either because men do not know where God's greatest glory is to be found or because they do not desire it. Now Mary, to whom we surrender the value and merit of our good actions, knows perfectly well where God's greatest glory lies and she works only to promote that glory. The devout servant of our Lady, having entirely consecrated himself to her as I have described above, can boldly claim that the value of all his actions, words, and thoughts is used for the greatest glory of God, unless he has explicitly retracted his offering. For one who loves God with a pure and unselfish love and prizes God's glory and interests far above his own, could anything be more consoling?

[Fifth Motive. It leads to union with our Lord]

152 This devotion is a smooth, short, perfect and sure way of attaining union with our Lord, in which Christian perfection consists.

a **This devotion is a smooth way.** It is the path which Jesus Christ opened up in coming to us and in which there is no obstruction to prevent our reaching him. It is quite true that we can attain to divine union by other roads,[232] but these involve many more crosses and exceptional setbacks and many difficulties that we cannot easily overcome. We would have to pass through spiritual darkness, engage in struggles for which we are not prepared, endure bitter agonies, scale precipitous mountains, tread upon painful thorns, and cross frightful deserts. But when we take the path of Mary, we walk smoothly and calmly.

It is true that on our way we have hard battles to fight and serious obstacles to overcome, but Mary, our Mother and Queen, stays close to her faithful servants. She is always at hand to brighten their darkness, clear away their doubts, strengthen them in their fears, sustain them in their combats and trials.[233] Truly, in comparison with other ways, this virgin road to Jesus is a path of roses and sweet delights. There have been some saints, not very many, such as St. Ephrem, St. John Damascene, St. Bernard, St. Bernardine, St. Bonaventure, and St. Francis de Sales, who have taken this smooth path to Jesus Christ, because the Holy Spirit, the faithful Spouse of

Mary, made it known to them by a special grace. The other saints, who are the greater number, while having a devotion to Mary, either did not enter or did not go very far along this path. That is why they had to undergo harder and more dangerous trials.

153 Why is it then, a servant of Mary might ask, that devoted servants of this good Mother are called upon to suffer much more than those who serve her less generously?[234] They are opposed, persecuted, slandered, and treated with intolerance. They may also have to walk in interior darkness and through spiritual deserts without being given from heaven a single drop of the dew of consolation. If this devotion to the Blessed Virgin makes the path to Jesus smoother, how can we explain why Mary's loyal servants are so ill-treated?

154 I reply that it is quite true that the most faithful servants of the Blessed Virgin, being her greatest favorites, receive from her the best graces and favors from heaven, which are crosses. But I maintain too that these servants of Mary bear their crosses with greater ease and gain more merit and glory. What could check another's progress a thousand times over, or possibly bring about his downfall, does not balk them at all, but even helps them on their way. For this good Mother, filled with the grace and unction of the Holy Spirit, dips all the crosses she prepares for them in the honey of her maternal sweetness and the unction of pure love. They then readily swallow them as they would sugared almonds, though the crosses may be very bitter. I believe that anyone who wishes to be devout and live piously in Jesus will suffer persecution[235] and will have a daily cross to carry. But he will never manage to carry a heavy cross, or carry it joyfully and perseveringly, without a trusting devotion to Our Lady, who is the very sweetness of the cross. It is obvious that a person could not keep on eating without great effort unripe fruit which has not been sweetened.[236]

155 b **This devotion is a short way** to discover Jesus, either because it is a road we do not wander from, or because, as we have just said, we walk along this road with greater ease and joy, and consequently with greater speed. We advance more in a brief period of submission to Mary and dependence on her than in whole years of self-will and self-reliance. A man who is obedient and submissive to Mary will sing of glorious victories over his enemies.[237] It is true, his enemies will try to impede his progress, force him to retreat or try to make him fall. But with Mary's help, support and guidance, he will go forward towards our Lord. Without falling, retreating and even without being delayed, he will advance with giant strides towards Jesus along the same road which, as is written,[238] Jesus took to come to us with giant strides and in a short time.

156 Why do you think our Lord spent only a few years here on earth and nearly all of them in submission and obedience to his

Mother? The reason is that "attaining perfection in a short time, he lived a long time,"[239] even longer than Adam, whose losses he had come to make good. Yet Adam lived more than nine hundred years!

Jesus lived a long time, because he lived in complete submission to his Mother and in union with her, which obedience to his Father required. The Holy Spirit tells us that the man who honors his mother is like a man who stores up a treasure. In other words, the man who honors Mary, his Mother, to the extent of subjecting himself to her and obeying her in all things will soon become very rich, because he is amassing riches every day through Mary who has become his secret philosopher's stone.[240]

There is another quotation from Holy Scripture, "My old age will be found in the mercy of the bosom."[241] According to the mystical interpretation of these words it is in the bosom of Mary that people who are young grow mature in enlightenment, in holiness, in experience and in wisdom, and in a short time reach the fullness of the age of Christ.[242] For it was Mary's womb which encompassed and produced a perfect man.[243] That same womb held the one whom the whole universe can neither encompass nor contain.[244]

157 c **This devotion is a perfect way** to reach our Lord and be united to him, for Mary is the most perfect and the most holy of all creatures, and Jesus, who came to us in a perfect manner, chose no other road for his great and wonderful journey.[245] The Most High, the Incomprehensible One, the Inaccessible One, He who is, deigned to come down to us poor earthly creatures who are nothing at all. How was this done?

The Most High God came down to us in a perfect way through the humble Virgin Mary, without losing anything of his divinity or holiness. It is likewise through Mary that we poor creatures must ascend to almighty God in a perfect manner without having anything to fear.

God, the Incomprehensible, allowed himself to be perfectly comprehended and contained by the humble Virgin Mary without losing anything of his immensity. So we must let ourselves be perfectly contained and led by the humble Virgin without any reserve on our part.

God, the Inaccessible, drew near to us and united himself closely, perfectly and even personally to our humanity through Mary without losing anything of his majesty. So it is also through Mary that we must draw near to God and unite ourselves to him perfectly, intimately and without fear of being rejected.

Lastly, He Who Is deigned to come down to us who are not and turned our nothingness into God, or He Who Is. He did this perfectly by giving and submitting himself entirely to the young Virgin Mary, without ceasing to be in time He Who Is from all eternity. Likewise it is through Mary that we, who are nothing, may become like God by grace and glory. We accomplish this by giving ourselves to her so perfectly and so completely as to remain nothing, as far as self is concerned, and to be everything in her, without any fear of illusion.

158 Show me a new road to our Lord, pave it with all the merits of the saints, adorn it with their heroic virtues, illuminate and enhance it with the splendor and beauty of the angels, have all the angels and saints there to guide and protect those who wish to follow it. Give me such a road and truly, truly, I boldly say—and I am telling the truth—that instead of this road, perfect though it be, I would still choose the immaculate way of Mary.[246] It is a way, a road without stain or spot, without original sin or actual sin, without shadow or darkness. When our loving Jesus comes in glory once again to reign upon earth—as he certainly will—he will choose no other way than the Blessed Virgin, by whom he came so surely and so perfectly the first time. The difference between his first and his second coming is that the first was secret and hidden, but the second will be glorious and resplendent. Both are perfect because both are through Mary. Alas, this is a mystery which we cannot understand. "Here let every tongue be silent."

159 d **This devotion to our Lady is a sure way** to go to Jesus and to acquire holiness through union with him.

1 The devotion which I teach is not new.[247] Its history goes back so far that the time of its origin cannot be ascertained with any precision, as Fr. Boudon, who died a short time ago in the odor of sanctity, states in a book[248] which he wrote on this devotion. It is however certain that for more than seven hundred years we find traces of it in the Church.[249]

St. Odilo, abbot of Cluny, who lived about the year 1040, was one of the first to practice it publicly in France as is told in his life.[250]

Cardinal Peter Damian[251] relates that in the year 1076 his brother, Blessed Marino, made himself the slave of the Blessed Virgin in the presence of his spiritual director in a most edifying manner. He placed a rope around his neck, scourged himself and placed on the altar a sum of money as a token of his devotion and consecration to our Lady. He remained so faithful to this consecration all his life that he merited to be visited and consoled on his deathbed by his dear Queen and hear from her lips the promise of paradise in reward for his service.

Caesarius Bollandus[252] mentions a famous knight, Vautier de Birbak, a close relative of the Dukes of Louvain, who about the year 1300 consecrated himself to the Blessed Virgin.

This devotion was also practiced privately by many people up to the seventeenth century, when it became publicly known.[253]

160 Father Simon de Rojas[254] of the order of the Holy Trinity for the Redemption of Captives, court preacher to Philip III, made this devotion popular throughout Spain and Germany. Through the intervention of Philip III, he obtained from Gregory XV valuable indulgences for those who practiced it.

Father de los Rios,[255] of the order of St. Augustine, together with his intimate friend, Father de Rojas, worked hard, propagating it throughout Spain and Germany by preaching and writing. He composed a large volume entitled *Hierarchia Mariana,* where he treats of the antiquity, the excellence and the soundness of this devotion, with as much devotion as learning.

The Theatine Fathers in the seventeenth century established this devotion in Italy, Sicily and Savoy.[256]

161 Father Stanislaus Phalacius of the Society of Jesus spread this devotion widely in Poland.[257]

Father de los Rios in the book quoted above mentions the names of princes and princesses, bishops and cardinals of different countries who embraced this devotion.

Father Cornelius a Lapide,[258] noted both for holiness and profound learning, was commissioned by several bishops and theologians to examine it. The praise he gave it after mature examination, is a worthy tribute to his own holiness. Many other eminent men followed his example.

The Jesuit Fathers, ever zealous in the service of Our Blessed Lady, presented on behalf of the sodalities of Cologne to Duke Ferdinand of Bavaria, the then archbishop of Cologne, a little treatise on the devotion, and he gave it his approval and granted permission to have it printed. He exhorted all priests and religious of his diocese to do their utmost to spread this solid devotion.

162 Cardinal de Bérulle, whose memory is venerated throughout France, was outstandingly zealous in furthering the devotion in France, despite the calumnies and persecution he suffered at the hands of critics and evil men. They accused him of introducing novelty and superstition. They composed and published a libelous tract against him and they—or rather the devil in them—used a thousand stratagems to prevent him from spreading the devotion in France. But this eminent and saintly man responded to the calumnies with calm patience. He wrote a little book in reply to their libel and forcefully refuted the objections contained in it. He pointed out that this devotion is founded on the example given by Jesus Christ, on the obligations we have towards him and on the promises we made in holy baptism. It was mainly this last reason which silenced his enemies. He made clear to them that his consecration to the Blessed Virgin, and through her to Jesus, is nothing less than a perfect renewal of the promises and vows of baptism. He said many beautiful things concerning this devotion which can be read in his works.

163 In Fr. Boudon's book[260] we read of the different popes who gave their approval to this devotion, the theologians who examined it, the hostility it encountered and overcame, the thousands who made it their own without censure from any pope.[261] Indeed it could not be condemned without overthrowing the foundations of Christianity.

It is obvious then that this devotion is not new. If it is not commonly practiced, the reason is that it is too sublime to be appreciated and undertaken by everyone.

164 2 This devotion is a safe means of going to Jesus Christ, because it is Mary's role to lead us safely to her Son; just as it is the role of Our Lord to lead us to the eternal Father.[262] Those who are spiritually-minded should not fall into the error of thinking that Mary hinders our union with God. How could this possibly happen? How could Mary, who found grace with God for everyone in general and each one in particular, prevent a soul from obtaining the supreme grace of union with him? Is it possible that she who was so completely filled with grace to overflowing, so united to Christ and transformed in God that it became necessary for him to be made flesh in her,[263] should prevent a soul from being perfectly united to him?

It is quite true that the example of other people, no matter how holy, can sometimes impair union with God, but not so Our Blessed Lady, as I have said[264] and shall never weary of repeating. One reason why so few souls come to the fullness of the age of Jesus[265] is that Mary who is still as much as ever his Mother and the fruitful spouse of the Holy Spirit is not formed well enough in their hearts. If we desire a ripe and perfectly formed fruit, we must possess the tree that bears it. If we desire the fruit of life, Jesus Christ, we must possess the tree of life which is Mary.[266] If we desire to have the Holy Spirit working within us, we must possess his faithful and inseparable spouse, Mary the divinely-favored one, whom as I have said elsewhere,[267] he can make fruitful.

165 Rest assured that the more you turn to Mary in your prayers, meditations, actions and sufferings, seeing her, if not perhaps clearly and distinctly, at least in a general and indistinct way, the more surely will you discover Jesus. For he is always greater, more powerful, more active, and more mysterious when acting through Mary than he is in any other creature in the universe, or even in heaven. Thus Mary, so divinely-favored and so lost in God, is far from being an obstacle to good people who are striving for union with him. There has never been and there never will be a creature so ready to help us in achieving that union more effectively, for she will dispense to us all the graces to attain that end. As a saint once remarked,[268] "Only Mary knows how to fill our minds with the thought of God" (St. Germanus). Moreover Mary will safeguard us against the deception and cunning of the evil one.

166 Where Mary is present, the evil one is absent. One of the unmistakable signs that a person is led by the spirit of God is the devotion he has to Mary, and his habit of thinking and speaking of her. This is the opinion of a saint,[269] who goes on to say that just as breathing is a proof that the body is not dead, so the habitual thought of Mary and loving converse with her is a proof that the soul is not spiritually dead in sin.

167 Since Mary alone has crushed all heresies, as we are told by the Church under the guidance of the Holy Spirit (Office of B.V.M.), a devoted servant of hers will never fall into formal heresy or error, though critics may contest this. He may very well err materially, mistaking lies for truth or an evil spirit for a good one, but he will be less likely to do this than others. Sooner or later he will discover his error and will not go on stubbornly believing and maintaining what he mistakenly thought was the truth.[270]

168 Whoever then wishes to advance along the road to holiness and be sure of encountering the true Christ, without fear of the illusions which afflict many devout people, should take up with valiant heart and willing spirit[271] this devotion to Mary which perhaps he had not previously heard about. Even if it is new to him, let him enter upon this excellent way which I am now revealing to him. "I will show you a more excellent way."[272]

It was opened up by Jesus Christ, the Incarnate Wisdom. He is our one and only Head, and we, his members, cannot go wrong in following him. It is a smooth way made easy by the fullness of grace, the unction of the Holy Spirit. In our progress along this road, we do not weaken or turn back. It is a *quick* way and leads us to Jesus in a short time. It is a *perfect* way without mud or dust or any vileness of sin. Finally, it is a reliable way, for it is *direct* and *sure,* having no turnings to right or left but leading us straight to Jesus and to life eternal.

Let us then take this road and travel along it night and day until we arrive at the fullness of the age of Jesus Christ.[273]

[Sixth Motive. The practice of this devotion gives great liberty of spirit – the freedom of the children of God[274] – to those who faithfully practice it.]

169 For through this devotion we make ourselves slaves of Jesus by consecrating ourselves entirely to him. To reward us for this enslavement of love, our Lord frees us from every scruple and servile fear which might restrict, imprison or confuse us; he opens our hearts and fills them with holy confidence in God, helping us to regard God as our Father; he inspires us with a generous and filial love.

170 Without stopping to prove this truth, I shall simply relate an incident which I read in the life of Mother Agnes of Jesus, a Dominican nun[275] of the convent of Langeac in Auvergne, who died there in the odor of sanctity in 1634.

When she was only seven years old and was suffering great spiritual anguish, she heard a voice telling her that if she wished to be delivered from her anguish and protected against all her enemies, she should make herself the slave of our Lord and his Blessed Mother as soon as possible. No sooner had she returned home than she gave herself completely to Jesus and Mary as their slave, although she had never known anything about this devotion before. She found an iron chain, put it around her waist and wore it till the day she died.[276] After this, all her sufferings and scruples disappeared and she found great peace of soul.

This led her to teach this devotion to many others who made rapid progress in it—among them, Father Olier, the founder of the Seminary of St. Sulpice, and several other priests and students from the same seminary. One day the Blessed Virgin appeared to Mother Agnes and put a gold chain around her neck to show her how happy she was that Mother Agnes had become the slave of both her and her Son. And St. Cecilia, who accompanied our Lady, said to her, "Happy are the faithful slaves of the Queen of heaven, for they will enjoy true freedom." *Tibi servire libertas.*[277]

[Seventh Motive. It is of great benefit to our neighbor.]

171 Another consideration which may bring us to embrace this practice is the great good which our neighbor receives from it. For by it we show love for our neighbor in an outstanding way, since we give him through Mary's hands all that we prize most highly – that is, the satisfactory and prayer value of all our good works, down to the least good thought and the least little suffering. We give our consent that all we have already acquired or will acquire until death should be used in accordance with our Lady's will for the conversion of sinners or the deliverance of souls from purgatory.

Is this not perfect love of our neighbor? Is this not being a true disciple of our Lord, one who should always be recognized by his love?[278] Is this not the way to convert sinners without any danger of vainglory, and deliver souls from purgatory by doing hardly anything more than what we are obliged to do by our state of life?

172 To appreciate the excellence of this motive we must understand what a wonderful thing it is to convert a sinner or to deliver a soul from purgatory. It is an infinite good, greater than the creation of heaven and earth, since it gives a soul the possession of God.[279] If by this devotion we secured the release of only one soul from purgatory or converted only one sinner in our whole lifetime, would that not be enough to induce any person who really loves his neighbor to practice this devotion?

It must be noted that our good works, passing through Mary's hands, are progressively purified. Consequently, their merit and their satisfactory and prayer value is also increased. That is why they become much more effective in relieving the souls in purgatory and in converting sinners than if they did not pass through the virginal and liberal hands of Mary. Stripped of self-will and clothed with disinterested love,[280] the little that we give to the Blessed Virgin is truly powerful enough to appease the anger of God and draw down his mercy. It may well be that at the hour of death a person who has been faithful to this devotion will find that he has freed many souls from purgatory and converted many sinners, even though he performed only the ordinary actions of his state of life. Great will be his joy at the judgment. Great will be his glory throughout eternity.

[Eighth Motive. Finally, what draws us in a sense more compellingly to take up this devotion to the most Blessed Virgin is the fact that it is a wonderful means of persevering in the practice of virtue and of remaining steadfast.]

173 Why is it that most conversions of sinners are not lasting? Why do they relapse so easily into sin? Why is it that most of the faithful, instead of making progress in one virtue after another and so acquiring new graces, often lose the little grace and virtue they have? This misfortune arises, as I have already shown,[281] from the fact that man, so prone to evil, so weak and changeable, trusts himself too much, relies on his own strength, and wrongly presumes he is able to safeguard his precious graces, virtues and merits.

By this devotion we entrust all we possess to Mary, the faithful Virgin. We choose her as the guardian of all our possessions in the natural and supernatural sphere. We trust her because she is faithful, we rely on her strength, we count on her mercy and charity to preserve and increase our virtues and merits in spite of the efforts of the devil, the world, and the flesh to rob us of them. We say to her as a good child would say to its mother or a faithful servant to the mistress of the house,[282] "My dear Mother and Mistress, I realize that up to now I have received from God through your intercession more graces than I deserve. But bitter experience has taught me that I carry these riches in a very fragile vessel and that I am too weak and sinful[283] to guard them by myself. Please accept in trust everything I possess, and in your faithfulness and power keep it for me. If you watch over me, I shall lose nothing. If you support me, I shall not fail. If you protect me, I shall be safe from my enemies."

174 This is exactly what St. Bernard clearly pointed out to encourage us to take up this devotion, "When Mary supports you, you will not fail. With her as your protector, you will have nothing to fear.

With her as your guide you will not grow weary. When you win her favor, you will reach the port of heaven."[284] St. Bonaventure seems to say the same thing in even more explicit terms, "The Blessed Virgin," he says, "not only preserves the fullness enjoyed by the saints, but she maintains the saints in their fullness so that it does not diminish. She prevents their virtues from fading away, their merits from being wasted and their graces from being lost. She prevents the devils from doing them harm and she so influences them that her divine Son has no need to punish them when they sin."[285]

175 Mary is the Virgin most faithful who by her fidelity to God makes good the losses caused by Eve's unfaithfulness. She obtains fidelity to God and final perseverance for those who commit themselves to her. For this reason, St. John Damascene compared her to a firm anchor which holds them fast[286] and saves them from shipwreck in the raging seas of the world where so many people perish through lack of such a firm anchor. "We fasten souls," he said, "to Mary, our hope, as to a firm anchor." It was to Mary that the saints who attained salvation most firmly anchored themselves as did others who wanted to ensure their perseverance in holiness.

Blessed, indeed, are those Christians who bind themselves faithfully and completely to her as to a secure anchor! The violent storms of the world will not make them founder or carry away their heavenly riches. Blessed are those who enter into her as into another Noah's ark! The flood waters of sin which engulf so many will not harm them because, as the Church makes Mary say in the words of divine Wisdom, "Those who work with my help—for their salvation—shall not sin."[287] Blessed are the unfaithful children of unhappy Eve who commit themselves to Mary, the ever-faithful Virgin and Mother who never wavers in her fidelity and never goes back on her trust![288] She always loves those who love her,[289] not only with deep affection, but with a love that is active and generous.[290] By an abundant outpouring of grace she keeps them from relaxing their effort in the practice of virtue or falling by the wayside through the loss of divine grace.

176 Moved by pure love, this good Mother always accepts whatever is given her in trust, and, once she accepts something, she binds herself in justice by a contract of trusteeship to keep it safe. Is not someone to whom I entrust the sum of a thousand francs obliged to keep it safe for me, so that if it were lost through his negligence he would be responsible for it in strict justice? But nothing we entrust to the faithful Virgin will ever be lost through her negligence. Heaven and earth would pass away sooner than Mary would neglect or betray those who trusted in her.

177 Poor children of Mary, you are extremely weak and changeable. Your human nature is deeply impaired. It is sadly true that you have been fashioned from the same corrupted nature as the other children of Adam and Eve. But do not let that discourage you. Rejoice and be glad! Here is a secret[291] which I am revealing to you, a secret unknown to most Christians, even the most devout.

Do not leave your gold and silver in your own safes which have already been broken into and rifled many times by the evil one. They are too small, too flimsy and too old to contain such great and priceless possessions. Do not put pure and clear water from the spring into vessels fouled and infected by sin. Even if sin is no longer there, its odor persists and the water would be contaminated. You do not put choice wine into old casks that have contained sour wine. You would spoil the good wine and run the risk of losing it.[292]

178 Chosen souls, although you may already understand me, I shall express myself still more clearly. Do not commit the gold of your charity, the silver of your purity to a threadbare sack or a battered old chest, or the waters of heavenly grace or the wines of your merits and virtues to a tainted and fetid cask, such as you are. Otherwise you will be robbed by thieving devils who are on the look-out day and night waiting for a favorable opportunity to plunder. If you do so, all those pure gifts from God will be spoiled by the unwholesome presence of self-love, inordinate self-reliance, and self-will.

Pour into the bosom and heart of Mary all your precious possessions, all your graces and virtues. She is a spiritual vessel, a vessel of honor, a singular vessel of devotion.[293] Ever since God personally hid himself with all his perfections in this vessel, it has become completely spiritual, and the spiritual abode of all spiritual souls. It has become honorable and has been the throne of honor for the greatest saints in heaven. It has become outstanding in devotion and the home of those renowned for gentleness, grace and virtue. Moreover, it has become as rich as a house of gold, as strong as a tower of David and as pure as a tower of ivory.

179 Blessed is the man who has given everything to Mary, who at all times and in all things trusts in her, and loses himself in her. He belongs to Mary and Mary belongs to him. With David he can boldly say, "She was created for me,"[294] or with the beloved disciple, "I have taken her for my own,"[295] or with our Lord himself, "All that is mine is yours and all that is yours is mine."

180 If any critic reading this should imagine that I am exaggerating or speaking from an excess of devotion, he has not, alas, understood what I have said. Either he is a carnal man who has no taste for the spiritual; or he is a worldly man who has cut himself off from the Holy Spirit;[297] or he is a proud and critical man who ridicules and condemns anything he does not understand. But those who are born not of blood, nor of flesh, nor of the will of man,[248] but of God and of Mary, understand and appreciate what I have to say. It is for them that I am writing.

181 Nevertheless after this digression, I say to both the critics and the devout that the Blessed Virgin, the most reliable and generous of all God's creatures, never lets herself be surpassed by anyone in love and generosity. For the little that is given to her, she gives generously of what she has received from God. Consequently, if a person gives himself to her without reserve, she gives herself also without reserve to that person provided his confidence in her is not presumptuous and he does his best to practice virtue and curb his passions.

182 So the faithful servants of the Blessed Virgin may confidently say with St. John Damascene, "If I confide in you, Mother of God, I shall be saved. Under your protection I shall fear nothing. With your help I shall rout all my enemies. For devotion to you is a weapon of salvation which God gives to those he wishes to save."[299]

[Chapter 5: Biblical Figure of This Perfect Devotion: Rebecca and Jacob]

183 The Holy Spirit gives us, in Sacred Scripture,[300] a striking allegorical figure of all the truths I have been explaining concerning the Blessed Virgin and her children and servants. It is the story of Jacob who received the blessing of his father Isaac through the care and ingenuity of his mother Rebecca.

Here is the story as the Holy Spirit tells it. I shall expound it further later on.

[The Story of Jacob]

184 Several years after Esau had sold his birthright[301] to Jacob, Rebecca, their mother, who loved Jacob tenderly, secured this blessing for him by a holy strategem full of mystery for us.[302]

Isaac, realizing that he was getting old, wished to bless his children before he died. He summoned Esau, who was his favorite son, and told him to go out hunting and bring him something to eat, in order that he might then give him his blessing. Rebecca immediately told Jacob what was happening and sent him to fetch two small goats from the flock. When Jacob gave them to his mother, she cooked them in the way Isaac liked them. Then she dressed Jacob in Esau's clothes which she had in her keeping, and covered his hands and neck with the goat-skin. The father, who was blind, although hearing the voice of Jacob, would think that it was Esau when he touched the skin on his hands.

Isaac was of course surprised at the voice which he thought was Jacob's and told him to come closer. Isaac felt the hair on the skin covering Jacob's hands and said that the voice was really like Jacob's but the hands were Esau's. After he had eaten, Isaac kissed Jacob and smelled the fragrance of his scented clothes. He blessed him and called down on him the dew of heaven and the fruitfulness of earth. He made him master of all his brothers and concluded his blessing with these words, "Cursed be those who curse you and blessed be those who bless you."

Isaac had scarcely finished speaking when Esau came in, bringing what he had caught while out hunting. He wanted his father to bless him after he had eaten. The holy patriarch was shocked when he realized what had happened. But far from retracting what he had done, he confirmed it because he clearly saw the finger of God in it all. Then as Holy Scripture relates, Esau began to protest loudly against the treachery of his brother. He then asked his father if he had only one blessing to give. In so doing, as the early Fathers point out, Esau was the symbol of those who are too ready to imagine that there is an alliance between God and the world, because they themselves are eager to enjoy, at one and the same time, the blessings of heaven and the blessings of the earth. Isaac was touched by Esau's cries and finally blessed him but only with a blessing of the earth, and he subjected him to his brother. Because of this Esau conceived such a venomous hatred for Jacob that he could hardly wait for his father's death to kill him. And Jacob would not have escaped death if his dear mother Rebecca had not saved him by her ingenuity and her good advice.

[Interpretation of the story]

185 Before explaining this beautiful story, let me remind you that, according to the early Fathers and the interpreters of Holy Scripture,[305] Jacob is the type of Our Lord and of souls who are saved, and Esau is the type of souls who are condemned.[304] We have only to examine the actions and conduct of both in order to judge each one.

1 Esau, the elder brother, was strong and robust, clever, and skillful with the bow and very successful at hunting.

2 He seldom stayed at home and, relying only on his own strength and skill, worked out of doors.

3 He never went out of his way to please his mother Rebecca, and did little or nothing for her.

4 He was such a glutton and so fond of eating that he sold his birthright for a dish of lentils.

5 Like Cain,[305] he was extremely jealous of his brother and persecuted him relentlessly.

186 This is the usual conduct of sinners:

1 They rely upon their own strength and skill in temporal affairs. They are very energetic, clever and well-informed about things of this world but very dull and ignorant about things of heaven.[306]

187 2 And so they are never or very seldom at home, in their own house, that is, in their own interior, the inner, essential abode that God has given to every man to dwell in, after his own example, for God always abides within himself. Sinners have no liking for solitude or the spiritual life or interior devotion. They consider those who live an interior life, secluded from the world, and who work more interiorly than exteriorly, as narrow-minded, bigoted and uncivilized.

188 3 Sinners care little or nothing about devotion to Mary the Mother of the elect. It is true that they do not really hate her. Indeed, they even speak well of her sometimes. They say they love her and they practice some devotion in her honor. Nevertheless they cannot bear to see anyone love her tenderly, for they do not have for her any of the affection of Jacob; they find fault with the honor which her good children and servants faithfully pay her to win her affection. They think this kind of devotion is not necessary for salvation, and as long as they do not go as far as hating her or openly ridiculing devotion to her they believe they have done all they need to win her good graces. Because they recite or mumble a few prayers to her without any affection and without even thinking of amending their lives, they consider they are our Lady's servants.

189 4 Sinners sell their birthright, that is, the joys of paradise, for a dish of lentils, that is, the pleasures of this world. They laugh, they drink, they eat, they have a good time, they gamble, they dance and so forth, without taking any more trouble than Esau to make themselves worthy of their heavenly Father's blessing. Briefly, they think only of this world, love only the world, speak and act only for the world and its pleasures. For a passing moment of pleasure, for a fleeting wisp of honor, for a piece of hard earth, yellow or white,[308] they barter away their baptismal grace, their robe of innocence and their heavenly inheritance.

190 5 Finally, sinners continually hate and persecute the elect, openly and secretly. The elect are a burden to them. They despise them, criticize them, ridicule them, insult them, rob them, deceive them, impoverish them, hunt them down and trample them into the dust; while they themselves are making fortunes, enjoying themselves, getting good positions for themselves, enriching themselves, rising to power and living in comfort.

191 Jacob, the younger son, was of a frail constitution, gentle and peaceable and usually stayed at home to please his mother, whom he loved so much. If he did go out it was not through any personal desire of his, nor from any confidence in his own ability, but simply out of obedience to his mother.

192 He loved and honored his mother. That is why he remained at home close to her. He was never happier than when he was in her presence. He avoided everything that might displease her, and did everything he thought would please her. This made Rebecca love him all the more.

193 He was submissive to his mother in all things. He obeyed her entirely in everything, promptly without delay and lovingly without complaint. At the least indication of her will, young Jacob hastened to comply with it. He accepted whatever she told him without questioning. For instance, when she told him to get two small goats and bring them to her so that she might prepare something for his father Isaac to eat, Jacob did not reply that one would be enough for one man, but without arguing he did exactly what she told him to do.

194 He had the utmost confidence in his mother. He did not rely on his own ability; he relied solely on his mother's care and protection. He went to her in all his needs and consulted her in all his doubts. For instance, when he asked her if his father, instead of blessing him, would curse him, he believed her and trusted her when she said she would take the curse upon herself.

195 Finally, he adopted, as much as he could, the virtues he saw in his mother. It seems that one of the reasons why he spent so much time at home was to imitate his dear mother, who was so virtuous, and to keep away from evil companions—who might lead him into sin. In this way, he made himself worthy to receive the double blessing of his beloved father.

196 It is in a similar manner that God's chosen ones usually act. They stay at home with their mother—that is, they have an esteem for quietness, love the interior life, and are assiduous in prayer. They always remain in the company of the Blessed Virgin, their Mother and Model, whose glory is wholly interior and who during her whole life dearly loved seclusion and prayer. It is true, at times they do venture out into the world, but only to fulfill the duties of their state of life, in obedience to the will of God and the will of their Mother.

No matter how great their accomplishments may appear to others, they attach far more importance to what they do within themselves in their interior life, in the company of the Blessed Virgin. For there they work at the great task of perfection, compared to which all other work is mere child's play. At times their brothers and sisters are working outside with great energy, skill and success, and win the praise and approbation of the world. But they know by the light of the Holy Spirit, that there is far more good, more glory and more joy in remaining hidden and recollected with our Lord, in complete and perfect submission to Mary, than there is in performing by themselves marvelous works of nature and grace in the world, like so many Esaus and sinners. Glory for God and riches for men are in her house.

Lord Jesus, how lovely is your dwelling place! The sparrow has found a house to dwell in, and the turtle-dove a nest for her little ones! How happy is the man who dwells in the house of Mary, where you were the first to dwell! Here in this home of the elect, he draws from you alone the help he needs to climb the stairway of virtue he has built in his heart to the highest possible points of perfection while in this vale of tears. "How lovely is your dwelling place, Lord, God of hosts!"[309]

197 The elect have a great love for our Lady and honor her truly as their Mother and Queen. They love her not merely in word but in deed. They honor her not just outwardly, but from the depths of their heart. Like Jacob, they avoid the least thing that might displease her, and eagerly do whatever they think might win her favor. Jacob brought Rebecca two young goats. They bring Mary their body and their soul, with all their faculties, symbolized by Jacob's two young goats, 1) so that she may accept them as her own; 2) that she may make them die to sin and self by divesting them of self-love, in order to please Jesus her Son, who wishes to have as friends and disciples only those who are dead to sin and self; 3) that she may clothe them according to their heavenly Father's taste and for his greater glory, which she knows better than any other creature; 4) that through her care and intercession, this body and soul of theirs, thoroughly cleansed from every stain, thoroughly dead to self, thoroughly stripped and well-prepared, may be pleasing to the heavenly Father and deserving of his blessing.

Is this not what those chosen souls do who, to prove to Jesus and Mary how effective and courageous is their love, live and esteem the perfect consecration to Jesus through Mary which we are now teaching them?

Sinners may say that they love Jesus, that they love and honor Mary, but they do not do so with their whole heart and soul.[310] Unlike the elect, they do not love Jesus and Mary enough to consecrate to them their body with its senses and their soul with its passions.

198 They are subject and obedient to our Lady, their good Mother, and here they are simply following the example set by our Lord himself, who spent thirty of the thirty-three years he lived on earth glorifying God his Father in perfect and entire submission to his holy Mother. They obey her, following her advice to the letter, just as Jacob followed that of Rebecca, when she said to him,[311] "My son, follow my advice"; or like the stewards at the wedding in Cana, to whom our Lady said, "Do whatever he tells you."[312]

Through obedience to his Mother, Jacob received the blessing almost by a miracle, because in the natural course of events he should not have received it. As a reward for following the advice of our Lady, the stewards at the wedding in Cana were honored with the first of our Lord's miracles when, at her request he changed water into wine. In the same way, until the end of time, all who are to receive the blessing of our heavenly Father and who are to be honored with his wondrous graces will receive them only as a result of their perfect obedience to Mary. On the other hand the "Esaus" will lose their blessing because of their lack of submission to the Blessed Virgin.

199 They have great confidence in the goodness and power of the Blessed Virgin, their dear Mother, and incessantly implore her help. They take her for their pole-star to lead them safely into harbor. They open their hearts to her and tell her their troubles and their needs. They rely on her mercy and kindness to obtain forgiveness for their sins through her intercession and to experience her motherly comfort in their troubles and anxieties. They even cast themselves into her virginal bosom, hide and lose themselves there in a wonderful manner. There they are filled with pure love, they are purified from the least stain of sin, and they find Jesus in all his fullness. For he reigns in Mary as if on the most glorious of thrones. What incomparable happiness! Abbot Guerric says, "Do not imagine there is more joy in dwelling in Abraham's bosom than in Mary's, for it is in her that our Lord placed his throne."[313]

Sinners, on the other hand, put all their confidence in themselves. Like the prodigal son, they eat with the swine. Like toads they feed on earth. Like all worldlings, they love only visible and external things. They do not know the sweetness of Mary's bosom. They do not have that reliance and confidence which the elect have for the Blessed Virgin, their Mother. Deplorably they choose to satisfy their hunger elsewhere, as St. Gregory says,[314] because they do not want to taste the sweetness already prepared within themselves and within Jesus and Mary.

200 Finally, chosen souls keep to the ways of the Blessed Virgin, their loving Mother—that is, they imitate her and so are sincerely happy and devout and bear the infallible sign of God's chosen ones. This loving Mother says to them, "Happy are those who keep my ways,"[315] which means, happy are those who practice my virtues and who, with the help of God's grace, follow the path of my life. They are happy in this world because of the abundance of grace and sweetness I impart to them out of my fullness, and which they receive more abundantly than others who do not imitate me so closely. They are happy at the hour of death which is sweet and peaceful for I am usually there myself to lead them home to everlasting joy. Finally, they will be happy for all eternity, because no servant of mine who imitated my virtues during life has ever been lost.

On the other hand, sinners are unhappy during their life, at their death, and throughout eternity, because they do not imitate the virtues of our Lady. They are satisfied with going no further than joining her confraternities, reciting a few prayers in her honor, or performing other exterior devotional exercises.

O Blessed Virgin, my dear Mother, how happy are those who faithfully keep your ways, your counsels and your commands; who never allow themselves to be led astray by a false devotion to you! But how unhappy and accursed are those who abuse devotion to you by not keeping the commandments of your Son. "They are accursed who stray from your commandments."[316]

[Services of our Lady to her faithful servants]

201 Here now are the services which the Virgin Mary, as the best of all mothers,[317] lovingly renders to those loyal servants who have given themselves entirely to her in the manner I have described and following the figurative meaning of the story of Jacob and Rebecca.

1 *She loves them.*

"I love those who love me." She loves them:

a Because she is truly their Mother. What mother does not love her child, the fruit of her womb?

b She loves them in gratitude for the active love they show to her, their beloved Mother.

c She loves them because they are loved by God and destined for heaven. "Jacob I loved, but Esau I hated."[319]

d She loves them because they have consecrated themselves entirely to her and belong to her portion, her inheritance. "In Israel receive your inheritance."[320]

202 She loves them tenderly, more tenderly than all the mothers in the world together. Take the maternal love of all the mothers of the world for their children. Pour all that love into the heart of one mother for an only child. That mother's love would certainly be immense. Yet Mary's love for each of her children has more tenderness than the love of that mother for her child.

She loves them not only affectively but effectively, that is, her love is active and productive of good like Rebecca's love for Jacob—and even more so, for Rebecca was, after all, only a symbolic figure of Mary. Here is what this loving Mother does for her children to obtain for them the blessings of their heavenly Father:

203 1 Like Rebecca she looks out for favorable opportunities to promote their interests, to ennoble and enrich them. She sees clearly in God all that is good and all that is evil; fortunate and unfortunate events; the blessings and condemnations of God. She arranges things in advance so as to divert evils from her servants and put them in the way of abundant blessings. If there is any special benefit to be gained in God's sight by the faithful discharge of an important work, Mary will certainly obtain this opportunity for a beloved child and servant and at the same time, give him the grace to persevere in it to the end. "She personally manages our affairs," says a saintly man (Raymundus Jordanus).[321]

204 2 She gives them excellent advice, as Rebecca did to Jacob. "My son, follow my counsels."[322] Among other things, she persuades them to bring her the two young goats, that is, their body and soul, and to confide them to her so that she can prepare them as a dish pleasing to God. She inspires them to observe whatever Jesus Christ, her Son, has taught by word and by example. When she does not give these counsels herself in person, she gives them through the ministry of angels who are always pleased and honored to go at her request to assist one of her faithful servants on earth.

205 3 What does this good Mother do when we have presented and consecrated to her our soul and body and all that pertains to them without excepting anything? Just what Rebecca of old did to the little goats Jacob brought her. (a) She kills them, that is, makes them die to the life of the old Adam. (b) She strips them of their skin, that is, of their natural inclinations, their self-love and self-will and their every attachment to creatures. (c) She cleanses them from all stain, impurity and sin. (d) She prepares them to God's taste and to his greater glory. As she alone knows perfectly what the divine taste is and where the greatest glory of God is to be found, she alone without any fear of mistake can prepare and garnish our body and soul to satisfy that infinitely refined taste and promote that infinitely hidden glory.[323]

206 4 Once this good Mother has received our complete offering with our merits and satisfactions through the devotion I have been speaking about,[324] and has stripped us of our own garments, she cleanses us and makes us worthy to appear without shame before our heavenly Father.

She clothes us in the clean, new, precious and fragrant garments of Esau, the first born, namely, her Son Jesus Christ. She keeps these garments in her house, that is to say, she has them at her disposal. For she is treasurer and universal dispenser of the merits and virtues of Jesus her Son. She gives and distributes them to whom she pleases, when she pleases, as she pleases and as much as she pleases, as we have said above.[325]

She covers the neck and hands of her servants with the skins of the goats that have been killed and flayed, that is, she adorns them with the merits and worth of their own good actions. In truth, she destroys and nullifies all that is impure and imperfect in them, but at the same time keeps the good that grace has produced in them. She preserves and enhances this good so that it adorns and strengthens their neck and hands, that is, she gives them the strength to carry the yoke of the Lord and the skill to do great things for the glory of God and the salvation of their poor brothers.

She imparts new perfume and fresh grace to those garments and adornments by adding to them the garments of her own wardrobe of merits and virtues. She bequeathed these to them before her departure for heaven, as was revealed to a holy nun of the last century,[326] who died in the odor of sanctity (Mary of Agreda). Thus all her domestics, that is, all her servants and slaves, are clothed with double garments, her own and those of her Son.[327] Now they have nothing to fear from that cold which sinners, naked and stripped as they are of the merits of Jesus and Mary, will be unable to endure.

207 5 Finally, Mary obtains for them the heavenly Father's blessing. As they are the youngest born and adopted, they are not really entitled to it. Clad in new, precious, and sweet-smelling garments, with body and soul well-prepared and dressed, they confidently approach their heavenly Father. He hears their voice and recognizes it as the voice of a sinner. He feels their hands covered with skins, inhales the aroma of their garments. He partakes with joy of what Mary, their Mother, has prepared for him, recognizing in it the merits and good odor of his Son and his Blessed Mother,

a He gives them a twofold blessing, the blessing of the dew of heaven,[328] namely, divine grace, which is the seed of glory. "God has blessed us in Christ with every spiritual blessing,"[329] and also the blessing of the fertility of the earth,[330] for as a provident Father, he gives them their daily bread and an ample supply of the goods of the earth.

b He makes them masters of their other brothers, the reprobate sinners. This domination does not always show in this fleeting world,[331] where sinners often have the upper hand. "How long shall the wicked glory, mouthing insolent speeches?" "I have seen the wicked triumphant and lifted up like the cedars of Lebanon."[332] But the supremacy of the just is real and will be seen clearly for all eternity in the next world, where the just, as the Holy Spirit tells us, will dominate and command all peoples.[333]

c The God of all majesty is not satisfied with blessing them in their persons and their possessions, he blesses all who bless them and curses all who curse and persecute them.

2 [*She provides for all their needs.*]

208 The second charitable duty that Our Lady fulfills toward her faithful servants is that she provides them with everything they need for body and soul. We have just seen[334] that she gives them double garments. She also nourishes them with the most delicious food from the banquet table of God. She gives them the Son she has borne, the Bread of Life,[335] to be their food, "Dear children,"[336] she says, in the words of Divine Wisdom, "take your fill of my fruits," that is to say, of the Fruit of Life, Jesus, "whom I brought into the world for you." "Come," she repeats in another passage, "eat the bread which is Jesus. Drink the wine of his love which I have mixed[337] for you with the milk of my breasts."[338]

As Mary is the treasurer and dispenser of the gifts and graces of the Most High God,[339] she reserves a choice portion, indeed the choicest portion, to nourish and sustain her children and servants. They grow strong on the Bread of Life; they are made joyful with the wine that brings forth virgins.[340] They are carried at her breast.[341] They bear with ease the yoke of Christ scarcely feeling its weight[342] because of the oil of devotion with which she has softened its wood.[343]

3 *[She leads and guides them.]*

209 A third service which Our Lady renders her faithful servants is to lead and direct them according to the will of her Son. Rebecca guided her little son Jacob and gave him good advice from time to time, which helped him obtain the blessing of his Father and saved him from the hatred and persecution of his brother Esau. Mary, Star of the sea,[344] guides all her faithful servants into safe harbor. She shows them the path to eternal life and helps them avoid dangerous pitfalls. She leads them by the hand along the path of holiness,[345] steadies them when they are liable to fall and helps them rise when they have fallen. She chides them like a loving mother when they are remiss and sometimes she even lovingly chastises them. How could a child that follows such a mother and such an enlightened guide as Mary take the wrong path to heaven?[346] Follow her and you cannot go wrong, says St. Bernard. There is no danger of a true child of Mary being led astray by the devil and falling into heresy. Where Mary leads, Satan with his deceptions and heretics with their subtleties are not encountered. "When she upholds you, you will not fall."[347]

4 *[She defends and protects them.]*

210 The fourth good office our Lady performs for her children and faithful servants is to defend and protect them against their enemies. By her care and ingenuity Rebecca delivered Jacob from all dangers that beset him and particularly from dying at the hands of his brother, as he apparently would have done, since Esau hated and envied him just as Cain hated his brother, Abel.[348]

Mary, the beloved Mother of chosen souls, shelters them under her protecting wings as a hen does her chicks.[349] She speaks to them, coming down to their level and accommodating herself to all their weaknesses. To ensure their safety from the hawk and vulture, she becomes their escort, surrounding them as an army in battle array.[350] Could anyone surrounded by a well-ordered army of, say, a hundred thousand men fear his enemies? No, and still less would a faithful servant of Mary, protected on all sides by her imperial forces, fear his enemy. This powerful Queen of heaven would sooner despatch millions of angels to help one of her servants than have it said that a single faithful and trusting servant of hers[351] had fallen victim to the malice, number and power of his enemies.

5 *[She intercedes for them.]*

211 Finally the fifth and greatest service which this loving Mother renders her faithful followers is to intercede for them with her Son. She appeases him with her prayers, brings her servants into closest union with him and maintains that union.[352]

Rebecca made Jacob approach the bed of his father. His father touched him, embraced him and even joyfully kissed him after having satisfied his hunger with the well-prepared dishes which Jacob had brought him. Then inhaling most joyfully the exquisite perfume of his garments, he cried: "Behold the fragrance of my son is as the fragrance of a field of plenty which the Lord has blessed.[353] The fragrance of this rich field which so captivated the heart of the father, is none other than the fragrance of the merits and virtues of Mary who is the plentiful field of grace in which God the Father has sown the grain of wheat of the elect,[354] his only Son.

How welcome to Jesus Christ, the Father of the world to come,[355] is a child perfumed with the fragrance of Mary![356] How readily and how intimately does he unite himself to that child! But this we have already shown at length.[357]

212 Furthermore, once Mary has heaped her favors upon her children and her faithful servants and has secured for them the blessing of the heavenly Father and union with Jesus Christ, she keeps them in Jesus and keeps Jesus in them.[358] She guards them, watching over them unceasingly, lest they lose the grace of God and fall into the snares of their enemies. "She keeps the saints in their fullness"[359] (St. Bonaventure), and inspires them to persevere to the end, as we have already said.[360]

Such is the explanation given to this ancient allegory which typifies the mystery of predestination and reprobation.

[Chapter 6:] Wonderful Effects of This Devotion

213 My dear friend, be sure that if you remain faithful to the interior and exterior practices of this devotion which I will point out,[361] the following effects will be produced in your soul:

1 *[Knowledge of our unworthiness]*

By the light which the Holy Spirit will give you through Mary, his faithful spouse, you will perceive the evil inclinations of your fallen nature and how incapable you are of any good apart from that which God produces in you as Author of nature and of grace. As a consequence of this knowledge you will despise yourself and think of yourself as a snail that soils everything with its slime, as a toad that poisons everything with its venom, as a malevolent serpent seeking only to deceive. Finally, the humble Virgin Mary will share her humility with you so that, although you regard yourself with distaste and desire to be disregarded by others, you will not look down slightingly upon anyone.

2 *[A share in Mary's faith]*

214 Mary will share her faith with you. Her faith on earth was stronger than that of all the patriarchs, prophets, apostles and saints. Now that she is reigning in heaven she no longer has this faith, since she sees everything clearly in God by the light of glory. However, with the consent of almighty God she did not lose it when entering heaven. She has preserved it for her faithful servants in the Church Militant.[362] Therefore, the more you gain the friendship of this noble Queen and faithful Virgin, the more you will be inspired by faith in your daily life. It will cause you to depend less upon sensible and extraordinary feelings. For it is a lively faith animated by love enabling you to do everything from no other motive than that of pure love. It is a firm faith, unshakeable as a rock, prompting you to remain firm and steadfast in the midst of storms and tempests. It is an active and probing faith which like some mysterious pass-key admits you into the mysteries of Jesus Christ and of man's final destiny and into the very heart of God himself. It is a courageous faith which inspires you to undertake and carry out without hesitation great things for God and the salvation of souls. Lastly, this faith will be your flaming torch, your very life with God, your secret fund of divine Wisdom, and an all-powerful weapon for you to enlighten those who sit in darkness and the shadow of death. It inflames those who are lukewarm and need the gold of fervent love.

It restores life to those who are dead through sin. It moves and transforms hearts of marble and cedars of Lebanon by gentle and convincing argument. Finally, this faith will strengthen you to resist the devil and the other enemies of salvation.[363]

3 *[The gift of pure love]*

215 The Mother of fair love will rid your heart of all scruples and inordinate servile fear. She will open and enlarge it to obey the commandments of her Son with alacrity and with the holy freedom of the children of God. She will fill your heart with pure love of which she is the treasury. You will then cease to act as you did before, out of fear of the God who is love, but rather out of pure love.[364] You will look upon him as a loving Father and endeavor to please him at all times. You will speak trustfully to him as a child does to its Father. If you should have the misfortune to offend him you will abase yourself before him and humbly beg his pardon. You will offer your hand to him with simplicity and lovingly rise from your sin. Then, peaceful and relaxed and buoyed up with hope you will continue on your way to him.

4 *[Great confidence in God and in Mary]*

216 Our Blessed Lady will fill you with unbounded confidence in God and in herself:

1 Because you will no longer approach Jesus by yourself but always through Mary your loving Mother.[365]

2 Since you have given her all your merits, graces and satisfactions to dispose of as she pleases, she imparts to you her own virtues and clothes you in her own merits. So you will be able to say confidently to God: "Behold Mary, your handmaid, be it done unto me according to your word."[366]

3 Since you have now given yourself completely to Mary, body and soul, she, who is generous to the generous, and more generous than even the kindest benefactor, will in return give herself to you in a marvelous but real manner. Indeed, you may without hesitation say to her, "I am yours, O Blessed Virgin, obtain salvation for me,"[367] or with the beloved disciple,[368] St. John, "I have taken you, Blessed Mother, for my all." Or again you may say with St. Bonaventure, "Dear Mother of saving grace, I will do everything with confidence and without fear because you are my strength and my boast in the Lord,"[369] or in another place, "I am all yours and all that I have is yours, O glorious Virgin, blessed above all created things. Let me place you as a seal upon my heart, for your love is as strong as death."[370] Or adopting the sentiments of the prophet, "Lord, my heart has no reason to be exalted nor should my looks be proud; I have not sought things of great moment nor wonders

beyond my reach, nevertheless, I am still not humble. But I have roused my soul and taken courage. I am as a child, weaned from earthly pleasures and resting on its mother's breast. It is upon this breast that all good things come to me."[371]

4 What will still further increase your confidence in her is that, after having given her in trust[372] all that you possess to use or keep as she pleases, you will place less trust in yourself and much more in her whom you have made your treasury. How comforting and how consoling when a person can say, "The treasury of God, where he has placed all that he holds most precious, is also my treasury." "She is," says a saintly man, "the treasury of the Lord."[373]

5 *[Communication of the spirit of Mary]*

217 The soul of Mary will be communicated to you to glorify the Lord. Her spirit will take the place of yours to rejoice in God, her Savior,[374] but only if you are faithful to the practices of this devotion. As St. Ambrose says, "May the soul of Mary be in each one of us to glorify the Lord! May the spirit of Mary be in each one of us to rejoice in God!"[375] "When will that happy day come," asks a saintly man of our own day[376] whose life was completely wrapped up in Mary, "when God's Mother is enthroned in men's hearts as Queen, subjecting them to the dominion of her great and princely Son? When will souls breathe Mary as the body breathes air?" When that time comes wonderful things will happen on earth. The Holy Spirit, finding his dear Spouse present again in souls, will come down into them with great power. He will fill them with his gifts, especially wisdom, by which they will produce wonders of grace.[377] My dear friend, when will that happy time come, that age of Mary, when many souls, chosen by Mary and given her by the most High God, will hide themselves completely in the depths of her soul, becoming living copies of her, loving and glorifying Jesus? That day will dawn only when the devotion I teach is understood and put into practice. *Ut adveniat regnum tuum, adveniat regnum Mariae.* "Lord, that your kingdom may come, may the reign of Mary come!"

6 *[Transformation into the likeness of Jesus]*

218 If Mary, the Tree of Life,[378] is well cultivated in our soul by fidelity to this devotion, she will in due time bring forth her fruit which is none other than Jesus.[379] I have seen many devout souls searching for Jesus in one way or another, and so often when they have worked hard throughout the night, all they can say is, "Despite our having worked all night, we have caught nothing."[380] To them we can say,[381] "You have worked hard and gained little; Jesus can only be recognized faintly in you." But if we follow the immaculate path of Mary, living the devotion that I teach, we will always work in daylight, we will work in a holy place, and we will work but little. There is no darkness in Mary, not even the slightest shadow since there was never any sin in her. She is a holy place, a holy of holies, in which saints are formed and molded.[382]

219 Please note that I say that saints are molded in Mary. There is a vast difference between carving a statue by blows of hammer and chisel and making a statue by using a mold. Sculptors and statue-makers work hard and need plenty of time to make statues by the first method. But the second method does not involve much work and takes very little time. St. Augustine speaking to our Blessed Lady says, "You are worthy to be called the mold of God."[383] Mary is a mold capable of forming people into the image of the God-man.[384] Anyone who is cast into this divine mold is quickly shaped and molded into Jesus and Jesus into him. At little cost and in a short time he will become Christ-like since he is cast into the very same mold that fashioned a God-man.

220 I think I can very well compare some spiritual directors and devout persons to sculptors who wish to produce Jesus in themselves and in others by methods other than this. Many of them rely on their own skill, ingenuity and art and chip away endlessly with mallet and chisel at hard stone or badly-prepared wood, in an effort to produce a likeness of our Lord. At times, they do not manage to produce a recognizable likeness either because they lack knowledge and experience of the person of Jesus or because a clumsy stroke has spoiled the whole work. But those who accept this little known secret of grace[385] which I offer them can rightly be compared to smelters and molders who have discovered the beautiful mold of Mary where Jesus was so divinely and so naturally formed.[386] They do not rely on their own skill but on the perfection of the mold. They cast and lose themselves in Mary where they become true models of her Son.

221 You may think this is a beautiful and convincing comparison. But how many understand it? I would like you, my dear friend, to understand it. But remember that only molten and liquified substances may be poured into a mold. That means that you must crush and melt down the old Adam in you if you wish to acquire the likeness of the new Adam in Mary.[387]

7 *[The greater glory of Christ]*

222 If you live this devotion sincerely, you will give more glory to Jesus in a month than in many years of a more demanding devotion. Here are my reasons for saying this:

1 Since you do everything through the Blessed Virgin as required by this devotion, you naturally lay aside your own intentions no matter how good they appear to you. You abandon yourself to our Lady's intentions even though you do not know what they are.

Thus, you share in the high quality of her intentions,[388] which are so pure that she gave more glory to God by the smallest of her actions, say, twirling her distaff, or making a stitch, than did St. Laurence suffering his cruel martyrdom on the gridiron, and even more than all the saints together in all their most heroic deeds![389] Mary amassed such a multitude of merits and graces during her sojourn on earth that it would be easier to count the stars in heaven,[390] the drops of water in the ocean or the sands of the seashore than count her merits and graces. She thus gave more glory to God than all the angels and saints have given or will ever give him. Mary, wonder of God, when souls abandon themselves to you, you cannot but work wonders in them!

223 2 In this devotion we set no store on our own thoughts and actions but are content to rely on Mary's dispositions when approaching and even speaking to Jesus. We then act with far greater humility than others who, imperceptibly rely on their own dispositions and are self-satisfied about them; and consequently we give greater glory to God, for perfect glory is given to him only by the lowly and humble of heart.

224 3 Our Blessed Lady, in her immense love for us, is eager to receive into her virginal hands the gift of our actions, imparting to them a marvelous beauty and splendor, and presenting them herself to Jesus most willingly. More glory is given to our Lord in this way than when we make our offering with our own guilty hands.[391]

225 4 Lastly, you never think of Mary without Mary thinking of God for you. You never praise or honor Mary without Mary joining you in praising and honoring God. Mary is entirely relative to God. Indeed I would say that she was relative only to God, because she exists uniquely in reference to him.[392]

She is an echo of God, speaking and repeating only God. If you say "Mary" she says "God." When St. Elizabeth praised Mary calling her blessed because she had believed, Mary, the faithful echo of God, responded with her Canticle, "My soul glorifies the Lord."[393] What Mary did on that day, she does every day. When we praise her, when we love and honor her, when we present anything to her, then God is praised, honored and loved and receives our gift through Mary and in Mary.

[Chapter 7] *Particular Practices of This Devotion*

[1.] *Exterior Practices*

True Devotion to Mary

226 Although this devotion is essentially an interior one,[395] this does not prevent it from having exterior practices which should not be neglected. "These must be done but those not omitted."[396] If properly performed, exterior acts help to foster interior ones. Man is always guided by his senses and such practices remind him of what he has done or should do. Let no worldling or critic intervene to assert that true devotion is essentially in the heart and therefore externals should be avoided as inspiring vanity, or that real devotion should be hidden and private. I answer in the words of our Lord, "Let men see your good works that they may glorify your Father who is in heaven."[397] As St. Gregory says,[398] this does not mean that they should perform external actions to please men or to seek praise; that certainly would be vanity. It simply means that we do these things before men only to please and glorify God without worrying about either the contempt or the approval of men.

I shall briefly mention some practices which I call exterior, not because they are performed without inner attention but because they have an exterior element as distinct from those which are purely interior.

1 *[Preparation and Consecration]*

227 Those who desire to take up this special devotion, (which has not been erected into a confraternity, although this would be desirable),[399] should spend at least twelve days in emptying themselves of the spirit of the world, which is opposed to the spirit of Jesus, as I have recommended in the first part of this preparation for the reign of Jesus Christ. They should then spend three weeks imbuing themselves with the spirit of Jesus through the most Blessed Virgin. Here is a program they might follow:

228 During the first week they should offer up all their prayers and acts of devotion to acquire knowledge of themselves and sorrow for their sins.

Let them perform all their actions in a spirit of humility. With this end in view they may, if they wish, meditate on what I have said concerning our corrupted nature,[400] and consider themselves during six days of the week as nothing but snails, slugs, toads, swine, snakes and goats.[401] Or else they may meditate on the following three considerations of St. Bernard: "Remember what you were—corrupted seed; what you are—a body destined for decay; what you will be—food for worms."[402]

They will ask our Lord and the Holy Spirit to enlighten them saying, "Lord, that I may see,"[403] or "Lord, let me know myself,"[404] or the "Come Holy Spirit." Every day they should say the Litany of the Holy Spirit, with the prayer that follows, as indicated in the first part of this work. They will turn to our Blessed Lady and beg her to obtain for them that great grace which is the foundation of all others, the grace of self-knowledge. For this intention they will say each day the *Ave Maris Stella* and the Litany of the Blessed Virgin.

229 Each day of the second week they should endeavor in all their prayers and works to acquire an understanding of the Blessed Virgin and ask the Holy Spirit for this grace. They may read and meditate upon what we have already said about her.[405] They should recite daily the Litany of the Holy Spirit and the *Ave Maris Stella* as during the first week. In addition they will say at least five decades of the Rosary for greater understanding of Mary.

230 During the third week they should seek to understand Jesus Christ better. They may read and meditate on what we have already said about him.[406] They may say the prayer of St. Augustine which they will find at the beginning of the second part of this book.[407] Again, with St. Augustine, they may pray repeatedly, "Lord, that I may know you," or "Lord, that I may see."[408] As during the previous week, they should recite the Litany of the Holy Spirit and the *Ave Maris Stella,* adding every day the Litany of the Holy Name of Jesus.

231 At the end of these three weeks they should go to confession[410] and Holy Communion with the intention of consecrating themselves to Jesus through Mary as his slaves of love. When receiving Holy Communion they could follow the method given later on.[411] They then recite the act of consecration which is given at the end of this book.[412] If they do not have a printed copy of the act, they should write it out or have it copied and then sign it on the very day they make it.[413]

232 It would be very becoming if on that day they offered some tribute to Jesus and his Mother, either as a penance for past unfaithfulness to the promises made in baptism or as a sign of their submission to the sovereignty of Jesus and Mary.[414] Such a tribute would be in accordance with each one's ability and fervor and may take the form of fasting, an act of self-denial, the gift of an alms or the offering of a votive candle. If they gave only a pin as a token of their homage, provided it were given with a good heart, it would satisfy Jesus who considers only the good intention.

233 Every year at least, on the same date, they should renew the consecration following the same exercises for three weeks. They might also renew it every month or even every day by saying this short prayer: "I am all yours and all I have is yours, O dear Jesus, through Mary, your holy Mother."[415]

2 [The Little Crown of the Blessed Virgin]

234 If it is not too inconvenient, they should recite every day of their lives the Little Crown of the Blessed Virgin, which is composed of three Our Fathers and twelve Hail Marys in honor of the twelve glorious privileges of Mary.[416] This prayer is very old and is based on Holy Scripture. St. John saw in a vision a woman crowned with twelve stars, clothed with the sun and standing upon the moon.[417] According to biblical commentators, this woman is the Blessed Virgin.[418]

235 There are several ways of saying the Little Crown but it would take too long to explain them here. The Holy Spirit will teach them to those who live this devotion conscientiously. However, here is a simple way to recite it. As an introduction say: "Virgin most holy, accept my praise; give me strength to fight your foes," then say the Creed. Next, say the following sequence of prayers three times: one Our Father, four Hail Marys and one Glory be to the Father. In conclusion, say the prayer, *Sub tuum*—"We fly to thy patronage."

3 [The Wearing of Little Chains]

236 It is very praiseworthy and helpful for those who have become slaves of Jesus in Mary to wear, in token of their slavery of love, a little chain[419] blessed with a special blessing.[420]

It is perfectly true these external tokens are not essential and may very well be dispensed with by those who have made this consecration. Nevertheless, I cannot help but give the warmest approval to those who wear them. They show they have shaken off the shameful chains of the slavery of the devil, in which original sin and perhaps actual sin had bound them, and have willingly taken upon themselves the glorious slavery of Jesus Christ. Like St. Paul, they glory in the chains they wear for Christ.[421] For though these chains are made only of iron they are far more glorious and precious than all the gold ornaments worn by monarchs.

237 At one time, nothing was considered more contemptible than the Cross. Now this sacred wood has become the most glorious symbol of the Christian faith.[422] Similarly, nothing was more ignoble in the sight of the ancients, and even today nothing is more degrading among unbelievers than the chains of Jesus Christ. But among Christians nothing is more glorious than these chains, because by them Christians are liberated and kept free from the ignoble shackles of sin and the devil.[423] Thus set free, we are bound to Jesus and Mary not by compulsion and force like galley-slaves, but by charity and love as children are to their parents. "I shall draw them to me by chains of love" said God Most High speaking through the prophet.[424] Consequently, these chains are as strong as

death, and in a way stronger than death,[425] for those who wear them faithfully till the end of their life. For though death destroys and corrupts their body, it will not destroy the chains of their slavery, since these, being of metal, will not easily corrupt. It may be that on the day of their resurrection, that momentous day of final judgment, these chains, still clinging to their bones, will contribute to their glorification and be transformed into chains of light and splendor. Happy then, a thousand times happy, are the illustrious slaves of Jesus in Mary who bear their chains even to the grave.

238 Here are the reasons for wearing these chains:

a They remind a Christian of the promises of his baptism and the perfect renewal of these commitments made in his consecration. They remind him of his strict obligation to adhere faithfully to them.[426] A man's actions are prompted more frequently by his senses than by pure faith and so he can easily forget his duties towards God if he has no external reminder of them. These little chains are a wonderful aid in recalling the bonds of sin and the slavery of the devil from which baptism has freed him.[427] At the same time, they remind him of the dependence on Jesus promised at baptism and ratified when by consecration he renewed these promises. Why is it that so many Christians do not think of their baptismal vows and behave with as much license as unbelievers who have promised nothing to God? One explanation is that they do not wear external signs to remind them of these vows.

239 b These chains prove they are not ashamed of being the servants and slaves of Jesus and that they reject the deadly bondage of the world, of sin and of the devil.

c They are a guarantee and protection against enslavement by sin and the devil. For we must of necessity choose to wear either the chains of sin and damnation or the chains of love and salvation.[428]

240 Dear friend, break the chains of sin and of sinners, of the world and the worldly, of the devil and his satellites. "Cast their yoke of death far from us."[429] To use the words of the Holy Spirit let us put our feet into his glorious shackles and our neck into his chains. Let us bow down our shoulders in submission to the yoke of Wisdom incarnate, Jesus Christ, and let us not be upset by the burden of his chains.[430] Notice how before saying these words the Holy Spirit prepares us to accept his serious advice, "Hearken, my son," he says, "receive a counsel of understanding and do not spurn this counsel of mine."[431]

241 Allow me here, my dear friend, to join the Holy Spirit in giving you the same counsel. "These chains are the chains of salvation."[432] As our Lord on the cross draws all men to himself,[433] whether they will it or not, he will draw sinners by the fetters of their sins and submit them like galley-slaves and devils to his eternal anger and avenging justice. But he will draw the just, especially in these latter days, by the chains of love.[434]

242 These loving slaves of Christ may wear their chains around the neck, on their arms, round the waist or round the ankles. Fr. Vincent Caraffa, seventh General of the Society of Jesus, who died in the odor of sanctity in 1643, carried an iron band round his ankles as a symbol of his holy servitude and he used to say that his greatest regret was that he could not drag a chain around in public.[435] Mother Agnes of Jesus, of whom we have already spoken,[436] wore a chain around her waist. Others have worn it round the neck, in atonement for the pearl necklaces they wore in the world. Others have worn chains round their arms to remind them, as they worked with their hands, that they are the slaves of Jesus.

4 *[Honoring the mystery of the Incarnation]*

243 Loving slaves of Jesus in Mary should hold in high esteem devotion to Jesus, the Word of God, in the great mystery of the Incarnation, March 25th, which is the mystery proper to this devotion, because it was inspired by the Holy Spirit for the following reasons:

a That we might honor and imitate the wondrous dependence which God the Son chose to have on Mary, for the glory of his Father and for the redemption of man. This dependence is revealed especially in this mystery where Jesus becomes a captive and slave in the womb of his Blessed Mother, depending on her for everything.[437]

b That we might thank God for the incomparable graces he has conferred upon Mary and especially that of choosing her to be his most worthy Mother. This choice was made in the mystery of the Incarnation. These are the two principal ends of the slavery of Jesus in Mary.

244 Please note that I usually say "slave of Jesus in Mary," "slavery of Jesus in Mary." We might indeed say, as some have already been saying, "slave of Mary," "slavery of Mary." But I think it preferable to say, "slave of Jesus in Mary." This is the opinion of Fr. Tronson,[438] Superior General of the Seminary of St. Sulpice, a man renowned for his exceptional prudence and remarkable holiness. He gave this advice when consulted upon this subject by a priest.

Here are the reasons for it:

245 a Since we live in an age of pride when a great number of haughty scholars, with proud and critical minds,[439] find fault even with long-established and sound devotions, it is better to speak of "slavery of Jesus in Mary" and to call oneself "slave of Jesus" rather than "slave of Mary." We then avoid giving any pretext for criticism. In this way, we name this devotion after its ultimate end which is Jesus, rather than after the way and the means to arrive there, which is Mary.[440] However we can very well use either term without any scruple, as I myself do. If a man goes from Orleans to Tours, by way of Amboise, he can quite truthfully say that he is going to Amboise and equally truthfully say that he is going to Tours. The only difference is that Amboise is simply a place on the direct road to Tours, and Tours alone is his final destination.

246 b Since the principal mystery celebrated and honored in this devotion is the mystery of the Incarnation where we find Jesus only in Mary, having become incarnate in her womb, it is more appropriate for us to say, "slavery of Jesus in Mary," of Jesus dwelling and reigning in Mary, according to the beautiful prayer, recited by so many great souls, "O Jesus, living in Mary."[441]

247 c These expressions show more clearly the intimate union existing between Jesus and Mary.[442] So closely are they united that one is wholly in the other. Jesus is all in Mary and Mary is all in Jesus. Or rather, it is no longer she who lives, but Jesus alone who lives in her. It would be easier to separate light from the sun than Mary from Jesus. So united are they that our Lord may be called, "Jesus of Mary," and his Mother "Mary of Jesus."

248 Time does not permit me to linger here and elaborate on the perfections and wonders of the mystery of Jesus living and reigning in Mary, or the Incarnation of the Word. I shall confine myself to the following brief remarks. The Incarnation is the first mystery of Jesus Christ; it is the most hidden; and it is the most exalted and the least known.

It was in this mystery that Jesus, in the womb of Mary and with her co-operation, chose all the elect. For this reason the saints called her womb the throne-room of God's mysteries.[443]

It was in this mystery that Jesus anticipated all subsequent mysteries of his life by his willing acceptance of them.[444] Consequently, this mystery is a summary of all his mysteries since it contains the intention and the grace of them all.

Lastly, this mystery is the seat of the mercy, the liberality, and the glory of God. It is the seat of his *mercy* for us, since we can approach and speak to Jesus through Mary. We need her intervention to see or speak to him. Here, ever responsive to the prayer of his Mother, Jesus unfailingly grants grace and mercy to all poor sinners. "Let us come boldly then before the throne of grace."[445]

It is the seat of *liberality* for Mary, because while the new Adam dwelt in this truly earthly paradise[446] God performed there so many hidden marvels beyond the understanding of men and angels. For this reason, the saints call Mary "the magnificence of God,"[447] as if God showed his magnificence only in Mary.[448]

It is the seat of *glory* for his Father, because it was in Mary that

Jesus perfectly atoned to his Father on behalf of mankind. It was here that he perfectly restored the glory that sin had taken from his Father. It was here again that our Lord, by the sacrifice of himself and of his will, gave more glory to God than he would have given had he offered all the sacrifices of the Old Law. Finally, in Mary he gave his Father infinite glory, such as his Father had never received from man.[449]

5 *[Saying the Hail Mary and the Rosary]*

249 Those who accept this devotion should have a great love for the Hail Mary, or, as it is called, the Angelic Salutation.

Few Christians, however enlightened, understand the value, merit, excellence and necessity of the Hail Mary.[450] Our Blessed Lady herself had to appear on several occasions to men of great holiness and insight, such as St. Dominic,[451] St. John Capistran and Blessed Alan de Rupe,[452] to convince them of the richness of this prayer.

They composed whole books on the wonders it had worked and its efficacy in converting sinners. They earnestly proclaimed and publicly preached that just as the salvation of the world began with the Hail Mary, so the salvation of each individual is bound up with it. This prayer, they said, brought to a dry and barren world the Fruit of Life, and if well said, will cause the Word of God to take root in the soul[453] and bring forth Jesus, the Fruit of Life. They also tell us that the Hail Mary is a heavenly dew which waters the earth[454] of our soul and makes it bear its fruit in due season. The soul which is not watered by this heavenly dew bears no fruit but only thorns and briars, and merits only God's condemnation.[455]

250 Here is what our Blessed Lady revealed to Blessed Alan de Rupe as recorded in his book, *The Dignity of the Rosary,* and as told again by Cartagena: "Know, my son, and make it known to all, that lukewarmness or negligence in saying the Hail Mary, or a distaste for it, is a probable and proximate sign of eternal damnation, for by this prayer the whole world was restored."

These are terrible words but at the same time they are consoling. We should find it hard to believe them. were we not assured of their truth by Blessed Alan and by St. Dominic before him, and by so many great men since his time. The experience of many centuries is there to prove it, for it has always been common knowledge that those who bear the sign of reprobation, as all formal heretics, evildoers, the proud and the worldly, hate and spurn the Hail Mary and the Rosary.[456] True, heretics learn to say the Our Father but they will not countenance the Hail Mary and the Rosary and they would rather carry a snake around with them than a rosary. And there are even Catholics, who, sharing the proud tendencies of their father Lucifer, despise the Hail Mary or look upon it with indifference. The Rosary, they say, is a devotion suitable only for ignorant and illiterate people.

On the other hand, we know from experience that those who show positive signs of being among the elect, appreciate and love the Hail Mary and are always glad to say it. The closer they are to God, the more they love this prayer, as our Blessed Lady went on to tell Blessed Alan.

251 I do not know how this should be, but it is perfectly true; and I know no surer way of discovering whether a person belongs to God than by finding out if he loves saying the Hail Mary and the Rosary. I say, "if he loves," for it can happen that a person for some reason may be unable[457] to say the Rosary, but this does not prevent him from loving it and inspiring others to say it.

252 Chosen souls, slaves of Jesus in Mary, understand that after the Our Father,[458] the Hail Mary is the most beautiful of all prayers. It is the perfect compliment the most High God paid to Mary through his archangel in order to win her heart. So powerful was the effect of this greeting upon her, on account of its hidden delights, that despite her great humility, she gave her consent to the incarnation of the Word. If you say the Hail Mary properly, this compliment will infallibly earn you Mary's good will.

253 When the Hail Mary is well said, that is, with attention, devotion and humility, it is, according to the saints, the enemy of Satan, putting him to flight; it is the hammer that crushes him, a source of holiness for souls, a joy to the angels and a sweet melody for the devout. It is the Canticle of the New Testament, a delight for Mary and glory for the most Blessed Trinity.[459] The Hail Mary is dew falling from heaven to make the soul fruitful.[460] It is a pure kiss of love we give to Mary. It is a crimson rose, a precious pearl that we offer to her. It is a cup of ambrosia, of divine nectar that we offer her. These are comparisons made by the saints.

254 I earnestly beg of you, then, by the love I bear you in Jesus and Mary, not to be content with saying the Little Crown of the Blessed Virgin, but say the Rosary too, and if time permits, all its fifteen decades, every day. Then when death draws near, you will bless the day and hour when you took to heart what I told you, for having sown the blessings of Jesus and Mary, you will reap eternal blessings in heaven.[461]

6 *[Praying the Magnificat]*

255 To thank God for the graces he has given to our Lady, her consecrated ones will frequently say the *Magnificat,* following the example of Blessed Marie d'Oignies[462] and several other saints. The *Magnificat* is the only prayer we have which was composed by our Lady, or rather, composed by Jesus in her, for it was he who spoke through her lips. It is the greatest offering of praise that God ever received under the law of grace. On the one hand, it is the most humble hymn of thanksgiving and, on the other, it is the most sublime and exalted. Contained in it are mysteries so great and so hidden that even the angels do not understand them.[463]

Gerson,[464] a pious and learned scholar, spent the greater part of his life writing tracts full of erudition and love on the most profound subjects. Even so, it was with apprehension that he undertook towards the end of his life to write a commentary on the *Magnificat* which was the crowning point of all his works. In a large volume on the subject he says many wonderful things about this beautiful and divine canticle. Among other things he tells us that Mary herself frequently recited it, especially as thanksgiving after Holy Communion.[465] The learned Benzonius,[466] in his commentary on the *Magnificat,* cites several miracles worked through the power of this prayer. The devils, he declares, take to flight when they hear these words, "He puts forth his arm in strength and scatters the proud-hearted."[467]

7 *[Contempt of the world]*

256 Mary's faithful servants must despise this corrupted world. They should hate and shun its allurements, and follow the exercises of the contempt of the world[468] which we have given in the first part of this treatise.

[2.] *Special interior practices for those who wish to be perfect*

257 The exterior practices of this devotion which I have just dealt with should be observed as far as one's circumstances and state of life permit. They should not be omitted through negligence or deliberate disregard. In addition to them, here are some very sanctifying interior practices for those souls who feel called by the Holy Spirit to a high degree of perfection.[469] They may be expressed in four words, doing everything THROUGH Mary, WITH Mary, IN Mary and FOR Mary, in order to do it more perfectly *through* Jesus, *with* Jesus, *in* Jesus and *for* Jesus.

1 *[Through Mary]*

258 We must do everything through Mary, that is, we must obey her always and be led in all things by her spirit, which is the Holy Spirit of God. "Those who are led by the Spirit of God are children of God,"[470] says St. Paul. Those who are led by the spirit of Mary are children of Mary, and, consequently children of God, as we have already shown.[471] Among the many servants of Mary only those who are truly and faithfully devoted to her are led by her spirit.
I have said[472] that the spirit of Mary is the spirit of God because

she was never led by her own spirit, but always by the spirit of God, who made himself master of her to such an extent that he became her very spirit. That is why St. Ambrose says, "May the soul of Mary be in each one of us to glorify the Lord. May the spirit of Mary be in each one of us to rejoice in God."[473] Happy is the man who follows the example of the good Jesuit Brother Rodriguez,[474] who died in the odor of sanctity, because he will be completely possessed and governed by the spirit of Mary, a spirit which is gentle yet strong, zealous yet prudent, humble yet courageous, pure yet fruitful.

259 The person who wishes to be led by this spirit of Mary:

1 Should renounce his own spirit, his own views and his own will before doing anything, for example, before making meditation, celebrating or attending Mass, before Communion. For the darkness of our own spirit and the evil tendencies of our own will and actions, good as they may seem to us, would hinder the holy spirit of Mary were we to follow them.

2 We should give ourselves up to the spirit of Mary to be moved and directed as she wishes. We should place and leave ourselves in her virginal hands, like a tool in the hands of a craftsman or a lute in the hands of a good musician. We should cast ourselves into her like a stone thrown into the sea. This is done easily and quickly by a mere thought, a slight movement of the will or just a few words as—"I renounce myself and give myself to you, my dear Mother." And even if we do not experience any emotional fervor in this spiritual encounter, it is none the less real. It is just as if a person with equal sincerity were to say—which God forbid!—"I give myself to the devil." Even though this were said without feeling any emotion, he would no less really belong to the devil.

3 From time to time during an action and after it, we should renew this same act of offering and of union. The more we do so, the quicker we shall grow in holiness and the sooner we shall reach union with Christ, which necessarily follows upon union with Mary, since the spirit of Mary is the spirit of Jesus.

2 *[With Mary]*

260 We must do everything with Mary,[475] that is to say, in all our actions we must look upon Mary, although a simple human being, as the perfect model of every virtue and perfection, fashioned by the Holy Spirit for us to imitate, as far as our limited capacity allows.[476] In every action then we should consider how Mary performed it or how she would perform it if she were in our place. For this reason, we must examine and meditate on the great virtues she practised during her life,[477] especially:

1 Her lively faith,[478] by which she believed the angel's word

without the least hesitation, and believed faithfully and constantly even to the foot of the Cross on Calvary.[479]

2 Her deep humility,[480] which made her prefer seclusion, maintain silence, submit to every eventuality and put herself in the last place.

3 Her truly divine purity, which never had and never will have its equal on this side of heaven.

And so on for her other virtues.

Remember what I told you before, that Mary is the great, unique mould of God, designed to make living images of God at little expense and in a short time. Anyone who finds this mould and casts himself into it, is soon transformed into our Lord because it is the true likeness of him.[481]

3 *[In Mary]*

261 We must do everything in Mary. To understand this we must realize that the Blessed Virgin is the true earthly paradise of the new Adam and that the ancient paradise was only a symbol of her.[482] There are in this earthly paradise untold riches, beauties, rarities and delights, which the new Adam, Jesus Christ, has left there. It is in this paradise that he "took his delights" for nine months, worked his wonders and displayed his riches with the magnificence of God himself. This most holy place consists of only virgin and immaculate soil from which the new Adam was formed with neither spot nor stain by the operation of the Holy Spirit who dwells there. In this earthly paradise grows the real Tree of Life which bore our Lord, the fruit of Life, the tree of knowledge of good and evil, which bore the Light of the world.

In this divine place there are trees planted by the hand of God and watered by his divine unction which have borne and continue to bear fruit that is pleasing to him. There are flowerbeds studded with a variety of beautiful flowers of virtue, diffusing a fragrance which delights even the angels. Here, there are meadows verdant with hope, impregnable towers of fortitude, enchanting mansions of confidence and many other delights.

Only the Holy Spirit can teach us the truths that these material objects symbolize. In this place the air is perfectly pure. There is no night, but only the brilliant day of the sacred humanity, the resplendent, spotless sun of the Divinity, the blazing furnace of love, melting all the base metal thrown into it and changing it into gold. There the river of humility gushes forth from the soil, divides into four branches and irrigates the whole of this enchanted place. These branches are the four cardinal virtues.

262 The Holy Spirit speaking through the Fathers of the Church, also calls our Lady the Eastern Gate, through which the High

Priest, Jesus Christ, enters and goes out into the world.[483] Through this gate he entered the world the first time and through this same gate he will come the second time.

The Holy Spirit also calls her the Sanctuary of the Divinity, the Resting-place of the Holy Trinity, the Throne of God, the City of God, the Altar of God, the Temple of God, the World of God. All these titles and expressions of praise are very real when related to the different wonders the Almighty worked in her and the graces which he bestowed on her. What wealth and what glory! What a joy and a privilege for us to enter and dwell in Mary, in whom almighty God has set up the throne of his supreme glory!

263 But how difficult it is for us to have the freedom, the ability and the light to enter such an exalted and holy place. This place is guarded not by a cherub, like the first earthly paradise[484] but by the Holy Spirit himself who has become its absolute Master. Referring to her, he says: "You are an enclosed garden, my sister, my bride, an enclosed garden and a sealed fountain."[485] Mary is enclosed. Mary is sealed. The unfortunate children of Adam and Eve, driven from the earthly paradise, can enter this new paradise only by a special grace of the Holy Spirit which they have to merit.[486]

264 When we have obtained this remarkable grace by our fidelity, we should be delighted to remain in Mary. We should rest there peacefully, rely on her confidently, hide ourselves there with safety, and abandon ourselves unconditionally to her, so that within her virginal bosom:

1 We may be nourished with the milk of her grace and her motherly compassion.

2 We may be delivered from all anxiety, fear and scruples.[487]

3 We may be safeguarded from all our enemies, the devil, the world and sin which have never gained admittance there. That is why our Lady says that those who work in her will not sin,[488] that is, those who dwell spiritually in our Lady will never commit serious sin.

4 We may be formed in our Lord and our Lord formed in us,[489] because her womb is, as the early Fathers call it, the house of the divine secrets[490] where Jesus and all the elect have been conceived. "This one and that one were born in her."[491]

4 *[For Mary]*

265 Finally we must do everything for Mary. Since we have given ourselves completely to her service, it is only right that we should do everything for her as if we were her personal servant and slave. This does not mean that we take her for the ultimate end of our service for Jesus alone is our ultimate end. But we take Mary for our proximate end, our mysterious intermediary and the easiest way of reaching him.[492]

Like every good servant and slave we must not remain idle, but, relying on her protection, we should undertake and carry out great things for our noble Queen.[493] We must defend her privileges when they are questioned[494] and uphold her good name when it is under attack. We must attract everyone, if possible, to her service and to this true and sound devotion.[495] We must speak up and denounce those who distort devotion to her by outraging her Son, and at the same time we must apply ourselves to spreading this true devotion.[496] As a reward for these little services, we should expect nothing in return save the honor of belonging to such a lovable Queen and the joy of being united through her to Jesus, her Son, by a bond that is indissoluble in time and in eternity. Glory to Jesus in Mary! Glory to Mary in Jesus! Glory to God alone!"

[Supplement]

This Devotion at Holy Communion

Before Holy Communion[497]

266 1 Place yourself humbly in the presence of God.

2 Renounce your corrupt nature and dispositions, no matter how good self-love makes them appear to you.

3 Renew your consecration saying, "I belong entirely to you, dear Mother, and all that I have is yours."[498]

4 Implore Mary to lend you her heart so that you may receive her Son with her dispositions. Remind her that her Son's glory requires that he should not come into a heart so sullied and so fickle as your own, which could not fail to diminish his glory and might cause him to leave. Tell her that if she will take up her abode in you to receive her Son—which she can do because of the sovereignty she has over all hearts[499]—he will be received by her in a perfect manner without danger of being affronted or being forced to depart. "God is in the midst of her. She shall not be moved."[500]

Tell her with confidence that all you have given her of your possessions is little enough to honor her, but that in Holy Communion you wish to give her the same gifts as the eternal Father gave her. Thus, she will feel more honored than if you gave her all the wealth in the world. Tell her, finally, that Jesus, whose love for her is unique, still wishes to take his delight and his repose in her even in your soul, even though it is poorer and less clean than the stable which he readily entered because she was there. Beg her to lend you her heart, saying, "O Mary, I take you for my all; give me your heart."[501]

During Holy Communion

267 After the Our Father, when you are about to receive our Lord, say to him three times the prayer, "Lord, I am not worthy."[502] Say it the first time as if you were telling the eternal Father that because of your evil thoughts and your ingratitude to such a good Father, you are unworthy to receive his only-begotten Son, but that here is Mary, his handmaid,[503] who acts for you and whose presence gives you a special confidence and hope in him.[504]

268 Say to God the Son, "Lord I am not worthy," meaning that you are not worthy to receive him because of your useless and evil words and your carelessness in his service, but nevertheless you ask him to have pity on you because you are going to usher him into the house of his Mother and yours, and you will not let him go until he has made it his home.[505] Implore him to rise and come to the place of his repose and the ark of his sanctification.[506] Tell him that you have no faith in your own merits, strength and preparedness, like Esau, but only in Mary, your Mother, just as Jacob had trust only in Rebecca his mother. Tell him that although you are a great sinner you still presume to approach him, supported by his holy Mother and adorned with her merits and virtues.[507]

269 Say to the Holy Spirit, "Lord, I am not worthy." Tell him that you are not worthy to receive the masterpiece of his love because of your lukewarmness, wickedness and resistance to his inspirations. But, nonetheless, you put all your confidence in Mary, his faithful Spouse, and you say with St. Bernard, "She is my greatest safeguard, the whole foundation of my hope."[508] Beg him to overshadow Mary, his inseparable Spouse, once again. Her womb is as pure and her heart is as ardent as ever. Tell him that if he does not enter your soul neither Jesus nor Mary will be formed there nor will it be a worthy dwelling for them.

After Holy Communion

270 After Holy Communion, close your eyes and recollect yourself. Then usher Jesus into the heart of Mary: You are giving him to his Mother who will receive him with great love and give him the place of honor, adore him profoundly, show him perfect love, embrace him intimately in spirit and in truth,[509] and perform many offices for him of which we, in our ignorance, would know nothing.

271 Or, maintain a profoundly humble heart in the presence of

Jesus dwelling in Mary. Or be in attendance like a slave at the gate of the royal palace, where the King is speaking with the Queen. While they are talking to each other, with no need of you, go in spirit to heaven and to the whole world, and call upon all creatures to thank, adore and love Jesus and Mary for you. "Come, let us adore."[510]

272 Or, ask Jesus living in Mary that his kingdom may come upon earth through his holy Mother. Ask for divine Wisdom, divine love, the forgiveness of your sins, or any other grace, but always through Mary and in Mary. Cast a look of reproach upon yourself and say, "Lord, do not look at my sins, let your eyes see nothing in me but the virtues and merits of Mary."[511] Remembering your sins, you may add, "I am my own worst enemy and I am guilty of all these sins."[512] Or, "Deliver me from the unjust and deceitful man."[513] Or again, "Dear Jesus, you must increase in my soul and I must decrease."[514] "Mary, you must increase in me and I must always go on decreasing." "O Jesus and Mary, increase in me and increase in others around me."[515]

273 There are innumerable other thoughts with which the Holy Spirit will inspire you, which he will make yours if you are thoroughly recollected and mortified, and constantly faithful to the great and sublime devotion which I have been teaching you. But remember the more you let Mary act in your Communion the more Jesus will be glorified. The more you humble yourself and listen to Jesus and Mary in peace and silence—with no desire to see, taste or feel—then the more freedom you will give to Mary to act in Jesus' name and the more Jesus will act in Mary. For the just man lives everywhere by faith, but especially in Holy Communion, which is an action of faith.[516]

Footnotes to The True Devotion to the Blessed Virgin

1 According to ST. JEROME, that is the meaning of the word "almah" (In Is. Proph. 3, 7).

2 Song 3:6; 8:5.

3 Cf. St. Thom. III, q. 27, a. 5, ad 3.

4 Concerning the title "Spouse of the Holy Spirit," cf. LEO XIII, *Divinum illud munus,* 1897; and PIUS XII, *Broadcast Message for Crowning of Statue of our Lady of Fatima,* 1946; *Marialis Cultus,* No. 26; and JOHN PAUL II: "I beg on my knees that, through the intercession of Mary, holy spouse of the Holy Spirit, and Mother of the Church, we may all receive the light of the Holy Spirit" (*Letter to all the bishops of the Church,* 1980).

5 Cf. LEW 106. This idea is from St. BERNARDINE OF SIENA, *Serm. de Concept. B.V.M.,* art. 3, c. 1.

6 Jn. 2:4; 19: 26.
7 Song 4:12; cf. TD 263.
8 Cf. TD 261-263.
9 A Marian accommodation of Gen. 2:8, made by many Fathers including St. Ephrem, St. Proclus, St. Ambrose, St. John Damascene.
10 Cf. RICHARD a Sancto Laurentio, *De laudibus B.V.M.*, and ST. BERNARDINE OF SIENA, *Serm. XII.*
11 Lk. 1:49.
12 Cf. ST. GREGORY THE GREAT, *In I Regum expos.*, bk. I, c. 1.
13 Cf. TD 37, 76.
14 Cf. Eph. 3; 18; Apoc. 21:15, 16.
15 From ST. BONAVENTURE. Marian accommodation of Is. 6:3.
16 Cf. Dan. 10:13; Heb. 1:14.
17 Continues the Marian application of Is. 6:3.
18 Cf. BOUDON, *Immaculée,* preface: "If we were to say that there are enough books on devotion to the Virgin Mary, the holy Fathers would answer that we can never praise her enough. St. Bernard assures us that if all men undertook to speak of her, never could they say enough . . ."
19 Ps. 44:14.
20 Cf. SM 1.
21 1 Cor. 2:9.
22 This expression is found in ST. ISIDORE of Thess., *Serm. in Praes. B.V.M.;* also in ST. GERMAIN of Constantinople and ST. JOHN DAMASCENE.
23 Montfort speaks here of practical knowledge which is opposed to knowledge that is purely academic, dry and sterile.
24 Ex. 3:14.
25 Cf. TD 39.
26 Heb. 1:12; Ps. 102:26.
27 Cf. Lk. 1:30; ST. AMBROSE, *Expos. in Luke 2;* ST. BERNARD, *Hom. 3 super Missus est,* No. 10.
28 ST. AUGUSTINE (inter subditia), *Serm. 215 in Redditione Symb.*, No.
29 Cf. ARGENTAN, 11th confer., art. 5, vol. 1.
30 Cf. TD 6.
31 Cf. BENEDICT XV: "Mary suffered and almost died with her suffering and dying Son. She abdicated her maternal rights for the salvation of men and, as much as she could, immolated her Son to appease the justice of God to such an extent that we can justifiably say that she redeemed the human race with her Son" *(Inter Sodalicia).*

II VATICAN COUNCIL: "Mary stood by the Cross suffering grievously with her only-begotten Son. There she united herself with a maternal heart to his sacrifice and lovingly consented to the immolation of this victim which she herself had brought forth and also was offering to the eternal Father" (*Lumen Gentium,* No. 58). Cf. *Marialis Cultus,* No. 20.
32 Cf. Gen. 22:2.
33 Cf. Lk. 2:51; ST. BERNARD, *Hom. 1 super Missus est.*

34 Cf. TD 27, 139, 156.
35 Cf. Lk. 1:41; LEO XIII, *Jucunda semper,* 1894.
36 Cf. Jn. 2:1-12; PIUS XII, *Mystici Corporis,* 1943.
37 Cf. ARGENTAN, 1st conf., art. 4; 3rd conf., art. 3.
38 Cf. POIRÉ, *Crown of excellence,* 6th star; ARGENTAN, 12th conf., art. 3.
39 Cf. TD 216.
40 RICHARD a Sancto Laurentio, *De laudibus B.V.M.,* bk. 2; RAYMOND JORDAN (Idiota), *Piae lectiones seu contemplationes de B.V.M.* in proem.; cf. POIRÉ, *Crown of power,* 9th star: "She is the treasurer and dispenser of the graces of God."
41 RICHARD a Sancto Laurentio, *ibid.;* ST. BERNARD, *In Nativ. B.V.M.,* Serm. de aquaeductu.
42 ST. BERNARDINE OF SIENA, *Serm. de 12 Prov.; Serm. in Nativ. B.V.M.*
43 Cf. TD 141; PIUS XII: "She gives us her Son and with him all the helps we need for God has willed us to have everything through Mary" (*Mediator Dei,* 1947). ST. BERNARD, *in Nativ. B.V.M.,* 7.
44 FRANÇOIS POIRÉ (1584-1637), of the Society of Jesus, one time rector of the college of Lyons and afterwards that of Dole. His most important work was *The Triple Crown of the Blessed Virgin Mary, Mother of God, merging together her sublime gifts of excellence, power and goodness* which first appeared in Paris in 1630.
45 Cf. TD 76.
46 Cf. Ex. 32:10-14.
47 Statement made by Suarez, quoted by ARGENTAN, 15th conf.
48 Cf. CONRAD of Saxony, *Speculum B.V.M., lect. 11, No. 6, who bases his assertion on a text of ST. ANSELM, Or. 52.*
49 Cf. Lk. 1:52.
50 ST. BONAVENTURE, *Psalt. majus,* Cant. ad instar illius trium puerorum.
51 This long series of Marian praises is a re-statement of the titles of many of the stars of the *Crown of Power* of POIRÉ.
52 Sir. 24:8.
53 This text seems to re-echo the words of ST. CYPRIAN in *De Unitate Ecclesiae:* "He cannot have God for father who has not the Church for mother." Montfort, following BOISSIEU (p. 438), relates the maternity of Mary to the paternity of God.
54 Cf. TD 63-65.
55 Sir. 24:8.
56 Ps. 86:5. The interpretation in a Marian sense of this verse is suggested by Letter 119 of OLIER.
57 "born in her." Cf. PIUS X: "We must consider ourselves as having our origin in Mary's womb, whence we were born as a body attached to the head" (*Ad diem illum,* 1903). PIUS XII: "She who was mother of our Head according to the flesh became by a new title of sorrow and of glory the spiritual Mother of all his members" (*Mystici Corporis,* No. 110). PAUL VI: "The faithful will be brought to a deeper realization of the brotherhood which unites all of them as sons and daughters of the Virgin Mary, who with a

mother's love has co-operated in their rebirth and spiritual formation" (*Marialis Cultus,* No. 28).

58 Gal. 4:19. Montfort quotes from memory. (Cf. LEW 214; SM 56.) The Marian application of this text was provided by POIRÉ (*Crown of goodness,* 2nd star).

59 Cf. Eph. 4:13. This expression was very dear to Montfort and he used it on many occasions (cf. LEW 214, 226; SM 67; TD 119, 156, 164, 168).

60 St. AUGUSTINE, *De Virg.,* 1. c. 6; *De Symb. ad catech.,* serm. 4.

61 Sir. 24:12. POIRÉ gives an extensive commentary on this text and Montfort also comments upon it in his notebook. The two commentaries, however, are entirely different.

62 Cf. TD 214.

63 Cf. TD 108.

64 Cf. TD 47-49.

65 Cf. TD 76. Cf. PIUS XII: "Her kingdom is as vast as that of her Son and of God since nothing is excluded from her sovereignty" (*Radio Message to Fatima,* 1946). Cf. II VATICAN COUNCIL: "She has been exalted by the Lord as Queen of all" (*Lumen Gentium,* No. 59).

66 Cf. PIUS XII: "Jesus is the king of eternal ages by nature and by conquest. Through him, with him and subordinate to him, Mary is Queen by grace, by divine alliance, by special election" *(Radio Message to Fatima).*

67 Cf. PIUS XII: "The Blessed Virgin received not only the highest degree of excellence and perfection after Christ but also a share in that influence which warrants our saying that her Son, our Savior, is King over the minds and hearts of men" (*Ad Coeli Reginam,* 1954).

68 Cf. a prayer indulgenced by the Sacred Penitentiary, 1924: "Take and accept my whole being, O Mary, Queen of all hearts, and make me your slave with chains of love, that I may belong to you and may repeat in all truth, 'I belong entirely to Jesus through Mary.' "

69 Cf. TD 14.

70 Devotion to our Lady as a sign of predestination was a theme very much favored by authors in the seventeenth century. Montfort quotes many of them, e.g. POIRÉ, CRASSET, GRENIER, ARGENTAN and BOISSIEU. Cf. PIUS XII: "Devotion to the Blessed Virgin Mary, Mother of God, which is regarded by the saints as a sign of predestination . . ." (*Mediator Dei,* 1947).

71 Cf. TD 40.

72 Cf. *I Fioretti,* c. 10. Montfort has probably borrowed the story from BOISSIEU, pp. 114, 115.

73 Cf. SR 101-104.

74 Lk. 1:30.

75 Lk. 1:28.

76 Cf. Lk. 1:35.

77 Cf. TD 24, 25.

78 Cf. SM 70.

79 Cf. Song 1:3; GERSON, *Collect. in cant. Magnificat;* ST. JOHN

OF THE CROSS, *Spiritual Canticle,* 25.
80 Cf. TD 261. Cf. Nehem. 4:17.
81 Cf. Ps. 44:13. Cf. ST. BERNARD, *Serm. 4 in antiph. Salve Regina.*
82 The "holy soul" was MARIE DES VALLÉES, a celebrated mystic who died in 1656. Her biographer was M. de Renty and her confessor was St. John Eudes.
83 PM 11.
84 This prophecy is obscure and does not relate to our Lady.
85 Ps. 58:13, 14. Literally this psalm refers to the conversion of the Jews or the preaching of the gospel at the end of the world.
86 Cf. Ps. 86:3.
87 Cf. TD 2-5.
88 This text is borrowed from POIRÉ, *Crown of excellence,* 5th star. At the time of St. Louis Marie this apocryphal letter to St. Paul was generally considered authentic.
89 Cf. Prov. 8:35.
90 Cf. Jn. 14:6.
91 Cf. Song 6:3. Quoted again in TD 210.
92 Apoc. 12:12.
93 Cf. PM 13.
94 Cf. TD 42.
95 This is a theme particularly favored by the early Fathers. Cf. PIUS XII: "In the work of our redemption Mary was, by God's will, associated with Jesus Christ, the source of salvation. She was, moreover, associated with him in a way parallel to the way in which Eve was associated with Adam, the source of death. It may therefore be said that the work of our salvation was wrought by the inclusion, in some way, of the many in one. So, just as the human race was committed to death through a virgin, it is saved by means of a Virgin" (*Ad Caeli Reginam,* 1954).
96 Cf. Gen. 4:8; Cf. TD 185, 210.
97 Cf. TD 184-212 (development of biblical example).
98 Cf. TD 152-168.
99 Ps. 104:4; Heb. 1:7; for the description of the apostles of the latter times cf. TD 56-59 and PM 7-25.
100 Ps. 127:4.
101 Cf. Mal. 3:3; 1 Cor. 6:17.
102 Cf. 2 Cor. 2:15-16.
103 Cf. Is. 60:8.
104 Cf. Heb. 4:12; Eph. 6:17.
105 All this number is a commentary on verses 13, 14 of Psalm 68 and a further development can be found in PM 17-25.
106 Cf. Rom. 13:10.
107 Matt. 22:16.
108 Cf. Heb. 4:12; Eph. 6:17.
109 Cf. FC 19; PM 8.
110 Ps. 39:2.
111 These fundamental truths are no different from those of all authentic Christian living and therefore of all authentic Marian devotion.

Here, however, they represent the remote preparation for the most perfect practice of true Marian devotion (cf. TD 118, ff.).

112 This number abounds in biblical references.

113 End of Eucharistic Prayer.

114 "Already shown," cf. TD 24, 31-33, 50. "Will show again later," cf. TD 75, 83-86, 120, 152-168.

115 Cf. TD 13; cf. II VATICAN COUNCIL: "The faithful must bear in mind that real devotion does not consist in sterile, transitory emotion nor in idle credulity . . ." (*Lumen Gentium,* No. 67).

116 An allusion to Jansenists and to the book *Avis salutaires* of ADAM WIDENFELT, published in 1673 and placed on the Index in 1676. Cf. TD 93.

117 Cf. SM 1.

118 ST. BONAVENTURE, *Psalt. majus,* Ps. 79.

119 WILLIAM of Paris, *De rhetorica divina.*

120 The prayer of ST. AUGUSTINE, which the author gives in Latin, seems to have been composed of different extracts from the works of ST. AUGUSTINE or those attributed to him. The original compiler is unknown.

121 Cf. 1 Cor. 6:19; 12:27.

122 Cf. ST. THOMAS III, qu. 48, art. 4; TD 126.

123 Cf. Rom. 7:4; 1 Pet. 2:9.

124 Cf. Ps. 1:3; Jn 15:5; 10:1-6; 15:1; Mt. 13:8.

125 Cf. Mt. 21:19; 25:24-30.

126 Eph. 2:10 quoted from memory.

127 Cf. ST. THOM. III, qu. 48, art. 1. St. Augustine distinguishes four kinds of slavery: that of nature, of compulsion, of fear, of choice. Montfort's immediate source for all this number is GRENIER.

128 Ps. 23:1.

129 1 Sam. 16:7; Ps. 73:26; Prov. 23:26.

130 Cf. BOUDON, *Slavery,* tr. 1, c. 2, t. 2, col. 380. In giving his explanation of this difference, Montfort considers the two terms purely from the point of view of their historical existence without justifying them. His aim is to prove that the term "slave" emphasizes our belonging to God and our total dependence upon him.

131 Textually from BOUDON.

132 Phil. 2:7.

133 Lk. 1:38.

134 Rom. 1:1; Gal. 1:10; Philem. 1:1.

135 1 Cor. 7:22; 2 Tim. 2:24.

136 Probable allusion to PIERRE GRENIER who wrote a book on this subject entitled *Apologia of devotees of the Blessed Virgin,* which Montfort resumes in his notebook.

137 Cf. TD 129.

138 Cf. TD 126.

139 Magnificent résumé of TD 18, 19, 24, 37.

140 This principle of "fittingness" was particularly brought out by SUAREZ, *In III partem D. Thomae,* qu. 27, art. 2. Cf. PIUS XII: "(The great Suarez) used to teach in mariology that, keeping in mind the standards of propriety and where there is no repugnance

on the part of Scripture, the mysteries of grace which God has wrought in the Virgin Mary must be measured not by ordinary laws but by the divine omnipotence" (*Munificentissimus Deus,* 1950).

141 ST. JOHN DAMASCENE, *Hom. 22 in Dorm. B.V.M.*

142 Among those whose teaching is explicit on the subject is ST. ILDEPHONSUS, *Liber de virginitate perpetua S. Mariae,* c. 12.

143 Cf. TD 164.

144 ST. BONAVENTURE, *Psalt. majus,* Ps. 117.

145 Cf. TD 27, 37-38.

146 Cf. TD 71.

147 Cf. 1 Kings 2:19; Esther 5:6, 7.

148 Cf. TD 244, 245.

149 TD 120 ff.

150 In giving these comparisons Montfort does not mean to invalidate the graces and gifts of God nor affirm that our actions can spoil them. He desires only to stress that even our best actions are generally imperfect because of self-love and an "unconscious attachment to creatures which slips unnoticed into our best actions" (cf. TD 146). Cf. Parallel texts in FC 47; TD 146, 173, 213, 228.

151 Cf. Rom. 6:6; Ps. 50:7.

152 Gen. 6:12.

153 "We have nothing in us but lies and sin": cf. II Council of Orange can. 22. As regards the series of comparisons, "prouder than peacocks, etc.," which offend some modern readers, ST. JOHN CHRYSOSTOM gives a longer and more uncomplimentary list (*Hom. 4 in Matt.,* 8).

154 Cf. Eph. 2:3.

155 Cf. Matt. 16:24; Lk. 8:23; Jn. 12:25.

156 Cf. 1 Cor. 7:31.

157 1 Cor. 15:31.

158 Jn. 12:24.

159 Col. 3:3.

160 Cf. TD 218-221.

161 Cf. SM 1.

162 Cf. TD 78, 79.

163 Cf. ST. BERNARD, *Sermo de Assumpt.: Signum magnum,* Nos. 1, 2.

164 This number is full of biblical references: 1 Jn. 2:1; 1 Tim. 2:5; Rom. 13:14; Gen. 27.

165 ST. BERNARD, *Hom. 5 in Assumpt.: Signum magnum,* No. 2. This statement of St. Bernard can be clarified by No. 62 of *Lumen Gentium:* "The unique mediation of the Redeemer does not exclude but rather stimulates among creatures a participation and co-operation which is varied but which originates from a single source. The Church has no hesitation in admitting this subordinate office of Mary. It is the subject of her constant experience and she recommends it to the faithful for their heartfelt attention."

166 ST. BERNARD, *Sermo in Nativ. B.V.M.:* de aquaeductu, No. 7.

167 Cf. LEO XIII: "Just as we cannot go to the Father except through the Son, so we cannot go to Christ except through his Mother" (*Oc-*

tobri mense, 1891).

168 Cf. TD 120 ff.

169 2 Cor. 4:7.

170 Cf. 2 Pet. 5:8.

171 "that I shall later explain": from TD 120 onwards.

172 ST. LEO THE GREAT, *Serm. 42, De Quadr.*, 4.

173 After having explained the "fundamental truths" Montfort broaches the question: What does this devotion consist in? (TD 60). The following number (91) gives the subdivisions of this latter theme.

174 Cf. TD 135.

175 When dealing with false devotions Montfort is inspired by CRASSET's *La Véritable Dévotion* and by TRONSON (*Works*, vol. 1: Particular examens, 74th examen). However he follows them quite freely for his presentation is more constructive and he directs the reader towards the choice of the true devotion and its most perfect practice.

176 Cf. TD 64.

177 Lk. 1:42.

178 Cf. TD 224-225.

179 Cf. SM 25, 26.

180 Cf. Sir. 27:22; Apoc. 12:1.

181 Cf. LEW 215-216.

182 A list of Mary's virtues was given in TD 34. This number gives a complete list of the "principal virtues." In TD 260 three virtues are particularly stressed: faith, humility and purity.

183 Cf. Heb. 10:38 and TD 214.

184 Cf. Jn. 1:13.

185 Note the association of these three terms: children, servants, slaves. The *Catechism of the Council of Trent* points this out in part I, c. 3: "Although Jesus holds us in his power and under his dominion as slaves he has ransomed by his blood, he shows us such love that he deigns to call us his friends and brothers and not his slaves. Here we have surely one of the strongest, and perhaps the most convincing, reason why we should always acknowledge, honor and serve Jesus as our true Lord."

186 This prediction was literally fulfilled. The manuscript of the book was hidden away in a chest during the French Revolution. It was discovered in 1842 and published for the first time in 1843.

187 Mt. 24:15; 19:12.

188 As he had previously announced in TD 91 Montfort, after having pointed out the false devotions to be avoided and the true one to be embraced, goes on to describe the "practices" of true devotion. Following his plan he presents first the different interior practices and then embarks on that which, he believes, realizes perfectly the aim of true Marian devotion (cf. TD 91, 116, 118).

189 Cf. SM 1. This affirmation contains a twofold restriction: "nearly every book," and those "on devotion to the Blessed Virgin." Montfort obviously refers to the works of his day and especially those he was able to consult in the library at Saint-Sulpice where he had been librarian.

After having presented the interior and exterior practices common to every true devotion to Mary, Montfort approaches the question of the "most perfect" practice (TD 110). He himself gives the titles to the different sections: "The perfect consecration to Jesus Christ" (TD 120), "The effects" (TD 213), the "Particular practices" (TD 226, 257). He leaves out only one title, that of "Motives" but remedies this in TD 134.

190 Cf. SM 1.

191 Cf. Eph. 4:13; TD 33.

192 Heading: This is the first heading given in the manuscript; Montfort wrote it in large letters (Cf. TD 118, Note 189).

193 Montfort recalls here the first fundamental truth (cf. TD 61, 62) to show that it is verified perfectly in this perfect practice.

194 Cf. TD 126 ff.

195 Cf. TD 146 ff.

196 Cf. TD 120. The arguments that Montfort intends to put forward (126, 127, 129) are taken from BÉRULLE, *Narré.* In TD 162 Montfort speaks glowingly of Bérulle and his writings which he found in the library at Saint-Sulpice.

197 That is, by his seductions and snares.

198 Cf. Introduction to this book.

199 The promises of baptism are an act of latria, i.e., due only to God, as is also their renewal; but this does not prevent us from offering an act of latria to God through and with Mary.

200 Cf. ST. THOMAS, II-II, qu. 88, art. 2.

201 Cf. ST. AUGUSTINE, *Ep. 149 ad Paulinum,* No. 16.

202 Canonist J. CALVINUS (1553).

203 This number is taken from a résumé of one of Montfort's sermons and is a transcript of a passage from a sermon of Fr. Leschassier on the obligations of baptism. The COUNCIL OF SENS (6th Council of Paris) was held in 829 at Paris, which was then a suffragan see of Sens.

204 Cf. *Catechismus Conc. Trid.,* part I, c. 3: "The pastor must exhort the faithful never to lose sight of the fact that it is from Jesus Christ that we receive the name of Christian and that we cannot ignore the immense benefits he has heaped upon us since he himself chose to make them known by faith and therefore we are obliged in conscience more than all men to dedicate and consecrate ourselves for ever to our Redeemer and Lord as his slaves."

205 Montfort was inspired by BOUDON in these responses: *Slavery,* tr. 1, c. 6, t. 2.

206 Cf. TD 138, 144, 201 ff., 213 ff.

207 Cf. TD 118. This is a transitional number introducing a new section of the treatise (134).

208 Cf. BOUDON, *Slavery,* tr. 1, c. 2, vol. 2.

209 Cf. TD 110.

210 Cf. Mt. 19:29.

211 ST. BERNARD, *Serm. 22 de Diversis, De quadruplici debito,* No. 6.

212 Allusion made to what he said in TD 118.

213 Cf. TD 14-39.
214 Cf. TD 32.
215 ST. BERNARD, *Serm. in Nativ. B.V.M.: de aquaeductu,* Nos. 7, 6.
216 Cf. TD 25.
217 ST. BERNARD, *Serm. 3 in Vigilia Nativ. Domini,* No. 10.
218 ST. BERNARD, *Serm. in Nativ. B.V.M.: de aquaeductu,* No. 18. Montfort "borrows" many of these texts of St. Bernard from CRASSET. Cf. TD 149; SM 35.
219 Jas. 4:6.
220 Cf. TD 108.
221 Jn. 19:27; cf. TD 179.
222 Reference here to the 1st, 3rd and 4th effect (TD 213, 215, 216).
223 Cf. Gen. 32:24.
224 ABBOT RUPERT, proemium *In Cantica Cant. de Incarn. Domini.* Text borrowed from POIRÉ, *Crown of power.*
225 ST. AUGUSTINE (inter opera), *In fest. Assumpt. B.M.*
226 Cf. SM 37.
227 Lk. 1:46; cf. TD 225.
228 ST. BERNARD, *Serm. in Nativ. B.V.M.: de aquaeductu,* No. 18. Cf. TD 142; SM 37.
229 Cf. TD 147.
230 Cf. TD 183-212.
231 Cf. BOUDON, *Slavery,* tr. 1, c. 5, vol. 2.
232 Montfort is not speaking here of devotion to Mary which is necessary to all men but of the perfect practice of true devotion. He is not contradicting what he said in TD 39.
233 Cf. TD 107.
234 Cf. SM 22.
235 Cf. 2 Tim. 3:12.
236 Cf. BOISSIEU, p. 87.
237 Once a common interpretation of Prov. 21:28 but now proved to be erroneous.
238 Ps. 18:6.
239 Cf. Wis. 4:13.
240 Sir. 3:5. Concerning the philosopher's stone cf. LEW 86, 87.
241 Ps. 91:11. Interpretation now proved to be erroneous.
242 Cf. Eph. 4:13; TD 33.
243 Jer. 31:22.
244 Cf. Responsory of the Reading of the Office of the Blessed Virgin Mary. Cf. Kings 8:27.
245 Cf. TD 85.
246 Ps. 17:33. Cf. TD 50, 218.
247 Cf. SM 1.
248 HENRI-MARIE BOUDON (1624-1702), archdeacon of Evreux. The book referred to is *God alone or the Holy Slavery of the admirable Mother of God,* which first appeared in Paris in 1667. (Boudon mentions in his book that English Catholics were noted for the practice of this devotion.) Montfort refers to it again in TD 163 which leads us to believe that he had consulted it especially when preparing the historical survey he is about to give. Certain di-

vergences, concerning dates for example, lead us to believe that he consulted another source which was perhaps Louis Jobert's work *The devotion of the Holy Slavery of the Mother of God, a great help in the working out of one's salvation.*

249 This assertion is exact if we accept the formulas of Consecration as we know them today. There are, however, explicit texts much more ancient indicating devotion of slavery to our Lady (Cf. ST. ILDEPHONSUS OF TOLEDO).

We find the term "doulos" (slave) with reference to the Mother of God on the ancient seals of the Empire of the East dating from the first centuries; on the ambo of the church of Santa Maria Antiqua in the Roman Forum and on mosaics which once belonged to the former basilica of St. Peter. One wonders, however, if in these instances the term had the same meaning as Montfort gives to the word "slave" in his writings.

250 ST. ODILO (962-1048) was abbot of Cluny from 994. Here is the text of his consecration: "O most holy Virgin, Mother of the everlasting Savior, from this day forward take me into your service and be my advocate in all the affairs of my life. After God nothing is more precious to me than you and I most willingly deliver myself for ever to your service as your slave."

251 This incident, described by Montfort is recorded by ST. PETER DAMIAN (1007-1072) in the *Opusc. 13 ad Desiderium abbatem cassinensem,* c. 4. The date (1072) given by Montfort is inaccurate. St. Peter Damian, who died in 1072, speaks of the death of his brother and of the consecration he made whilst in good health and therefore before 1072.

252 CAESARIUS D'HEISTERBACH (born before 1188; died c. 1210) of the Cistercian Order, in a book written in 1222 tells the story of Vautier de Bierbeek whom he had known.

253 Cf. HENRI BREMOND, *Histoire littéraire du sentiment religieux en France,* 1923, vol. 6, p. 266, and the letter written by Mme de Sévigné to the count of Guitaux. The earliest known confraternity was founded by a Conceptionist Franciscan nun, Inés de San Pablo, in agreement with her religious Sisters in the monastery of the Conception of our Lady at Alcalâ de Henares (Spain). From the register we learn that the date of its foundation was August 2, 1595.

254 SIMON DE ROJAS (1552-1624), a Spanish Trinitarian, was confessor of the convent of Alcalâ de Henares. He founded the Confraternity of the Slaves of the Virgin Mother of God and propagated Marian slavery in Spain and the Indies through the monasteries of his Order.

255 BARTHOLOMEW DE LOS RIOS (1580-1652) was appointed in 1622, at the suggestion of Simon de Rojas, preacher to the Infanta Isabel, daughter of Philip II and wife of the Archduke Albert, governor of the Netherlands. It was thought that Los Rios had more than a passing influence on Montfort but this is disputed. LAURENTIN, (Bulletin marial, in *Vie spirituelle,* Suppl. No. 51) came to the conclusion there was no dependence but from a historical

point of view the question remains open.

256 Cf. SILOS, *Historiarum Clericorum Regularium* (1665), second part, p. 119.

257 STANISLAUS FENICKI (1592-1652) spread the devotion of the holy slavery in Poland with other Jesuit Fathers at the request of King Wladislas IV and published his book *Mariae mancipatus.* His name is latinised diversely by different authors: "Phoenicius," "Thanicius," "Phalacius."

258 CORNELIUS VAN DEN STEEN (1567-1637) was commissioned to examine the orthodoxy of the holy slavery when Fr. Stanislaus Fenicki was spreading it in Poland. One can derive from what he wrote in his *Comment. in Eccli.,* c. 6, v. 6, that his judgment was favorable.

259 BÉRULLE (1575-1629). Did Bérulle adopt this devotion in Spain where he spent some time in 1604? Between 1611 and 1613 he composed a number of short writings for the priests of the Oratory. On the occasion of a visitation he made in his capacity as Superior in the Carmel of Chalons-sur-Saône, he imposed the "vow" upon the Carmelites. This was followed by a "pamphlet" controversy which led ultimately to a condemnation of a "formulary of a fourth vow" by the theologians of Louvain and Douai and by Fr. Lessius, S.J. Bérulle answered the allegations made in the pamphlets by explaining that the "vow" simply meant the baptismal promises. Montfort falls in with this explanation, and those persons he stigmatises as "critics and evil men" were members of the clergy and especially Carmelite Fathers.

260 Cf. TD 3; BOUDON, tr. 1, c. 7, vol. 2.

261 GRENIER asserts that "Popes Clement VIII, Urban VIII and Alexander VII approved it and attached indulgences to it . . . and that no pope had ever condemned it." (*Apologia,* 1675, pp. 312-316.)

262 Cf. TD 86.

263 Cf. ST. THOM. III, qu. 2, art. II.

264 Cf. TD 75; SM 21.

265 Cf. TD 33.

266 Cf. SM 70.

267 Cf. TD 20, 21, 34, 36.

268 ST. GERMAIN of Constantinople, *Serm. 2 in Dormit. Deip.*

269 ST. GERMAIN of Constantinople, *Orat. in sanctae Deip. Zonam.*

270 Cf. TD 209.

271 2 Macc. 1:3.

272 1 Cor. 12:31. The text that follows gives a résumé of the whole of the 5th motive (TD 152-168).

273 Cf. TD 33.

274 Cf. Rom. 8:21. This motive expands TD 107 and already anticipates the 3rd effect (TD 215).

275 AGNES DE LANGEAC (1602-1634) was prioress of the Dominican Sisters of the convent of Saint-Catherine of Langeac. Up to the time of the French Revolution the religious of the order of St. Dominic were called "Jacobins" after their convent of Saint-Jacques in Paris.

276 Not quite true. In obedience to her confessor, Fr. Boyre S.J., she relinquished the chain in 1618. Fr. Boyre himself seemingly became a slave of love after asking the advice of Suarez.

277 Cf. LANTAGES, *Life of Mother Agnes of Langeac,* p. 581. It would seem that Montfort is quoting from memory, having probably heard the story told often enough at Saint-Sulpice.

278 Cf. Jn. 13:35.

279 Cf. ST. AUGUSTINE, *Tract. 72 in Joann.*

280 Cf. TD 146-147, 151.

281 Cf. TD 87-89.

282 1 Tim. 6:20. Cf. SM 40.

283 Ps. 118:141.

284 ST. BERNARD, *Hom. 2 super Missus est,* No. 17.

285 ST. BONAVENTURE, *Speculum B.V.M., lect. 7, par. 6. Cf. SM 40; TD 212.*

286 ST. JOHN DAMASCENE, Hom. in Dorm. B.V.M., No. 14.

287 Sir. 24:22. Cf. TD 264, (3).

288 2 Tim. 2:13 speaks of God; Montfort refers it to Mary.

289 Prov. 8:17.

290 Cf. TD 201.

291 Cf. SM 1.

292 The three numbers (TD 177-179) of the 8th motive constitute a perfect response to the 3rd truth (TD 78-81).

293 Invocations of the Litany of Loreto.

294 Ps. 118:56. Cf. SM 66.

295 Accommodation to 1st person of Jn. 19: 27. Same interpretation in SM 66 and TD 216, 266.

296 Quotation from memory of the prayer of Jesus to his Father. Jn. 17:10.

297 Allusion to Mt. 16:23; Jn. 14:17.

298 Cf. Jn. 1:13.

299 This text cannot be traced in the Sermon on the Annunciation.

300 The story is found in Gen. 27 but Montfort uses other biblical passages to present his "explanation," e.g., Mal. 1:2, 3; Heb. 11:20; 12:16.

301 Cf. Gen. 25:33.

302 Especially the mystery of predestination of Jacob who "from his mother's womb superseded his brother" (Hos. 12:3). All that happened afterwards, i.e., the selling of the birthright, the blessing of Isaac, merely fulfilled the plan of God.

303 Among them ST. AMBROSE, *De Jacob et vita beata,* bk. 2, c. 2. (but here Rebecca is a type of the Church); ST. BERNARD, *Serm. 28 in cant.;* ST. ANTONINUS, *Summa theol.,* part 4, tit. 15, c. 14, par. 3.

304 Esau can also be considered as a figure of Jesus Christ, as Montfort himself states in TD 206.

305 Cf. Gen. 4:8; same allusion in TD 52, 210.

306 ST. GREGORY THE GREAT, *Moralium,* bk. 32, c. 22, No. 46. Montfort borrowed this text from CRASSET. In explaining this story Montfort applies in an original manner to the reprobate sym-

bolized by Esau the marks of false devotions (cf. TD 92-104); to the predestinate, symbolized by Jacob, the marks of true devotion (cf. TD 105-110); and to Mary, prefigured by Rebecca, the motherly care shown to her slaves of love (cf. TD 144-149).

308 This is a favorite expression of Montfort's for designating gold and silver (cf. PM 27).

309 Ps. 83:2.

310 Cf. Prov. 3:9.

311 Gen. 27:8.

312 Jn. 2:5.

313 GUERRICUS, *Serm. in Assumpt.*, No. 4. Montfort borrowed this text from POIRÉ, *Crown of goodness,* 8th star.

314 ST. GREGORY THE GREAT, *Hom. 36 in Evang.*, bk. 2. Cf. the end of TD 48.

315 Prov. 8:32.

316 Ps. 118:21.

317 Cf. JOHN XXIII: "We are all protected by the sheltering and tender motherhood of the Virgin Mary, who performs for us the same services as every mother performs for her children. She loves us, she watches over us, she protects us, she intercedes for us" (*Radio message, Lisieux,* 1961).

318 Prov. 8:17.

319 Rom. 9:13.

320 Sir. 24:13; Cf. TD 31.

321 RAYMOND JORDAN (Idiota), *Piae lectiones seu contemplationes de B.M.*

322 Gen. 27:8.

323 Cf. TD 151.

324 Especially in TD 121-125.

325 Cf. TD 24, 25, 141.

326 The holy nun referred to was MARY OF AGREDA (1602-1665) who speaks of a revelation on this subject in her book *The Mystical City of God.*

327 Prov. 31:21. This same interpretation is given by CORNELIUS A. LAPIDE, *Comm. in Prov.* 31:21. An extensive commentary on Mary's services to her children, whom she adorns with her virtues, is given by RICHARD of Saint-Laurence, *In laudibus B.V.M.*, bk. 2.

328 Gen. 27:28.

329 Eph. 1:3.

330 Gen. 27:28.

331 Cf. 1 Cor. 7:29-31.

332 Ps. 93:3-4; Ps. 36:35.

333 Wis. 3:8.

334 Cf. TD 206; SM 38.

335 Cf. Jn. 6:35.

336 Sir. 24:26.

337 Prov. 9:5. Cf. end of SM 20.

338 Song 5:1.

339 Here he again recalls what he has written in TD 23-25.

340 Cf. Zech. 9:17.
341 Is. 66:12.
342 Cf. Mt. 11:30; TD 154.
343 Is. 10:27.
344 Cf. ST. BERNARD, *Hom. 2 super Missus est,* No. 17.
345 Cf. Ps. 22:3.
346 Brief commentary of a text already given in TD 174.
347 Continuation of the preceding text.
348 Cf. Gen. 4:8; same comparison in TD 54, 185.
349 Cf. Ps. 90:4; Mt. 23:37.
350 Song 6:3. Cf. TD 50, 7th.
351 Reference to Ps. 90:11; Mt. 26:53 with Marian application.
352 She "maintains that union": Montfort added this last phrase to complete his thought: conversion, union, perseverance. These three benefits which constitute the greatest good refer back to TD 39-48, where he speaks of the necessity of devotion to Mary; also to the 3rd, 4th and 5th fundamental truths (TD 78-88). The second benefit ("union with her Son") refers back to the 5th motive (TD 152-158). The third benefit ("maintains that union") refers back to the 8th motive (TD 173-182).
353 Gen. 27:27. The Marian interpretation of this passage is also given by RICHARD of Saint-Laurence, *De laudibus B.V.M.,* bk. 8.
354 Cf. Zech. 9:17.
355 Cf. Is. 9:6.
356 Cf. TD 206 (4).
357 Cf. TD 152-168.
358 Cf. Jn. 14:20.
359 Cf. TD 174.
360 Cf. TD 173-182.
361 Cf. the "exterior practices," TD 226-256, and the "interior practices," TD 257-265. In the preceding numbers Montfort has explained the action of Mary in souls consecrated to her. He now goes on to describe the effects which this action produces in the same souls that show their faithfulness by performing special practices. These effects (the "wonders of grace" foretold in TD 35) are presented according to a certain progressive order of the spiritual life.
362 Now that our Lady is in heaven enjoying the beatific vision of God she does not possess the virtue of faith. St. Louis Marie merely means that as she has been commissioned to distribute to men all graces and heavenly gifts, so likewise, with God's consent, she imparts to our faith the qualities her faith had on earth, that is she makes them pure, lively, active, firm, and so on. One must read this whole passage in the context of TD 34.
363 All Nos. 214 and 215 are rich in biblical allusions.
364 Sir. 24:24.
365 Cf. TD 85.
366 Lk. 1:38. Mary's action in the soul gives to the person consecrated to her a Marian attitude to God, so that the person can say like Mary, "Behold the servant of the Lord . . ."

God alone

367 Ps. 118:94.
368 Cf. TD 179.
369 ST. BONAVENTURE, *Psalt. Majus,* Canticum ad instar illius, Is. 12.
370 ST. BONAVENTURE, *Psalt. Majus,* Cant. instar illius Moisis Ex. 15.
371 Ps. 130:1, 2. The text is slightly changed.
372 Cf. TD 173.
373 Originally from RAYMOND JORDAN but text taken from POIRÉ, *Crown of Power,* 9th star.
374 Cf. Lk. 1:47.
375 ST. AMBROSE, *Expos. in Luc.* II, No. 26. Quoted also in SM 54 and TD 258.
376 The saintly man mentioned here seems to have been Fr. RIGOLEUC, a disciple of Fr. Louis Lallemant.
377 Cf. TD 20, 34, 36, 37, 38, 166.
378 Cf. SM 70.
379 Cf. Lk. 1:42; Ps. 1:3.
380 Lk. 5:5.
381 Hag. 1:6.
382 Biblical allusions: Ps. 17:33; Jn. 9:4; 1 Jn. 1:5; Ex. 26:34.
383 Cf. SM 16.
384 Allusion made to Ps. 81:6.
385 SM 1.
386 "Divinely," that is, by the operation of the Holy Spirit. "Naturally," that is, in human nature and by voluntary collaboration.
387 This beautiful and convincing comparison has already been alluded to in TD 82. Cf. ST. THOMAS I-II, qu. 38, art. 5.
388 Cf. TD 151.
389 Cf. ST-JURE, *Connaissance et amour de Notre Seigneur Jésus Christ.*
390 Cf. Little Crown of the Blessed Virgin.
391 Résumé of TD 146-149.
392 This expression is found in BÉRULLE, vol. 2, *Works of Piety.* Montfort's thought finds its place in the mainstream of the French school of spirituality. Cf. PAUL VI: "In the Virgin Mary everything is relative to Christ and dependent upon him" (*Marialis Cultus,* No. 25). II VATICAN COUNCIL: "The functions and the privileges of the Blessed Virgin are always relative to Christ, the origin of all truth, holiness and piety" (*Lumen Gentium,* No. 67).
393 Lk. 1:46.
394 Cf. TD 118, 213.
395 Cf. TD 119.
396 Mt. 23:23.
397 Mt. 3:16.
398 ST. GREGORY THE GREAT, *Hom. II in Evang.,* No. 1.
399 In 1899, the first Confraternity of Mary, Queen of All Hearts, was erected in Ottawa. In 1913, Pius X erected the confraternity in Rome into an Archconfraternity. In 1955, the Holy See established two distinct associations, for the faithful and for priests. The asso-

ciation for the faithful possesses today 140 centres spread throughout the world. The headquarters are at Rome, Viale dei Monfortani 65. Monte Mario, 00135 Rome, Italy.

400 Cf. TD 78-79.

401 Cf. TD 79.

402 Cf. ST. BERNARD (inter opera), *Meditationes piissimae de cognitione humanae conditionis,* c. 3, No. 8: *Cogita quid fueris, semen putridum; quid sis vas stercorum; quid futurus sis, esca vermium.*

403 Cf. Lk. 18:41.

404 ST. AUGUSTINE, *Soliloquia,* bk. 2, c. 1: *Deus semper idem, noverim me, noverim te.*

405 Especially in TD 16-36, 83-89.

406 Especially in TD 61-77.

407 TD 67.

408 Cf. TD 228 (Notes 1 & 2).

410 Cf. PIUS XII: "Your pastors have already called on you to do so and you are now preparing to recite the solemn formula. May you be suitably prepared by fulfilling all the conditions such a great act requires. The first one is that you should be in a state of grace, for anyone who is not cannot consecrate himself to Jesus. The consecration is an act of love for Jesus; how can anyone make it who is far away from him or remains indifferent to him or even positively offends him? You cannot consecrate yourself unless you become reconciled with Jesus first . . ." (*Radio Message to the faithful of Emilia on the occasion of their consecration to the Sacred Heart,* 28 October 1956.

411 Cf. TD 266-273.

412 In the manuscript as we have it, there is no formula of consecration at the end. The formula which has always been used is the one given at the end of the manuscript of LEW.

413 At the end of his missions, it was Montfort's custom to have a covenant signed which contained in substance the elements of the act of consecration as a renewal of the baptismal promises.

414 This tribute is suggested by JOBERT, *The devotion of the holy slavery.* In SM 62 Montfort suggests that it should be repeated "every year on the same day."

415 *Tuus totus ego sum, et omnia mea tua sunt.* Formula taken from ST. BONAVENTURE (inter opera), *Psalt. majus,* cant. ad instar illius Moisis.

416 Cf. SM 64. This text is suggested by JOBERT, who adds that the Little Crown "is what is called the rosary of the holy slavery."

417 Cf. Apoc. 12:1.

418 This interpretation is supported by many Scripture scholars. Montfort certainly alludes to the list given by POIRÉ in the introduction to *the Triple Crown.* PIUS X sums up the traditional view as follows: "*A great sign*—it is in these words that St. John describes a divine vision—*has appeared in heaven: a woman clothed with the sun, with the moon under her feet and a crown of twelve stars round her head.* And St. John goes on to say: *She was pregnant, and in the anguish of her labor cried out to be delivered.* So St.

John saw the most holy Mother of God in eternal bliss and yet in mysterious childbirth. Who is she giving birth to? Undoubtedly to us who are still in exile and need to be brought forth into the perfect love of God and eternal happiness. As for the birth pangs, they suggest the eagerness and love with which Mary watches over us from on high and, through her tireless prayers, works to bring the number of the elect to its fulness" (*Ad diem illum,* 1904).

419 Cf. SM 65. The Holy See has condemned the wearing of chains on several occasions. However, these decrees were directed against specific abuses. Other confraternities of holy slavery were granted indulgences. In Montfort associations a chain is sometimes worn round the neck withy the medal of "Mary, Queen of All Hearts."

420 The formula of blessing is not found in the manuscript.

421 Cf. Eph. 3:1; Philem. 1:1, 9.

422 Cf. Gen. 6:14.

423 Cf. Rom. 6:22; TD 68, 73.

424 Hos. 11:4. Cf. SM 65; TD 241.

425 Cf. Song 8:6; TD 216.

426 Cf. TD 126-130.

427 Cf. Rom. 6:17.

428 *Vincula peccatorum; in vinculis caritatis.* The first few words are in line with some Scripture passages (cf. Is. 5:18); the rest is in Hos. 11:4.

429 *Dirumpamus vincula eorum et projiciamus a nobis jugum ipsorum.* Ps. 2:3.

430 *Injice pedem tuum in compedes illius, et in torques illius collum tuum.* Sir. 6:25.

431 *Audi, fili, et accipe consilium intellectus, et ne abjicias consilium meum.* Sir. 6:24. RICHARD of Saint-Laurence has made the same Marian application in *De laudibus B.V.M., bk. I, c. 2.*

432 *Vincula illius alligatura salutis.* Sir. 6:31.

433 *Omnia traham ad meipsum.* Jn. 12:32.

434 *Traham eos in vinculis caritatis.* Hos. 11:4. Same text in SM 65; TD 237.

435 VINCENT CARAFFA (1585-1649), 7th Superior General of the Society of Jesus from 1646.

436 Cf. TD 170.

437 Cf. TD 139.

438 LOUIS TRONSON (1622-1700), 3rd Superior of Saint-Sulpice from 1676. The priest referred to may have been Montfort himself.

439 Cf. TD 93.

440 Cf. TD 61-62, 120.

441 Here is the prayer in its entirety: "O Jesus living in Mary, come and live in us in your spirit of holiness, in the fulness of your power, in the perfection of your ways, in the truth of your virtues, in the communion of your divine mysteries; subdue in us our powerful enemies, the devil, the world, and the flesh, in the strength of your spirit and for the glory of your Father."

442 Cf. TD 63.

443 ST. AMBROSE, *De institut. Virgin. et S. Mariae Virg. perpetua,*

ad Eusebium, c. 7.
444 Heb. 10:5-9.
445 Heb. 4:16.
446 Cf. TD 6.
447 Cf. TD 6.
448 Is. 33:21.
449 Concerning the last consideration, cf. ST. THOMAS, III, qu. 48, art. 6.
450 Cf. SR 44-52.
451 Cf. SR 11-17.
452 Cf. SR 18-20.
453 Cf. Lk. 8:11-15.
454 Cf. Zech. 8:12; SR 51.
455 Cf. Gen. 3:17-18; Heb. 6:8.
456 Cf. SR 50, 77.
457 "natural inability," that is, physically or morally unable to say it; "or even supernatural inability," that is, unable to use external senses, which is the case in a state of ecstasy.
458 Cf. SR 44, 45.
459 Cf. SR 46-48.
460 Cf. SR 51.
461 2 Cor. 9:6.
462 Blessed MARIE D'OIGNIES (1177-1212), a recluse buried at Oignies, in northern France.
463 These ideas were inspired by ARGENTAN, part 2, confer. 16.
464 JEAN LE CHARLIER DE GERSON (1363-1429), chancellor of the university of Paris. The book Montfort alludes to is the *Tractatus XII super Magnificat.*
465 This is an allusion to the *Tractatus IX* in which Gerson recalls how the Mother of Jesus was constantly at prayer with the faithful in the Upper Room (Acts 1:14) and received the food of the Eucharist every day with joy and simplicity of heart, praising God and meditating on the words, "You have filled the hungry with good things" of her Magnificat.
466 BENZONIUS RUTILIUS (d. 1613), bishop of Loreto. The passage Montfort alludes to is found in the *Dissertationes et commentaria in cant. Magnificat . . . libri quinque,* bk. 1, c. 21.
467 Lk. 1:51.
468 Cf. LEW 194-200.
469 Cf. TD 119, 226. In SM 60, Montfort calls the four formulas simply "the interior practice."
470 Rom. 8:14.
471 Cf. TD 29-30.
472 Montfort develops here what he only hinted at in TD 217, 225.
473 Cf. TD 217.
474 ST. ALPHONSUS RODRIGUEZ (1531-1617), a co-adjutor brother of the Society of Jesus canonized by Leo XIII on 15 January 1888 (not to be confused with his namesake, Fr. Alphonsus Rodriguez, who died in 1616 and is the author of the *Practice of Christian Perfection*).

475 Cf. SM 45-46, in which Montfort emphasizes the importance of this interior practice which he calls "essential."

476 Cf. PIUS X: "But, generally speaking, our weakness is such that this sublime exemplar (Christ) easily disheartens us. It was therefore an entirely providential kindness on the part of God that he should have provided us with another one as close to Jesus Christ as human nature can be, and yet wonderfully suited to our weakness. This exemplar is no other than the Mother of God" (*Ad diem illum,* 1904).

477 Cf. TD 108.

478 Cf. TD 214.

479 Cf. Lk. 1:45; Jn. 19; 25.

480 Cf. TD 2-5.

481 Cf. SM 16-18; TD 219-221.

482 This whole number is a commentary on Gen. 2:8-10. Cf. TD 6.

483 Cf. Ez. 44:1-3; Ps. 86:1; Is. 6:1-4. The Latin and Greek Fathers of the Church abound in Marian interpretations and applications of these biblical symbols; Montfort has mentioned some of them which he borrowed from POIRÉ, *Crown of Excellence,* 12th star, and from SPINELLI, c. 2, and c. 5.

484 Cf. Gen. 3:24.

485 Song 4:12. ST. JEROME gives the same interpretation in *Adversus Jovinianum,* bk. 1, No. 31.

486 Cf. SM 52.

487 Cf. TD 168-169.

488 Sir. 24:30; the same text occurs in TD 175.

489 Cf. TD 219.

490 Cf. TD 248.

491 Ps. 86:5; cf. TD 32.

492 Cf. TD 61-62, 74-77, 168.

493 Cf. PIUS XII, *Discourse for the crowning of Mary, "Salus Populi Romani,"* 1 November 1954.

494 Cf. TD 93, against critical devotees.

495 Cf. TD 94-95, against scrupulous devotees.

496 Cf. TD 97-99, against presumptuous devotees.

497 The title and sub-titles are taken from the manuscript. Montfort had done a great deal of research work before presenting this method. The borrowing he did, however, is hardly noticeable and the method preserves its originality as compared with his predecessors'.

498 Cf. TD 233.

499 Cf. TD 37-38.

500 Ps. 45:6.

501 Adaptation of two biblical passages: Jn. 19:27 and Prov. 23:26.

502 Mt. 8:8; Lk. 7:6: the humble prayer is addressed to each Person of the Blessed Trinity. Cf. Nos. 268, 269.

503 Lk. 1:38.

504 Ps. 4:10.

505 Song 3:4.

506 Ps. 131:8.

507 Cf. TD 205, 206.

508 *Haec maxima mea fiducia; haec tota ratio spei meae.* ST. BERNARD, *Serm. de acquaeductu,* No. 7.

509 Cf. Jn. 4:24.

510 Ps. 94:6.

511 Ps. 16:2. Montfort has added the last two words.

512 Mt. 13:28.

513 Ps. 42:1.

514 Jn. 3:30.

515 Gen. 1:28.

516 Heb. 10:38; Rom. 1:17; Gal. 3:11. Cf. ST. THOMAS III, qu. 78, art. 3. The Eucharist is an act of faith: "the mystery of faith," as it is called in the canon of the Mass.

VRAI
DEVO
TION
S.LVD.M
MONTFORT

Prayer For Missionaries

The Rule of the Missionaries of the Company of Mary

Letter to the Members of the Company of Mary

Introduction

These three texts form a sort of trilogy and refer very specifically to the Missionaries of the Company of Mary, (Montfort Missionaries) and all three have been handwritten by St. Louis Marie. The first two pages of the manuscript have been lost, and so we are left without an introduction and title, if indeed these actually existed. The missing part at the beginning of the Prayer for Missionaries (i.e. No. 1 and part of No. 2) has been supplied by Grandet, one of Louis Marie's biographers, but the actual manuscript begins with the words "through the prophetic insight."[2]

The second part of the trilogy, "The Rule of the Missionaries of the Company of Mary," is found in its entirety in the manuscript, including title and subtitles.

The third part, addressed to the members of the Company of Mary, ends abruptly in the middle of a sentence. There is no means of knowing how much of the text is missing and one cannot even try to reconstruct the missing part.

It is not easy to fix a date for these writings. We know that soon after his ordination, Montfort conceived the idea of founding a society of missionaries. He made an agreement in 1707 with Fr. Poullart des Places, founder of the Holy Ghost Fathers, who promised that, God willing, he would supply Montfort with priests. Poullart died in 1709 but the Holy Ghost Fathers continued to honor the agreement. Montfort offered the successors of Poullart a programme and set of rules he had composed for the students who were destined to join him, and it was probably at that time that the Rule was drawn up.

It is not known when the two other works were composed but, as they seem to form a continuity even to the numbering of the pages, one can only assume that they were written at the same time as the Rule.

8 Prayer for Missionaries

Introduction

1 Memento, Domine,
Congregationis tuae,
quam possedisti
ab initio.[1]

Remember, Lord, this Congregation, which you have possessed from all eternity. You made it your own from the beginning, *ab initio,* when your mind dwelt on it before time began. You made it your own from the beginning, *ab initio,* when you held it in your hand as you created the world out of nothing. You made it your own when you took it to your heart while your dear Son, dying on the cross, bedewed it with his blood, consecrated it by his death and entrusted it to his holy Mother's keeping.

2 Give free rein, then, O Lord, to your merciful intent and raise up men of your right-hand whom you revealed through the prophetic insight of some of your greatest servants—Francis of Paola, Vincent Ferrer, Catherine of Siena and so many others during the last century and even in our day.

3 *Memento.* Ever keep this Congregation in mind, Almighty God, and, by the power of your right arm which has lost nothing of its strength,[2] make it a living reaiity and lead it to perfection. *Innova signa, immuta mirabilia,*[3] *sentiamus adjutorium brachii tui:* Great God, who can change lifeless stones into sons of Abraham,[4] say but one word and it will be enough to send good workers to gather in your harvest, and missionaries worthy of the name to work in your Church.

4 *Memento.* God of all goodness, remember your mercy of times past, and, in that same mercy, be ever mindful of this Congregation. Remember the promises you made to us, time and again, through your prophets and through your divine Son, that you would grant our just petitions.

Remember also the prayers of your servants in past ages. May their longings, their tearful pleadings, and the blood which they shed for your sake be ever in your sight and become a powerful claim on your mercy. But above all, bear in mind your dear Son: *respice in faciem Christi tui.*[5] Look upon the face of your anointed one. The agony he suffered, the shame he endured, the loving complaint he uttered in the Garden of Olives: *quae utilitas in sanguine meo,*[6] "Of what use is my death to you?", his cruel death and the blood he shed, all these cry out to you for mercy, so that, by this Congregation, his kingdom may bring down the empire of his enemies and rise upon its ruins.

5 *Memento.* Be mindful, Lord, of your Congregation, when you come to dispense your justice. *Tempus faciendi, Domine, dissipaverunt legem tuam:*[7] it is time to act, O Lord, they have rejected your law. It is indeed time to fulfill your promise. Your divine commandments are broken, your Gospel is thrown aside, torrents of iniquity flood the whole earth carrying away even your servants. The whole land is desolate,[8] ungodliness reigns supreme, your sanctuary is desecrated and the abomination of desolation has even contaminated the holy place.[9] God of Justice, God of Vengeance, will you let everything, then, go the same way? Will everything come to the same end as Sodom and Gomorrah? Will you never break your silence? Will you tolerate all this forever? Is it not true that your will must be done on earth as it is in heaven? Is it not true that your kingdom must come?[10] Did you not give to some souls, dear to you, a vision of the future renewal of the Church? Are not the Jews to be converted to the truth and is this not what the Church is waiting for? All the blessed in heaven cry out for justice to be done: *vindica*[11] and the faithful on earth join in with them and cry out: *amen, veni, Domine,*[12] amen, come, Lord. All creatures, even the most insensitive, lie groaning under the burden of Babylon's countless sins and plead with you to come and renew all things: *omnis creatura ingemiscit,* etc.[13] the whole creation is groaning. . . .

6 Lord Jesus, *memento Congregationis tuae:* be mindful of your Congregation. Give your Mother this new company so that you may renew all things through her and bring the era of grace to a close through Mary just as you began it through her. *Da Matri tuae liberos, alioquin moriar:*[14] to this end, increase the number of those who call her Mother and serve her. If this is not to be so, let me die.

Da Matri tuae: it is for your Mother's sake that I make this request. It was she who gave you birth and nurtured you. Remembering this, how can you refuse me? Remember whose Son you are and grant my plea. Remember what she means to you and what you mean to her, and fulfill my holy desires.

It is no personal favor that I ask, but something which concerns your glory alone, something you can and, I make bold to say, you must grant since not only are you truly God having all power in heaven and on earth,[15] but you are also the most dutiful of sons with an infinite love for your Mother.

7 What, then, am I asking for? *Liberos,* men who are free, priests who are free with the freedom that comes from you, detached from everything, without father, mother, brothers, sisters or relatives and friends as the world and the flesh understand them, without worldly possessions to encumber or distract them, and devoid of all self-interest.[16]

8 *Liberos:* men who are free but still in bondage to your love and your will; men after your own heart who, without taint or impediment of self-love, will carry out your will to the full and, like David of old, lay low all your enemies, with the Cross for their staff and the Rosary for their sling: *in baculo Cruce et in virga Virgine.*[17]

9 *Liberos:* men as free as the clouds that sail high above the earth, filled with the dew of heaven, and moving, without let or hindrance, according to the inspiration of the Spirit. They are included among those whom the prophet had in mind when he asked: *qui sunt isti qui sicut nubes volant?*[18] *Ubi erat impetus spiritus illuc gradiebantur,*[19], What men are these who move like clouds in the sky, wherever the Spirit leads them?

10 *Liberos:* free men. Men always available, always ready to obey you when those in authority speak. Always with the words of Samuel on their lips: *praesto sum,*[20] here I am; always ready to be on the move and to suffer with you and for you, just as the Apostles were: *eamus et moriamur cum illo*[21], let us go and die along with him.

11 *Liberos:* true children of Mary whom she has conceived and begotten by her love,[22] nurtured and reared, upheld by her and enriched with her graces.

12 *Liberos:* true servants of the Blessed Virgin who, like a Dominic of old, will range far and wide, with the holy Gospel issuing from their mouths like a bright and burning flame, and the Rosary in their hands, and bay like your watchdogs, burn like fire and dispel the darkness of the world like a sun.[23] Their inspiration will be their authentic devotion to Mary which will be interior and devoid of all hypocrisy, exterior but not critical, prudent and well-informed, tender without indifference, constant without fickleness, holy without presumption. In this way, they will crush the head of the serpent wherever they go and ensure that the curse you have laid upon it of old will be fulfilled to the letter: *inimicitias ponam inter te et mulierem, inter semen tuum et semen ipsius et ipsa conteret*

caput tuum,[24] I will put enmity between you and the woman and between your seed and her seed and he shall bruise your head.

13 True it is, indeed, great God, as you yourself have foretold, that the devil will lie in wait to attack the heel of this mysterious woman, that is, the little company of her children who will come towards the end of time. There will be great enmity between the blessed posterity of Mary and the accursed issue of Satan, the only enmity which you have instigated. The children of Belial will wage war against the children of your blessed Mother and afflict them with persecutions which will have no other outcome than to make more manifest, in a striking manner, the power of your grace, their courage and virtue and the reality of your Mother's authority. It cannot be otherwise since, from the beginning of time, you have appointed this humble Virgin to crush this proud spirit under her heel: *Ipsa conteret caput tuum.*

14 *Alioquin moriar:* otherwise, I would be better dead. Would it not be better for me to be dead, Lord, than to see you offended daily so deliberately and with such impunity and, daily, to stand, myself, in ever-increasing danger of being swept away by the ever-swelling flood of iniquity? I would rather die a thousand deaths than endure such a fate. Send me your help from heaven or let me die.

Were it not for the hope that I have that, sooner or later, the interests of your glory will prevail and that you will hear this poor sinner's prayer, as you have heard so many others: *iste pauper clamavit et Dominus exaudivit eum*[25] I would make mine the ultimate plea of your prophet: *tolle animam meam,*[26] take away my life. Yet, my trust in you is so great that I am inspired to cry out like another of your prophets: *non moriar sed vivam et narrabo opera Domini,*[27] I will live and proclaim the Lord's mighty works. This I will do until the time comes when I can say with Simeon: *nunc dimittis servum tuum in pace, quia viderunt oculi mei,* etc.,[28] now, O Lord, you let your servant depart in peace because my eyes have seen your salvation.

15 *Memento:* Holy Spirit, be ever mindful that it is you who, with Mary as your faithful spouse, are to bring forth and fashion the children of God. In her and with her, you brought forth the Head of the Church and, in the same way, you will bring all his members into being. Within the Trinity, none of the divine Persons is begotten by you. Outside the Trinity, you are the begetter of all the children of God. All the saints who have ever existed or will exist until the end of time, will be the outcome of your love working through Mary.

16 The reign especially attributed to God the Father lasted until the Flood and ended in a deluge of water. The reign of Jesus Christ ended in a deluge of blood, but your reign, Spirit of the Father and the Son, is still unended and will come to a close with a deluge of fire, love and justice.[29]

17 When will it happen, this fiery deluge of pure love with which you are to set the whole world ablaze and which is to come, so gently yet so forcefully, that all nations, Muslims, idolators and even Jews, will be caught up in its flames and be converted? *Non est qui se abscondat a calore ejus.*[30] *Accendatur:* none can shield himself from the heat it gives, so let its flames rise. Rather let this divine fire which Jesus Christ came to bring on earth be enkindled before the all-consuming fire of your anger comes down and reduces the whole world to ashes. *Emitte Spiritum tuum et creabuntur et renovabis faciem terrae:*[31] when you breathe your Spirit into them, they are restored and the face of the earth is renewed. Send this all-consuming Spirit upon the earth to create priests who burn with this same fire and whose ministry will renew the face of the earth and reform your Church.

18 *Memento Congregationis tuae:* it is to be a congregation, a gathering, a selection, a picked handful of predestined men to be chosen by you from among those who are in the world: *Ego elegi vos de mundo,*[32] I have chosen you from amidst the world.

You are to select from all these fierce wolves[33] a flock of peaceful sheep; from all these ugly crows, a flight of pure doves and royal eagles; from all these buzzing hornets, a swarm of honey-bees; from all these slow-moving tortoises, a herd of nimble deer; from all these timid hares, a pride of bold lions.

Lord, *congrega nos de nationibus,*[34] gather us in from every nation. Bring us together and unite us and may all the glory be given to your holy and mighty name!

19 You revealed the coming of this noble company to one of your prophets who concealed the secret of this revelation under the cloak of obscure but divinely inspired words:

1 *Pluviam voluntariam segregabis, Deus, haereditati tuae et infirmata est, tu vero perfecisti eam.*

2 *Animalia tua habitabunt in ea. Parasti in dulcedine tua pauperi, Deus.*

3 *Dominus dabit verbum evangelizantibus virtute multa.*

4 *Rex virtutum dilecti dilecti et speciei dividere spolia.*

5 *Si dormiatis inter medios cleros, pennae columbae deargentatae et posteriora dorsi ejus in pallore auri.*

6 *Dum discernit coelestis reges super eam, nive dealbabuntur in Selmon; mons Dei, mons pinguis.*

7 *Mons coagulatus, mons pinguis: ut quid suspicamini montes coagulatos.*

8 *Mons in quo beneplacitum est Deo habitare in eo, etenim Deus habitabit in finem.*[35]

20 What is meant, Lord, by this abundant rain that you have stored up for your languishing heritage, if not these holy missionaries, Mary's children, whom you are to gather together and set apart from the rest of men for the good of your Church, at present so weakened and besmirched by the crimes of her children?

21 And who are these creatures and these poor folk who will dwell in the heritage you have given them and, there feed on the divine sweetness you have prepared for them? They are none other than the poor missionaries, entirely dependent on Providence, who will feast to their heart's content on the spiritual delights you provide for them. They are none other than those mysterious animals described by Ezekiel[36] who have the kindly nature of a man—witness their selfless and beneficent love of their neighbor; the face and boldness of a lion—witness their holy anger, their burning and prudent zeal against the devil and the children of Babylon; the strength of an ox—witness their apostolic labors and their self-mortification; the soaring flight of an eagle—witness the height of their contemplation. Such will be the missionaries you have in mind for your Church. They will look kindly on their fellowmen, fearlessly on your enemies, impartially on themselves and, when they look on you, they will be carried away in contemplation.

22 These followers of the apostles will preach with great power and effect. So powerful will their impact be that they will stir the minds and hearts of all who hear them. It is to them that you will give your word—*dabit verbum;* the very words of your own mouth and wisdom: *dabo vobis os et sapientiam cui non poterunt resistere omnes adversarii vestri,*[37] and none of their enemies will be able to withstand them.

23 It is among these men so dear to you, that you, Holy Spirit, as the greatest gift that Jesus Christ, the beloved Son, has made to men, will be pleased to dwell since, in all the missions they undertake, their sole aim will be to give glory to you for the spoils they have won from your enemies: *Rex virtutum dilecti dilecti et speciei domus dividere spolia.*

24 The silver wings of the dove will be theirs because of their total dependence on Providence and their devotion to Mary; *inter medios cleros pennae columbae deargentatae,* they shall be covered with silver like the wings of a dove, by the purity of the doctrine they teach and their irreproachable life; *et posteriora dorsi ejus in pallore auri,* for them the silvered pinions of the dove will be the perfect love they have for their neighbor which enables them to bear with his shortcomings, and their great love for Jesus Christ which enables them to carry his cross.

25 You alone, King of heaven and King of kings, will set these men apart like kings and make them purer than the snows on Zalmon, the mountain of God, where all good things grow in abundance, this strong and compact mountain where God delights to dwell, and dwell forever.

Lord, God of truth, who is symbolized by this mysterious mountain of which so many marvels are told if not Mary, your beloved spouse, whose beginnings you established on the heights: *Fundamenta ejus in montibus sanctis.*[38] *Mons in vertice montium,*[39] where all other mountains end.

Blessed, a thousandfold blessed, are those priests whom you have chosen with such care to dwell with you on this divine mountain of all delights. There they will become kings for eternity by their contempt of the world and their nearness to God, and purer than snow by their union with Mary, your beautiful, pure and immaculate spouse. They will be enriched by the dew of heaven above and the fat of the earth beneath, and all the blessings of time and eternity which Mary possesses in such abundance will be theirs.

From the summit of this mountain, they will, like Moses of old, address their ardent prayers to heaven, turning them into the weapons which will overcome or convert their enemies.[40]

This is the mountain on which Jesus Christ, who dwells there forever, will teach them in his own words the meaning of the eight beatitudes.[41]

It is on this mountain that they will be transfigured as he was on Mount Thabor; that they will die with him as he died on Calvary, and from it, they will ascend to heaven as he did from the Mount of Olives.

26 *Memento Congregationis tuae. Tuae:* be mindful of this your Congregation, for it is you alone who must, by your grace, make it a living reality. If man is the first to put his hand to the work, nothing will come of it. If he contributes anything of his own to what you are doing, the entire undertaking will be warped and come down in ruins.

Tuae Congregationis: your own Congregation. *Opus tuum fac,* it is your work, great God. Make your divine purpose a reality. Muster your chosen men from every corner of your dominions. Call them and gather them together. Mobilize them and make of them an army to fight against your enemies.

27 Look, Lord God of hosts, the captains of war are forming companies, each with its full complement of soldiers; and potentates have recruited vast armies. The ship-owners have whole fleets at their disposal, and the merchants are thronging to the markets and fairs. What a motley assembly of ungodly men! Thieves, drunkards, and profligates gather together every day under the flimsiest pretexts in order to oppose you! Blow a whistle, beat a drum, show the blunt point of a sword, promise a withered laurel branch as a reward, offer a piece of gold or silver; in short, a whiff of fame, a worthless reward, a vile beastly pleasure and, in the twinkling of an

eye, along come the thieves, soldiers rally by battalions and merchants flock together. Gambling dens and market places are crammed full and the whole of land and sea is covered with an innumerable multitude of reprobates. These people, although at variance among themselves for reasons of distance, temperament or personal interest, are nevertheless all unanimously resolved to wage war to the death against you, under the banner and leadership of the devil.

28 How is it, then, great God, that although it is so glorious, so satisfying and so profitable to serve you, hardly anyone will support your cause? Scarcely one soldier lines up under your standard. Scarcely anyone fired with zeal for your glory will stand up and cry out, like St. Michael in the midst of his fellow-angels: *Quis ut Deus?* Who is like to God? Let me then raise the cry of alarm: "The House of God is on fire! Souls are perishing in the flames! The sanctuary itself is ablaze! Help! Help! Good people! Help our brother who is being murdered. Help our children who are being massacred. Help our kind father who is being done to death!"

29 *Qui Domini est jungatur mihi:*[43] if anyone has the Lord's cause at heart, let him stand side by side with me. Let all those worthy priests who are to be found throughout the world, those still in the fight and those who have withdrawn to deserts and secluded places, let them, I say, come and join us. In unity there is strength. With the cross as our standard, let us form a strongly disciplined army drawn up in lines of battle. Let us make a concerted attack on the enemies of God who have already sounded the call to arms: *sonuerunt, frenduerunt, fremuerunt, multiplicati sunt.*[44] *Dirumpamus vincula eorum et projiciamus a nobis jugum ipsorum. Qui habitat in caelis irridebit eos.*[45] They have sounded the alarm, vented their anger and become a mighty army. Let us break their bonds asunder and throw away their yoke. He who dwells in heaven will laugh them to scorn.

30
Exsurgat Deus
et dissipentur inimici ejus![46]
Exsurge, Domine,
quare obdormis? Exsurge.[47]

Let the Lord arise and let his enemies be scattered. Arise, Lord. Why is it you appear to be like one asleep? Arise in your might, your mercy and your justice and create this bodyguard of handpicked men who will protect your house, defend your glory and save the souls that are yours. Thus, there will be but one sheepfold and one shepherd and all will make your temple resound with their praise of your glory: *et in templo ejus omnes dicent gloriam.*[45] Amen.

Prayer for Missionaries

God Alone!

Footnotes to the Prayer for Missionaries

1 Cf. Ps. 73:2.
2 Cf. Is. 59:1.
3 Sir. 36:6. Cf. Wis. 5:17.
4 Cf. Mt. 3:9.
5 Ps. 83:10.
6 Ps. 29:10.
7 Ps. 118:126.
8 Jer. 12:11.
9 Cf. Dan. 9:27; Mt. 24:15; Mk. 13:14.
10 Cf. Mt. 6:10.
11 Cf. Rev. 6:10.
12 Cf. Rev. 22:20.
13 Cf. Rom. 8:22.
14 Cf. Gen. 30:1.
15 Cf. Mt. 28:18.
16 Cf. Mk. 10:29; Lk. 14:26.
17 Cf. 1 Kgs. 17:40 and Ps. 22:4; SAINT PETER DAMIAN, *Sermo in Assumpt.*
18 Is. 60:8.
19 Ezek. 1:12.
20 1 Kgs. 3:16.
21 Cf. Jn. 11:16.
22 Cf. SAINT AUGUSTINE, *Enarratio in Psalmum* 147, No. 14.
23 Cf. JORDAN OF SAXONY, *Libellus de principiis ordinis praedicatorum,* Rome, 1935.
24 Cf. Gen. 3:15.
25 Ps. 33:7.
26 Ki: 19:4.
27 Ps. 117:17.
28 Lk. 2:29-30.
29 Cf. Jn. 5:8.
30 Ps. 18:7.
31 Ps. 103:30.
32 Jn. 15:19.
33 Cf. Lk. 10:3.
34 Ps. 105:47.
35 Ps. 67:10-17. Saint Louis Marie does not give a complete translation of this psalm which is a notoriously difficult one. Hebrew scholars say the original text is very corrupt and this is why it has always been a problem for biblical translators. Restoration of the text and some inspired guesswork have given it a fairly coherent meaning. St. Louis Marie's translation of portions of the psalm and their application are very much his own. (Translators' note.)

1 You have set aside, Lord, an abundant rain for your heritage;
it was languishing but you have restored it.

2 Your creatures will dwell in it. In your goodness, O Lord,
you have provided for those in need.
3 The Lord gave the command and the news was announced with
great power.
4 Kings and their armies were routed and the women at home
shared out the spoils.
5 They are covered with silver like the wings of a dove and
with gold like the dove's pinions.
6 While God scatters the kings, snow fell on Zalmon, Mountain
of God! Mountain of Bashan!
7 A mountain of many peaks is Bashan's hill. But why, hill
of many peaks, gaze in envy
8 at the hill where the Lord delights to dwell and where he
will dwell forever? (Translation: R.S.V. and N.E.B.)

36 Cf. Ezek. 1:5-14.
37 Cf. Lk. 21:15.
38 Ps. 86:1.
39 Is. 2:2. Cf. Mic. 4:1.
40 Cf. Exod. 17:8-13.
41 Cf. Mt. 5:3-11.
42 Cf. SAINT GREGORY, *Homil. 34 in Evang.*
43 Cf. Exod. 32:26.
44 Cf. Ps. *passim* (Ps. 2:1, 24:19; 45:4; 34:16; 37:20).
45 Ps. 2:3-4.
46 Ps. 67:1.
47 Ps. 43:23.
48 Ps. 28:9.

9 Rule of the Missionary Priests of the Company of Mary

The Special Aim of the Company

1 Only priests who have already completed their seminary training are to be admitted to the Company. Therefore clerics in minor orders are excluded until such time as they have been ordained priests. However, there is a seminary in Paris where young clerical students who are called to the mission in the Company receive academic and spiritual training to prepare them to become members.
2 The priests who enter must be called by God to preach missions in the steps of the apostles who were poor, and not be curates, parish priests, teachers in colleges or seminaries, as so many other good priests are, God having called them to this good work.

The members of the Company, therefore, avoid such work as being contrary to their missionary vocation so as to feel free at all times to repeat after Jesus Christ: *pauperibus evangelizare misit me Dominus,*[1] the Lord has sent me to preach good news to the poor, or, as the Apostle said: *non misit me Dominus baptizare sed evangelizare,*[2] Christ did not send me to baptize but to preach the gospel. They look upon the occasions which occur of helping people in these various ways as a very subtle temptation. Unfortunately, this is the change or deviation which has occurred in several good communities which were established in recent times by the holy inspiration of their founders for the purpose of preaching missions. The pretext given was that they could thus do more good. Some turned to educational work, others to the training of priests and clerics. If they still give a few missions, these are only incidental and unplanned. In these communities, the majority of the members live a sedentary or even solitary life in their town or country residences. Their motto is *habitatores quietis*[3] (lovers of the quiet life) whereas the motto of the true missionary is one which enables him to say in all truth like St. Paul: *Instabiles sumus,* we have no permanent home of our own.

3 Priests in poor health or men over sixty are not admitted since they are not equal to the struggles which missionaries, as valiant champions of Jesus Christ, must wage increasingly against the enemies of our salvation. If, however, a priest of the Company becomes incapable, through age or infirmity, of continuing missionary work, he can retire to a house which the Company has set aside for such cases.

4 Lay Brothers are admitted into the Company to take care of temporal affairs provided they are detached, robust and obedient, ready to do all they are told to do.

5 Priests and Brothers alike must not accept even simple benefices and temporal possessions, even those they may inherit. If they did have any before entering the Company, they must return the benefices to those who presented them. What they inherited must be given to their relatives or the poor, having first taken the advice of a good counsellor. They thus exchange their paternal inheritance for one which God himself gives them, namely, the inexhaustible inheritance of his divine Providence.

6 So, free from every other occupation and unimpeded by the administration of any temporal possessions which might hold them back, they stand ready, like St. Paul, St. Vincent Ferrer, St. Francis Xavier and other apostles, to run wherever God may call them. Whether the call be to the city or the country, to a market-town or village, to one diocese or another, near or far, they will always be ready to answer, when obedience calls: *paratum cor meum, Deus,*[5] *ecce adsum,*[6] *ecce venio*[7], My heart is ready, O God, here I am, behold I come. Never will they have the heart to say what is said daily by all those worldly priests, those well-fed beneficed clerics, those pleasure-seeking ecclesiastics and those lovers of ease: *emi, emi . . . duxi, etc., ideo non possum, no possum. Habe me excusatum,*[8] I have bought a field . . . I have bought five yoke of oxen . . . have me excused . . . I cannot come.

7 Although they do not confine the grace of God or their own zeal to rural areas alone, as do M. Vincent's missionaries,[9] but go to preach missions, whether in town or country, according to the will of God, manifested through their Superior, they will nevertheless share in the most tender inclinations of the heart of Jesus, their model, who said: *pauperibus evangelizare misit Dominus,* The Lord sent me to preach the good news to the poor. Consequently, they will, in general, prefer rural areas to the towns and the poor to the rich.

8 To be accepted as permanent members of the Company, they must, first, in the presence of the Superior, make simple vows of poverty and obedience for one year. These vows are renewable annually. Then, if, at the end of an unbroken five-year period spent in the Company, they themselves feel they are truly called by God to belong to the Company and are judged to be so called, they take the two vows of poverty and obedience in perpetuity. These being only simple vows, a dispensation from them in order to leave the Company for legitimate reasons can be obtained from the bishop. For its part, the Company, in accordance with the right it reserves to itself, can dismiss one of its members, even after final vows, should his behavior become an occasion of scandal, rather than edification, in spite of the steps taken to correct him. These two conditions are implicitly contained in this second profession, as is the case with the vows of many other communities.

9 The Company never undertakes responsibility for students or boarders, clerical or lay, not even if one of them wishes to make over all his worldly goods to it.

Detachment or Evangelical Poverty

10 1 As already stated, they are to have neither inherited possessions nor income from a benefice as this is contrary to apostolic detachment. Their sole resource must be God's providence. God will decide who will provide for them and the manner in which this provision will be made.

11 2 The members of the Company are to have no money or possessions of their own either openly or in secret. The Community will supply all that is necessary in the way of food and clothing, depending on what Providence supplies to the community.

12 3 Within the realm of France, the Company will own two houses and never more than two. The first will be in Paris for the training of clerics in the apostolate. The second will be situated outside Paris, one of the provinces of the realm. There, the members of the Company who have retired from the fray may rest and end their days in retirement and solitude after having spent the best years of their lives in the conquest of souls.

The Company may accept, as coming from the hands of divine Providence, any other houses which may be donated to them in the various dioceses where God calls them. It will, however, accept only the use of these premises and the missionaries will consider themselves as tenants who have rented a house or as travellers who lodge at an inn. If no one donates a house, the Company will not ask for one but will lease one, preferably in the country. If, however, some kind person makes over a house to the Company, the latter will by deed convey the ownership of these premises to the bishop of the place, and his successors, and retain only the use. Consequently, the said bishop and his successors will have every right and authority to take this house from the missionaries if, in the course of time, the latter remain idle and do not fulfill their duties. The bishop and his successors may divert the use of the house to other charitable purposes more beneficial to the people but they may not appropriate the revenues accruing from it.

In this way, the missionaries will not become settled in any one place, as communities, even the most regular, normally do. Instead of this undesirable stability they will be more solidly grounded in God alone, provided they always yield themselves without reserve to the care of his Providence. They will not be distracted from their apostolic work by questions of rates and rents, and the disputes that seem to follow inevitably on the ownership of houses and land. They then become more aware that they are to consider themselves strangers and pilgrims,[10] looking upon the houses where they are received simply as hostels to be left when their work is done. Thus they can always be on the move: *posui vos ut eatis,*[11] I appointed you that you should go and bear fruit.

13 4 During a mission, they may not receive any money as alms from those to whom they are preaching. However, when the mission is ended, they may accept through their Superior whatever has been given out of pure charity or gratitude.

14 5 It is strictly forbidden, either during the mission or after, to ask anyone, directly or indirectly, for money, food or anything else whatsoever. They must rely entirely on divine Providence for all things. God would sooner work a miracle than fail to supply the needs of those who trust in Him. They are not, however, forbidden to mention in public or in private their state of dependence on Providence and the rules they follow in this matter.

15 6 They will say all their masses *gratis* for all who ask them to do so, following the practice of the members of the Society of Jesus; they may undertake to say up to thirty such masses but no more. If, however, anyone wishes to give them a sum of money as a token of thanks or a stipend, they will arrange for it to be handed to the director or bursar.

The Director of the mission must, as a general rule, offer his masses only for the benefactors of the missionaries and for the poor. He must not fail to inform the people of this.

16 7 When they go to give a mission, the Director or Bursar will, if possible, bring along a sum of money for almsgiving, to help repair the churches and feed the poor of the localities where they are going. In the case where people, because of their lack of charity or their poverty, fail to provide for the needs of the missionaries, the latter may use part of this money for their upkeep. This self-supporting thrift of theirs, far from contradicting their dependence on Providence, will on the contrary, turn to the advantage of the missionaries and inspire the people to contribute towards the repairing of churches and the maintenance of the poor. Moreover, having one common purse, *pro suis pauperumque usibus,*[12] to provide for their own needs and those of the poor, is an example given to us by Jesus Christ himself.

17 8 Should any priest who enters the Company be in possession of money, he must deposit the entire sum into this "purse of Providence." If, after he enters, his relatives or friends give him an unsolicited donation or mass stipend, he must deposit this also in the common purse so that it may be used for the needs of the whole community. This contribution does not entitle him to claim any particular advantage or personal privilege any more than if he had brought nothing with him and had not been asked to contribute anything.

18 9 If, either before or after making his vows, one of the missionaries on his own leaves the Company without permission or through formal disobedience, he has no right to ask for even a partial refund or for any compensation for what he may have donated as alms to the Company, which is committed to voluntary poverty. On the other hand, if he did not leave of his own accord but was dismissed for some serious fault, other than formal disobedience, account will be taken, at least pro rata, of what he brought with him, expenditure on his upkeep having been deducted.

Obedience

19 1 They will obey their superiors wholeheartedly, without reservation; readily without delay; joyfully without irritation; blindly without raising objections; and holily for God alone. This is easier said than done, especially when we see how the world, including the world of ecclesiastics, is bent on doing its own will, and when we see the disorders brought about by those whose self-will insists on doing only what suits them because such is their good pleasure. Nevertheless, in this Company, as in the Society of Jesus, it is obedience as we have described it, which is the foundation and unshakable support of all its holiness and of all the blessings which God confers or will confer through its ministry.

20 2 Their spiritual director must always be a member of the Company and they will obey him in matters pertaining to their conscience, and open their hearts to him in all simplicity and confidence. They should neither undertake nor omit anything important without informing him and obtaining his approval and permission.

21 3 They will obey the Superior of the Company in all things, great and small, whether prescribed by the Rule or not, in both matters concerning the allocation of work and the good order of the Company.

22 4 They will obey the bishop of the diocese to which they belong, the Vicars-General and other ecclesiastical superiors who represent the bishop, and the parish priest of the locality where they are giving the mission. They will obey them in all things which concern the external organization of the mission, such as the place, the time and other such circumstances. These matters, of no great consequence in themselves, take on a very helpful and important aspect when regulated by obedience.

Should any ecclesiastical superior command something which runs counter to their most important rules or vows, they would not be obliged to obey him. If, however, he commands or forbids or even strongly advises them to do things which in themselves are not very important, they will follow his decision without hesitation even though they are not in the habit of either omitting or doing such things. Their obedience in such circumstances will make the action more sanctifying and of greater consequence.

23 5 Each member must faithfully discharge the duties entrusted to him and will not, unless directed to do so by obedience, pry into the work of another in order to find out what he is doing or how he is doing it.

24 6 They will obey the least important of the community's rules with perfect fidelity and consider them all as being as dear to Jesus Christ as the apple of his eye. It is fidelity of this kind which shows that they are led by the Holy Spirit and not by the spirit of the world which, even where virtue is concerned, has no use for anything unless it is showy and has a high-sounding name.

25 7 They will look upon formal or obdurate disobedience to a superior, even in unimportant things, as the greatest offense that can be committed in the Company and as perhaps the only one which merits exclusion from the community, no matter how old or holy the offender may otherwise be.

26 8 They must be so penetrated with love and respect for this divine virtue that they will be ready to sacrifice their bodies, their health, their lives and all else when obedience commands them to do something both good and feasible, however difficult and distasteful it may appear to human nature.

Therefore, when they happen to discover any faults, public or private, which they may have committed by surprise or temptation, against this heavenly virtue, they will punish themselves immediately and ask their superior to impose a penance on them.

27 9 They are, however, permitted to state openly and straightforwardly the reasons they may have for omitting or for not undertaking what is commanded. Once they have done so, they must, if their reasons have not prevailed, obey blindly and promptly, without asking the why or wherefore. Their obedience must involve not only their will but also their mind and their understanding, and they must believe, in spite of their own personal views, that what the superior has commanded or forbidden is absolutely what is best in the eyes of God.

Prayers and Spiritual Exercises

28 1 All year round, they will make daily morning meditation, lasting at least half an hour.

29 2 Every day they will say all fifteen decades of the Rosary, and also the Little Crown of the Blessed Virgin at a convenient time. The purpose of these heaven-sent devotions is to call down the blessing of God on themselves and their ministry. They experience daily the efficacy of these prayers.

30 3 Normally, they will celebrate Holy Mass daily, having first suitably prepared themselves. After Mass, they will spend at least half an hour in thanksgiving. They will consider as a subtle and common temptation anything which might prevent them from devoting this time to thanksgiving. As the saying has it, *qui sibi nequam, cui alii bonus erit,*[13] how can a man who does no good to himself do any good to others?

31 4 They will use the Roman Breviary and say it together as far as their work permits. If they have to say it in private, they should do so with exemplary modesty, attention and devotion.

32 5 Every day before their midday meal, they will make their particular examen together. It should last about a quarter of an hour.

33 6 After they have returned from their missions, they will hold at least one day of recollection every month, spending the whole day in prayer and penance.

34 7 Their meals will be taken in silence and will be marked by charity, reserve and sobriety. If they have to speak during meals, it must be quietly and briefly.

35 8 When they have completed their mission schedule and return to enjoy the rest which divine Providence provides for them and counsels them to take, *venite seorsum et requiescite pusillum,*[14] come aside and rest a little, they will apply themselves to study in order to perfect themselves more and more in the art of preaching and hearing confessions.

36 9 The Rule does not prescribe any corporal penances. This is left to their own fervor controlled by obedience. They will, however, abstain from meat on Wednesdays and fast on Fridays or Saturdays, and, on the evenings of these two days only a light meal is to be served.

Contempt of the World

37 1 Their minds will be swayed neither by the sentiments of the world nor their hearts by its maxims nor their conduct by its ways.

38 2 Their motto will be: *nolite conformari huic seculo nequam,*[15] do not follow the ways of the world. Consequently, they will avoid, as far as is consistent with charity and obedience, whatever might savor of worldliness, such as, wearing wigs and skullcaps, muffs and gloves, long-flowing sashes, fancy shoes, expensive materials, glossy hats, or using tobacco as snuff or in any other way, etc.

39 3 They must not condemn out of hand those worldlings, who for reasons of propriety or necessity, make use of these things, but they reply to those who wish to persuade them to do the same, *nos talem consuetudinem non habemus,*[16] such is not our custom. Since by their ministry they profess publicly opposition to the world of Antichrist, they keep as far away from it as possible, even in matters indifferent in themselves, but which could lead them little by little to conform to it: *qui spernit modica paulatim decidet,*[17] the man who despises little things will gradually be brought to his ruin.

40 4 Nevertheless, they must not affect any singularity in their appearance but try, insofar as divine Providence with motherly care makes provision for them, to dress like ordinary ecclesiastics of good standing, especially those of the seminary of St. Sulpice in Paris, and their collar, hat, cape and other articles of clothing will be of the same style as theirs.

41 5 During their missions, they never go out to dine in private houses except once or twice at the local parish priest's house. When they are not engaged in mission work, they may do so only very rarely and with special permission from the Superior.

42 6 They are not to send or receive letters without first handing them to the Superior who will read them if he thinks it opportune.

43 7 Whenever possible, they travel to their missions on foot, following the example given by Jesus Christ and apostolic men.

If, however, their health is poor or the roads are bad, they have no qualms about accepting any help which God's providence may provide.

Their Charity towards Their Neighbor

44 1 Their charity to one another will be attentive and full of good will, and they will look for opportunities to do one another a good turn. It will be marked by mutual respect which inclines them to give precedence to others[18] and by patience, which enables them to bear with one another's faults.[19]

45 2 Charity is the queen and superior, who governs the Company with her golden scepter. She is its life-blood, its guardian, and the bond which holds it together; pride, self-conceit and self-seeking being banished from it: *limen obi, vivax imperat intus amor,* cross the threshold, life-giving love reigns within.

46 3 Their charity towards everyone, especially their enemies, will be joyful and sincere. They will return good for evil[20] and, far from complaining about anyone who has done them a notable injury, or speaking ill of him or taking revenge, they will pray to God for him for a week.

47 4 Whether during the time of their missions or not, the poor are to be the especial objects of their care. They must never refuse to help them, materially when possible, and spiritually, even if they say only one Hail Mary.

48 5 After each catechetical instruction, they will provide a meal for all the poor of the parish who have attended the instruction and every morning and evening they will bring one of them to eat at their table.

49 6 They will strive to implement faithfully the words which express so well the charity of the great Apostle: *omnibus omnia factus sum,*[21] becoming out of love all things to all men, even in indifferent matters, without getting caught up in the ways of the world or in any way becoming slack in the observance of their duty.

Directives to be Followed during their Missions

50 1 They will give all their missions in complete dependence on Providence and must not accept any endowment for future missions as do some communities of missionaries founded by the King or by private persons.

There are four main reasons for this:

i It is the example which Jesus Christ, the apostles and apostolic men have handed down to us.

ii God repays a hundredfold even in this world[22] those who show charity to the missionaries and often (as experience proves) he gives them the grace of conversion as a reward for their alms-giving: *date et dabitur vobis,* give and it will be given to you.

iii This mutual charity brings with it its own recompense in the form of a wonderful union of hearts between the faithful and the missionaries who are preaching to them. Charity begets charity.

iv The grace of a mission thus founded on Providence and on complete dependence on the people (a state of affairs most repugnant to proud nature) is, by far, the most effective and powerful means of converting sinners. In endowed missions, the missionaries are set up by their independence on a kind of pedestal and this, while flattering their pride and heaping honor on them, does not win for them the love of their neighbor or the grace of God. Only those who have tried both these ways of giving missions can appreciate how true this is.

51 2 Should some kind person wish to defray alone all the expenses of the mission, they will thank him for this generous offer without, however, accepting it. They will simply ask this person to give what he pleases during the time of the mission when they are entirely dependent on the generosity of the faithful. They do this because it is not right that any one person should by a monopoly of giving deprive the missionaries of that total dependence on divine Providence which they have undertaken precisely for the good of the people themselves.

52 3 About two weeks before the mission is due to begin, one or two of the missionaries should go, whenever possible, to give advance notice to the people of the locality. This announcement should take the form of an appeal to the people's feelings so that the missionaries may

a persuade them to give up their sinful ways;

b prepare the way for Jesus Christ as did the disciples whom Jesus sent two by two to the places where He was to go;[24]

c devote themselves to prayer in order to be worthy of the grace of the mission. For this purpose, they urge the people to recite daily the whole Rosary or at least five decades. In this way, the missionaries on their arrival will find the ground well-prepared.

53 4 They must adjust the number of the people to whom they give the mission to the number of missionaries available and not "bite off more than they can chew." Consequently, they should take on only one parish if it is a big one, whereas, if there are several small adjoining parishes, they can preach the mission in all of them simultaneously.

Unless the Superior gives special permission, they must not admit people from parishes which are not included in the mission program. By this I do not mean such people should be prevented from attending the sermons since the church and the word of God are for everybody. Nevertheless, the missionaries must not hear the confessions of such people, so that the people of the parish which provides for their upkeep may have a stronger spiritual incentive for coming to confession without being able to complain, and rightly so, that people from other parishes are being heard before those to whom the mission is being preached.

54 5 As a rule, they will preach in the morning and evening on weekdays at times best suited to the people they are striving to convert. Under ordinary circumstances, their sermons should not last more than three-quarters of an hour and never more than one hour. On feast days, in addition to the two sermons already mentioned, they will preach again at High Mass and, at about one o'clock, will give a conference for the people's instruction.

55 6 This conference should be an informal instruction in question-and-answer form on the truths of our religion. The missionaries may choose a particular topic and, after a brief expository introduction, one of them may ask brief and serious questions of a practical nature on the topic under discussion. They may also allow the members of the congregation to bring up their own problems on this or any other subject, provided that the missionary who gives the conference is prepared to deal with any matter that may arise. This is the boldest method of all and the one which does the most good to the people.

56 7 The purpose of these missions is to renew the spirit of Christianity among the faithful. Therefore, the missionaries will see to it that, as the Pope has commanded, the baptismal vows are renewed with the greatest solemnity. They are not to give absolution or communion to any penitent who has not first renewed his baptismal promises with the rest of the parishioners. Only those who have seen the results of this practice can appreciate its value.

57 8 During the whole of the mission, they must do all they can by the morning readings and by the conferences and sermons, to establish the great devotion of the daily Rosary and they will enroll (they have the faculties for this) as many as possible in the Rosary confraternity.

They will explain the prayers and mysteries of the Rosary either by instructions or by pictures and statues which they have for this purpose. They will give the people the example by having the Rosary recited aloud every day of the mission, saying all fifteen decades in French with the offering of the mysteries at three different times of the day. The first five decades are to be said in the morning during Mass before the sermon, the second five decades before the catechism class while the children are assembling, and the last five in the evening before the last sermon. This is one of the greatest secrets to have come down from heaven. Its heavenly dew refreshes men's hearts and makes God's word operative within them.[25] Everyday experience brings this fact home to them.

58 9 They should see to it that almost everyone makes a general confession. Even if the penitent's past confessions were not invalid, it is always extremely beneficial because of the humility it demands. It is not to be imposed on people who suffer from scruples. These, however, are rarely met with.

59 10 They must not be either too strict or too lax in imposing penances or granting absolution but must hold to the golden mean of wisdom and truth as described in detail in the *Méthode Uniforme que les Missionnaires Doivent Garder dans l'Administration du Sacrament de Pénitence pour Renouveler l'Esprit du Christianisme* (Uniform Procedure to be Followed by Missionaries in Administering the Sacrament of Penance in order to Bring about a Renewal of the Christian Spirit.) There is also a little manuscript book of greater length entitled the *Veni-mecum du Bon Missionnaire* (The Good Missionary's Companion)[26] which they should keep handy.

60 11 The preaching of God's word is the most far-reaching, the most effective and also the most difficult ministry of all. The missionaries will, therefore, study and pray unceasingly that they may obtain from God the gift of wisdom so necessary to a true preacher for knowing and relishing the truth and getting others to relish it.

It is the easiest thing in the world to be a fashionable preacher. It is a difficult but sublime thing to be able to preach with the inspiration of an apostle, to speak like the wise man, *ex sententia*[27] (with true understanding) or, as Jesus Christ says, *ex abundantia cordis*[28] (from the fullness of one's heart), to have received from God as a reward for one's labors and prayers, a tongue, a mouth and a wisdom which the enemies of truth cannot withstand: *mercedem linguam*[29] . . . *os et sapientiam cui non poterunt resistere omnes adversarii vestri,*[30] your reward—a mouth, a tongue and a wisdom which none of your enemies will be able to withstand.

Out of a thousand preachers—I could say ten thousand without telling a lie—there is scarcely one who has this great gift of the Holy Spirit. The majority have only the tongue, mouth and wisdom of men. That is why, even though these preachers quote Holy Scripture and the Fathers of the Church, only a few people are enlightened or moved and converted by their words. And this in spite of the fact that all they say is founded on reason, clearly proven, well-arranged and beautifully delivered before a receptive and admiring audience. Their sermons are well-composed and their words most carefully chosen. Their ideas are expressed with great ingenuity, and quotations from Holy Scripture and the Fathers come readily to their lips. Their gestures are well-coordinated and their eloquence is stimulating. Unfortunately, nothing of all this rises above the purely human and natural level and so, as a result, produces only what is human and natural.

A well-dissimulated complacency on the part of the preacher in his beautifully composed and elaborate sermon provides the dart with which the proud and cunning Lucifer blinds him. All the preacher gets for his trouble and effort is popular admiration which occupies the mind of worldly people during the sermon and provides them with a subject of conversation when they meet socially after church.

Since such preachers only beat the air[31] and titillate the ears, we must not be surprised if no one attacks them and if the father of lies does not utter a word, *in pace quae possidet,*[32] all that he possesses remains undisturbed. Since the fashionable preacher does not strike at the heart, the citadel where the tyrant has locked himself in, the latter is not unduly alarmed by all the hubbub going on outside.

61 But let a preacher full of God's word and spirit merely open his mouth and all the powers of hell sound the alarm and do their utmost to defend themselves. A fierce battle ensues between the truth which issues from the mouth of the preacher and the lies which originate in hell; between those listeners whose faith has made them friends of the truth and those whose unbelief has made them the friends of the father of lies.

A preacher of this caliber can, by a simple, unpretentious statement of the truth, rouse a whole city or province by the conflict he stirs up there. This is a continuation of the tremendous battle which was fought out in heaven between truth, with St. Michael as its champion, and falsehood represented by Lucifer.[33] It is a result of the enmities which God himself has established between the blessed children of his Mother and the accursed issue of the serpent.[34]

Do not then be surprised at the bogus peace which fashionable preachers enjoy nor at the extraordinary persecutions and calumnies directed against the preachers who have received the gift of proclaiming God's eternal word, for all the members of the Company of Mary must one day be preachers of this caliber. *Evangelizantibus virtute multa,*[35] great is the host of those who bore the tidings.

62 12 The apostolic missionary should, therefore, preach the simple truth, avoiding all pretentiousness and discarding all fables, false statements and dissembling. He must be bold and speak with authority, showing neither fear nor human respect. He must preach with all charity and give offense to none. His intention must be holy and centered on God alone. God's glory must be his sole preoccupation and he must first practice what he preaches: *coepit Jesus facere et docere,*[36] Jesus began by doing and then teaching.

63 13 In the pulpit, they must avoid several snares which the devil, under the cloak of zeal, sets for inexperienced preachers and a few others. These are:

1 Self-complacency about what they have said or in the

good results they have obtained.

2 Soliciting compliments, directly or indirectly, after they have delivered their sermon.

3 Being envious of others who have larger audiences or who preach with greater feeling, etc.

4 Criticizing another preacher whom they have heard or been told about.

5 Losing their temper. This is natural enough and they can easily give way to anger when the congregation provokes this response during the sermon.

6 Referring directly or indirectly to an individual in the audience, either by looking straight at him or by pointing at him or by saying things which can refer only to him.

7 A barrage of affected or exaggerated condemnations of rich or important people, of public officials or of officers of the law.

8 Censuring and criticizing priests and giving detailed accounts of their sins.

All these excesses are blameworthy because they shock people and can explain why a missionary, however holy or well-intentioned he may be, can neutralize to a great extent, if not completely, the effect of the word of God.

64 14 In the pulpit, a good preacher must look upon himself as an innocent man condemned to the pillory. Without any thought of getting his own back, he must suffer the false judgments of an entire congregation often ill-disposed towards him, the censures of proud scholars and the unfavorable interpretation they put on what he says, the jests, mockery and contempt of the ungodly and, lastly, the load of calumny which the entire population lays at his door. He must understand that the strength which underlies his zeal comes not only from the forcefulness of his preaching but also from the way he stands unshaken and undisturbed like a rock, weathering all the storms which rage around him.

He must leave to the truth which he preaches and which of its nature provokes hatred, the care of delivering him from false accusations: *veritas liberabit me,*[38] the truth will set me free. It will never fail to do so provided it is allowed to take its course.

65 15 Finally, let them remember that it is Jesus Christ who is sending them just as He sent the apostles, *sicut agnos inter lupos,*[38] like lambs among wolves. Consequently, they must imitate the lamb's gentleness, patience and charity so that, in this heavenly-inspired way, they may change the wolves into lambs.

Their Timetable during Missions

 66 1 Unless they are indisposed and holy obedience ordains otherwise, they will get up at 4 a.m. all year round as do the missionaries of the Society of Jesus and the Society of Monsieur Vincent.

67 2 At 4:30 a.m. they will make half an hour's mental prayer unless the Director gives them something else to do such as celebrating Mass, teaching hymns to the people, reading to them, etc.

68 3 At 6 a.m. or thereabouts, according to the season of the year, they will celebrate Holy Mass one after the other according to the order drawn up by the Director.

69 4 They will take their places in the confessional as soon as they can before or after the sermon and remain there until 11 a.m. precisely.

70 5 In winter, the time for the sermon is normally between seven and eight o'clock; in summer, between six and seven o'clock. The people's convenience must be taken into consideration in fixing these times.

71 6 At 11 a.m. on a signal from the Director they leave their confessional promptly even though there are people waiting. They then make their examen together before their midday meal.

72 7 They take all their meals together and in silence while listening to readings from Holy Scripture or from some sound book of moral cases. For reasons of charity and propriety, the Director may stop the reading towards the end of the meal to enable them to indulge in edifying conversation.

73 8 After grace, they take recreation together and no one must be absent without special permission. During recreation they may discuss cases of conscience which have come up in the place where they are giving the mission without divulging the names of the people concerned.

74 9 Recreation ends at one o'clock sharp and then they say Vespers and Compline together. After Vespers, they return to the confessional, unless the Director gives them other work to do, and they remain there until about five o'clock, depending on the season of the year. After that, they return to their residence and recite Matins together.

75 10 After Matins, they take their supper and a period of recreation as at midday.

76 11 After one hour's recreation, they say prayers together, listen to the reading of the subject for mental prayer and then go to bed.

77 12 By about nine o'clock, they should have retired to bed quietly and modestly.

78 13 Outside the times when they are giving missions, their timetable is about the same but with these exceptions: they do not get up until five o'clock and the time allotted during the mission for preaching and hearing confessions is devoted to study, prayer and retreat.

God alone

Rules for Catechetical Instruction

79 1 The catechist has the most important function of the whole mission, and the one who is appointed catechist by obedience must do all he can to fulfill his function worthily.

It is more difficult to find an accomplished catechist than it is to find a perfect preacher.

80 2 He must endeavor to make himself both loved and feared at the same time but in such a way that the oil of love predominates over the vinegar of fear. Consequently, while he inspires a certain fear in the children, as an experienced teacher does, by warnings and punishments which humble them, he must also, like a kind teacher, encourage them by praising them, by promising and giving them rewards and by showing them affection. He must never strike them either with his hand or with the cane. If a child should prove incorrigible, the catechist should send him to his parents to be given ten or twelve strokes of the whip or cane.

81 3 He must be very firm and not allow the children to talk or play during the catechism lesson. If he lets them off the first time they misbehave, he must warn them the second time; the third time, he gives them a penance and the fourth time he sends them away to receive suitable punishment.

82 4 Children are naturally inclined to laugh a lot and so the catechist must always try to be very serious and not say anything which might incite them to laugh boisterously. He can, however, and indeed must, enliven the catechism lesson (of its nature a rather dry subject) by adopting a pleasant manner, making little jokes or telling interesting little stories which entertain the children and bring their attention back to the lesson.

83 5 One great principle he should follow is to put a lot of questions to the children while saying very little himself. Afterwards, at the end of the lesson, he or another missionary can give a talk of about fifteen minutes. The topic of this talk will be one of the great truths of our faith so that, after the children's minds have been enlightened by the questions on the catechism, their hearts may be softened and touched by this exhortation.

It is a fact of experience that this is the best of all methods for teaching catechism in a short time and for turning the children's hearts to God.

84 6 As regards the time and circumstances of the catechism class, the following rules are to be observed:

The catechist will take his dinner at 11 a.m. promptly. After the midday Angelus he will go to church and say the Rosary aloud together with the children as they assemble. When this is done, he will sing two or three verses of a hymn.

85 7 At the first or second instruction, he will get the children to sit side by side in a set order according to age and in a manner symbolizing the nine choirs of angels in heaven. The children must keep to this order for the whole time of the mission, always sitting in the same place and next to the same companions, each row being named after one of the nine choirs of angels, seraphim, cherubim, thrones, etc. This method is ideal:

i for keeping the children in order and the God of order in the children;

ii for making the children attentive and regular in their attendance, each child being obliged to inform the catechist of the absence of the one who sits next to him;

iii for shortening the duration of the lesson, since the catechist does not have to write down the children's names or call the register since he can see at a glance who is missing or present.

86 8 After the rosary has been said and the children have taken their places, the catechism class begins. First, the catechist gets the children to make an act of faith in the presence of God and then the acts of hope, charity and contrition, the offering of the catechism class to Jesus, an invocation to the Holy Spirit and a prayer to the Blessed Virgin and the Guardian Angel to ask for their help.

87 9 He then has one child repeat all that was taught in the previous lesson and puts a question which is repeated by several of the children in turn according to the seating arrangement. He can frequently do this without saying a word—merely indicating the child with his finger or with the pointer. In this way, he can, without any great fatigue to himself, question four or five hundred children in an hour and a half.

88 10 The catechism class should not normally take more than one hour and a half. After the final exhortation, he lets the children out, row by row, if the class is a large one, in an orderly manner without tolerating the shouting and rushing for the door which are so common at the end of catechism classes.

89 11 After the catechism, the poor children who attended are to be brought two by two to the Providence where they will be given their dinner which they will eat in humble silence. During the meal, the catechist will have something read to them or perhaps put some questions to them on the catechism since we have a greater obligation to the poor than to the rich.

90 12 Responsibility for proficiency in the catechism of the children who have been chosen to make their first communion lies with the catechist. Here he must abide by the rules which have been drawn up, i.e.,

i He must give them sound instruction.

ii He must discuss the matter with the children's parents.

iii He must examine them closely on their knowledge of the catechism.

iv He must make sure that the confessor has given the children absolution. The confessors must give a certain password to those children whom they have absolved, warning them not to repeat it to the other children. The purpose of this precaution and many other similar ones is to prevent the children from making bad communions since they are easily led astray by the example of others and by the suggestions of the evil one.

91 13 In general, they are to use only the "Catéchisme Abrégé des Missionnaires" (Abridged Catechism for the Use of Missionaries)[39] from which the children can learn in seven short lessons all that is necessary for salvation.

I say "in general," because, in the case where the parish priest of the locality has given the children a sound instruction based on another catechism with a different wording, the missionary must use this catechism. He thus avoids confusing the minds of the children who learn more by rote than by reasoning.

Footnotes to the Rule of the Missionary Priests of the Company of Mary

1 Cf. Lk. 4:18.
2 Cf. 1 Cor. 1:17.
3 Cf. Is. 38:11.
4 1 Cor. 4:11.
5 Ps. 107:2.
6 Gen. 46:2.
7 Ps. 39:8.
8 Cf. Lk. 14:18-20.
9 Cf. *Regulae seu Constitutiones communes Congregationis missionis, ch. 1, 2.*
10 Cf. 1 Chr. 29:15; Ps. 38:13.
11 Jn. 15:16.
12 Cf. VENERABLE BEDE, *In Lucae Evangelium exposito* IV, ch. 12.
13 Sir. 14:5.
14 Mk. 6:31.
15 Cf. Rom. 12:2.
16 1 Cor. 11:16.
17 Sir. 19:1.
18 Rom. 12:10.
19 Col. 3:13; Eph. 4:2.
20 Cf. 1 Pet. 3:9.
21 1 Cor. 9:22.
22 Cf. Mk. 10:30.
23 Lk. 6:38.
24 Cf. Lk. 10:1.

25 Cf. Gen. 27:28.
26 This manuscript has not been found.
27 Wis. 7:15.
28 Mt. 12:34.
29 Cf. Sir. 51:30.
30 Lk. 21:15.
31 Cf. 1 Cor. 9:26.
32 Lk. 11:21.
33 Cf. Rev. 12:7.
34 Cf. Gen. 3:15.
35 Ps. 67:12.
36 Acts 1:1.
37 Cf. Jn. 8:32.
38 Lk. 10:3.
39 This "Abridged Catechism" has not been found.

10 Letter to the Members of the Company of Mary

Nolite timere	**Fear not,**
pusillus grex	**little flock,**
quia complacuit	**because it has pleased**
patri vestro	**your Father**
dare vobis regnum.	**to bestow a kingdom**
	on you.

1 Fear not, although humanly speaking, you have every cause for fear. You are only a little flock, so few in numbers that a child can count you, *puer scribet eos.*[2] Ranged in opposition against you are nations, worldlings, misers, pleasure-seekers and profligates, all banded together in their thousands ready to fight you with mockery, calumnies, contempt and violence, *convenerunt in unum.*[3] They have united with this in mind.

2 You are of little account. They are influential. You are poor. They are rich. You have no influence. They have the backing of all who matter. You are weak. They are men in positions of authority. But let me repeat: *nolite timere,*[4] have no fear, at least, no deliberate fear. Listen to Jesus Christ who tells you: *Ego sum, nolite timere,* It is I, do not be afraid. It is I who have chosen you, *ego elegi vos;*[5] I am your good shepherd and I know you for my sheep, *ego sum pastor bonus; ego cognosco,* etc.[6] *Nolite mirari si odit vos mundus, scitote,*[7] Do not be surprised if the world hates you, but know that it began by hating me.[8] If you belonged to the world, it would hold you dear as something of its very own, but because you do not belong to the world,[9] you must endure its hatred, calumnies, insults, contempt and outrages.

3 *Ego protector tuus sum*[10] *in manibus meis descripsi te,*[11] I am your protector; I hold you in my hands, little Company,

says our Eternal Father. I have graven you on my heart and on the palms of my hands in order to cherish and defend you because you have put your trust in me and not in men, in my Providence and not in wealth. I will deliver you from the snares they set for you, from the calumnies they spread about you, from the terrors of the night and from the devil who roams at noonday to seduce you.

I will shelter you under my wings; I will carry you on my shoulders. I will provide your sustenance. I will arm you with my truth and you will find it such a powerful weapon that you will see with your very eyes your enemies falling by the thousands around you: a thousand wicked paupers on your left hand and ten thousand evil rich on your right. You yourselves have nothing to fear from my avenging power. It will not even come near you.

You will trample on the asp and on the basilisk with all its envy and calumny. You will crush underfoot the lion and the dragon of ungodliness with its proud fury. I will hear you when you pray and I will be at your side when you suffer. I will deliver you from all the evils that beset you. All the glory that I have will be yours and will be revealed to you after I have given you length of days and abundant blessings upon earth.[12]

4 Dear little Company of Mary, these are the marvelous promises which God has made to you through his prophets. They will be yours provided you put all your trust in him through Mary.

Entirely dependent as you are on God's Providence, it is up to Him to support you and to increase your numbers, saying to you: *crescite et multiplicamini et replete terram,*[13] increase and multiply and fill the earth. Do not, therefore, be discouraged because you are few in number. God will be your defender, so do not be afraid of your enemies. God will provide all that is necessary for your bodily needs. Do not, then, be afraid that you will lack the necessities of life in these hard times which are hard only because people do not have enough trust in God.[14] It is God who will glorify you, *glorificabo,*[15] and have no fear that anyone will take this glory from you. In a word, fear nothing whatsoever and sleep in peace in your Father's arms.

5 But it is not enough simply to be unafraid. God wants you to hope for great things from Him and to be filled with joy by reason of this hope. Our bountiful Father wants to give you the kingdom of his grace. He has made you his kings and priests, *fecisti nos Deo nostro reges et sacerdotes,*[16] by the Christian faith and the priestly ordination he has conferred on you; and your voluntary poverty gives you an additional right to be called kings, for blessed are the poor in spirit theirs is the kingdom of heaven: *beati pauperes spiritu, quoniam ipsorum est regnum caelorum.*[17] Our Lord does not merely promise the kingdom of heaven [in the future[18]] but states that, because you are poor in spirit, you possess it now. How is this to be explained?

6 1 The blessed in heaven feel no need of the things of this world since they have a superabundance of all things, spiritual and eternal. God is theirs in his fullness. Likewise, men such as you who profess voluntary poverty feel no need for the things of this world because they neither want nor desire them. If they did, they would not be truly poor in spirit. As the wise man says: *substantia inopis secundum cor ejus,*[19] the poor man's riches are proportionate to the desires of his mind and heart. If his heart is contented, he is rich and wants for nothing.

7 2 The poor in spirit are rich in faith and the other virtues. *Pauperes in hoc saeculo divites in fide; affatim dives est qui cum Christo pauper est,*[20] In this world, says St. Jerome, the poor are rich in faith and he who is poor with Jesus is rich beyond measure. He is rich in divine consolations, *parasti in dulcedine tua pauperi, Deus.*[21] He does not have to live the thorny life of the rich nor share their urge for riches. Like one who reigns in heaven, he has turned away from the enjoyment of earthly consolations in order to enjoy those which God has provided for him in such abundance, *praebebit delicias regibus.*[22] He even counts heavenly glory as part of his wealth in spite of his not yet being in heaven. One can say that what has the value of gold is gold, and, by analogy, that which is equivalent to heaven is heaven. What is poverty of spirit worth? The kingdom of heaven and heavenly glory.

8 3 The man who is truly poor in spirit possesses God himself in his heart. *Quid enim gloriosus homini quam sua vendere et Christum emere,* What is more glorious for a man than to sell all he has in exchange for Christ Jesus? says St. Augustine. What a profitable sale and what a good bargain! *Nescit homo praetium ejus,* Man does not realize its worth.

Understand this, dear brothers, no man realizes the value of your evangelical poverty, *semper ergo dives est christiana paupertas, quia plus est quod habet quam quod non habet; nec timet in hoc mundo indigentia laborare cui donatum est in omnium rerum Domino omnia possidere.*[25] The man who embraces the poverty of Christ is always rich because what he possesses more than offsets what he lacks. He is not afraid of being deprived of anything in this world since he has been given the grace of possessing all things by possessing the Lord of all.

9 To increase the rich treasure your poverty brings you and remain in possession of the kingdom you have conquered, there are three things you must put into practice:

i You must truly value this real and effective poverty to which you have committed yourself and have a real love for it. No one becomes rich more easily or knows the best use to make of these riches, says a holy bishop, than the man who is truly poor in spirit. He knows that wealth only serves to reduce to poverty and misery those whose heart is centered on it; whereas those who give up this wealth through a holy and praiseworthy contempt for it become rich and happy in the truest sense of the word: *divitiae pauperem faciunt et miserum, si diligantur, beatum et divitem, si pro Christo contemnantur,*[26] Riches make a man poor and miserable if he loves them. If he despises them for Christ's sake, they make him rich and happy.

Be careful then and do not look back at the patrimony or benefice you have given up: *nemo mittens manum ad aratrum et respiciens post se est aptus regno Dei,*[27] No one putting his hand to the plow and looking behind is fit for the kingdom of God. Be careful, too, not to glance enviously around you at the thousand and one benefits, ecclesiastical or otherwise, which you could acquire with as much right as anyone else, for they arouse the fool's concupiscence, *quae concupiscentiam praebent insensato.*[28]

10 ii Experience, then, for yourselves the effects of poverty, for instance, (1) the labor it entails in the pulpit or the confessional by which you earn your bread by the sweat of your brow; (2) the humiliation and disdain which are usually shown to poor clerics; (3) other discomforts which poverty brings with it: lack of suitable clothing, of proper food and accommodations, and the fatigue and traveling it imposes.

11 iii Let all your longings be centered on eternal things. Knock on the door which opens to you the mercy of Jesus Christ who recognizes and hears without fail those who are dressed in the livery of his poverty.

The man truly poor in spirit sees the world as a frightful wilderness and turns his heart from it. He avoids getting involved in worldly affairs, *nemo militans Deo implicat se negotiis:*[29] No man enlisted in God's army gets involved in other business. To his relatives and friends in the world he only . . .

The original MS ends here with this incomplete sentence. The final pages have been lost. The following conclusion is given in the Rule of Fr. Deshayes of 1837.

In the same way, therefore, that a traveler bent on reaching some royal city, towards which he is directing his swift passage, and who, totally taken up with this one idea, passes on indifferently without stopping to consider the beauty of the countries through which he is passing, so the missionary, carefree like St. Francis, walks with great haste towards the heavenly Jerusalem, solely taken up with the charms of the immortal city of peace and glory; he has eyes only for its contemplation. He cannot consider painful what it has cost him to get there, nor pleasurable what could turn him away from it. Like another St. Paul, he doesn't consider things visible but the invisible, because he tells himself, the visible are passing and perishable; death takes them away just when one expects to enjoy them; indeed, they are often lost in anguish before death; while invisible goods, those intangible treasures, which are only tasted in the possession of God, are eternal.

And so, at last, the missionary, sustained and spurred on by this noble hope, which beats high in his breast, can't deceive himself, and persevering in his holy and sublime vocation, he will have the happiness of being able to repeat with confidence when he is dying, those beautiful, consoling words of Jesus Christ's most zealous missionary: *'Bonum certamen certavi cursum consummavi, fidem servavi; in reliquo reposita est mihi corona iustitiae quam reddet mihi Dominus in illa die iustus iudex. Amen.* I have fought the good fight, I have finished my course, I have kept the faith. As to the rest, there is laid up for me a crown of justice, which the Lord, the just judge, will render to me on that day.

Amen.'

Footnotes to a Letter to the Members of the Company of Mary

1 Lk. 12:32.
2 Is. 10:19.
3 Ps. 2:2.
4 Lk. 24:36.
5 Jn. 15:16.
6 Cf. Jn. 10:14.
7 1 Jn. 3:13.
8 Cf. Jn. 15:18.
9 Cf. Jn. 15:19.
10 Gen. 15:1.
11 Is. 49:16.
12 Cf. Ps. 90.
13 Gen. 1:28.
14 Cf. Mt. 6:26-34.
15 Cf. Ps. 90:15.
16 Cf. Rev. 5:10.
17 Mt. 5:3.
18 The manuscript does not contain these three words. Compare this passage and the following with NOUET, *L'homme d'oraison,* 60th meditation.
19 Sir. 38:20.
20 SAINT JEROME, *Ad Heliodorum Monachum,* Letter XIV.
21 Ps. 67:11.

God alone

22 Gen. 49:20.

23 SAINT AUGUSTINE, *Serm. ult. de diversis.*

24 Job 28:13.

25 Similar ideas, though not identically expressed, are to be found in SAINT AUGUSTINE, *Sermo 78* and *Sermo 85.*

26 HUMBERTUS OF ROMANS, *Epistola de tribus votis substantialibus religionis.*

27 Cf. Lk. 9:62.

28 Cf. Wis. 15:5.

29 2 Tim. 2:4.

11 The 'Wisdom' Cross of Poitiers

Introduction

When Fr. de Montfort was chaplain at the poorhouse at Poitiers from 1701-1703, he formed a group of young girls who gathered together regularly in a house which he called "La Sagesse" (Wisdom). Soon afterwards Marie Louise Trichet and Catherine Brunet, who were to become the first Daughters of Wisdom, joined them.

Montfort composed for them a program of the spiritual life based upon the words of Jesus Christ, Incarnate Wisdom: "We must renounce self and carry our cross after Jesus Christ, under Mary's guidance."

He wrote this program in a very simple way on a cross, which has been preserved by the community of the Daughters of Wisdom in Rome.

DENY
ONESELF
CARRY
ONE'S CROSS
TO FOLLOW
JESUS CHRIST

IF YOU ARE ASHAMED OF THE CROSS
OF JESUS CHRIST, HE WILL BE
ASHAMED OF YOU BEFORE HIS FATHER.

LOVE
THE CROSS
DESIRE:
CROSSES
CONTEMPT
PAIN
ABUSE
INSULTS
DISGRACE
PERSECUTION
HUMILIATIONS
CALUMNIES
ILLNESS
INJURIES.

MAY JESUS PREVAIL
MAY HIS CROSS PREVAIL

DIVINE LOVE
HUMILITY
SUBMISSION
PATIENCE
OBEDIENCE:
COMPLETE
PROMPT
JOYFUL
BLIND
PERSEVERING

SAGES

12 Original Rule of the Daughters of Wisdom

Introduction

The manuscript of St. Louis Marie upon which the following text is based is kept in the archives of the Daughters of Wisdom. It is in the form of a booklet of sixty-two pages, all numbered and enclosed in a folder of parchment. Montfort's text finishes towards the middle of p. 61 and is followed by seven episcopal approvals given over a period from 1715 to 1739.

The first of these approvals, that of Bishop Champflour, is most valuable since it enables us to determine a time when the manuscript was composed: "I approve the above rules of the Daughters of Wisdom," Etienne, Bishop of La Rochelle, August 1st, 1715. Montfort must have personally presented his manuscript to the bishop because the latter gave only his signature to the document and the actual formula of approbation was written by Montfort.

There are a number of corrections, erasures and over-written words in the text. Where a word is hard to decipher, it is clearly given in a note. It is impossible to identify the author of these changes which the first edition of the Rule, published in 1750, has reproduced. It would seem, therefore, that the changes were made before the death of Marie Louise of Jesus, the first Daughter of Wisdom, who died in 1750.

In 1760, the Constitutions of the Congregation were published. They were drawn up by Marie Louise before her death, and it is curious that they quote a passage of the Rule which was not in the

1715 text, which would seem to indicate that there existed a text earlier than that of 1715.

It seems certain that one source of inspiration for Montfort was St. Francis de Sales, who is quoted textually in two places. A fleeting allusion is made to the Sisters of Charity of St. Vincent de Paul and it is probable that the ideas of Vincent de Paul had appealed to Louis Marie. Fr. Tronson, one-time Superior of the Seminary of St. Sulpice, also had an influence over him, and Montfort borrowed a whole chapter from him. Other passages clearly reflect Tronson's inspiration.

But these sources do not destroy the originality of Louis Marie's vision for the Congregation of the Daughters of Wisdom.

Rules of the Daughters of Wisdom[1]

1 The interior aim of the Congregation of the Daughters of Wisdom[2] is the acquisition of Divine Wisdom. The exterior aim is threefold, in keeping with the talents of its members: 1. the instruction of children in charitable schools, both in the town and in country places; 2. the proper care of the poor, whether in hospitals or not, sick or not, incurable or not; 3. the conducting of retreat houses to which the Sisters may be called.

2 As all the Sisters have their particular aptitudes, the Superior assigns them accordingly to various charges at the end of their novitiate year. However, should this time prove insufficient to reveal their aptitudes, their assignment may be deferred for several years.

Counsels

3 My dear daughters, beware of the temptations of the evil spirit with regard to the end you should have in view on entering community life.

4 1 Do not take for principal end either your personal comfort or the practice of charity towards your neighbor. You should not aim at a life of natural or even interior repose, according to the inclinations of nature, because obedience, which often prescribes exterior duties contrary to your taste, will thus upset your plans. It would also be a mistake to make charity towards your neighbor your chief end, for if in time you were not engaged in serving your neighbor, you would become troubled, sad, and discouraged. If, however, your primary purpose is your own sanctification achieved by the accomplishment of the will of God as indicated by obedience, then you will remain at peace, no matter what happens.

5 2 Since our Lord commands us not to think of the morrow,[3] not only with regard to our corporal, but especially our spiritual needs, do not deliberately think of what might happen to you in the future regarding the kind of life you have chosen. Consider these thoughts of a possible and conditional future as subtle temptations of the devil who wants you to lose heart by showing you a long succession of years to be spent in silence, penance, obedience, and poverty. His aim is to make you lose your peace of soul or at least your time, by inspiring idle imaginings of things which do not as yet exist and may never come to pass. These contingencies are, for example, "If my father or mother were to die, what would I do? If this person, this Superior, this Director should leave, what would become of the house?"

6 3 You may be sure that the devil will tempt you in a thousand ways, either before or after profession, to make you change your resolves and the purposes for which you work. He will magnify and increase your fears, difficulties and dislikes. He will arouse your passions and darken your understanding. Finally, he will resort to all kinds of diabolical tricks in order to make you change your mind. But you will be victorious and happy if you disclose your difficulties to your Director and your Superior and obey them blindly.

Admission to the Novitiate

7 1 Only respectable young girls or widows from the age of sixteen to forty are received among the Daughters of Wisdom. Persons too old or too infirm are not accepted.

8 2 Poor and rich alike are received, provided their intentions are good and their vocation sincere, that is, if they are docile and poor in spirit.

9 3 No money or board is required of them; however, should they bring money, it is accepted as an alms and placed in the common purse to supply the needs of the whole community.

10 4 Boarders, i.e. girls or women who have no intention of making profession, are rarely accepted; but, in extraordinary cases, if an exception is made in favor of some person of great merit, these persons are required to follow all the common rules without exception and no board is required of them.

11 5 The novices and boarders may leave the house only in case of urgent necessity and with a special permission of the Superior. If there is no chapel in the community, they go out to hear holy Mass and receive the Sacraments. They do not assume charge of, or burden themselves with, temporal affairs. However, if they are involved in any temporal matters before entering the novitiate or becoming boarders, they must terminate them before being admitted. If, after their entrance, they should acquire temporal goods, they do not manage them personally but entrust their administration to some competent secular person.

12 6 The first novitiate begins with the taking of the habit and lasts at least one year. It may be prolonged if the disposition of the novice requires it. During the novitiate the novices are trained in the practice of every virtue to rid them of their bad habits, evil inclinations, changing moods, and their smallest imperfections. Therefore, the Mistress of novices trains them in the practice of obedience, silence, modesty, mortification, meditation, contempt of world and self.

13 7 The second novitiate lasts at least a year, during which period, apart from the time devoted to the exercises of piety common to the community, they apply themselves according to their attitudes to the study of proper methods of teaching catechism, conducting elementary schools, and the arts of reading and writing, as well as manual skills.

Counsels

14 Beware of the different temptations by which the evil spirit tries to ensnare novices. Having been unable to prevent their entrance into the novitiate by using worldly relatives, selfish friends, vain fears, human respect and by suggesting a thousand false reasons against entering, he tries to nullify the effect of this step, which is the sanctification of the person concerned:

1 by showing her what she has left in the world;

2 by making her disregard the minor rules and devotional practices traditional in the community;

3 by afflicting her with troubles and anxieties;

4 by suggesting that she should receive more consideration than others because of her rank, the amount of money she brought with her, or some physical or mental quality she possesses;

5 by prompting her to be cold towards others and even towards her Superiors, and making her believe that they have something against her;

6 by keeping her from the sacraments under the most specious pretexts.

There are many other snares that the devil, together with the world, sets for the novices, either to make them leave, to induce them to sin, or to retard their perfection. Candor and blind obedience are the infallible remedies and all-powerful arms in these trials and struggles.

Original Rule La Sagesse

Profession and Vows

15 1 At the end of the year of first novitiate, or later, if the novice is so inclined, she makes profession by pronouncing the three simple vows of obedience, poverty and chastity for one year. This profession, made privately, in secret and without exterior ceremony, is preceded by ten days of retreat and silence, during which she communicates with no one except the Superior and the Director.

16 2 She renews her vows every year if she willingly and wholeheartedly perseveres in her vocation; otherwise, when the year of vows has expired, she may without hindrance leave the Congregation.

17 3 Likewise, if the Superior, in agreement with the community, is not satisfied with a professed religious because of grave and repeated faults, she may dismiss her.

18 4 If the religious leaves at the end of the year of her own accord or is dismissed because of an act of formal disobedience, the money or other gifts she may have donated as alms on entering are retained by the community. However, if the community dismisses her at the end of the year for some good reason, all she brought with her is returned, her expenses deducted.

19 5 If, however, the departing Sister had given all her goods to the community, the latter should return these, after her board has been deducted.

20 6 At the end of each of the five consecutive years after their profession, the novices renew the three vows for one year. If, at the end of five years, the professed are convinced that they have a true vocation, they pronounce their perpetual vows, after having obtained the consent of the community.

Counsels

21 1 When the thought of leaving the community comes to you after profession, reveal it immediately to your Director or Superior, and wait a considerable time in order to determine if the thought is just a mere temptation.

22 2 Beware of occasioning these temptations by frequent association with outsiders or people following pious fads, or by seeking counsel from persons other than your Director or Superior.

23 3 On the first Saturday of each month, renew your vows to God through the hands of the Blessed Virgin in a Communion offered for this intention.

Their Poverty

24 1 They have nothing they may call their own, not even a

penny, a habit, an office book, piece of furniture or article of devotion; everything is in common, and after their profession the community is obliged to give them whatever food, care and clothing they need.

25 2 Unless the Sisters so desire, they do not renounce the revenue from their patrimony, if they have any; nor the radical domain thereof, but the usufruct and use of these goods are completely at the disposition of their Superiors, to use as they see fit for the needs of the community without distinction as to rich or poor.

26 3 Being poor, they dress in the grey habit of the poor of the hospitals and countryside. This habit resembles somewhat that of the Daughters of Monsieur Vincent; moreover, for greater religious modesty, they wear a black mantle which enshrouds them from head to foot.

27 4 The only furnishings of their little cells are: 1) a wooden bed with pallet of straw, a mattress and curtains; 2) a table; 3) a chair; 4) a crucifix; 5) a picture of the Blessed Virgin; 6) a box without a lock; 7) a clothes rack, some dusters, a candlestick and a broom; everything else should be excluded as useless and superfluous.

28 5 They engage in manual work, but of their own accord, they do not seek work outside the house. They do not set their wages or receive personally the payment thereof. They derive no benefit from this work except what they receive in common with the rest of the community, for all funds are placed in the common purse by the Bursar or the Superior.

29 6 In their temporal needs they ask alms of no one, neither of parents nor of strangers, directly or indirectly, neither for the community in general nor for themselves in particular. They abandon themselves to the care of God's divine Providence, confident He will aid them in all their necessities when and how He sees fit. Their trust is so absolute that it is as though they expected to receive food and care directly from an angel sent from heaven. Yet, they undertake manual work to help earn their living, as though they expected nothing from God.

30 7 When, according to their talents, they are sent to teach catechism or to direct town or country schools, they consider the modest salary received yearly for their work and labors in such wise that if, through negligence, they do not fulfill their duty, they commit a grave injustice by using money they have not earned. Since they are given as salary only what is absolutely necessary to live on, they do not spend it carelessly. If they realize a profit during the year, they are not allowed to give it either to their parents or friends without an explicit permission.

31 8 They ask nothing, either directly or indirectly, of their pupils, but if the parents of a rich child wish of their own accord to offer an alms through gratitude, the Sisters ask them to present it to the Superior of the Mother-Community or the novitiate. They never receive gifts personally unless they are teaching at a distance from the Mother House.

32 9 If God calls them to take charge of a hospital, they content themselves with a modest and frugal way of living, sharing, if need be, the food of the poor. As for the board and alms given to them, they follow the directives mentioned above for the teachers and do the work out of charity.

33 10 Every year the Superior has them change cells, furniture, and even habits, if the Sisters have shown too much attachment to these things. Twice a year they have their hair cut.

Counsels

34 1 Beware of possessing anything personal unless there is a real need and always with permission. The devil is ever eagerly inspiring religious with countless false pretexts and a thousand specious reasons for transgressing their vow of poverty, or at least diminishing its merit.

35 2 Beware then of the least attachment. When you feel a strong liking for anything, set it aside for a while or deprive yourself of it altogether.

36 3 The evil spirit will tempt you, under the pretense of piety, to keep in your room pictures and devotional objects for yourself and others. Scarcely one religious in a hundred succeeds in overcoming this subtle temptation.

37 4 On the other hand, it is also a subtle temptation not to reveal to your Superior your temporal needs through fear of a refusal or through capriciousness.

38 5 Do not deliberately think of the morrow without real necessity. God does not wish this[4] and the devil inspires it only to upset you or make you waste time.

39 6 If you see one of your Sisters better dressed or better cared for than you, beware of jealousy and murmuring. The evil spirit will not hesitate to exaggerate the advantages enjoyed by others and denied you, in order to upset and alienate you from the Sisters, at least interiorly. For this reason he will remind you that you brought more to the community, that you are a greater asset and that you work harder. He will remind you of the comforts you enjoyed when you disposed of your own possessions, and he will awaken in you a desire to return to the world.

40 7 I advise you to choose, whenever possible and through a spirit of poverty and humility, the worst in all things: the least palatable food, the oldest and coarsest habits, the most menial offices, etc.

41 8 Deprive yourself readily of something that others will not do

without, showing outwardly no regret at what you have done.

42 9 Never speak highly of the goods of this world. Never say, "If I were given such a sum of money, . . ." "If some rich person gave us . . .", etc. These are the desires of pagans[5] and worldlings, and are unworthy of the truly wise, who, far from desiring temporal goods even for pious purposes, leave even their legitimate possessions to follow more closely Incarnate Wisdom.[6]

43 10 Beware of telling others of the comforts you enjoyed in the world and of what you brought to the community. Never speak of your skill or ability to do different types of work.

44 11 Set no store by what is merely exterior and imposing, no matter how great and important it may seem from a natural standpoint. And esteem greatly those Sisters who are seemingly the poorest and least capable.

45 12 If you have a request regarding your health or other material needs, before making it known to the Superior, pray to God for at least a quarter of an hour to see if in his light the need is real and in keeping with perfection. If so, ask simply and fearlessly. If you are refused or rebuffed in your request, remain as peaceful as if Jesus Christ in person had refused you.

Their Obedience

46 1 Holy obedience, practices with all possible perfection, is the special virtue that should characterize the Daughters of Wisdom. Just as divine Wisdom, who reigned in the heavens, came down to earth to obey from the first moment of his incarnation to his death,[7] so, following his example, his daughters have left the world to subject their mind and will to the yoke of obedience.

47 2 They obey their Rule and all their Superiors

1 Entirely, without reservations;
2 Promptly, without delay;
3 Cheerfully, without sadness;
4 Holily, without human respect;
5 Blindly, without reasoning;
6 And continuously, without inconstancy.

48 3 The Sisters should be faithful to their Rule even in the smallest details, and when their Rule does not prescribe an action, they ask permission if they want to do it so that obedience may purge their actions of the poison of self-will.

49 4 They should obey their Superior in all things, prescribed or not. If, on certain occasions or under certain circumstances, the practice of the Rule becomes impossible or difficult, they should ask the Superior for an exemption or an interpretation.

50 5 They may, and often should, present their reasons for doing or not doing a certain action, but they should do so with calm and

indifference, not taking offense at the refusal of a request which they consider most reasonable.

51 6 They try to obey all persons for the love of God, when the command is not opposed to any other will but their own.

52 7 They ask all their permissions of their Superior on their knees and in all humility because they see only Jesus Christ in her. They never kneel to ask permissions in the presence of outsiders.

53 8 They do not fail to make public reparation for any fault against holy obedience committed in public.

54 9 With regard to the government of the community, they obey the bishop and his representative, as well as the pastors of the parishes to which they are assigned. In hospitals they are subject to the chaplains in all spiritual matters concerning the patients, and to the Directors in all questions of administration.

Counsels

55 As the devil is proud and disobedient, he will assail you, my dear daughters, with strong and subtle temptations, to turn you against the holy obedience that you owe your Rule, your Superior and your Director.

56 1 Beware of disregarding minor rules and devout practices, and transgressing them without scruple, for anyone who despises minor duties will fall little by little.[8]

57 2 To deter you from obeying your Superior, the evil spirit will suggest:

1 that she does not like you, and even that she seeks to accuse you of faults and holds a grudge against you;

2 that she is not capable of giving orders;

3 that she assumes an air of domination and superiority;

4 that there is no sense in what she commands;

5 that she does not contradict others as she does you;

6 that she has all kinds of defects, that what she says is not worth your attention and that she does not deserve your confidence.

58 3 If the devil cannot make you disobey outright, he will make you obey reluctantly, with delays, complaints, grumblings, murmurings, and with a vexed and disdainful air.

59 4 Reveal all your interior dispositions to your Director. Hide nothing that will help him to know your temperament. Make known your good and evil tendencies, your plans and undertakings. Think neither well nor ill of yourself; leave this judgment entirely to your Superior and your Director.

60 5 Consider as a shrewd temptation the thought of not consulting your Director about something very simple you wish to do, under the pretext that he is not sufficiently enlightened on the subject, or that you have no doubts about the goodness of the action

or the truth of the matter.

61 6 After a refusal by your Superior, beware of complaining to an equal or subordinates. Beware of resorting to artifice or evasion to extort a permission from Superiors.

62 7 Do not fear to offend worldly ways when obeying promptly a small point of the Rule or a minor order of your Superior. If a community exercise calls you, promptly leave the people you are with, unless it is absolutely necessary to remain.

63 8 To perfect yourself quickly in obedience, that great virtue of Divine Wisdom, do not hesitate to submit your judgment and will to your equals and subordinates in indifferent matters.

64 9 Note that you are entirely free to disclose your interior dispositions to either your Director or Superior, as you choose. However, we must admit that those Sisters who are humble and obedient enough to open their hearts to their Superiors are performing an heroic act, and through this practice, which is common in fervent communities, will make more progress in virtue than others.

65 10 Remember this admirable statement found in the Rule of Saint Francis de Sales: "In proportion as you prefer what is common to what is personal, you will perceive the progress you have made."[9]

Their Chastity

66 1 At their profession the Daughters of Wisdom make a simple vow of chastity for one year, and every year they renew it with the other vows if they decide to do so. This ceremony takes place privately, as mentioned above.

67 2 No man is allowed to enter their rooms or cells except when absolutely necessary, as is the case of a doctor or workman, etc.

68 3 When they leave the house, it is only to render service to the poor, and they faithfully observe the following rules: 1) whenever possible, they take a companion for their guardian angel; 2) they walk modestly through the city streets, their eyes cast down and avoid looking to the right or left into shop windows; 3) they never look men directly in the face while speaking to them but turn a little to the side; 4) as much as possible, they cover their face and hands with their mantle; 5) when visited, they never remain alone with a man in a room with the door closed. When they are obliged through charity or necessity to converse with a man, whether layman, cleric or religious, it must be, if at all possible, in an open place, or indoors with the door of the room left open; 6) to obtain from God the preservation of the treasure of purity and the grace to fulfill their duties of charity, they never enter their own room or that of another person without saying a Hail Mary, either kneeling or standing, before or after entering; 7) they accept no present per-

sonally without explicit permission; 8) they never return to a house where insulting words have been addressed to them, and should this happen, they are careful not to laugh it off, but quietly reprimand the offenders, or at least show their disapproval by quickly leaving the place. Should this happen in the street, they pass on in silence, making an act of contrition in their heart.

69 4 Unlike worldly persons, who are not sufficiently careful in this matter, they avoid anything that might in the least tarnish the beautiful flower of purity, such as, too much familiarity with one another, mutual kissing, fondly holding one another's hands.

70 5 They are very careful, while rising or retiring, that no part of the body may be seen, and they never sleep two in a bed without necessity.

Counsels

71 1 Since you wish with the help of a special grace to preserve your virginity and chastity for our Lord Jesus Christ, obtain this grace through persevering prayer and cultivate a great devotion to the Blessed Virgin, the Mother, Queen and Model of all true virgins.

72 2 Distrust yourself greatly, no matter how strong you may be or how many victories you may have won. Therefore, avoid the slightest occasion of sin contrary to this divine virtue, as if you had never won a victory, and frankly reveal your temptations in this matter.

73 3 Resist vigorously the first promptings of temptations, for if you delay, you will yield.

74 4 Never give your body all it demands. With permission, refuse it from time to time even some lawful satisfaction. The rose blossoms among thorns, and chastity in the midst of discipline and mortification.

Their Silence

75 1 They faithfully observe silence at all times save during the two hours of recreation after meals and whenever charity, obedience or the duties of their office require them to do otherwise.

76 2 When they are obliged to speak in the community, in schools or in homes for the poor, they always do so in a low voice and as briefly as possible, thus conforming as perfectly as they can to the rule of silence.

77 3 For this reason they avoid calling a person from afar or through a window, preferring to take a hundred steps rather than violate the rules of silence or religious modesty.

78 4 When permitted to speak with visitors, they observe the rules of religious modesty in speech, and never remain more than a half hour without special permission.

79 5 They make no visits but those which obedience, charity or Christian courtesy requires, and these visits should be as rare as possible.

80 6 They do not speak in their Superior's presence unless questioned or asked to speak.

81 7 If they have some necessary information to impart, they wait, if possible, until recreation to do so.

Counsels

82 1 Remember that if you observe silence carefully at the specified times, despite the longing women ordinarily have to talk, you will win a great victory over yourself, the world, and the devil, and you will soon be wise and perfect.

83 2 Speak little at those times when you may speak, and speak with due decorum without passion, vanity, dissembling or self-seeking.

84 3 Speak of worldly things only to condemn them. Never discuss news of the town, the court, the army, etc.

85 4 Sanctify your silence by vocal or mental prayer, according to your inclination.

Their Contempt of the World

86 1 They look upon their grey habit covered with the black mantle as their shroud and as the livery of the poverty of Jesus Christ, which the world abhors; therefore, they kiss it lovingly as they put it on. Far from introducing any worldly fashion into their habit, they choose rather materials of the coarsest texture, repulsive both to nature and to the spirit of the world, a feature often noticed among devout persons.

87 2 They shun as they would a subtle poison the hundred and one fashions and manners of the world, anathematized by the Holy Spirit when He says, "Do not be conformed to this present and corrupt world."[10]

88 3 They take no heed of the rash judgments, the stinging mockeries, the calumnies, and harsh maltreatment which they may have to suffer from the world; nay, they even rejoice when for the sake of Jesus Christ they are an object of contempt before the world, his own greatest enemy.

89 4 Under the pretext of securing temporal gain for the commu-

nity, they never become involved in worldly affairs, such as, taking on social obligations, taking part in lotteries, etc. He who is truly poor in spirit has no desire for what he does not possess.

90 5 They avoid becoming involved in the temporal affairs of their relatives; they undertake no lawsuit, even when justified in doing so, preferring to lose their habit or mantle rather than lose their peace of soul and offend against charity and the spirit of poverty in keeping them.

91 6 Like the poor, they have no mirror in their cell; no lace, ribbons or gold material in their clothing; no snuff boxes or colored handkerchiefs in their pockets; no gold or silver in their spoons, forks, knives, watches, crosses, reliquaries, etc. They avoid the use of these and a hundred other things, loved and coveted by the worldly and so opposed to the poverty of Jesus Christ.

Counsels

92 1 Beware of people tainted with worldliness, enemies of the poverty and the cross of Jesus Christ. No matter what mask of holiness disguises them, they are more dangerous in their conversation, language and counsel than the most outspoken freethinker, of whom one is naturally distrustful.

93 2 Deprive yourself, when among outsiders, of some small unnecessary gratifications in order to avoid those that are forbidden and to edify your neighbor.

94 3 Guided by your spiritual director, try to practice all that is most humiliating and contrary to nature, in order to combat the world, which daily opposes and always has opposed our Lord Jesus Christ in his teaching, his example, and his faithful followers.

95 4 When in doubt of the truth or the goodness of a thing, do not say, "What do people think? What do they say of such and such a thing?" but "What does faith teach me? What does Jesus Christ say?"

96 5 Always consider the desire to see your relatives, to have news of them, or to lend them assistance in their education or temporal concerns as a great temptation and a real obstacle to your perfection and salvation.

97 6 Be strictly on your guard against worldliness in religious life, which is prevalent in most religious institutes. This spirit consists in:

1 desiring news of one's relatives and being concerned about their affairs;

2 valuing, cherishing and seeking money and temporal revenues in order to open a house, build a chapel, etc., just as worldly people avidly seek money to make a name and a fortune for themselves, to build their houses, etc.;

3 seeking the entry of a rich person into the community, setting more store by her gold or silver, which is the open sesame of worldlings, than by Christ's spirit of poverty, which is the key to the kingdom of heaven;

4 complaining inside or outside the convent of the poverty and inconveniences of community life;

5 seeking and scheming to get honorable positions and offices in the community as the worldlings do those of the world;

6 speaking highly of natural talents and the goods of this world, and manifesting a desire to possess them;

7 despising those who lack these natural talents, for example, those who have little intelligence, health, ability, industry, knowledge, wealth, etc.;

8 seeking in the community all one's comforts in dress, lodging, furniture, meals, etc.;

9 finally, worldliness in religious life consists in doing one's own will as much as possible, imposing one's opinions on others, and seeking to make oneself indispensable to the community by one's intelligence, knowledge, and ability.

This, my dear daughters, is a brief explanation of the most subtle poison of religious communities. Preserve yourselves from it, for the love of Jesus.

98 7 When God, wishing to purify and reward you, permits someone to calumniate and persecute you, do not fail, out of gratitude, to pray for him for eight days and to receive Communion for him at least once.

Their Charity towards their Neighbor

99 1 Pure charity is, as has been said, the aim of the Institute of the Daughters of Wisdom, whether they are engaged, according to their talents and the call of holy obedience, in conducting charitable schools in towns and in country places, in administering hospitals, in directing retreat houses, or in caring for and nursing poor incurable people.

100 2 When God calls them to conduct primary schools, they faithfully observe all the rules which are given later and are motivated only by charity.

101 3 If God calls them to take charge of hospitals, they observe the rules of prudence and charity contained in the following paragraphs.

102 4 They render the poor of the hospitals every service possible, whether spiritual or temporal. For the spiritual care, they are dependent upon the chaplains or the parish priests, and for the corporal, upon the administrators of the hospital, doing neither more nor less than their ecclesiastical and lay superiors permit.

103 5 They must be prepared to endure much opposition in hospitals which are governed by many administrators; hence they must arm themselves with patience in order to bear these trials without being discouraged.

104 6 If the Board of Administration wishes to force them to disregard some rule essential to their Institute, they should not only refuse to comply, but should be ready to leave the hospital, should their major Superiors judge it necessary. However, if in the judgment of the Superiors, the rule or regulation which the Board wishes to add or suppress is not essential or contrary to the Constitutions, the Sisters accede in all charity and obedience to its request.

105 7 They ordinarily go to confession to one confessor, who is the mutual choice of both the Superior and the Sisters, whether it be the chaplain of the hospital, the parish priest or some other priest. Should this confessor imprudently counsel them to transgress any of their rules, they will choose another, but they never take this step without a serious reason.

106 8 In temporal matters, they obey the administrators of the hospitals and other authorized persons who have requested their services and upon whom they depend for their subsistence.

107 9 They consider themselves as belonging to the poor class, as they do in reality, and they rarely and very reluctantly interfere in the temporal affairs of the hospitals where they are employed.

108 10 Their Superior alone has the right to appeal to the Board in regard to the temporal needs of the poor or the Sisters; however, should the Board disregard these requests or openly oppose them, they show no discontent. They complain to no one, either in or outside the hospital, and do not seek to enlist the services of a friendly administrator to win their cause.

109 11 They may have control of funds in the wards over which they have charge, but as they receive directly from their Superior, who assigned them to their charge, and not from the administrators, the money necessary for their needs, it is to her that they render an account of these funds and have recourse in all their necessities. The Superior in her turn gives an account of her administration to the Board or Bursar appointed by the Board for the administration of temporal goods. If the Superior refuses the Sisters' request, however just, they do not appeal to anyone, whether of the hospital or not, to obtain what they want. Such a procedure, by causing division, would destroy all peace and obedience.

110 12 They try to act in such a way that the goods of the houses to which they are assigned be rightly used and not exposed to theft and waste. However, should this happen through no fault of their own, they are not held accountable since out of charity they have tried to prevent the loss of these goods.

God alone

Rules of Prudence, Firmness and Charity towards One Another, towards the Poor and Children

Interior Rules

111 1 They never interpret as evil what has only an appearance of evil; they excuse as due to weakness, ignorance or passion, what is evidently wrong, believing that God permits the evil that they see to bring about a greater good that they do not see for want of sufficient light.

112 2 They are slow to believe evil reports about another even though such reports are made with the charitable intention of righting some wrong. They charitably suspend their judgment until they are better informed, preferring to be duped through excessive charity rather than judge rashly through too little charity and prudence.

113 3 They never consciously reflect on the evil conduct and the faults of their neighbor or on the wrongs they may have suffered from them.

114 4 Contrary to the promptings of self-love, they are honestly convinced that they are the most imprudent, most ignorant and most worthless of all.

115 5 In things indifferent in themselves or not clearly wrong, they readily sacrifice their own interior lights and renounce their views, however valid, to submit out of humility and charity to those of others.

116 6 They never entertain any secret aversion or coldness towards anyone, but when, in spite of themselves, such feelings arise, they always reveal them to their Director.

Exterior Rules

117 1 They obey with a joyful countenance, even though the commands of their Superiors may be contrary to their natural inclinations.

118 2 They never complain of, or take offense at, their Superior's way of acting, in the presence of someone who cannot remedy the situation; they never seek approval of their opinions and conduct when these are in opposition to the opinion of their Superior.

119 3 They never try to make their opinion prevail over that of others, but after simply stating their views, they readily adopt those of others.
120 4 Each one concerns herself with her own work and does not take upon herself the supervision of another's.
121 5 They never listen to the complaints of inferiors against the Superiors; or if they do, they try to make the subordinates understand, at least outwardly, that their complaints are not justified, gently accusing them of impatience, pride, grumbling, etc., and expressing their approval of the Superiors in so far as truth permits.
122 6 They never reveal to the poor whom they direct, however trustworthy they may be, the secrets and rules of the community, and in their trials and troubles never unburden their hearts to them.
123 7 They show great affability, candor, respect, and affection towards one another. They avoid, on one hand, that haughty, reserved or distant air incompatible with true charity; and on the other, all immoderate familiarity, bantering and childish conduct, which breeds contempt.
124 8 They excuse one another when they are at fault, and uphold and defend one another against rumors, detraction, calumnies and persecution.
125 9 They avoid all duplicity, and their mutual relations are characterized by great candor and openness of heart.
126 10 They charitably point out to one another their faults in private, and they take the proffered correction in good part.
127 11 They avoid using haughty and arrogant words, shouting, making odious comparisons and a host of other defects which violate charity, or at least impair it.
128 12 They endeavor to be both kind and firm towards the poor. They are charitable, bearing with them and excusing them in their frailties, ignorance, defects of body and mind, and even in their sins. They are, likewise, firm, punishing them without fear of what people may say for their wrongdoings, pride and stubbornness, for their disobedience to the regulations and the Superiors, particularly when these faults are public and give scandal. If they let such faults go unpunished in individual persons, their charity will degenerate into blameworthy connivance, thus destroying law and order in the community and giving occasion to the wicked to commit the same faults or worse. Oh, how difficult it is to find the happy mean between kindly charity and strict firmness, and yet, how necessary it is to find it if one is to govern the poor and the young well. If those who govern are too indulgent and are content with merely warning the offenders instead of applying a prudent chastisement, they increase the evil by weak compromise; on the other hand, if they are too severe, chastising with rigor, they will aggravate the evil. Therefore, in schools and hospitals, they ordinarily mingle oil with vine-

gar, reward with chastisement, in such a way that the oil of pardon always rises above the vinegar of punishment.

129 13 They render the poor every service within their power, both spiritual and corporal, becoming all things to all men[11] and even to the least among them, convinced that the first among themselves is not the richest, the most exalted and the wisest, but the one who believes and places herself the last of all.

130 14 Should a Sister so forget herself as to address harsh, disdainful or reproachful words to another Sister, she should ask pardon on her knees and kiss the floor. The offended Sister shall do likewise through humility, sealing their reconciliation with a few cordial words. This shall be done in the presence of the Superior and never in her absence.

131 15 They give their Superior the simple title of Mother and the two Sisters who replace her, Mother Assistants; they call each other Sister, treating one another with honor and respect and bowing as they pass one another.

132 16 They carefully avoid all singularity, that is, they do nothing in public that is out of the ordinary, purposely, or under the pretext of greater perfection.

Their Prayers and Meditations

133 1 Every morning from four-thirty until five-thirty and every evening from five-thirty until six, they meditate; they recite the holy Rosary every day in its entirety. When they are in community, they chant it in two choirs at three different times; when absent on some work of charity, they say it whenever they can, but never omit it.

134 2 Each week they make at least an hour of adoration of the Blessed Sacrament; each month they make a retreat of one day; and every year a retreat of ten days.

Counsels

135 1 Beware of giving up meditation because of distractions, worries and cares, or because you feel you are doing nothing, or you are too ignorant, or it is not your calling, or that your vocation is manual work and action and not contemplation and meditation. These are temptations of the evil spirit.

136 2 When you pray, nourish your soul as much as possible on pure faith, without depending on visible and exterior things. Spiritual consolations are to be esteemed, but do not think highly of yourself when you have made them, and, on the other hand, do not think everything is lost when you no longer enjoy them.

137 3 Beware of over-activity in your meditations, not giving enough place to the action of God, who works only where peace reigns.

138 4 To do all your work in the presence of God and for Him alone is to pray without ceasing. Do not fail to say daily the entire Rosary to honor the life, death and passion and glory of Jesus and Mary.

Their Devotion to the Blessed Virgin

139 1 They look upon the Blessed Virgin as the Superior and Mother of the whole Congregation. To honor her, they recite the holy Rosary daily; they feed a poor person every day; they fast, in so far as their health permits, one day a week, ordinarily on Saturday.

140 2 When they have time, they recite the Little Office in her honor.

141 3 They strive to imitate all her virtues, particularly her charity, humility, purity, fidelity and modesty.

142 4 They often speak of her great dignity and her compassion, and they defend devotion to her against freethinkers, critics, and heretics.

143 5 When the clock strikes the hour, they say a Hail Mary in her honor.

144 6 Their devotion to the Blessed Virgin is interior, without hypocrisy; exterior without criticism; tender without distrust; constant without fickleness; and holy without presumption. They are not of those devotees: 1) who are scrupulous and fear to dishonor the Son in honoring the mother: 2) who are critical, finding fault with exterior and well-grounded practices of devotion to the Blessed Virgin; 3) who are inconstant, being devoted to her only for a time; 4) who are presumptuous, joining sin with devotion to the Blessed Virgin, dishonoring and crucifying the Son under the mantle of the Mother.

Reception of the Sacraments

145 1 They go to confession regularly every week to the confessor chosen by the community.

146 2 With the permission of the Superior, however, they may go to confession to another confessor, when necessity requires.

147 3 They are not bound to receive Holy Communion on any specified days; however, they communicate as often as possible, according to their own desires and the advice of their Director and their Superior.

148 4 They do not withdraw themselves from the community to pursue other devotions, but make every effort to assist at Mass and receive Holy Communion with the community.

149 5 They never fail to make at least a half hour of thanksgiving after Holy Communion unless a real necessity compels them to

leave God for God.

150 6 Though their Director may permit them to receive Holy Communion, they do not do so without their Superior's permission, which they ask kneeling. On the eve of the important feasts of the year, which are general Communion days, they kneel to ask this permission of the Superior, who may accord or refuse it as she sees fit.

151 7 They never criticize one another or anyone else with regard to the reception of Holy Communion, and are never jealous of their Sisters who receive Holy Communion more frequently.

Counsels

152 1 Never be so attached to Holy Communion that the refusal of your Superior troubles and vexes you; for an act of obedience is of more value than Holy Communion.

153 2 Never fail to ask your Director and your Superior for permission to receive Holy Communion when you feel the desire, even though you may have been refused several times. Often it is pride which fears a refusal and is the cause of reluctance to ask.

154 3 Be careful to receive Communion through routine, human respect, self-love, vanity or a spirit of singularity.

155 4 Do not receive Communion to enjoy the spiritual consolations that accompany this divine action, but to sacrifice all things to Jesus crucified and annihilated.

156 5 If, before or after holy Communion, some thought troubles or disturbs you, reject it promptly, for the devil is its instigator, and not the Holy Spirit, who is the author of peace.

157 6 Never carry out immediately, without the advice of your Director, the good inspirations that God gives you in Holy Communion. As experience proves daily, the illusions of the evil spirit are to be feared as much in Holy Communion as in other spiritual actions.

158 7 Always try to receive Communion in union with the Blessed Virgin, renouncing your own dispositions and adopting those of the Blessed Virgin, even though they are unknown to you. Thus, in spirit and in truth, Jesus will once more repose in her virginal bosom.

159 8 Guard yourself against scruples in Confession and Communion. Self-will, attachment to one's judgment and secret pride engender and increase scruples. Blind obedience on the other hand, is the only way to overcome them.

160 9 When preparing for confession, strive more to rouse yourself to contrition than to recall all your sins, and when receiving holy Communion, take more pleasure in self-abhorrence and self-annihilation than in interior consolations, spiritual enlightenment and a feeling of tranquility.

Their Manual Work

161 1 They do different kinds of manual work when the Rule prescribes no other exercise.
162 2 They receive their piecework from the Sisters in charge, and return it to them, without asking to whom it belongs and how much is being paid for it.
163 3 They never become totally absorbed in their work but only, as it were, lend themselves to it, avoiding haste, curiosity, vanity, and worldliness. For this reason, they do not make articles of a worldly nature, invented by fashion only to satisfy vanity and pride. They never work outside the house.

Counsels

164 1 While working, beware of haste and undue attachment to what you are doing; likewise, avoid vanity and self-complacency, when the work is completed.
165 2 Take care not to work like the people of the world, who are motivated by self-interest, pleasure and honors, but work rather through a spirit of penance and charity.
166 3 Choose the work for which you feel the least natural inclination, and when the devil tempts you to hurry, stop working for a time.
167 4 Take care never to use for meditation the time assigned for work.

Their Mortification

168 1 No exterior mortification is required by the Rule. All mortifications such as the discipline, the hair shirt, the pointed cincture, etc., are entirely voluntary and are used under the guidance of the Director and the Superior.
169 2 However, when they are in good health, they fast on Saturday and abstain from meat on Wednesday.
170 3 They courageously apply themselves to the mortification of their senses and faculties, mortifying their eyes, sense of smell and taste, their faculties of mind and will, etc., in their inordinate and useless affections.
171 4 Every week during the novitiate the novices render an account of their interior life to the Mistress of Novices. Each month the professed Sisters render a like account to the Director or Mother Superior.

God alone

Counsels

172 1 Beware of thinking that bodily mortification is not necessary to acquire Wisdom, for Wisdom is never found in those who live a life of ease and who gratify their senses.
173 2 Be convinced that you will make progress in virtue only insofar as you do violence to yourself by doing or enduring that which goes against your natural inclinations.
174 3 Do not neglect little mortifications, which are often more meritorious than great ones and are less apt to give rise to vanity.
175 4 Mortify your eyes and you will be modest; mortify your ears and you will be charitable; mortify your senses of smell and taste and you will be temperate; mortify your tongue and you will be wise; finally, mortify your sense of touch and you will be chaste.
176 5 Mortify:

1 a certain natural activity that inclines you to hurry and to accomplish much;

2 changing moods that rule you and displease your neighbor;

3 your tongue, which always wishes to talk, laugh, mock, etc.;

4 a tendency to lack religious modesty in your bearing, which makes you act like a child, laugh like a fool, jump around like a juggler, and eat and drink like an animal.

177 6 Carefully avoid excess and indiscretion in the practice of mortification, due to lack of obedience, and also tepidity through lack of mortification.
178 7 Be assured that the smallest mortification made for God, for example, to repress useless words and glances or to check a movement of anger or impatience, etc., is a greater victory than to conquer the universe and a greater action than to create a world; so say the saints.
179 8 Above all, apply yourself to the mortification of your self-will by submitting to obedience in all instances for the love of God.

Their Meals

180 1 In schools, hospitals or other houses to which they are assigned, they have dinner and supper at an appropriate time, after the poor have eaten or school is dismissed, that is ordinarily between eleven and twelve o'clock; in the community they always dine at eleven thirty.
181 2 They eat any kind of food whatsoever, as Divine Providence, their Mother, provides. Their love of mortification will inspire them to deprive themselves during their meals of what is naturally most pleasing to them.

182 3 They never eat outside the community nor between meals without real necessity and only with explicit permission. This will happen rarely.
183 4 They listen attentively to the reading at table without talking or looking around. When they need something, they ask the one who serves by sign or in a low voice, observing all the rules of religious modesty which are given further on.
184 5 They avoid singularity when they eat in community, either by asking for a particular dish or specially prepared food, or by refusing every dish provided. They may, however, let some dish pass if they can do so without this being too noticeable.
185 6 If a dish is not to their liking or not well prepared, they show no dissatisfaction by word, look or sign, either at table or afterwards during recreation; if they are not mortified enough to eat food that is not to their taste, at least they do not complain about it.
186 7 All those who read well take their turn in reading at table, and each in turn, even the Superior, waits on table.

Counsels

187 1 When you go for your meals, deplore the fact that because of your lower nature you are obliged to partake of food as the animals do. In order not to resemble them altogether, renounce the sense of pleasure that nature necessarily finds in eating, and raise your heart to Jesus Christ to unite your meals with his.
188 2 Never, like the people of the world, speak of what was served at table, whether it pleased your taste or not. Never say at recreation,"Oh, but that food was good. How I enjoyed this or that! It gave me an appetite," etc.
189 3 Take care not to look with greediness and envy at the portions of those near you to see how they compare with yours.
190 4 In spirit, dip the first morsel you eat in the blood of Jesus Christ, and unite with the Bread of angels, Jesus Christ, whom you received in your last Communion.
191 5 Beware of a fault common to people living in community, that is, saying grace before and after meals without attention or devotion, simply through routine, thinking sometimes of what they have eaten, or what they have to do after the meal, picking their teeth, and sometimes standing in an undignified manner.

Their Recreation

192 1 They have two hours of recreation a day, the first after dinner and the second after supper, during which they converse with freedom, gaiety, and as religious persons.

193 2 They take recreation with freedom and merriment, but at the same time observing religious modesty, avoiding immoderate laughter, childish amusements and unseemly postures. On the other hand, they also avoid a too severe or scrupulous reserve; somber, dreamy and melancholy airs; a singular and critical spirit; and a haughty and proud demeanor.
194 3 They take recreation in all holiness, having no other intention than to take their rest piously in God, and as God did when he created the world,[12] or as Jesus Christ did when he rested at the well of Jacob[13] or as the saints did who performed this action with holy motives. At times they perform this exercise through a motive of charity, in order to gladden their Sisters and to become more capable of serving the poor and aiding their neighbor; at other times they take humility as their motive, acknowledging that they are weak and have need of some relaxation; finally, they take recreation to encourage their neighbor in the joyful practice of virtue in a life which otherwise might seem too austere.
195 4 During recreation, more than at any other time, they carefully avoid offending charity by mockery, reproaches, open suspicion, criticism, scornful gestures, harsh words, etc.
196 5 They should ordinarily speak only of God and the things of God, and never of the world, its news and vanities.
197 6 They spend their recreation in common and remain together, unless excused by necessity or permission. They avoid particular friendships, never seeking to converse more often with one than with another.

Counsels

198 1 Before recreation, as before meals, renounce all natural satisfaction and raise your heart to God.
199 2 Do not hesitate to enjoy yourselves quietly and give joy to your Sisters, who are the children of God your Father. Remember that He has charged you with making them happy during recreation in order that they may be more capable of doing His work.
200 3 Should one of your Sisters cause you sorrow, bear it in silence. If she disagrees with you, give in, and you will have gained the victory.
201 4 From time to time during recreation raise your heart to God.

Their Faith

202 1 As faith is the foundation of all religion, so is it the basis of all wisdom and perfection; hence faith, the daily bread of the Daughters of Wisdom, is the motivating force of all their thoughts, words and actions.

203 2 They perform all their actions for the greater glory of God in union with Jesus and Mary; in longer actions they renew this intention from time to time.
204 3 They strive to banish from their actions all vanity, sensuality, human respect, passion, natural motives, and routine, and seek instead to act from a motive of faith, which animates and sustains them, so that should anyone ask why they perform a certain action, they would be able to answer truthfully: it is for God alone, through such and such a Christian motive.
205 4 In their doubts they do not turn to human wisdom, custom, interested friends or relatives, but rather to the holy gospel and their Rule, as explained by their Director.
206 5 They do not desire visions, revelations or extraordinary lights since faith alone is sufficient for them; should God, however, favor them with such graces, they should reveal them to their Director, placing no reliance whatever on them, for fear of illusions which generally creep in when there is question of extraordinary occurrences.
207 6 They pray to God in the words of the Apostles, "Lord, increase our faith";[14] or they use the prayer of clients of the Blessed Virgin, "Virgin most faithful, pray for us"; or that of the Church, "I believe."

Their Humility

208 1 They attribute to themselves only sin and wretchedness, placing no trust in their own thoughts or will, their own actions or plans; they renounce, even in their best actions, their evil nature which spoils everything.
209 2 In spite of the promptings of self-love, they believe others to be better than themselves, even though, through want of enlightenment, they do not clearly perceive the good qualities of others.
210 3 They banish all pride and vanity from their thoughts and words, never reflecting consciously on their virtues and good works, and never speaking either well or ill of themselves.
211 4 They do not respond to praises, deserved or undeserved, which may be given them, but in their hearts they humble themselves before God, allowing those who praise them to interpret their silence as they wish.
212 5 Wherever they are, they always choose the last place, particularly in the company of those who are not of the Community. At table they take the last place, which is ordinarily nearest the door, and are never the first to express their opinion in a conversation. When there are three together, they avoid the middle place, which is the most honorable; in the street, they take the place nearest the road. When they enter a church, they remain in the rear.

213 6 However, among themselves, a cordial simplicity should prevail over exterior humility, inducing them to take the nearest place and avoid all worldly formalities.
214 7 They willingly choose the most menial and undesired occupations.
215 8 When they are accused unjustly, they do not try to defend themselves, and they never dispute with anyone.

Their Modesty[15]

216 1 They comport themselves, in private as well as in public, without affectation or hypocrisy, in such a way as to please God and edify their neighbor.
217 2 As modesty is, according to the saints, a God-like quality, a reflection of the Holy Spirit and a veritable treasure before God,[16] the Sisters practice this virtue in all their bodily movements and make a very special study of it.

Their Modesty of Face and Eyes

218 1 Ordinarily they hold their head erect; they avoid lifting or lowering it too much, tilting it to one side or the other, holding it up with the hands, shaking it at every word, and turning it from side to side on the slightest pretext.
219 2 They do not stare at anyone nor permit their eyes to wander but keep them slightly lowered, and their movements are neither too frequent nor too abrupt. Their gaze is meek, humble and respectful, never rude, contemptuous, bold or sullen.
220 3 They avoid holding the mouth open, tightening the lips too much, blowing the nose or expectorating in an offensive manner, or yawning in front of anyone.
221 4 They avoid wrinkling their forehead, frowning, biting their nails, cleaning their nose or ears with their fingers.
222 5 They refrain from all outburst of laughter or laughing too frequently; but at the same time they are not sad, gloomy, overserious or too solemn.
223 6 They are careful not to make grimaces or assume affected airs and they avoid anything that might denote artificiality or dissimulation. They try to cultivate an expression that is joyful, serene, open, tranquil, unaffected and unrestrained, and so give an impression of goodness, meekness and piety, which tends to win hearts and lead them to God.

Their Modesty in Posture

224 1 As a general rule, they stand erect, not stooping or leaning

to one side, without, however, showing constraint or affectation.
225 2 When standing they do not shift from one foot to the other, changing at every moment their position and their posture, which denotes, according to the saints, a certain fickleness.[17]
226 3 They do not place their hands on their hips or behind their backs, nor do they touch the face or other part of the body without necessity.
227 4 They refrain from stretching out their arms and legs in a careless and lazy manner, which denotes a negligent and indolent nature.
228 5 They do not lean on their elbows or against anything, neither do they bend over in an unseemly manner nor cross their feet or legs.

Their Modesty in Speech

229 1 They speak neither too much nor too little. They avoid, on one hand, being so loquacious and tedious as never to give others the chance to speak, and on the other, being so taciturn by their misplaced silence that they become ordinarily burdensome in any conversation.
230 2 They never interrupt those who are speaking, nor do they anticipate with a hurried answer those who wish to question them.
231 3 They regulate the tone of their voice in such a manner that it will be neither too loud nor too low, unduly harsh nor affectedly mild, rude nor effeminate, boorish nor languid; they do not use an authoritative, imperious, contemptuous or passionate tone of voice.
232 4 They avoid words savoring of falsehood, mockery, contempt, clownishness, flattery, vanity and anything that could offend decorum or charity.
233 5 They are reluctant to be the first to express an opinion on any subject, as if they were more capable of judging than others, and when, upon request, they do give an opinion, it is always with simplicity; should the question seem doubtful, they do not speak in too decisive and bold a manner.
234 6 They avoid all kinds of arguments and disputes; they prefer to gain the victory by yielding, as if they had been mistaken, rather than by contesting with passion and pride.
235 7 Finally, they weigh all their words before speaking.

(Modesty in the wearing of the habit has been discussed.)

Their Modesty in Walking

236 1 They do not walk too quickly or with great haste, never running except in case of necessity. In accordance with this rule,

when going up or down the stairs, they do not take more than one step at a time.

237 2 They do not walk too slowly, dragging their feet or lifting them carelessly.

238 3 They avoid walking with an affectedly springy step, or at a calculated and studied pace.

239 4 While walking, they avoid all unnecessary movements of the head, hands, arms, shoulders and body, a fault which the saints condemn as levity.

240 5 When they are obliged to make visits to town, they avoid talking too loudly, laughing boisterously, dallying, and acting unbecomingly, looking curiously into shop windows, vehicles, and other places, and stopping on street corners to read the posters or to see masquerades or listen to charlatans; finally, as much as possible, they avoid fairs, public squares, and all other places where vanity reigns and where Jesus Christ is not ordinarily found.

Their Modesty in Church

241 1 They go to church properly dressed, that is, wearing their mantle, their heads modestly covered.

242 2 When they enter a church, they comport themselves piously and religiously, taking holy water as they go in and kneeling ordinarily at the back of the church out of humility.

243 3 When passing before the Blessed Sacrament, they make a genuflection, whereas before another altar or an image of a saint, they make only a moderate bow.

244 4 They never pass through a church to shorten their way; they talk in church only when necessary and then in few words and in a low voice; they also observe this rule in the sacristy, which is part of the church.

245 5 In church they are particularly careful to control their eyes, countenance and posture, but in so doing they avoid all unnatural and unbecoming attitudes and extraordinary gestures or movements of the body. They ordinarily assist at Holy Mass kneeling, their eyes modestly lowered or fixed on the altar, their hands crossed on their breast under their mantle; they may either sit or stand during the sermon. When weakness or weariness does not allow them to kneel, they simply sit down.

Domestic Enclosure

246 1 Although they cannot observe strict enclosure as in monasteries since they are obliged by their charitable duties to work outside their houses, they must nevertheless maintain a kind of personal enclosure, which is all the more difficult as they are surrounded

by the world and in daily contact with people.

247 2 No matter where they live, the Sisters have their own cells, and their quarters have no communication with those of outsiders, not even with those of the poor of hospitals or school children.

248 3 As mentioned above, no outsiders, whether men or women, are admitted to the Sisters' quarters without absolute necessity and explicit permission.

249 4 When they receive visitors, the Sisters leave their apartments to speak to them in a room set aside for this purpose on a lower floor. They may, however, through love of enclosure and with the Superior's permission, refuse to go to the parlor.

250 5 Before going to the parlor, they say the "Come, Holy Spirit" and a Hail Mary in the public oratory or chapel. They then converse with the visitors politely, prudently and briefly, and always take the initiative in shortening the meeting.

251 6 They never go to the parlor or walk in the streets without their mantle, which covers them as with a shroud.

252 7 They neither receive nor write letters without the permission of their Superior; they submit to her all their correspondence.

253 8 Upon returning from town or from the parlor, they spend a few moments of recollection in the oratory or chapel.

The Chapter of Faults

254 1 The Chapter of Faults is held every week on the day that is most convenient, namely, Sunday or a feast day.

255 2 As soon as the Sisters hear the bell, they go promptly to the room assigned, kneel, say the customary prayers, and on the Superior's signal take their places, after kissing the floor.

256 3 The object of this exercise, which is common to all well-regulated Communities, is to make the spirit humble and to mortify the flesh by acknowledging one's faults anew.

257 4 They never confess faults that are purely interior, but only those committed in the presence of the Sisters.

258 5 They accuse themselves simply and briefly; sincerely, hiding nothing; humbly, not excusing themselves; charitably, not accusing others nor revealing their faults.

259 6 When they are accused by the Superior of exterior faults of which they are not guilty, they do not excuse themselves in public but receive the penance with humility. With all the more reason shall they remain silent when scolded or reprimanded for faults they have really committed. If, however, the Superior tells them to speak or questions them, they answer with simplicity.

260 7 The Sisters accusing themselves of their faults kneel in a determined place, with downcast eyes and hands joined. After listening to the admonition and receiving the penance from the Mother

Superior, they kiss the floor and, on a signal from her, return to their places.

261 8 The Sisters will have a higher opinion of and greater esteem for a religious who accuses herself with simplicity, even when her faults are serious; for though the Sisters never doubted that she was a sinner, they know now by her confession that she is humble, that she esteems humiliation, and that she has made amends for her faults by her humility.

262 9 Those Sisters who by reason of their charge are obliged to violate some points of the Rule, such as silence, do not accuse themselves of those faults, as they could not have done otherwise.

263 10 They never speak outside the Chapter of what has occurred therein. This secrecy is so binding that it resembles somewhat that of Confession; therefore, they may not break it without sinning.

264 11 Every evening, at night prayer, they may accuse themselves of faults committed in public during the day.

Various Offices

265 With the Sisters of Wisdom, as in all other well-regulated Communities, there are several offices which are given to Sisters by the Superior and from which they receive their title. Among these are 1) the infirmarian, 2) the sacristan, 3) the sister supervisor, 4) the time-keeper, 5) the cook, 6) the bursar, as well as Mother Superior and her two counselors. Each of these offices has its own particular rules which are only made known to them when obedience gives them that duty.

Daily Time-table

266 1 They rise in all seasons at four o'clock and have half an hour to dress, make their bed and put their room in order.

267 2 From half-past four till half-past five they make an hour's meditation; from half-past five till six, they chant the first Rosary, standing.[18]

268 3 They are careful to observe the rules of silence and modesty as they go into holy Mass; on returning, if they wish to take breakfast, they take it in silence.

269 4 After breakfast, each one applies herself until 11:30 to the work and charge marked out for her by obedience.

270 5 At a quarter-past-eleven they make the particular examen for fifteen minutes; they then take their dinner, observing the rules of silence and religious modesty.

271 6 After this meal they take recreation till one o'clock.

272 7 At one o'clock sharp, they chant the second Rosary as they did the first and return to work until 5:30.

273 8 At 5:30, they make a half-hour's meditation, after which the third Rosary is chanted as the others; they then go to supper.
274 9 After supper they take recreation till eight o'clock; then follows night prayers, the reading of the subject of meditation or an instruction until 8:30; they are in bed by nine o'clock at the latest.

Rules for the Schoolmistresses

275 1 They must be capable of reading and writing well and of teaching catechism. It would be useful if they were proficient in arithmetic.
276 2 They are to begin school at eight o'clock in the morning and continue till ten o'clock. They re-start at two o'clock and continue till four, except on Thursday which is a free day. They take the children to Mass every day at ten o'clock and they have them say the Rosary at four o'clock in the afternoon.
277 3 If they live in community, they leave the house every morning a little before eight o'clock and return for lunch after having assisted at holy Mass with the children. In the afternoon, they go to school after having chanted the Rosary, i.e. at about half-past one and return to the community at half-past four, after the children have said the Rosary.
278 4 If they conduct school in a town or country parish at a distance from the community, they perform their religious duties in the place where they are, just as if they were in community.
279 5 When they conduct their school in a town or country parish they close the school from the day after the Assumption of the Blessed Virgin to the day after the feast of St. Matthew. During this month's interval they are called by their Superior into the community to give an account of the year and to make a ten-day retreat to recoup their strength in order to work better.
280 6 This holiday period is chosen because in the country districts it is harvest time and the children are given work by their parents and so the rest period for the Sisters fits in with the circumstances of the place where they work.

Rules to be observed in the Charity Schools of the Daughters of Wisdom

281 1 The purpose of the schools of charity is to instruct and promote their spiritual welfare, a task performed out of pure charity with no self-seeking, but only for the greater glory of God, the salvation of souls and one's own spiritual progress.
282 2 To attain this noble end it is absolutely necessary that order and silence be well observed, for their absence could become a

source of sin both to pupils and mistresses.
283 3 For the sake of order that is pleasing to God, rules must be laid down 1) concerning the teachers who are conducting the school, 2) the children being taught there, 3) the time spent there, 4) the places where classes are held, 5) the study and spiritual exercises customary there, 6) the rewards to be given, 7) the punishments to be meted out.
284 4 The schoolmistresses should be capable of doing this good work, and should have made religious profession in their Community.
285 5 Girls only, whether they be rich or poor, up to the age of twenty and who are well-behaved and docile, are accepted into these schools. The following are not accepted: 1) boys; 2) married women and widows; girls of ill-fame or who are intractable or too young to be teachable.
286 6 The Sisters conduct the schools out of pure charity, neither asking nor receiving directly or indirectly anything from the children. If, however, a child or parent, out of gratitude and without being solicited, makes a contribution the Sisters may not accept it themselves but direct the donors to give it to the superior of the Daughters of Wisdom to be used for the upkeep of the community.
287 7 The children, after having breakfasted at home, must arrive promptly at eight o'clock at school. At ten o'clock they go to attend holy Mass. They come to school on all weekdays, except Thursday which is a free day.
288 8 The room where the class is held should be oblong in shape. The chair of the mistress is placed at one end and above her on the wall a list of the pupils is displayed. Nine benches are placed in the schoolroom and their size should conform to the shape of the room and the number of children, four at one side, four at the other and one at the base. The first is called the bench of the Seraphim and the children who have made their first Communion are placed in it. The second is that of the Cherubim and is occupied by those who, by age and good behavior, are preparing for their first Holy Communion. The third, that of the Thrones, contains those aged thirteen, fourteen, etc., who have not yet received Holy Communion and are judged not mature enough to warrant immediate preparation. The fourth bench is that of the Dominations and children twelve years old are placed in it. The fifth, that of the Virtues, is occupied by children eleven years old. The sixth, that of the Powers, seats the ten-year-olds. The seventh, that of the Principalities, seats the nine-year-olds. The eighth, that of the Archangels, seats the eight-year-olds. The ninth, that of the Angels, is occupied by the young seven-year-olds.
289 The whole school is divided into four classes when no second school exists for the very young. The first is called "Reading";

the second is called "Assembling the Letters"; the third is called "Naming the Letters"; and the fourth the "A B C." If any child aged ten or under is clever enough to be placed in the first class among the Seraphim, Cherubim and Thrones, he/she should be placed there, for knowledge must be considered more important than age.

When there are two separate rooms in the school, those who are learning to read and write fluently are placed in the first and those who are only learning to recognize, name and assemble letters are placed in the second.

290 The children learn to read and write for an hour and a half in the morning and an hour and a half in the afternoon. The other two hours are spent teaching them their prayers and catechism, attending Mass in the morning and saying the Rosary in the evening. All this amounts to five hours a day.

291 The children are admitted into the school building only when the bell is rung at eight o'clock and they must enter in an orderly manner, two by two and in silence. As they enter they take holy water, saying aloud, *Deo gratias,* and then go to kneel down each in her place, remaining there in silence with hands joined until the schoolmistress begins the morning prayer. When all are assembled the Sister intones the hymn:

"O Holy Spirit enlighten us.
Come, inflame each one of us.
Rule us, inspire our prayers.
For we can do nothing without you."

She then gives a signal for the children to stand and a second signal for them to bow to Jesus and Mary, and a third for them to sit down with their hands joined.

292 The Sister begins the prayers by inviting the children to make the sign of the cross twice to remind them of the presence of God. They then recite the following prayers:

1 My God, I firmly believe that you are here present. I adore you and acknowledge you as my sovereign Lord and Master upon whom alone I depend.

2 My God, I believe all that the Holy, Roman Catholic and Apostolic Church believes and teaches because you have said it and your word is always true.

3 My God, I trust in the assistance of your grace to obtain salvation through the merits of Jesus Christ, my Savior.

4 My God and my all, I love you above all things and for your sake. I also love my neighbor as myself out of love for you.

5 My God, I am heartily sorry for having offended you because you are infinitely good and infinitely lovable and because sin displeases you. I firmly resolve with your grace never to offend you

again. I would prefer to die at this moment rather than commit a single mortal sin.

6 Infant Jesus, we offer you this our school day and with your holy Mother please bestow your blessings upon it.

7 Holy Guardian Angels, we greet you and pray that you protect us in this school. Preserve us from the devil's influence and may no harm come to us.

The Election of the Superior and her two Assistants

293 1 All the community, after having made a novena of Communions and fasted for three days to request the help of the Holy Spirit, proceed to elect the Superior in the following manner:
294 2 The person being considered for superiorship should possess the following qualities: she should be outstandingly mature and prudent, poor in spirit, detached from the world and family, dead to self, exact in observing silence and other rules, a lover of recollection, most desirous of receiving Holy Communion, advanced in prayer and mortification, most charitable though generally firm, and so present a shining example of virtue. She is therefore not to be chosen because of wealth or nobility.
295 3 Three Sisters, noted for these virtues and qualities, are presented for election. On the morning of Saturday, the Eve of Pentecost, the *Veni Creator* is sung and the Sisters advance in line to vote secretly for the one who in their eyes is the most worthy to be God's representative. This is done by placing a tiny pea in the box which bears the name of the one they are choosing.
296 4 The one who receives the most votes is elected Superior. The one who comes next becomes the first assistant and the one who has least votes becomes second assistant.
297 5 The elected Superior remains for 33 days without exercising her functions in order to make herself more docile and obedient than ever before. She therefore considers herself the last of the community and performs the most menial work as, for example, serving at table, sweeping the floor, kissing the feet of others, etc. She should perform these offices with joy and in obedience to the former Superior. She assumes the reins of the government of the community in the following manner:
298 6 The Sisters assemble in Chapter and the former Superior invites the new Superior to kneel down before her and, in the presence of the others who are seated around, puts first this question to her: "My dear Sister, what do you wish to do in this community?" She answers in one word, "Obey." A second question is then put to her, "What place do you want to occupy?" She answers, "The last."

Then the former Superior tells her she must obey God alone and that the Holy Spirit when choosing her as Superior wishes her to govern the others and occupy His place in the community. Then the outgoing Superior kneels down and before all the Sisters asks pardon for all the faults she has committed and the bad example she has given.

The new Superior then makes the sign of the cross, saying aloud, "Our help is in the name of the Lord," and takes the place of the outgoing Superior. The latter then kneels before her and says to her, "I firmly believe that you hold the place of God among us and therefore I submit to all your commands out of love for God, and I trust, with the help of his grace, to remain faithful to them." To this, the Sisters on their knees answer "Amen." They then advance one by one to kiss the feet of the new Superior, who begins her office by a gesture of love embracing each Sister with warm affection. The *Te Deum* and the *Magnificat* are then sung.

299 7 The Superior General may hold the office for life. However, every three years she must be confirmed by a general assembly and if she is considered by a majority of the community not to have done her duty, the assembly will proceed to elect another.

300 8 When the Mother General is absent, the first assistant takes her place, and the second assistant in turn replaces the first.

For the guidance of the Superior:

Special Rules of Prudence and Charity which the Superior should Observe

301 1 She should become a model of all virtue, especially of humility and the spirit of recollection, which are the virtues most difficult for a Superior to practice although in her efforts she will be helped by the Holy Spirit. Consequently, she should meditate every day upon the following two directives of Wisdom:

1 Humble yourselves in the measure that you are exalted, and if you are made Superior in a house, be as humble as those placed under you (cf. Sir. 3:20);

2 Martha, Martha, you are troubled about many things. There is only one thing necessary (Lk. 10:42).

302 2 She should not introduce anything new and of consequence without asking advice from the spiritual director and her two Assistants. If she is of different opinion from them, she should decide to follow their opinion. By so doing, she will act humbly and therefore wisely and prudently, for God gives his grace to those who are humble and who, in spite of their own lights, submit their judgment to others in peace and obedience even when their own judgment would seem to be the right one, and God will receive glory and honor from this submission. However, she listens to her two Assistants in such a way that she makes her decision privately and in their absence, after having had recourse to God in prayer.

303 3 She should endeavor to foster love more than fear and so govern with the golden rod of charity and not with the iron rod of fear. Love shown by the Superior opens wonderfully the hearts of the subordinates and inspires and strengthens them to do better. On the other hand, the spirit of fear created by harsh, repulsive, severe and high-handed attitudes on the part of the Superior causes the heart of the inferiors to close and makes them feel faint-hearted and depressed.

304 4 She should, as much as possible, keep an eye on all that goes on without appearing to do so. She lets it be seen that she has a deep desire to please them and a strong resolve to see them intent on well-doing. She must avoid therefore those domineering ways by which many Superiors govern, who, led by too great a desire to have the rules observed, go around probing into trivial matters, suspicious of all that is done by others, interpreting wrongly the smallest faults, reproving unwisely and severely delinquents who, at the time, are incapable of accepting in a fruitful manner the bitter medicine of correction, or imposing penances upon them which only dishearten them. This manner of governing may work with subjects who are cowed and servile and who can only be led by fear and force, but it will not accomplish any good in those who have voluntarily bound themselves and are guided by love.

305 5 This kindly approach should not prevent Superiors from being just and firm in reproving and correcting those at fault. But they must learn to distinguish faults due to weakness and ignorance from those arising from malice and stubbornness. The former, they should forgive easily and sometimes act as if they did not notice them; the latter they must correct most firmly but always blending gentleness with firmness letting it be seen that they are administering the correction against their will and only for the good of the community. If they say nothing or only put up a weak resistance when a Sister, throwing off restraints, deliberately commits a serious public fault against the rule, for example, by breaking silence or by open disobedience, she would then be guilty of culpable connivance and weakness and would have to answer to God for the transgression of the rules and for the laxity that could ensue.

306 6 If one of the Sisters should commit a public fault witnessed by the others and if the Superior believes this Sister possesses enough virtue to accept a public reprimand, she will administer it. If the defaulter, carried away by passion, is not in a mood to profit by a reprimand, the Superior will ask the community not to be scandalized, that things in due time will be put right. Then some time afterwards she will correct the Sister in question and will require her to perform a public act of penance as atonement for her public fault.

307 7 She will never publicly correct faults which have been committed in private and have therefore been an occasion of scandal to no one.

308 8 When speaking to the Sisters she must beware of being over-familiar, or of speaking insultingly to them, or publicly reproaching them concerning Communion, or of arguing with them or shouting at them. She must speak to them both in public and in private with all humility and charity. When she has a legitimate reason to reproach them she does it always in a courteous manner. If a Sister objects to being corrected, the Superior gives way for a time but afterwards reprimands her and imposes an act of penance.

309 9 When a Sister, or one of the poor of the hospital, or a schoolchild comes to her to complain about a Sister placed over them, she listens calmly and charitably but does not show approval and so imply condemnation of the Sister in question. On the contrary she strives to speak well of the Sister in the presence of the complainant even if actually the Sister was wrong. Later she will speak privately to this Sister to uncover the truth and settle the matter.

310 10 She must be on her guard against believing too readily unfavorable reports concerning her Sisters. She should suspend judgment and never openly condemn the accused person until she has learned the complete truth concerning the matter. She must be careful not to make public what happens in the community and she should require the same discretion of all her Sisters, correcting firmly those who gossip and do not control their tongues.

311 11 Here is something St. Francis de Sales says[19] which is worth remembering: “As the soul and the heart give assistance, movement and action to all the parts of the body, so the Superior should animate with her charity, care and example the whole of her community. She should inspire with her zeal all the Sisters over whom she is placed, see that the rules are as strictly observed as possible and foster mutual charity and a holy friendliness in the house. To attain this she should show warm, motherly affection equally to all her daughters so that they will turn to her with full confidence in all their doubts, difficulties, scruples, troubles and temptations.

312 “The Superior should do her best to observe faithfully the rules and constitutions without making herself in any way different from others, or claiming or receiving any advantages in clothing, food, etc., except when she would permit the same to other Sisters.

313 “When she commands her Sisters either individually or as a community she speaks seriously and with assurance but at the same time shows herself pleasant, gentle and humble, filled with love for them and desirous to help them as she commands them.

314 "She keeps an attentive eye on the little section of the Congregation over which she is placed so that the whole Community may show forth the peace, harmony, union and generosity of Jesus Christ himself. When every month the Sisters give an account to her of their souls, she may discreetly inquire about their spiritual life so as to be able afterwards to help and stimulate them, as well as correct and console them.

315 "She will show a special care for the needs of the sick and will often tend personally those who are seriously ill.

316 "She will support with tender love those Sisters who, like little children, are still weak in devotional practice, remembering what St. Bernard says to those who are called to save souls: "Robust souls do not require special care, but only those who are weak. For if anyone helps you more than you help him, acknowledge that you cannot be his superior but his equal. The just and the perfect do not need a superior and guide. They are themselves by the grace of God their own law and director and are capable of doing what is required of them without being commanded."

"The Superior, while giving particular attention to the weak and feeble, should not neglect the stronger ones, but help them to persevere and not become lukewarm. In short, she should see to the needs of the Sisters as required by sincere Christian love and not through any natural consideration, based upon the birth or parentage of the Sisters or their social status, their good looks or other attractive traits. She should not become too familiar with certain ones and so arouse envy in others.

317 "She should avoid correcting faults at the moment they are committed and in the presence of others but do so in private and with charity, unless the fault is such that for the edification of those who witnessed it, it requires a prompt expression of disapproval which she will show in such a way that, whilst condemning the fault, she shows consideration for the one at fault and thus, whilst striving to be justly feared, she becomes loved all the more.

318 "Let her not give permission easily for too frequent reception of the sacraments, i.e. above what is permitted by the Constitutions, for the Sisters, instead of being moved by love and reverence, may approach Holy Communion only to copy others, or through jealousy, self-love or vanity."

319 She should choose a good friend among her Sisters to advise her on her defects, one whom other Sisters can approach easily to tell of their complaints when they have not the courage to approach the Superior directly because of the respect they have for her. She should listen with satisfaction when she is thus being informed privately of her defects.

320 12 The Superior possesses the power to dispense from the rules in particular cases when prudence, charity and necessity require it

either because of sickness or because of the nature of the work; but she must never dispense any Sister for an indefinite period or for reasons based upon the status of the person.

Footnotes to the Original Rule of the Daughters of Wisdom

1 Montfort had crossed out "or of Providence."
2 Montfort here and in many places has erased "Providence" and written "Sagesse" (Wisdom) in its place.
3 Cf. Mt. 6:34.
4 Cf. Mt. 6:34.
5 Cf. Mt. 6:32.
6 Cf. Mt. 19:21.
7 Cf. Phil. 2:68.
8 Cf. Sir. 19:1.
9 FRANCIS DE SALES, *Rules of the Sisters of the Congregation of St. Augustine.*
10 Cf. Rom. 12:2.
11 Cf. 1 Cor. 9:22.
12 Cf. Gen. 2:2.
13 Cf. Jn. 4:6.
14 Cf. Lk. 17:5.
15 Cf. TRONSON, *Examens particuliers.* Most of this chapter on modesty is borrowed from Tronson.
16 Tronson attributes these words to SAINT AMBROSE, *De Officiis,* bk. 1, ch. 18.
17 Cf. Clement of Alexandria, quoted by Tronson who always justifies his teaching by references to the Fathers.
18 The manuscript shows that the time-table has been changed several times.
19 SAINT FRANCIS DE SALES, *Constitutions of the Religious Sisters of the Visitation,* ch. 29. This whole passage, from Nos. 311 to 318, is borrowed literally from St. Francis de Sales.

Sedes Sapientiae

13 Maxims and Lessons of Divine Wisdom

Introduction

Montfort inscribed on the "Cross of Wisdom" at Poitiers a concise program of the spiritual life. He enlarged upon this program for the benefit of the Daughters of Wisdom and wrote this small book of maxims and lessons which contains the same message as that given in chapter twelve of the "Love of the Eternal Wisdom," which is entitled "Principal Oracles of Divine Wisdom."

The original manuscript of this booklet has not been found but the text which is given here is an accurate rendition of the 1761 edition entitled, "Spiritual Instructions to the Daughters of Wisdom." At the beginning of pg. 47 of this book we find the following note: "Maxims and lessons of Divine Wisdom that Father de Montfort wrote for his Daughters with the recommendation that they conform their life to them if they sincerely wish to acquire the spirit of true Wisdom."

First Maxim

1 True happiness on earth consists in voluntary poverty and imitation of Me.

1 My daughter, guided by the judgment of your Superior, who stands in my place, you must forsake all your earthly possessions.

2 2 You must not be attached to anything created, however holy it is, whether interior or exterior, whether spiritual or corporal.

3 3 Be especially careful in matters where your human affections are involved.

4 4 Do not underestimate the danger of natural friendships, whether with your relatives or friends.

5 5 If, in order to carry your cross as I carried mine, you have to offend or displease them, do not be afraid of doing so.

6 6 Following my example, you must daily carry your cross of opposition, persecution, self-denial, scorn, etc.

7 7 Do not be ashamed of performing an act of virtue, whatever company you may be in, and never leave undone any good act through fear of scorn or even of praise, when you believe God wants it of you.

8 8 Prefer to give rather than receive, and prefer the loss of what is lawfully yours to the claiming of your rights.

Second Maxim

9 You are indeed blessed when the world opposes you and strives to thwart your plans, however good, misjudging your intentions, condemning your conduct, taking away your reputation and your worldly possessions.

10 1 My daughter, be careful not to complain to anyone but Me, when you are treated unkindly, and make no effort to justify yourself, especially if it is you alone who suffer.

11 2 Rather pray for those who bring you the good fortune of persecution.

12 3 Thank me for treating you as I was treated on earth since I myself was a sign of contradiction.

13 4 Do not let yourself be discouraged from doing any good work because of opposition; this is a sign of future victory. Any good work which is not marked with the sign of the cross has little value in my sight and will not endure.

14 5 Consider your persecutors as your best friends, for they can gain you great merit on earth and great glory in heaven.

15 6 Understand that the people to be pitied are the rich, those who live well, those who seek the company of high society, those who are money-makers, and all those who live in constant pursuit of enjoyment.

16 7 Never do anything, good or evil, out of human respect, to avoid criticism, insult, mockery or even praise.

17 8 Whenever you are responsible for some loss or when you fall into disfavor, do not worry about it. Be humbled before God and accept from Him the punishment for your failure.

Third Maxim

18 Detest your own soul and so lead it to life everlasting.

1 You must, then, my daughter, hate your own turn of mind by distrusting your thoughts, rejecting them if they are bad, danger-

ous, or frivolous, and submitting them to the judgment of your Superior if they are good.

19 2 Never rely on your own ideas, thoughts, knowledge, visions, contemplations, and do not set yourself up as the final judge of their value or harmfulness.

20 3 Believe that other people's judgment on unimportant matters is always more accurate and reliable than your own, however much you would like to believe the opposite.

21 4 Detest your imagination and your memory by putting away unpleasant imaginings and fanciful and useless schemes. Reject empty, dangerous or even useless thoughts of the past or of the future.

22 5 Free your memory of everything but the presence of God.

23 6 Be careful not to think deliberately of the harm you have suffered or of the good you have done.

24 7 Detest your own will by subjecting it to your Superiors and by renouncing it, even when you have the best intentions.

25 8 Do nothing of any importance without advice, so that later you will not regret having done it.

26 9 Do not harbor in your soul restless desires for things you do not possess, however useful to your neighbor or pleasing to My majesty.

27 10 Ask earnestly for special graces, but ask them only because I want you to, and let agreement with my will be at the heart of your request.

Fourth Maxim

28 Take up your cross daily and follow me.

1 Deny yourself, my daughter, all the pleasures of the senses, innocent though they be.

29 2 Mortify your sight by not looking at things which are harmful or arouse curiosity, and keep your glance modestly lowered.

30 3 Mortify your hearing by not listening to bad, empty or useless talk.

31 4 Mortify your tongue by speaking little, and then only of Me or of things that concern Me. If possible, do not speak of the good you have done, or of the weaknesses of your neighbor, or of any special qualities you may have.

32 5 Mortify your sense of taste by not eating between meals. Fast through obedience. Eat things you do not like. Take your meals with quiet restraint when healthy appetite or hunger urges you to take food.

33 6 Mortify your sense of smell. Do not use unnecessary scents and perfumes. Avoid smelling flowers, taking snuff, or using scented powder.

34 7 Mortify your hands by avoiding unnecessary and extravagant gestures. Keep your hands still or make few gestures when you are talking.

35 8 Mortify your feet by walking modestly and avoiding haste. Avoid visits or outings that are merely for pleasure. When you are standing, do not shift from one leg to the other. Do not cross your legs when sitting. When you are walking, do so simply and modestly, with easy restraint and without affectation.

36 9 Mortify your sense of touch by wearing rough clothes. Sleep on a hard bed and use instruments of penance as far as obedience to your Superior or your confessor allows.

37 10 Mortify your whole body by working in a spirit of penance and by accepting the hardships of the weather and the various ailments which affect your health.

Fifth Maxim

38 The way to heaven and the gate thereof are narrow; few there are who find the way and enter by that gate.

39 1 So, my daughter, wage unceasing war on your disposition and your moods, so that you may be among the few who find the way of life and who enter heaven by the narrow gate.

40 2 Be careful not to follow the majority or the ordinary run of men; these are among those who are lost.

41 3 Make no mistake, there are only two roads: one which leads to life, and is narrow; the other which leads to death and is wide. There is no middle way.

42 4 If your eye or your hand or your foot scandalizes you, cut it off without delay, lest it should cause your ruin. In other words, flee occasions of sin, even though they are as necessary to you as one of your limbs.

Sixth Maxim

43 Watch and pray without ceasing.

1 My daughter, you must apply yourself unceasingly to prayer, both vocal and mental.

44 2 Do everything you do in a spirit of prayer, that is, for the love of God and in his holy presence.

45 3 Never give up meditation, no matter what difficulty or dryness you experience in it.

46 4 Do not direct your heart to what is outside yourself for the kingdom of God is within you.

47 5 Value what is in your heart much more than anything that is exterior.

48 6 Unless you have a special call from God, do not burden

yourself with exterior or temporal matters, however charitable they seem, for the exterior exercise of charity has for some people been the cause of their losing the spirit of prayer and recollection.

49 7 Do believe that the greatest things on earth are done interiorly in the hearts of faithful souls.

50 8 Act through faith in everything you do, and let faith provide the food of your mental prayer and your rule of conduct.

Seventh Maxim

51 Love your enemies, do good to those who wrong you.

1 Pray, then, my daughter, for those who persecute you, insult you, or rob you of your good name or your possessions.

52 2 Do not do to others what you would not want them to do to you.

53 3 Bear with everybody's failings for the love of God, who bears with yours.

54 4 Reprove those who offend Me without fear of what they may do to you.

Eighth Maxim

55 I speak easily to simple people. I make known my secrets only to little ones.

56 1 So, my daughter, be as simple as a dove, without any bitterness, deceit or hypocrisy.

57 2 The higher the position you hold, the more you must practice humility, that is to say, become the servant of others, choosing the lowest place, the lowliest task, the poorest clothes.

58 3 As God gives his grace to the humble, do all your actions with great humility of heart; in this way you will obtain my grace and friendship.

59 4 Keep away from what men view as great, important and brilliant; such things are loathsome in my sight.

60 5 Love the life that is hidden, poor, and totally annihilated, for it is the object of my delight.

61 6 If you want to get to heaven, you must become as a little child, that is, you must be simple, innocent and gentle as a little child.

62 7 Those whom men consider the least and the servants of others are the first and the noblest in my sight, if they love their condition.

63 8 If, of your own strength, you raise yourself higher than is my will for you, you will be humbled further than you wish, both in this world and in the other. On the other hand, if you humble yourself more than others, I will raise you above others, even in this world.

Ninth Maxim

64 He who is faithful in little things will be faithful in greater things; he who is unfaithful in little things will be unfaithful also in greater things.

65 1 So, my daughter, be faithful to little points of the Rule, to small promptings of grace, and to little practices of virtue.

66 2 Neglect nothing that can help you to reach perfection.

67 3 If you are faithful in little things, I assure you that I shall set you over many things. In other words, if I see that you are corresponding faithfully to the few inspirations that you possess and to the slight fervor that you feel, I will give you an abundance of graces, inspirations, and other such favors.

68 4 Take care not to neglect small things, for you will gradually fall into laxity and tepidity, and little by little you will lose your spiritual insights, your piety, your merits and your graces.

Tenth Maxim

69 I choose what is meanest and lowliest to confound and destroy what is most exalted.

70 1 Despise yourself, my daughter, and be poor and humble, and I shall make something of you.

71 2 Give your coat to the thief who steals your cloak.

72 3 Turn the other cheek to those who strike you.

73 4 Endure everything without complaint.

74 5 Be first in accusing yourself and in taking blame.

75 6 Believe the best of others and the worst of yourself.

76 7 Choose the worst in everything.

77 8 Rejoice when you face all kinds of difficulties and opposition, and when you are deemed worthy of suffering something for Me.

78 9 Never lose hope or be troubled when you fall into sin, but be humbled and ask my forgiveness.

Eleventh Maxim

79 Beware of false prophets.

My daughter, you must strongly distrust:

1 The inspirations of your own mind, however spiritual you are;

80 2 The feelings of your own heart, even if they seem righteous and sincere;

81 3 The spiritual maxims of people who are lax;
82 4 Fine and lofty thoughts and holy plans inspired by the devil because this wicked and deceitful spirit, transformed into an angel of light, often deceives the most zealous and most spiritual people by his false light, and in this way brings about their downfall.
83 5 In order to recognize and avoid the subtle snares of self-love, of the flesh and of the devil, here are some important counsels which I give you:
84 1 Never consciously rely on your own powers, and even less on your ideas, fantasies and resolves. You who are the slave of Mary, place your confidence and trust in her merits and intercession with Jesus. Rely on the blood and merits of Jesus with his Father, and trust in the infinite mercy of God, your Father.
85 2 Do not set yourself up as your own judge, for no one is an admissible lawful judge in his own cause. Disclose your thoughts, your ideas, etc., to your Superiors; hide from them nothing that you consider important, or that has affected you, etc.
86 3 Obey your Confessor who has been chosen for you by your Superior; take advantage of his advice, and follow the rules of conduct, and the maxims and lessons of divine Wisdom, which I have just made known to you.

REGINA CORDIVM

14 Letter to the People of Montbernage

Introduction

Grignion de Montfort, having been released from his post as chaplain of the general hospital of Poitiers in 1705, obtained from Mgr. de la Poype, Bishop of Poitiers, permission to preach missions in the town and suburbs of Poitiers.

He began by concentrating on those districts where the ordinary people lived. He immediately met with great success but at the same time encountered serious opposition, especially from the Vicar-General, M. de Villeroi. For the sake of peace the bishop chose to sacrifice Louis Marie who was forced to leave the town at the beginning of Lent 1706. Before leaving Poitiers, he wrote a circular letter to the people of the parishes where he had preached a mission. (cf. Besnard.)

The original manuscript of this letter has disappeared, but we possess two very early texts given by his biographers, Grandet and Besnard, which are almost identical. The text given here is that of Besnard who introduces it with these words: "I have no hesitation in including it (the letter) here, for it is an exact copy of the text which has been juridically compared with the original before being passed on to me."

Letter to the People of Montbernage

1 God Alone
Dear People of Montbernage,[1]
St. Saturnin, St. Simplicien,
La Resurrection and others[2]

who profited from the mission
which Jesus Christ, my Master,
has just given you,
greetings in Jesus and Mary.

Not being able to speak to you personally, since holy obedience prevents me,[3] I take the liberty of writing to you on my departure, as a father writing to his children, not to teach you anything new, but to confirm you in the truths I have already taught you.

The Christian and fatherly love I bear you is so great that you will always have a place in my heart as long as I live and even into eternity. I would rather lose my right hand than forget you wherever I may be, whether at the altar, or far away at the end of the earth or even at death's door. You can be sure of my remembrance as long as you are faithful to what Jesus Christ has taught you through his missionaries[4] and through my unworthy self, in spite of the devil, the world and the flesh.

2 Remember, then, my dear children, my joy, my glory and my crown (Phil. 4:1), to have a great love for Jesus and to love him through Mary. Let your true devotion to your loving Mother Mary be manifest everywhere and to everyone, so that you may spread everywhere the fragrance of Jesus and, carrying your cross steadfastly after our good Master, gain the crown and kingdom which is waiting for you. So, do not fail to fulfill your baptismal promises and all that they entail, say your rosary every day either alone or in public and receive the sacraments at least once a month.[5]

3 I beg my dear friends of Montbernage, who possess the statue of Our Lady, my good Mother and my heart,[6] to continue praying even more fervently and not to allow into their district those who swear and blaspheme, sing ribald songs and drunkards, without doing something about it.

When I say, "without doing something about it," I mean that if you can't prevent them from sinning by reproving them zealously but kindly, at least let some godly man or woman undertake to do penance, even in public be it only by saying a Hail Mary in the street where they say their prayers, or even to hold a lighted candle in their room or in the church. This is what you have to do and keep on doing and so with God's help persevere in his service. I give this same advice to the other districts.

4 My dear children, you must be living examples to all Poitiers and district. Let no one work on Sundays or Holydays. Let no one lay out his wares or even half-open his shop, and so counter the general practice of bakers, butchers, second-hand dealers and other shopkeepers of Poitiers who rob God of his day and are sadly damning themselves in spite of the fine excuses they may offer. If, under necessity you must do otherwise, then receive the approval of your parish priest. Do not work, then, in any way on Holydays and God, I promise you, will bless you both in body and soul, and you will never be short of what you need.

5 I ask my dear women of St. Simplicien who sell fish and meat, and other shopkeepers and retailers, to continue giving good example to the whole town by living what they learned during the mission.

6 I ask you all, in general and individually, to follow me with your prayers on the pilgrimage[7] which I am going to make for you and many others. I say, "for you," because I am undertaking this long and difficult journey in dependence on the Providence of God to obtain from him through the prayers of Mary, your perseverance.

I say, "for many others," because I bear in my heart all the poor sinners of Poitou and elsewhere, who are sadly placing their salvation at risk. They are so dear to my God that he gave all his blood for them and would I give nothing? He undertook such long and arduous journeys for them, and would I undertake none? He went so far as to risk his own life and wouldn't I risk mine too? Only a pagan or a bad Christian could fail to be affected at the immense loss of the infinite treasure of souls which Jesus Christ redeemed. So pray for that intention, my dear friends, and pray also for me, that my sinfulness and unworthiness do not hinder what God and his holy Mother wish to accomplish through my ministry.

I am seeking divine Wisdom; help me to find it. I am faced with many enemies. All those who love and esteem transitory and perishable things of this world treat me with contempt, mock and persecute me, and the powers of evil have conspired together to incite against me everywhere all those in authority. Surrounded by all this I am very weak, even weakness personified; I am ignorant, even ignorance personified and even worse besides which I do not dare to speak of.

Alone and poor (cf. Ps. 24:16) as I am, I would certainly perish were I not supported by Our Lady and the prayers of good people, especially your own. These are obtaining for me from God the gift of speech or divine Wisdom, which will be the remedy for all my ills and a powerful weapon against all my enemies (cf. LEW 95-97).

With Mary it is easy. I place all confidence in her, despite the snarls of the devil and the world and I say with St. Bernard, "In her I have placed unbounded confidence; she is the whole reason for my hope."[9] Have these words explained to you for I would not have dared to propose them on my own authority. Through Mary I will seek and find Jesus; I will crush the serpent's head and overcome all my enemies as well as myself, for the greater glory of God.

Farewell but not goodbye, for if God spares me, I shall pass this way again, either to stay for a short while, subject to the obedience I owe to your good bishop who is so zealous for the salvation of men and so compassionate to us in our weakness, or while on my way to some other place; for since God is my Father, wherever he is offended by sinners, there is my dwelling-place.

"Let those who do good, go on doing good.
Let the unclean continue to be unclean (Rev. 22:11).
For some the smell of death leads to death,
For others the sweet smell of life leads to life" (2 Cor. 2:16).

I am all yours,

Louis Marie de Montfort,
priest and unworthy slave of Jesus in Mary.[10]

Footnotes to the Letter to the People of Montbernage

1 Montbernage was a suburban area of Poitiers inhabited by the poorer classes. It was here that Montfort gave his first mission in the diocese of Poitiers. The district was in the parish of St. Radegonde but situated at a fair distance from the church. Montfort succeeded in transforming a local dance hall, called "Grange de la Bergerie" into an oratory, which he furnished with a crucifix and "fifteen standards" of the rosary.

2 These were probably the people who had attended the missions Montfort gave at St. Catherine, St. Savin and in the churches of the Penitents during several months of the year 1705 and 1706.

3 This is a respectful reference to the order he received from the bishop to quit in disgrace the diocese of Poitiers.

4 Montfort had several priests working with him in these missions. One of them was Fr. de Revol, the Vicar-General of Poitiers who later on in 1706 was appointed bishop of Óleŕon.

5 This whole paragraph reflects the main aims of a Montfortian mission, namely, love for Jesus through Mary; carrying one's cross; living a sacramental life; saying the Rosary regularly (cf. Covenant pact).

6 As a farewell gift Montfort placed in the "Grange de la Bergerie" a statue of the Virgin Mary under the title of "Mary Queen of all hearts." Suspended from it was a golden heart, which explains the expression "my heart." This statue still exists in the chapel of Montbernage.

7 Montfort is alluding here to the pilgrimage he is about to make to Rome and in the following passage he is underlining its penitential character. He had other intentions, too. He saw how difficult it was to do any good in France in the face of so much opposition from all quarters, even from those who should have supported him, and he wondered if he should leave France and go elsewhere to exercise a more fruitful and promising ministry. He therefore set out for Rome to consult Clement XI, place himself at his disposal and express his readiness to go anywhere the Pope wished to send him (cf. Blain). Fr. de la Tour, S.J., who was the saint's confessor at this time, informs us that the pilgrim believed "that by journeying to Rome he could receive faculties to make his ministry more effective" (cf. Grandet, p. 457). Montfort returned from Rome with the title of "Apostolic Missionary."

8 At this time in the north of Italy the armies of Louis XIV and Joseph I, emperor of Germany, were confronting each other and the soldiers of both armies were plundering the area. Foreigners, travellers and pilgrims ran the risk of being molested. Was the pilgrim told of these dangers before he set out? What did happen was that he was taken for an enemy dressed as a priest (cf. Besnard, "Montfort," Bk. 2, p. 56).

9 St. Bernard, "in Nat. B.M.V., de Aquaeductu" No. 7.

10 Montfort uses different forms of signature; the one given here is the usual one.

15 The Rules

Introduction

St. Louis Marie composed several Rules for the "Associations" which he established during his missions. Some of them, including that of "The Soldiers of St. Michael," have not been preserved. The three texts presented here come down to us from his two early biographers, Grandet and Besnard.

The first two are taken from Grandet and they show the aims and the significance of the confraternity of Penitents and that of Virgins. Grandet writes, "Fr. de Montfort set up in his missions special groups or confraternities; one for men called the 'White Penitents,' and another for girls called the 'Society of Virgins.' "

The aim of the "White Penitents" was to deter men from giving way to drunkenness, immorality, swearing and slander. The "Society of Virgins" was formed to protect girls from the corrupting influence of the world and the temptations arising from attending dances, seeking the company of boys, keeping late nights and all such occasions of offending God.

Confraternities of penitents began in Italy and spread widely in the south of France. There were the White Penitents of Nimes and Sète, the Black Penitents of Marseilles, the Blue Penitents of Toulouse and the Grey Penitents in other places. Montfort may have been the first to introduce them into the West of France, or again he may have got the idea from the Marian congregation of the "Cruciger" which had existed under the direction of the Jesuits at La Rochelle since 1706 or even earlier.

The "Society of Virgins" would seem to be something new in the diocese of La Rochelle. In fact, people were critical of it as we gather from a letter of Mgr. Champflour, Bishop of La Rochelle, to Fr. Mulot, the first successor of Montfort. The Bishop wrote: "They are wrong to force me to speak out, for I have never disapproved of the temporary vow of chastity that Fr. de Montfort re-

quired of these girls. On the contrary, I have always considered it a holy undertaking. Do not be surprised at these evil accusations made against this poor deceased priest." (Grandet) The Rules composed by Montfort conformed to the pattern of confraternities authorized in the diocese of La Rochelle at the time.

Concerning the third set of Rules, Grandet gives us some details of Fr. de Montfort's plan for a pilgrimage which a group of White Penitents of Saint Pompain were about to make on foot to the shrine of Our Lady of Saumur. "1) He placed two priests at the head of the group to lead them; 2) He gave them a rule to be followed on the way; 3) He stressed the purpose of the pilgrimage which was to ask God, through Mary's intercession, for the grace to reject sin, to have a happy death and to send good missionaries to continue Montfort's own mission work." Besnard, after giving Grandet's account, furnishes us with the text of the Rule and informs us that it is taken from the original as composed by Fr. de Montfort. The text given here can therefore be accepted as a faithful reproduction of that of St. Louis Marie.

1 RULE of the Forty-four Virgins

1 They will not be more than forty-four in number. When one dies or otherwise leaves, the parish priest will appoint a replacement. He will choose a steady, good-living person who will take a vow not to marry for one year.

2 Those who are called by God to marry will ask the advice of their spiritual director and when they have completed the time for which their vow was binding, they will give up their veils and rings before marrying. The director will refund the cost of these articles, if desired, and they will be sold again to new members.

3 The virgins will be specially faithful to saying the Rosary every day. They will avoid the smallest fault against purity or anything at all which might in the least sully their holy state, such as dances, parties and the company of the opposite sex.

4 They will meet in church four times a year on the following feasts of Our Lady: the Annunciation, the Sunday within the octave of the Assumption, the Immaculate Conception and the Purification. They will dress in white, receive Holy Communion at High Mass and after Vespers they will carry Our Lady's statue in procession. Then either the parish priest or his deputy will give them an instruction in the rosary chapel.

5 They will obey their mother mistress and her two assistants

and will accept their advice with respect and submit when ordered or forbidden to do something for the general good.

6 If, after receiving two admonitions, one of the virgins should continue to give bad example, her name will be removed from the list of members and a more suitable person will be chosen to take her place.

7 Each year on the feast of the Annunciation they will renew their vow for one year.

2 RULE of The White Penitents

1 They will be men of high moral standard who say the Rosary regularly.

2 They will go to Confession frequently especially on the first Sunday of the month and the principal feasts of the year.

3 Four times in the year they will walk in procession, barefoot and dressed in white.

4 Each week they will practice some act of bodily mortification in keeping with their strength and on the advice of a wise director.

5 They will edify the faithful of both sexes by their example of Christian virtue.

6 They will not engage in any lawsuit. Should there be differences to regulate, they will consult prudent and informed people so as to settle the matter out of court.

7 In order to avoid scandal and moral corruption, they will go to taverns only by necessity.

8 When one of their members dies, they will assist at his funeral and pray for the repose of his soul.

9 They will meet frequently, as arranged by their director, to receive the instructions he will see fit to give them.

10 To be accepted into the congregation, the aspirant must receive a majority vote.

3 The Pilgrimage to Our Lady of Saumur[2] made by the Penitents to obtain from God good Missionaries.

1 You will make this pilgrimage for the following intentions: Firstly, to obtain from God through Mary's intercession good missionaries, who will follow the example of the apostles by complete abandonment to divine Providence and the practice of virtue under the protection of Our Lady.

Secondly, to obtain the gift of wisdom in order to know, love and practice the truths of our faith and to lead others to Christ.

2 You will not have anything to distinguish you from others, except your modest demeanor, your holy silence and your continual prayer. You could, however, without making yourselves conspicuous, have a rosary in your hand and a crucifix around your neck to show that you are on a pilgrimage and not making an ordinary journey.

3 In the villages and towns you will walk two by two to edify, but in the country you will keep together and not separate into groups except through necessity or obedience. If through fatigue anyone falls behind, the others in their charity wait for him and, if necessary, put him on a horse,[3] thus keeping each other as members of one body.

4 On the journey they will sing hymns, say the Rosary or engage in silent prayer. They will not speak to each other except for one hour in the morning about ten o'clock and again after dinner between one and two o'clock.

5 The day's time-table is as follows:

1 As far as possible they will stay in the same inn; the weaker men will sleep in beds, the more penitent on hay and straw. They will observe silence and say the evening prayer together.

2 They will all get up at daybreak when the superior gives the signal. They will say together the Our Father, Hail Mary, creed, the commandments of God and the Church.

3 Then if there is a church fairly near, they will visit the Blessed Sacrament and sing the Tantum Ergo with its prayer.[4]

4 As they resume their journey, they will sing hymns and say the Little Crown of the Blessed Virgin, then they will keep silent for half an hour meditating on the Passion and Death of Our Lord.

5 Meditation finished, they will say the first rosary in two choirs. To facilitate this, they will try, as far as possible, to walk in twos or fours.

6 After the rosary, they will sing hymns for about an hour until, at a signal from the superior, they will talk together until dinner, unless they are passing through a town or village when they will again sing hymns.

7 If there is a church close to where they stop for dinner, they will pay a visit to the Blessed Sacrament before going to the inn.

8 At the inn, if it is possible, they will either all go to an upstairs room or group together in a room on the ground floor. They will kneel down and after having sung, "O Holy Spirit, give us your

light," and said a Hail Mary, they will sit at table.

9 When grace has been said, one of them will read a short passage to which they will listen in silence. At the end of the reading, the superior, whom they obey for the love of Jesus Christ, will give them permission to talk.

10 Before leaving the inn, they will sing, "Mother of God, you are our Mother," and "Lord, graciously reward our benefactors," then they will say a Hail Mary.

11 After dinner they will take recreation for an hour, at the end of which the superior will give the signal for the second rosary which they will say in two choirs. They will then sing hymns for an hour, keep silent for an hour and then talk quietly until they reach their night's lodging.

12 On their arrival, while the one appointed prepares a meal, they say the third rosary to edify anyone who might see or hear them. Finally they take their evening meal and go to bed in the manner mentioned above.

6 Unless they are prevented by sickness they try to fast[5] during the whole pilgrimage.

7 They will never leave the group nor do anything out of the ordinary without the permission of the one whom they have chosen as their leader and superior. Thus they will be blessed more by their obedience than by their penance.

8 About a quarter of an hour before arriving at Saumur,[6] they may take off their shoes and go into the Lady Chapel barefoot, two by two, singing hymns. But if they arrive in the morning when Mass is being celebrated, they must stop singing at the door. At the end of Mass or in the evening when the office is not being sung, the superior may ask permission of the sacristan to say the Rosary aloud and to sing hymns before the statue of Our Lady. If this is not permitted they will be content to pray silently for as long as the superior wishes. No one must leave without necessity or without his permission. In this way they will altogether defeat God's enemies, the devil, the world and the flesh, in their united effort to separate and subvert the pilgrims.

9 All the pilgrims will go to Confession and each will receive Holy Communion at least once and all the group together will receive Communion at ten o'clock the day after their arrival. They will spend the rest of the day at Saumur, not sight-seeing like tourists, but praying and thanking God like genuine penitents.

10 They will leave the following day after having been to Mass and again receiving Holy Communion, provided they have not committed any serious sin and have obeyed this rule and their superior.

11 The superior will allow them to go just once to buy devotional articles[7] but they must return to the inn and not go elsewhere.

12 After Mass and half an hour's prayer, they will leave the town of Saumur, walking two by two, singing hymns. They will ignore the jeers of the irreligious; their only answer will be their modesty, their silence and their songs of spiritual joy.

13 If they make the pilgrimage in this way, I am sure they will be seen to be worthy of God, of angels and of men;[8] and they will obtain from God through the intercession of his Blessed Mother great graces not only for themselves but for the whole Church of God.

14 It would be befitting that they do not mention the names of the missionaries who have drawn up this present rule so as to ensure that the glory go to God alone; since he alone inspired this undertaking, he alone must be the reward.

15 On their return they will render an account of all the trials they have had to face as well as everything else that has happened to them, and in thanksgiving a solemn High Mass will be offered for them.[9]

Footnotes to The Rules

1 "They should be only forty-four in number in honor of the 144,000 virgins of whom St. John speaks in the Apocalypse" (Rule of the ladies of this parish who are consecrated to the Blessed Virgin Mary; manuscript preserved at Contré and inscribed in the register of 1716 by Francis Guillemot in 1722 after a mission given by one of Montfort's successors).

2 Our Lady of Pity of Ardilliers which Montfort visited several times.

3 "We accompanied thirty-three penitents all on foot and often barefoot, except for one good old man suffering from gout, who virtuously joined us and who was on horseback." Account given by Fr. Mulot (BESNARD, *Montfort,* bk. 8, p. 238). Frs. Mulot and Vatel were the two priests who led the pilgrims who, according to Grandet, numbered thirty-six.

4 "The parish priest of St. John of Thouars dressed in surplice gave an address at the entrance to the church." Report of Fr. Mulot (BESNARD, *Montfort,* bk. 8, p. 238).

5 Fr. Mulot notes that it was Lent (cf. BESNARD, *Montfort,* bk. 8, p. 238). "In the month of March," says Grandet.

6 Saumur is about 80 kilometres from Saint-Pompain. Fr. Mulot records that the journey there took three days (BESNARD, *Montfort,* p. 238).

7 Makers and sellers of rosaries. The business of making rosaries developed around the sanctuary of Our Lady of Ardilliers at the end of the 16th century. The "industry" was situated in the main thoroughfare of the suburb of Fenette and at the beginning of the Revolution employed 1,000-2,000 persons.

8 Cf. 1 Cor. 4:9.

9 Fr. Mulot reported that the pilgrimage concluded with Benediction

of the Blessed Sacrament on the Sunday after the pilgrims had arrived back (cf. BESNARD, *Montfort,* bk. 8, p. 239). Grandet, however, writes that the whole exercise lasted seven days and terminated with the planting of a cross, and although there had been a heavy fall of snow the penitents did not hesitate to walk barefooted.

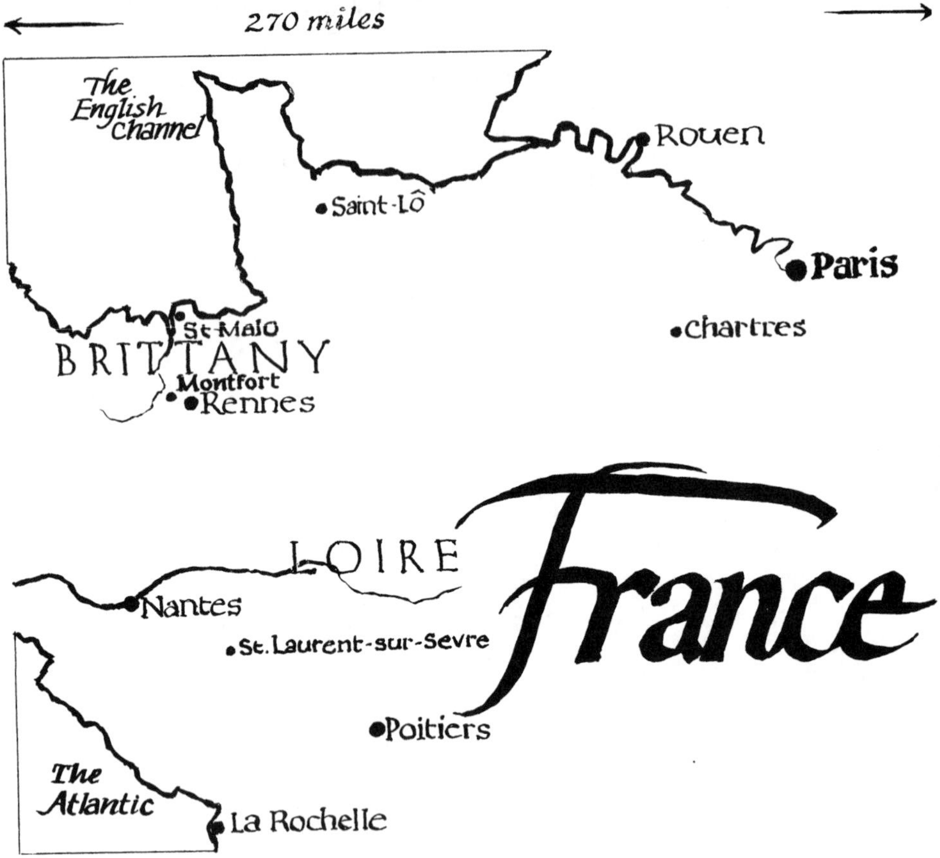

270 miles

The English Channel

Rouen

Saint-Lô

Paris

Chartres

St Malo

BRITTANY

Montfort

Rennes

France

LOIRE

Nantes

St. Laurent-sur-Sevre

Poitiers

The Atlantic

La Rochelle

16 Covenant with God

Introduction

According to Grandet, Montfort's aim in his missions was "to revive the Christian spirit through the renewal of the baptismal promises," and to this Grandet adds, "and to help them (Christians) remember their undertakings, he had a formula of renewal printed and those who could write were required to sign it," and he goes on to describe at some length the ceremony into which this act of renewal was inserted.

Four printed copies have been preserved. They are mementos of missions at Pontchâteau (1709), Croissac (1709), Fontenay (1715), and Vouvant (1715). These four copies indicate that there were at least two different versions and, although they are substantially the same, the variations are interesting and so the two versions are given.

1st Formula

Vows or Promises of Holy Baptism

1 1 I firmly believe all the truths of the Holy Gospel of Jesus Christ.

2 I renounce forever Satan, the world, sin and myself.

3 With the help of God's grace, which will never be wanting to me, I promise to keep faithfully all the commandments of God and of the Church, and avoid mortal sin and its occasions, especially bad company.

4 I give myself entirely to Jesus Christ by the hands of Mary to carry my cross after him all the days of my life.

5 I believe that if I keep these promises faithfully until death, I shall be eternally saved, but that if I do not keep them, I will be eternally damned.

In testimony of this I affix my signature.

Signed in the presence of the Church in the parish of Pont-château, on this 4th day of May in the year 1709.

L. M. de Montfort[1]

Practices to be adopted by those who have renewed their baptismal vows.

2 1 They will say at least once a day the Little Crown of the Blessed Virgin, which comprises three Our Fathers and twelve Hail Marys.

2 They will go to Confession at least once a month.

3 They will avoid like the plague drinking-houses, gambling-places, dances, theatres, and other worldly spectacles.

4 Every year on the 2nd of February, they will renew the vows they made in baptism, recite the holy Rosary and make a visit to the Blessed Sacrament.

5 They will treasure with affection the cross given to them when renewing their promises in this contract.

6 They will shun vanity and extravagance in their clothes.

7 They will say every day 5 Our Fathers and 5 Hail Marys in honor of the 5 Names enclosed in the Cross[2] given to them, and in honor of the 5 wounds of Jesus crucified, their head and their model.

2nd Formula

Vows and Promises of Holy Baptism

3 1 I firmly believe all the truths contained in the holy Gospel of Jesus Christ.

2 I renounce forever the devil, the world, sin and myself.

3 With the help of God's grace, which will never be wanting, I

promise to keep faithfully all the commandments of God and of the Church, and to avoid mortal sin and the occasions of mortal sin, especially bad company.

4 I give myself entirely to Jesus through the hands of Mary, to carry my cross after him all the days of my life.

5 I believe that those who break these vows without any repentance will be condemned, and that those who keep them up to death will be saved.

In testimony of this I have signed hereunder.

Written in the presence of the Church, in the parish of Vouvant, on this third day of December 1715.

L. M. de Montfort

Practices of Christian living for those who have renewed the Promises of Baptism.

4 1 I shall avoid dances, theatres, and other public spectacles, games of chance, luxurious living, vanity, bad books and songs.

2 I will never frequent, except when necessary, drinking houses and other such places of temptation.

3 I will go to Confession once a month, and even oftener as guided by a good director.

4 Every year on the 4th of July, I will renew privately the vows of my Baptism. I will say the Rosary, I will visit the Blessed Sacrament for half-an-hour, and endeavor to go to Communion on that day.

5 I will say every day the Little Crown of the Blessed Virgin, and five Our Fathers and five Hail Marys in honor of the Holy Name of JESUS, a habit I will faithfully adhere to as long as I live.

Footnotes to Covenant with God

1 There is reason to doubt the authenticity of this signature. Was it really written by St. Louis Marie? On the Croissac copy the signature of the missionary is preceded by that of Guillaume Guigan.

2 Grandet writes (p. 101): "The pope granted him permission to bless little crosses of paper and cloth bearing the names of Jesus and Mary, which he distributed at the end of each mission to those who had assisted at thirty-three sermons." None of these crosses have survived.

SUR
LA TOMBE
GABY

17 Last Will and Testament

Introduction

On the first of April 1716, Fr. de Montfort, accompanied by several Brothers, arrived at St. Laurent-sur-Sèvre to begin a mission. He had previously made a pilgrimage to Our Lady of Ardilliers at Saumur to confide to the Queen of heaven his future apostolate and those foundations which he had previously begun. After a short time two other missionaries joined him, Fr. Thomas le Bourhis who had been associated with him since 1712, and Fr. Clisson concerning whom nothing is known. He was joined also by the Prior and parish priest of Saint Pompain, Jean Mulot, who had decided to accompany his brother René, a young priest thirty years of age. René had joined Fr. de Montfort in October 1715 and during those few months had become Montfort's friend, confidant and confessor.

During the mission which began on April 5th, the bishop of the diocese of La Rochelle arrived to make a canonical visitation. Montfort, as the leader of the mission, worked hard to prepare an enthusiastic reception for the bishop, but he was not able to be present at the bishop's arrival, being laid low by a feverish illness. However, later on in the day he went into the pulpit and preached a moving sermon on the love of Jesus Christ.

After the sermon he was forced again to take to his bed from which he was not to rise. From the 23rd of April onwards the illness made rapid progress and nothing could give him relief—certainly not the bleedings and the medicines of the doctors. On the 27th of April, sensing that death was approaching, he decided to dictate his last will and testament and dispose of all he possessed. He charged René Mulot, his confessor, to write down his last wishes. Then with a trembling hand the dying man traced his signature on the docu-

ment, which was followed by the signatures of René Felix Rougeau, dean of Saint Laurent, and Francis Triault, curate of the parish, who acted as witnesses required for the validity of the document.

I, the undersigned, the greatest of sinners, will that my body be buried in the cemetery and my heart under the step of the altar of the Blessed Virgin. I confide to His Lordship the Bishop of La Rochelle and to Father Mulot my small pieces of furniture and my mission books, to be preserved for the use of the four Brothers who joined me in a life of obedience and poverty; namely, Brother Nicholas of Poitiers, Brother Philip of Nantes, Brother Louis of La Rochelle, and Brother Gabriel, who is at present with me, for as long as they continue to renew their annual vows, and for the use of those whom divine Providence will call into the same community of the Holy Spirit. I give all the statues of the Calvary and the cross to the house of the Sisters of the Incurables at Nantes. I have no private money belonging to me, but there are 135 pounds belonging to Nicholas of Poitiers to pay for his keep after he has finished his stay with us.

Fr. Mulot will give the following monies from the common fund: ten crowns to James, if he decides to leave; ten crowns to John, if he also decides to leave; ten crowns to Mathurin, if he decides to leave and not renew the vows of poverty and obedience. If there is anything remaining in the purse, Fr. Mulot will use it like a good father for the Brothers and for himself. As the house at La Rochelle is reverting to its natural heirs, there will only be left for the community of the Holy Spirit the house at Vouvant, which was given to me by Madame de la Brulerie by an agreement, the conditions of which Fr. Mulot must fulfill; and the two pieces of land given by the Lieutenant of Vouvant's wife, and a small house given by a good lady of rank. If there is no possibility of building there, it should be put at the disposal of the Brothers of the community of the Holy Spirit to conduct charity schools.

I give three of my banners to Our Lady of Patience at La Séguinière, and the other four to Our Lady of Victories at La Garnache, and to every parish of Aunis where the Rosary is still being said I give one of the banners of the holy Rosary. I give to Fr. Bouris the six volumes of sermons of La Volpillière, and to Fr. Clisson the four volumes of the "Catechism for Country People." If there is anything owing to the printer, he can be paid from the fund. Should there be anything over, Fr. Vatel must be given what belongs to him, if His Lordship decides that this is right.

This is my Last Will, and I make Fr. Mulot my executor giving him full right to dispose as it seems good to him of the chasubles, chalice and other church and mission articles, for the benefit of the community of the Holy Spirit.

Written during the mission at St. Laurent-sur-Sèvre, this 27th day of the month of April, one thousand seven hundred and sixteen. All the pieces of furniture at present at Nantes are for the use of the Brothers who run the school, as long as the school remains there.

Louis Marie
de Montfort Grignion

N. F. Rougeou, Dean of Saint-Laurent
F. Triault, priest, curate

18 Morning and Night Prayers

Introduction

In the original rules of the Daughters of Wisdom and the Missionary Priests, Fr. de Montfort speaks of prayers that both Congregations must say, but he does not give any further details.

We do not possess the original manuscript of the prayers. However, in the report of the general chapter of the Company of Mary held on the 4th and 5th of June 1859, we find this note: "The chapter, desiring to adhere as closely as possible to the wishes of the Venerable Founder, prescribes that the morning and night prayers, recently published on the 14th of April, be said throughout the Congregation. They are a faithful copy of the author's own manuscript." (General archives of the Company of Mary.)

We can therefore safely accept the text we give here, taken from the edition of 1859, as a reliable version, especially as it is followed by this confirmation: "Conformed to the manuscript of the Venerable Montfort which has recently been printed"—Denis, Superior-General, St. Laurent 16th of April 1859.

The "Little Crown," prescribed for morning prayer, is given in Latin, to which we append an English translation.

The question arises, how much of this text is Montfort's own composition?

The "Little Crown," which is inspired by the text of the book of Revelation, Chapter 12, 1-18, is a form of prayer which was currently used in the 17th century. Among its promoters were: St. Joseph Calasanctius (d. 1648), St. Andrew Avellino (d. 1630), Alexis of Salo, Francis Olimpio (d. 1639). The Jesuits commended it to the members of their Marian congregations. Blessed Julian Maunoir put it into verse, and had it sung during his missions in Brittany.

The sermon of St. Bernard, "In signum magnum," or "De duodecim stellis," served as a basis for some versions. That of Fr. de Montfort, however, derives its structure from the work of Fr. Poiré, entitled, "The Triple Crown."

The source of the final prayer of the Little Crown is uncertain; it evokes ideas and contains expressions reminiscent of ecclesiastical writers of the Middle Ages, and adopted by other authors of the seventeenth century.

As regards the Night Prayer, its structure was commonly used at that time and has persisted until the twentieth century. The part which is most original is that relating to the theme of rest and sleep, which one associates with the French school of spirituality.

MORNING PRAYERS

1 Veni, Sancte Spiritus; reple tuorum corda fidelium, et tui amoris in eis ignem accende.
Emitte Spiritum tuum, et creabuntur;
Et renovabis faciem terrae.

Oremus. Deus, qui corda fidelium Sancti Spiritus illustratione docuisti: da nobis in eodem Spiritu recta sapere, et de ejus semper consolatione gaudere. Per Christum Dominum nostrum.

Amen.

The Little Crown of the Blessed Virgin

2 Dignare me laudare te, Virgo sacrata.
Da mihi virtutem contrà hostes tuos.

1 *Pater noster.*

2 *Ave, Maria.*

Beata es, Virgo Maria, quae Dominum portasti Creatorem mundi, genuisti qui te fecit, et in aeternum permanes virgo.
Gaude, Maria Virgo;
Gaude millies!

2 *Ave, Maria.*

Sancta et immaculata Virginitas, quibus te laudibus efferam nescio; quià quem coeli capere non poterant tuo gremio contulisti.
Gaude, Maria Virgo;
Gaude millies!

3 *Ave, Maria.*

Tota pulchra es, Virgo Maria, et macula non est in te.
Gaude, Maria Virgo;
Gaude millies!

4 *Ave, Maria.*

Plu(re)s tibi sunt dotes, Virgo, quàm sidera coelo.

Gaude, Maria Virgo;
Gaude millies!

Gloria Patri, et Filio, etc.

3 2 *Pater noster.*

5 *Ave, Maria.*

Gloria tibi sit, Imperatrix poli! Tecum nos perducas ad gaudia Coeli.

Gaude, Maria Virgo;
Gaude millies!

6 *Ave, Maria.*

Gloria tibi sit, Thesauraria gratiarum Domini! Fac nos participes thesauri tui.

Gaude, Maria Virgo;
Gaude millies!

7 *Ave, Maria.*

Gloria tibi sit, Mediatrix inter Deum et hominem! Fac nobis propitium Omnipotentem.

Gaude, Maria Virgo;
Gaude millies!

8 *Ave, Maria.*

Gloria tibi sit, haeresum et doemonum Interemptrix! Sis pia nostra gubernatrix.

Gaude, Maria Virgo;
Gaude millies!

Gloria Patri, et Filio, etc.

4 3 *Pater noster.*

9 *Ave, Maria.*

Gloria tibi sit, Refugium peccatorum! Intercede pro nobis ad Dominum.

Gaude, Maria Virgo;
Gaude millies!

10 *Ave, Maria.*

Gloria tibi sit, orphanorum Mater! Fac nobis propitius sit omnipotens Pater.

Gaude, Maria Virgo;
Gaude millies!

11 *Ave, Maria.*

Gloria tibi sit, Laetitia justorum! Tecum nos perducas ad gaudia Coelorum.

Gaude, Maria Virgo;
Gaude millies!

12 *Ave, Maria.*

Gloria tibi sit, in vitâ et in morte Adjutrix praesentissima! Tecum nos perducas ad Coelorum regna.

Gaude, Maria Virgo;
Gaude millies!
Gloria Patri, et Filio, etc.

5 *Oremus*

Ave, Maria, filia Dei Patris; ave, Maria, mater Dei Fillii; ave, Maria, sponsa Spiritus Sancti; ave, Maria, templum totius sanctissimae Trinitatis; ave, Maria, domina mea, bona mea, rosa mea, regina cordis mei, mater, vita, dulcedo, et spes mea carissima, imo, cor meum et anima mea: tuus totus ego sum, et omnia mea tua sunt, o Virgo super omnia benedicta. Sit ergo in me anima tua, ut magnificet Dominum; sit in me spiritus tuus, ut exultet in Deo. Pone te, Virgo fidelis, ut signaculum super cor meum, ut in te et per te Deo fidelis inveniar. Largire, o Benigna, ut illis annumerer quos tanquam filios amas, doces, dirigis, foves, protegis. Fac ut, amore tui, terrenas omnes spernens consolationes, coelestibus semper inhaeream, donec in me per Spiritum Sanctum sponsum tuum fidelissimum, et te fidelissimam ejus sponsam, formetur Jesus Christus filius tuus, ad gloriam Patris. Amen.

(For translation, see No. 10 ff.)

Morning Prayers
For the Daughters of Wisdom

6 In the name of the Father, and of the Son, and of the Holy Spirit.

Amen.

Veni, Sancte Spiritus, reple tuorum corda fidelium, et tui amoris in eis ignem accende.
Emitte Spiritum tuum et creabuntur.
Et renovabis faciem terrae.

Oremus. Deus qui corda fidelium Sancti Spiritus illustratione docuisti, da nobis in eodem Spiritu recta sapere, et de ejus semper consolatione gaudere. Per Christum Dominum nostrum.

Amen.

7 *Let us place ourselves in the presence of God and bow in adoration before him.*

My God, I firmly believe that you are here present; I adore you and acknowledge you as my sovereign Lord and Master upon whom I wholly depend.

Amen.

8 *Let us ask God for all that is necessary for our salvation.*

My God, grant me sorrow to lament my sins, strength to overcome temptations, zeal to practice the virtues of my state of life, submission to my superiors, charity towards my Sisters, compassion for my neighbor especially for the poor and the sick, and may I never fail to be attentive to my prayers, exact in my duties, and persevering in my resolves.
Amen.

9 *Let us offer all our actions to God.*

My God, just as I wish to love nothing more than you, so I wish to live only for you. I offer you all my thoughts, all my words, all my actions and all my sufferings this day; please bestow your holy blessing upon them.
Amen.

Let us say The Little Crown of the Blessed Virgin *to obtain from God through Mary's intercession the grace not to offend him today.*

The Little Crown of the Blessed Virgin

10 Virgin most holy, accept my praise.
And give me strength to fight your foes.
Our Father. Hail Mary.
You are indeed blessed, Virgin Mary, in having brought forth the Creator of the universe.
You gave birth to the one who made you, while ever remaining a virgin.
Rejoice, O Virgin Mary.
Rejoice forever and ever.
Hail Mary.
Virgin holy and immaculate, no tongue can praise you worthily.
For you bore in your womb the God whom the very heavens cannot enclose.
Rejoice, O Virgin Mary.
Rejoice forever and ever.
Hail Mary.
You are all beautiful, O Mary.
And free from every stain of sin.
Rejoice, O Virgin Mary.

Rejoice forever and ever.
Hail Mary.
The gifts bestowed on you, Virgin Mary.
Outnumber the stars of heaven.
Rejoice, O Virgin Mary.
Rejoice forever and ever..
Glory be to the Father.
11 Our Father. Hail Mary.
Queen of the whole world, we praise you.
Lead us to the joys of heaven.
Rejoice, O Virgin Mary.
Rejoice forever and ever.
Hail Mary.
Treasury of all God's graces, we praise you.
Grant us a share in your heavenly gifts.
Rejoice, O Virgin Mary.
Rejoice forever and ever.
Hail Mary.
Mediatrix between God and man, we praise you.
Through your intercession may the Almighty be favorable to us.
Rejoice, O Virgin Mary.
Rejoice forever and ever.
Hail Mary.
Victor over heresies and all that is evil, we praise you.
Guide us lovingly in the way of truth.
Rejoice, O Virgin Mary.
Rejoice forever and ever.
Glory be to the Father.
12 Our Father. Hail Mary.
Refuge of sinners, we praise you.
Reconcile us with Almighty God.
Rejoice, O Virgin Mary.
Rejoice forever and ever.
Hail Mary.
Mother of orphans, we praise you.
Make us beloved children of our Father.
Rejoice, O Virgin Mary.
Rejoice forever and ever.
Hail Mary.
Joy of those who serve the Lord, we praise you.
Lead us with you to the happiness of heaven.
Rejoice, O Virgin Mary.
Rejoice forever and ever.
Hail Mary.
Advocate ever near us in life and in death, we praise you.
Lead us with you to the kingdom of God.

Rejoice, O Virgin Mary.
Rejoice forever and ever.
Glory be to the Father.

13 *Let us pray.*

Hail, Mary, daughter of God the Father, mother of God the Son, spouse of the Holy Spirit, temple of the Blessed Trinity.

Hail, Mary, my mistress, my wealth, my joy; Queen of my heart, my Mother and my life; my consolation, my dearest hope, my very heart and soul.

I belong to you entirely, and all that I possess is yours, Virgin blessed above all. May your soul be in me to glorify God; may your spirit be in me to rejoice in God.

Virgin most faithful, set your seal upon my heart, so that in you and through you I may be found faithful to God.

Grant, gracious Mother, that I may be numbered among those whom you love and instruct, whom you guide, cherish, and protect as your children. O Queen of heaven, I renounce from this moment anything in me that does not belong to you. O daughter of the King of kings, whose principal glory is within, do not allow me to be distracted by things that are visible and transitory; grant, rather, that through God's abundant grace, I may always be intent on the life within me, where I may find in God my delight, my wealth, my honor, my glory and my rest. Thus, through the Holy Spirit, your faithful spouse, and through you, his faithful spouse, Jesus Christ, your beloved Son may be perfectly formed in our hearts for the greater glory of God our Father, forever and ever.

Amen.

Night Prayers

14 Veni, Sancte Spiritus, etc.

Benedicta sit sancta atque individua Trinitas, nunc et semper, et per infinita saecula saeculorum.

Amen.

15 *Let us place ourselves in the presence of God.*

My God, I firmly believe that you are here present; I adore you, and acknowledge you as my sovereign Lord and Master. Amen.

My God, I love you with all my heart, above all things, because you are infinitely worthy of my love; I also love my neighbor as myself for your sake. Amen.

My God, I hope for the assistance of your grace to obtain life everlasting through the merits of Jesus Christ, my Savior. Amen.

My God, I firmly believe all that the Catholic, Roman and Apostolic Church believes and teaches, because you, the sovereign Truth, have revealed it. Amen.

God alone

My God, I thank you with all my heart for all the graces you have bestowed on me during my whole life, and especially for those of this day. Amen.

My God, I beseech you to enlighten me now as if it were the hour of my death, so that I may know the sins by which I have offended you. Amen.

16 *Let us examine the sins we have committed this day by thought, word and deed.*

(Pause for a short while.)

Let us beg pardon of God, with great sorrow for having offended him.

My God, I am very sorry for having offended you, because you are infinitely good and most worthy of my love, and because sin is so displeasing to you; I firmly resolve by the help of your grace never more to offend you. Amen.

17 *(Here follow the Confiteor, Misereatur and Indulgentiam.)*

My God, forgive us our sins through the intercession and merits of the Blessed Virgin and of all the Saints; through the praise and adoration they offer you in heaven; through the Precious Blood of your dear Son, and through your infinite goodness.

Amen.

18 *Let us say an Our Father and a Hail Mary for our penance.*

Our Father. Hail mary.

Holy Guardian Angel, I thank you for your care and protection; watch over me, I beseech you, to the end of my life. Amen.

My God, I beseech you to grant contrition and pardon to all poor sinners, perseverance to the just, eternal rest to the souls in Purgatory, peace among Christian rulers, a hundredfold reward to our benefactors, and the grace of a good life and a happy death.

Amen.

19 *To obtain all these graces, let us ask our Lady to intercede for us by saying devoutly the Litany of Loreto.*

(Here follows the Litany of Loreto and concluding prayer.)

20 O Jesus living in Mary, come and dwell in your servants in the spirit of your holiness, in the fullness of your power, in the perfection of your ways, in the truth of your virtues, in the communion of your mysteries. Subdue your enemies, the devil, the world and the flesh, in the strength of your Spirit, for the glory of your Father.

Amen.

My God, we offer you the rest we are about to take in honor of the eternal rest which you take in yourself, in your Son and your Holy Spirit, in the Blessed Virgin, in all the Saints in heaven and on earth.

Amen.

Savior Jesus, we offer you our sleep in honor of, and in union with your sleep, your death and burial; and our awakening tomorrow in honor of and in union with your holy resurrection. We adore your holy dispositions in these actions, and we beg of you the grace to obtain the same.

Amen.

21 *Let us pray for our dead relations, friends and benefactors. Let us say the De Profundis for our dear departed.*

(Here follows the De Profundis and concluding prayer.)

Jesus, Mary, Joseph.
Help us.
God grant us his peace, his love and his grace.
And life everlasting.

22 *Let us thank God for the graces he has bestowed on us today by saying the Magnificat.*

(Here follows the Magnificat.)

23 *After the Magnificat has been said in two choirs, the subject of mental prayer is read. Then the following verses are said kneeling:*

Maria, Mater gratiae,
Dulcis parens clementiae,
Tu nos ab hoste protege,
Et mortis hora suscipe.

Jesu, tibi sit gloria,
Qui natus es de Virgine,
Cum Patre et almo Spiritu
In sempiterna saecula. Amen.

Praised and blessed be at every moment.
The most holy and divine Sacrament.
Nos, cum prole pia, benedicat Virgo Maria!
Amen.

God Alone

19 The Hymns

Introduction

Montfort could be called a missionary singer.

With the intuition of a zealous evangelizer he saw immediately the immense importance of song as supportive of his teaching, either as a preparation for it or as its continuation in the minds and hearts of simple people to whom he always gave apostolic preference. For their benefit he composed nearly 200 hymns on a great variety of subjects, hymns which could be sung to tunes of songs already well-known. Not that our missionary was the first to use this device; he simply adopted a practice already in vogue in his time but brought to bear on it his own genius and flair for composing.

Popular hymns occupied an important place in parish missions. They were sermons in rhyme and song that poet-preachers composed, basing the metre and tunes on existing songs of the day.

Fr. de Montfort, who desired so much an effective apostolate and who would seize upon any medium that would bear fruit, saw it as an obligation to put his natural gifts at the service of a method of apostolate that experience had proved so acceptable to simple country folk and calculated to enlighten and convert them. He saw here a marvelous means of opening hearts to the lessons of the gospel and extending its message to the highways and into the homes of the faithful.

Grandet, Montfort's first biographer, wrote eight years after the death of the missionary: "The third means was the singing of hymns of which he composed a whole volume." M. Blain, Montfort's friend of his student days at the seminary, tells us that even at St. Sulpice Louis Marie Grignion "busied himself composing spiritual songs which he intended to use in his missions later on." This was only the beginning. It is difficult, with a few exceptions, to put a date to the different items of his compositions, but we can safely say that the poetic career of Montfort extended over the whole of his missionary life.

He brought, however, to this medium his personal touch, especially his fiery zeal. It is interesting to read on this subject Hymns 1 and 2, where he gives the justification for what he calls "my verses and my songs." His real aim was to communicate the teaching of the gospel in a form easy to retain and not to compose fine poetry; to give clear lessons and not to seek admiration. We can safely affirm that he has succeeded since many of his compositions have been handed down from generation to generation even to our own day.

That special aim which Fr. de Montfort set for himself explains the characteristics of his popular poetry and, at the same time, its drawbacks. It explains the subjects chosen and, at the same time, the licenses he allowed himself in versification and in the bluntness of certain expressions. Having said this, we cannot overlook the talented and fertile mind of a man whose life, apart from writing hymns, was totally absorbed in apostolic work, and we cannot fail to admire his direct, clear, simple and easy style and even the poetic beauty of certain hymns.

Nor can we fail to appreciate the diversity of the subjects chosen, beginning with God, Jesus Christ, the Blessed Virgin and then moving into the virtues and the various states of the Christian life. One cannot help but notice also the orthodoxy of his doctrine. He often gives, in the margin, the theological basis of what he is saying.

In short, the mission hymns were for Montfort the extension of his pulpit preaching. Whether he spoke, wrote or sang, the holy missionary intended only to preach the gospel and turn people to Jesus Christ. It would be unfair to expect, or require, anything more than this.

In the archives of the Montfort Fathers are carefully preserved four manuscripts of the "Cantiques" of Louis Marie and these contain 164 hymns. There is no doubt about the authenticity of this collection of hymns. Besides the fact that many hymns and series of hymns are preceded by the note "new hymns," we are sure that Montfort would not have given himself the trouble of re-copying hymns that had already been published. The comparison with other hymnals of the period provides another argument in favor of their authenticity. Fr. Fradet had studied a considerable number of hymn collections of Montfort's time and declares that he could not find any of Montfort's hymns in any other collection.

The hymns have been published frequently over the years, and most publishers have respected the text, although sometimes correcting it.

The first collection was published by Montfort himself, in 1711, at La Rochelle, but unfortunately we do not possess a copy of it. We know of its existence through a description given by Pauvert, one of the saint's biographers, who possessed a copy. He described it in detail pointing out that it comprised five parts: one dealing with the Christian virtues, a second and third with parish hymns, a fourth with hymns in honor of our Lady and a fifth with hymns to the Sacred Heart.

Other editions were published by the Montfort Fathers, beginning with that of M. Vatel, in 1725, and followed by others down to the present day. Many of these collections were destined for use during missions and, in general, they have reproduced faithfully the original text. But in some of them, verses and sometimes even entire hymns have been re-cast in a manner which was customary, but nonetheless regrettable. In these same collections some compositions of other authors have been mistakenly attributed to the saintly missionary.

It is only when we come to Fr. Fradet, in 1929, that we have the first complete edition of St. Louis Marie's hymns. For many years, Fr. Fradet devoted himself to a most careful study of the four manuscripts preserved in the archieves and of other collections of hymns before, during, and after Montfort's time. He restored to their pristine state the hymns that had been re-cast and included many others which traditionally had been attributed to Montfort, i.e. those which in all probability were his composition, nearly forty of them. Fr. Fradet's edition was published in 1929 under the title of, "The works of Blessed de Montfort—popular and mystical poet—his hymns with critical study and notes."

Unfortunately, very few of Montfort's hymns have been translated into English as of this date. We here present a translation of a handful of them on a representative number of subjects from which, we hope, the reader will be able to elicit something of the Saint's clear and simple presentation of the gospel.

The Cries of the Poor

"Riches, réveillez-vous" No. 18

1 Awake, you rich in this world's goods,
And listen to our cries;
We, poor, depend on you for help
In our great miseries.
We are one Christian family,
All brothers in the Lord;
From your abundant store you can
A mite to us accord.

God Alone

2 Our God has only made you great
To be our fathers dear,
Our God has furnished you with power
So you our pleas can hear.
In comfort you enjoy yourselves
With all you can desire,
While you expect us to survive
On scraps we can acquire.

3 You have fine clothes to keep you warm,
Sleep on a feather bed,
But rags protect us from the cold,
We have to beg for bread.
Men bless you, pay you great respect,
And show you courtesy,
While we are cursed and knocked about
And treated shamefully.

4 They give us nothing when we ask
Save looks of cold disdain;
They think it's for the common good
To treat us as insane.
They chase us and lay hands on us
And put us into chains,
They even disallow us poor
To advertize our pains.

5 The rich man says to us: I've not
A penny piece to spare;
To nobles we are riff-raff all,
At whom they curse and swear.
"Behold those downright layabouts,
Those rascals, one and all,"
In company with the common mob
So many shout and bawl.

6 Lord God, come to our aid, we pray,
By many ills beset;
You surely can't forget our needs
As mortal men forget.
Look down on us from Paradise,
O Father whom we trust,
And come and grace our lowly home
Down in the very dust.

God

7 Dear poor in heart, your just complaints
Forever rise to me,
I share your sorrows and I feel
The same indignity.
Have patience for a while and then
My anger will reply;
Though I am God, almighty Lord,
Your Father, too, am I.

8 My eldest children are you poor,
You truly are my friends,
All called to share my wealth with me
In life that never ends.
The evil which men do to you
Is done to me anew,
And when they satisfy your wants,
They show they love me too.

The Poor

9 You who are rich, how good it is
To give an alms for love,
A corner nook allowed to us
will bring a throne above,
A few old clothes obtains for you
God's robe of grace and gold,
And all the joys of Paradise
Just for some water cold.

10 If you resolve to smile on us
And not be miserly,
The secret of true wealth is yours,
Great riches yours will be.
The Lord has promised his reward,
Even a hundredfold,
To all who give to those in want
And leave his friends consoled.

11 Such charity wins o'er God's heart,
Great favors will ensue;
An alms extinguishes the fire
Of all his judgments true.
Almsgiving by the sinner brings
The certain hope possessed,

To gain one day a glorious crown
From his dear Savior blest.

The Triumph of the Cross

"La croix est un mystère" No. 19

1 The Cross in mystery
Is veiled for us below;
Without great light to see,
Who shall its splendor know?
Alone the lofty mind
Shall this high secret trace;
And none shall heaven find
Who grasps it not by grace.

2 Nature the Cross abhors;
Reason gives it a frown;
The learned man ignores
It. Satan tears it down.
Despite a pious art,
Even the fervent soul
Oft takes it not to heart,
But plays the liar's role.

3 Essential is the Tree,
And we who know its cost
Must mount to Calvary
Or languish and be lost.
As Saint Augustine states
With outcry ominous,
We all are reprobates
Unless God chasten us.

Its necessity

4 One road to heaven runs:
The highway of the Cross.
It was the royal Son's,
His road to life from loss.
And every stone of it
That guides the pilgrim's feet
Is chiselled fair to fit
In Zion's holy street.

5 Vain is the victory
Of him who, conquering

The world, lacks mastery
Of self through suffering;
Vain if he has not Christ,
Slain Christ, for exemplar,
Or spurns the Sacrificed
For dread of wound and scar.

Its Victories

6 Christ's Cross, restraining hell,
Has conquered Eden's curse,
Stormed Satan's citadel,
And won the universe.
Now to His faithful band
He gives that weapon bright
To arm both heart and hand
Against the evil sprite.

7 In this auspicious Sign
Thou shalt be conqueror,
Said He to Constantine,
Who that proud Standard bore;
A glorious augury,
Of whose prodigious worth
The records all agree
In heaven and on earth!

Its Glory and Merit

8 Despite deceitful sense
And reason's fickle shift,
The Cross with confidence
We take as Truth's own gift.
A princess there we see
In whom, let faith confess,
We find all charity,
Grace, wisdom, holiness.

9 God's love could not resist
Such beauty or its plea,
Which bade Him keep a tryst
With our humanity.
Coming to earth, He said:
This, Lord, and nothing more:
Thy saving Cross imbed
Here in My bosom's core.

10 He took it, found it fair,

An object not of shame
But honor, made it share
His love's most tender flame.
From childhood's morning hour
His longing kept in sight
As beauty would a flower
The Cross of His delight.

11 At last in its caress
Long sought for eagerly,
He died of tenderness
And love's totality.
That dear supreme baptism
For which His heart had cried,
The Cross became His chrism,
Love's object undenied.

12 Christ called the Fisherman
A Satan scandalous
When he but winced to scan
What Christ would bear for us.
Christ's Cross we may adore,
His Mother we may not.
O mystery and more!
O marvel beyond thought!

13 This Cross, now scattered wide
On earth, shall one day rise
Transported, glorified,
To the celestial skies.
Upon a cloudy height
The Cross, full-brillianted,
Shall, by its very sight,
Judge both the quick and dead.

14 Revenge, the Cross will cry
Against its sullen foes;
Pardon and joy on high
And blessedness for those
Of proved fidelity
In the immortal throng,
Singing its victory
With universal song.

15 In life the saints aspired
To nothing but the Cross;
'Twas all that they desired,

Counting all else but loss.
Each one, in discontent
With such afflictions sore
As chastening heaven sent,
Condemned himself no more.

16 St. Peter, prison-chained,
Had greater glory there
Than when at Rome he gained
The first Christ-Vicar's chair.
Saint Andrew, faithful, cried:
O good Cross, let me yield
To thee and in thee hide,
Where death in Life is sealed.

17 See how the great St. Paul
Depicts with meagre gloss
His rapture mystical,
But glories in the Cross.
More admirable far
More merit-rich is he,
Behind his dungeon bar
Than in his ecstasy.

Its Effects

18 Without a Cross, the soul
Is cowardly and tame;
Like fire to a coal
The Cross sets it aflame.
One who has suffered not,
In ignorance is bound;
Only in pain's hard lot
Is holy wisdom found.

19 A soul untried is poor
In value; new, untrained,
With destiny unsure
And little wisdom gained.
O sweetness sovereign
Which the afflicted feels
When pleased that to his pain
No human solace steals!

20 'Tis by the Cross alone
God's blessing is conferred,
And His forgiveness known
In the absolving word.

He wants all things to bear
The mark of that great seal;
Without it, nought is fair
To Him, no beauty real.

21 Wherever place is given
The Cross, things once profane
Become instinct with heaven
And shed away their stain.
On breast and brow, God's sign,
Worn proudly for His sake,
Will bless with Power divine
Each task we undertake.

22 It is our surety,
Our one protection,
Our hope's white purity,
Our soul's perfection.
So precious is its worth
That angels fain would bring
The blest soul back to earth
To share our suffering.

23 This Sign has such a charm
That at the altar-stone
The priest can God disarm
And draw Him from His throne.
Over the sacred Host
This mighty Sign he plays,
Signals the Holy Ghost,
And the Divine obeys.

24 With this adorable Sign
A fragrance is diffused
Most exquisite and fine,
A perfume rarely used.
The consecrated priest
Makes him this offering
As incense from the East,
Meet crown for heaven's King.

25 Eternal Wisdom still
Sifts our poor human dross
For one whose heart and will
Is worthy of the Cross,
Still seeks one spirit rare
Whose every pulse and breath

Is fortitude to bear
The Christ-Cross until death.

Ardent Apostrophe

26 O Cross, let me be hushed;
In speech I thee abase.
Let my presumption, crushed,
Its insolence erase.
Since thee I have received
Imperfectly, in part,
Forgive me, friend aggrieved,
For my unwilling heart!

27 Dear Cross, here in this hour,
I bow to thee in awe.
Abide with me in power
And teach me all thy law.
My princess, let me glow
With ardor in thine arms;
Grant me to chastely know
The secret of thy charms.

28 In seeing thee so fair,
I hunger to possess
Thy beauty, but I dare
Not in my faithlessness.
Come, mistress, by thy will
Arouse my feeble soul
And I will give thee still
A heart renewed and whole.

29 For life I choose thee now,
My pleasure, honor, friend,
Sole object of my vow,
Sole joy to which I tend.
For mercy's sake, print, trace
Yourself upon my heart,
My arm, my forehead, face;
And not one blush will start.

30 Above all I possess
I choose thy poverty;
And for my tenderness
Thy sweet austerity.
Now be thy folly wise
And all thy holy shame

As grandeur in my eyes,
My glory and my fame.

31 When, by your majesty,
And for your glory's sake,
You shall have vanquished me,
That conquest I shall take
As final victory,
Though worthy not to fall
Beneath thy blows, or be
A mockery to all.

Maxims of the World

"Vous convertir? Tout beau, tout beau" No. 39

1 Oh! You converted? Steady now!
Trustworthy people never change;
This sudden fervor can't be good,
And everyone will find it strange.

Beware, though we such wiles enjoy,
Their hidden poison can destroy.

2 Too scrupulous is what you are,
This zeal of yours will pass away;
Would you have people think you odd
And make a joke of how you pray?

Beware . . .

3 That priest you have is far too strict,
He's always preaching on our sins;
They'll treat you as a fool like him,
And welcome you with hidden grins.

Beware . . .

4 The Lord does not demand of you
Those penances or that good work:
Beneath them over-weening pride,
Self-love, and self-conceit all lurk.

Beware . . .

5 Lord, save us! What piosity!
What ostentatious zeal!
You know you're being led astray

By Satan every time you kneel.
Beware . . .

6 That Meditation must be dropped,
For you it is a dangerous thing:
Temptation for the idle soul
Is all the fruit that it will bring.

Beware . . .

7 Of what use all those Rosaries?
Much better do your work each day;
Content yourself to say no more
Than prayers that other people pray.

Beware . . .

8 Avoid this singularity,
True virtue loves to hide itself;
You show too much of what you do,
Be on your guard against yourself.

Beware . . .

9 You have so many talents, friend,
Your place is in society;
Conduct yourself with elegance,
Your critics then will leave you free.

Beware . . .

10 Even your clothes are most bizarre,
To everyone a smile they bring;
You are the subject of their songs,
I dare not tell you everything.

Beware . . .

11 If you will walk with eyes cast down
And in unsocial ways engage,
You might as well become a monk
Or go into a hermitage.

Beware . . .

12 I am your friend, believe me, do,
Must you behave like pious fools?
It is absurd without a doubt
To turn mere trifles into rules.

God Alone

Beware . . .

13 It's not what I alone believe,
Your friends and your relations shun
Such over-zealous practices;
They surely know what is not done.

Beware . . .

14 All this and more the world proclaims
To sanction its deceitful ways,
And many volumes I would need
To tell of all the snares it lays,
And to reveal its tricks and lies,
Its sins in such attractive guise.

Beware . . .

15 O cursed love of earthly things,
O cursed brood of vipers, ye,
Ye cursed offspring of the damned,
O cursed source of misery,
Destroyer of all good intent,
O scourge of all the innocent.

Beware . . .

16 Accurst by God eternally,
You and I declare to be my foe;
To God alone I now profess,
In spite of all I undergo,
That I will be his servant true,
No matter what you try to do.

Beware . . .

17 Inspired by Jesus' holy life,
Henceforth I now resolve again
To always do that which is right,
without regard or fear of men,
So as to earn the blessed name
Of warrior who the world o'ercame.

Beware . . .

18 Come to my help, O Queen of Heaven,
Come to my help, O Virgin, pray,
That I might fight this wretched world,
Against its fear of what men say,

That I might triumph with your Son,
With all its perils overcome.

Beware . . .

19 Great God, support me with your strength,
Take not your powerful hand away,
That I may overcome this beast,
This fear of what the world will say.
Dear Jesus, on whom I rely,
With you I will the world defy.

Beware . . .

Reparation to the Heart of Jesus

Amende Honorable au Coeur de Jésus No. 47

1 O Heart of God, adorable Heart!
Heart, object of my total love,
Worthy of boundless love Thou art
Who lovest me all bounds above.

2 Here, wretched in my poverty,
The worst of sinners, let me start
At least to make amends to Thee,
O loving and majestic heart!

3 Pardon all the unfaithful—those
Who, made to serve Thee, in spite
Of all Thy love, become Thy foes,
Thus turning toward eternal night.

4 Pardon those who in schisms break
The bond of Christian unity;
Forgive those teachers who forsake
Thy changeless Truth's integrity.

5 Pardon their rude affronts, their rage,
Their deeds unseemly, scandal-fraught;
Forgive the dreadful heritage
Of harm their heresies have wrought.

6 Pardon, O Sacred Heart, those who
Neglect Thy Blessed Sacrament.

Pardon Thy false recipients, too,
  Partaking, yet impenitent.

7 Thy Heart of Hearts is pierced thereby—
  Something the Devil cannot do.
Though anguished by such blasphemy,
  Let still Thy pardon carry through.

8 Lord, pardon all unfaithful priests,
  Betrayers false to Thy embrace;
Forgive the thousands at Thy Feasts
  Who come ungarmented in grace.

9 Pardon my lack of quickened sense
  To savor well Thy banquet spread,
My languid, dull indifference
  Though by the Bread of Angels fed.

10 Savior, Thy mercy show to me
  For sins wherein my will has crossed
Thy will. Without Thy clemency
  My soul must forever lost.

11 I love Thee, Heart all lovable;
  I long, yes ardently I thirst
To love Thee wholly, knowing well
  That Thou indeed didst love me first.

12 Have pity on my poor deserts,
  So frequently approaching Thee
With callous coldness, even hurts
  When sin beguiles and burdens me.

13 Pardon that base ingratitude.
  Having received from Thee so much,
My heart is reprobate and rude
  To risk Thy grace and lose Thy touch.

14 O foolish heart, could you thus spurn
  Unfeelingly the Heart of Christ?
Could you not love the Heart in turn
  That for your sake was sacrificed?

15 To Thee through Mary's purity,
  O Heart of God, my heart I raise.
Jesus, my soul's security,
  To Thee all honor, love and praise.

The True Devotee of Mary

"J'aime ardemment Marie" No. 76

1 God first, my Ransomer,
Then Mary ardently
I love. To win for her
One heart I'd gladly die.
O Mistress good, O Queen!
If we but knew her well
We'd hasten to be seen
In her best clientele.

2 Assuming here on earth
Our nature, God became
Docile to her from birth;
Let me then do the same.
Virgin most faithful, she
Shows to my steps the way.
Through her, grace comes to me;
To her, then, I must pray.

3 Jesus is glorified
By honors paid to her.
In error those abide
Who otherwise aver.
To iove her Son the less
For loving her would be
An insult pardonless
To Christian piety.

4 Away then, heretic
With scruples overblown!
Away your false critique
And its presumptuous tone!
Unceasingly I'll pray
To her, my Paragon
Of grace, and in that way
Be pleasing to her Son.

5 In mercy she excels;
Great is her gentleness.
Not one soul she repels
That seeks her tenderness.
Jesus himself constrains
My soul to grasp and prize

The grace her suffrage gains.
Dare I do otherwise?

6 She is Queen-Sovereign
Of all the universe.
Heaven is her domain;
Her heel is Satan's curse.
She is the treasurer
Of all Christ's goods. She lifts
Sin's bar and bids us share
The Holy Spirit's gifts.

7 She is the cloister-cell
Where God became a Child;
Where man, O miracle,
With God was reconciled.
She is God's daughter fair,
Mother of Grace Divine,
Made by her *fiat*-prayer
The Holy Spirit's shrine.

8 Unique while on this sphere,
The purest and the best,
She now is without peer
Among the Heaven-blest.
She is the greatest foe
Of Satan, hell's dark prince;
Her very name is woe
To him and makes him wince.

9 St. Augustine makes clear
With total verity:
She is the image sheer
Of the Divinity.
Through her and her consents
The Lord has set us free.
She is the sea immense
Of all His Majesty.

10 Although enthroned in light
Near God, her very Son,
She witnesses our plight
And pleads for everyone.
Purgation's fire severe
She enters, setting free
The chained, while demons hear
Her chant of victory.

11 She is more radiant
Than all the Cherubim;
She is more luminant
Than all the Seraphim.
Outside the Trinity
And solely by God's grace
In Heaven's galaxy
She holds the highest place.

12 Under her queenly sway
I'll never be afraid
To beg her: Do away
With Satan's dark charade!
As her devoted liege,
My hope is to be given
After this pilgrimage
A higher place in Heaven.

13 My gracious Queen, accept
These accents unbeguiled,
These pleadings so inept.
I'm but a simple child.
Better than I can do,
Let others take your part.
May all men offer you
A present of their heart.

The Devout Slave of Jesus in Mary

"Que mon âme chante et publie" No. 77

1 Let this my song declare
  (Thus honoring her Son)
Our Lady's boundless care
  Toward her poor serving-one.

2 O that my voice might say
  Thunder-loud east to west
Far happiest are they
  On earth who serve her best.

3 Predestined ones, prepare
  Your ears. I tell things true,

Marvels sublime and rare
   Of her who mothered you.

4 Mary is my great wealth;
   With Christ she is my all,
My tenderness, my health,
   My honor's treasure-hall.

5 She is the covenant-ark
   Of purity's defense;
My refuge from the dark,
   My robe of innocence.

6 She is the chaste retreat
   Where I can always pray
In Jesus' presence sweet
   And not be turned away.

7 She is the citadel
   Where I am safe from harm;
Amidst the deluge-swell
   She takes me by the arm.

8 Depending on her care
   The better to depend
On Jesus, I stake there
   This life and its last end.

9 When from the Tempter's stings
   I struggle up toward God,
It is on Mary's wings
   I mount, no more a clod.

10 My just Redeemer's ire
   By Mary's plea is eased.
"Behold," I cry, "your Mother!"
   At once He is appeased.

11 This Mistress, when I call,
   Comes to my aid with power.
If, being weak, I fall
   She helps me in that hour.

12 At times when like a plague
   Some daily sin assails,
"O Mary, help!" I beg,
   And grace once more prevails.

13 She answers when I cry

For strength God's will to do:
"Have courage, son, for I,
Shall not abandon you."

14 When as a nursing child
I seek her breast's pure milk,
This Virgin chaste and mild
Feeds me celestial milk.

15 Here is a mystery:
By Mary's motherhood
I carry her in me;
Her goodness is my good.

16 She fructifies my soul
By her fecundity;
She makes me meek and whole
By her humility.

17 She is the limpid pool
Wherein my sores show plain,
Wherein, refreshed, I cool
My passions and their pain.

18 Through Jesus I must go
To see His Father's face;
Through Mary's help, just so,
I seek to gain that grace.

19 I do all things through her.
This is the surest way
To do God's will, the spur
And key to sanctity.

20 Christians, arise! Outrun
My laggard constancy.
Love Mary, love her Son
Now and eternally.

Desire for Holy Communion

"Mille fois mon coeur vous désire" No. 112

1 My Jesus, I long ardently
For you to come to me this day;
Without you life is misery.
Come to me soon, I pray.

God Alone

2 Without the fervor that you bring,
O Love, I languish night and day;
And do you not desire my love?
Inflame my heart, I pray.

3 Good Shepherd, bear your lost sheep home
Within your arms, whene'er I stray;
From ravening wolves that round me roam
Oh, keep me safe, I pray.

4 O bread of Life, for you I sigh,
Give me yourself without delay;
For otherwise my soul must die.
Give me to eat, I pray.

5 O fount of living waters clear,
How long and weary is the way;
Refresh my soul which thirsts for you.
Give me to drink, I pray.

6 O loving Lord, my soul is chilled
By icy winds that round me play;
O fire of love, let me be filled
With warmth from you, I pray.

7 Like the blind man who cried to you:
Have mercy on me, Lord, I say,
O Mary's son, that I may see;
Increase my faith, I pray.

8 Lord, I am sick beyond all cure,
But with a word you can display
Your power; without you death is sure.
O heal me, Lord, I pray.

9 My Lord, I knock upon your door;
Your favors I can ne'er repay,
Yet in my want I beg for more.
Fulfill my needs, I pray.

10 I am not worthy, Lord, that you
Should come into my house today
As heavenly food; say but the word
And heal my soul, I pray.

11 Lord, you alone are my true friend,
My treasure which can ne'er decay;
All earthly joys do you transcend.
Do visit me this day.

Come, O Wisdom, Come!

"O Sagesse, venez" No. 124

1 Come, O Wisdom, come! Hear this, a beggar's plea
By Mary's womb, by every gush
Of Blood her Jesus shed for me,
Confound me not, nor bid me hush.

2 Why do you so prolong my painful martyrdom?
For you I languish night and day;
My heart keeps calling to you, "Come!"
My soul grows faint with you away.

3 Open, O longed-for one. I knock here at your door.
Not as an alien fugitive
But as a suitor, heart-sick, sore
Whose only home is where you live.

4 Perhaps you do not want me in your retinue.
At least allow me in that case
The privilege of seeking you
Though finding not your hiding-place.

5 I cast myself in spirit before your lofty throne.
If I have come unbidden there
At least do not my love disown:
Help thou my need lest I despair.

6 Wisdom, I am beset by fears and dangers still;
Much cowardice enfeebles me.
I need a bolder faith and will,
A will to love you boundlessly.

7 Worthy Mother of God, Virgin all-faithful, pure,
Lend me your faith; lift me on wings
Of faith, that I may mount secure
To Wisdom's height, and have all things.

8 By Mary's faith then come, O Wisdom heaven-sent!
You leapt to her as light to flame;
She gave you your embodiment,
In her Incarnate you became.

9 My faith no longer flags; I know it shall avail
Against all odds to win my plea
That you, O Wisdom, come to me,
Since God has said and cannot fail:

"Who prays with faith, his boon shall win;
"Who knocks with faith shall enter in;
"Who seeks with faith shall find." *Amen.*

Act of Reparation to the Blessed Sacrament

"Soupirons, gémissons, pleurons amèrement" No. 136

1 Let me cry, let me weep bitter tears to God above,
For Jesus is abandoned in his Sacrament of love;
Forgotten and insulted in the dwelling of the Lord,
Derided and rejected where once he was adored.

2 The mansions of the nobles are all clean and set with care,
Yet the house of God's forgotten, its altars standing bare;
The floor is all broken, the roof lets in the rain,
The crumbling walls are marked with holes and every kind of stain.

3 The crucifix is broken, the pictures green with damp,
The altar cloths are rotting, no light burns in the lamp,
The missals torn and battered, the brasswork stained with rust,
The things of God are thrown about and scattered in the dust.

4 The ciborium is tarnished, the chalice turning black,
The monstrance, which is made of tin, is mouldy at the back;
From font right up to sacristy the picture is the same,
Such disorder in the house of God is our reproach and shame.

5 The pagans in their temples dare not spit upon the floor,
But in our church a crowd of dogs run in and out the door;
They bark and fight continually and fill the place with slime,
But no one cares enough of this to avenge the dreadful crime,

6 There is just one exception in all this sorry scene:
My Lord and Lady's special pew is always neat and clean;
And standing out in bright new paint upon the dingy wall
Their gaily-colored coat-of-arms looks down upon it all.

7 Above the Lord's own altar, instead of the Lord's own name,
The banners of his Lordship a place of honor claim;

Both priest and mule are flaunting the badges of their thrall,
The former at the altar, the latter in his stall.

8 The houses of the nobles are so crowded and gay,
And fashionable young ladies are courted night and day;
But the church of God's deserted, unless they condescend
To go to church for one short Mass they think will never end.

9 Behold the worldly cleric coming in with haughty face.
How his lady friends admire him as he bows with courtly grace!
He bobs a genuflection, then seeks whom he should greet;
He strolls about and chatters as though walking in the street.

10 Still worse, he has a snuff-box, which he opens with a jest,
And delicately takes a pinch, then passes around the rest.
Puffed up with self-importance and with his graceful ways,
He squirms about and poses, making faces as he prays.

11 Alas, it's often happened, the way to church he's trod
To pay reverence to Venus, to a goddess not to God;
Every thought and aspiration, every word and loving glance
Are but homage to a creature, a prayer to find romance.

12 Behold upon the other side a sorry scene is played,
A shameless hussy sitting in all her fine brocade;
In her dainty little slippers and head-dress trimmed with lace,
Come simply to parade herself within the holy place.

13 This empty-headed madam, with an impudence unknown,
Up to the very altar ostentatiously is shown,
And poses on a bench in front, so to be seen by all,
To captivate the eyes of men and hold their hearts in thrall.

14 To think this devil's agent, while her knee to Jesus bends,
Must rob him of his glory and lead astray his friends!
The splendor of her finery the thought of Jesus harms,
Forgotten is the altar in the presence of her charms.

15 And if the time seems tedious, she always has her fan,
Her dog and gloves, to pass the time, and often her young man;
She'll read a bit, and roll her eyes, and fix her hat with care,
Then look around the chapel to see who's watching her.

16 O strike them, God almighty, strike this ungrateful lot!
At least let them respect thee, if they will love thee not.
Too long hast thou been patient; thy justice let them see;
Let fear replace that insolence with which they now mock thee.

17 Thy glory has been ravished, dishonored is thy name,
Such sinners against thy majesty must bow their heads in shame.
And yet restrain thy anger, at least a while, I pray;
The greatness of their wickedness with greater good repay.

18 Forgive them, dearest Jesus, for they know not what they do;
Remember thy great Passion, and have mercy on us too.
And if we are unable to atone for all our guilt,
Accept our feeble homage, and treat us as thou wilt.

19 We confess before thy altar that we are sinners still;
Thou canst punish us or spare us according to thy will.
But remember thy great mercy and the tears that we have shed,
And hear our cries for pardon, for our hearts are full of dread.

To the Sisters of Wisdom

"O Filles de la Sagesse" No. 149

1 Dearest Sisters of Christ-Wisdom,
In your life it is your aim
To assist the poor, the outcasts,
The despairing and the lame.
All those by the world rejected
On your love have greater claim.
Let our love on all men rest,
Where God dwells a loving guest.

2 Taking Providence as guardian,
Do not future wants ensure,
And depend not on that prudence
Which requires to be secure,
Nor repose your firm reliance
On what you yourselves procure.
Let our love, etc. . . .

3 Wonderful our God who fashions
All he wishes out of naught.
Do not think, then, my dear daughters,
Entry to the convent's bought
With the key of gold or silver,
Contrary to what Christ taught.
Let our love, etc. . . .

4 Take that girl who has no money:
Willing and detached is she.

But refuse that rich young lady,
Though prized in society,
If, besides, she lacks the spirit
Which our Lord expects to see.
Let our love, etc. . . .

5 Be the servants of God's people,
Give them all with all your power.
Such will be a source of treasure
Which no moths can e'er devour.
Such your letters of approval
Before which your foes will cower.
Let our love, etc. . . .

6 Vast must be your heart's devotion
With a boundless love for all,
But your loving must be guided
By obedience's call,
Lest its beauty should be tarnished
When imprudent acts befall.
Let our love, etc. . . .

7 That your victory be perfect,
Shining like the sun on high,
You should choose, in God, a Father
Who will guide your mind and eye.
Him consult in all that matters
And on his advice rely.
Let our love, etc. . . .

The Call to the Mission

"Mon cher parent, mon cher voisin" No. 163

1 Arise, dear brother, come, my friend,
Let us arise before the sun,
God calls us to his festival,
The mission has begun.
So be there ice or be there snow,
To gain God's grace, to church we'll go.

2 In spite of every obstacle,
In spite of cold and winter's sting,
In spite of all the body's groans,
The mission hymn we'll sing.
So be there wind or be there rain,
Off to the church, God's grace to gain.

3 The family, they all call it mad,
The devil and world protest:
"Stay by the fireside, stay in bed."
But in the church we'll rest.
And be there ice or be there frost,
The mission grace must not be lost.

4 Leave troubled Martha on her own,
Leave all the timid ones in bed.
As we march boldly on, our God
Counts every step we tread.
So be there rain or be there ice,
We'll seek the grace of Paradise.

5 You workmen, cease to labor now;
Complete your lawsuit, you in court;
You sinners, leave your sinful ways,
And be deterred by naught.
So be there mist or be there rain,
The grace of God we will attain.

6 All that you ask you will receive,
Says Jesus. Seek and you will find.
The door will open if you knock.
So do not stay behind.
In spite of frost, in spite of rain,
Seek for my grace and you'll obtain.

7 You joiners, lay aside your wood,
Put down your iron, you smiths, for now,
Let craftsmen leave their work a while,
That grace may all endow.
And be there thunder, be there frost,
We'll seek that grace, whate'er the cost.

8 Let us arise, both great and small,
Awake from all our sluggishness,
To seek the gifts of priceless worth
And blessings numberless.
So be there snow or be there ice,
Let us seek grace and Paradise.

9 For heaven is the pearl we seek,
Our harbor and our resting-place,
The prize for which we pray and toil.
Let us, then, seek God's grace.
And be there ice or be there snow,
We'll not the mission grace forego.

10 To reach the heavenly harbor, we
Must toil and fight against the waves.
So to the sails and to the ropes
To earn the grace that saves.
Then be there snow or be there frost,
We'll persevere, not count the cost.

11 Bestir yourselves, you lazy ones.
Although the way is long and cold,
We will not shrink or spare ourselves.
Our need will make us bold.
So be there wind or be there rain,
We'll seek a heavenly throne to gain.

12 Wake up, you people wrapped in sleep.
We seek, despite our many foes,
The pardon of our sins, which God
Through his great grace bestows.
So be it wet or be it cold,
Reward we'll gain a hundredfold.

13 Now off you go to hear our Lord,
Who in the sermon speaks to you,
To try to touch your hearts once more
And offers grace anew.
Its call is brief, its passing swift;
Let us not miss this precious gift.

14 The mission is the chosen time
When we find pardon for our sins,
Despite the devil and the world,
And when new life begins.
Grace calls us once, then passes on,
So to the church let us be gone.

15 If we must bear the cross in life,
Our heavenly prize is worth the pain;
That is our inspiration now,
The great reward we gain.
Grace comes, then leaves us if ignored;
Let us seek grace and God's reward.

16 It is for heaven that we strive,
But for God's glory, his alone.
To rise to heaven, above the skies,
And to a glorious throne—
Though wind and rain display their might—
Up to a crown of glory bright.

20 Rules on Voluntary Poverty in the Early Church

Introduction

This text, found in Montfort's Notebook, appears quite abruptly among pages which had been left blank. The subject treated is unrelated to other matters of the Notebook, which concentrates in its first part on the Blessed Virgin and in the second on Jesus Christ. Montfort must have written these notes at a time when the theme of poverty for lay people living in community presented itself to him with a certain immediacy. The rules are addressed to Brothers who, though living in community, still remained in close relationship with their environment and their families.

We do not know who these Brothers were, nor can we identify the author of the original work from which Montfort draws his material. Certain archaisms in the spelling would indicate that it was written at the beginning of the 17th century.

Rules on voluntary poverty in the early church

Basic truths regarding poverty of spirit.

1 We cannot serve both God and money.

2 1 Money is the god of the wicked. 2 The desire for money is the root and source of all evils. 3 It is a misfortune to be rich.

3 Those who wish to acquire riches, even though their intentions are good 1 will make shipwreck of their faith; 2 will gradually succumb to the snares of the devil; 3 act contrary to the example of Christ, his apostles and his true disciples; 4 are accepting the corrupt standards of the modern world.

4 Poverty of spirit is absolutely necessary for salvation, whether we be very rich or very poor. But in either case it is so rare that many, both rich and poor, lose their souls.

5 True voluntary poverty gives great glory to God, assures one's salvation, is most useful to one's neighbor and most dreaded by the devil.

6 It gives great glory to God: 1 He gave us the example of it. 2 It is the gospel's hidden treasure, the pearl of great price. 3 It is in keeping with the teaching and example of the great saints.

7 It assures our salvation: 1 Poverty destroys covetousness and self-love, the root of all evils. 2 The words 'yours' and 'mine,' which chill the most ardent love, are effaced. 3 Through and upon poverty all other virtues are founded, engendered and acquired. 4 Poverty reduces the dangerous occasions when our arch-enemy the devil attacks us and strives to vanquish us. 5 It models us on Jesus Christ. 6 It makes us judges of the world.

8 Poverty is most helpful to our neighbor: 1 By it we share all our possessions with him. 2 Our neighbor is edified by our detachment and by the other virtues it helps to cultivate.

9 Poverty is most dreaded by the devil for it diminishes the dangerous occasions and the snares which he sends to entrap us and by which he plans to bring about our ruin.

10 People, even living in the world, may take a vow of poverty for one year (but always in the presence of a priest) for several reasons. In the first place, the vow gives glory to God and helps the soul towards perfection more than any other practice of devotion. Secondly, this vow gives stability and strengthens the will. Thirdly, it wards off temptations against detachment which assail us either from the world or from the devil himself.

11 It would seem best that persons living in the world should take this vow for only one year: 1) So as not to tempt God or test themselves beyond their strength. 2) That their good will might accompany the obligation it imposes.

12 Those wishing to take this voluntary vow of poverty must keep the following rules:

1) They must declare exactly what they possess whether in property, goods or money;

2) They must not be in debt, at least for any long-standing or considerable sums. If they are, they must begin to repay them.

3) Having paid their debts, they must put into the common purse all the money they actually possess. Once a month they must hand

in the money they have earned or acquired, having subtracted what is necessary for their upkeep.

4) Holy obedience, which, together with the vow of poverty, removes selfishness in the necessary use of material possessions, will nevertheless allow them to draw on the small personal income arising from their patrimony or work, (i) for their own upkeep and the maintenance of their family, (ii) for almsgiving, (iii) for the maintenance of their essential possessions.

5) When they die they must leave all their possessions, property and goods to their relatives, if they have any. Otherwise their belongings will be given to the Society of the voluntary poor.

6) Their burial will be like that of the poor, inexpensive, without any pomp, in the cemetery and never in the church. They must make their will in good time and show it to their superior.

7) In keeping with their vow, when any one of the Brothers is in need of something, he is obliged by his vow to ask the bursar for what he needs, whether it be for his upkeep, clothing or apostolic work. But if what he wants is either costly, or not absolutely necessary, then the rest of the community must be consulted.

On these conditions, we, the undersigned, in order the more perfectly to imitate Jesus Christ, take for one year the vow of poverty according to the above rules into the hands of one of our Brothers. We ask our Blessed Lady and St. Francis of Assisi, whom we take as our patrons and protectors, to obtain for us from God the grace of complete fidelity to this vow.

Signed

21 Four Short Meditations on the Religious Life

Introduction

The manuscript of 'The Secret of Mary' ends in the middle of a page. The final, 'qui tenet, teneat,' *is followed by a large GOD ALONE which introduces four summaries of meditations on poverty, chastity, obedience, and Religious Rules. This text is not necessarily a copy of Montfort's original manuscript but could be a copy of personal notes taken by someone who heard his talks.*

Four Short Meditations on the Religious Life

I Meditation on Religious Poverty

1st Point Consider that in virtue of the vow of poverty you can neither take, receive, give, keep, return, or lend anything whatsoever without permission. The penalties laid down by Canon Law for infringements are severe.

2nd Point These are the degrees of poverty: 1) to give up all one's possessions; 2) to give up all attachment to them; 3) to be content with mere necessities; 4) to be ready to endure privations; 5) to be in want of something necessary at this present moment; 6) to suffer with patience and joy both sickness and health.

3rd Point Consider the teaching and example of the Son of God;

what he said, what he did, how he lived, how he died, what he has promised to the poor in spirit.

Examine yourself to see if you have committed any fault against this vow, if you have hidden anything as did the wicked Achan (Josh. 7.1.) who caused God's army to be defeated. Convince yourself that you will receive nothing from God as long as you hold on to any possession.

II Meditation on Religious Chastity

1st Point Consider that the virtue of chastity makes a soul resemble the angels and even God himself. By this vow we become the spouse of Christ. Thus a religious cannot share his love with another nor have a divided heart. Arouse sentiments of joy, gratitude, and shame for the past, and promise unshaken fidelity for the future.
2nd Point Consider the esteem which our Lord had for this virtue. He willed to have a virgin Mother on earth, as he had a virgin Father in heaven. His beloved disciple was a virgin; he is surrounded by virgins in heaven; he was accused of every sin except the sin of impurity. Of the eight beatitudes it is only the pure of heart who are promised they will see God; consequently it follows that those who are not pure will never see him.
3rd Point Here are the means for remaining chaste: 1) fidelity to mental prayer; 2) humility, for God allows the proud to fall to the lowest depths; 3) obedience, for the flesh will never obey its master, the spirit, if the spirit is not obedient to its master; 4) avoidance of dangerous occasions, visits and conversations, for he who loves the danger will perish in the danger; 5) vigilance over one's heart, mortification of the senses and making known one's temptations to those who can help to overcome them.

III Meditation on the Vow of Obedience

1st Point Consider both the excellence and the use of the vow of obedience. 1) It is the source and root of all other virtues; 2) It is the noblest of the three vows because it sacrifices the mind and the will to God; 3) it makes us holy and in a sense sinless; 4) it consecrates our actions and gives them a priceless value; 5) it helps to overcome all temptations, since it encompasses every virtue. On the other hand a disobedient religious has to strive against every vice, especially that of impurity which attacks mainly the proud; for it is not possible that a man who refuses to submit his will to God should be master of his body.

Finally, obedience brings to a soul peace and security both in life and in death, since through it one has the certainty of doing the will of God, while rebellious souls find neither peace, joy, nor merit. God opposes their will because they oppose his.

2nd Point Consider what Our Lord had to say about this virtue and to what degree he practised it. He commanded men to obey those seated on the chair of Moses. He declared that those who obey their superiors obey him and that those who despise their superiors despise him. So, if I criticize my superior, I criticize Jesus Christ. Secondly, he taught us the meaning of this virtue by his own example; he obeyed his parents, his enemies, his executioners, indeed all his creatures. He chose death rather than disobey. Arouse in yourself sentiments of abasement and shame for being proud and ambitious in the presence of this humble and obedient God.

3rd Point Consider the four essentials of perfect obedience: 1) we must obey all our superiors; 2) we must obey in everything that is not sinful; 3) we must obey willingly and joyfully; 4) we must obey blindly and wholeheartedly.

Examine yourself, feel ashamed, be converted and convince yourself that you cannot be a true religious if you are not obedient.

IV Meditation on the Rules

1 Consider

1 A religious is not a good religious unless he keeps the rules of his Order; just as a Christian is not a good Christian unless he keeps the laws of Christ.

2 Our perfection is rooted in our obedience to the rules since these are channels of God's grace as well as the chains which bind us to him according to his words, 'If you love me, keep my commandments.'

3 Whatever you do in the religious life, you will do nothing and merit nothing if you do not keep your rules, for it will lack the seal of obedience and love, being contrary to the will of God as shown in the rules.

4 A disorderly life cannot bring peace. We cannot be secure from temptation if we are not protected by our rules, for the devil is powerful where there is lack of order. Moreover, we endanger our salvation, for grace comes to us from our rules and we commit grave sin when we violate them through contempt.

Indeed, how can we continually break a rule without coming to despise it? However small the rule, its transgression is always dangerous. He who is unfaithful in small things will soon be unfaithful in great things. What ensures our peace, and our salvation, and our perfection, as well as what has cost our holy Founder much sorrow and anxiety can surely never be called small.

2 Consider that when we despise our rules we despise the authority of God himself who gave them to us through our holy Founder; just as formerly he gave his divine law through Moses and the rules of St. Pachomius through an angel. Moreover, to disregard our rules is to stray from the path of perfection for the devil never harms a man who keeps his rules. 'Keep your Rule and your Rule

will keep you,' says St. Augustine, 'but if you do not keep it, it will destroy you.'

Arouse sorrow in your heart for having despised God's commands and resolve to obey them more faithfully in the future.

3 Consider that on the observance of the Rules depends the stability of the religious life. It is its very texture, its support, its foundation, its rampart. Those therefore who are unfaithful to the Rule are the bane of religious life and a source of scandal. They are like parricides, children who kill their parents and dishonor and afflict the spirit of the Founder.

Examine yourself and see if you have really lived as a religious up to now; if you have a sincere desire to tend towards perfection; or if you have despised your God-given means of salvation, like the unfaithful Jew whom Scripture calls a fugitive from the Law, an enemy of his country, one held in abhorrence by his brothers.

Humility is a virtue which suppresses our excessive desire for honors and prestige and makes us want to be despised, because through it we realise that of ourselves we are nothing but evil; that we have received everything from God; that we can do nothing without his help; and that we have gravely offended him.

The practice of obedience consists in:

1 Submitting our judgement to the decrees of God, of his Church, and of our superiors.

2 Avoiding innovations, schisms and heresies.

3 Never complaining about the sufferings God sends us, knowing that we deserve infinitely more.

4 Avoiding honors, dignities, distinguished offices, praise and empty applause, which we do not deserve as there is nothing but evil in us.

5 Never speaking to our advantage.

6 Despising no one.

7 Accepting every kind of insult and injury.

8 Excusing our neighbor's faults.

9 Speaking in a low voice and not giving way to anger as if we were being treated unjustly; undertaking everything with self-distrust and not letting ourselves be upset by our faults and failings.

Amen.

22 Sermons

Introduction

This manuscript contains 478 pages. The oldest part is made up of 150 pages numbered by Montfort himself 1-150. Later on, the pages have been numbered from 91-384. Subsequently, additions were made:—at the beginning 90 pages (55 written and 35 blank) and at the end 94 pages (384-478). There are therefore three distinct parts in the manuscript.

The first part contains a series of sermons entirely composed according to a pre-arranged plan. It is the work of a missionary preparing to meet his congregation. In this present work we give a list of the subjects treated and include two of the sermons.

The second part, which is the oldest part, contains a considerable number of sermon plans (293) taken from reputable preachers of the time, including Biroat, Laselva, Loriot, Reina and the Jesuit Texier. It also contains several items borrowed from the directors of St. Sulpice, such as Frs. Leschassier, d'Oursel and d'Outrecolles. The subjects treated are in alphabetical order from AMOUR p. 91 to ZELE p. 384. This is the typical work of a seminarian preparing for the important ministry of preaching. Fr. Blain, a student with Louis Marie in the seminary, stated, in 1724, that "the remainder of the time at the seminary after his ordination, Montfort was engaged in compiling and preparing subject-matter for sermons and in amassing a fund of material enabling him to speak later on as a missionary on a great variety of subjects."

The publication in full of this second part would be of little interest. However, to enlighten the reader concerning Montfort's work of preparation for the missionary apostolate, and to give some idea of the manner in which the seminarian condensed sermons into rough schemas, we reproduce a plan on a theme which particularly interested him, namely baptism and the promises of baptism.

In keeping with his objective, the seminarian set out to draw up plans for a mission from sermons of different authors. These pages contain numerous extracts from the works of St. John Eudes, St. Francis de Sales and St. Charles Borromeo. One piece, which is certainly a later addition, has as title, 'Concerning heretics.' Here he gives a method which, if followed, would make it easier to explain the truths of the faith to one of the 'reformed' religion. This is a proof that the missionary made a point of informing himself on the procedure for winning over the Protestants who were particularly numerous at La Rochelle and in the adjoining neighborhood.

The third part of the book is concerned with a variety of subjects. We even find in it a whole treatise in verse on the holy angels. Montfort also inserted here two methods for saying the Rosary devoutly, which we have placed at the end of the "Secret of the Holy Rosary," with the other methods.

The last pages of the manuscript are of exceptional interest. They deal with a special feature of Montfort's apostolate: 'The Return of the Mission.' It was his custom, a year after a mission, to return to the parish and preach for a week on the four last things. From page 458 to 477, he gives a sermon for each day of the week and also treats of the 'Remote Dispositions for a Happy Death,' which is found also in a shorter work bearing this title, and which we have inserted after the sermons.

The Book of Sermons

(First Part: Complete List of Subjects treated)

God[1]

Who is like to God?

1 God exists: We must know him and believe in him.
2 God is great: We must serve him and adore him.
3 God is just: We must fear him, but with filial fear.
4 God is good: We must love him with all our heart.
5 God is truthful: We must believe him and live according to his word.

1st Sermon: God exists
2nd Sermon: God is great.
3rd Sermon: God is just.
4th Sermon: God is truth[2].

Command to preach the word of God

5th Sermon: Supreme value of the word of God.
6th Sermon: Abuse of the word of God.
7th Sermon: God is good and must be loved with all one's heart.
8th Sermon: Excellence of charity.
9th Sermon: Love and gentleness of Jesus Christ.[3]

10th Sermon: On grace.
11th Sermon: On humility (9 talks).
12th Sermon: Examination of conscience.

8th Sermon

The Excellence of Charity[4]

1. Point: The excellence of charity.
2. Point: Its qualities.

(1st point—Excellence of charity.)

1st Motive: It comes from the heart of God. God is love. Explain what is meant by God living in us. Explain the meaning of charity.
2nd. It is the predominant virtue of God. . . . Charity was the motive for the Incarnation. 'Who for us men and for our salvation, etc. . . .'
3rd. It is the first and greatest of the commandments.
The first
1 Because it was the first he gave us.
2 It is the first thing we have to do.
3 It should occupy the first place in our heart.
Nothing can be greater than charity.
1st. It is the concern of all men, for all men can and must love God. . . . Some are not able to fast . . . others are not able to give alms . . .
2nd. We cannot do anything greater in heaven or on earth . . . It is golden, it is the sun, it is heaven.
3rd. Charity makes us great in this world and in the next and it transforms us into God.
1 It is the fulfillment of the whole law. 2 It is for all time. It is eternal. In heaven there is no longer faith or hope or patience but charity persists. . . .
4th. It fulfils all the demands of the law. (Rom. 13.10) 'Love and then do what you want.' (St. Augustine)
5th. It is the queen, the life, the truth, the merit or stimulus and the charm of all the virtues.
1 The queen: 'The greatest of these is charity.' (1 Cor. 13.13)
2 The life: 'If I do not possess charity I am nothing.' (1 Cor. 13, 1) 'He who does not love, remains dead.' (1 Jn. 3.14)
3 The truth: 'If I should have faith . . . if I should understand all mysteries . . . if I should give away . . . I am nothing . . . an empty appearance of virtue.'
4 The stimulus, charm and bond: 'Where there is love, there is no labor, or if there is labor, the labor is loved.' (Imit. Christ, bk.1.)
5 The bond: 'The bond of perfection." (Col. 3.14)
5th (Repeated) It is the great machine which makes all things easy, no matter how difficult they may be. The machine of the mind is

that power of love which takes one from the world and carries one to God. (St. Gregory)

1 It enables us to do everything with ease.

2 It gives us the courage to leave everything.

3 It enables us to suffer everything with joy.

The example of the saints: "They lived by faith, they conquered kingdoms, they performed works of justice, they inherited the promises." They said with St. Paul: "For him I have accepted the loss of everything and I look on everything as so much refuse," (Phil. 3.8) or with St. Ignatius the Martyr: "Let fire, beasts, crosses, torments of the devil come to me as long as I have the joy of possessing Christ," or "nothing will come between me and the love of God, neither persecution . . . nor troubles or worries . . . nor princes . . . neither height nor depth . . . nor danger." (Rom. 8.38, 39)

6 It is the sign and mark of the elect: "the sons of God cannot be distinguished from the sons of the devil except by charity." (St. Augustine)

7 It unites and transforms the soul into God. "God is love and what is more precious? He who dwells in love, dwells in God; what is more secure? God is within the soul; what could be more joy-giving?" (St. Bernard) "Your value as a person depends upon the quality of your love. If you love the world, you are of the world; if you love God you are of God." (St. Augustine). "I live, yet not I, but Christ lives in me." (Gal. 2.20)

8 Nothing is so easy, so useful and at the same time, so necessary.

So easy: our heart is made to love; nothing can prevent it from loving.

So necessary: "If you wish to enter into life, keep the commandments." (Matt. 19.17) "Those things God has prepared for them that love him." (1 Cor. 2.9.) So useful: "I show you a more excellent way." (1 Cor. 12.31)

"The value of a soul is assessed according to its measure of love. If it possesses much love, it is of great value; if it possesses little love, it is of little value; if it has no love, it is nothing, as the Apostle says, if I have not love, I am nothing." (St. Bernard)

"I can affirm that if any virtue is to lead us to the life of the Blessed, it can only be a supremely great love of God." (St. Augustine)

"The true patience of the saints can only come from their love of God and the false patience of the wicked can only come from the cupidity of the world." (St. Augustine)

(2nd point—Qualities of divine love)

Everyone claims that he loves God. (St. Gregory) However,

nothing is more rare. "Do not be deceived, Brothers." (1 Cor. 6.9.) Among the metals are gold and silver. Charity is gold.

True charity is:

1 full of action as a fire. It is a seed that germinates, a root that sprouts, water that flows, a fire that burns: "never is the love of God idle. If it is a great love, it will always be active; if there is no action it does not exist." (St. Gregory)

All the virtues operate through the commandment of charity, "faith which operates through charity." (Gal. 5.6.)

2 strong as death: "love is as strong as death . . . o unsurpassable virtue of charity, that overcomes the invincible." (St. Bernard)

When we love God, we imitate him in his love which, according to Richard of St. Victor: is a love which never tires; a love which is never the first to break off; a love which is not deterred by our rebelliousness.

3 sweet as honey: "O yoke of holy love which you accept so readily, and bear so triumphantly; which presses so lightly upon you and whose burden brings you joy." (St. Bernard) "My work lasts hardly an hour, but even if there were more work, I would not feel it because of love." (St. Bernard)

4 attractive as a magnet: "His love of God is all the greater who attracts many to God's love." (St. Gregory) "The frigid heart cannot understand the burning speech of love . . . the language of love is foreign to one who does not love and is just booming brass and tinkling cymbals." (St. Bernard)

5 it lasts throughout eternity. . . .

6 it is infinite like God: "the measure of our love of God is to love him without measure." (St. Bernard)

7 pure as gold. There are three sorts of love:

1 that of a mercenary;

2 that of a slave;

3 that of a child:

"mercenaries are greedy, slaves are fearful, sons are loving. Each has his own law: mercenaries are impelled by cupidity; slaves are moved by fear, sons are inspired by love. All seek what is proper to them."

8 finally, faithful to the law of God. It is by a show of deeds that charity is proven. "Simon, do you love me? Feed . . . feed . . ." (Jn. 21.15) "It is your own selves that you should be testing." (11 Cor. 13.5.)

"We do not love by word or lips (1. Jn. 3.18)," but by deeds and truth. "See the cloud of witnesses" (Heb. 12.1) . . . "they have drunk of the chalice of the Lord and have been made friends of God." "We do not live in love without there be sorrow . . . roses are gathered among thorns." Love with all one's heart: that is, courageously in spite of obstacles.

Love with all one's mind: that is, with every thought, supremely and discreetly, for love is discerning.
Love with all one's soul: that is, totally without reservations, deeply without hypocrisy for love is tender.
Love with all one's strength: that is, courageously, doing all, abandoning all, suffering all for God, for love is powerful.

Conclusion:

1. When we do not love God, even if we perform marvels, it is a waste of life's precious time. "Life is lost, if God is not loved." (St. Augustine)

2. The immense wealth we acquire when we produce acts of love of God which have the effect of effacing sin and increasing our reward.

"Through and with charity you will become capable of possessing blessedness, but without it you will never see God. Charity is the summit of all the virtues, it contains the promise of the kingdom and is the supreme reward of the saints in heaven." (St. Augustine)

"Become a lover and experience what I tell you. Be a person of desires, be a hungry person, be a pilgrim in the solitudes of love, be a thirsty person seeking the waters of your eternal home. Be warm as the sun and you will understand what I say, for if I speak to a cold person, he will not understand my message." (St. Augustine)

9th Sermon On the Love and Gentleness of Jesus.

Introduction: I go fishing, etc. . . . or: this is eternal life . . . the world did not know him . . . they thought it was a ghost. . . . It is I, do not fear . . . no one knows the Son except the Father and him to whom the Father chooses to reveal him . . . let us add: except the Mother and him to whom she chooses . . . sinners, you are mistaken . . . they understood wrongly and they spoke wrongly, so cry those who know him. You did not know me, cries Jesus Christ himself. Who is Jesus Christ? He is love, gentleness, kindness, humanity itself: love appeared . . . St. John . . . kindness and humanity appeared. St. Paul . . . What we have heard and what we have seen with our own eyes, what we have perceived and touched with our hands, as the beloved apostle of Jesus Christ has told us. (1 John 1, 1)

Jesus is Gentle.

1 According to the prophets who foretold him long before his birth.
2 According to his origins.
3 According to the name which was given to him.
4 According to the manner of his coming.
5 He is gentle in countenance.
6 He is gentle in speech.
7 He is gentle in his deeds.

8 In his conduct: –
1 During his life . . .
1 Humble with children.
2 Familiar with the poor.
3 Charitable towards the apostles.
4 Merciful towards sinners.
5 Patient towards his enemies.
2 During his passion.
3 After his Resurrection.
4 Gentle more than ever at the present time.

1 Jesus is gentle according to the prophets. 'My soul finds its delight in him,' says God. Why?

1 He shall not cry out and his voice will not be heard out of doors.

2 He will not be sad nor agitated.

3 He will not crush the broken reed nor quench the smoking flax.

4 As a lamb before the shearer he was silent . . . he was led as a sheep to the slaughter (Is. 42) etc.

2 Jesus is gentle in his origins.

1 In the bosom of the Father where he was from all eternity and where he abode, says St. Bernard, in the source of holiness to whom gentleness is natural. . . . "In heaven as the Father is, so is the Son, on earth as the Mother is, so is the Son." (Hugo of St. Victor)

2 By the gift he has given to us out of pure love. "God so loved the world, etc."

3 Conceived by the operation of the Holy Spirit, who is love itself and as the Church proclaims: Father of the poor, perfect consoler, gentle guest of the soul, gentle, cool refreshment.

4 Born of Mary who is the gentlest of all creatures: 'Gentlest of the gentle' . . . nothing austere in her, etc.

5 He is the uncreated and incarnate Wisdom. What gentleness!

3 Jesus is gentle in his name . . . 'Gentle lamb' . . . 'sheep' . . . say the prophets. Gentleness of a lamb: "Behold the Lamb of God," said his Precursor who knew him better than any man on earth. "Behold . . . I am Jesus," he said . . . Gentleness of the name of Jesus.

4 Gentle in the way he came.

1 How fearful he was before the Incarnation!

1 No one dare approach the place where he was. Examples of Mount Sinai and the burning bush.

2 No one dare listen to his voice. Adam said, "I heard your voice and I was afraid." . . . "Do not let the Lord speak to us," said the Israelites.

3. No one dared look at him. "No man will see me and live."

"We will probably die because we have seen the Lord."

4 No one dared approach his living seat which was the Ark and which bore everywhere the dismal traces of death. He punished Osa because of his temerity and the fifty thousand Bethsamites because of their curiosity and the Philistines because of their ungodliness.

5 He is the God of vengeance, sensitive to any show of contempt and ready to be wrathful with sinners . . . not ready to put up with them. Hardly had sin been committed when there followed the punishment, either the earth opened up or fire came down or snakes appeared to eat up the sinner. Even his favorite ones were not immune from his vengeance . . . example of Moses.

6 They did not dare to speak to him; witness Abraham: "I will speak to the Lord although I am but dust and ashes." Jacob believed he would die of fright after having seen in his sleep that mysterious ladder and could only swear "through fear of Isaac his father" . . . and not "through love." But since his Incarnation he has laid aside all fearsomeness. He has made himself so familiar and so approachable that everyone can look upon him without being dazzled. Out of love he shed his brilliance . . . we can now speak to him without fear, approach him and converse with him.

2 The Son of God, Jesus Christ, came:

1 As a rain falling on fleece and not with pomp, noise and thunder.

2 As a gentle breeze . . . for it was thus that he showed the prophet Elijah the gentleness of his soul by the manner in which he would come: "the Lord is not in a whirlwind." "The Lord is not in a great noise, the Lord is not in fire."

3 As a gentle dawn . . . do not fear, he comes not with firearms, not to punish but to save . . . he became a child bound to his Mother by tender bonds yet full of fear. (St. Bernard)

4 Jesus Christ calls shepherds and kings to his crib and all are charmed and won over by the gentleness of his face and the attractiveness of his presence.

5 Jesus is gentle to gaze upon . . . At his birth he enraptured the shepherds in spite of their roughness and the kings in spite of their pride . . . Children vied with one another to visit him as a growing child.

6 Jesus is gentle in his speech: "The rule of clemency was on his tongue" . . . "His lips were as a distilling honeycomb . . . honey and milk upon his tongue."

7 Jesus is gentle in all his actions.

1 During his life

1 Humble with the children. "Suffer little children to come unto me."

2 Tender towards the afflicted: 'Come to me all . . .'

3 Familiar with the poor: "He sent me to bring good news to the poor" . . . They followed him devotedly . . . all the people were so attracted to him that the pharisees were jealous that so many followed him and said, "See, we can do nothing about it; all the world follows him." Even gentiles came to see him, "We wish to see Jesus."

4 He was charitable and condescending towards the apostles he had chosen, who were simple, rough and ignorant, without goods, money or manners, full of imperfections and faults. "Such a Lord and such a Master was he among them, these men of the lowest class, fishermen . . . sinners, that he mingled among them and ministered to them." (Claud. Aquavi) "How gently did the Lord Jesus treat with men!" (St. Bernard)

5 Merciful towards poor sinners:

1 He never used his power to take revenge, except on a figtree when he made an example of it. "Crushed reed, etc."

2 He reproved his apostles who wanted fire to come down from heaven . . . "you do not know what spirit is moving you . . . I have not come to condemn men but to save them."

3 His kind words: "I have not come to call the just but sinners . . . to heal those who have sorrow in their hearts . . . to seek out and to save what was lost . . . how often I wanted to gather." His tears of compassion: "Jesus wept; see how he loved."

4 Examples of his goodness and his mercy:

a towards the Samaritan woman even when tired . . . "Jesus was weary."

b With Mary Magdalene.

c With the woman taken in adultery . . . "Lord Jesus, we hasten to follow you especially because of your gentleness as we hear you say that you do not despise the poor, that you do not hate the sinner, that you did not reject the repentant thief nor the tearful, repentant woman, nor the pleading Canaanite woman, nor the woman taken in adultery, nor the man sitting in the custom-house, nor the pleading publican, nor the disciple who denied you, nor the persecutor of the disciples, nor your executioners . . . we hasten to you as they did." (St. Bernard) (Sermon 22 on Song of Songs)

2 During his Passion . . . at the washing of the feet: "Do you wash my feet?"; in the garden of olives: "Simon, are you sleeping? . . . The spirit is willing, but the flesh is weak" . . . at the kiss of Judas: O Judas, how monstrous and shameful is your treachery! You approach as a friend, '*Amice*'; you greet him as a disciple greets his master, 'Hail, Master'; you kiss him as a child kisses his father: "You betray the Son of Man with a kiss?" as a cruel serpent you poison him with your breath. Jesus says to him, "Friend, if my enemy had cursed me . . ." . . . during all his passion . . . "Jesus remained silent" . . . on the Cross: "Father, forgive them . . . today

you will be with me in paradise."

3 After his Resurrection: 'a lamb in a manger, a lamb born among tax-collectors and sinners, a lamb on the Cross, a lamb in bloody sacrifice and what is more marvellous, a lamb on a kingly throne.' (Claud. Aquavi.) After his Resurrection, out of charity he remained forty days with his apostles. "Greetings"! he said to the women who sought him and he permitted them to kiss his feet. "Mary," he said to Mary. . . . What joy he gave to St. Peter!: "He appeared to Peter" . . . to the disciples of Emmaus, "Was not our heart . . . ". . . Was there anything more moving than his appearance to the apostles in the cenacle on the very day of his resurrection. Recall Joseph who made himself known to his brothers and who, throwing himself on their necks embraced them . . . "I am Joseph, your brother" . . . What great clemency he showed when he returned eight days afterwards to free Thomas from unbelief . . . the sin of this apostle was great. There was unbelief, pride, contempt of others, stubbornness, for he was determined not to believe unless he saw with his own eyes and touched with his hands. . . . O unbelieving disciple! If an angel came from heaven, would you not believe him? "Unless I see, I shall not believe." Even if the Blessed Virgin . . . "I will not believe." Let it be. A 'fiat' allows us to believe without touching. His appearance to St. Paul: "I am Jesus. . . ."

4 (at present)

Finally, he is still at this moment as merciful as ever . . . He went up to heaven to open its gates and invite us to join him: "I wish that where I am. . . ."

If he is all-powerful it is so that he can help us: "Jesus standing at the right hand . . . the lamb that was slain" . . .

If he possesses immortality, it is so that he can make unceasing intercession for us.

Example of the good priest Carpus.

Appearance of a child in the Blessed Sacrament.

'The kindness of God leads us to repentance.'

If there is here some poor Magdalene. . . . "Here I am, do not fear." "O God, your merciful anger exists only to assist; threatens only to spare; takes away only to restore; accuses only to release; destroys only to reward; rejects only to accept." (Berengs, abbot, sermon 1 in Nat. Martyr)

"Already they strike me: I am indeed ready yet again to suffer that men may be saved." (St. Denis)

"I wish always to enter but not to rush in uninvited." (St. Ambrose)

It is mercy that I want.

Example of father of prodigal son.

Sermons

Order of Sermons for a Lenten Mission

2nd Sunday of Lent.	1 The greatness of God and the service given to him. 2 The Word of God.
Monday	1 Necessity of penitence. 2 The marks of false penitence.
Tuesday:	1 The beauty, the price and the life of the soul. 2 The importance of salvation.
Wednesday	1 Necessity and difficulty of a good examination of conscience. 2 Particular examination of conscience.
Thursday	1 Examination of conscience. 2 Examination of conscience.
Friday	1 Examination of conscience. 2 General consideration of death.
Saturday	1 Dying as one has lived. 2 Happy death.
3rd Sunday	1 Qualities of a good penitent. 2 Further qualities. 3 Restitution.
Monday	1 Particular judgment. 2 Dignity of the Christian.
Tuesday	1 Hell. 2 Eternity of unhappiness.
Wesnesday	1 The security of penitence. 2 Sorrow and tears.
Thursday mid-Lent	1 Heaven. 2 Ways of going there.
Friday	1 Scandal. 2 Fraternal correction and good example.
Saturday	1 The necessity of actual grace. 2 Devotion to Mary.
4th Sunday	1 Reconciliation. 2 Forgiveness of sins. 3 Marriage.
Monday	1 Love of Jesus Christ. 2 Humility.
Tuesday	1 Lying. 2 Slander.
Wednesday	1 Gentleness and anger. 2 Obedience.
Thursday	1 Purity. 2 Impurity.
Friday	1 Patience. 2 Reparation to the Blessed Sacrament.
Saturday	1 Prayer.

	2 Qualities of devotion to Mary.
5th Sunday	1 Occasions of sin.
	2 Lawsuits.
	3 Dancing.
Monday	1 Faith.
	2 Almsgiving.
Tuesday	1 The devil and his temptations.
	2 The guardian angel and devotion to him.
Wednesday	1 Contempt of the world.
	2 The maxims of the world.
Thursday	1 The love of God.
	2
Friday	1 The name of Jesus.
	2 The crucifix.
Saturday	Renewal.
5th Sunday	1 Fervent Communion.
	2 The unworthy Communion.
	3 The holy Rosary.
Monday	1 Time.
	2 Good works.
Tuesday	1 Qualities of good works.
	2 The rule of life.
Wednesday	1 Duties of mother and father.
	2 Duties of children.
Thursday	
Friday:	1 The Passion.
Saturday	1 The passion of the Blessed Virgin Mary.
	2
Sunday	1 The Resurrection of Jesus Christ.
	2 The resurrection of the Christian.
	3 The resurrection of the body and general judgment.
Monday	1 Priests
	2
Tuesday	1 Faithfulness and perseverance.
	2 Farewell discourse.

Program of a four weeks' Mission.

Sunday	God	Word of God
Monday	Penance	Salvation.
Tuesday	General Examination	Particular examination.
Wednesday	Particular examination	Particular examination.
Thursday	Prayer	Contrition
Friday	Death in general	Dying as one has lived.
Saturday	Particular judgment	Devotion to Mary
Sunday	Hell	Restitution

Monday	Heaven	Heaven
Tuesday	Love of Jesus	Love of the poor
Wednesday	Lying	Slander
Thursday	Purity	The 'ugly' sin.
Friday	Fasting	Reparation
Saturday	Small number of elect	Devotion to Mary
Sunday	Reconciliation	Lawsuits 3 Marriage
Monday	Christianity	Faith
Tuesday	Devil	Guardian angel
Wednesday	World	Venial sin
Thursday	Qualities of penance	Qualities of good penitent
Friday	Scandal	Crucifix
Saturday	Renewal	
Sunday	Unworthy Communion	General judgment
Monday	Time	Laziness
Tuesday	Qualities of good works	Same continued
Wednesday	Humility	Gentleness
Thursday	Thanksgiving	Obedience
Friday	Passion	Same continued

Sermon-matter for a Mission, or a Retreat, or the Renewal of Baptismal Promises.

'I renounce the devil, his pomps and his works and I unite myself with you, my Jesus.'

'I renounce the devil'

1st sermon

1 From God's side. From the devil's side: freedom, 'carte blanche.'

2 Opposition between them. Understanding of what God is in himself and with regard to us; what the devil is in himself and with regard to God and with regard to us.

3 Conclusion arrived at from both sides. Examination. Contrition.

2nd sermon

The devil's hatred for man; the temptations of the devil:

1 Necessity of temptation;

2 Quantity and quality;

3 Utility.

3rd sermon

The devil's hatred for man (continued)

1 As a means of waging war against God and

2 To win our soul over to him.

Supreme value of soul! . . .

1 It is beautiful,

2 It is immortal,

3 It is precious: in its principle, its value and its purpose.

4th sermon

1 its principle;
2 its essence;
3 its end. 'The importance of salvation.'
'I renounce his pomps'

6th sermon
The world is
1 the enemy of God and must be rejected;
2 the enemy of truth and must be despised;
3 the enemy of virtue and must be hated;
4 the enemy of man and must be shunned.

7th sermon
1 Futility of riches.
2 Futility of pleasure.
3 Futility of honors.
'I renounce his works'

8th sermon.
Horror of mortal sin:
1 in itself;
2 with regard to God;
3 with regard to man.

9th sermon
Consequences of mortal sin:
1 unhappy death
2 dreadful judgment – particular and general;
3 eternal suffering.

10th sermon
Speaking of specific mortal sins:
1 pride;
2 avarice;
3 drunkenness;
4 impurity, etc.

11th sermon
Necessity of devotion to the Blessed Virgin for a true and prudent (?) repentance.
1 the Blessed Virgin in relation to God;
2 in herself;
3 in relation to us.

12th sermon
Importance of interior and exterior penance.

13th sermon
A good Confession
1 its necessity;
2 its rarity
3 its qualities.

14th sermon

Holy Communion:
 1 unworthy;
 2 lukewarm;
 3 fervent.
15th sermon
Good works:
 their necessity;
 their qualities;
 and their reward.
16th sermon
Heaven
 'I unite with Jesus my Savior'
17th sermon
 1 The treasure we have in Jesus Christ.
 2 The love Jesus has for us.
18th sermon
The love we must have for Jesus Christ and gratitude for his gifts.
19th sermon
Union with Jesus Christ:
 1 its necessity;
 2 its excellence;
 3 its qualities and effects.
20th sermon
To preserve this union, practice the virtues of Jesus Christ. One can give several talks on this:
 1 on love for God;
 2 on charity towards our neighbor;
 3 on giving alms to the poor;
 4 on contempt of the world;
 5 on humility, purity, self-denial.
21st sermon
 the promises of Baptism:
 their justification;
 their necessity and their practice.
22nd sermon
 1 Necessity of renewing them: from the writings of the Fathers, from the Councils and from our own experience.
 2 The manner of renewal through the Blessed Virgin Mary: Mother of the Head, Mother of the members, treasurer, advocate, terror of the devil, refuge, faithful virgin.
23rd sermon
Renewal.
24th sermon
Perseverance.
 3 To rob man of his grace and his baptismal innocence:

Footnotes to The Book of Sermons

1 The nine first sermons in this book are detailed plans ready for preaching.

2 Montfort has interchanged Nos. 5 and 4 in the introduction. The sermons 4, 5 and 6 refer to 5, and the sermons 7, 8, 9, refer to 4.

3 In sermon 9, Montfort had written 'On the love and the gentleness' and then added in darker ink 'of Jesus Christ.' This was Montfort's last sermon and was preached at the mission of St. Laurent-sur-Sèvre.

4 The main ideas of this sermon are borrowed from *The knowledge and love of Jesus Christ* of SAINT-JURE, S.J.

23 Dispositions for a Happy Death

Introduction

On the eve of the death of St. Louis Marie, a copy of the 'Dispositions for a Happy Death' was found among the effects of the missionaries accompanying the Saint. On a few blank pages of this little book, Fr. Mulot wrote the Last Will and Testament that the dying man had dictated to him, and this fact explains why the copy of this little work, the only one extant, has come down to us. It is preserved in the general archives of the Company of Mary.

This short writing comprises five parts, of which the last three were re-edited in 1868 by Fr. G. Denis S.M.M., in his book, 'Life in Union with Jesus and Mary,' or, 'Interior Life of a Daughter of Wisdom.' 'It can be reasonably presumed,' he says in an introduction, that they were composed by the Venerable Fr. de Montfort himself.' It has since emerged that this is not so and that the three sections in question are the work of Fr. J. Nouet, S.J., who died in 1680.

The second section, 'Vast Expanse of Paradise,' appears obviously to be a borrowing.

This leaves us with the first part entitled, 'Dispositions for a Happy Death,' a title which has been extended to the whole work. Was this section, which seems to be fundamental, really written by Fr. de Montfort? We have no firm proof that it was, but certain factors favor an affirmative answer. There exists in the Book of Sermons (of St. Louis Marie) seven drafts of sermons, or meditations, which develop in the same order the six points of the first remote disposition. Much more significant is the place reserved in this first section to the Blessed Virgin and the renewal of baptismal promises—themes which, as we know, were dear to St. Louis Marie. Also the fact that this short work was printed at La Ro-

chelle, where Montfort is said to have published the first edition of his hymns, is an added argument in favor of its authenticity.

If, then, the 'Dispositions' is placed among the works of the Saint it is done with the reservations called for in the case.

Remote Dispositions

1 I. Think of Death every day.
1. Death is certain. 2. It is near. 3. It is deceptive. 4. It is awe-inspiring. 5. It is painful. 6. It follows the pattern of life.

2 II. Live a good life.
1. Avoid grave sin and deliberate venial sin. 2. Combat your dominant fault. 3. Love the cross. 4. Receive the sacraments frequently. 5. Practice mental prayer and obedience. 6. Have a great devotion to the Blessed Virgin.

3 III. Make your Will as soon as you can.
1. Have Masses said before you die. 2. Present your Will in proper form. 3. Return everything wrongfully acquired. 4. Pay your debts.

4 IV. Follow some of these practices of the saints to remind you of death and to prepare for it.
1. When you go to bed, take the position of a dead person. 2. At every meal remember that one day your body will be the food of worms. 3. Consider sickness as the companion of death. 4. Keep a skull in your room and meditate on what that person was, what he did, said, and thought. Think of what this skull is now and what will become of it, and then reflect on your own life. 5. Prepare your coffin and your grave, and embrace them in spirit every day.

Proximate Dispositions

5 I. Endure sickness patiently for these reasons:
1. God sends it to you. 2. It can free you from this exile of yours. 3. It helps you to expiate your sins. 4. Firmly believe that you will die of this illness.

6 II. Receive the sacraments of Penance, Holy Eucharist and Extreme Unction.
1. Receive them as soon as possible, and sooner than your friends and relatives want you to. 2. Receive them with contrition, humility and gratitude. 3. Receive them with fervor.

7 III. Choose two good friends to help you.
1. They can keep out of your room relatives, friends and other people who can be of no help to you. 2. They will

help you to make acts of faith, hope and love. 3. They will help you to receive the Sacraments. 4. They will help you to withstand temptation.

8 IV. Resist the temptations of the devil.
1. If you are tempted against faith, simply say 'I believe in God,' or 'I believe everything the Catholic Church teaches.' 2. If you are tempted to despair, put all your trust in the infinite merits of our Lord and the all-powerful intercession of Mary. 3. If you are tempted to impatience, think of the sufferings of Jesus, the reward he promises, the sufferings of the next life, the seriousness of your sins.

9 V. Resist any temptation to vainglory and presumption by considering the number and gravity of your past sins in the face of the infinite holiness of God.

10 VI. Do not be misled by the comforting words of your friends and relatives, and keep them away from you as much as you can. Do not share their natural grief; do not listen to their anxious advice or their deceptive reassurances.

Final Dispositions

11 1. Follow the example of Jesus and forgive all your enemies from the depths of your heart.

12 2. Ask pardon of those you have offended, and of those you caused to offend God.

13 3. Commit your soul into the hands of God.

14 4. Commit your body to the earth, and willingly accept that it become the food of worms.

15 5. Pray to God for yourself and for others.

16 6. Commit all your relatives and friends to the care of the Blessed Virgin.

17 7. Exhort your whole family to true devotion to the Blessed Virgin.

18 8. Renew your baptismal promises, and bid goodbye to everyone here below.

19 9. Thank God for his infinite mercy and for all his benefits, and then rely on him alone.

20 10. Adore God's judgment of you, no matter what it may be.

21 11. Offer yourself to the Justice of God in union with Jesus, no matter where he may put you, provided that there you may be able to love God.

22 12. Ardently desire the joyous possession of Jesus and of his kingdom.

23 13. Have the prayers for the dying said, and give the responses yourself. Have the Passion of our Lord read or the Prayer he offered before he died, in the 17th Chapter of the Gospel according to Saint John.

24 14. Recite, if you can, the *Magnificat*[1] and the Psalm 'I rejoiced because they said to me, "We will go up to God's house." '

25 15. Finally, in union with Jesus and Mary, with nothing more to worry about, with no one near you but your two friends, wait for the hour of death with joy. Often repeat the words 'Jesus, Mary, Joseph,' to gain the indulgences of the confraternities you belong to, kiss your crucifix, look at the image of the Blessed Virgin, make the sign of the cross, and sprinkle your bed with holy water.

Vast Expanse of Paradise

26 According to astrologers, the stars which are to be found in the eighth heaven are all larger than the earth. They are divided into six different groups. Those in the first group are seventeen times larger than the earth, and there are seventeen of them. Those in the second group are 90 times larger than the earth, and there are 45 of them. Those in the third group are 54 times larger than the earth, and there are 264 of them. Those in the fourth group are 35 times larger, and there are 217 of them. Those in the fifth group are 18 times larger, and they are numberless. The sky or the firmament where they are located has a circumference of 125,000,000 miles; and yet Heaven is still greater than that.

Prayers for the Seven Anointings of Extreme Unction

The Eyes

27 Dear Jesus, by the tears you shed, I beg you to forgive the sins I have committed by the wrong use of my sight, so that when I have finished my life's course, I may see the beauty of your face, the sight of which will be my heaven.

The Ears

28 Dear Jesus, I beg you, by the heavenly purity of your sense of hearing, to wash away the impurity of mine, so that at the hour of death I will have no fear of a dreadful sentence, but may joyfully present myself before your throne, to receive my crown and to hear those consoling words, 'Come, you who have my Father's blessing, take possession of the Kingdom which has been prepared for you ever since the beginning of the world.'

The Nostrils

29 Dear Jesus, I beg you, by the sweet odor of your virtues, and by the patience with which you suffered the fetid atmosphere of Calvary, deliver me from the stench of hell. Forgive the sins I have

committed by my fastidiousness and my extravagant spending to satisfy my sense of smell, so that at the hour of death I may say to you, 'Draw us to you, we run in the odor of your perfume.'

The Mouth

30 Dear Jesus, by the power of the sacred words of your mouth, I beg you to forgive my intemperate words and my uncontrolled tongue, so that, as I leave this place of exile, I may enter the temple of your glory, there to sing your praises for all eternity.

The Hands

31 Dear Jesus, by the sacred wounds in your hands I pray you to wipe away all the sins I have committed through the misuse of my hands, so that after my death I may embrace you tenderly and bind myself to you for all eternity.

The Feet

32 Dear Jesus, by the sacred wounds in your feet, I beg you to forgive all the steps I have taken in the direction of evil, so that my soul, delivered from the weight of this mortal body, may take its flight to you, its centre and place of rest.

The Back

33 Dear Jesus, by the loving wound in your Sacred Heart and by the innocence of your most holy life, I beg you to forgive the shameful excesses of my body. I implore you to bathe me in your blood, in which alone I place all my hope. Instil into me power from the water which issued from your sacred side, washing away the stains of my body and soul, so that, being completely cleansed as I leave this wretched place of captivity, I may joyfully find myself with you, who are the true paradise of eternal joy. 'Create a clean heart for me, O God. Thoroughly wash me from my guilt and cleanse me from my sin.'[3]

The Seven Last Words of Jesus

34 First Word. "Father, forgive them; they do not know what they do."[4]

Prayer

O Jesus, you prayed for your enemies as they crucified you. Forgive me my offences as with all my heart I forgive those who have offended me.

35 Second Word. "In truth, I declare, this day you will be with me in paradise."[5]

Prayer

O Jesus, you promised paradise to the repentant thief. I

implore you in your infinite goodness to remember me at the hour of my death, and to grant me true sorrow for my sins.

36 Third Word. "Woman, behold your son. . . . Behold your mother."[6]

Prayer

O Jesus, when you were dying, you manifested the tenderness of your heart for your Blessed Mother, and you confided to her all your disciples in the person of Saint John. Place me, I beg you, under her protection and give me the heart of a son to honor her. Remember that your Son on the tree of the Cross confided my soul to you. Show him that you are a good mother, and that you are taking my salvation into your care: 'Show yourself a mother.'[7]

37 Fourth Word. "My God, my God, why have you abandoned me?"[8]

Prayer

O Jesus, in an excess of love you consented to be forsaken by your Father, to prevent sinners being abandoned; do not forsake me, I implore you, at the hour of my death, when everyone else abandons me. You are my sole refuge. Hide me in your wounds, and grant that there I may find my consolation and my salvation.

38 Fifth Word. "I am thirsty."[9]

Prayer

O Jesus, you willed to drink vinegar and gall. By your burning thirst for the glory of your Father and for my perfection, I beseech you to make reparation for my coldness in the past, and to enkindle in my heart an ardent desire to serve you and to glorify you eternally. Amen.

39 Sixth Word. "All is accomplished."[10]

Prayer

O Jesus, you have entirely accomplished the will of your Father in everything, and completed by your death the work of our redemption. Grant me the grace before I die to fulfil and accomplish perfectly all the plans which, for your glory and my own good, you have in store for me.

40 Seventh Word. "Father, into your hands I commit my spirit."[11]

Prayer

O Jesus, you committed your spirit into your Father's hands before you died. I implore you, receive my soul into your merciful arms at the last moment of my life. Hide me in the tabernacle of your loving heart at that fearful hour when I am in danger of being lost. Protect me in that divine sanctuary against all the efforts of my enemies. Shower down upon me the marvels of your grace, for you save with your all-powerful arm those who hope in you. Shield me as the apple of your eye against those who resist you and want to upset the plan you have to save me. Hide me in the shadow of your wings from those who persecute me.

My Spiritual Will

41 In the name of the Father and of the Son and of the Holy Spirit. Most loving Savior, now that I am about to die, with my mind, due to your mercy, still completely clear, I declare to you, in the presence of the holy angel you gave me to watch over me, that I wish to die in the faith and the sentiments of the Catholic, Roman and Apostolic Church, in which all your Saints and your friends have died.

42 1. My God, I firmly believe everything you have revealed, and from this moment I renounce every temptation to unbelief and despair which might come my way through the malice of the devil and the waywardness of my mind.

43 2. From this moment I accept death out of love for you, not just to be freed from the sorrows of this life or the sooner to enjoy the glory of heaven, but only to accomplish your holy will.

44 3. I submit to everything you wish me to endure in body and soul, and I offer it to you in union with your most holy agony to satisfy the demands of your justice and to make reparation for the loss I have caused to your glory.

45 4. From now on I renounce the world, the flesh, my present life, the use of my senses, the company of living people, and every natural comfort, because you will it and because I deserve to be deprived of them.

46 5. O Saviour most kind and merciful, I trust that in your goodness you will forgive all my sins, because I know for certain that your mercy is infinitely greater than the enormity of my offenses. And so, my God, I have confidence in your infinite mercy and the merits of your death, the source of all heavenly blessings, and I await the forgiveness for which you have pleaded with tears of blood, and the grace to keep myself in your love until the very end of my life. “In you, O Lord, I have hoped; let me never be put to shame.”[12]

47 6. O my God, my supreme good and my last end, you have commanded me to love you. I declare in your divine presence that I wish to love you with all my heart, and I desire that my soul remain purified and free of every other love but yours. With all my strength I renounce every other interest, throughout time and eternity and I do not wish to be concerned with anything but you, my God and my all! May I be entirely, completely yours, as you are entirely mine. How I regret that I have loved you so little and so late! “Late have I loved you, O ageless beauty, late have I loved you.”[13]

48 7. O God, my blessedness, my light, my life, I long for you.

With inconceivable ardor I want to see myself one day united with you, to love you and to glorify you in the purest and most perfect way possible. That is why I beg you, O God of my heart, to deliver my soul from the prison of my body, and in your kindness to break the shackles which hold it captive, and to give it the liberty of your children, so that it may sing for ever songs of love and blessings in the land of the living,[14] for it is there, and not in the land of the dying, that I shall give you perfect praise and love. And there, my God, I shall please you without ever causing you sorrow, and there too shall I contemplate you in all your brilliance, love you unceasingly, and perform every service faultlessly. "My soul thirsts for God, the God of my life.[15] How lovely is your dwelling place, O Lord of hosts![16] I shall be satisfied when your glory appears."[17] Until then, dear Lord, I will take no rest, I will languish out of love. My heart will beat continually within me, for you have made it for yourself, and it will never find rest until it finally rests in you.[18]

49 8. Eternal Father, Father of mercy, Father of light, from whom every best gift comes, by the loving heart of Jesus Christ our Lord, I offer you countless acts of thanksgiving for all the blessings you were pleased to bestow upon me purely out of your goodness at every moment of my life. I now give back that life to you with a heart full of gratitude and love. In all humility I thank you once again for the use of that life you gave me. I thank you, too, for every moment of the eternal blessedness and all the joys of the glory which I hope will be mine through the merits of the wounds of my Savior, who obtained them for me with so much suffering. I invite all the saints and all creatures to praise you for me. "Let everything that breathes praise the Lord."[19]

50 But when I consider the ill-use I have made of all these blessings, and for which I have returned only ingratitude, I am profoundly sorry, and I sincerely regret the wickedness of my past life. Very humbly I ask your forgiveness and beg you to wipe away the stains from my soul with the blood of your dear Son. I beg you to forget the neglect which so often in the past led me away from the paths of your Holy Spirit, and frustrated the plans which in your goodness you had made for me. Do not enter into judgement against your poor servant, O God. But since you never reject the sacrifice of a contrite and humble heart, grant me the grace to weep for my sins during the little time I have left, and like your saints to die in the spirit of repentance.

51 Lord Jesus, by that ardent love which separated your most holy soul from your sacred body, may my heart, wounded with love and crushed with sorrow, appease your anger. O Blessed Mother, happy Gate of Heaven, give me just one of the tears of your Son and just one of the sighs of your heart pierced with sorrow at the foot of the Cross, to make up for my lack of contrition. Receive my soul among the number of those who obtain by your intercession forgiveness for their sins and life everlasting. Dear Guardian Angel, take care of the last moments of my life, and assist me with your power against all my enemies, so that I may emerge victorious from this final combat, and die in the love and out of love for my God, and my most loving Savior. Amen.

Footnotes to Dispositions for a Happy Death

1 Lk. 1:46-55.
2 Ps. 122(121).
3 Ps. 50; 12:4.
4 Lk. 23:34.
5 Lk. 23:43.
6 Jn. 19:26,27.
7 From the hymn 'Ave Maris Stella' (Hail thou star of Ocean).
8 Mt. 27:46; Mk. 15:34.
9 Jn. 19:28.
10 Jn. 19:30.
11 Lk. 23:46.
12 Ps. 31:2; 70:1.
13 SAINT AUGUSTINE, *Confessions.*
14 Ps. 116:9.
15 Ps. 42:2.
16 Ps. 84:2.
17 Cf. Ps. 16:15.
18 Cf. SAINT AUGUSTINE, *Confessions.*
19 Ps. 150:6.

24 Index of subjects

God Alone

Index of Subjects

Index of Subjects

Index of Subjects

Index of Subjects

Index of Subjects

Index of Subjects

Index of Subjects

Index of Subjects

Index of Subjects

of proper names

Abogar, Abgar V or Khama, king of Edessa (c. A.D. 750)	legend has it that he sent a letter to Christ. Cf. Eusebius, *Ecclesiastical History* I, XIII, 5. LEW 121.
Agreda, Mary of, (1602-1665)	mystic of the Order of the Poor Clares; author of *The Mystical City of God.* TD 206 (note).
Alain Robert	uncle of Louis Marie, priest of Saint Saviour parish in Rennes. L 1, 2, 3, 4.
Alan De La Roche, O.P. (1428-1475)	born in Brittany, died at Zwolle, Holland. Most of his writings are concerned with the Rosary: *De Psalterio B. Virginis Mariae . . . ; Compendium psalterii B. Trinitatis . . . ; De immensa et ineffabili dignitate et utilitate psalterii precelse ac intemerate semper virginis Mariae.* Works very much edited by Coppenstein in the seventeenth century. SR 11 and *passim;* TD 249, 250.
Alègre, Madame d'	a lady who agreed to bequeath the sum of 160 livres to the seminary of Saint-Sulpice to cover Montfort's annual fees. She paid this sum to Fr. de la Barmondière. L 3.
Arsenius the Great, St. (c. 354-412)	monk; private tutor of the sons of Theodosius I, later hermit in the Egyptian desert. LEW 200.
Augustine, St. (354-430)	Bishop of Hippo. LEW 30, 213; FC 58; SR 37, 40, 53, 88; SM 14; TD 8, 33, 40, 67, 127, 145, 219, 230; LCM 8, H 76:9.
Barin (or Barrin), Fr.	Vicar-General at Nantes; author of the epitaph in French on the tomb of Father de Montfort, whose friend he was. L 33.
Barmondière, Fr. Claude de la (d. 1694)	Superior of the "Community of poor students," near Saint-Sulpice; it was he who admitted Montfort to this community. L 2, 3.
Baronius (1538-1607)	Cardinal, and Superior of the Oratory; author of the very erudite ecclesiastical annals. LEW 112.
Barry, Paul, S.J., (1587-1661)	author of *Paradise opened to Philagia* by means of a hundred easy practices of devotion to the Mother of God. TD 117.
Benzonius, Rutilius (d. 1613)	Bishop of Loreto; author of the *Dissertationes et Commentaria in Canticum Magnificat et in Salutationem Angelicam.* TD 255.
Bérulle, Cardinal Pierre de (1575-1629)	founder of the French Oratory. The French School of Spirituality owed a lot to his influence and teaching. He supported the custom of making a vow of servitude to Jesus and Mary. TD 162; SR 133.
Blain, Jean-Baptiste	Canon of Rouen, school-friend of Montfort; author

Index of Proper Names

of a Memoir on Saint Louis Marie and probably also of the Latin epitaph on his tomb. Also author of a biography of Saint John Baptist de la Salle.

Blosius, Venerable François-Louis, (1506-1566) — (Louis de Blois); Benedictine abbot; author of *Speculum Monacorum* and *Paradisus animae.* SR 91.

Bollandus, Caesarius d' Heisterbach (c. 1188-1240) — religious of the Cistercian Order; author of several spiritual books. TD 159.

Bonaventure, St., O.F.M. (1221-1274) — It is now accepted that he is not the author of the *Mirror of the Blessed Virgin,* as was formerly believed. SR 30, 52; TD 8, 27, 40, 75, 76, 85, 86, 116, 152, 174.

Boudon, Henri-Marie, Archdeacon of Evreux (1624-1702) — his writings on the Blessed Virgin and the Holy Slavery, as well as *The Holy Way of the Cross* were studied assiduously by Montfort. TD 159, 163.

Brenier — Superior of the Minor Seminary of Saint-Sulpice. L 5, 6 (P.S.), 10, 11 (P.S.).

Brunet, Catherine — Sister of the Conception, first companion of Marie Louise of Jesus. L 27, 31.

Cajetan, (Thomas de Vio), O.P. (1460-1533) — author of commentaries on St. Thomas Aquinas. SR 76. (Not to be confused with St. Cajetan, who lived about same time.)

Caraffa, Fr. Vincent (1585-1649) — seventh Superior General of the Jesuits; wore chains on his ankles as a sign of his slavery to the Mother of God. TD 242.

Carpus, St. — Bishop of Beroea according to the Menologies; mentioned by St. Paul in 2 Tim. 4:13. LEW 130.

Carthagena, John de, O.F.M. (1563-1617) — author of *Homeliae Catholicae.* SR 14, 15, 27, 32; TD 250.

Conception, Sister of the — Cf. Brunet, Catherine.

Cornelius A Lapide, S.J. (1567-1637) — a famous Scripture scholar. TD 161.

Daughters of the Blessed Sacrament (Benedictine Nuns) — founded by Mother Mechtilde. During his stay in Paris (1703-1704), Montfort used to go to their house, accompanied by a poor man, to have the meal which was reserved for the poor in honor of our Lady. He got them to admit his sister, Guyonne-Jeanne, as one of their members (at Rambervilliers). His sister took the name of Sister Catherine of Saint Bernard. L 18.

Daughters of Wisdom — founded by Saint Louis Marie Grignion de Montfort, at Poitiers in 1703. L 28, 29, 30, 32, 33; H 149.

Dauvaise, Mademoiselle Elisabeth — Superior of the Home for Incurables in Nantes. With Sister Mathurine she undertook the expenses of the small mausoleum above the tomb of Montfort. L 33.

Delanoue, St. — foundress of the Daughters of Providence, in

Jeanne (1660-1736) Saumur. Met Montfort in 1705.

Del Rio, Martin-Antoine, S.J. (1551-1608) born at Antwerp. Friend of Justus Lipsius; wrote *Disquisitiones magicae*. LEW 88.

Denis the Areopagite, of Athens lived in the first century A.D., was converted by St. Paul, Acts 17:34. In the Middle Ages he was identified with St. Denis of Paris. The *De Coelesti Hierarchia* was ascribed to him (Pseudo-Denis the Aeropagite). However, the author of the works ascribed to the Areopagite appears to be another Denis (Pseudo-Denis) living at the end of the fifth century or at the beginning of the sixth century. LEW 130; TD 49.

Dominic, St. (c. 1170-1221) founder of the Dominicans. SR 11, 16, 19, 20, 22, 26, 31, 51, 61, 66, 79, 90; TD 42, 249, 250; PM 12.

Dominic of Prussia, Fr. (1384-1460) Carthusian; author, among other books, of the *Corona B. Mariae*. SR 89, 94.

Doorlant, Pierre (1568-1658) author of the *Chronicon Cartusiense,* (Cologne, 1606). SR 89.

Fathers of the Church ecclesiastical writers distinguished by their orthodox doctrine and their holy lives. (1) Period from the beginning to the Council of Nicea (325): apostolic Fathers and apologetic Fathers. (2) Golden Age: from 325 to the death of St. Augustine (431). (3) Period of decline: from 431 to St. Bernard (d. 1153). LEW 163, 207, 208; TD 25, 26, 40, 41, 75, 93, 130.

Fontevrault, near Saumur abbey founded in 1099 by Robert d' Arbrissel. In 1701 the abbess was Gabrielle de Rochechouart-Mortemart. Her sister, Madame de Montespan, who was a benefactress of Montfort's sisters, had a long conversation with the saint (1701). L 6.

Francis De Sales, St. (1567-1622) Bishop and Doctor of the Church; founder, with St. Jane Frances de Chantal, of the Visitation Sisters. Author of *The Devout Life* and of the *Treatise on the Love of God.* SR 80, 130; TD 152.

Francis of Assisi, St. (1182-1226) founder of the Friars Minor, the Poor Clares and the Franciscan Third Order. LEW 166; TD 42.

Geoffroy, Madame she offered hospitality to Marie Louise of Jesus when the latter arrived at La Rochelle. Her daughter took the habit of the Daughters of Wisdom but did not persevere. L 29.

Germanus, St. (633?-733) Patriarch of Constantinople; wrote several letters particularly valuable for Mariology, especially with regard to the Assumption. TD 40.

Gerson, John (1363-1429) theologian and chancellor of the University of Paris. Wrote in support of the Immaculate Conception. TD 255.

Grignion, Joseph-Pierre (1674-1714) brother of Saint Louis Marie; was ordained priest in 1698. In a letter to his uncle, Louis Marie recom-

Index of Proper Names

	mends him to place his studies under the protection of our Lady. L 1.
Guerric, Blessed (1075-1154)	Cistercian abbot; friend of St. Bernard, he was abbot of Clairvaux, then of Isigny. SM 54; TD 199.
Hermann, Joseph, Blessed	Premonstratensian monk (c. 1150-1241); had a great devotion to the Blessed Virgin. SR 121.
Hugues De Saint-Cher, O.P.	Cardinal; died in 1263 at Orvieto. SR 84, 118.
Humbertus	Cf. Umbertus.
Jesus, Society of	TD 161; RM 15, 19.
John, Brother	one of the co-adjutor Brothers of Montfort. L 27, 29; W 5.
Joseau, Brother	taught at Saint-Laurent-sur-Sèvre until his death in 1759. Copied the works of Montfort which had been passed on to him by Brother Jacques. He began a chronicle of events in the life of the two communities of Saint-Laurent, which was continued by Sister Florence after his death. SM, introduction.
Justus Lipsius (1547-1606)	Flemish humanist. Wrote on the shrines of Montaigu and Halle in Belgium. TD 40.
Lepanto	town and port in Greece. Scene of the victory of the Christian fleet over the Turks on 7 October 1571. SR 132.
Leschassier, François	Superior of the Saint-Sulpice seminary and spiritual director of Montfort. L 5, 6, 8-11.
Leuduger, Fr. (1649-1722)	in charge of diocesan missions of St. Brieuc. He founded the "Daughters of the Holy Spirit." Montfort placed himself under his guidance in 1706. L 5.
Lévêque, Fr. René	disciple of Fr. Olier, founder of the community of Saint Clement in Nantes. L 5, 8, 9, 11 and postscript.
Lopez, John, O.P.	died in 1632; Bishop of Corrone in Calabria and of Monopoli. Author of *Rosario de Nuestra Señora* (1584). SR 95.
Louise, Guyonne-Jeanne	sister of Louis Marie. Cf. Daughters of the Blessed Sacrament.
Louise Trichet	Cf. Marie Louise of Jesus.
Lull, Raymond (1235-1315)	born at Palma, Majorca, author of *Ars Magna*. LEW 87.
Marie D'Oignies, Blessed (1177-1213)	a Beguine well known for her devotion to the Blessed Virgin and the Eucharist. TD 255.
Marie Louise of Jesus (7 May 1684-28 April 1759)	first Daughter of Wisdom. L 15, 16, 25, 27-29, 34.
Marie Reine (Roy)	a penitent of Father de Montfort at La Rochelle, who ran a small dressmaking workshop. Montfort sent Marie Louise and Catherine Brunet to stay with her. L 29.
Mathurin Rangeard, Brother (1686-1760)	the first Brother, a faithful companion of Montfort and his successors in missions. L 21.

Michel De Lisle	Bishop of Salubre, disciple and colleague of Blessed Alan de la Roche who worked with him in spreading devotion to the Holy Rosary. SR 56.
Montbernage (Suburb of Poitiers)	part of the parish of St. Radegonde. The "Grange de la Bergerie" was turned into a chapel by Montfort which he called "Our Lady of All Hearts." LPM.
Montespan, Madame de	Françoise Athénais, Marquise de Rochechouart. She ended her unedifying life in the practice of penance. She took Louis Marie and his sisters under her protection. L 6, 9.
Montfort, Saint Louis Marie Grignion de (1673-1716)	second child by Jean-Baptiste Grignion and Jeanne Robert. Was declared Venerable by Gregory XVI on 7 September 1838, beatified by Leo XIII on 22 January 1888, and canonized by Pius XII on 20 July 1947.
Montigny, Mademoiselle de	was given accommodation by the Grignion family in Rennes and obtained a place for Louis in the house for poor students founded by Fr. de la Barmondière. L 3.
Mulot, Fr. René (1686-1749)	the second recruit of Montfort for his "little Company." Confessor of Louis Marie and his immediate successor. W.
Navarre, Martin Navarrinus de Azpilcueta (1492-1586)	theologian, moralist and canonist. SR 27.
Nicolas, Brother	one of Montfort's first co-adjutor Brothers. He accompanied the missionary to the last. Is mentioned in the Saint's last will and testament together with Brothers Philip, Louis and Gabriel.
Odilo, St. (c. 962-1049)	Abbot of Cluny. He organized the great movement of monastic reform of his time in the main Cluniac monasteries in France, Lombardy and Spain. Friend and adviser of popes and princes. TD 159.
Oecolampadius, Jean (1482-1531)	one of the Reformers, of aggressive temperament, who fought Luther, Benz, Servet and the Anabaptists. TD 40.
Olier, Jean-Jacques (1608-1657)	founder of the Society of Saint-Sulpice; his spiritual director was St. Vincent de Paul who fostered his zeal and attended him at his death. TD 170.
Penitents of Saint-Pompain	to obtain members for his Company of Mary Montfort sent 33 White Penitents on a pilgrimage to our Lady of Ardilliers in Saumur. The Penitents were led by Father Mulot and Father Vatel. PS.
Phalacius, Fr. Stanislaus, S.J. (1591-1652)	through his preaching and writings he spread the Holy Slavery to Mary in Poland at the request of King Ladislas IV. TD 161.
Popes	SM 42; TD 163; RM 56.
Renty, Gaston-Jean-Baptiste, Baron	disciple of Bérulle and Condren. He spread devotion to the Child Jesus and had a number of missions

(1611-1649)	given in the provinces at his own expense; he wrote a life of Marie des Vallées. TD 47.
Rios, Bartholomew de los (1580-1652)	hermit of St. Augustine, preacher to the Infanta Isabella, governor of the Netherlands. He spread "Slavery to the Name of Mary," wrote *Hierarchia Mariana* (1641). TD 160, 161.
Robert, Jeanne (1649-1718)	mother of Louis Marie; was the daughter of a sheriff of Rennes and sister of three priests. L 20.
Rochefoucauld, François de la (1558-1645)	Cardinal, was very zealous for the conversion of heretics. He had the canons of the Council of Trent accepted in France. SR 133.
Rojas, Fr. Simon (1552-1624)	Trinitarian. Founded the famous Congregation of the Slaves of the Most Lovable Name of Mary, more generally known as the *Ave Maria.* TD 160.
Rupert, of Deutz (1075-1130)	Benedictine abbot, theologian, author of *In Canticum Canticorum,* etc. LEW 164; TD 145.
Saint-Laurent-Sur-Sèvre	Parish in Vendée where Montfort gave his last mission begun on 5 April 1716. He died on 28 April 1716. Tomb of the holy Missionary. Basilica dedicated to him. L 33, date.
Saint-Sulpice	Parish in Paris which became fervent thanks to the zeal of Fr. Olier. Near the parish church Fr. Olier established the Seminary in 1642. Montfort was a theological student there from 1693 to 1700. L *passim.*
Sorbonne	the famous university in Paris, founded by Canon Robert de Sorbon in 1255 and endowed by St. Louis IX. FC 26.
Sprenger, Fr. James, O.P. (c. 1436-1495)	zealous promoter of the Rosary, founder of the famous first Confraternity of the Rosary of Cologne in 1475; author of the book *Rosenkransbuchlein.* SR 32.
Suarez, Francis (1548-1617)	well-known Jesuit theologian. SR 54; TD 40.
Suso, Blessed Henry (1295 or 1300-1366)	German Dominican. Author of *Horologium Sapientiae,* etc. LEW 101, 102, 132.
Thomas Aquinas, St., O.P. (1225-1274)	eminent theologian. LEW 94, 163; SR 69, 76, 88; SM 23; TD 40, 127.
Trent, Council of	The Catechism of the Council of Trent. TD 72, 129.
Tronson, Louis (1622-1700)	third Superior General of the Sulpicians. Under the direction of Fr. Olier, he exercised his ministry in the parish of Saint-Sulpice. First superior of the seminary. Works: *Règlement de Saint-Sulpice; Forma Cleri; Les Examens particuliers.* TD 244.
Umbertus, O.P. (c. 1200-1277)	fifth Superior General of the Dominicans, disciple of Hugues de St-Cher. Author of *Epistola de tribus votis substantialibus religiosis.* LCM 9.
Vatel, Adrien	The first priest of the Company of Mary. He had met Montfort at the seminary of the Holy Spirit in Paris in 1713. When he was on his way to the for-

eign missions in the West Indies, he stopped at La Rochelle, where he was called by Montfort. He remained with Montfort and died at Rennes in 1748.

Vautier De Bierbeek, Walterius (d. 1222) knight, relative of the Dukes of Louvain. "Fuit cultor egregius Mariae; Virginis studiosissimus" (Bourassé) TD 159.

Vincent Ferrer, St., O.P. (1350-1419) great preacher and miracle-worker. He travelled through France, Spain, Italy, England and Ireland. In 1417, while preaching in the moorland of La Ferrière near La Chèze, he had predicted that an apostolic man would one day renovate the chapel dedicated to our Lady of Mercy (a prophecy which, in fact, was realized in 1707 by Father de Montfort). TD 48; PM 2; RM 6.

# of biblical references

This listing covers the whole of De Montfort's writings, singling out the word-for-word quotations as well as the most characteristic biblical references. It was not possible to cite all the allusions or the countless biblical texts and facts, so numerous are they and so integrated with De Montfort's own words. We therefore had to make a selection. To facilitate matters for the reader, we have placed an asterisk before the literal citations, which are taken from the Vulgate edition of the Bible. The following are the abbreviations used.

Books Quoted

Old Testament

Gen.	Genesis	Song	Song of Solomon
Ex.	Exodus	Wis.	Wisdom
Lev.	Leviticus	Sir.	Ecclesiasticus (Sirach)
Num.	Numbers	Is.	Isaiah
Deut.	Deuteronomy	Jer.	Jeremiah
Kgs.	Kings	Lamen.	Lamentations
Chron.	Chronicles	Ezek.	Ezekiel
Esd.	Esdras	Dan.	Daniel
Tob.	Tobit	Hos.	Hosea
Esther	Esther	Mic.	Micah
Mac.	Maccabees	Hab.	Habakkuk
Job	Job	Hag.	Haggai
Ps.	Psalms	Zech.	Zechariah
Prov.	Proverbs	Mal.	Malachi
Eccles.	Ecclesiastes		

New Testament

Mt.	Matthew	Thess.	Thessalonians
Mk.	Mark	Tim.	Timothy
Lk.	Luke	Tit.	Titus
Jn.	John	Philem.	Philemon
Acts	Acts of the Apostles	Heb.	Hebrews
Rom.	Romans	Jas.	James
Cor.	Corinthians	Pet.	Peter
Gal.	Galatians	Jn.	John
Eph.	Ephesians	Jude	Jude
Phil.	Philippians	Apoc.	Apocalypse
Col.	Colossians		

God Alone

Index of Biblical References

Index of Biblical References

Index of Biblical References

God Alone

Index of Biblical References

God Alone

Index of Biblical References

Index of Biblical References

Index of Biblical References